THE LOGIC OF CONSENT

To

Jonathan, Carla, and Anna,
Remembering a bear in Istanbul, an Inca bridge in Peru
and other marvels we have shared.

The Logic of Consent

The Diversity and Deceptiveness of Consent as a Defense to Criminal Conduct

PETER WESTEN
University of Michigan Law School, USA

Routledge
Taylor & Francis Group
LONDON AND NEW YORK

First published 2004 by Ashgate Publishing

Published 2016 by Routledge
2 Park Square, Milton Park, Abingdon, Oxfordshire OX14 4RN
711 Third Avenue, New York, NY 10017, USA

Routledge is an imprint of the Taylor & Francis Group, an informa business

British Library Cataloguing in Publication Data
Westen, Peter, 1943-
The logic of consent : the diversity and deceptiveness of consent as a defense to criminal conduct. - (Law, justice and power)
1.Consent (Law) 2.Defense (Criminal procedure)
I. Title
345'.04

Library of Congress Cataloging-in-Publication Data
Westen, Peter, 1943-
The logic of consent : the diversity and deceptiveness of consent as a defense to criminal conduct / Peter Westen.
p. cm. -- (Law, justice, and power)
Includes bibliographical references and index.
ISBN 0-7546-2407-2
1. Consent (Law)--United States. 2. Criminal liability--United States. 3. Defense (Criminal procedure)--United States. 4.Rape--United States. I. Title. II. Series.

KF9248.W47 2003
345.73'04--dc22

2003063821

ISBN 13: 978-0-7546-2407-3 (hbk)

Contents

Preface *vii*

INTRODUCTION 1

PART I FACTUAL CONSENT

Introduction 15

1. A Core Conception of Consent: An Attitude of Factual Acquiescence 25

2. An Expression of Factual Acquiescence 65

PART II LEGAL CONSENT

Introduction 107

3. Offenses to Which Consent is a Defense 111

4. Prescriptive Consent: An Attitude or an Expression? 139

5. Prescriptive Attitudinal Consent 177

6. Non-contemporaneous Prescriptive Consent 247

7. Imputed Consent 269

PART III THE CONSEQUENCES OF CONCEPTUAL COMPLEXITY

Introduction 307

8. The Confusions of Consent 309

Conclusion *337*

Bibliography *351*

Index of Cases *367*

Index *371*

Preface

My interest in consent is a response to years of feeling confused about it. For a time I thought I was the only one who was struggling to understand consent because judges and commentators who wrote about it, particularly in the context of rape, confidently treated it as a matter of common sense. Moreover, they seemed justified in their confidence because 'consent' is a commonplace term that people regularly employ on the unstated assumption that everyone knows what it means. In time, however, I concluded that this shared confidence about the transparent meaning of consent is seriously misplaced. We tend to invoke 'consent' to talk about personal subjects that matter a great deal to us. And we are able to do so because consent is a protean concept that takes diverse and shifting shapes depending upon the context. Yet because we are often only dimly aware of the shifting content of consent, we end up talking past one another—and, even worse, contradicting one another—without being aware of it.

My engagement with consent began in the mid-1980s with feminist critiques of rape laws. Commentators who agreed on little else joined then in criticizing the widespread practice of defining rape as sexual intercourse with a woman *by force* and *without her consent*. Yet at the same time they emphatically disagreed about the solution. Some of them argued that rape should be defined solely in terms of force without any reference to consent; others argued that it should be defined solely in terms of non-consent without any reference to force; and still others argued that it should be defined alternatively in terms of either force or non-consent. As I sought to understand the dispute, I found myself floundering over what these commentators meant by 'force' and 'non-consent'. I could see that they were loading the terms with meaning, but I could not restate what they meant, at least not well enough to explain it to myself or to others. So I turned to the underlying concepts of force and consent that appeared to be doing all the heavy lifting. In doing so, I have come to the conclusion that although commentators then and now differ among themselves about what ought to count as rape, their differences do not turn in any significant way upon whether rape statutes are framed in terms of 'force' or in terms of 'non-consent'. They may believe they disagree about force and non-consent, but in reality they disagree about what is being masked by their references to force and non-consent.

This book is an exercise in conceptual analysis. It is an effort to clarify what we mean when we talk about consent in criminal cases. I hasten to say that it is not an effort to reduce all references to consent to a single concept. To the contrary, I am seeking to identify the many forms that consent takes and the diverse consequences the differing forms entail. I sympathize with commentators who are tempted to dismiss conceptual analysis in favor of directly addressing the task of making criminal statutes more just. I am tempted to do so myself. But I have come to believe from my own experience that we cannot resolve the justice of statutes regarding offenses of non-consent without first clarifying to ourselves and to others the diverse and potentially deceptive meanings of consent.

I am profoundly grateful to many who have contributed to this project: to Dean Jeffrey Lehman and Terry Elkes for supporting a semester of leave at a point at which the project might otherwise have foundered; to my seminar students for vetting my ideas; to the faculty of the University of Michigan for creating an environment in which scholarship may flourish; to Paula Payton for masterfully organizing and meticulously formatting the manuscript for publication; to Larry Alexander, Antony Duff, Sandy Kadish, Heidi Malm, Sandra Marshall, Kenneth Simons, Lloyd Weinreb, Alan Wertheimer, and Christina Whitman for thoughtfully and meticulously commenting on earlier drafts; to Jonathan, Carla, and Anna for encouraging me to continue when there seemed no end in sight; and, most of all, to Marianne for enabling me to immerse myself in an undertaking to which she must have wondered whether she had consented.

INTRODUCTION

> Evidentiary considerations aside, consent appears to be a conceptually simple issue. Either the female assented to intercourse, or she did not (*Model Penal Code*, 1980, pt. I, vol. 1, sec. 213.1, p. 302).

> Now the problem with this word is that it's short enough for headlines, and memorable and evocative, and everybody thinks they know what it means—sexual intercourse 'without consent'. But 'consent' is the word that sets . . . lawyers slaverying. How can it be proved or disproved? What does it mean? (Appleyard, 'Sleazy Legal Dance Round the Minefield of Date-Rape', *Sunday Times*, 2 Feb. 1992).

> It is characteristic not only of the use of legal concepts, but also of many concepts in other disciplines and in ordinary life, that we may have adequate mastery of them for the purpose of their day-to-day use; and yet they may still require elucidation; for we are puzzled when we try to understand our own conceptual apparatus. We may know how to use these concepts, but we cannot *say* how or describe how we do this in ways which are intelligible to others and indeed to ourselves. We know, and yet do not fully understand. . . . This surely is the predicament which makes the philosophical elucidation of concepts necessary (Hart, 'Analytical Jurisprudence in Mid-Twentieth Century', p. 964).

> One would not expect a book on scientific method to do the work of science itself; and one must not expect to find [in an analytic study in ethics] any conclusions about what conduct is right or wrong. The purpose of an analytical study, whether of science or ethics, is always indirect. It hopes to send others to their tasks with clearer heads and less wasteful habits of investigation (Stevenson, *Ethics and Language*, p. 1).

A grand jury in Travis County, Texas, sitting in a seemingly ordinary case, returned a judgment in September 1992 that shocked the nation.[1] The county district attorney had sought to persuade the grand jury that a stranger, Joel Valdez, 27, had broken into Elizabeth Wilson's apartment and raped her at knife point. The prosecution's uncontested evidence showed that in the early hours of the morning of September 17, 1992, Ms. Wilson, a 25-year-old artist, returned home after a party and went to bed. Ms. Wilson was awakened at 3:00 a.m. by a noise. When she turned on the light, she was confronted by Valdez, who was approaching her with a knife. She fled to the bathroom, where she locked the door and was dialing 911 when Valdez broke down the door, knocked the phone from her hand, and, knife in hand, ordered her to take off his pants. Ms. Wilson, fearing that Valdez would stab her if she resisted and that he would infect her with HIV if she submitted, agreed to submit to sexual intercourse with Valdez if he put on a condom. Valdez put the condom on and had sexual intercourse with Wilson over the course of an hour until she fled naked from the apartment and sought help from a neighbor. At the close of the prosecution's case, the grand jury was instructed that under Texas law rape is a crime of sexual intercourse for which consent is a defense. As is customary everywhere, the grand jury deliberated in secret and returned a ruling without explanation. The grand jury's ruling was not to indict Valdez for rape. An unnamed 'participant' said later that several grand jurors believed that Ms. Wilson's willingness to submit to sexual intercourse in return for Valdez's wearing a condom constituted 'consent' on her part.[2]

The public reacted to the grand jury ruling with outrage. The prosecutor was stunned by the ruling and resolved to overturn it.[3] Elizabeth Wilson herself said, 'I was raped by a man and now I'm being raped by society'.[4] Women's rights groups joined Ms. Wilson in condemning the grand jury for a ruling that they regarded as morally and legally perverse. Ms. Wilson and her supporters may have been right to condemn the grand jury for being perverse because the grand jury may, indeed, have consisted of people with distorted moral and legal attitudes. Nevertheless, there is an alternative explanation for what the Travis County grand jury did. When lawful authorities like the Travis County grand jury reach problematic judgments that they do not explain, it is possible that, rather than being perverse, they are simply *confused*. They may consist of people of good faith who share the moral and legal views of the community and yet, because of conceptual fallacies in the way they reason about norms, they unwittingly render normative judgments that misrepresent their true moral and legal views.

There is no way to be certain whether the Travis County grand jury was conceptually confused rather than normatively perverse because the grand jury did not explain its ruling. Nevertheless, circumstantial evidence suggests that the former is the more likely possibility. The seven women and five men on the Travis County grand jury had no reason to be, or any history of being, perverse. They were drawn from the city of Austin, a city that prided itself on being politically progressive and socially enlightened, possessed a woman police chief and a woman city manager, and possessed one of the nation's most sophisticated networks for dealing with sexual assault. The district attorney, who was instrumental in selecting the grand jury, regarded the jurors as 'actually . . . a pretty good group'.[5] At the same time, the grand jurors had reason to be confused in their deliberations because of what they were deliberating about—namely, the nature of consent. These grand jurors may have unwittingly rendered a legal judgment that did not reflect their true legal views because of conceptual confusion about what it means to 'consent' to another's conduct.

To be sure, we all have a general sense of what consent means. To 'consent', in the words of the dictionary, is to 'voluntarily acquiesce in what another proposes or desires'.[6] We also generally understand that consent can refer to a change in moral and legal relationships that acquiescence can bring about—specifically, a change in the moral or legal rights that an actor, *A*, has vis-à-vis a subject, *S*, by virtue of *S*'s having acquiesced to the conduct *x* in which *A* engages.[a] Beyond that, however, we have only vague and conflicting notions of what we mean by consent.

---

[a] I shall use 'A' to refer to an actor who is accused of subjecting an alleged victim, 'S' to conduct that is criminal for an actor to impose upon S without her consent.

As H.L.A. Hart has said about concepts like consent, '[W]e may have adequate mastery of them for the purpose of their day-to-day use; and yet they still require elucidation; for we are puzzled when we try to understand our own conceptual apparatus. We may know how to *use* these concepts, but we cannot *say* how or describe how we do this in ways which are intelligible to others and indeed to ourselves'.[7] Like other concepts, consent is a mental category by which we organize our experiences of the world. Some concepts (*e.g.*, concepts of 'grams', 'meters', and 'liters') present no risk of confounding our normative judgments because they exist only to organize natural events. In contrast, concepts like 'freedom' and 'equality' and 'consent' have very different purposes: they operate in whole or in part to organize the way we reason and talk about norms and events of normative significance. Consequently, to the extent we are puzzled about how such concepts organize our thinking about norms and events, we run the risk of confusing ourselves normatively. We run the risk of failing to think and communicate clearly about normative values to which we are committed.

To illustrate a kind of normative confusion that is conceptual in nature, consider the disagreement among some advocates of rape reform about the relationship between 'consent', on the one hand, and 'force', on the other. Some reformers, such as Susan Estrich, argue that the best way to enhance the autonomy of women through rape reform is to base reform upon revitalized standards of consent.[8] In contrast, and just as emphatically, other reformers, such as Catharine MacKinnon, reject the use of consent and argue instead that rape reform ought to be based on prohibitions of force.[9] From the intensity of the dispute, one would infer that the scope of prohibited conduct turns significantly upon whether prohibitions are framed in terms of 'non-consent' or in terms of 'force'. In reality, the differences are rhetorical not substantive. There is no form of sexual conduct that MacKinnon would prohibit that is incapable of being proscribed in terms of non-consent; by the same token, there is no form of sexual conduct that Estrich would prohibit that is incapable of being proscribed in terminology of 'force'. The very real substantive differences between Estrich and MacKinnon are differences between competing ***conceptions*** of consent (and competing conceptions of force), rather than differences between consent and something other than consent. If their dispute suggests otherwise, it is because the conceptual apparatus of consent, which exists to facilitate understanding of interpersonal relationships, is itself poorly understood and, being poorly understood, creates a false impression of normative disagreement—just as it elsewhere creates a false impression of normative consensus.

This study is an effort to illuminate 'our conceptual apparatus' of consent in criminal law, not for the purpose of changing people's normative views but for the purpose of clarifying the way people think and converse about their respective normative views. Consent comes in two co-existing forms: it exists as a single and generic concept; and at the same time, it takes the form of more specific and sometimes conflicting conceptions. Generically, consent consists of all instances in which persons are found or deemed to acquiesce to, or choose for themselves, what other persons do to them. At the same time, however, consent can be reduced to one or another discrete conception of choice—discrete notions of what it is to acquiesce to something—each of which possesses its own conceptual boundaries and configurations. Consent derives conceptual power from this relationship between its generic and specific forms. The generic concept of consent gives 'consent' its scope, enabling it to range over and encompass every instance in which a person can be found or deemed to acquiesce to something, whether in actual fact, hypothetically, or constructively. The specific conceptions of consent, in turn, give 'consent' its particularity, identifying subsets of acquiescence and distinguishing them from one another. Unfortunately, the interplay between consent's generic and specific forms also creates confusion by causing people to confound one specific conception of acquiescence with another.

The key to thinking clearly about consent lies in understanding its various conceptions. At its core, consent consists of a basic conception—or 'core conception'—with respect to which other conceptions are derivative. Some derivative conceptions of consent (including several of the most commonplace and legally significant conceptions of consent) *incorporate* the core conception of consent in the way that nesting dolls incorporate smaller, inner dolls. Other derivative conceptions simply *make necessary reference* to the core conception without actually incorporating it. And still others constitute *fictions* of the core conception—either fictions of conceptions that themselves incorporate the core conception of consent, or fictions of conceptions that make reference to the core conception. Although each of these various conceptions differs from the others, together they constitute the totality of what it means to consent in criminal law.

A Core Conception of Consent: Factual Attitudinal Consent

The core conception of consent consists of a factual state of mind of acquiescence. By a 'state of mind' I mean a subjective attitude or feeling that one experiences internally on a first-person basis, as opposed to something one manifests externally to third persons. A state of mind of acquiescence, in turn, is a felt willingness to agree with—or to choose—what another person seeks or proposes. One uses consent in this sense, for example, when one says of a child *S*, '*S* pretended to be asleep when her grandmother leaned over and kissed her, but she was secretly consenting the entire while'. Clearly, in saying *S* 'secretly consented', one is using consent to refer to a welcoming state of mind on *S*'s part rather than to an expression of such a state of mind; otherwise, one would be contradicting oneself in describing the consent as secret.

The core conception of consent, as I have said, is also factual in nature. A 'factual' concept is one that organizes our experiences with natural events without constituting a normative judgment about people's ensuing moral or legal relationship to others. Grams and meters are factual concepts because they function to organize our empirical experiences of the world without embodying normative judgments about people's moral or legal rights. The core conception of consent is factual because it embraces an empirical experience on *S*'s part without itself constituting a moral or legal judgment about *S*'s relationship to others. Assume, for example, that a judge makes the following statement in the course of a bank-robbery trial:

> The defendant insists that the bank teller consented to give him the money by eagerly handing it to him. But the teller consented to hand over the money only when the defendant thrust a gun in her face. Consent that is extorted at the point of a gun is invalid as a defense to robbery. Therefore, the bank teller's consent no more authorized the defendant to take the bank's money than if the defendant had abruptly grabbed the money without the teller's consent.

Clearly, the judge is using consent in a factual sense; if she were using consent normatively, she would be contradicting herself in stating that the bank teller's consent had no effect on her or the bank's legal relationship to the defendant.

All remaining conceptions of consent are derivative of the core conception. To say they are derivative, however, is to say nothing of the frequency with which they are invoked or the normative significance they possess. They are derivative solely in respect of their *logical relationship* to the core conception of consent. They are derivative in that they incorporate, or refer to, or construct fictions, of the core concept.

Factual Expressive Consent

Consider the conception of consent as an *expression* rather than a state of mind. Just as people sometimes use consent to refer to a mental state or subjective attitude on *S*'s part (i.e., 'attitudinal' consent), they sometimes use consent to refer to something *S* objectively does—namely, to words or conduct by which *S* expresses her choices to others ('expressive' consent). Thus, when we say '*S* may have consented, but she did not mean to', we are using consent to refer to a choice *S* objectively manifested, rather than a choice she subjectively experienced; if we were using consent to refer to a subjective experience on *S*'s part, we would be contradicting ourselves in contrasting her consent with what she subjectively felt. Nevertheless, expressive consent is conceptually derivative of attitudinal consent because the former makes necessary *reference* to the latter: expressions of consent are expressions *of* something, namely, of subjective attitudes of acquiescence, whether genuine or not.[10] A person may express a mental state that she does not subjectively feel (just as a person may possess subjective attitudes that she does not express). But a person cannot express acquiescence without making reference to her subjective attitudes because expressions of acquiescence are expressions of subjective attitudes, whether genuine or not.

Legal Consent

The two aforementioned conceptions of consent are both factual in nature. The core conception is factual, as we have seen, because it consists of an empirical attitude on *S*'s part that, in itself, represents no necessary change in *S*'s legal relationships to others. Similarly, expressive consent can also be factual because it can consist of an expression of factual acquiescence that, in itself, constitutes no necessary change in *S*'s legal relationships to others. In contrast, some conceptions of consent are inherently legal in nature. 'Legal' concepts and conceptions (as I shall define them) are ones that constitute, or embody, legal judgments about people's relationship to others. Thus, 'rights' and 'duties', as used in law, are legal concepts because they function solely to constitute legal judgments about people's relationships to one another. Similarly, while the core conception of consent is factual (much like the factual concepts of 'grams' and 'meters'), some conceptions of consent are legal in nature (much like legal concepts of 'rights' and 'duties'). Assume, for example, that a judge makes the following statement in the course of a trial for theft:

> The defendant is charged with the criminal offense of theft, namely, taking a bank's money without its consent. The defendant emphasizes in his defense that the bank teller acquiesced to his taking the money by eagerly handing it over on the basis of the papers he presented. However, the papers that the defendant presented were fraudulent. Acquiescence that is based upon fraud is not 'consent' within the meaning of the law of theft and, hence, is not a defense to theft.

Clearly, the judge is using 'consent' in a legal rather than a factual sense because she invokes a conception of consent that derives its content from norms of criminal law that, when present, change a defendant's legal relationship to a bank from that of a thief to a lawful transferee.

Prescriptive Consent

Legal conceptions of consent, in turn, fall into two subsets that I shall call 'prescriptive' and 'imputed'. Prescriptive conceptions of consent incorporate within themselves the elements of factual consent—much in the way that a larger nesting doll incorporates a smaller doll. To illustrate prescriptive consent, imagine that the judge in the embezzlement trial expands upon her prior statement in the following way:

> The defendant is charged with taking the bank's money without its consent. He emphasizes in his defense that the bank teller not only subjectively acquiesced to his taking the money, but objectively expressed her acquiescence as well. But acquiescence is 'consent' for purposes of the criminal law only if it consists of an attitude or expression of acquiescence that is competent, informed, and free. Because the defendant misled the bank teller about the withdrawal, her acquiescence was not

> informed. Not being informed, her acquiescence does not amount to 'consent' within the meaning of the law and, hence, is not a defense.

As before, the 'consent' to which the judge refers is legal rather than factual, because it is a legal conception that embodies a judgment in law about *S*'s legal relationship to *A*, namely, that *S* is adjudged not to have been a victim of theft by *A*. In addition, however, the consent to which the judge refers is an instance of a particular subset of legal consent: it is an instance of legal consent that incorporates elements of factual consent—namely, an attitude or expression of factual acquiescence on *S*'s part. Thus, just as factual consent *wholly* consists of either an attitude of factual acquiescence or an expression of factual acquiescence, so, too, prescriptive consent consists *partly* of such attitudes or expressions. Thus, prescriptive *attitudinal* consent by *S* vis-à-vis *A* consists of an attitude of factual acquiescence by *S* under conditions of a certain kind—namely, such conditions of competence, knowledge, freedom, and motivation to acquiesce as are deemed necessary to change *S*'s legal relationship to *A*. Similarly, prescriptive *expressive* consent on *S*'s part consists of an empirical expression of acquiescence by *S* in the context of such apparent competence, knowledge, freedom, and motivation to acquiesce as are deemed necessary to give the expression legal effect. In either event, whether it takes the form of an attitude or expression, prescriptive consent incorporates within itself the elements of one or the other of the two factual conceptions of consent previously discussed.

Imputed Consent

In contrast to prescriptive consent, 'imputed consent' is a subset of legal consent that does *not* achieve legal effect by incorporating elements of factual consent. Rather, imputed consent consists of fictions of prescriptive consent that are attributed to *S* without *S*'s otherwise experiencing or expressing such factual consent. Consider, for example, how some jurisdictions conceptualize the criminal responsibility of athletes for injuries that they inflict upon their opponents in the course of athletic play. Every jurisdiction makes it a criminal offense to inflict physical injury on persons without their legal consent. Some jurisdictions, however, take the position that, regardless of what athletes in organized competitions may actually be thinking or saying, they are deemed in law to consent legally to certain classes of physical injury inflicted upon them in the course of play, even if inflicted in flagrant violation of rules of the game. Thus, Canadian courts have held that amateur ice hockey players who participate in industrial league play in which body-checking is prohibited are nonetheless deemed to legally consent to a certain amount of body-checking, provided it is not excessive.[11] In so holding, however, the Canadian courts do not mean that amateur hockey players take to the ice actually thinking or saying, 'Yes, I know I am about to be body-checked in violation of the rules, and that's fine with me.' Rather, the Canadian courts attribute to amateur hockey players the fiction that they prescriptively consent to body-checking, a fiction based either upon the willingness of amateur hockey players to run the *risk* of body-checking or upon their mere willingness to engage in amateur hockey itself. The courts treat hockey players *as if* they had prescriptively consented to body-checking—as if they had factually acquiesced in mind or expression to a certain amount of prohibited body-checking under such conditions as suffice to give their acquiescence legal effect—in order to mimic the rights and duties that would have existed if the players had, indeed, prescriptively consented to it. To be sure, because imputed consent is a legal fiction, courts and legislatures could achieve the results that the fiction achieves without making reference to consent. Thus, the Canadian courts could simply rule that the law which makes it an offense to inflict physical injuries on a person without his consent does not apply to amateur hockey players in the course of body-checking. Instead, the Canadian courts prefer, first, to treat the law against non-consensual battery as applicable to hockey players and, then, to construct the fiction that amateur hockey players factually acquiesce in mind or expression to prohibited body-checking. The fact that imputed consent is an avoidable fiction, however, does not mean that it lacks conceptual importance. It plays a surprisingly significant role in matters of legal consent, as we shall see.

'Hypothetical consent' is another variety of imputed consent. Like the consent that Canada attributes to amateur hockey players, hypothetical consent is a fiction of prescriptive consent. Yet in contrast to varieties of imputed consent that operate without regard to *S*'s felt and expressed wishes, hypothetical consent is predicated on what is known about *S*'s personal values. Consider, for example, the way some courts conceptualize the so-called right to refuse treatment. Every jurisdiction in the United States adheres to the view that persons who find themselves in a permanently vegetative state (PVS) have a right to the removal of unwanted life support, provided that they validly acquiesce to its removal. Jurisdictions differ, however, with respect to the kinds of consent which they legally require. Some jurisdictions take the position that persons in PVS have no right to the withdrawal of life support unless they prescriptively consent beforehand either by executing a 'living will' or by leaving other 'clear . . . convincing [and] inherently reliable evidence' that that is what they actually 'wish'.[12] Yet other jurisdictions take the view that, even in the absence of prescriptive consent, a subject *S* in PVS will be deemed to legally consent to the withdrawal of life support if, hypothetically, *S* *would* have prescriptively consented—that is, if, based upon everything that surrogate decisionmakers know about *S*'s personal values, withdrawal appears to be what *S* personally would have wished for herself under the circumstances.[13]

These multiplicitous conceptions of consent do not confuse participants who are fully conscious of them. Unfortunately, many of us tend to talk about consent without realizing that we mean different things by it. Sometimes we mean to refer to a factual state of mind; at other times, an expression of a factual state of mind; at still other times, a 'constructed' state of mind or expression. Sometimes we mean to describe an event without legally evaluating it; at other times, we mean to describe an event *and* legally evaluate it; at still other times, we mean to construct or hypothesize an event in order to convey a legal evaluation. What constitutes consent by one measure may fail by another. As a consequence, we not only run the risk of misleading one another, we also risk confusing ourselves.

With that in mind, let us revisit the *Valdez* case. The issues of consent are conceptually more complex in *Valdez* than in typical stranger rape cases. Stranger rape typically present either no legal issues at all regarding the nature of consent or, at least, none of any complexity. Consider, for example, the sensational stranger rape of the Central Park jogger in 1989. The Central Park assault was too sudden and frightful, too violent and brutal, for the victim to consent in any form. The 28-year-old victim was jogging alone in Central Park at night when she was suddenly and viciously attacked by at least one and perhaps more assailants. She was struck by hand and with a metal pipe wrapped in tape, fracturing her skull and cutting and bruising her arms, legs, and chest. Tearing off her clothes, her assailant dragged her 200 feet to the bottom of a ravine where he held her down and had sexual intercourse with her. She appears to have fought back as best she could because when, after losing three-quarters of the blood in her body, she was found in a coma, she was still reflexively flailing at her assailant. No one, much less the victim herself, hazarded to suggest that she consented in any form, whether factual, legal, attitudinal, expressive, constructive, or hypothetical.[14]

Valdez differs from the Central Park case because there is an important sense in which Elizabeth Wilson *did* consent to sexual intercourse with Joel Valdez. She consented to sexual intercourse with Joel Valdez in the same sense that consent is frequently used in statutory definitions of rape. Consider, for example, the way the Delaware legislature defines 'consent' for purposes of the law of rape. Delaware states: '[C]onsent of the victim does not constitute a defense if . . . [i]t is induced by force, duress, or deception'.[15] Obviously, when Delaware refers to consent that is induced by 'force, duress, or deception', Delaware is not using 'consent' prescriptively to refer to instances of acquiescence that constitute a defense. Rather, it is using consent in a factual sense to include instances in which victims are forced to acquiesce at the point of a gun or knife. It is possible, therefore, that the Travis County grand jurors understood consent in that same way. If so, they were right to refuse to indict Valdez because Elizabeth Wilson did factually consent to sexual intercourse with Valdez. She consciously chose to engage in sexual intercourse with Valdez in the sense that she preferred sexual intercourse to the risks of death, injury, and disease she feared she would otherwise face.

As unsettling as it is, the Travis County grand jurors may have believed in good faith that they were doing what they were charged to do. That is, the jurors may well have made what Gilbert Ryle calls a 'category mistake'[16]—the mistake, in their case, of taking the term consent, which the Texas judge intended them to understand *legally*, and interpreting it *factually*. Given the latter interpretation of consent, it was natural for the jurors to conclude that, in so far as Ms. Wilson agreed to submit to sexual intercourse in turn for Valdez's wearing a condom, she 'consented' to the intercourse. If that is what the grand jurors did, their confusion is unusual in one respect and, yet, not so unusual in another. What is unusual is the degree to which their confusion led them astray. Typically, grand jurors realize that, because they are being instructed to exercise legal authority, *e.g.*, to decide whether Joel Valdez should stand trial for raping Ms. Wilson, they cannot be expected to interpret consent factually. What is not so unusual is *that* the Travis County grand jurors were confused. The field of consent is rife with categories, and, hence, rife with possibilities for category mistakes, particularly in cases in which mistakes are less egregious than those in Travis County and, therefore, less likely to alert persons of good faith to the possibility of confusion.

I come to this analysis of consent in somewhat of a dilemma. I believe that a proper analysis ought to clarify the logic of consent in all areas in which it operates—in moral and political discourse as well as in law, and, in law, in contracts, torts, and procedure as well as in criminal law. For a time, I considered trying to follow Alan Wertheimer's model study of coercion by giving equal attention to all areas in which consent operates.[17] My training, however, is in law rather than moral philosophy; and in law it is primarily in substantive criminal law rather than torts, contracts, or procedure. Consent differs considerably across these areas, partly because criminal law is uniquely a condemnatory institution, and partly because contracts are predicated on something that has no counterpart elsewhere, namely, promise-making. For those reasons I have chosen to focus on the concept of consent exclusively within substantive criminal law and, within it, largely (though not exclusively) on the area in which consent is most frequently and fervently contested, *viz.*, the law of rape.[18] Legal consent in criminal law is consent by a subject *S* to conduct *x* on the part of an actor *A* that constitutes either a complete or a partial criminal defense for *A* to subjecting *S* to *x*. The purpose of this study is to clarify defenses of consent in criminal law by illuminating the various forms they can take, and by distinguishing consent that is a defense to criminal liability from consent that is not.

I start in Part I with factual consent because I believe understanding consent in its non-normative forms helps clarify what *more* and (in some cases) what *else* is required to constitute consent in its legal forms. I address two conceptions of factual consent in Part I: a core conception of consent as a mental state of factual acquiescence; and a derivative conception of consent as a communication of factual acquiescence. Each is factual in nature because each consists of empirical acquiescence by *S* in *A*'s conduct, *x*, without regard to the presence or absence of such further considerations as are required in law for *S*'s acquiescence to *x* to constitute a complete or partial criminal defense for *A*. Part II addresses several conceptions of legal consent, that is, several varieties of consent by *S* to *A*'s conduct x that constitute a criminal defense for *A* to subjecting *S* to *x*. They include legal consent as a state of mind, legal consent as an expression of a mental state, prospective and retrospective forms of each, and fictions of each. Part III broadens the framework beyond these basic conceptions of consent by discussing various ways in which confusions about the conceptual apparatus of consent can lead to normative confusion, especially in the area of sexual assault.

Notes

1. *Houston Chronicle*, 10 Oct. 1992, p. 30; *New York Times*, 25 Oct. 1992, p. 18.
2. *New York Times*, 25 Oct. 1992, p. 18.
3. The prosecutor later brought the same charges to another grand jury that did indict Valdez, producing a trial in which he was convicted. *Detroit Free Press*, 28 Oct. 1992, p. 3A.
4. *Detroit Free Press*, 10 October 1992, p. 5A.
5. *New York Times*, 25 Oct. 1992, p. 18.
6. *Oxford English Dictionary*, 1989, vol. 3, pp. 760-61.
7. Hart, 'Analytical Jurisprudence in Mid-Twentieth Century', p. 964.
8. Estrich argues in favor of defining rape in terms of 'non-consent' rather than in terms of 'force'. Estrich, 'Rape', pp. 1095-96, 1132-33; Estrich, *Real Rape*, p. 63. For commentators who take similar positions, *see* Schulhofer, *Unwanted Sex*, pp. 11, 32-33; Bogart, 'Commodification and Phenomenology: Evading Consent in Theory Regarding Rape', p. 258; Henderson, 'Rape and Responsibility', p. 158.
9. MacKinnon, 'Feminism, Marxism, Method and the State', pp. 650, 655; MacKinnon, *Toward A Feminist Theory of the State*, p. 245 (arguing that 'rape should be defined as sex by compulsion, of which physical force is one form'). For commentators who take similar positions, *see* West, 'Legitimating the Illegitimate', p.1459; Note, 'Focusing on the Offender's Forceful Conduct', pp. 399-401; and commentators cited in Sherwin, 'Infelicitous Sex', p. 214 n. 17.
10. Harrison, 'Rape', p. 52:

    What principally distinguishes rape from normal sexual activity is the consent of the raped woman. Of course, in law, the intention of the man is also very important. However, what the man's intention is, and hence what action the man takes himself to be undertaking, depends upon what he understands the intention of the woman to be. So the central feature here again is what the woman is intending to do, even if reflected through the man's perception of this intention rather than what the intention actually is.
11. Regina v. Leclerc, (1991) 67 CCC (3d) 563, relying upon Regina v. Cey, (1989) 48 CCC (3d) 480. *See* McCutcheon, 'Sports Violence, Consent, and the Criminal Law'.
12. *See* Cruzan v. McCanse, 760 S. 2d 408, 425-26 (Missouri, 1988), *affirmed sub nom*, Cruzan v. Director, Missouri Department of Health, 497 U. S. 261 (1989).
13. *See* In re Nancy Ellen Jobes, 108 N. J. 394, 413-14, 529 A. 2d 434, 444 (1987) (citations and footnotes omitted).
14. The best accounts of the Central Park jogging cases are law-reporter Sullivan's *Unequal Verdicts*, and Didion's essay, 'Sentimental Journeys'. Benedict, in her critical account of how the press covers rape stories, 'The Jogger and the Wolfpack', devotes an important chapter to the case. Several of the teenage suspects, having recanted their confessions, argued at trial that it was the victim's boyfriend who had battered her and left her for dead in the park. However, none of them suggested that she consented to being battered.
15. Delaware Code tit. 11, §§ 453, 772 (2001).
16. Gilbert Ryle discusses 'categories', and 'category mistakes', in *The Concept of Mind*, pp. 18-24.
17. Wertheimer, *Coercion*.

18. I shall use the term 'rape' to refer to what jurisdictions variously denominate 'rape', 'sexual assault', 'sexual battery', 'sexual abuse', 'sexual intercourse without consent', 'criminal sexual penetration', 'gross sexual imposition', and 'criminal sexual conduct'. For discussion of the various terms for denominating sexual offenses, *see* Remick, 'Read Her Lips', p. 1109 n. 22 (citing Patricia Searles and Ronald J. Berger, 'The Current Status of Rape Reform Legislation', pp. 25, 31).

PART I
FACTUAL CONSENT

Introduction

Consent matters because of the normative work it does. Consent possesses what Heidi Hurd calls 'moral magic'.[1] Its moral magic—as well as its legal magic—consists of its power to change moral and legal relationships between persons who engage in consent and persons to whom the consent is directed. In criminal law, consent can transform the most horrific crimes into noncrimes, turning 'rape' into sexual intercourse, 'maiming' into therapeutic surgery, 'kidnapping' into vacation, 'trespass' into hospitality, and 'theft' into gift-giving.[2] Even when it does not transform crimes into noncrimes, consent can mitigate the severity of crimes by reducing them from aggravated offenses to nonaggravated offenses, as it does, for example, in reducing murder to assisted suicide, and rape to adultery or fornication in jurisdictions that continue to criminalize the latter.

Yet not every conception of consent is legally transformative in the aforementioned way. Only certain conceptions of consent—only conceptions of legal consent—operate to transform crimes into non-crimes and aggravated offenses into lesser offenses. 'Legal consent', as I define it, is consent by a subject, *S*, to conduct, *x*, on the part of an actor, *A*, that either exonerates *A* of criminal responsibility for *x* or mitigates *A*'s responsibility for *x* by fulfilling or signaling the fulfillment[a] of whatever interests on *S*'s part the jurisdiction deems *S* to possess with respect to *x*. The law of rape uses 'consent' in a legal sense, for example, when it defines the offense as 'sexual intercourse without consent'.[3] Courts use consent legally when they distinguish it from mere 'acquiescence' or 'submission'.[4] Susan Estrich uses consent legally when she states that force and coercion '*negate*' consent; John Harman uses consent legally when he emphasizes that the law must specify what '*counts*' as consent; Leigh Bienen uses consent legally when she writes of rape cases in which 'force, injury, and the relationship of the parties' establish that 'there was *no consent*'.[5]

Legal consent, as we shall see in Part II, comes in the form of three distinct conceptions: (1) a certain *mental state* of acquiescence by *S* to *A*'s conduct; (2) a certain *expression* by *S* of such a mental state on her part; and (3) a *legal fiction* of one or the other (or both) of the two prior conceptions of legal consent. Significantly, the first two conceptions of legal consent (of which the third in turn is a legal fiction) both consist in part of more fundamental conceptions of consent that are non-normative in nature. These more fundamental conceptions of consent are non-normative in that, although they constitute *component parts* of what

[a] Chapter 4 examines whether consent operates by actually protecting *S*'s interests or merely signaling their protection.

together constitutes complete or partial defenses to criminal responsibility, they do not alone suffice to constitute such defenses.

To illustrate the relationship between legal conceptions of consent, on the one hand, and the simpler, non-normative conceptions of consent they incorporate, consider the 1969 Canadian statute that decriminalized the crime of sodomy among consenting adults:

> (1) The offense of sodomy does not apply to any act committed in private between . . . any two persons, each of whom is 21 years or more of age, both of whom consent [$consent_{legal}$] to the commission of the act.
>
> (2) For purposes of subsection (1) . . . a person shall be deemed not to consent [$consent_{legal}$] to the commission of the act if the consent [$consent_{factual}$] is extorted by force, threats or fear of bodily harm or is obtained by false and fraudulent misrepresentation as to the nature and quality of the act.[6]

The word 'consent' appears in the Canadian statute three times. However, the first two usages of consent, *i.e.*, '$consent_{legal}$', differ significantly from the third, '$consent_{factual}$'; and I have marked them accordingly. $Consent_{legal}$ is legal in nature, because it is consent by adults that suffices under Canadian law to relieve their sexual partners of criminal responsibility for sodomy. Yet $consent_{legal}$ differs significantly from $consent_{factual,}$ because $consent_{legal}$ is defined in *terms* of $consent_{factual}$: $consent_{legal}$ is defined as consisting of some but not all instances of $consent_{factual}$, namely, only such instances of $consent_{factual}$ that are not the product of 'force', 'fear', or 'fraud' within the meaning of Canadian law. $Consent_{factual}$ thus refers to a kind of consent that is *necessary* to legal consent but that, because it may include events that do not amount to legal consent (*i.e.*, instances of $consent_{factual}$ induced by force, fear or fraud), is not *sufficient* to constitute legal consent. Therefore, in contrast to $consent_{legal}$, the usage of 'consent' in $consent_{factual}$ is non-normative because it is consent that does not itself suffice to constitute a complete or partial defense to criminal responsibility under the Canadian statute.

Given their differences, it is important to be able to distinguish non-normative conceptions of consent from legal conceptions of consent. The term I shall use for non-normative conceptions of consent is 'factual'. With respect to conduct *x* with which an actor, *A*, is criminally charged, a subject, *S*, 'factually consents' to *x* when her acquiescence to *x*—whether in mind or expression—does not necessarily constitute a complete or partial criminal defense to *A* for subjecting *S* to *x*. Unfortunately, because 'factual' is a term that is used differently by different people, some of whom claim more for it than I do here, I should emphasize what I do *not* mean. By 'factual consent' I do not mean consent that is uninfluenced by culture, context, market pressures, gender relations, socialization, or social institutions. Nor do I mean consent that is emptied of all value judgments, or consent that serves no human ends, or consent that possesses no legal significance. On the contrary, 'factual consent', as I use it, is invariably a product of social context, can be highly value-laden, and is explicitly a subject of criminal law. By

S's 'factual consent' to *A*'s conduct *x*, I refer to mental states of acquiescence by *S* in *x*, or objective expressions by *S* of such mental states, that—however much they may be influenced by social context, and however value-laden they may be—are not themselves complete or partial defenses to *A* for subjecting *S* to *x*.

To illustrate what I do, and do not, mean by factual consent, consider the relationship in *Regina v. Carmen M.*[7] between an anonymous 13-year-old Ontario girl, whom I shall call 'Mary', and a 23-year-old young man, Carmen M. Mary was eleven years-old in 1986 and living with her aunt when Carmen M., then 21-years-old, began dating Mary's aunt. Within two years, when Mary was 13, she became infatuated with Carmen M. and for the next five years engaged in what the Ontario court called 'consensual acts of vaginal intercourse, anal intercourse, and oral intercourse'. Mary regarded Carmen M. as her boyfriend, even after he became engaged to marry her aunt. It was not until Mary was 18 and Carmen M. actually married her aunt that (in the court's words) Mary 'realized' that Carmen's 'statements of love were lies'. Mary complained to the authorities; and Carmen was arrested and convicted of having sexual intercourse with Mary during the several months five years earlier when Mary was under the statutory age of 14.

All Anglo-American jurisdictions like Canada make it an offense for an adult to have sexual intercourse with girls under certain ages, but they conceptualize the prohibition in different ways. Some jurisdictions follow the *Model Penal Code* and, without ever mentioning consent, simply state that it is an offense for an adult to have sexual intercourse with an underage girl.[8] Other jurisdictions, like New York, invoke the language of consent by first declaring it to be sexual assault for a person to have sexual intercourse with a female without her consent and, then, defining sexual intercourse with an underage female to be without her consent:

> ***N.Y. Penal Code Section 130.20:*** A person is guilty of sexual misconduct when . . . being a male, he engages in sexual intercourse with a female without her consent [$\text{consent}_{\text{legal}}$]. . . .[9]

> ***N.Y. Penal Code Section 130.05:*** Lack of consent [$\text{consent}_{\text{legal}}$] results from . . . (b) Incapacity to consent [$\text{consent}_{\text{legal}}$]. A person is deemed incapable of consent [$\text{consent}_{\text{legal}}$] when he is . . . less than 17-years-old.[10]

In contrast, Canada achieves the same prohibition in a different way. Canada begins as New York does by defining it to be sexual assault for a person to have sexual intercourse with another person without the latter's consent. Yet rather than declaring sexual intercourse with underage persons to be *without* their consent, Canada takes the converse position that all sexual intercourse that is 'voluntarily agreed' to—including by underage persons—is *with* consent for purposes of sexual assault. Then, having declared voluntarily-agreed-to sexual intercourse by underage persons to be *with* their consent, Canada goes on to declare that it is 'no defense' to sexual assault on an underage person that the latter 'consented' to the sexual intercourse:

> ***Assault.*** A person commits an assault when, without the consent [$consent_{legal}$] of another person, he applies force intentionally to that other person, directly or indirectly. This section applies to all forms of assault, including sexual assault [section 271], sexual assault with a weapon [section 272], . . . and aggravated sexual assault [section 273].
>
> ***Meaning of 'consent'.*** 'Consent' [$consent_{legal}$] means, for the purposes of sections 271, 272 and 273, the voluntary agreement of the complainant to engage in the sexual activity in question.
>
> ***Consent no defense.*** Where an accused is charged with an offence under . . . section 271, 272, or 273 in respect of a complainant under the age of 14 years, it is not a defense that the complainant consented [$consent_{factual}$] to the activity that forms the subject-matter of the charge.[11]

Thus, in contrast to the *Model Penal Code* which makes it an offense to have sexual intercourse with underage girls without mentioning consent, New York and Canada both do so by invoking the language of 'consent;' and they invoke consent in contrary senses. New York uses consent legally, that is, it uses consent to refer to acquiescence that when present constitutes a complete defense to the crime of sexual assault and, hence, it declares that sexual intercourse with underage girls is 'without' their consent. In contrast, Canada uses consent in two distinct ways. In defining the offense of sexual assault with respect to all persons *other* than those who are underage, Canada uses consent in a legal sense to refer to acquiescence by such persons that occurs under conditions of competence, knowledge, freedom, and motivation that suffice to protect the interests that Canada deems them to possess with respect to the offense of sexual assault and that, therefore, exonerate their partners of sexual assault. Yet in stating it to be an offense to have sexual assault with an underage person *with* her consent, Canada uses 'consent' factually because Canada uses it to refer to a mental state or expression of acquiescence on an underage victim's part that does *not* occur under conditions of competence, knowledge, freedom and motivation sufficient to fulfil her legal interests regarding sexual intercourse—and, hence, does not possess the legal 'magic' to exculpate her sexual partner of criminal assault. For, if it possessed such magic, the Canadian court would acquit defendants like Carmen M. who have sexual intercourse with underage girls.

Except for their ages, the mental state or expression that constitutes factual consent to sexual intercourse on the part of, say, a 13-year-old girl may be identical to the mental state and/or expression that constitutes legal consent on the part of, say, an 18-year-old girl, namely, 'voluntary agreement to engage in the sexual activity in question'. Yet, because two such girls differ in age, they differ precisely in their legal competence under Canadian law to assess their interests regarding sexual intercourse and, hence, in their legal competence to exonerate their sexual partners of sexual assault. Canada would say that both girls 'consented'. But because Canada regards only the 18-year-old girl's consent as sufficient in itself to protect her interests regarding sexual intercourse, only the 18-year-old girl's 'consent' is legal consent. And because only the 18-year-old girl's consent is legal, the 13-year-old girl's 'consent' is factual consent.

With respect to 13-year-old Mary and her adult lover, the Canadian court described Mary's intercourse with Carmen M. as 'consensual', because it adjudged Mary to have 'voluntarily agreed' to have sexual intercourse with Carmen M. In our terminology, Mary's consent was factual because it consisted of a mental state and/or expression by Mary of acquiescence to sexual intercourse that, though genuine, fell short of constituting a complete or partial defense to Carmen M's crime of sexual assault. Calling it 'factual consent', however, does nothing to deny either the complex social forces that influenced Mary or the value judgments inherent in its constituting consent under Canadian law. Mary's acquiescence was surely a product in part of her socialization, the social meaning of her age difference with Carmen M., her perception of gender roles, her socially-constructed relationship to her aunt, and her understanding of 'love'. Her acquiescence was also heavily value-laden, considering that, had Mary been a few months older when Carmen M. seduced her, her age would have sufficed under Canadian law to exonerate him of criminal assault. Yet her acquiescence nevertheless constituted factual consent because it consisted of subjective and/or expressive acquiescence on her part to sexual intercourse with Carmen M. that, given her age, did not suffice to protect the interests that Canada deemed her to possess with respect to sexual intercourse and hence did not negate or mitigate Carmen M.'s criminal responsibility for seducing her.

We shall see in Chapter 3 that the conditions of competence, knowledge, freedom and motivation that jurisdictions deem necessary to transmute *S*'s factual consent into legal consent will differ depending upon the offense at issue. Consequently, a given instance of acquiescence to *x* may occur under conditions that suffice to render it a defense for purposes of one offense and, yet, fail to render it a defense for purposes of another statute. To avoid confusion, therefore, I shall treat the statutory offense with which an actor *A* is *charged* as the measure of whether *S*'s acquiescence is a defense (and, hence, legal) or not a defense (and, hence, factual). Thus, for purposes of this discussion, a given instance of acquiescence by *S* constitutes legal consent if it completely or partially negates *A*'s criminal responsibility for the statutory offense with which he is charged; otherwise it constitutes factual consent.

To illustrate the aforementioned standard, consider two jurisdictions, 'Opala' and 'Rubia', that both make it to be an offense for *A* to subject an underage girl to sexual intercourse, but use different statutory schemes to do so:

> ***OPALA*[12] *Section 100.*** Rape: It is a felony to have sexual intercourse with a woman without her consent. Sexual intercourse with a woman is 'without her consent' for purposes of this section if the woman is induced to submit to it by threats of violence or fraud.

> ***OPALA Section 105.*** Sex With A Minor. It is a felony to have sexual intercourse with a woman without her consent. Sexual intercourse with a woman is 'without her consent' for purposes of this section if the woman is underage at the time.

> ***RUBIA***[13] ***Section 200.*** Rape: It is a felony to have sexual intercourse with a woman without her consent. Sexual intercourse with a woman is 'without her consent' for purposes of this section if the woman either is induced to submit to it by threats of violence or fraud or is underage at the time.

Suppose now that two actors, A_1 and A_2, have sexual intercourse with their respective underage girlfriends, S_1 and S_2, in Opala and Rubia, respectively. Suppose further that the evidence shows that S_1 and S_2 both eagerly engaged in the sexual intercourse with their boyfriends without either of them having been threatened or defrauded in any way. Suppose finally that Opala charges A_1 with Section 100 'Rape' (and *not* with Section 105 'Sex with a Minor'), while Rubia charges A_2 with Section 200 'Rape'. In that event, we could say that, while both girls 'consented' to sexual intercourse with their boyfriends, S_1's consent was legal because, not having been threatened or defrauded, S_1 consented under conditions that sufficed to constitute a defense to the particular offense with which Opala charged the accused, A_1 (*i.e.*, *'Rape'* under section 100). In contrast, S_2 only factually consented because, being underage, S_2 failed to consent under conditions that sufficed to constitute a defense to the particular offense of 'Rape' under section 200 with which Rubia charged the accused, A_2.

The purpose of Part I is to identify the minimal elements that are invariably present when persons are referred to as factually 'consenting' to certain conduct, *x*. Specifically, it is to identify the minimal elements of the subjective mental states of acquiescence to *x* (Chapter 1) and the objective expressions of acquiescence to *x* (Chapter 2) that, though insufficient in themselves to constitute complete or partial defenses to criminal responsibility for *x*, are, nonetheless, components of two of the three respective conceptions of legal consent that do constitute such defenses (as well as being fictional components of the third conception of legal consent).

Now it might be thought that I could simplify my statement of purpose as being this: to identify the minimal elements that are necessarily present when lawmakers refer to a person's consent to *x* as being 'void', 'unlawful', 'invalid', 'ineffective', 'fraudulent', 'coerced', 'involuntary', 'vitiated' or otherwise legally deficient as a criminal defense to *x*.[14] For when lawmakers make such references to consent, they are, indeed, referring to mental states of acquiescence to *x* or expressions thereof that fall short of constituting complete or partial defenses to *x*. Nevertheless, to state the purpose in that way is misleading because it falsely suggests that 'consent' is used factually only in the event that it refers to acquiescence that occurs under conditions that are insufficient to render it a defense. In reality, 'consent' is also used factually when it is conjoined with adjectives that signify that acquiescence occurs under conditions that, combined with it, *suffice* to render it a defense. Thus, consent is used factually in phrases such as 'valid consent', 'meaningful consent', 'lawful consent', 'effective consent', 'excusing consent', 'consent in law', 'informed consent', 'free consent', 'voluntary consent', 'real consent', 'genuine consent', and 'true consent'.[15] The term 'consent' in those phrases is factual because if the 'consent' alone sufficed to constitute a defense, the accompanying adjectives (*e.g.*, 'valid', 'meaningful', 'lawful') would be superfluous. To be sure, *as phrases*, 'valid consent, 'lawful consent', etc., are legal in nature because, as phrases, they refer to mental states or expressions of acquiescence that occur under conditions that suffice to constitute complete or partial defenses to crime. But the constituent word 'consent' in each phrase occurs factually; because if consent were being used in a legal sense, the phrases 'valid consent', 'lawful consent', etc., would be redundant.

Alternatively, it might be thought that the purpose of this Part is to identify, not the minimal elements that are invariably present in instances of factual consent, but the single thing to which factual usages of consent always refer—or, perhaps, the two things depending upon whether consent is used to refer to a mental state of acquiescence or an expression thereof. But that is not so, because there is no single thing, nor two single things, that consent always means when it is used factually. Contrast, for example, what the Canadian court in *Carmen M.* meant in calling Mary's lovemaking 'consensual' with what the Missouri Supreme Court in *Davis v. Missouri* (1977)[16] meant in stating that Davis' victim 'consent[ed]' out of fear. The defendant in *Davis* was convicted of rape, based on testimony by a woman that she was dragged into the defendant's basement and beaten by two male acquaintances until she was willing to comply with their sexual demands. The woman consciously submitted to sexual intercourse, first with the two men and then, after they left, with the defendant who had entered the room in the midst of the beating, fearing throughout that if she did not submit she would be beaten further. The defendant argued at trial that because he did not personally beat the woman and because the woman submitted without resistance, she should be deemed to have 'consented' within the meaning of the law prohibiting sexual intercourse without consent. The court rejected the argument, ruling that a man who has sexual intercourse with a woman whom he knows is submitting for fear of physical violence is guilty of rape, even though he neither inflicts physical violence himself nor threatens her with it. The court stated: '*Consent* [consent$_{factual}$] to intercourse induced by fear is no *consent* [consent$_{legal}$]'.[17]

I have marked *Davis*' two references to consent as 'consent$_{factual}$' and 'consent$_{legal}$', respectively, to show that, although the *Davis* court uses the former factually, the *Davis* court means something quite different from what the Canadian court meant in describing Mary's lovemaking as 'consensual'. The consent to which the *Davis* court refers in speaking of 'consent to sexual intercourse induced by fear' is factual in nature; because it consists of a woman's acquiescence to sexual intercourse (whether in the form of a mental state of willed submission, or an expression of willed submission, or both) that is no defense to rape. In contrast, of course, the consent to which the *Davis* court refers in 'consent$_{legal}$' is legal in nature, because it consists of such acquiescence as changes a woman's legal relationship from that of a victim to a nonvictim of rape. It follows, therefore, that when the Canadian court in *Carmen M.* referred to Mary's lovemaking as 'consensual', and when the Missouri court referred to Davis' victim's 'consent to sexual intercourse induced by fear', both courts were using consent factually; for they were both using it to refer to acquiescence to sexual intercourse that itself constituted no defense to rape. Yet the two courts also meant different things by consent. The *Davis* court used 'consent$_{factual}$' to refer to a kind of acquiescence to sexual intercourse that it regarded as being compatible with unlawful force, because the *Davis* court recognized that such consent can be elicited by means of unlawful force. In contrast, the Canadian court used 'consensual'to refer to a kind of acquiescence to sexual intercourse on Mary's part that, though it was compatible with Mary's being underage, was not compatible with unlawful force, because Canada defines consent to consist of 'voluntary agreement' of a kind that, had Mary been of age, would have constituted legal consent. Our task, therefore, is not to identify the single thing that the *Davis* and *Carmen M.* courts both meant when they used 'consent' factually (for they meant different things by it), but, rather, to identify the minimal elements that both usages share in common.

The purpose of Part I is to examine the minimal elements that are present when consent is stripped of its legal connotations and is used to describe instances of empirical acquiescence, whether in the form of subjective mental states of acquiescence or objective expressions of acquiescence, without connoting that they occur under conditions sufficient to constitute criminal defenses. I shall discuss two factual conceptions of consent: a core conception of consent as a subjective mental state of acquiescence in Chapter 1; and a derivative conception of consent as an expression of such mental acquiescence in Chapter 2—derivative in that what expressive consent *expresses* is that the consenting party possesses a mental state of acquiescence.

Notes

1. Hurd, 'The Moral Magic of Consent'.
2. Consent always transforms what would otherwise be the crime of rape into a noncrime, but it does not necessarily transform it into the blessing of lovemaking, because what the criminal law regards as *tolerable* sexual intercourse may fall far short of what women regard as *fulfilling* sexual intercourse. *See* West, 'A Comment on Consent, Sex, and Rape', pp. 249-50.
3. *See, e.g.*, Alaska Statutes § 11.41.410(a) (2000)('An offender commits the crime of sexual assault in the first degree if . . . the offender engages in sexual penetration with another person without consent of that person').
4. *See, e.g.*, New Jersey v. Harris, 70 N.J. Super. 9, 16, 174 A.2d 645, 648-49 (1961) ('The fact that a victim finally submits does not necessarily imply that she consented. Submission to a compelling force, or as a result of being put in fear, is not consent'); Fla. Stat. § 794.011(1) (2000) ('As used in this chapter . . . "Consent" means intelligent, knowing, and voluntary consent and does not include coerced submission'); Connecticut v. Brown, 59 Conn. App. 243, 251, 756 A.2d 860, 865 (2000) ('[C]onsent must have been actual and not simply acquiescence brought by force or fear. The fact that a victim submits to a defendant's demands after the use of force does not amount to consent on her part'); Harley v. United States, 373 A.2d 898, 902 (D.C. Court of Appeals, 1977) ('if no force is used and the girl in fact acquiesces, the acquiescence may nevertheless be deemed to be non-consent if it is induced by fear').

5. Estrich, 'Rape', p. 1182; Harman, 'Harm, Consent, and Distress', p. 295; Bienen, 'Mistakes', p. 227.
6. Criminal Code, Revised Statutes of Canada 1970, c. C-34, § 158. The 1969 offense of nonconsensual sodomy, Revised Statutes of Canada 1970, c. C-34, § 155, was replaced by a different version in the Criminal Code of 1985, and the age of consent was lowered to 18 (*see* Criminal Code, Revised Statutes of Canada 1985, c. C-46, § 159). The amended offense of sodomy was later declared unconstitutional. *See* Regina v. Carmen M., (1992) 11 C.R.R. (2d) 363.
7. (1992) 11 C.R.R. (2d) 363.
8. *See, e.g.*, *Model Penal Code* § 213.1(1)('Rape. A male who has sexual intercourse with a female . . . is guilty of rape if . . . (d) the female is less than 10 years old').
9. New York Penal Code § 130.20 (2000).
10. New York Penal Code §§ 130.05(1.and 2.) (2000).
11. Revised Statutes of Canada 1985, c. C-46, §§ 265, 273.1, and 150.1.
12. For a jurisdiction with a statutory scheme that approximates this model, *see* California Penal Code §§ 261, 261.5 (2001); California v. Tobias, 25 Cal. 4th 327, 338-43, 21 P.3d 758, 765-68 (2001) (George, J., concurring).
13. For a jurisdiction that adopts essentially this model, *see* New York Penal Code §§ 130.05, 130.20 (2001).
14. *See, e.g.*, Paul v. Florida, 110 So. 2d 388, 395 (1959) ('It is a well established principle of law that consent of the woman from fear of personal violence is void'); Louisiana v. Collins, 242 La. 704, 734-35, 138 So. 2d 546, 557 (1962) ('unlawful'); Montana v. Garn, 274 Mon. 296, 300, 871 P.2d 878, 880 (1994) ('invalid'); Montana Code § 45-2-211 (2000):

    (1) The consent of the victim to conduct charged to constitute an offense or to the result thereof is a defense.

    (2) Consent is ineffective if . . . (c) it is induced by force, duress, or deception.

    Regina v. Diggs, 1987 W.C.B.J. 10646, 1 W.C.B. (2d) 429 ('The elements of the offence of sexual assault are . . . the intentional application of force to another . . . without the other's consent, or with an extorted or fraudulent consent'); Washington v. Ieremia, 78 Wash. App. 746, 757, 899 P.2d 16, 21 (1996):

    > [A]lthough the victim [in Bright] testified that she did not struggle or otherwise indicate a lack of consent, the jury was presented with evidence that her consent, even if given, was coerced by the fact that the rapist was an armed officer of the law. Since coerced consent is equivalent to non-consent, that evidence was sufficient to warrant an instruction on the lesser degree crime of third degree rape.

    Regina v. O'Connor, (1988) 159 D.L.R. (4th) 304, para. 27 ('involuntary consent'); California v. Cicero, 157 Cal. App. 3d 465, 478, 204 Cal.Rptr. 582, 592 (1984) ('vitiated').
15. *See, e.g.*, McArtor v. Wyoming, 699 P.2d 288, 294 (1985) ('valid'); Louisiana v. Adkins, 721 So.2d 1090, 1093 (1998) ('Rape is defined as the act of anal or vaginal sexual intercourse with a male or female person committed without a person's lawful consent'); North Carolina v. Anthony, 351 N.C. 611, 618, 528 S.E.2d 321, 325 (2000) ('meaningful'); California v. Rivera, 44 Cal. App. 4th 466, 483, 41 Cal.Rptr. 2d 421, 431 (1995) ('effective consent'); Arizona v. Denton, 101 Ariz. 455, 459, 420 P.2d 930, 934 (1966) ('consent induced by force or fear and intimidation does not amount to consent in law and does not prevent the intercourse from being rape'); Arizona v.

Bartlett, 171 Ariz. 302, 309, 830 P.2d 823, 830 ('these cases involve violent sexual crimes against young children who were incapable of giving actual, let alone legal, consent'); Pierson v. Wyoming, 956 P.2d 1119, 1125 (1998) ('informed consent'); New Jersey v. Martin, 235 N.J. Super. 47, 57, 561 A.2d 631, 636 (1989) ('If someone in Mary's position was "detained", she was legally incapable of giving knowing and free consent to proscribed sexual conduct with her supervisors who held power over her'); Bennett v. Alabama, 31 Ala. App. 435, 436, 18 So. 2d 291, 292 (1944) ('voluntary'); Regina v. Stoll, 1999 W.C.B.J. 286, 41 W.C.B. (2d) 54, para. 158 ('real consent'); California v. McKellar, 146 Cal.Rptr. 327, 329 (1978) ('Appellant has conceded that the state has a compelling interest in preventing and punishing all cases of sexual intercourse with victims who are minors when there is not free, full and genuine consent'); Regina v. Cuerrier, [1998] 2 S.C.R. 371, para. 127 (opinion of Cory, J.) ('true consent'); Comment § 211, *Model Penal Code*, pt. I, vol. 1, pp. 398 ('excusing consent'). But *see* Hubin and Haely, who in their article, 'Rape and the Reasonable Man', p. 116, appear to conflate factual with legal usages of 'consent' by stating that 'the phrase "informed, voluntary consent" . . . is, strictly speaking, redundant'.

16. 557 S.W.2d 41 (1977).
17. 557 S.W.2d at 43. *See* also Jackson v. Georgia, 225 Ga. 553, 560, 170 S.E.2d 281, 287 (1969) ('Consent to sexual intercourse obtained through a present and immediate fear of bodily injury to the female involved is the equivalent of no consent at all'); Thomas v. Georgia, 159 Ga. App. 249, 251, 249 S.E.2d 37, 39 (1981) ('consent induced by force or fear and intimidation does not amount to consent in law').

Chapter One

A Core Conception of Consent: An Attitude of Factual Acquiescence

All incidents of legal consent by a subject, *S*, to conduct, *x*, by another person, *A*, are predicated upon empirical events on *S*'s part. Sometimes the underlying empirical event consists of an attitude or action or omission by *S* upon which the courts, in turn, construct the legal fiction that *S* actually acquiesced to *x* in her mind and/or expression. More often, however, the underlying empirical event consists of actual acquiescence by *S* to *x* in mind and/or expression—acquiescence that, though insufficient in itself to constitute a defense to criminal wrongdoing by *A*, is nevertheless a necessary component of such a defense. Thus, consider what is meant in rape cases when it is said: 'Every consent involves a submission, but it by no means follows that submission involves consent.'[1] The reference to 'consent' is legal because it is a reference to that which constitutes a defense to rape. The reference to 'submission' is to an empirical event that is necessary but not sufficient to a defense to rape, namely, an act of conscious, even if reluctant, acquiescence to sexual intercourse on *S*'s part, whether in mind or expression. *S*'s actual acquiescence to sexual intercourse is a ***necessary*** component of her legally consenting to it because sexual intercourse that takes place without it is invariably rape, ***e.g.***, when *S* is unconscious or asleep. But *S*'s actual acquiescence is not ***sufficient*** to constitute legal consent because it can occur under conditions that fail to suffice to satisfy her interests regarding sexual intercourse, ***e.g.***, when it occurs at the point of a gun.

Lawmakers thus use 'consent' in contradistinction to terms like 'submission' and 'assent'[2] in order to contrast legal consent to *x*, on the one hand, with the component elements of factual acquiescence to *x* that are necessary for legal consent but not sufficient, on the other. Significantly, however, other lawmakers commonly use 'consent' in an opposite sense: they use it in a factual sense to refer precisely to what the former lawmakers call 'submission', that is, to the element of factual acquiescence that is necessary but not sufficient to constitute a defense. Consider, for example, another provision from the Canadian Criminal Code, this one defining the offense of rape. The provision, now superseded, made it an offense to have sexual intercourse with a woman either ***without*** her consent or, in the event the consent was the product of force or fraud, ***with*** her consent:

> A male person commits rape when he has sexual intercourse with a female person who is not his wife,
> (a) without her consent, or
> (b) with her consent if the consent

(i) is extorted by threats or fear of bodily harm,
(ii) is obtained by impersonating her husband, or
(iii) is obtained by false and fraudulent representations as to the nature and quality of the act.[3]

Section 143 does not use the term 'consent' in a legal sense. For if it did, section 143(a) alone would suffice to define the offense; and section 143(b) would be a contradiction in terms. (By definition, a person who has sexual intercourse *with* a woman's legal consent cannot be guilty of rape, regardless of how he elicits her acquiescence.) Rather, section 143 uses 'consent' as a synonym for what other jurisdictions call 'submission'. That is, section 143 uses consent to refer to something that is necessary to a defense of rape but not sufficient, namely, an instance of actual acquiescence to sexual intercourse on her part. If a man has sexual intercourse with a woman *without* such acquiescence on her part (say, by subjecting her to sexual intercourse when she was unconscious or asleep), he lacks a defense under the statute. Moreover, even if a man has sexual intercourse with a woman *with* such acquiescence, he still lacks a defense if he elicits her acquiescence by 'force' or 'fraud'. In order for a man who has sexual intercourse with a woman to possess a defense under section 143, two things must occur: first, the woman must submit or acquiesce to sexual intercourse (or, in Canada's words, 'consent' to sexual intercourse); and second, her consent must be free of 'force', 'impersonation', or 'fraud'.

Section 143 does not explicitly state whether the 'consent' to which it refers consisted of a subjective mental state of acquiescence on a woman's part, on the one hand, or an objective expression by her of such acquiescence, on the other. Nevertheless, the Canadian courts interpreted the term 'consent' in section 143 to consist of a subjective mental state of acquiescence to sexual intercourse.[4] Canada is not alone in holding that in order to legally consent to sexual intercourse, a woman must subjectively acquiesce to it in her mind. Many jurisdictions take the view that legal consent to sexual intercourse presupposes a component element of subjective acquiescence to sexual intercourse. The *Model Penal Code*, for example, takes the position that the inquiry into the defense of consent in rape cases 'is an inquiry into the victim's subjective state of mind'.[5] California takes the view that what underlies the defense of consent in rape cases is what the putative victim 'subjectively' feels, rather than what she objectively does.[6] Florida states that the defense of consent is a 'subjective state of mind' of which the defendant may or may not be aware.[7] Hawaii states that 'consent' in rape cases 'is an operation of the mind rather than one of the body, . . . impl[ying] a positive mental attitude on the part of the person granting consent'.[8] Louisiana defines 'consent' in rape cases in term of 'the beliefs' of the putative victim.[9] Michigan courts rule that the defense of consent to criminal sexual conduct under Michigan law is a woman's 'subjective consent', not her external manifestations of acquiescence.[10] English courts rule that 'consent' in rape cases consists not of something that is 'demonstrated' or 'communicated' but of a 'state of mind'.[11] Other jurisdictions take the same position.[12a]

[a] Chapter 4 examines whether jurisdictions are justified in putting such legal weight on subjective acquiescence as opposed to expressive acquiescence.

To be sure, in stating consent to be a mental state, some of the aforementioned jurisdictions are using 'consent' legally to refer to mental states of acquiescence to sexual intercourse that by their standards are sufficiently competent, informed, and free to constitute a defense to rape—rather than using 'consent' factually, as Canada does in section 143, to refer to the underlying mental acquiescence to sexual intercourse that may or may not constitute a defense. Nevertheless, although these jurisdictions may not all use 'consent' to refer to underlying mental acquiescence that may or may not constitute a defense, they agree with Canada that such underlying mental acquiescence is a necessary component of legal consent. Moreover, the minimal elements of the underlying mental acquiescence to sexual intercourse that they all require—the event that Canada calls 'consent' and other jurisdiction call 'submission'—are the same for all of them. They are elements of subjective acquiescence that, if they occur under such conditions of competence, knowledge, freedom and motivation as the jurisdiction requires, constitute a defense to rape and, otherwise, do not.

The purpose of this chapter is to identify the minimal elements of what I regard as a core conception of consent in criminal law on the part of a person *S* whom an actor *A* is subjecting to conduct *x*—namely, a mental state or subjective 'attitude'[13] of factual acquiescence on *S*'s part that may or may not constitute a defense to *A*, depending upon whether *S* further possessed the competence, knowledge, freedom and motivation that the jurisdiction at hand regards as necessary in order for *S* to take responsibility for acquiescing to *x*. Needless to say, this core conception of consent as an attitude of factual acquiescence is essential in jurisdictions like Canada that explicitly refer to such attitudes as 'consent'. Yet it is also relevant in jurisdictions like England that, while referring to these attitudes as instances of 'submission' and 'assent' rather than 'consent', nevertheless agree with Canada in regarding them as necessary (albeit not sufficient) components of legal consent. Significantly, however, the role that such attitudes possess as a 'core conception' of consent is not confined to jurisdictions like Canada and England that predicate legal consent upon them. It also extends to jurisdictions that define legal consent as consisting of expressive acts of acquiescence (rather than of subjective attitudes of acquiescence), as well to jurisdictions that define legal consent in terms of fictions of attitudinal or expressive acquiescence. It is a core conception of consent in that other conceptions of consent are conceptually derivative of it—including factual *expressive* consent (Chapter 2), *legal* expressive consent (Chapter 4), legal *attitudinal* consent (Chapters 5 and 6), and legal consent in the form of *fictions* of attitudinal or expressive consent (Chapter 7). For regardless of whether a jurisdiction defines consent as *wholly consisting* of such an attitude of factual acquiescence (as Canada does), or as *partly consisting* of such an attitude (as England does), or as wholly or partly consisting of an *expression* of such an attitude, or as consisting of a *fiction* of such an attitude or expression, a jurisdiction invariably makes reference to such attitudes of factual acquiescence.

We shall address the following questions: Across the range of instances in which 'consent' is used as a synonym for 'submission' to refer to a subjective attitude of factual acquiescence to the conduct of others under conditions that may or may not constitute a defense, what minimum constituent features, if any, do such instances of factual attitudinal consent share? What is the mental content of the underlying attitude? Is it an attitude of desire, enthusiasm, preference, or even indifference, or is it an attitude of authorization? What minimal capacities, if any, does such attitudinal consent presuppose? Can a person who is mentally ill nonetheless factually consent in her mind, albeit under conditions of incompetence that might invalidate her consent as a legal defense? (Or does the answer depend upon the nature of the mental illness?) Can a person who is unaware of something nonetheless factually consent to it in her mind, albeit under conditions of ignorance that might well invalidate her consent as a defense? (Or does the answer depend upon the nature of her unawareness?) Can a person factually consent to something that he feels compelled to do, albeit under conditions of force that might well invalidate his consent as a defense? (Or does the answer depend upon the nature of the force?).

Mental Nature of Factual Attitudinal Consent

We have seen that jurisdictions like Canada use consent in sexual assault cases to refer to subjective attitudes of factual acquiescence on a woman's part that may or may not constitute a defense to her partner, depending upon the further conditions under which she forms her attitude. However, we have yet to examine the content of the attitude or attitudes that such jurisdictions have in mind. Is there any single mental state that they all have in mind? If not, is there any single mental state to which the mental states they have in mind can be reduced?

To address these questions, suppose that at various times over the years a woman *S* has sexual intercourse with a male acquaintance *A* with the following Mental States ('MS'):

> ***MS 1 Unconditional enthusiasm.*** 'I am overcome with yearning for having sexual intercourse with A. It's the only thing I can think of'.
>
> ***MS 2 Conditional preference.*** 'I hope A doesn't want to have sexual intercourse with me, because I have a headache and I'm not feeling very well. But if he makes sexual overtures, I would rather go along with it than disappoint him by refusing'.
>
> ***MS 3 Indifference.*** 'I don't care one way or another whether we have sexual intercourse or not. I am fine with whichever he chooses to do'.
>
> ***MS 4 Authorization.*** 'I know that A may not lawfully have sexual intercourse with me unless I allow him to, and, knowing that, I permit him to'.
>
> ***MS 5 Unconditional repugnance.*** 'I abhor having sexual intercourse with A, and I am doing everything I can to prevent it'.

As a candidate for what jurisdictions like Canada appear to mean by 'consent', MS 5 can be dismissed out of hand. MS 5 cannot possibly be regarded as a subjective attitude of acquiescence by *S* in *A*'s having sexual intercourse with her, because *S* cannot in any way be regarded as subjectively choosing to have sexual intercourse with *A*. *S* and *A* may be husband and wife and in that event jurisdictions might say (as jurisdictions have indeed said in the past) that by virtue of marrying and remaining married to *A*, *S* constructively consents to have sexual intercourse with him at his pleasure, regardless of how she may have felt about such sexual intercourse at the time of the marriage and regardless of how she may feel about it now. But constructive consent is a fiction as to how a person actually feels about conduct, not an instance of how she actually feels about it. Constructive consent is a fiction by which the law treats a person *as if* she had subjectively acquiesced to conduct in her mind, knowing full well that she had not.

In ordinary language, at least, the remaining mental states are all instances of subjective acquiescence to sexual intercourse. They are all instances in which *S* subjectively chooses to have sexual intercourse with *A*. Yet the four mental states also differ from one another in significant ways. The major difference is between MS 1 to 3 and MS 4. Although all four mental states consist of subjective choosing, MS 1 to 3 are mental states of mere *desire* for sexual intercourse under the circumstances, while MS 4 is a mental state in which *S* both desires sexual intercourse under the circumstances and consciously *authorizes* or *permits* it. The differences among these mental states thus raise the question as to which one or more of them suffice to constitute what jurisdictions like Canada mean by factual attitudinal 'consent'.

Mental States of Mere Desire

MS 1 to 3 are all mental states of desire for sexual intercourse, though the desires differ from one another. MS 1 ('unconditional enthusiasm') is a mental state of unconditional desire in that it is a subjective choosing of sexual intercourse that *S* does not experience as being conditioned upon the existence of constraining circumstances that she wished did not obtain. In contrast, MS 2 ('conditional preference') is a mental state of desire for sexual intercourse, *all things considered*: *S* is aware that she would not desire sexual intercourse under counterfactual circumstances that she wished existed (*i.e.*, that she could refuse to have sexual intercourse with *A* without disappointing him); and yet given the circumstances that she believes exist, she consciously prefers sexual intercourse to what she believes to be the alternative (*i.e.*, that *A* will be disappointed).[14] MS 3 ('indifference'), in turn, is also a mental state of desire, though it is one that is entirely derivative of another's desire: *S* subjectively desires sexual intercourse in the sense that, although she has no preference for sexual intercourse vis-à-vis what she believes to be the alternatives, she nevertheless consciously chooses to accept it in the event that he desires it under the circumstances.

Having seen that MS 1 to 3 all count as subjective acquiescence in ordinary language, we must examine whether they also constitute in law the kind of factual attitudinal consent to which jurisdictions like Canada refer when they require, as a precondition to a woman's legally consenting to sexual intercourse, that she subjectively 'consent' to it in fact. Now it might be thought that a person cannot factually consent to conduct in her mind unless she feels unconditional desire for it. But that cannot be true, for if it were, jurisdictions like Canada would have to say of a woman like *S* in MS 2 who acquiesces in sexual intercourse to avoid disappointing her husband, 'She is a victim of criminal sexual assault, because her husband subjected her to sexual intercourse without her consent'. To be sure, to say that women who consciously acquiesce in sexual intercourse under the felt pressure of circumstances subjectively 'consent' to it does not necessarily mean that their consent is valid as a defense. On the contrary, Canada explicitly makes it an offense to induce women to consent to sexual intercourse by means of 'threats or fears' of certain kinds. Significantly, however, Canada does *not* say of victims of such threats and fears that they do not 'consent' to sexual intercourse. It says of them that they *do* 'consent' to sexual intercourse, albeit under pressures that render their consent invalid as a defense to rape.

The more interesting question is whether jurisdictions like Canada would say that MS 3 (*i.e.*, a mental state of indifference) is also among the kinds of consent that are necessary albeit not sufficient to a defense to rape. Notice that *indifference* is not the same as *indecisiveness*. A person who is indecisive about *x* is someone who feels that it matters or may matter to her whether *x* occurs but cannot come to one mind about it. An indecisive person does not in any way consent to *x* in her mind because she is unable to form a subjective judgment as to how she feels about its occurrence. In contrast a person who is indifferent as to whether *x* occurs knows how she feels about *x*: she feels that it does not matter to her in one way or another whether it occurs and, hence, she is willing to delegate the decision about it to her partner.[15] Accordingly, a jurisdiction like Canada might well conclude that a person who is indifferent as to whether sexual intercourse occurs *does* factually consent to it in her mind because by virtue of being willing to delegate the decision to *A*, she is willing to engage in sexual intercourse if her partner initiates it.[16]

To say that a jurisdiction *might* equate indifference to *x* with the kind of factual attitudinal consent to *x* that lies at the core of legal conceptions of consent does not mean that it *must*. Depending upon its normative views regarding *x*, a jurisdiction might well conclude that a person does not even factually consent to *x* in her mind unless she affirmatively *prefers* *x* to the alternatives under the circumstances.[17] Consider the 'Termination of Life on Request' statute that the Netherlands recently enacted.[18] While the statute generally makes it an offense to terminate a patient's life, the statute permits a physician to terminate the life of a patient who suffers from unremitting and unbearable suffering for which there is no reasonable alternative, provided that the patient voluntarily 'request[s]' it.[19] Much depends, of course, upon the normative criteria that determine whether a patient's request is voluntary for purposes of the statute. But regardless of how voluntary a patient's decision may be, a decision exculpates a physician only if the underlying decision constitutes a 'request'. A request, in turn, is an expression of a state of mind on a patient's part. What state of mind, then, must a patient express herself to have in order to 'request' a termination of life under the statute? Does it suffice to express indifference as to whether she lives or dies? Or must she express an affirmative preference for death vis-à-vis the alternatives? We do not know for certain how the Dutch courts will resolve these questions, but the courts might well rule that a 'request' is an expression of affirmative preference for death, not merely an expression of indifference toward death.

What, then, can we say thus far about the content of factual attitudinal consent that lies at the core of legal conceptions of consent? The most we can say is that although unconditional and conditional preferences for *x* *always* suffice to constitute factual attitudinal consent, mere indifference to *x* *sometimes* suffices, too, depending upon the jurisdiction's normative views regarding *x*. Stated differently, no single mental state lies at the core of all conceptions of legal consent. Rather, the core conception of factual attitudinal consent to *x*—that is, the core conception that all conceptions of legal consent to *x* variously incorporate, refer to, or fictionalize—consists alternatively of *either* affirmative preferences for *x* *or* mere indifference to *x*, depending upon a jurisdiction's normative views regarding *x*.

Mental States of Authorization

Interestingly, several commentators have argued that regardless of how offenses of non-consent may currently be defined, the mental state that *ought* to underlie conceptions of legal consent in criminal law is not a mental state of mere desire for *x* under the circumstances, but a mental state in which one consciously authorizes *x* under the circumstances. Thus, Larry Alexander argues that in order for *S* legally to consent to an act by *A* that is otherwise an offense, *S* ought to be required to possess a subjective intention 'to forgo [her] moral complaint against [*A*'s] act'.[20] Similarly, Emily Sherwin argues that for *S* legally to consent to an act, *S* must express that she is engaging in 'a particular mental act', namely, a 'decision' on her part 'to confer a privilege and forgo a right'.[21] They and others take the position that it does not suffice for *S* to feel or to say to *A*, 'I wish you to do *x*'. Rather, they say, the criminal law ought to require that *S* also know that she has a right to determine the lawfulness of *x* and that she possess the feeling—or, according to some commentators, that she express the feeling—'You have my permission to do *x*'.

Now it is true that legal consent in all its forms has the *effect* of permitting an actor *A* to do what would otherwise infringe *S*'s legal rights. Thus, regardless of whether it consists of a mental state or an expression of a mental state or a fiction of a mental state, *S*'s legal consent operates as a Hohfeldian 'privilege' to allow *A* to do what *S* would otherwise have a 'claim right' to foreclose *A* from doing.[22] It does not follow, however, that because *S*'s legal consent has the legal effect of granting *A* legal permission to do *x*, *S*'s underlying state of mind (whether it is possessed or expressed or fictionalized) must itself consist of *S*'s consciously granting *A* legal permission. Nor is it true that the underlying state of mind *ought* to consist of *S*'s consciously granting *A* legal permission. Imagine, for example, the following case:

> ***Sharon the Unwitting Adult.*** Sharon is a 16-year-old high school student in a state in which 16-year-olds are legally competent to consent to sex with boys their own age or even a few years older. However, she and her family just arrived from a state in which she knew that 16-year-olds were not legally competent to consent to sexual intercourse; and she mistakenly believes that the same is true of her new home. Sharon develops a crush on an 18-year-old football player who asks her on a date. Sharon hopes the boy will want to have

> sexual intercourse with her, and she does everything she can to bring it about. As she has sexual intercourse with the boy, she thinks to herself and says, 'I know I am too young to give you permission, but I really want you to make love to me'.

Alexander and Sherwin would say that although Sharon unconditionally desired to have sexual intercourse with the boy, she did not possess nor express the state of mind that the law ought to require as a prerequisite of legal consent, namely, a state of mind of granting a legal privilege. Yet it is hard to see why Sharon's conscious choice of sexual intercourse ought not to have the effect of granting her boyfriend a legal privilege. Sharon made her choice freely, and in the eyes of the state, she made it at an age in which she was old enough to take responsibility for her choice. To be sure, she was not aware of her legal authority to grant a privilege. Nevertheless, she possessed and expressed consciousness of everything that appears to have a bearing upon her being able to take responsibility for her decision.

This is not to say that mental states of authorizing are never normatively relevant to the lawfulness of person's consent. A person's awareness of her right to confer a privilege can be relevant when, in contrast to Sharon, her ignorance causes her to submit to conduct to which she would not otherwise acquiesce and, in doing so, undermines important interests that the privilege is designed to serve.[23] Consider, for example, the police practice of inducing suspects to consent to searches of homes for which the police lack probable cause to search. The absence of legal consent renders such searches both unlawful and criminal, while the presence of legal consent renders them entirely lawful. The U.S. Supreme Court has held that a police officer's failure to apprise a homeowner of her right to withhold consent and a homeowner's ignorance thereof do not preclude a homeowner from legally consenting for fourth amendment purposes.[24] Nevertheless, some jurisdictions take the opposite view for purposes of state constitutional law. These jurisdictions take the position that a person who is unexpectedly confronted on her doorstep by police officers who wish to search her home and who may believe that she has no authority to refuse cannot make a decision that adequately serves her privacy interests unless she aware that she has a legal right to withhold the permission to search.[25]

Given that individual jurisdictions sometimes do and sometimes do not require as conditions of legal consent that persons be aware of their right under the law to withhold privileges, what conclusions follow regarding the content of factual attitudinal consent? Can factual attitudinal consent be reduced to either one or the other? One thing seems clear: factual attitudinal consent cannot be reduced exclusively to mental states of authorizing, for it sometimes consists of mental states of desire (*e.g.*, 'Sharon the Unwitting Adult'). Now it might be thought that the converse is true, too. That is, it might be thought that just as factual attitudinal consent cannot be reduced exclusively to mental states of authorizing, it cannot be reduced exclusively to mental states of desire either. But the latter does not necessarily follow. On the contrary, factual attitudinal consent can be conceptualized—and, I believe, ought to be conceptualized—as consisting invariably of mental states of desire alone, for a combination of two reasons. First of all, mental states of authorizing are *subsets* of mental states of desire: to subjectively authorize x is to desire x under the circumstances (whether by virtue of unconditionally desiring *x*, or preferring *x* under the circumstances, or being indifferent to *x* under the circumstances) *while being aware of ones right to withhold the privilege of x.* Mental states of authorizing are nothing more than mental states of desire, plus awareness of one's right to refuse. To illustrate, suppose that the following case arises within a jurisdiction that makes it an offense to touch a person without the latter's voluntary consent and that defines 'consent' to be a mental state of authorizing:

> Young Man: 'I want to kiss you, but I am reluctant until you say I may.'
>
> Young Woman: 'You're right to hesitate, because you are not allowed to kiss me in this state unless I subjectively authorize it. And I can tell you, I'm not subjectively authorizing it. But I can also tell you this: I find you really attractive, and I really want you to kiss me—now!'

The case is revealing because the young woman contradicts herself about what she is feeling. She says that she has a mental state of desire rather than a mental state of authorizing. But given that she is aware of her legal rights, she cannot possess a metal state of desire to be kissed under the circumstances without also having a mental state of authorizing the kissing. For the sentiment 'I desire *x* under the circumstances' is functionally equivalent to the sentiment 'I allow *x* under the circumstances' with respect to any person who is aware of her right to withhold the privilege of *x*.

Second, the feature that distinguishes mental states of authorizing *x* from all other mental states of desire for *x*, *i.e.*, that the person is aware of his right to withhold the legal privilege of *x*, can be fully accommodated within a framework in which factual attitudinal consent is defined as a mental state of desire. It can be accommodated by conceptualizing it as among the separate conditions of voluntariness that are legally required if the factual attitudinal 'consent' of a person is to be *valid*. Thus, to the extent that a jurisdiction requires as a condition of *S*'s legal consent to *x* that *S* subjectively authorize *x*, its requirement can be conceptualized as consisting of two elements: (1) a requirement of factual attitudinal consent consisting of a desire on *S*'s part for *x* (whether in the form of an unconditional desire for *x*, a preference for *x* under the circumstances, or indifference toward *x* under the circumstances); and (2) a further requirement that *S* form her desire with knowledge of certain kind, namely, knowledge of her right to deny her partner the privilege of engaging in *x*. Conceptualizing *S*'s knowledge of her legal rights as part of step #2 that comes into play after step #1 is useful because, as we shall see in Chapter 5, the validity of *S*'s factual attitudinal consent under step #2 typically depends upon what she knows about the circumstances that accompany *x*.

To illustrate, suppose that a jurisdiction follows the model for defining 'consent' that Canada adopts in section 143 by defining consent for purposes of trespass as a factual attitude, and by further providing that consent is not valid as a defense unless it is properly informed. Suppose, too, that the jurisdiction also takes the view that a homeowner does not privilege the police to search his home for purposes of the laws against trespass unless the police inform him of his right to withhold the privilege.

Suppose finally that a police officer within the jurisdiction induces a homeowner *S* to submit to a search without informing him of his right to refuse. How would the courts of the jurisdiction frame what is criminal about the police officer's search? The courts would presumably conclude that although the homeowner 'consented' to the search by virtue of his subjectively preferring the search to the alternatives of which he was aware at the time, his consent was not valid as a defense to trespass because the police officer failed to inform him of his right to refuse.

Minimum Conditions for Factual Attitudinal Consent

We have seen thus far that consent can be used in law as a synonym for mental states of conscious submission, whether they take the form of conscious preferences under the circumstances or indifference under the circumstances. We shall now turn to the minimum conditions of capacity, awareness, and freedom, if any, that must obtain upon a person's part in order for her to possess such mental states of preference or indifference. We shall see that there is a difference between capacity and awareness, on the one hand, and freedom, on the other. For in order to describe *S* as factually 'consenting to *x*' in her mind, she must possess certain mental capacities and a certain awareness of *x*. But, significantly, she need *not* possess any freedom to avoid *x*.

Minimum Capacity Required for Factual Attitudinal Consent

Patricia Noble, a first-year student at North Carolina State University, went drinking with friends during the evening of August 31, 1984. Returning alone to her room after midnight, she turned on the radio to low volume, lay down on her bed fully clothed, and fell asleep. When she awoke, she found a man, whom she later recognized as a friend of her roommate, lying on top of and astride her. The man had already inserted his penis into her vagina and was engaged in active sexual intercourse. The man was arrested, charged, and convicted of rape, and sentenced to twelve-years imprisonment. In sustaining the charge of rape, North Carolina Supreme Court held that sexual intercourse with a woman who is asleep is necessarily without her 'consent', because 'it is easily recognized and universally understood that a person who is unconscious by reason of intoxication, drugs, or sleep, is incapable of exercising any judgment in any matter whatsoever.'[26]

What makes Patricia Noble's case unique, as we shall soon see, is not that she was subjected to sexual intercourse while she was asleep. Sadly to say, law reports are rife with cases in which men are accused of having sexual intercourse with women who were asleep or otherwise unconscious at the time. In many such cases, the women are unconscious as a result of intoxication of one kind or another, sometimes self-induced, sometimes not. Whatever the cause, the law's response is everywhere the same: a person may be able to consent to sexual intercourse before losing consciousness or even after regaining consciousness; but a person cannot consent to sexual intercourse *while being* unconscious, because a person who is unconscious lacks the 'capacity to consent'.[27]

It seemed obvious to the North Carolina court that sleeping persons cannot consent to sexual intercourse in the sense of subjectively acquiescing to it, because sleep seems inconsistent with several essential elements of subjective acquiescence. One is consciousness. A state of mind of acquiescence to *x*, after all, is a state of mind *of* something, namely, a certain accepting of *x* as that which one either chooses for oneself under the circumstances or is indifferent about. Unconsciousness, in turn, is either an absence of a state of mind or a state of mind of nothingness. In either event, unconsciousness is not a subjective state of acquiescence. In that sense, the courts are surely correct in saying that it is 'easily understood and universally recognized' that unconsciousness precludes attitudinal consent.

Consciousness is not the only capacity that subjective acquiescence requires. It also requires what the North Carolina court calls a capacity for 'judgment', *i.e.*, a minimal capacity to adjudge what one desires for oneself under the circumstances as one perceives them to be. Persons who lack the capacity to make judgments—whether because they suffer pathological 'absences of will' or because they are too terrified or otherwise subjectively disoriented to decide what they want—are persons who cannot subjectively acquiesce, any more than persons who are unconscious.[28] Consider what happened to Starr Copithorne, a hospital technician in Massachusetts who sought help from a neurosurgeon for pain she was suffering in her back. Offering to make a house call, the doctor examined Ms. Copithorne on her bed. He told her that she had a muscle spasm and recommended an injection of Valium to relax her muscles. He then administered an injection of five to ten milligrams of Valium, causing her, first, to become '[v]ery groggy, very out of it, very heavy . . . like I couldn't move my arms or my legs' and, then, to lose consciousness. When she regained consciousness, she found that he had undressed her and was lying naked beside her, fondling her and commencing sexual intercourse. She testified that her mind was 'in a fog . . . like it wasn't real. . . . Like I was in like a Twilight Zone'. She drifted in and out of consciousness, waking and asking at one point 'why he was doing it, because wouldn't it hurt my back?'[29] Like most victims of sexual intercourse during sleep, Ms. Copithorne was unconscious for periods of time and was incapable then of experiencing any state of mind, much less a state of mind of acquiescence. During some of the time, however, she was conscious, including, significantly, at the time the doctor was first commencing sexual intercourse. Yet even then she lacked an acquiescing state of mind because, apart from feeling physically helpless, she lacked the capacity to make a judgment of acquiescence. Feeling herself 'in a fog', she was incapable of forming a mental picture of what was happening to her or how she felt about it. Indeed, the doctor administered the Valium for precisely that purpose. As the court observed in affirming the doctor's conviction for rape, Valium, when administered intravenously, 'sedates people physically'. A dose of five to ten milligrams, the dosage Ms. Copithorne received, causes patients to 'become very tranquil and fall spontaneously off to sleep' and causes 'their decisionmaking capacity, thought processes, physical coordination and speech [to become] impaired'.

In order to be described as factually 'consenting' to sexual intercourse in her mind, a subject *S* must not only possess a capacity for judgment, she must also *exercise* the capacity in a certain way—namely, by subjectively acquiescing to sexual intercourse as opposed to *not* subjectively acquiescing to it. A person subjectively acquiesces in conduct, *x*, when she subjectively chooses *x* for herself under the circumstances in which she perceives herself to be either by affirmatively preferring that *x* occur or by being so indifferent as to whether it occurs as to be willing to leave its occurrence to *A*. It is not enough, therefore, that *S* is conscious of *A*'s conduct, or even conscious that she is physically complying with *A*'s wishes. *S* must subjectively acquiesce to the conduct by subjectively accepting it for herself under the circumstances.[30] Suppose, for example, that a doctor injects a patient with a mind-altering 'Hypnotic Drug' that, like hypnosis, makes the patient highly susceptible to suggestion, with the difference that the patient remains conscious the whole time that her body is responding to the doctor's hypnotic will rather than to her own.[31] Once the Hypnotic Drug takes effect, the doctor directs the patient to engage in sexual intercourse with him. Though finding the request repugnant, the patient observes in horror as her body, from which she is subjectively estranged, complies with the doctor's directives. The patient in this fanciful hypothetical may physically comply with the doctor's wishes, but she cannot in any way be described as consenting to them in her mind because she does not experience her compliance as a product of her willed acquiescence.[32]

Nor is it enough, moreover, that *S* has a longing for sexual intercourse. She must subjectively choose it for herself under the circumstances. A woman can subjectively repudiate acts of sexual intercourse that she knows will bring her sexual pleasure. She can even subjectively repudiate acts of sexual intercourse at the very moment they bring her sexual pleasure. It occasionally happens, for example, that victims of violent rapes report experiencing sexual orgasms during sexual assaults they find abhorrent. Although some courts seem troubled by such testimony,[33] most courts respond in the way they should, namely, by ruling that a person can experience somatic arousal in sexual intercourse without in any way consenting to sexual intercourse in her mind.[34]

Nor is it enough, finally, that some detached part of a person chooses to engage in sexual intercourse. The choice must be *hers*, and for that, she must possess a dominant and continuing self capable of making choices for herself.[35] To illustrate the absence of such a self, consider Sarah, a 28-year-old woman in Oshkosh, Wisconsin, who allegedly suffered from multiple personality disorder (MPD), possessing as many as 46 'alternate' personalities (so-called 'alters'). Mark, a young man her age who was aware that Sarah suffered from MPD and who had been warned by neighbors not to 'take advantage' of her, had sexual intercourse in a local park with what Sarah described as one of her many alters, *i.e.*, 'a 20-year old who enjoyed having fun but who had no knowledge of sex'. Mark was prosecuted and convicted of rape on the ground that Sarah herself, to the extent there *was* such a thing as Sarah herself, had never consented in her mind to sexual intercourse with Mark. Sarah's case is a rarity, of course, in part because many in the psychiatric community harbor doubts about whether MPD truly exists and, if it does, whether persons suffering from it lack continuing and dominant personalities that can control their alters.[36] Nevertheless, the case is illustrative because given the expert testimony that the jury heard in support of MPD, the jury was justified in concluding that Sarah lacked a dominant and continuing self who was capable of choosing sexual intercourse for Sarah as a whole.[37]

This brings us back to Patricia Noble, the young woman at North Carolina State who was subjected to sexual intercourse while asleep. What makes Patricia Noble's case unique is that though she was sleeping at the time sexual intercourse occurred, she was not unconscious of sexual intercourse because she testified to having been 'dreaming' that she was having sexual intercourse at the time it occurred.[38] The report of the case does not reveal how she felt in her dream about the sexual intercourse and, hence, does not reveal whether she welcomed it or abhorred it. But it nevertheless suggests the question: if in her dream Patricia Noble welcomed the sexual intercourse about which she was dreaming, and if the sexual intercourse about which she was dreaming was the sexual intercourse that was then occurring, can Patricia be said to have 'submitted' to the sexual intercourse in her mind C and, hence, as Canada uses the term in section 143, to have 'consented' to it in her mind? Notice that the foregoing question is narrower than it may seem. We are not asking whether Patricia must be subjectively aware of the *identity* of the person with whom she is having sexual intercourse in order to be described as consenting to sexual intercourse in her mind. (That is a question that will be addressed in the following section of this chapter.) Nor are we asking whether Patricia *legally* consented to the sexual intercourse in a way that negated its being an offense—that is, whether her subjective acquiescence occurred under such conditions of competence, knowledge, freedom and motivation as sufficed to render it valid as a defense to rape. (Those are matters to be discussed in Chapter 5.) The question, rather, is whether by virtue of dreaming favorably of the sexual intercourse that was actually occurring, Patricia can be described as acquiescing to it in her mind, albeit under conditions that might well fail to render it a defense to rape. If so, she experienced the kind of attitudinal consent in which we are interested here—namely, a *subjective choosing* of sexual intercourse *without which* the defendant's conduct necessarily constitutes rape in jurisdictions like Canada that define consent as a mental state of acquiescence in sexual intercourse, and *with which* his conduct may also constitute rape, depending upon whether her subjective choosing of it is adjudged to be sufficiently competent, informed, and free on her part to protect the interests that the state deems her to possess with respect to sexual intercourse.

Now it might be argued that a dream-state is a separate personality, much like the alters manifested by persons with MPD. Thus, if Sarah's childlike alter (*i.e.*, the '20-year-old who enjoyed having fun but who had no knowledge of sex') was a rogue personality who could not consent on Sarah's behalf, the argument goes, then a dreaming Patricia Noble could not consent for an awakened Patricia Noble. Nevertheless, the analogy between Patricia Noble and Sarah is questionable. The issue is not whether a dreaming Patricia Noble could *legally* consent for an awakened Patricia Noble. The issue is whether Patricia, once she awakened, experienced her dream as a subjective experience of her own. In that respect, people with MPD, like Sarah, may differ from people like Patricia Noble who remember their dreams. People with MPD presumably lack dominant and continuing selves that direct and oversee the actions of their alters. Either they are unaware of what their alters are doing; or, if they are aware, they are aware of them in the way one is aware of third persons.[39] In contrast, Patricia Noble not only remembered her dream, she also recognized her dreaming self as *her* self.[40]

The more difficult question is the significance, if any, of the fact that, objectively speaking, Patricia Noble seemed to have had no control over her dreaming self's subjective choices. Again, it is important to distinguish the minimum conditions necessary to describe Patricia as *factually* consenting to sexual intercourse in her mind from the conditions necessary to *legal* consent. Control clearly has significance for purposes of legal consent because the justice or injustice of holding a person to her subjective choices by virtue of their being her choices depends upon her ability to control them. It is less clear, however, that a person's objective control over her subjective choices has any bearing upon whether she can be described as factually consenting in her mind. It may suffice that she actually experience the choices as her own.

To illustrate with another fanciful example, suppose that pharmacologists develop a 'Desire Drug' that, without causing people to lose consciousness, nonetheless affects them in two ways. Like the Hypnotic Drug, the Desire Drug invariably reduces people's psychological resistances to zero, rendering their bodies entirely susceptible to the suggestions of others. Unlike the Hypnotic Drug, however, the Desire Drug *usually* works to cause people also to subjectively welcome whatever is suggested to them.[41] Unfortunately, no one can tell until after the drug dissipates whether subjects happily complied with the suggestions they received or, like the victims of the Hypnotic Drug, complied while subjectively rejecting what they were doing. Suppose, too, that a married woman who was sexually abused as a child wishes to use the Desire Drug to overcome continuing phobias regarding sexual intercourse. In consultation with a physician who warms her of the risks, and in accord with her husband, she takes the Desire Drug and, thereafter, at her husband's suggestion, pliantly engages in sexual intercourse with him. As the drug wears off, she remembers everything, including how she felt at the time. 'Don't worry', she reassures her husband, 'I wanted to make love—I was consenting the whole time'. Notice that we know perfectly well what the woman means in saying she was 'consenting' to the sexual intercourse, and we feel that she is using the word 'consent' correctly. And yet we also know—and, indeed, *she* knows, too—that she had no control over how she felt about the sexual intimacy. Her subjective experience of willed acquiescence constituted her 'consent' despite her being unable to control it. True, she decided in advance to deprive herself of control, and her prior decision would have important bearing upon whether her attitudinal consent sufficed to exonerate her husband in the event he was charged with rape. But her prior decision did not affect the psychological content of what she subsequently experienced, or prevent her from meaningfully saying of the experience, 'Don't worry . . . I was consenting the whole time'.

Ultimately, we need not decide whether a woman who subjectively welcomes sexual intercourse while in the sleep-like state of dreaming can be described as factually consenting to it in her mind because, with the exception of some kinds of post-hypnotic suggestion, such events are extremely rare. The purpose of the discussion is to emphasize that when people speak of 'consent' to *x* they are sometimes using consent non-normatively, or 'factually', to refer to a subjective experience of conscious acquiescence to *x*—conscious acquiescence that may or may not occur under such conditions of motivation, freedom, knowledge, and competence as the jurisdiction requires to render it a defense.

Minimum Awareness Required for Factual Attitudinal Consent

It occasionally happens that a person subjectively acquiesces to something only to discover afterwards that she misunderstood what was occurring. Thus, a woman may acquiesce to a gynecological examination only to learn later that the doctor also engaged her in sexual intercourse. She might acquiesce to sexual intercourse with a man only to learn later that the man is actually her boyfriend's identical twin brother; or to sexual intercourse with her boyfriend only to discover later that he is infected with a contagious venereal disease; or to sexual intercourse with her husband only to learn later that he has filed for divorce, or is planning to file for divorce, or is having an affair. Can *all* of these women be said to have consented to sexual intercourse in their minds? Can *any* of them be said to have consented to it in their minds? What minimum awareness of conduct involving sexual intercourse must a person possess, if any, before she can be said to have factually consented to the sexual intercourse in her mind, even if she is perhaps deemed to have done so as a result of fraud?

The answer lies in what it means to factually 'consent' to something, say, *x*, in one's mind. We have seen that to factually consent to something in one's mind is to choose it, whether by virtue of subjectively preferring it or by being indifferent to it under the circumstances. Yet a person cannot subjectively choose something for herself without being aware of it.[42] The *x* of which the person is conscious may be something that actually exists or something that she mistakenly believes to exist. She factually consents in her mind to something that actually exists by *accurately* believing it to exist—that is, by *knowing it*—and thereupon choosing it for herself under the circumstances. She factually consents in her mind to something that does not exist by mistakenly believing it to exist and choosing it for herself in her mind. Suppose, for example, that a dentist administers general anesthesia to a patient under the pretense of removing a tooth and instead subjects her to sexual intercourse without even attempting to remove her tooth. In that event, the dental patient subjectively consents to two things—one of which actually exists, and the other of which does not. She subjectively consents to general anesthesia because while accurately believing that the dentist was administering it to her, she consciously chooses general anesthesia as that which she prefers for herself under the circumstances. She also subjectively chooses a tooth extraction because while she mistakenly believes that the extraction is imminent, she consciously chooses the extraction as that which she prefers for herself under the circumstances. But the patient does not in any way subjectively consent to sexual intercourse because she does not in any way believe, either accurately or inaccurately, that she is submitting to sexual intercourse.

A person can also consent in her mind to conduct *x* that she knows may or may not eventually occur, provided that she hopes that it occurs or is indifferent as to its occurring. But that does not mean that a person can consent in her mind to *x* merely by subjectively consenting to a *risk* of *x*. A person who subjectively consents to a risk of *x* does just that—she subjectively consents to a risk, not to *x* itself.[43] Whether she also subjectively consents to *x* depends upon how she feels about the possible occurrence of *x*. If she hopes for or is indifferent to *x*, she does, indeed, subjectively consent to *x*. Otherwise she does not. To illustrate, assume for a moment that the dental patient submits to anesthesia in the following state of mind: she realizes that the dentist will not extract the tooth if an intervening emergency demands his immediate attention, but she is willing to run the risk of an intervening emergency in the hope that the tooth extraction goes as planned. At the same time, while she also realizes that the dentist may sexually molest her during the operation, and while she is willing to run the risk of sexual contact because of the dentist's skill as a surgeon, she is repelled by the thought of sexual contact and does not wish it to occur. Under those circumstances, she factually consents in her mind to the tooth extraction, even though she realizes it may not occur. And she also factually consents in her mind to the risk of sexual molestation because she prefers running the risk of sexual molestation to what she believes to be the alternative (*i.e.*, that of having no chance of having her tooth removed). But except as a metaphor or legal fiction, she cannot be said to factually consent in her mind to sexual contact with the dentist when she does nothing more than subjectively consent to the *risk* of sexual contact.

The answer to the question 'What minimum awareness of conduct *x* must a person possess, if any, before she can be said to factually consent to *x* in her mind?' is evident: where *x* consists of something that actually exists, she must know that *x* exists; and where *x* consists of something that does not exist, she must believe that *x* exists; and where *x* consists of something that has a chance of existing, she must realize that it has a chance of existing and hope that it exists. The answer is evident, because subjective 'consent *to x*' *means* a subjective choosing of *x* and because subjective 'choosing' of *x* requires consciousness of *x*. Unfortunately, this resolution of the question raises a further problem that is inherent in the relationship between attitudes of factual consent to conduct, on the one hand, and the multiple ways in which conduct can be described, on the other. We have thus far referred to conduct as 'conduct *x*', as if given conduct could always be reduced to a single description, or as if the multiple descriptions to which given conduct lends itself were interchangeable for purposes of factual attitudinal consent. Neither is true. A person's attitude toward conduct can depend upon which of the conduct's multiple and equally valid descriptions she has in mind. That is what it means to say that propositional attitudes are 'opaque'.[44] Propositional attitudes, which include attitudes of preference and indifference, are mental states of belief or emotion (*e.g.*, desire, hope, and fear) that are predicated upon the assumptions about the nature of world. To say that propositional attitudes are opaque means that a person may possess a certain attitude toward an event or state of affairs as described in one way and, yet, *not* possess that attitude toward the *very same* event or state of affairs described differently. It means that a person may subjectively prefer or be indifferent toward conduct under one description and yet subjectively disprefer the same event under a different but equally valid description. As Onora O'Neill puts it, 'When we consent to another's proposals, we consent, even when 'fully' informed, only to some specific formulation of what the other has it in mind to do. We may remain ignorant of further, perhaps equally pertinent accounts of what is proposed, including some to which we would not consent'.[45]

To illustrate how subjective attitudes toward conduct can depend upon how the conduct is described, consider the New York case of 'Lenny Hough's Girlfriend'.[46] Lenny Hough had a girlfriend with whom he was sexually intimate. Lenny also had an identical twin, Lamont. One evening, after Lenny's girlfriend had fallen asleep, Lamont went to her apartment and, without turning on the light, climbed into her bed. Passing himself off as his twin brother Lenny, Lamont began to fondle Lenny's girlfriend and to cajole her into having sexual intercourse. Addressing him as 'Lenny', she told Lamont to 'make it quick' because she had 'to work in the morning'. They had sexual intercourse for several minutes during which she did not look at his face. It was not until Lamont said 'Are you going to tell Lenny?' that she realized that she had just had sexual intercourse not with her boyfriend, but with his twin brother.[47] Lenny's girlfriend's conduct can be accurately described in at least two ways: (#1) sexual intercourse with the man who entered her bed; (#2) sexual intercourse with Lamont. In reality, #1 and #2 describe one and the same conduct because Lamont and the man who entered the bed are one and the same. Yet Lenny's girlfriend consciously chose the conduct only as described in #1, because the conduct as described in #2 remained opaque to her. Lenny's girlfriend factually consented in her mind to #1 and not to #2, even though #1 and #2 constitute equally valid descriptions of the same event.

This means that when the underlying conduct is subject to multiple descriptions, and when a person's attitude toward underlying conduct depends upon its description, determining whether a person factually consents to the underlying conduct depends upon which of the multiple descriptions is the *relevant* description of it. Thus, determining whether Lenny's girlfriend consented to what happened to her depends upon whether #1 or #2 is the relevant description of what happened to her. The relevance of descriptions in *criminal law*, in turn, is a function of how the criminal law describes the conduct it means to prohibit in the absence of legal consent. A person factually consents to conduct in her mind if, and only if, the description of the conduct she has in mind is an instance of what the criminal statute at issue describes to be the conduct that it prohibits in the absence of legal consent.

To illustrate, consider another case in which a person factually consented to conduct under a certain description of it but not under a different yet equally valid description of it. Dr. McNair, a Nevada gynecologist, had given his patient Elizabeth a breast, pelvic, and rectal examination for suspected cancer. Elizabeth was so relieved to hear that the examination was negative that she impulsively hugged the gynecologist. In reaction, Dr. McNair told her that he wanted to see if he had lacerated her during the pelvic exam and asked her to bend over a chair and open her gown from the back. He then put on a glove and, with her back turned toward him, penetrated her rectum first with a finger and then with something else that Elizabeth only later realized to her revulsion was his penis.[48] The conduct to which Dr. McNair subjected Elizabeth can be described in two ways: (1) the forcible penetration of her rectum with, first, a finger and, then, a hard rubber-like object; (2) the forcible penetration of her rectum with, first, a finger and, then, a penis. Elizabeth subjectively consented to the conduct under description #1 in that she consciously submitted to those penetrations; but she did not subjectively consent to the conduct under description #2, even though #1 and #2 are accurate descriptions of the same underlying conduct, because she did not consciously submit to penile penetration. To determine whether Elizabeth subjectively consented to the underlying conduct for purposes of the criminal law, one must determine whether either description is an instance of what the criminal statutes at issue describe to be the conduct that they prohibit in the absence of legal consent. It happens that Nevada possesses two pertinent offenses of non-consensual physical contact:

> ***Battery.*** Nevada defines it to be an offense of 'battery' for an actor to subject a person to physical 'force' without the latter's legal consent.[49]

> ***Sexual Assault.*** Nevada also defines it to be an offense of 'sexual assault' for an actor to subject another person to 'sexual penetration', including 'penile penetration', without the latter's legal consent.[50]

Elizabeth factually consented in her mind to what Dr. McNair did to her for purposes of the Nevada battery statute, because every forcible penetration of a person's rectum with a hard rubber-like object is an instance of physical 'force' for purposes of the battery statute; and, hence, by factually consenting to the former, Elizabeth factually consented to conduct that the battery statute describes. Yet not every forcible penetration of a person's rectum with a hard rubber-like object is an instance of 'penile' penetration for purposes of the Nevada sexual assault statute; and, hence, by factually consenting to the former, Elizabeth did not factually consent to the conduct that the sexual assault statute describes.

This is not to say that by factually consenting to Dr. McNair's conduct for purposes of the battery statute, Elizabeth also *legally* consented to it. On the contrary, Nevada might well take the position that Elizabeth's acquiescence to the forcible penetration of her rectum did not constitute legal consent to it, given that Dr. McNair profoundly misled her as to its nature and purpose. Nevertheless, if it chose to speak in the language of factual consent, Nevada could say of Elizabeth's relationship to the battery statute what it could not say of her relationship to the sexual assault statute. Nevada could plausibly say of Elizabeth, 'She subjectively consented to the forcible penetration of her rectum with a hard rubber-like object, but her subjective consent was induced by fraud and, hence, is no defense to a charge of battery'. But Nevada could not say of Elizabeth, 'She subjectively consented to the forcible penetration of her rectum with a penis, but her subjective consent was induced by fraud', because the prospect of being penetrated by a penis never entered her mind.

Minimum Freedom Required for Factual Attitudinal Consent

We have previously seen that, in order to be described as factually consenting to conduct x in her mind, a subject S must possess certain capacities and certain awareness of x. The present question is whether such factual consent by S also presupposes a certain self-perceived freedom on S's part to prevent x from occurring.

Notice that the question is whether *S* must subjectively *perceive* herself to be free to avoid *x*, and not whether she must objectively be free to avoid *x*. A woman may subjectively perceive a constraint to exist that does not in fact exist, just as she may fail to perceive a constraint to exist that does in fact exist. For example, contrast two women: (1) Ruth who, in terror, submits to sado-masochistic sexual intercourse in the mistaken belief that, if she does not, she will be killed; and (2) Sadie who cheerfully submits to such intercourse without realizing that, if she does not, she will be killed. With respect to their objective situations, Ruth possesses freedom that Sadie lacks, namely, the freedom to eschew sexual intercourse without being killed. With respect to their subjective experience, however, their situations are precisely the opposite: Sadie experiences freedom that Ruth does not. We are concerned here with what persons like Ruth and Sadie subjectively believe their options to be because as a state of mind, the core conception of consent consists of what people subjectively experience, not what objectively exists.

We shall see that, in contrast to capacity and awareness, perceived freedom to avoid *x* is not a prerequisite to being able to describe a person as factually 'consenting to *x*' in her mind. Persons like Ruth can factually consent to *x* in their minds, regardless of how much they perceive themselves to be pressured to engage in *x*. Obviously, this does not mean that such persons also legally consent to *x*; for we shall see in Chapter 5 that legal consent invariably presupposes certain freedom from pressure. Rather, it means that people who possess the capacity to decide what they desire under the circumstances can elect in their minds to 'submit' to it C or, in Canada's usage in section 143, subjectively 'consent' to it C regardless of how much they may feel themselves pressured to engage in *x*.

To say that attitudinal consent to *x can* coexist in the face of perceived pressure of all kinds, however, does not mean that it invariably *does*. People who feel pressured to engage in *x* (say, sexual intercourse) may, or may not, respond to the perceived pressure by factually consenting to the sexual intercourse in their minds. How they respond to perceived pressure is a function of which of the two following situations they are in: Situation 1, *infra*, in which they consciously feel that they possess no influence at all over whether sexual intercourse occurs; or Situation 2, *infra*, in which they consciously feel that, though they may possess some influence over whether sexual intercourse occurs, their influence is constrained.[51] The distinction between Situations 1 and 2 is significant. For although persons are capable of factually consenting to sexual intercourse in their minds in both situations, the very fact that sexual intercourse eventually occurs in Situation 2 is itself *evidence* that a person did, indeed, factually consent to it in her mind, albeit under conditions that may render her consent invalid as a defense to rape.

Situation 1: *Where persons believe they possess no influence over whether sexual intercourse occurs.* Meir Dan-Cohen, in his essay 'Conceptions of Choice and Conceptions of Autonomy', examines the kinds of freedom, if any, that are required in moral and political theory for a person truly to 'choose' something for himself. He asks us to imagine a woman, S, who has no influence over whom she must marry—that is, who is being compelled to marry A—and, yet, upon meeting A, finds that she 'falls in love with him' such that she fervently desires to marry him. Dan-Cohen uses the example to help resolve whether a person can be said to 'choose' what she cannot prevent, if the latter happens to be what she desires under the circumstances:

> Our intuitions seem to be split. On the one hand, it is felt, how can I be said to choose x, when x is the only thing I can do? On the other hand, what more can a person want than to do precisely what he wants to do (or to have precisely what he wants to have, etc.)?'[52]

The resolution, Dan-Cohen argues, depends upon which of two 'conceptions of choice' in moral and political theory one invokes: *S* is able to choose to marry *A*, if 'choosing' means 'willing', because *S* fervently desires to marry *A*. However, *S* is *not* able to choose to marry *S* if 'choosing' means selecting from within a set of genuine options, because *S* has no option but to marry *A*.[53]

Dan-Cohen is right that we possess two competing conceptions of choice in moral and political theory, one of which is inconsistent with a person's choosing what he cannot prevent. It is also true (or, at least, so I have argued) that factual attitudinal consent is a kind of choosing. Nevertheless, it does not follow that a person cannot possess an attitude of factual consent toward conduct that he cannot prevent. The choosing that constitutes factual attitudinal consent falls within the first of Dan-Cohen's conceptions: it is a subjective experience of 'willing' *x*, whether the willing consists of an unconditional desire for *x*, or a conditional preference for *x* under the circumstances, or such indifference as to be willing to leave *x*'s occurrence to others. Because attitudinal consent consists entirely of subjective willing, one can unambiguously say of a person, 'She subjectively consented to *x* even though she could not prevent *x*'.

As an illustration, consider the story of Snow White. In the story, Snow White is placed under an evil spell that causes her to fall into a sleep that will last until she is kissed by a prince. Snow White is asleep when the prince kisses her and, hence, is unable subjectively to consent to being kissed. Suppose, however, that instead of actually inducing sleep, the spell merely causes the appearance of sleep, leaving Snow White (whom we shall call 'Snow Blanche') conscious of everything about her circumstances, including her need to be kissed to escape the spell. Suppose, too, that when the prince appears, he turns out to be someone whom she would wish to kiss her even if she were not under a spell. Consequently, as she perceives the prince to be vacillating as to whether to kiss her, she prays, silently and unconditionally, 'Please, please, let him kiss me!' And he does. Now consider the difference between merely saying that she 'chose' to be kissed, and saying that she subjectively 'consented' to be kissed. For the reasons Dan-Cohen gives, one may hesitate to say that Snow Blanche 'chose' to be kissed, because there is one conception of choice (*i.e.*, choice as selecting among genuine options) by reference to which she was incapable of choosing. But one does not hesitate to say that Snow Blanche subjectively 'consented' to be kissed, because the freedom that attitudinal consent requires is the freedom to decide how one feels about *x*, not freedom to influence the occurrence of *x*.[54]

Significantly, this analysis is consistent with our earlier discussion of the 'Desire Drug', the hypothetical case of the woman who took a mind-altering drug that caused her to desire to have sexual intimacy with her husband. The drugged woman, it will be recalled, was conscious of two constraints: (1) she was conscious that she had no control over her actions and was going to do what her attending physician suggested to her, say, *x*; and (2) she was also conscious that she had no control over her desires and, yet, that she fervently desired *x* for herself under the circumstances. Despite her being conscious of constraints (1) and (2), we nonetheless concluded that by virtue of her subjectively experiencing her desire for *x* as what she wanted for herself under the circumstances, she could plausibly be described as 'consenting' to *x* in her mind. The same must also be true, then, of a person like Snow Blanche who is conscious solely of constraint (1). That is to say, if a drugged woman, who knows that she cannot influence *either* the occurrence of *x* *or* her subjective feelings about *x*, can nevertheless be described as consenting to *x*, so, too, can Snow Blanche who, though having no influence over the occurrence of *x*, consciously believes that she *is* in control of her subjective desires for *x*.

Admittedly, 'Snow Blanche' is an easier case for attitudinal consent than most cases, because Snow Blanche's desire to be kissed was unconditional. It would be a harder, and more realistic, case if her desire to be kissed were *conditional*—that is, if she consciously felt that her desire to be kissed was conditioned upon the situation in which she found herself. To examine the harder case, therefore, let us imagine a 'Snow Bianca' who finds herself in the identical situation as Snow Blanche, except that she has the following feelings: (1) Snow Bianca wishes above all that she could be released from paralysis without suffering the unpleasantness of a man's kissing her; (2) yet she abhors having to remain in perpetual paralysis; (3) given that a man's kiss is the only thing that will release her from her perpetual paralysis, she would rather be kissed than not kissed, and she would rather be kissed by a prince than by a commoner. Whereupon, a prince and a commoner both appear, and both seem eager to kiss her. The prince announces that he will kiss Snow Bianca first, and that the commoner may kiss her afterwards. Hearing the conversation, Snow Bianca thinks, 'Once the prince's kiss awakens me from perpetual paralysis, I will make sure that no man ever kisses me again'.

Now what about Snow Bianca? Does she 'desire' the kiss she receives from the prince? If so, does she desire it in ways that are relevant to attitudinal consent? The answers are more complex for her than for a person whose desires are unconditional, because her desires occur in the context of ranked preferences. To say that a person 'desires' something, say, *x*, in the context of ranked preferences means that the person has compared *x* to a certain baseline alternative and, given her preferences, prefers *x* to the baseline alternative. Clearly, Snow Bianca desires to be released from paralysis without being kissed because she prefers that to every baseline alternative that she imagines for herself. As for being kissed by the prince, however, she both does and does not desire it: she desires it as compared to the baseline alternative of 'remaining in perpetual paralysis'; but she does not desire it as compared to the baseline alternative of being 'released from paralysis without any man's kissing her'.

The more important question is the relationship of Snow Bianca's conflicting desires to her attitudinal consent. We have seen that Snow Bianca both does and does not desire the prince to kiss her, depending upon the baseline alternative. What does that signify regarding her attitudinal consent? Does that mean that she *can* be described as consenting in her mind to be kissed by the prince? Or does it mean that she *cannot* be described as consenting in her mind to be kissed by the prince? Or does it mean that, as with desire, she both can and cannot be described as consenting in her mind to be kissed by the prince? Let us consider the last possibility first. The reason that Snow Bianca can have conflicting desires is that the concept of 'desire' is not predicated upon a single and exclusive baseline for comparing ranked preferences. Desires are a function of a baseline, but the baselines can vary from one inquiry to another. That is why one can say of Snow Bianca that she both does and does not desire to be kissed by the prince: she desires it by reference to some baselines and not by reference to others. In contrast, although attitudinal consent is also a function of a baseline, the baseline does not vary. For if it did, it would mean that, if the commoner stole the first kiss from Snow Bianca by forcibly pushing the prince aside as the prince struggles to kiss her, we would have to say she 'consented' to the stolen kiss (even though she clearly did not), merely because she would have preferred the commoner's kiss to the baseline of not being kissed by anyone. By the same token, we would have to say of Snow Bianca that she did *not* consent to be kissed by the prince (even though she clearly did), merely because she would have dispreferred the prince's kiss to the baseline of being released from paralysis without being kissed by anyone.

If we are correct, then, that Snow Bianca *did* subjectively consent to be kissed by the prince and *did not* subjectively consent to be kissed by the commoner, it means that the concept of factual attitudinal consent itself specifies a baseline for comparing ranked preferences. The example of Snow Bianca also helps illuminate what the baseline is: persons with ranked preferences factually consent to *x* in their minds if, all things considered, either they prefer *x* to what they believe to be the alternatives or (within jurisdictions that equate indifference with preference) they are so indifferent as to whether *x* occurs as to be willing to leave its occurrence to *A*.[55] Thus, Snow Bianca does, indeed, subjectively consent to being kissed by the prince, because she prefers it to what she believes to be the alternatives, *viz.*, that she will remain paralyzed. By the same token, she does not subjectively consent to be kissed by the commoner, because she neither prefers it to what she believes to be the alternatives (*i.e.*, that she will be kissed by the prince) nor is she indifferent as to which occurs.[56]

To be sure, some people may perceive themselves to be so much a captive of events that they regard as inevitable, and are so resigned to them, that they do not know how they feel about them. Thus, recall Dan-Cohen's hypothetical woman, who believes it to be inevitable that she will marry whomever her father selects for her as a husband. Dan-Cohen supposes that once the woman discovers whom she must marry, she also discovers that she wants to marry him. But it is also possible to imagine a woman who is so accustomed to lacking control over life decisions, and so unaccustomed to consulting her own desires, that she cannot be said to have any personal view at all about a marriage she regards as inevitable—not even the personal view that, having consulted her feelings, she does not care one way or another whether she marries. In that event, she cannot be said to have consented to the marriage in her mind, because she does not unconditionally desire the marriage, nor does she prefer it to what she believes to be the alternatives, nor is she so indifferent as to be willing to leave its occurrence to *A*.[57]

Situation 2: Where persons believe they may possess influence over whether sexual intercourse occurs. In contrast to the way Snow Blanche and Snow Bianca felt about being kissed, most people who desire to engage in sexual intimacy probably feel that there is a causal connection between their desires, on the one hand, and whether sexual intercourse occurs, on the other. Many of them pursue sexual intercourse so fervently that they are oblivious to alternatives, except, perhaps, for the unwanted alternative of forgoing the sexual intimacy altogether. Persons in that frame of mind can be described as factually consenting to sexual intercourse in their minds, because they feel unconditional desire for it. Others, however, consciously choose to submit to sexual intercourse with mixed feelings. Their willingness to allow sexual intercourse to take place is a ranked preference, a preference that they rank above some of the alternatives they believe are at their disposal, and below others. If they choose to submit to sexual intercourse—that is, if they refrain from exercising the influence they believe they may have to preclude or forestall sexual intercourse from taking place—they do so because their desires are constrained by their circumstances. They choose to submit to sexual intercourse, something that they would otherwise rebuff if more favorable circumstances existed, because they believe that it is the best they can do under present circumstances. They prefer it to what they believe to be the alternatives.

Take the experience that Diana Russell attributes to 'Mrs. Norman' in her book *Rape in Marriage*. Mrs. Norman found sexual intercourse with her husband physically repellent during all of her 18 years of marriage. If the choice had been entirely hers, she would have abstained. At the same time, however, although her husband did not resort to physical or emotional threats, she felt she 'had to do it because I was his wife'.[58] Forced by circumstance to rank her preferences, she reluctantly submitted to acts of marital intercourse, which she felt she might have avoided, because she preferred engaging in repugnant sexual intercourse with her husband to feeling that she had failed in her marital duties. Other women do the same thing. They reluctantly engage in sexual intercourse to avoid what they regard as greater evils under the circumstances, *e.g.*, losing a chance to gratify a man they love, losing an opportunity to become pregnant, disappointing a potential boyfriend, alienating a long-time companion, being exposed to public ridicule as a 'tease' or 'frigid', losing a job, being physically battered, being mortally wounded, being deliberately killed. Thus, in contrast to a woman who does everything she can to prevent sexual intercourse from taking place, even at the risk of being killed, they consciously *refrain* from doing all they believe they can to thwart sexual intercourse because they prefer sexual intercourse to the alternatives they believe they would face under the circumstances.

Admittedly, there are significant legal differences between sexual intercourse induced by a threat of violent death and sexual intercourse induced by reluctance to disappoint a loved one. The former is a criminal wrong in every society; the latter is not. Consequently, when subjective 'consent' is used in a legal sense to legitimate sexual intercourse, it does require a certain measure of freedom, namely, whatever freedom to reject sexual intercourse the society believes a woman must possess if her choice of sexual intercourse is to satisfy her legitimate interests in it. Thus, legally, a woman does not subjectively consent to sexual intercourse at the point of a gun because, regardless of how much she may desire the man to have sexual intercourse with her rather than kill her, society does not permit a man to elicit a woman's acquiescence by threatening otherwise to kill her. Nor can a woman be described, even factually, as consenting to sexual intercourse in her mind when she is too paralyzed by fear to assess her preferences under the circumstances.[59] Nevertheless, just as a person who chooses sexual intercourse as the lesser of two evils under the circumstances can be described as 'submitting' to it, she can also be described as factually 'consenting' to it. For, used factually, 'consent' conveys precisely what distinguishes her state of mind from that of persons who suffer sexual intercourse *without* preferring sexual intercourse to what they believe to be the alternatives.

To illustrate this factual usage of 'consent' as the mere choosing of *x* as the lesser of two evils, contrast Christy M., on the one hand, with Samuel Whittaker's victim, on the other. Christy was walking at noon in Los Angeles with her infant daughter trailing a few steps behind when the defendant, a stranger, slowed down and asked her if she wanted a ride. She said 'No' and continued walking. She realized a few moments later that her daughter was no longer behind her. Turning, she saw her daughter's legs protruding from the passenger window of the car into which the defendant was pulling her. Christy ran to the car to get her daughter, but the defendant told her, 'If you want her, you have to get in the car with me'. Christy was afraid to get into the car, but she did because, as a court later put it, 'although she was afraid to get into the car, she was more afraid not to get in, because of what could happen to her daughter; she felt she had no choice but to cooperate'. The defendant thereupon drove to an alley between two buildings where he made the little girl get out. He told Christy to take off her pants and get into the back seat. She did, and the defendant had sexual intercourse with her there. She later explained why she complied with his sexual demands: 'Because I was thinking of where my daughter was, and I was concerned about where she was; and I just felt like if whatever he wanted to do, that the quicker he did it and it was done with, that I could get out and find her. I didn't want to argue with him or get him mad to where he might hurt me'. The California court rejected the defendant's claim that Christy 'voluntarily' consented to sexual intercourse. Christy was 'forced to consent to the defendant's demands', the court said, because 'she was afraid he would harm her [child] if she did not accede to his demands'.[60]

Now consider Samuel Whittaker's victim in *Whittaker v. State.*[61] We do not know the woman's name because, to protect her privacy, the court refers to her anonymously as 'the prosecutrix'. But we do know that she did everything that she believed was in her power to prevent Whittaker from having sexual intercourse with her, even at the risk of being killed. When the assault began, she did a number of things to frustrate it. She struggled against Whittaker, who was armed with a revolver. She called for help. Even after he threatened to kill her if she did not 'shut up', she continued to cry for help. She continued to resist 'to the utmost extent of her physical ability', until she 'couldn't do any more'. What distinguishes Christy from Whittaker's victim is her state of mind under the circumstances. Both women experienced terrible fears: Whittaker's victim feared that she would be shot; Christy feared that her daughter would be killed or lost. Both women were also compelled by circumstances to choose between facing their fears and yielding to sexual intercourse. Both women were subjected to sexual intercourse that amounted to rape. They differed, however, in their preferences under the circumstances and, hence, in the way they were raped. Whittaker's victim preferred death to sexual intercourse with Whittaker and, hence, struggled till the end, despite the risk of being killed. Christy preferred sexual intercourse to the loss of her child and, hence, complied with the stranger's demands, despite her repugnance. This difference in attitude toward sexual intercourse is reflected in the language of consent. Although one can easily say that Whittaker's victim was *forced* to have sexual intercourse, one cannot possibly say that she was 'forced *to consent*' to sexual intercourse, because she is not reported to have done or experienced anything that could be characterized as acquiescence to sexual intercourse. In contrast, one can say that Christy was 'forced to consent' to sexual intercourse—indeed, that is precisely what the court in Christy's case *said* of her, that she was forced to 'consent'—because Christy did experience a form of acquiescence: she consciously submitted to sexual intercourse because she preferred it to her alternatives under the circumstances.

Of course, the Christy court could have used consent differently. It could have used consent in a legal sense: it could have said that because Christy lacked the freedom of choice that she ought to have had, she did *not* consent to the sexual intercourse. But, instead, the court framed the issue differently. It said that Christy *did* 'consent', albeit out of fear. In saying so, the court could not have been using consent legally because if Christy legally consented, Samuel Whittaker would have been acquitted. Rather, the *Whittaker* court used consent in the same way that Canada used 'consent' in section 143 when it is stated that a man commits rape who has sexual intercourse with a woman *with* her 'consent' if the man elicits her 'consent' by 'force'. The Christy court used consent to refer to a certain mental state on Christy's part, *i.e.*, the mental state of mind of preferring sexual intercourse to the alternatives, without in any way suggesting that her mental state constituted a defense to what her assailant did.

This leaves one remaining question: Why distinguish between persons based upon whether or not they feel they can influence the course of events? That is, why distinguish between Snow Blanche, who knew she had no control over whether the prince would kiss her, and Diana Russell's subject, Mrs. Norman, who felt she had some control over whether she would have sexual intercourse with her husband? The distinction, after all, does not *determine* whether persons can be described as factually consenting to conduct x in their minds. Persons can be described as consenting in either event. And, in either event, the nature of their consent is the same: persons factually consent to x in their minds if they either unconditionally desire x or prefer x to what they believe to be the alternatives. Rather, the distinction is significant for *evidentiary* reasons in that it tends to *reveal* whether persons in fact subjectively consent to x—specifically, whether, in fact, they prefer x to what they believe to be the alternatives. With respect to Snow Blanche, and others who feel they possess no alternatives. With respect to Snow Blanche, and others who feel they possess no control over whether a sexual encounter occur, we cannot ascertain whether they subjectively consent except by inquiring directly into their states of mind. With respect to persons like Mrs. Norman who feel that they possess control over whether sexual intercourse occurs, however, we have circumstantial evidence of attitudinal consent. We know that unless they are too disoriented to assess their preferences under the circumstances, or too paralyzed by panic to act accordingly,[62] the fact that they do not resort to the measures which they believe are at their disposal to foreclose sexual intercourse means that they prefer sexual intercourse to the risk associated with trying to stop it. And the fact that they prefer sexual intercourse to the risk associated with trying to stop it means that they factually consent to it in their minds, for that is what factual attitudinal consent *is*.

The occurrence of sexual intercourse does not conclusively establish factual consent in persons who believe they can control whether sexual intercourse occurs. Persons may be too disoriented to assess their preferences under the circumstances, or too paralyzed to act on their preferences. Or they may believe they have control and try their best to exert it—only to discover, to their dismay, that the measures which they thought would succeed in preventing sexual intercourse are inadequate. Samuel Whittaker's victim believed till the end, albeit mistakenly, that if she continued to struggle, she could thwart Whittaker's sexual designs. Obviously, such women do not factually consent to sexual intercourse merely because they fight to the end mistakenly believing that they can escape it. Nevertheless, the very fact that a person was subjected to sexual intercourse that she appears to have been capable of preventing is circumstantial evidence of factual attitudinal consent, because it means she *did* factually consent to it in her mind, unless she was too disoriented or paralyzed to resist or she mistakenly believed her resistance would succeed.

Conclusion

The criminal law uses the term consent in various ways, including what I call 'legal consent'. Legal consent is any consent by a person that suffices in law to constitute a complete or partial defense to conduct that is otherwise a criminal violation of the person's interests. Thus, the law uses consent in a legal sense when it defines rape as the crime of having sexual intercourse with a person without her 'consent'. We shall see in later chapters that legal consent comes in three distinct forms depending upon how criminal statutes are framed: (1) mental states of voluntary acquiescence to conduct; (2) expressions of voluntary acquiescence to conduct; and (3) legal fictions of mental states or expressions of voluntary acquiescence to conduct. Whichever form they take, however, definitions of legal consent are invariably complex.

Yet at the same time, the criminal law also uses the term 'consent' in a quite different sense. It uses consent as a synonym for what it also refers to as 'submission' or 'assent', namely, for simpler instances of factual acquiescence that are necessary components of certain forms of legal consent but that do not themselves suffice to constitute legal consent. In order to distinguish these simpler instances of factual acquiescence from the more complex forms of legal consent of which they are a necessary part, I refer to them as 'factual consent'—'factual', because they consist of instances of empirical acquiescence that may or may not be accompanied by such additional elements of voluntariness as are legally required for legal consent; and 'consent', because legislatures and courts frequently refer to these simpler instances of factual acquiescence as 'consent'. Factual consent in turn comes in two forms. Factual *attitudinal* consent consists of a mental state of factual acquiescence on a person's part that may or may not be accompanied by the additional elements of voluntariness that are legally required to render it a defense. Factual *expressive* consent consists of an expression of factual acquiescence that may, or may not, be accompanied by the additional elements of voluntariness that are legally required to render it a defense.

I have devoted this first chapter to factual attitudinal consent because, conceptually speaking, it is central to all conceptions of consent. Factual attitudinal consent is essential to conceptions of legal consent that are predicated upon the possession of mental states of acquiescence, because it is a necessary *component* of such legal consent. Factual attitudinal consent is also closely related to all conceptions of expressive consent, because attitudes of acquiescence are precisely what persons who express consent are *making reference to*. Finally, factual attitudinal consent is conceptually connected to all fictions of legal consent by virtue of what the latter are fictions *of*—namely, attitudes of acquiescence and expressions of attitudes of acquiescence.

To illustrate the role that conceptions of factual attitudinal consent can play in analyzing disputes, let us recall Canadian Penal Code section 143:

> A male person commits rape when he has sexual intercourse with a female person who is not his wife,
> (a) without her consent, or
> (b) with her consent if the consent
> (i) is extorted by threats or fear of bodily harm,
> (ii) is obtained by impersonating her husband, or
> (iii) is obtained by false and fraudulent representations as to the nature and quality of the act.

Section 143's usage of consent is factual rather than legal, because if its usage of consent were legal, subsection (b) would not only be superfluous, it would be contradictory. Section 143's usage is also attitudinal rather than expressive, because the Canadian courts have interpreted it to be a reference to a mental state rather than to an expression. Now let us consider how section 143 would apply to three cases that we previously discussed in other contexts:

> (1) ***No consent (Elizabeth).*** Elizabeth, a gynecology patient, submits to what she thinks is a rectal examination, only to discover afterwards that her gynecologist had actually subjected her to anal intercourse.

(2) ***Invalid consent (Christy).*** Christy, being accosted on the street while walking with her child, submitted to her assailant's sexual demands for fear that if she did not, he would injure her child.

(3) ***Valid consent (Mrs. Norman).*** Mrs. Norman, being in a loveless marriage, submitted to marital intercourse that gave her no physical pleasure, not because her husband ever threatened or coerced her in any way that the criminal law regards as illicit, but because she simply believed it to be her duty.

Section 143's usage of consent in a factual sense is significant, because this usage does something that cannot be done by using consent in a legal sense: it highlights what is present in both Christy's and Mrs. Norman's cases and yet lacking in Elizabeth's case, namely, that Christy and Mrs. Norman subjectively acquiesced in sexual intercourse as the best they believed they could do for themselves under the circumstances, while Elizabeth did not. Consent cannot be used in a legal sense to highlight that element, because when consent is used in a legal sense, it classifies Christy's mental state with Elizabeth's as an instance of 'non-consent', rather than classifying Christy's mental state with Mrs. Norman's as an instance of consent. Moreover, it is important for several reasons to be able to identify the subjective acquiescence that Christy and Mrs. Norman share and that Elizabeth lacks. For one thing, subjective acquiescence is a necessary and integral component of legal attitudinal consent. Indeed, it is precisely the absence in Elizabeth of subjective acquiescence to sexual intercourse that precludes Elizabeth from legally consenting to what the gynecologist did to her. For another, by using 'consent' to refer to the subjective acquiescence that Christy and Mrs. Norman share, Canada obliges itself to make explicit what is sometimes masked when 'consent' is used in a legal sense, namely, the additional elements of voluntariness that are legally required for such subjective consent to be *valid.* Having used consent in a factual sense to refer to subject acquiescence, Canada goes on to specify that for subjective consent to be valid, it must be untainted by force and fraud of certain specified kinds. In making those additional elements conditions explicit, Canada clarifies precisely what renders Mrs. Norman's consent valid and Christy's consent invalid under section 143—namely, that Mrs. Norman subjectively acquiesced in sexual intercourse without fear of bodily harm, while Christy did not.

To be sure, Canada could have achieved the same goals without using consent to refer to factual attitudinal consent. It could have stipulated that the term 'consent' referred to legal consent and used alternative words such 'submission' or 'assent' to refer to the underlying mental states of factual acquiescence that Christy and Mrs. Norman shared. Indeed, if all jurisdictions and commentators uniformly confined 'consent' to legal consent, and if they all used alternative words such as 'submission' for the underlying elements of factual acquiescence, they could eliminate the confusions that presently arise when factual consent is conflated with legal consent, as described in Chapter 8. In reality, however, jurisdictions commonly use consent to refer to acquiescence of all kinds, legal as well as factual, and they will probably continue to do so. As long as they do, Canada's usage is not only unobjectionable, but a healthy reminder of the normative significance of factual attitudinal 'consent'.

What, then, are the minimal elements of factual attitudinal consent? What does it mean to subjectively consent to conduct *x* under conditions that may or may not suffice for the consent to be a valid defense to the perpetrator of *x*? We have seen that to subjectively consent to *x*, one must at the very least possess the mental state of choosing *x* for oneself under the circumstances. Such mental states of choosing can take several alternative forms, any of which suffice. Thus, it is enough that a person possess an unconditional desire for *x*. It is also enough that a person possess a decided preference for *x* under the circumstances—that is, a desire for *x*, all things considered. It can also be enough that a person be so indifferent as to *x* as to be willing to leave it to others as to whether *x* occurs. (Whether such indifference is enough depends upon the jurisdiction's normative views regarding *x*—specifically, upon whether the statute at issue requires that a person possess an affirmative preference for *x* under the circumstances or whether it is satisfied that she be indifferent.) Needless to say, this does not mean such mental states also suffice in themselves to constitute criminal defenses to actors who subject persons to *x*. It means that such mental states are *necessary* for legal attitudinal consent, not *sufficient* for it. Without them, there can be no subjective consent to *x* of any kind. With them, there is *factual* attitudinal consent, though whether there is also *legal* attitudinal consent depends upon whether the person subjectively chose *x* under conditions of voluntariness that suffice to protect the interests the jurisdiction at issue deems her to possess with respect to conduct *x*.

We have also seen that factual attitudinal consent itself presupposes capacity on a person's part, and a certain awareness on her part. But it does not presuppose any additional freedom on her part. Thus, a person cannot subjectively choose *x*, unless she has the capacity to adjudge what she desires for herself under the circumstances as she perceives them to be. Nor can she subjectively choose *x* for purposes of the criminal law unless the description of *x* of which she is aware is an instance of what the criminal statute at issue describes to be the conduct that it prohibits in the absence of legal consent. However, a person can subjectively choose *x* as that which she desires for herself under the circumstances even if she has no control over whether *x* occurs, and even if she would not choose *x* but for the circumstances in which she finds herself.

Notes

1. Wisconsin v. Herfel, 49 Wis. 2d 513, 519, 182 N.W.2d 232, 236 (1971). *See* also Regina v. Olugboja, [1982] 1 Q.B. 320, 332.
2. For the contrast between consent and submission, and consent and acquiescence, *see* note 4 of Introduction to Part I. For the contrast between 'consent' and 'assent', *see, e.g.*, Code of Alabama § 13A-2-7(c) (2000) ('Unless otherwise provided by this Criminal Code or by the law defining the offense, assent does not constitute consent if . . . (4) It is induced by force, duress or deception'); Missouri Revised Statutes § 556.061(5) (1999) ('Consent or lack of consent may be expressed or implied. Assent does not constitute consent if . . . (c) It is induced by force, duress or deception'); Hartley v. Alaska, 653 P.2d 1052, 1054 (Alaska Ct. App., 1982) ('[The complaining witness] vehemently denied that she had

consented to perform fellatio and stated that she assented because she thought that if she did not, he would kill her').

3. Criminal Code, Revised Statutes of Canada, 1970, c. C-34, § 143 (repealed 1980-81). For the current version, *see* Criminal Code § 271. For a District of Columbia case that uses 'consent' in the same way as the Canadian Code, *see* McGuinn v. United States, 191 F.2d 477, 479 (D.C., Cir., 1951) ('[In prosecution for rape] there must be an absence of consent by the complaining witness to warrant a conviction, unless consent was induced by . . . fear').
4. *See* Regina v. Abraham, (1977) 30 C.C.C. (2d) 332 (quoting Regina v. Donovan, [1934] 2 K.B. 498, 504) ('Consent, being a state of mind, is to proved or negatived only after a full and careful review of the behaviour of the person who is alleged to have consented').
5. *See* the Comment to § 213.1, *Model Penal Code*, pt. II, vol. 1, p. 303.
6. *See* California v. Barnes, 42 Cal. 3d 284, 289, 721 P.2d 110, 119, 228 Cal. Rptr. 228, 299 (1986); California v. Bruce, 208 Cal. App. 3d 1099, 1104, 256 Cal. Rptr. 647, 649-50 (1989):

   > When asserting the defense of consent, the defendant focuses on the victim's state of mind alone.
   >
   > * * *
   >
   > This defense [of consent] is distinct from the Mayberry defense—the defense of reasonable, good faith belief that the victim consented. When a defendant claims that the victim consented, the jury must weigh the evidence and decide which of the two witnesses is telling the truth. The Mayberry defense permits the jury to conclude that both the victim and the accused are telling the truth. The jury first considers the victim's state of mind and decides whether she consented to the alleged acts. If she did not, the jury will view the events from the defendant's perspective to determine whether the manner in which the victim expressed her lack of consent was so equivocal as to cause the accused to reasonably believe that she consented when she did not.

7. Coley v. Florida, 616 So.2d 1017, 1023 (1994).
8. Hawaii v. Lira, 70 Haw. 23, 28, 759 P.2d 869, 872 (1988).
9. *See* Louisiana Revised Statutes § 14:43 (1992).
10. Michigan v. Hale, 142 Mich. App. 451, 453, 370 N.W.2d 382, 383 (1985).
11. Regina v. Malone, [1998] 2 Cr App Rep 447. *See* also Regina v. Olugboja, [1982] 1 Q.B. 320, 331 (consent is a 'state of mind').
12. *See, e.g.*, Dolchok v. Alaska, 763 P.2d 977 (1988) ('Dolchok's theory of defense was that [the complaining witness] consented to the act of sexual intercourse or, in the alternative, that she failed to manifest her lack of consent'); Iowa v. Sullivan, 298 N.W.2d 267 (1980) (stating that 'state of mind' of the victim matters to the defendant's guilt); Maine v. Ricci, 507 A.2d 587 (1986) ('The words in section 251(1)(E) "produces in that person a reasonable fear" set forth a subjective-objective test, in which the magnitude of the threat is measured using the victim's mental state. The victim must in fact fear that death, serious bodily injury, or kidnapping will occur, and that fear must be reasonable under the circumstances') (citations omitted); Mayes v. Maryland, 50 Md. App. 628, 440 A.2d 1093 (1982) (providing that, before a defendant can be convicted of rape by means of fear of serious physical injury, the court must make a determination regarding the victim's state of mind).

    For commentators who assert that consent in the law of rape is a state of mind, *see* Bronitt, 'Rape and Lack of Consent', p. 189 ('Lack of consent governs the framework for rape in the present law. The effect is that the victim's state of mind before and during intercourse is a central focus in many rape trials . . . '.); Dripps, 'Panel Discussion: Men, Women, and Rape', p. 141 ('At present, the law recognizes an absence of consent as a fact necessary to any conviction for rape, and understands consent as a mental state of the victim'); Dworkin, 'The Resistance Standard in Rape Legislation', p. 682 (referring to 'consent' as a 'subjective standard requiring examination of the victim's state of mind'); Estrich, 'Rape', p. 1099 and n.25 (1986) (referring to consent in rape cases as a 'state of mind' on the putative victim's part); Schulhofer, *Unwanted Sex*, p. 63 ('It might seem too obvious for discussion that consent means consent in the mind of the person who is supposed to be giving it B in this case, the woman'); Note, 'Forcible and Statutory Rape', pp. 54-55 (1952) ('If a woman is legally capable of granting consent, her subjective attitude toward the sexual act determines whether or not it is rape').

13. I take the term 'attitudinal' consent from McGregor, 'Force, Consent, and the Reasonable Woman', p. 253.
14. *See* Malm, 'The Ontological Status of Consent', p. 14 ('I need a way to refer to that mental state. I will call it "consent-related willingness" or "willingness", for short. This type of willing is more along the lines of "willing to go along with" or "accepting" than either "wanting" or "desiring"').
15. For a commentator who fallaciously conflates *indecisiveness* with *indifference*, *see* Brett, 'Sexual Offenses and Consent', p. 84 (attempting to buttress his view that conceptions of prescriptive *expressive* consent are normatively preferable to conceptions of prescriptive *attitudinal* consent by fallaciously juxtaposing the way prescriptive expressive consent treats instances of *indecisiveness* with the way prescriptive attitudinal consent treats instances of *indifference*).
16. Cf. Brett, 'Sexual Offenses', p. 84 ('[It is] unlikely... that anyone would actually lay serious criminal charges against someone for involving one in an act about which one is neutral').
17. *See, e.g.*, Queen v. Park, 1995 Can. Sup. Ct. LEXIS 43, para. 39 (Canadian Supreme Court, 1995) ('the mens rea of sexual assault is not only satisfied when it is shown that the accused knew that the complainant was essentially saying "no", but is also satisfied when it is shown that the accused knew that the complainant was essentially not saying "yes"').
18. Termination of Life on Request and Assistance with Suicide (Review Procedures) Act, Upper House of the States General, 2000-01, no. 137, 26 691 (28 Nov. 2000).
19. *Id.* at arts. 2(1)(a), 20.
20. Alexander, 'The Moral Magic of Consent (II)', p. 166:

    > I agree . . . that consent . . . must be the exercise of will and, thus, a subjective mental state . . . I, on the other hand, believe that to consent to the conduct in question is not to intend that conduct. Rather, when one consents to what would otherwise be a boundary-crossing act of another, one chooses to forgo or waive one's moral objection to the boundary crossing. One need not choose that the act occur: indeed, one cannot choose another's acts. One can choose, however, to forgo one's moral objections, or, put differently, to waive one's right correlative to the other's duty not to act. To consent is to form the intention to forgo one's moral complaint against another's act.

21. Sherwin, 'Infelicitous Sex', p. 217. *See* also Brett, 'Commentary', p. 255 ('To consent is to *communicate permission*. In particular, it is to communicate permission to another person to act where he or she would otherwise have an obligation to refrain'); McGregor, 'Force, Consent, and the Reasonable Woman', p. 242 ('One common understanding of consent is that one "authorizes" another to act.... Another way of thinking about consent is that of giving "permission" to another to cross over a boundary of one's own. . . . Consent must, then, be deliberate and voluntary since its "understood purpose is to change the structure of rights of the parties . . . "'.).

23. New Jersey takes the position, for example, that individuals do not possess competence to legally consent to sexual intercourse if they are 'incapable of *understanding* or exercising *the right to refuse* to engage in such conduct with another'. New Jersey v. Olivio, 123 N.J. 550, 564, 589 A.2d 597, 605 (1991) (emphasis added). *See* also the consent form that the California legislature recommends—but, significantly, does not prescribe—regarding a person's consent to a durable power of attorney to withdraw life support. *See* Brock, *Life and Death*, pp. 374-86.
24. *See* Schneckloth v. Bustamonte, 412 US 218 (1973).
25. *See, e.g.*, New Jersey v. Johnson, 68 N.J. 349, 346 A.2d 66 (1975); Washington v. Ferrier, 136 Wash.2d 103, 960 P.2d 927 (1998); Bradley, *Criminal Procedure*, pp. 192-95 (German law requires the police to advise persons of their right not to be searched).
26. North Carolina v. Moorman, 320 N.C. 387, 391, 358 S.E.2d 502, 505 (1987) (quoting In re Childers, 310 P. 2d 776, 778 (Okla. Crim. App. 1957)). The North Carolina state defines rape as sexual intercourse 'against' a woman's will', rather than 'without her consent', but the North Carolina courts have held that the statutory phrase 'against the will' is synonymous with—and *means*—sexual intercourse 'without . . . consent'. North Carolina v. Carter, 265 N.C. 626, 630, 144 S.E.2d 826, 829 (1965).
27. In a notorious recent case, five young men from upper-state New York serially had sexual intercourse in a barroom booth with a woman acquaintance who had fallen into a coma after drinking excessively. The case caused an outcry, less because of what the defendants did than because of the lenient sentence the judge imposed on the five defendants—a fine of $750 for each of the five defendants. *See Los Angeles Times*, April 15, 1994, pt. A, p. 1, col. 1. For an Australian case that also raised an outcry because the judge sentenced a rapist to a significantly shorter prison term than the maximum possible sentence on the ground that the victim, having first been knocked senseless by a blow to the head, was unconscious of the sexual intercourse at the time it occurred, *see The Independent*, May 20, 1993, p. 14. For a collection of cases on sexual intercourse with persons who are asleep, *see* Hom, *North Carolina v. Moorman: Can Sex With A Sleeping Woman Constitute Forcible Rape?*

    With respect to the criminality of having sexual intercourse with a woman whose judgment is *impaired* by intoxication, some jurisdictions distinguish for various purposes between self-induced intoxication, on the one hand, and involuntary intoxication, on the other; and some jurisdictions distinguish, or further distinguish, between intoxication induced by the defendant, on the one hand, and intoxication induced by strangers, on the other. *See* generally Kramer, 'Rule by Myth', pp. 124-32.

    With respect to sexual intercourse with a woman who is so intoxicated as to be *unconscious*, however, all jurisdictions agree that it is criminal, regardless of whether the intoxication is voluntary or involuntary, and regardless of whether the defendant or others administer the intoxicant. *See* also *Model Penal Code*, pt. II, § 213.1, at 317:

    > Common-law authorities treated intercourse with an unconscious woman as rape and occasionally expanded this rule to cases where the female was not technically unconscious but was so incapacitated by alcohol or drugs as to be in a condition of utter insensibility or stupefaction. Most current statutes, however, differentiate unconsciousness from lesser impairment and require in the latter case that the drug or intoxicant be administered by or with the privity of the defendant in order to constitute the highest degree of forcible rape.

    Indeed, rather than leaving it to interpretation regarding 'consent', a number of jurisdictions specifically provide in their rape statutes that it is an offense to have sexual intercourse with someone who is 'unconscious'. *See, e.g.*, Michigan Compiled Laws Annotation, §

720.520d(1), making it an offense of criminal sexual assault in the third degree to have sexual intercourse with anyone who is physically helpless, and defining as 'physically helpless' anyone who is 'unconscious [or] asleep'. But *see* Colorado Revised Statutes § 18-3-402(4)(e) (2000) (a person who knowingly has sexual intercourse with a person whom he knows to be 'physically helpless' is guilty of sexual assault only if the victim 'has not consented' to such intercourse). For the reference to 'capacity to consent', *see* Missouri v. Dighera, 617 S.E.2d 524, 533 n.8 (1981).

28. *See* Malm, 'The Ontological Status of Consent', p. 148:

> The willing [of a person who is subjectively consenting] must also be done by someone who has the capacity to choose among her options in light of her goals and values. Only then is it possible for the willing to be a reflection of a self, or, in other words, only then could it plausibly be said that *I* consent.

Oliver Sacks in his book *Awakenings*, p. 15, describes some victims of sleeping sickness as suffering from what in neurological parlance is called 'aboulia', or 'absence of will':

> This passivity [of victims of sleeping sickness] . . . is also seen in ordinary Parkinson's disease: countless patients have said to me, 'I don't walk—I *am* walked', or (especially of festination), 'I play no part in it—it happens by itself'. In the 'zombie-like' post-encephalitic syndromes, passivity may become absolute and universal: 'Lack of will', or 'aboulia', forms the empty heart of such states. Such zombie—like patients cannot say or feel 'I will', and since the sense of 'I' depends on willing or acting, these will-less patients have lost their 'I'.

More common are people who are too frightened to decide what they want under the circumstances. The Wisconsin Supreme Court in Whittaker v. Wisconsin, 50 Wis. 518, 7 N.W. 431 (1880), holds that a woman cannot consent to sexual intercourse who is so 'paralyzed . . . by fear . . . that her volition [cannot] be exercised either for or against the act of sexual connection', or who is 'so terrified. . .as to destroy or suspend, for the time being, all power of mental protest'. People can also be too startled to make a judgment of acquiescence. This appears to be what the Michigan legislature means in making it an offense of 'criminal sexual assault' for a person to 'overcome [a] victim' by means of 'the element of surprise'. Michigan Complied Laws Annotated § 750.520b(1)(f)(v). For a jurisdiction that reaches the same result without possessing a statutory provision for 'surprise', *see* Ash v. Indiana, 455 N.E.2d 965 (1983).

29. Massachusetts v. Helfant, 398 Mass. 214, 217, 496 N.E.2d 433, 437 (1986) ('in a fog'). Massachusetts law requires that the identify of rape victims be kept confidential in criminal cases and, hence, the case report in *Helfant* does not identify Starr Copithorne by name. Interestingly, however, her name became public as a matter of law when she brought a separate civil suit against the hospital for which she worked, and with which Dr. Helfant was affiliated, for failing to take disciplinary action against Helfant for previous reports of sexual misconduct with female patients. *See* Copithorne v. Framingham Union Hospital, 401 Mass. 860, 520 N.E.2d 139 (1987).

30. *See* Hurd, 'The Moral Magic of Consent', p. 126 ('one must conclude that consent is equivalent not to desire as such, but to the execution of a desire, namely, to choice'); Wertheimer, 'What Is Consent?', pp. 569-70.

31. Colombian thieves and rapists are reported to use a drug, called 'Burundanga', that appears to have this effect. Burundanga is a derivative of a Colombian species of the nightshade plant that, when refined and administered to victims, causes them to 'lose their will' and to do whatever they are told to do, including engage in sexual intercourse. *See Wall Street Journal*, July 3, 1995, section A, p.1, col. 4.

32. Cf. McIlwain v. Florida 2d 1194 (1981). The defendant in *McIlwain*, a dentist, administered nitrous oxide (or 'laughing gas') to a 17-year-old boy under the pretext of performing surgery and, after the drug had taken effect, sexually molested him. The boy was conscious the whole time. He was also repelled by the experience, which left him 'shaking, sobbing, and trembling' when he was returned to his parents. However, because the paralyzing effects of the nitrous oxide, he was unable to say or do anything to stop the molestation at the time it occurred:

    I couldn't believe that it was happening, but I knew it was happening. . . . I thought I could get up, but I couldn't. I felt kind of heavy. . . . I couldn't respond, you know. . . .Then I kind of got disgusted at myself because I wanted to get up, but I couldn't.

    The boy did not subjectively acquiesce in the sexual intimacy because, though conscious of remaining passive throughout the encounter, he did not subjectively choose it as something he desired under the circumstances. For an account of the extent to which choice presupposes 'cognitive' capacity, *see* Duff, 'Choice, Character, and Criminal Liability', pp. 355-56.
33. *See* California v. Morehead, 192 Cal. App. 3d 292, 238 Cal. Rptr. 570, 572 (1987) ('We do pause to express our revulsion at the suggestion in footnote 6 of the dissent that a rape victim might experience an orgasm').
34. For instances in which victims of rape testify to having sexual orgasms during the course of sexual assaults, *see* Massachusetts v. Bobilin, 25 Mass. App. Ct. 410, 519 N.E.2d 1349 (1988); Ohio v. Johnson, 1993 Ohio App. LEXIS 3677, *14 (July 21, 1993):

    [The defense counsel] further points out that [the complainant] first suggested that she remove her clothes, and that she experienced orgasms during the alleged rapes. He further points to the fact that no evidence of recent trauma to either Sherman's vagina or anal area was observed upon medical examination.

    In our judgment, all of these observations go to the weight rather than to the sufficiency of the evidence. . . .There is nothing inherently inconsistent between orgasm and forcible rape.

    Flannery v. Texas, 676 S.W.2d 369 (1984); West Virginia v. Pancake, 170 W. Va. 690, 296 S.E.2d 37 (1982). *See* also Curtis v. Georgia, 236 Ga. 362, 364, 223 S.E.2d 721, 723 (1976) ('The trial court did not err in refusing to allow Curtis' attorney to ask the prosecutrix whether she experienced orgasm during these acts of intercourse; the answer would have been legally irrelevant to the issue of consent').
35. Bernard Williams makes this point in a somewhat different context by arguing that a person cannot be held criminally responsible for a homicide that, while in a state of somnambulism, he agrees to commit, because *agreeing* with such a project of another's is not something that in his state he can perform:

    Even if the somnambulist does perform actions, he may very well not be criminally responsible for those actions. . . . [Consider] the criminal figure of Dr. Caligari, who in Robert Wiene's 1919 film . . . controlled a figure called Cesare . . . . Cesare is kept in a box, and, when roused and instructed by Caligari, moves somnambulistically at his bidding. Among other crimes, he kills . . . the town clerk with a dagger.

    * * *

    Cesare. . . stabbed the town clerk. But he did it when he was asleep. He did these things as a result of a very peculiar relations he had to Dr. Caligari, one that enabled Dr. Caligari to bring it about that he did those things without his agreed to do them. For suppose Caligari had said, 'You agree to do it?' and Cesare, in is somnambulistic state, had said 'Yes, I agree to do it'. Cesare would *not* have actually agreed to do it: *that* is not an act that in his state he can perform. The explanation is to be found in his dissociation from considerations that essentially bear on his doing so. In this state, he cannot summon up, for instance, thoughts that would relate the killing to the rest of his life.

Williams, 'The Actus Reus of Dr. Caligari', pp. 1670-71.

36. For the nature of the controversy as revealed in Sarah's case, *see* Grogan, 'The Six Faces of Sarah Bear Witness to a Sexual Assault':

[D]efense witness Darold Treffert, a psychiatrist who was an adviser to the movie Rain Man, described multiple personality disorder as the 'UFO of psychiatry' and questioned its validity as a diagnosis of mental illness. But Chicago psychiatrist Bennett Braun insisted the disorder is all too real and is almost always a result of severe child abuse at the hands of someone 'who is both abusive and loving in an unpredictable and inconsistent fashion'.

See also Smolowe, 'The 21 Faces of Sarah'.:

The most difficult challenge for prosecutors may be persuading the jury that Sarah's ailment is genuine. MPD is so difficult to diagnose that estimates of the number of U.S. cases vary wildly, from 7,000 to as many as 16,000. The American Psychiatric Association did not recognize the disorder as a legitimate mental illness until 1980. 'Multiple-personality disorder is a very, very rare condition. Because of TV talk shows, it has become the disease of the month and the plea of the year', says Dr. Darold Treffert, director of the Fond du Lac County Health Care Center, who is expected to testify for the defense.

For the supposed phenomenology of MPD, *see* Saks, *Jekyll On Trial*, pp. 8-20. For differing views of the psychological community as to whether such phenomenology exists, *see id.* at 20-38.

37. For an account of the trial, *see* Grogan, 'The Six Faces of Sarah Bear Witness to a Sexual Assault':

When she took the witness stand during a rape trial in Oshkosh, Wis., this month, the slender, dark-haired victim identified herself as Sarah, age 27. Sarah, the woman explained to the court, is 'the name of the body' which is inhabited by as many as 46 different personalities she calls insiders. Although she had no recollection herself of meeting a 29-year-old grocery bagger named Mark Peterson, Sarah testified, she was convinced he had violated 'the body' by having sex with the naive and fun-loving personality known as Jennifer. '[The insiders] told me', Sarah said. 'And I believed them'.

Sarah testified that she has no control over what happens 'when the insiders take over', but has learned in psychotherapy how to summon and converse with some of them. During the three hours she was on the stand, prosecutor Joe Paulus asked her to call up five other personalities. Each time, she closed her eyes and bowed her head; seconds later she would take on an altered facial expression and speak in a different voice. Judge Robert Hawley directed that each of Sarah's personalities be sworn in separately. Franny, a maternal insider who says she takes care of the 'children within', testified that she was fishing in the park with friends when Peterson approached her and asked her out. Two days later, Franny testified, she 'bumped Sarah to a dark place' and went with Peterson to a local café. Over coffee, Franny recalled, she told Peterson about the insiders, and on the way home he asked to talk to Jennifer, a naive 20-year-old personality who loves to dance to rock and roll.

> At Paulus' request, Jennifer replaced Franny on the stand. After waving to the jury, she testified in a high-pitched voice that he drove her to a park and 'poked a hole in me with this thing . . . I put my arms around him and said it was nice. Mark said, "Time to pull out. I don't want you pregnant."'
>
> Recalled to the stand, Franny spoke of her anger when Jennifer and Emily explained what had happened. 'I trusted that man and he did harm to the body', she testified. 'Sarah started to shake when we told her'.

The trial judge ruled that there was sufficient evidence of incompetency to go to the jury. Following the jury verdict of guilty, however, the trial judge set it aside on the ground that the defendant's expert-witness psychiatrist had been wrongly denied an opportunity to examine Sarah. Thereafter, the prosecutor dismissed charges against the defendant, stating that Sarah's doctors had advised him that she could not tolerate another trial. *See United Press International*, 20 December 1990.

For other rape cases involving multiple personality disorders, including one involving a *defendant* who also allegedly suffered from a multiple personality disorder, *see Dallas Morning News*, 27 November 1994, section: news, p. 15A; *The Atlanta Journal and Constitution*, 20 May 1992, section: state news, section D, p. 1; *Houston Chronicle*, 31 October 1992, section: A, p. 29.

Commentators disagree as to whether a person who is possessed by several distinct alters ought to be convicted on the basis of what just one of them does. *Compare* Radden, *Divided Minds and Successive Selves*, (contending that a person's criminal responsibility is a function of what any of his alters does) *with* Haji, 'Multiple Selves and Culpability', pp. 249-276 (contending that a person is not criminally responsible for what any rogue alter does). Since the criminal responsibility of an actor *A* with MPD involves different issues than the consent of a subject *S* with MPD, one cannot draw inferences from the former for the latter.

38. North Carolina v. Moorman, 320 N.C. 387, 389, 358 S.E.2d 502, 504 (1987).
39. Saks, *Jekyll On Trial*, p. 5:

> [When people with MPD commit crimes, they] manifest a dividedness that, in many cases, is inconsistent with viewing them as single agents. It is indeed as if one body housed more than one person, each with his or her own wishes, dreams, fears and goals....Alter personalities can thus act autonomously, with or without the consent, cooperation, or even knowledge of the other alter personalities.

40. True, there may have been a gap in consciousness between the dreaming and awakened Patricia. But the same thing happens to anyone who, having subjectively consented to something, remembers it all the next day despite the interruption of a night's sleep.
41. Tragically, this thought experiment regarding 'Desire Drugs' may mimic the actual experiences of some severely damaged neurological patients. Thus, Oliver Sacks states that some sleeping-sickness patients exhibit profound 'compliance' behavior, compliance that they both experience subjectively and exhibit externally in accord with whatever is suggested to them. *See* Oliver Sacks, *Awakenings*, pp. 16-17:

> The general forms . . . of [sleeping-sickness] catatonia were closely analogous to those of Parkinsonism, but were at a higher and more complex level, and were usually experienced as subjective states which had exactly the same form as the observable behavioral states. Thus some of these patients showed automatic compliance or 'obedience', maintaining (indefinitely, and apparently without effort) any posture in which they were put or found themselves, or 'echoing' words, phrases, thoughts, perceptions or actions in an unvarying circulate way, once these had been suggested to them.

42. This is what Aristotle means in saying that a person's action is 'involuntary' when, rather than acting merely *in* ignorance, he acts ***through*** ignorance—that is, when he is ignorant of the very circumstances and objects of his action. *See* Aristotle, ***Nichomachean Ethics***, III, 1110a-1111a. And it is what Joel Feinberg means in saying that an action is 'completely involuntary' when an actor is unaware of what he is in fact doing. *See* Feinberg, ***Harm To Self***, p. 104 ('One's "choice" is completely involuntary . . . when through ignorance one chooses something other than what one means to choose, for instance, thinking arsenic powder is table salt, and thus choosing to sprinkle it on one's scrambled eggs').
43. *See* Hurd, 'The Moral Magic of Consent', p. 126.
44. *See* Moore, 'Foreseeing Harm Opaquely', pp. 126-43 (discussing the opacity of propositional attitudes generally); O'Neill, 'Between Consenting Adults', p. 255 ('Like other propositional attitudes, consent is opaque').
45. O'Neill, 'Between Consenting Adults', p. 256. *See* also Anscombe, 'Two Kinds of Error in Action', p. 393 ('Consent is consent to something. [B]ecause consent is consent to something . . .you may consent to something under one description and not under another...'.).
46. I refer to the woman as 'Lenny's girlfriend' rather than by her name, because in order to preserve the privacy of rape victims, the New York courts that reported the case refer to alleged victims anonymously as 'complainants'.
47. New York v. Hough, 159 Misc. 2d 997, 607 N.Y.S.2d 884 (1994).
48. McNair v. Nevada, 108 Nev. 53, 825 P.2d 571 (1992).
49. Nevada Revised Statutes § 200.481 (2002).
50. Nevada Revised Statutes § 200.366(1) (2002).
51. The former rape statute of the state of Maine tracked this distinction. The statute made it an offense for a man to have sexual intercourse with a woman *either* by means of 'force and against the person's will' *or* by means of 'threat of death, serious bodily injury, or kidnapping'. Maine Revised Statutes Ann., tit. 17-A, § 252(1) (1980). The courts of Maine distinguished between the two forms of rape, treating 'force' as 'actual' overwhelming physical power that victims lack the physical strength to resist, and treating 'threats' as coercive propositions designed to elicit sexual compliance. *See* Maine v. Reed, 479 A.2d 1291 (1984).
52. Dan-Cohen, 'Conceptions of Choice and Conceptions of Autonomy', pp. 221-43, and esp. pp. 227, 230-31.
53. Dan-Cohen, 'Conceptions of Choice and Conceptions of Autonomy', pp. 227, 230-31.
54. Another example of factual consent to *x* by a person who feels he has no control over whether *x* occurs is the parachutist who subjectively welcomes it when a friend, sensing the parachutist's momentary panic, pushes him out the airplane doorway when the parachutist is too scared to jump. Notice that to say the parachutist 'factually' consents does not mean that his subjective acquiescence suffice in law to legitimate the friend's action. A jurisdiction make take the view that the risks of error that an actor, *A*, faces in trying to assess the subjective feelings of a paralyzed person, *S*, are so great that *A* ought to be prohibited from acting, regardless of what *B* later reveals his subjective feelings to have been. Thus, some jurisdictions, make it an offense to have sexual intercourse with any person who is 'physically unable to communicate unwillingness to an act [of sexual intercourse]', regardless of what the person later reveals her feelings to be. *See, e.g.*, Re: Jordan J., 1992 Conn. Super. LEXIS 2282 (1992).
55. This is what Emily Sherwin, in the context of sexual intercourse, refers to as 'willingness to have sex on the terms presented'. Sherwin, 'Infelicitous Sex', pp. 209-3, p. 220.

56. As Malm puts it, subjective consent can be thought of as a 'cluster concept':

    > [T]he mental state associated with consent comes in degrees. . . . As intimated earlier, my willingness to accept something may range from mere toleration to eager pursuit. The willing may also be stable and well-supported, quite in keeping with my core self, or it might be novel and somewhat fleeting. I might even desire or be willing to accept something *because* it is out of line with what I normally choose.
    >
    > * * *
    >
    > A supporter of the mental-state conception of consent might respond that consent is a cluster concept. That is, a person counts as having consented if she has any one of a number of mental states that fall under the umbrella of 'consent'. This view allow[s] us to compare the various mental states in terms of degrees of willingness, for example, without committing us to the view that consent itself is a matter of degree.

    Malm, The Ontological Status of Consent', pp. 147-64 , p. 149. *See* also Chamallas, 'Consent, Equality, and the Legal Control of Sexual Conduct', p. 795 ('Consent is a devilishly malleable term which may describe a wide spectrum of responsive behavior, ranging from the mere failure to engage in active resistance, to active participation in and encouragement of another's initiatives').
57. One can imagine still another case—one that falls somewhere in between Dan-Cohen's hypothetical, on the one hand, and the woman who does not know how she feels, on the other hand. Specifically, one can imagine a person who is faced with a marriage that she regards as inevitable and who is so self-effacing and self-abnegating that, though she possesses feelings about the marriage, she is not sufficiently *self*-conscious of her feelings to think of them as 'her' wishes. Whether such a person factually consents depends upon the feelings she is experiencing.

    To be sure, it is not easy to ascertain the feelings of a person who is not self-conscious of her feelings at the time she experiences them. One way of ascertaining her feelings, perhaps, is to ask her *afterwards* how they felt at the time. Another way is to ask, hypothetically, what she would have said about her feelings if she had been asked about them at the time. It should be pointed out that the hypothetical question, 'What would she have said about her feelings, if she been asked about them at the time', is not the question which one asks with respect to 'hypothetical consent'. We shall see in Chapter 7 that hypothetical consent turns, not on the question 'What would she have said about her feelings, if she had been asked about them at the time?', but upon the question, 'What would her feelings at the time have been, if, counterfactually, she had been capable of feelings at the time?'
58. Russell, *Rape In Marriage*, pp. 78-79.
59. Cf. Archard, *Sexual Consent* , p. 52. *See* also Idaho v. Gossett, 119 Idaho 581, 584, 808 P.2d 1326, 1329 (1991) ('I stopped feeling. I didn't feel anything. I couldn't think. It's hard to explain, you can't know what it's like to wake up and feel a stranger touching you. I didn't, I just stopped, my brain quit functioning').
60. California v. LaSalle, 103 Cal. App. 3d 139, 147, 162 Cal. Rptr. 816, 820 (1980). Although the *LaSalle* court does not specify that it is using 'consent' to refer to Christy's subjective state of mind (rather than her objective expression of her state of mind), the court can be assumed to mean the former, because California takes the position that 'consent' refers to a state of mind rather than an expression. *See* note 6 to the Introduction to Part I.
61. Whittaker v. Wisconsin, 50 Wis. 518, 7 N.W. 431 (1880).
62. *See, e.g.*, North Carolina v. Brown, 332 N.C. 262, 420 SE2d 147 (1992), in which the victim testified that, when the defendant came into her hospital room, pulled back the

sheets, pulled up her gown, and stuck his fingers into her vagina, she was 'in shock' and 'didn't know what to do'. *See* also Barnes:

> For example, some studies have demonstrated that while some women respond to sexual assault with active resistance, others 'freeze'....One researcher found that many women demonstrate 'psychological infantilism'—a frozen fright response—in the face of sexual assault. (Symonds, supra, 26 Am.J.Psychoanalysis at p. 30; *see* also QBF, supra, at pp. 18-20 [reporting that some women 'freeze' and become helpless from panic and numbing fear]).

In addition to precluding a subject *S* from *forming* a subjective judgment as to what she wishes under the circumstances, a paralyzing fear can prevent a subject who subjectively rejects *x* under the circumstances from *manifesting* her subjective nonacquiescence. *See, e.g.*, California v. Kuches, 120 Cal. 566, 568, 52 P. 1002, 1003 (1898), in which the victim testified that she tried to scream but no words came out: 'I wanted to holler out, but couldn't; I was just like something had struck me; I don't know why I could not holler out'. Panic of the latter sort may be relevant to whether silence signifies *expressive* consent; but it has no bearing on issues of subjective consent, because it only comes into play to prevent a person from manifesting what must be conceded to be a lack of subjective consent.

Chapter Two

An Expression of Factual Acquiescence

It is easy to imagine a person who factually acquiesces in his mind without expressing it, just as it is easy to imagine a person who expresses that he is factually acquiescing in his mind without subjectively experiencing the acquiescence. Thus, in our retelling of the story of Snow White, the protagonists 'Snow Blanche' and 'Snow Bianca' both subjectively acquiesced to being kissed without expressing their acquiescence: they were conscious of everything around them and, being conscious, desired to be kissed by the prince under the circumstances; yet at the same time they were frozen in the appearance of perpetual sleep and, hence, unable to communicate their desires to the prince. The sleeping-sickness patients whom Dr. Oliver Sacks describes in his book *Awakenings* found themselves in similar positions: they were conscious of their surroundings and, in their consciousness, they subjectively welcomed being touched by friends and relatives; yet they were also frozen in catatonic states of post-encephalitic Parkinsonism and, hence, could not express their wishes in any way.[1]

In practice, of course, people typically can and do express their desires for physical intimacy under the circumstances, whether they express their desires verbally or non-verbally, actively or passively.[2] And courts commonly refer to such expressions in the language of 'consent'. Yet courts appear to be unaware of how ambiguous the language of consent is in relation to expressions of subjective acquiescence. Thus, on the one hand, in referring to such expressions, courts sometimes start with the core conception of consent as subjective acquiescence and, then, conjoin it with transitive verbs to signify the expressing of subjective acquiescence. Thus, they say of persons that they '*communicate* consent', '*manifest* consent', '*express* consent', or '*convey* consent'.[3] In doing so, they are not using 'consent' as a synonym for expression or communication; for if they were, they would be speaking redundantly. Rather, they are using 'consent' in the way it is used in Chapter 1: they are using it to refer to that which is being expressed, to that which is being communicated, namely, a subjective or first-person experience of acquiescence, whether the acquiescence takes the form of unconditional desire for *x*, a conditional preference for *x* under the circumstances, or even indifference toward *x*.

On the other hand, courts also commonly use the language of consent in a very different sense. They use it to refer to something a person *does*, rather than something a person experiences—to something external and objective that a person manifests on a third-person basis, rather than something internal and subjective that she possesses on a first-person basis. Thus, courts say of persons, she 'affirmatively consented', 'verbally consented', 'explicitly consented', 'expressly consented', 'tacitly consented', or 'gave her consent'.[4] When they do so, they are not using consent to refer to a subjective experience because subjective acquiescence is not something that requires words or conduct to be given. Rather, they are using consent to refer to external ways in which persons convey their acquiescence to others, whether again the acquiescence consists of unconditional desire, conditional preference, or even indifference. The Wisconsin legislature uses consent in this way in defining consent to be a defense to rape: 'Consent', the statute states, 'means words or overt actions by a person . . . indicating a freely given agreement to have sexual intercourse or sexual contact'.[5] Interestingly, a defendant argued in 1980 that the Wisconsin defense of consent should be interpreted to encompass not only expressions of acquiescent states of mind but also acquiescing states of mind themselves. He argued that even though the complainant in his case did not use 'words' or 'overt actions' indicating acquiescence, she nonetheless 'consented' for purposes of the statute because she subjectively acquiesced to the sexual intercourse in her mind. The court rejected the argument, holding that the woman could not have consented without using words or conduct indicating acquiescence because consent *consists* of such words or conduct.[6]

A number of academic commentators agree with Wisconsin that for purposes of the law of sexual assault, if not for criminal offenses generally, consent ought to be defined to be an act that a subject performs rather than a state of mind that he or she experiences. Several of them make the point by invoking the terminology of contemporary speech-act theory to assert that consent is, or at least should be understood to be, what speech-act theorists call a 'performative', that is, something that one uses words (and, perhaps, also limited forms of nonverbal conduct) to *do*.[7] Thus, David Archard speaks for himself and numerous others when he says:

> Consent is an act rather than a state of mind. Consent is something I do rather than think or feel . . . .The view of consent as something that is done rather than as a state of mind is normally expressed by the statement that consent should be understood in 'performative' and not 'psychological' terms.[8]

To be sure, when the State of Wisconsin defines consent to be an expressive act, Wisconsin is using consent in a *legal* rather than a *factual* sense. That is, Wisconsin is using consent to refer to words or conduct by *S* that constitute a defense to rape by *A* by properly signifying that *S* possesses the kind of mental state of acquiescence to sexual intercourse that protects whatever interests Wisconsin believes *S* possesses regarding such intimacy. Similarly, when Archard asserts *S*'s consent to be a 'performative', he means that it performs the normative work of 'transforming' sexual intercourse from rape into non-rape.[9] Nevertheless, just as consent is often used in law in a purely factual sense to refer to mental states of factual acquiescence that may or may not constitute legal defenses (see Chapter 1), so, too, consent can be used in law in a factual sense to refer to expressions of factual acquiescence to *x* that do not themselves constitute defenses to *x* but rather are component parts of such defenses.

To illustrate the use of consent to refer to the mere *fact* of an expression of factual acquiescence, and not to its legal effect, consider the way Heidi Malm uses consent in her essay on the 'Ontological Status of Consent'.[10] Like Archard, Malm argues in favor of defining consent in criminal cases as an expressive act rather than a state of mind. 'Consent', she says, 'is the signification of a particular mental state through the performance of a conventionally recognized act (or set of acts)'.[11] Yet Malm believes it is a mistake to reserve the word 'consent' for normatively valid instances of such expressive acts—or, as Malm puts it, to 'buil[d] an assessment of moral legitimacy into the very concept of consent'. The disadvantage of a 'normatively-laden conception of consent', she says, is that it precludes speakers from using consent in linguistically useful ways. Specifically, a normative usage of consent precludes speakers from saying of a woman who expressly acquiesces to conduct *x* as a result of force, fraud, or exploitation that, yes, the woman 'consented' (*i.e.*, she expressly preferred *x* to the alternatives available to her under the circumstances) but, no, because of the means by which it was elicited, her consent does not 'count' as a '[l]egitimate' defense to the person who subjected her to *x*. Consequently, in order to be able to use consent to refer to expressions of acquiescence that are legally invalid, or 'illegitimate' as she puts it, Malm makes it clear that she is using consent in a factual rather than a legal sense.[12]

The purpose of this chapter is to identify the essential elements implicit in what I shall call 'factual expressive consent', that is, 'consent' in the form of expressions of factual acquiescence that may or may not also constitute a defense, depending upon the conditions under which the expressions manifestly occur. This purpose can be illustrated by an opinion in ***Parish v. Louisiana*** (1980).[13] Marvin Parish was convicted of attempted forcible rape, an offense defined as attempting to have sexual intercourse with a person by means of threats of great and immediate bodily harm. The evidence showed that Parish, who outweighed his victim by 130 pounds, gained entry to her apartment by a ruse, seized her by the throat, clasped her mouth, declared that he wanted to have sex, and warned that he would kill her if she screamed. Fearing that Parish would otherwise kill her, the victim nodded and, when he uncovered her mouth, agreed to submit to his demands. Fortunately, Parish fell while dragging her to the bedroom, giving his victim a chance to beg Parish to stop and eventually causing him to change his mind and to leave the apartment. The Louisiana Supreme Court affirmed Parish's conviction on the ground that his change of mind came too late to exonerate him of attempted forcible rape. In the course of his opinion, Justice Watson uses consent to describe the victim's response to Parish's threat: 'Parish threatened to kill her if she screamed when he removed his hand. After he . . . removed his hand, she *verbally consented* to sexual intercourse'.[14] Justice Watson's statement, that the victim 'verbally consented' to have sexual intercourse is significant, because Justice Watson is using consent to refer to what I call 'factual expressive consent'. His reference is to consent as an *expression*, because the adverb 'verbally' is a term that modifies a communicative act by Parish's victim, not a state of mind. And the reference to consent is *factual*, because Justice Watson concedes that in manifesting acquiescence, the victim manifestly feared for her life and, hence, her consent was not 'lawful' within the meaning of the Louisiana rape statute. Thus, the purpose of this chapter is to identify the essential elements that must be present to enable a judge like Justice Watson to say of a victim like Parish's, 'She consented to sexual intercourse, albeit in fear for her life'. This is not to say that jurisdictions that use 'consent' to refer to expressions of factual acquiescence always mean the same thing by it. Clearly they do not. Sometimes they mean to refer to expressions of factual acquiescence that, although they appear to be uttered *freely*, nonetheless fall short of constituting a defense because they are manifestly *uninformed*.[15] Sometimes they mean to refer to expressions of factual acquiescence that, though they appear to be competent and informed, nonetheless fall short of constituting a defense because they are manifestly *unfree* (*e.g.*, Justice Watson's reference to 'consent' elicited by force). And sometimes they mean to refer to expressions of factual acquiescence *simpliciter*, regardless of whether they appear to be sufficiently competent, informed, or free to constitute a defense. Nevertheless, although *all* of what they mean is not invariably the same, *some* of it is—namely, the elements that enable them to say of a subject whose expressed acquiescence falls short of constituting a defense that she nevertheless expressively 'consented' to the conduct at issue.

I should emphasize, too, that by expressions of factual consent, I do not mean ones that are disembodied from social contexts, conventions, and roles. All expressions, both factual and legal, presuppose social conventions and social roles. The kiss that Snow Blanche seeks is a social convention, and, perhaps, even a gendered one. The status of being a 'prince' is entirely the product of social construction.[16] The way Snow Blanche would communicate with the prince if she were awake is a function of social conventions. Indeed, the very tale of Snow White, the passive woman who is brought to life by a prince's kiss, is a prototype of traditional gender roles for men and women. All expressions, including factual expressions of acquiescence, are socially constructed in these senses. The point is that when people employ social roles and conventions to express acquiescence to *x*, they only *sometimes* do so in ways that cause their expressed acquiescence to constitute a defense to *x*. When courts and commentators invoke the term 'consent' to refer to such instances, they are using it in a legal sense. Otherwise, however, they are using 'consent' in a factual sense, whether they are using it to refer to expressions of factual acquiescence that do not constitute a defense, or to refer to expressions of factual acquiescence without regard to whether they constitute a defense.

I shall proceed by addressing the following questions regarding the elements of factual expressive consent:

(A) When a speaker *S* is described as expressively 'consenting' to *x* with respect to an actor-observer *A*, whose point of view of *S*'s attitude toward *x* is implicit in the description? The speaker *S*'s? The observer *A*'s? Both *S*'s and *A*'s? Or either *S*'s or *A*'s?

(B) What, at a minimum, constitutes factual expressive consent from an observer's standpoint? What the observer actually understands? What he should understand? Or both?

(C) What most fully constitutes factual expressive consent—any verbal or nonverbal communication of acquiescence, or only an explicit statement of 'yes'?

(D) What kind of maxim is 'no means no'—a description of what women actually mean, or a legal rule as to what the law conclusively presumes women to mean?

(E) How does a person's saying 'no' while submitting to *x* bear upon whether she expressively consents to *x*?

Whose Point of View—The Speaker's? The Observer's? Those of Both? Or That of Either?

Marvin Parish knew what his intended victim was thinking when, after he seized her by the throat and threatened to kill her, she said that she would submit to his sexual demands. The conflict of wills that thereafter ensued when Parish fell while dragging the victim to the bedroom did not result from miscommunication. If anything, the conflict was enhanced because each knew what the other was thinking. Sometimes, however, people fail to express their preferences in ways that others understand. In that event, one must ask whether references like Justice Watson's to a subject *S*'s expressive 'consent' refer at a minimum to what *S means* to express, or to what an actor in *A*'s position *understands S* to be expressing—or, perhaps, *either* to what *S* means to express *or* to what an actor in *A*'s position understands *S* to be expressing, or perhaps, *both* to what *S* means *and* to what an actor in *A*'s position understands.

To give the issue texture, consider another fable of a woman and a prince, Hans Christian Andersen's 'Little Mermaid'. Having fallen in love with a prince whom she saves from drowning, the Little Mermaid enters into a bargain with the Sea Witch: the Little Mermaid agrees to surrender her voice to the Sea Witch in return for being transformed from a mermaid into a terrestrial woman who will acquire an immortal soul if the prince marries her, but who will dissolve into sea foam if the prince marries another. The prince finds the Little Mermaid on the beach; but, being mute, she is unable to tell him that she was the one who just saved his life. Nor can she tell him how she loves him or how much she welcomes his kisses and embrace. She tries to convey her feelings through her expressive eyes and by a dance she performs for him, but the prince does not realize the depth of her love until much later, by which time he is fatefully betrothed to another. The story, in addition to what it suggests about gender roles and a woman's lack of voice, illustrates the disjunction between what a speaker intends in expressing acquiescence and what an observer understands. Hoping that the prince will make love to her, the Little Mermaid tries to convey through body language how much she welcomes his embrace. But the prince does not interpret her conduct as an expression of love and acquiescence to lovemaking.

What, then, can be said in the language of 'consent' about conduct such as the Little Mermaid's? Can we say that the Little Mermaid in fact gave the prince her consent—even though he had no way of knowing that she was trying to convey her subjective acquiescence? Or is 'consent' invariably reserved for expressions of subjective acquiescence that are or are likely to be understood as such? What if, while wishing only to be embraced and *not* to be kissed, the Little Mermaid unwittingly pursed lips in the shape of a kiss, leading the prince reasonably but mistakenly to believe that she wished to be both embraced *and* kissed? Can we say that she 'consented' to be kissed even though she did not want to be kissed? Or is 'consent' invariably reserved for expressions of acquiescence that are actually intended as such?

In ordinary language at least, 'consent' appears to be plastic enough to encompass all of the aforementioned usages. That is, consent can be used in a factual sense to refer solely to speaker-based expressions of factual acquiescence, solely to observer-based expressions of factual acquiescence, and to expressions that speakers intend as well as observers understand as factual acquiescence. Thus, using consent to refer to what a speaker intends rather than what an observer understands, one can sensibly say of the Little Mermaid's efforts to be kissed, 'She consented to be kissed in every way she could; but the prince didn't get it'. Alternatively, using consent to refer to what an observer understands rather than what a speaker intends, one can sensibly say of the Little Mermaid, 'She tried in every way she could think of to consent to be kissed; but she did not succeed'. The same is true of the Little Mermaid's efforts to be embraced but not kissed. Using consent from the speaker's standpoint, one can say, 'She did not consent to be kissed, but the prince mistakenly thought she did'. From the observer's standpoint, one can say, 'She consented to be kissed, but she didn't mean to'. Or using it as a combination of both, one can say, 'She consented only to be embraced, because being embraced was the only thing that he rightly understood her to be wishing for herself'.

Having thus seen that 'consent' can be used in ordinary language to refer to speaker-based expressions alone, to observer-based expressions alone, and to combinations of both, what about such usages in law? Is 'consent' also used in the same three ways in criminal law? What about jurisdictions like Wisconsin that define the defense of consent to rape as consisting of 'words or overt actions by a person . . . indicating a freely given agreement to have sexual intercourse or sexual contact'? Whose point of view is intended to control what a person's words or overt actions 'indicat[e]'? May we infer from Wisconsin's reference to consent that it could be referring to what the person *intends* her words or overt actions to 'indicat[e]'? Or that Wisconsin is referring to the combination of what the person intends her words or overt actions to indicate and what observers *understand* her words or actions to indicate? Or that it is referring solely to what observers understand the person's words or overt actions to indicate?

The answers to these questions depend not upon the use of consent in ordinary language but upon the purposes of the criminal law. If a jurisdiction wished to base a criminal defense solely upon what *S* intends to be an expression of factual acquiescence on her part, as opposed to upon what observers understand to be an expression of factual acquiescence on her part, a jurisdiction could use the term 'consent' to do so. Similarly, if a jurisdiction wished to base a criminal defense upon the combination of what *S* intends to be an expression of factual acquiescence on her part *and* what observers would understand as such, a jurisdiction could also do so in terms of 'consent'. To my knowledge, however, no jurisdiction adopts either policy with respect to rape or any other criminal offense. On the contrary, we shall see in Chapter 4 that defining consent by reference to mental states of acquiescence on *S*'s part (as many jurisdictions do) serves legitimate criminal-law purposes, just as defining consent instead by reference to what observers understand to be expressions of acquiescence on *S*'s part (as other jurisdictions do) also serves legitimate purposes. But defining consent by reference to what *S* subjectively *intends* to be expressions of acquiescence serves no legitimate purpose—no purpose, at least, that is not better served by defining consent directly in terms of *S*'s mental states of acquiescence—and to my knowledge, no jurisdiction does so. We shall also see that although jurisdictions could legitimately define consent by reference to *either* *S*'s mental states *or* what observers would understand to be expressions of subjective acquiescence on her part, the purposes served by defining consent by reference to what observers understand to be *S*'s subjective acquiescence would be defeated if it were defined by reference to *both* that *and* *S*'s mental states. It follows, therefore, that when consent is used in criminal law to refer to expressions of subjective acquiescence on *S*'s part (as opposed to mental states of such acquiescence), it can be regarded as defined exclusively by reference to what observers understand her words and conduct to mean, rather than by reference to what she intends her words and conduct to mean.[17]

What Measures Consent from an Observer's Standpoint—What He Actually Understands? Or Should Understand? Or Both?

It is both natural and commonplace to describe *S*'s words and conduct vis-à-vis *A* as 'consent' when all observers understand them to constitute expressions of subjective acquiescence on *S*'s part—that is, (i) when *A* understands *S*'s words and conduct as expressions of subjective acquiescence, and (ii) *A*'s interpretive community does so, too, or, at least, would do so if it were consulted. It is not obvious, however, how the term 'consent' applies in criminal law when *A* understands *S*'s words and conduct as expressions of subjective acquiescence on her part but *A*'s interpretive community does not, or when *A*'s interpretive community understands them as expressions of subjective acquiescence on *S*'s part but *A* himself does not. Thus, the question is: when 'consent' is used in criminal law to refer to expressions of subjective acquiescence on *S*'s part, what is its role when *A* disagrees with his interpretive community over what *S*'s words and conduct mean?

Let us start with an actor, *A*, who interprets *S*'s words and conduct as an expression of subjective acquiescence under circumstances in which his interpretive community would not. Consider the charge of rape that Trish Crawford brought against her husband Dale on the night of December 6, 1991. Trish called the police to say that her husband, Dale, had forcibly seized her by the throat, carried her to the bedroom, tied her to the bed with ropes, sealed her mouth with duct tape, and while she struggled and tried to scream, subjected her to sexual intercourse with her. More sensationally, she told the police that she had a videotape to prove it because Dale had videotaped the events in the bedroom before telling her, afterwards, that he was leaving her. The tape, indeed, showed what Trish said it would—that Dale had tied Trish to the bed with ropes, taped her mouth, and had sexual intercourse with her while she struggled and made muffled sounds. The prosecutor charged Dale with marital rape, based significantly on what the prosecutor concluded from observing the tape. At trial, however, Dale had another story to tell. He testified without contradiction that he and Trish had engaged in consensual sadomasochism throughout their marriage, including the use of ropes, and that he had prior videotapes to prove it. He further testified that before they entered the bedroom and before he turned on the videotape, Trish had agreed to engage in the encounter as a 'sex game', and that she accused him of rape only after he had announced that he was going to leave her. He told the jurors that, if they looked closely at the videotape in light of his testimony, they would see that what they were observing was a sex game, not rape. The jury apparently believed Dale's testimony or, at least, had doubts about Trish's testimony because it eventually acquitted Dale.[18]

We will never know for certain what happened between Trish and Dale Crawford that night. It is possible that the entire episode was consensual in thought and word, as Dale said it was. It is also possible, as Trish said, that Dale knew all along that he was subjecting her to sexual intercourse against her will. However, at least two other interesting possibilities exist:

> ***S&M Gone Unwittingly Awry.*** It is possible that Dale was telling the truth about how the encounter *began*. That is, it is possible that Trish agreed to engage in a ritualized 'sex play' involving bondage, and that she allowed Dale to carry her into the bedroom and bind her to the bed. Yet Trish could also be telling the truth when she said that, after she was bound and gagged, she wanted Dale to stop. In any event, Trish may have wanted Dale to stop but, being bound and gagged, may have been unable to convey her wishes under the circumstances, leaving him unaware of them.

> ***Unexpected Attack.*** It is possible that Trish was telling the truth about how the encounter began. Trish admitted that she had engaged in consensual bondage with Dale before, but emphasized that they had always agreed in advance on how the game would be played. Trish may be telling the truth when she said that Dale acted this time without any prior agreement on her part—and, hence, outside the rules—when he unexpectedly attacked her, seized her by the neck, and carried her, protesting and struggling, to the bed. Yet it is simultaneously possible that Dale honestly believed that Trish subjectively welcomed the attack.

In 'S&M Gone Unwittingly Awry', Dale infers from Trish's words and conduct that she is factually acquiescing in sexual intercourse in her mind, under circumstances in which observers (*i.e.*, the police and prosecutors) infer the opposite. However, 'S&M Gone Unwittingly Awry' is not an illustration of the interpretive gap that arises when an actor infers a person to be factually acquiescing when members of his interpretive community would not; because the police and prosecutor are not members of Dale's interpretive community for purposes of interpreting Trish's conduct. Dale's 'interpretive community' is a personified norm for assessing the appropriateness, or reasonableness, of his inference that Trish subjectively welcomed his assault. An actor's interpretive community consists of real or hypothetical observers who know (i) everything that the actor himself knows regarding *S*'s words and conduct, (ii) all social conventions for expressing desires, preferences, and choices of which the actor himself is aware, and (iii) any further words or conduct on *S*'s part, as well as any further conventions for expressing desires, preferences, and choices, of which the actor would be aware if he paid appropriate or 'reasonable' attention to the interests of others. The police and prosecutor in 'S&M Gone Unwittingly Awry' fall short of being such observers because, among other things, they did not know something of which Dale was aware, namely, Trish's communicative conduct before the videotape started. They may have known what Dale knew about Trish's communicative conduct once Trish was bound and gagged, but they did not know that Dale and Trish had previously engaged in mutually agreeable sadomasochism of this sort, and they did not know that she explicitly acquiesced to this particular episode. If they had known what Dale knew about the totality of Trish's communicative conduct, they would probably have inferred, as Dale did, that Trish was factually acquiescing in her mind.

A better example of interpretive gap, therefore, is 'Unexpected Attack', where Dale departs from S&M conventions and yet nevertheless believes that Trish is factually acquiescing in her mind. 'Unexpected Attack' illustrates an interpretive gap, because an observer who knew what Dale knew about Trish's prior conduct, who knew what Dale knew about social conventions for communicating desires for S&M, and who gave reasonable attention to Trish's interests would not have interpreted Trish's startled reaction and robust protests as factual acquiescence. Given that Dale did interpret her reactions as factual acquiescence, he must have either disregarded social conventions for communicating desires for S&M or failed to give reasonable attention to Trish's interests.

How, then, does 'consent' function in criminal law, when it is used in cases like 'Unexpected Attack' to refer to *expressions* of factual acquiescence (as opposed to mental states of factual acquiescence)? What, for example, would Justice Watson of *Parish* v. *Louisiana* say of Trish's interaction with Dale? Would he say that Trish 'consented' to have sexual intercourse with Dale, simply because Dale happened to understand her to have factually acquiesced? Or would he say that while Dale mistakenly thought Trish consented, she did not? The answers to these questions appear to be the same in both ordinary language and criminal law: when 'consent' is used to refer to what *third-party observers* understand to be expressions of factual acquiescence by a subject *S* to conduct by an actor *A* (as opposed to what *S herself* means by it), the third parties whose observations are determinative are not *A* himself but rather independent observers, whether real or hypothetical. Thus, when consent is used in ordinary language to refer to observed-based expressions of factual acquiescence, the observer it presupposes is not *A* himself; for if it were, one would be precluded from saying in Unexpected Attack, 'Dale thought Trish was consenting, but he was *mistaken*'. Indeed, one would be precluded from saying, 'Dale *thought* Trish was *consenting*', because that implies that Dale's thoughts could differ from the social meaning of Trish's expressions. Rather, one would be obliged to say that by virtue of what Dale thought, 'Trish consented'. With respect to criminal law, we shall see in Chapter 4 that the purpose of defining consent to be an expression in criminal law is to provide a basis for evaluating an actor's conduct by reference to what he *ought* to understand to be subjective acquiescence on a subject's part. Consent cannot perform that function if it is confined to whatever an actor happens to understand to be subjective acquiescence on a subject's part. Consent can perform the function only if it is defined by reference to what members of the actor's interpretive community would understand to be subjective acquiescence on a subject's part.

This means that in jurisdictions that define consent to consist of expressions of factual acquiescence, a subject like Trish would be adjudged *not* to have consented, regardless of the fact that Dale believed she did. It does not follow, however, that such jurisdictions would be obliged to hold Dale responsible for acting without Trish's consent. To the contrary, by defining consent to consist of an expression of factual acquiescence, a jurisdiction takes but a single step: it commits itself to assessing consent by reference to what Dale's interpretive community would understand to be factual subjective acquiescence on Trish's part. It does nothing more than take a position on the *actus reus* of rape, by taking the position that an actor like Dale, who has sexual intercourse with a woman without her having uttered words or engaged in conduct that observers would rightly interpret as subjective acquiescence, acts without her 'consent'. It does not take a position on whether an actor like Dale possesses a guilty mind, or *mens rea*, with respect to such non-consent. With respect to *mens rea*, the jurisdiction remains free to adopt at least two alternative positions. On the one hand, it can take the position that an actor possesses a guilty mind regarding a woman's lack of factual expressive consent if, measured by the standards of his interpretive community, he *should* realize that his sexual partner has not expressed a desire to have sexual intercourse with him under the circumstances. In a jurisdiction that takes that position, an actor who commits the *actus reus* of rape (*i.e.*, an actor who has sexual intercourse that his interpretive community would not understand to be with a woman's factual expressive consent) also possesses a guilty mind (*i.e.*, the guilty mind of either being aware of the woman's non-acquiescence or being unaware where by the standards of his interpretive community, he ought to have been aware of it). On the other hand, a jurisdiction can take the position that an actor possesses a guilty mind regarding his sexual partner's lack of factual expressive consent if, and only if, he *realizes* that she is not expressively consenting—that is, if and only if he infers from her words and conduct that she is not subjectively choosing sexual intercourse as that which she desires for herself under the circumstances. In a jurisdiction that takes that position, an actor may commit the *actus reus* of rape and, yet, lack a guilty mind about it.

Now what about the opposite sort of interpretive gap? When 'consent' is used in criminal law to refer to expressions of factual acquiescence, how does it function in cases in which *A*'s interpretive community interprets *S*'s conduct as an expression of factual acquiescence, but *A* does not? To illustrate, consider the following hypothetical case:

> ***The Swinger's Club.*** Mr. and Mrs. *S* are members of a club that engages in spouse-swapping. The club has devised a set of codes, or cues, by which members can signal sexual interest in other members of the club. Newcomer, *A*, who is not a member of the club and is unaware of its codes and cues, comes to the club as an invited guest. Without realizing that *A* is a newcomer, Mrs. *S* employs the usual codes and cues to signal to *A* that she is sexually interested in *A*. Everyone in the room understands Mrs. *S* to be signaling to *A* that she wishes to be sexually intimate with him, except *A*, who remains clueless. Unaware that *S* has signaled acquiescence, *A* maneuvers *S* into a bedroom and suddenly, with physical strength she could not resist if she wished to, kisses and fondles *S*.

What would Justice Watson say of the encounter? Would he say that *S* 'consented' to be kissed and fondled for purposes of the criminal law—that is, that she *expressed* that she subjectively chose to be kissed and fondled by *A*—given that everyone in the room except *A* understood her to that effect? Or would Justice Watson say that *S* did not 'consent', given that *A* himself did not understand her to be making that subjective choice? The answer follows from what is said above. *S* consented, if and only if members of *A*'s interpretive community would have understood *S* to be subjectively choosing to be kissed and fondled, *A*'s interpretive community being persons who know (i) everything that the actor himself knows regarding *S*'s words and conduct, (ii) all social conventions for expressing desires, preferences, and choices of which the actor himself is aware, and (iii) any further words or conduct on *S*'s part, as well as any further conventions for expressing desires, preferences, and choices, of which the actor would be aware if he paid appropriate or 'reasonable' attention to the interests of others. By those standards, *A*'s failure to understand what others in the room understood was either reasonable or not. If *A*'s failure to understand *S* to be subjectively acquiescing was reasonable, *S* did *not* give him consent. If, however, *A*'s failure to understand *S* to be subjectively acquiescing was unreasonable (that is, if he ought to have understood her to be subjectively acquiescing), then *S* did give him consent, though *A* remains guilty of *attempting* to kiss and fondle *S* without her consent, given that he kissed and fondled her in the belief that she was not consenting.

Notice that in addressing consent as an expression, we have been addressing consent as an expression of a certain kind—namely, an expression of *factual* subjective acquiescence, not an expression of *legal* subjective acquiescence. This is so with respect to every personage, whether real or hypothetical, whose expressive consent we have thus far discussed. Thus, when Justice Watson describes the victim in *Parish* as 'consenting', he means only that she expressed to Parish that she subjectively preferred to submit to sexual intercourse than to suffer the alternatives with which Parish threatened her. Justice Watson obviously does not mean that when Parish's victim expressed her choice to submit, she also manifested the kinds of competence, knowledge, and motivation that Louisiana requires to render her choice 'lawful' as a defense to rape. The same is also true of Trish in 'S&M Gone Unwittingly Awry' and Mrs. *S* in 'The Swinger's Club'. When we say that they both 'consented', we mean only that they manifested a subjective willingness to engage in S&M and adultery, respectively. We do not mean that they also manifested the competence, knowledge, freedom, and motivation that are required to validate their choice as a legal defense; for we do not know whether the jurisdictions in which they reside regard persons as legally competent to consent to S&M and adultery, much less anything about the knowledge, freedom, and motivation that these jurisdictions requires to validate such subjective choices. Admittedly, we concluded that factual expressive consent is measured by the standards of an actor *A*'s interpretive community, and that the latter contain a normative element, *i.e.*, the social conventions for communicating desires, preferences, and choices of which *A* would be aware if he paid appropriate, or 'reasonable', attention to *S*'s interests. Nevertheless, the fact that this normative element is necessary for factual expressive consent does not mean that it also suffices to constitute legal expressive consent. The normative element was present when Parish's victim 'verbally consented' to have sexual intercourse with him, because without it, Parish could not have reasonably understood her to be expressing willingness to submit. But it does not follow that because he reasonably understood her to be expressing a willingness to submit to sexual intercourse, he also reasonably understood her expressed willingness to be competent, informed, and free.

Any Verbal or Nonverbal Communication? Or Only a 'Yes'?

People communicate acquiescence in countless ways, through words, silences, body language, and passivity. Consider a person who seats himself in a Chinese dim sum restaurant and repeatedly serves himself dishes from the array of trays that pass by his table, without, however, saying anything about paying for what he is eating. Though he says nothing about payment, most would all say that he tacitly agrees to pay for what he eats by virtue of remaining silent about payment in a context in which conventionally persons who are unwilling to pay say so in advance.[19] Or consider the scene toward the end of the movie *Forrest Gump* in which Jenny comes into Forrest's room at night, slides into his bed, slips off her nightclothes, moves on top of him, and after saying 'Forrest, I love you', commences to kiss him as the camera leaves. Forrest does not say anything at all except to ask, 'Jenny?' as she comes into the room. Yet most people would say that Forrest not only subjectively acquiesces to Jenny's sexual advances but also communicates acquiescence to Jenny's kisses through a combination of his previous declarations of affection and his contemporaneous responses, including passivity.

At the same time, however, people are ambivalent about whether a person can ever express factual consent by any other means than saying 'yes. We understand what it means to say that Forrest Gump expresses factual consent to being kissed, even though his expressions were entirely nonverbal. It means that unless Forrest was too disoriented to decide what he wanted under the circumstances, he preferred being kissed to the alternative situation he thought would occur, and that he communicated his preference by refraining from trying to bring about the alternative. In that respect, a person who appears to have the ability to thwart sexual contact expresses factual consent merely by virtue of manifestly refraining from invoking that preventive power. Yet there is a nagging sense, not only that this is *not* consent, but that the only authentic form of consent is an explicit 'yes'.

An example of the view that consent consists of a 'yes' is the policy that Antioch College adopted to govern sexual contact among students. The Antioch policy not only requires that sexual contact be 'consensual', but also clearly states that consent be both verbal and explicitly affirmative:

> All sexual contact and conduct between any two people must be consensual.... Consent must be clear and verbal (*i.e.*, saying: yes, I want to kiss you also). [T]he person who initiates sexual contact/conduct is responsible for getting the verbal consent of the other individual(s) involved. Verbal consent should be obtained with each new level of . . . sexual contact/conduct in any given interaction, regardless of who initiates it. Asking 'Do you want to have sex with me?' is not enough. The request for consent must be specific to each act. If you have had a particular level of sexual intimacy before with someone, you must still ask each and every time.[20]

The significant feature of the Antioch policy for our purposes is less its requirement that consent be verbal than its requirement that consent take the form of affirmative verbal answers to specific questions about the degree of desired sexual intimacy. It does not suffice under the Antioch policy for a student who seeks another's consent to sexual intimacy to do what Jenny did vis-à-vis Forrest Gump. Nor would it have sufficed for Forrest if, in turn, he responded to Jenny's overtures by physically escalating intimacy 'to a higher level' (to quote the Antioch policy). Admittedly, as viewers we do not know exactly how Jenny and Forrest moved from merely kissing to having the sexual intercourse that resulted in Jenny's becoming pregnant, but we are free to imagine. We can imagine that it was Forrest who, in the words of the Antioch policy, 'initiate[d]' moving to a higher level of sexual intimacy. If so, then it would not have sufficed for him under the Antioch policy that Jenny had smilingly slid into his bed or, having taken off her clothes, had climbed on top of him, saying 'I love you, Forrest'. To consent, she would have had to answer affirmatively to the explicit question, 'Do you want to have sexual intercourse?'

To be sure, in requiring an affirmative answer to the question 'Do you want to have sexual intercourse?' Antioch has different purposes than we do in this chapter. Antioch is not seeking to identify the minimum components of factual expressive consent. Antioch College is formulating a normative standard of consent for purposes of the school's official code of student conduct: it is using consent to designate the sole form of expressive acquiescence that it believes suffices to legitimate sexual contact among students. In that respect, being normative in nature, the Antioch policy is not an apt illustration of factual expressive consent. Nonetheless, there is nagging sense that the *reason* Antioch requires a verbal 'yes' is that even factually, anything less than a 'yes' is merely a substitute or metaphor for expressive consent. The columnist Ellen Goodman nicely captures this persistent view of consent when she asserts in defense of the Antioch policy that 'only a yes *means* yes'.[21] Rape reformer Liz Kelly captures it when she says, 'I don't believe consent can be presumed in any circumstances other than a woman saying, "I want to have sex with you."'[22]

Interestingly, this persistent view that 'only yes means yes' finds some non-normative support in contemporary speech-act theory. Speech-act theory helps explain why an explicit 'yes' or 'yes, I want to have sex with you' remains such a paradigmatic form of expressive consent (without necessarily implying, however, that 'yes' ought to be granted any special normative significance in criminal law). The philosophy of language has undergone a transformation since J.L. Austin delivered his William James Lectures at Harvard in 1955 on 'How To Do Things With Words'.[23] Austin argued that sentences derive significant elements of their meaning from what speakers intend to be doing in uttering them. He argued that speech involves at least two distinct acts. The first, and the one upon which students of language focused entirely, is the speaker's 'locutionary act' of uttering a certain sentence with a certain sense and reference. The second and more interesting is the speaker's 'illocutionary act' of uttering a certain sentence for a certain purpose, *e.g.*, for the purpose of questioning, warning, asserting, promising, ordering, requesting, apologizing.[24] One cannot know all that a sentence means, Austin argued, without understanding the illocutionary force with which it is uttered, that is, without understanding the social function that the sentence is intended to *perform*. Austin uses the term 'performative'[25] to refer to this latter, illocutionary work that sentences perform.

Following Austin's death, his student John Searle revised and transformed Austin's tentative explorations into a general and well-accepted theory of speech acts.[26] Placing particular emphasis on the significance of illocutions, Searle argues that all illocutionary acts fall into five general categories. Two of Searle's five categories have no bearing on consent in criminal law, though one of them, the category of 'commissives', encompasses illocutionary acts of promising that are relevant to the law of contracts.[27] Three of the categories, however, are pertinent to the defense of consent in criminal law, namely, 'Assertives', 'Directives', and 'Declarations':

> ***Assertives.*** A speaker's purpose in uttering an 'assertive' is to commit himself to the truth of the uttered proposition. It is a feature of assertives that they can be assessed for being true or false. It is also a feature of assertives that the speaker represents himself to believe what he utters. Thus, one engages in an assertive illocutionary act when one uses words to assert, suggest, state, insist, claim, hypothesize, describe, complain, or boast, etc.
>
> ***Directives.*** The purpose of a 'directive' is to get an observer to do something. Thus, one engages in directive illocutionary acts when one uses words to request, order, command, beg, invite, permit, etc., an observer to do something.
>
> ***Declarations.*** The defining characteristic of 'declarations' is that they bring about the very states of affairs represented in the propositions uttered, merely by declaring them to be so. That is, they are illocutionary acts of which it can be said that 'saying makes it so'. Thus, one performs a declaration when one uses words to successfully nominate a candidate ('I hereby nominate _____'), or declare war ('We hereby declare war on _____'), or resign ('I hereby resign'), etc.[28]

This is not to say that the illocutionary acts that people perform always correspond with the locutions they utter. People often speak in ways that create gaps between what they mean their words to do and what the words literally state. People speak 'indirectly', for example, when in addition to intending to commit themselves to the truth of what their uttered sentences literally state, they also intend their words to do something else as well. Thus, a person who says 'The vase of flowers is about to fall!' means to be doing two things with words and, hence, performs two illocutionary acts. He incidentally means to be affirming the literal truth of the sentence he is uttering (*i.e.*, 'The vase of flowers is about to fall!'), and hence he is performing an 'assertive' act. In addition, he primarily means to be urging the observer to act to stop the vase from falling, and hence he is primarily performing a 'directive' act. In contrast, people speak 'figuratively' when they do not at all intend to commit themselves to the truth of what their uttered sentences literally state but rather intend to commit themselves to the truth of something altogether different, such as when they speak metaphorically or ironically. Thus, a person who states metaphorically, 'Sam is a pig', performs the assertive illocutionary act of stating indirectly that Sam is greedy; but she does not at all perform the assertive illocutionary act of affirming the literal truth of the sentence 'Sam is a pig', because she does not mean that Sam is literally a pig. Similarly, a person who says ironically of a tactless person, 'He's really funny', performs the illocutionary act of asserting the opposite of what the uttered sentence states.[29]

The significance of 'yes' is that when a speaker says 'yes' to a question and means it, his 'yes' is an instance of what Searle calls 'the simplest case' of meaning in language, that is, one in which 'the speaker utters a sentence' —albeit, in the case of 'yes', an implicit sentence— 'and means exactly and literally' what he implicitly says.[30] When Jenny slips into Forrest's bed and says, 'I love you, Forrest', she may be performing the illocutionary act of stating that she wants to be kissed (an assertive act), or even the illocutionary act of inviting Forrest to kiss her (a directive act). But if she is, she is doing so indirectly because the sentence she utters says literally nothing about a kiss. Similarly, if Jenny tried to elicit a kiss by saying, 'Forrest, you're an angel', she would be speaking figuratively, because she would be uttering a sentence that she did not literally mean at all (*i.e.*, that Forrest is literally an 'angel') in order to get Forrest to do something that she did not literally state (*i.e.*, 'Kiss me'). In contrast, a speaker who says 'yes' to the question 'Do you want to make love?' is speaking literally because she is performing an assertive illocutionary act of stating a preference of hers that is identical to the literal meaning of the sentence she is implicitly uttering.[31] Her illocutionary act maps onto the locution she utters by committing herself to its truth.

Speech act theory thus provides a non-normative account of the centrality of 'yes' as a form of expressive consent. The significance of 'yes' does not depend upon its being verbal as opposed to nonverbal, for people perform speech acts as much by nodding their heads affirmatively as by uttering 'yes'.[32] Rather, a verbal or nonverbal 'yes' is a salient form of expressive consent because, whether in response to questions about preferences (*e.g.*, 'Do you want to make love?') or questions about permission (*e.g.*, 'Is it OK with you if I kiss you?'), a sincere 'yes' literally embodies what the speaker means to be conveying.

Nevertheless, the fact that a 'yes' is the 'simplest' and most 'direct' instance of meaning, as Searle puts it, does not mean that it possesses any particular normative significance in law or morals. Whether it does or not depends upon the norms of criminal responsibility that jurisdictions choose to adopt. Thus, on the one hand, most rape reformers do not suggest that women be required to communicate a verbal 'yes' to an explicit question 'Do you want to have sexual intercourse?' if, like Jenny in *Forrest Gump*, the women are able to convey their acquiescence in other ways.[33] On the other hand, one commentator suggests that men may be required to do more than elicit a 'yes' from women who may become pregnant from sexual intercourse, such as adhering to a mandatory waiting period between a 'yes' and the inception of sexual intercourse.[34] The legal role of an explicit 'yes' thus ultimately depends, not upon its place in speech-act theory, but upon the kinds of conduct jurisdictions regard it as just to punish.[35]

What Kind of Maxim is 'No Means No'?

What I have said thus far about the locution 'yes' has strong parallels to the locution 'no'. As a speech act, 'no' is the opposite of 'yes'. We have seen that a person who says and means 'yes' to the question 'Do you want to make love?' is performing an assertive illocutionary act of stating a preference of hers that is identical to the literal meaning of the sentence she is implicitly uttering, namely, that under the circumstances she prefers to make love. Similarly, a person who says 'no' to the question 'Do you want to make love?' and means it, is also performing an assertive illocutionary act of stating a preference of hers that is identical to the literal meaning of the sentence she is implicitly uttering, namely, that under the circumstances she does not prefer to make love.

Similarly, just as legal norms differ from one community to another regarding the necessity of saying 'yes', so, too, legal norms differ regarding the sufficiency of saying 'no'. Thus, in some communities saying 'no' to sexual intercourse is of no legal significance, except perhaps as circumstantial evidence that the speaker is submitting to sexual intercourse for fear of death or serious injury.[36] In other communities, saying 'no' to sexual intercourse is evidence, but only evidence, of something that if ultimately shown to be true is dispositive—namely, that the speaker honestly wishes that sexual intercourse not occur.[37] In still other communities, saying 'no' to sexual intercourse suffices by itself to invalidate sexual intercourse that occurs immediately thereafter, regardless of its relationship to the speaker's honest wishes regarding sexual intercourse.[38]

Nevertheless, despite these parallels, 'no' has the distinction of being contested in a certain way in which 'yes' is not. Specifically, while advocates of rape reform may differ about whether and, if so, when a verbal 'yes' is required to legitimate sexual intercourse, they tend not to make an issue of what 'yes' itself *means*.[39] With respect to 'no', however, the controversy focuses precisely upon what 'no' means—or, as the issue is typically framed, upon whether 'no' indeed means 'no'. This controversy is reflected in the divergent ways in which John Leo and Susan Estrich speak about 'no'. John Leo takes the view that 'no' does not have inherent meaning but rather draws its various meanings from the settings in which it is uttered. As he puts it, '[Men] know that depending on context and nonverbal signals, "No" can mean "maybe," "convince me," "back off awhile," or "get lost"'.[40] In contrast, Susan Estrich takes the view that 'no' means 'no':

> As recently as five or six years ago, the no means yes philosophy held sway in many courts. As recently as five or six years ago, charges would not even have been filed against William Kennedy Smith . . . or Mike Tyson, because what they were alleged to have done would not have been considered a crime. The changes have come because we as a society have changed.
>
> [T]hese . . . women, if you credit their accounts, ultimately did say no. So, granted she was foolish, granted she never should have been there in the first place, if she said no, why isn't he required to stop?
>
> You have to adopt a truly 1950s approach to sexual relations to say that women don't know what they mean or mean what they say.[41]

This dispute about what 'no' means is, at its core, a dispute about which of two distinct classes of illocutionary acts is being performed when a speaker says 'no' to overtures to sexual intercourse. Although neither Leo nor Estrich frames the issue in terms of speech acts, Leo believes that, like most words, 'no' is the kind of locution that can mean many different things depending upon the illocutionary purpose for which the speaker is using it, while Estrich believes that in the context of sexual intercourse, 'no' is the kind of locution that, when properly performed, inherently brings about what it literally states. In Searle's terminology, Leo implicitly believes that a woman who says 'no' to sexual intercourse could be performing any one of several illocutionary acts, including an assertive illocutionary act or a directive illocutionary act, while Estrich implicitly believes that the woman is invariably performing a 'declaration'. The difference is significant because, in contrast to assertive and directive illocutions, declarations are inherently normative in nature: to perform a declaration is to change the person's legal relationships to others.

A 1991 incident in California illustrates Estrich's and Leo's different understandings of 'no'. Despite being an emphatic exponent of the view that 'no means no', Estrich took pains to bring the incident to national attention in order to argue that the woman's 'no' in her case did *not* mean no. The incident, which occurred at Pomona College, involved a first-year woman student and a sophomore male student who were acquaintances. They linked up at a campus party and had a lot to drink. They left the party together, went to his room, and engaged in a variety of sexual intimacies: they lay on his bed; they kissed one another; the woman took off her jacket; the man took off the rest of her clothes; and then he took off his own clothes as well. The woman later said she felt uncomfortable lying there naked, but she did not say anything. At his coaxing, she first lay on top of him and then slid down to engage him in oral sex because she did not 'feel comfortable refusing'. They kissed some more, this time with him on top. Then came the crucial exchange. He asked, 'Should I get a condom?' She motioned 'no' by shaking her head back and forth and saying 'uh-uh'. As she herself later said, he apparently believed that she was saying 'no' to the condom rather than to sexual intercourse, and proceeded to have sexual intercourse with her in that belief. She, however, meant to be saying 'no' to sexual intercourse and two years later accused him of having sexual intercourse without her consent in violation of college rules.[42]

The Pomona case is significant because Estrich denies that the woman's 'no' meant 'no', thereby casting light upon what Estrich means by 'no means no'. Let us begin, however, by considering the kind of case on which she and John Leo would disagree. Let us assume that instead of the question 'Should I get a condom?' the young man asked the question 'Do you want to make love?' or 'Is this all right with you?' and that the woman responded by saying 'no'. What would John Leo say about such a case? He would presumably say that although the woman literally said 'no' to the question, and obviously intended to say the word 'no', she was not necessarily using 'no' to convey what the word literally means in response to the question, namely, that she did not 'want to make love', or that sexual intercourse was not 'all right' with her.[43] Of course, the woman *might* have been using 'no' for that purpose, because, as Searle puts it, speakers often 'mean exactly and literally what [they] say'.[44] But she might also have been using it to convey a different message, *e.g.*, 'I wasn't planning to do this', or 'I don't do this all the time', or 'Just ask me again'.[45] In John Searle's terminology, she might have been using 'no' figuratively to mean something different from what she was literally uttering, just as a person does who says metaphorically 'Sam is a pig', or says ironically of a tactless person 'He's really funny', or says politely to a host 'I couldn't eat another bite'. Thus, if the woman was using 'no' to convey the message 'I don't do this all the time', she was using it figuratively to perform an assertive illocutionary act. If she was using it to convey the message 'Just ask me again', she was using it figuratively to perform a directive illocutionary act. In either event, she was using 'no' to do what people do all the time, namely, to perform illocutionary acts that differ from the literal meaning of the sentences they actually utter.

Estrich would disagree with Leo, but not because she thinks that the illocutionary acts people perform are always identical to the words they literally utter. Estrich knows that people do not always mean what they literally say, particularly in the context of sexual encounters. She also knows what interviews with college-age women show, *viz.*, that a significant number of women report saying 'no' to overtures of sexual intercourse in social situations in which they subjectively hope sexual intercourse transpires.[46] Rather, Estrich differs with Leo about something more fundamental: she differs with him about what 'no means no' *itself* means and, specifically, about what it is to 'mean no'. When Estrich says that 'no means no' (or, as we shall label it for sake of clarity, 'No means No_1'), Estrich does not mean that every time a woman says 'No' she is actually expressing a subjective desire to halt sexual intercourse. What 'No' means, when it means 'No_1', is not something speakers actually desire or intend.[47] To 'mean No_1' is to cause a state of affairs of 'No_1' to exist—namely, a state of affairs in law in which sexual intercourse is *not* okay, *not* permitted, and *not* right. By the same token, 'No' means 'No_1' when the mere utterance of 'No' brings about the aforementioned legal state of affairs.

Now it might be thought that Estrich means something less than that. Thus, it might be thought that she just wants men to make a greater effort to determine what women subjectively desire, and that she uses 'no means no' as a heuristic device to induce them to think twice before proceeding. If that were so, however, Estrich would have no objection if a man proceeded in spite of a woman's statement, 'No, I really don't want you to do this', provided that he were perceptive enough to realize that she secretly wished him to proceed. But Estrich does object to that. When she says 'no means no', she means that when a woman says no to sexual intercourse, the man is 'required to stop'.[48] Alternatively, it might be thought that Estrich means that men must always behave *as if* women who say 'no' always subjectively wished them to stop. But that is not true either, because there is no necessary connection between a man's knowing that a woman wishes him to stop and his being morally or legally 'required to stop'. Indeed, many states traditionally permitted men to have sexual intercourse with women who said 'no' and who were known to mean it, provided that the men did not resort to certain kinds of force or violence.[49] Rather, when Estrich says 'no means no', she means (1) that a man must accept as a given fact that a woman who says 'no' to sexual intercourse subjectively wishes him to stop, *and* (2) that a man who understands that a woman subjectively wishes him to stop is 'require[d]' by law 'to stop' or be guilty of rape.[50]

In speech-act terminology, Estrich believes that 'no' to overtures of sexual intercourse is a 'declaration', namely, a locution the mere uttering of which brings about the very state of affairs expressed (*e.g.*, a baseball umpire's uttering 'foul ball!'). A declaration is an utterance of which it may be said that 'saying makes it so'. As Searle explains:

> There is . . . an important class of cases, where the state of affairs represented in the proposition expressed is realized or brought into existence by the illocutionary force indicating device, cases where one bring a state of affairs into existence by declaring to exist . . . . Examples of thee cases are 'I resign', 'You're fired', 'I excommunicate you', 'I christen this ship the battleship Missouri', 'I appoint you chairman', and 'War is hereby declared'.
>
> It is the defining characteristic of this class that the successful performance of one of its members brings about [a] correspondence between the propositional content and reality . . . : if I successfully perform the act of appointing you chairman, then you are chairman; if I successfully perform the act of nominating you as a candidate, then you are the candidate; if I successfully perform the act of declaring a state of war, then war is on; if I successfully perform the act of marrying you, then you are married.[51]

For Estrich, the utterance 'no' is like the utterance 'I excommunicate you'. When a woman says 'no' to an overture of sexual intercourse, she is implicitly saying 'no, no sex'; 'no, stop'; 'no, you may not'; 'no, it is against my will'; 'no, I don't want to'. And by saying so, she brings about in law the very state of affairs that she is expressing: that the man may not lawfully have sexual intercourse with her; that in law he must stop; that in law sexual intercourse is against her will; and that in law sexual intercourse is not something she wants. Needless to say, a woman who says 'no' will not always succeed in preventing sexual intercourse from actually occurring, any more than an umpire who yells 'time out' always succeeds in preventing players from continuing to play. But just as an umpire by saying 'time out' can affect the validity of continued play, a woman by saying 'no' can affect the lawfulness of sexual intimacy by delegitimating sexual intercourse that occurs in spite of it. That is what Estrich means when she says that saying 'no' to sexual intercourse means that the man is 'required to stop'.

Estrich and Leo know, of course, that certain speech acts exist such that saying it makes it so, *e.g.*, 'I resign'. They also know that other locutions exist such that saying them does *not* make them so, *e.g.*, 'I'm a genius'. They differ, however, as to how 'no' should be treated—whether it should be treated as a declaration like 'I resign' or as a non-declaration like 'I'm a genius'. To determine whether a 'no' to overtures to sexual intercourse is indeed a declaration, therefore, we must probe more deeply into what it is that transforms some utterances, and not others, into declarations.

All declarations are locutions, the mere saying of which under appropriate conditions 'makes it so', in that they create a new fact that corresponds to the literal meaning of the locution.[52] Thus, an umpire who under appropriate conditions says 'You're out!' creates a new fact, *i.e.*, that the batter is 'out', that corresponds to the literal meaning of the utterance. Nevertheless, the new facts that declarations create fall into two significant subsets: 'linguistic' facts that are themselves speech acts, *e.g.*, the fact of a promise; and 'extra-linguistic' facts that are not themselves speech acts, *e.g.*, the fact of excommunication.[53] The new fact that a woman creates by saying 'no' to sexual intercourse (*i.e.*, the fact that such conduct is henceforth unlawful) is an extra-linguistic fact like the fact of excommunication. The distinction is important because what distinguishes extra-linguistic declarations from other illocutionary acts, including linguistic declarations, is that extra-linguistic declarations derive their authority from what Searle calls 'extra-linguistic' regimes of norms and laws, such as the regimes that constitute games, social organizations, and legal institutions.[54] Thus, the word 'out' in baseball is a declaration because, properly uttered, it brings about the very state of affairs it states, viz., that under the rules of the game the base runner is out of play. To succeed as a declaration, however, 'out' must be uttered in accord with the norms that constitute baseball, that is, by a duly authorized umpire during the course of play. If a spectator shouts 'out', or an off-duty umpire does so, or a duly authorized umpire does so outside the course of play, the utterance fails as a declaration—that is, under the rules of the game the base runner is *not* out of play—because the utterance lacks authority under the rules of baseball. The same is true of the clerical utterance 'You are excommunicated'. Catholic priests can excommunicate Catholics by saying 'I excommunicate you', because they have lawful authority under canon law to do so, but Unitarian ministers cannot excommunicate Unitarians because they possess no such legal authority.

Accordingly, for 'No' to 'mean No_1', that is, for a woman to be able lawfully to 'require' a man 'to stop' his sexual advances solely by virtue of saying 'no' to him, a regime of law or an institutional authority must exist that vests women with that lawful authority. Regimes of that kind do exist. Thus, some states have adopted criminal laws that make it an offense for a man to proceed with sexual intercourse in the face of a non-rescinded 'no', and some public and private institutions (like Pomona College) have adopted comparable institutional rules to that effect.[55] When Estrich invokes the maxim 'no means no', she is in part referring to communities where 'No' does, indeed, 'mean No_1'. She is also doing something more, however; she is also speaking didactically. By intoning 'no means no', she is endeavoring to create a legal climate in which public and private authorities are increasingly induced to give 'No' the legal effect of 'No_1'.

Ultimately, therefore, Estrich and Leo possess very different understandings of what 'no means no' itself means. For Leo, a woman 'means no' when she subjectively desires that sexual intercourse cease. For Estrich, a woman 'means no' when by virtue of saying 'no', she succeeds in forclosing lawful sexual intercourse from occurring. The difference is significant because the former kind of 'no' does not necessarily entail legal consequences, while the latter kind does. Leo's 'no' does not necessarily entail legal consequences because men in some states are allowed to have sexual intercourse with women who say 'no' and subjectively mean it, provided that they do not resort to violence. In contrast, Estrich's 'no' always implies legal consequences because, even when it is uttered by a speaker who does not subjectively mean it, 'no' derives its meaning from extra-linguistic institutions that give it legal effect.

How then do we explain Estrich's view of the Pomona College case? The male student persisted in having sexual intercourse with the woman student after she had said 'no', yet Estrich argues that he should not be adjudged to have acted impermissibly. The explanation of this seeming paradox has nothing to do with what the woman actually desired under the circumstances. When Estrich says that 'no means no', she is not stating that what women subjectively desire and what they express invariably concur. If she were, she would have to conclude that the Pomona student *did* say and mean 'no', because when the Pomona student said 'no', she did subjectively desire sexual intercourse to cease. Rather, Estrich is referring to a certain state of affairs in some jurisdictions that a woman brings about merely by saying 'No, this is not okay'. According to Estrich, the reason the Pomona student did not succeed in bringing about that state of affairs in law is that the student never explicitly or implicitly said what a woman must say to bring about that state of affairs. In that sense, she did *not* say 'no', at least not for purposes of the legal maxim, 'No means no'.[56] Admittedly, she would have said such a 'no' if she had uttered her 'uh-uh' in response to the question, 'Okay?' or even in response to her companion's physical overtures toward sexual intercourse. But, instead, she uttered it in response to her companion's explicit question 'Should I get a condom', thereby saying 'no' *not* to the acceptability of sexual intercourse, but to the need for a condom. In the terms of speech-act theory, she failed to perform the *declaration*, 'Sexual intercourse is not okay', because she failed to utter the locution, 'Sexual intercourse is not okay'. She failed in the speech act she perhaps intended, not because of a disjuncture between her subjective desires and her words, but because she failed to say the thing that a person must say if she is to bring that thing about as a state of affairs in law.

Saying 'No' While Submitting to *x*

We have seen that jurisdictions use 'consent' in criminal law to refer to expressions of factual subjective acquiescence. We have also seen that a person consents to *x* in the latter sense when she either manifests unconditional desire for *x* or manifestly chooses to submit to *x* as that which she subjectively prefers for herself under the circumstances or, in some cases, as that about which she is subjectively indifferent under the circumstances. It follows, therefore, that with respect to a woman who submits to sexual intercourse in manifest fear of what the man will otherwise do, a jurisdiction may say of her what Justice Watson said of Parish's victim, *i.e.*, she 'consented' for fear of what he would otherwise do. Now what about a woman who consciously and manifestly submits to sexual intercourse while simultaneously saying 'no' to her partner for the ostensible purpose of getting him to stop? What can be said of her within a jurisdiction that takes the view that a 'no' to sexual intercourse is an utterance the meaning of which depends upon the illocutionary act the woman appears to intend it to perform (rather than being a Searlean 'declaration' that brings about the very thing it states)? Can she be said to have consciously and manifestly 'consented', even though she repeatedly said 'no' in the course of submitting?

To address the question, let us imagine two students, Louise and Kate, both of whom possess the same mixed feelings about having sexual intercourse with their respective partners. Both of them have migraine headaches and prefer not to have sexual intercourse with their partners if they can do so without hurting their partners' feelings. Yet both of them also feel that if they cannot avoid sexual intimacy without hurting their partner's feelings, they prefer to go ahead and submit to sexual intercourse. The difference is that Louise is at least willing to venture a 'no' in the hope that her partner will desist, while Kate is not willing to say 'no'. Thus:

> ***Silent Kate.*** (i) Kate desires, above all, that her partner decide on his own initiative to postpone sexual intercourse until another day.
>
> (ii) If he decides not to postpone it, Kate prefers that some innocuous and independent event occur that forcloses their having sexual intercourse, *e.g.*, a telephone call from his mother.
>
> (iii) If that does not happen, Kate prefers to submit to sexual intercourse rather than hurt her partner's feelings by saying 'no' for the illocutionary purposes of informing him of her preferences (*i.e.*, an assertive) and getting him to desist (*i.e.*, a directive).[57]
>
> Result: Kate's partner makes sexual overtures. Nothing independently occurs to forclose their having sexual intercourse. And, hence, without having said 'no', Kate submits to sexual intercourse silently but with noticeable reluctance.[58]
>
> ***Assertive Louise.*** (i) Louise, too, desires, above all, that her partner decide on his own initiative to postpone sexual intercourse until another day.
>
> (ii) If he decides not to postpone it, Louise, too, prefers that some innocuous and independent event occur that forcloses their having sexual intercourse.
>
> (iii) If that does not happen, Louise prefers to say 'no' for the purposes of informing him of her preferences and getting him to desist.
>
> (iv) If he does not desist, however, Louise prefers to submit to sexual intercourse rather than resort to more emphatic and effective forms of resistance.
>
> Result: Louise's partner makes sexual overtures. Nothing independently occurs to forclose their having sexual intercourse. Louise says 'no, I don't want to' for the manifest purpose of getting her partner to stop. Her partner understands her preference and yet, nonetheless, persists in his sexual overtures. And, hence, Louise *stops* saying 'no' and submits to sexual intercourse with noticeable reluctance.

Silent Kate's conduct is an illustration of factual consent, including factual attitudinal consent (Chapter 1) as well as factual expressive consent (Chapter 2). Thus, in consciously submitting to sexual intercourse, she factually consents to it *in her mind*, because she consciously chooses sexual intercourse as that which she prefers herself under the circumstances. By the same token, she also engages in factual *expressive* consent, because by not resorting to resistance (including verbal resistance) under circumstances in which resistance appears possible and under which she appears to be capable of making a decision for herself, she manifests that she is factually acquiescing to sexual intercourse in her mind. Obviously, however, this does not mean that Kate also legally consents to sexual intercourse so as to exonerate her partner of condemnation. For we do not know whether in consciously and manifestly submitting, Kate also possesses or manifests the competence, knowledge, freedom, and motivation that the jurisdiction at hand requires in order for a person's conscious submission to constitute a defense to rape.

Significantly, Assertive Louise's conduct is identical to Silent Kate's at the moment at which each eventually submits to sexual intercourse. At that moment, they both factually consent to sexual intercourse in mind as well as expression, because they both subjectively prefer sexual intercourse to the alternatives they believe they otherwise face and because they both manifest that preference. The difference between Louise and Kate arises—and then vanishes—at the earlier moment when Louise says 'no' and Kate does not. At that moment, Louise does not factually consent to sexual intercourse, either subjectively or expressively. Louise does not factually consent because by virtue of saying 'no' for the purpose of informing her partner of her preference and getting him to desist, she manifests that she subjectively prefers to *resist* sexual intercourse rather than submit to it—her resistance taking the form of the verbal protestation 'no'. Later, however, when her partner responds by presenting her with the new and, for her, less acceptable alternatives of either saying 'no' a second time or resorting to even more emphatic expressions of resistance, Louise elects to submit to sexual intercourse and, hence, like Kate, factually consents to sexual intercourse both subjectively and expressively.

What, finally, of a woman who continues to say 'no' throughout the entire period, including both before and during sexual penetration, for the apparent purposes of informing her partner of her preference and getting him to desist? Can a jurisdiction also say of her that she factually consents to the sexual intercourse? The answer depends upon what the woman appears to believe she is accomplishing by saying 'no'. If she appears to believe that her saying 'no' may cause her partner to change his mind, she *cannot* be described as expressively consenting to sexual intercourse; rather, she is continuing to express resistance to sexual intercourse, albeit resistance that she will soon discover fails. If, however, she appears to realize that saying 'no' will not change her partner's mind and to be consciously refraining from resorting to more emphatic forms of resistance at her disposal that might succeed, she, like Kate and Louise, factually 'consents' to sexual intercourse in mind as well as expression, because she subjectively prefers sexual intercourse to the alternatives to which she believes she could resort, and she makes her preference manifest.

Conclusion

We shall see in Chapter 4 that while some jurisdictions take the position that a subject *S*'s legal consent to *x* consists of a certain mental state of acquiescence on her part, other jurisdictions take the position that *S*'s legal consent to *x* consists of a certain *expression* of subjective acquiescence on her part. We shall also see that in order for an expressive act on *S*'s part to constitute a defense to *x* in the latter jurisdictions, three elements must be present:

#1. *S* must express that she is subjectively acquiescing to *x*—that is, that she subjectively chooses *x*—whether because she unconditionally desires *x*, or because she conditionally prefers *x* to the alternatives she believes she otherwise faces, or, perhaps, because she is indifferent to *x* under the circumstances under which she finds herself.

#2. The subjective acquiescence that *S* expresses must be—or appear to be—sufficiently competent, informed and free under the circumstances to protect whatever interests the jurisdiction believes *S* possesses regarding *x*.

#3. The form and media by which *S* communicates her acquiescence must protect whatever further conditions the jurisdiction requires, if any, to ensure that the communication is effective.

The purpose of this chapter has been to lay a foundation for understanding elements 1-3 by analyzing *one* of the three elements alone, namely, element 1. The term I use to refer to element 1 is 'factual expressive consent': 'expressive', because it consists of an expression of acquiescence on *S*'s part; 'factual', because the acquiescence that *S* expresses herself to possess is factual rather than legal in nature; and 'consent', because jurisdictions and commentators commonly refer to it as 'consent'.

This chapter focuses on factual expressive consent alone for several reasons. For one thing, isolating element 1 is a reminder that although 'consent' is sometimes used in law to refer to the combination of elements 1-3, it is also used commonly used in law to refer to element 1 alone. Furthermore, isolating element 1 helps emphasize that although factual expressive consent by itself is not sufficient to constitute a defense, it is nevertheless necessary in any jurisdiction that treats the defense as an expressive act. And finally isolating element 1 helps distinguish the normative considerations that underlie it from the very different ones that underlie elements 2 and 3. Determinations of factual expressive consent do, indeed, involve normative judgments, for to determine that *S* 'expressed' factual acquiescence to *x* for purpose of a statute regulating an actor *A* is to determine that *S* engaged in conduct (whether verbal or nonverbal, active or passive) that members of *A*'s normative-defined interpretive community would interpret to mean that *S* subjectively chose *x* as that which she desired for herself, given the circumstances under which she found herself to be. Nevertheless, the normative judgments that underlie elements 2 and 3 are quite different. Thus, element 2 involves highly contestable judgments as to how 'competent', 'informed', and 'free' *S*'s expressed acquiescence in *x* must be, or appear to be, to satisfy her interests in *x*. And element 3 involves contestable judgments as to whether expressive consent to sexual intercourse must be verbal as opposed to non-verbal,[59] or active as opposed to passive,[60] in order to be legally valid as a defense. Decoupling element 1 from elements 2 and 3 helps focus separate attention upon the distinct and typically more contested normative issues that underlie elements 2 and 3.

To illustrate, consider the Minnesota rape statute. The Minnesota statute provides that in order for a subject *S* to consent to sexual intercourse for purposes of the offense, two elements are necessary: (1) *S* must utter words or perform overt actions that 'indicat[e]' a 'present agreement' on her part to engage in sexual intercourse with the actor; (2) she must do so under circumstances that also indicate that her agreement is 'freely given'. Thus, the purpose of this chapter has been to analyze element 1 alone, that is, to analyze what it is for *S* to *indicate* agreement, regardless of whether or not the agreement also satisfies the additional requirement of appearing to be *freely given*. To be sure, when Minnesota speaks of 'consent', Minnesota uses consent in a legal sense to refer to elements 1 and 2 together, rather than to element 1 alone. Nevertheless, it is common to use 'consent' to refer to element 1 alone. Thus, Nathan Brett uses consent to refer to element 1 alone when he writes that consent is an expressive 'act' that does 'not' necessarily 'suffic[e] to generate an actual change in . . . rights and obligations of non-interference'.[61]

Brett is one of a number of commentators who, in agreeing with Minnesota that defenses of consent ought to consist of expressive acts rather than mental states, undertake to clarify the moral foundations of such expressive acts by invoking a term that speech-act philosopher J.L. Austin coined—namely, the term 'performative'.[62] Some like Brett do so by using the term 'consent' in a factual sense, while others do so by using consent in a legal sense.[63] Regardless of whether they use consent in a factual or legal sense, however, they agree that consent is not a state of mind, but a 'performative'—that is, not something that a person subjectively experiences, but something that she objectively does. As Brett puts it, consent is 'not . . . a subjective attitude' but a 'performative concept'—something 'we do . . . with words'.[64]

This use of the term 'performative' to refer to defenses of consent like Minnesota's serves one useful function: it signals that consent is being used to refer to an act of acquiescence that a person performs, rather than an experience of acquiescence that a person feels. Nonetheless, using 'performative' in this way is misleading in several respects. For one thing, since 'performative' is a term of art in speech-act theory, using it to refer to defenses of consent like Minnesota's implies acts of expressive consent either are, or ought to be, acts of *speech*—that is, verbal locutions or, at least nonverbal equivalents of verbal locutions, *e.g.*, nodding one's head, shaking one's head, *etc.*[65] Yet very few, if any, of the commentators who characterize consent as a performative take the view that in order to express acquiescence to sexual intercourse, women ought to be required either to use words or to perform nonverbal equivalents like nodding. On the contrary, most if not all of them appear to concur with Heidi Malm who, while using the term 'performative' to describe expressive consent, nonetheless takes the position that expressive consent extends beyond words and their nonverbal equivalents to expressive behavior generally:

> [Insisting on a strictly verbal standard of consent] is so at odds with the experience of most people that its adoption would very likely constitute a setback to the cause of reform. That is, a great deal of clearly consensual sexual activity that occurs between adults was never preceded by a verbal 'Do you want to do x?', and even more was never agreed to with a verbal 'yes'. Some clearly consensual sexual encounters have no verbal exchange at all, and others have no distinction between a pursuer and pursued. A law that defined all sexual activity that is not preceded by a verbal question and answer period as rape would be so contrary to experience as to be farcical. Thus, rather than bringing extra protection to women, such a law might actually set back reform because jurors would be likely to disregard a standard so at odds with their own experience, and substitute their own ideas of what ought to be rape for the instructions.[66]

To avoid confusion, therefore, commentators ought at least to emphasize that in characterizing consent as a performative, they are using 'performative' not as a term of art in speech-act theory to state that consent is confined to speech acts, but as a way of stating that consent is communication that a subject 'performs', whether by means of words or their nonverbal equivalents or by means of conduct *other* than words and their nonverbal equivalents.[67]

Furthermore, 'performative' is misleading in the context of consent because speech-act theorists themselves differ in the way they define it. Austin, for example, defines performatives as I have defined them here, namely, as illocutions of all kinds, while Searle confines performatives to one class of illocutions alone, *i.e.*, declarations.[68] The difference is significant; because as discussed below, the illocutionary force of speech acts of consent in criminal law does not derive (or, if it does, it does so rarely) from their being declarations. In addition, the term performative is associated with disputes that are peculiar to speech-act theory and not necessarily applicable to criminal law. Speech theorists differ, for example, as to whether performatives ought to be defined by reference to what speakers intend their words to do, by reference to what listeners reasonablely understand speakers to be using words to do, or by reference to both. Thus, Peter Strawson takes the view that performance of an illocutionary act depends solely upon what the speaker intends his words to be doing, even if his audience misunderstands what the speaker intends to be doing.[69] Austin takes the view that performance of an illocutionary act depends solely upon its 'securing uptake' among its audience, that is, upon what its audience understands the speaker to intend the locution to do, even if the audience is mistaken about what the speaker intends to do.[70] And Searle takes the view that performance of an illocutionary act depends upon the audience's reasonable understanding of what the speaker actually intends his locution to do.[71] These respective positions may each serve a purpose in speech-act theory. Yet despite what some commentators suggest,[72] they are not necessarily applicable for purposes of criminal law. We shall see in Chapter 4 that, in contrast to what Searle asserts for the purposes of speech-act theory, no jurisdiction defines *S*'s expressive consent in criminal law (whether factual or legal) by reference to *both* what *S* subjectively intends to communicate *and* what *S*'s audience reasonably understands. And, in contrast to what Strawson asserts for the purposes of speech-act theory, no jurisdiction that defines consent in criminal law as an expression defines it by reference to what the speaker intends as opposed to what the audience reasonably understands.

More than anything else, however, the term 'performative' is a misleading way of talking about consent because it sidesteps the controlling question: across the range of illocutionary acts that speakers necessarily perform in purposefully using words, which *specific* illocutionary act, or acts, does a speaker perform by virtue of consenting? The question is important because performatives themselves are as commonplace as speech itself, and yet they also differ from one another in significant ways. Every time speakers do things with words, they engage in performatives.[73] Yet speakers can do very different kinds of things with words and, hence, engage in very different kinds of performatives. The question is, what kind of performative is expressive consent (whether factual or legal)? Is it an utterance by which *S* promises not to oppose *A*'s conduct (a Searle 'commissive')? Is it an utterance the very uttering of which brings about in law a state of affairs being uttered (a 'declaration')? Is it an utterance by *S* which is designed to get *A* to do something or to remove a barrier to *A*'s doing something (a 'directive'). Or is it an utterance by which *S* commits herself to the truth of something (an 'assertive')?

The answer lies in what Searle calls the 'sincerity conditions' that underlie all performatives except declarations.[74] By virtue of performing any illocutionary act (except a declaration), a speaker represents himself as having a psychological state of one kind or another, whether or not he actually possesses it. Thus, a person who makes a promise represents himself as having an intention; a person who performs a directive represents himself as having a wish; and a person who performs an assertive represents himself as having a belief. Now contrary to what some commentators suggest,[75] expressive consent is not a promise, although factual expressive consent can accompany a promise. It is not a promise because by virtue of expressively consenting to something, say, sexual intimacy, *S* does not intentionally pledge herself to engage in sexual intercourse in the future even if she changes her mind in the meantime. *S* can promise to engage in sexual intercourse if she chooses to do, though such a promise is not one that the law will enforce.[76] And by virtue of promising to engage in sexual intercourse, *S* also necessarily expressively consents to sexual intercourse, at least until she changes her mind. But if *S* does change her mind, and is reproached for doing so, the reproach is predicated upon *S*'s having broken a promise, not upon her having also expressively consented, because expressive consent alone does not bind a subject not to change her mind. When *S* promises *A* to do *x*, *S* at most grants *A* what Wesley Hohfeld would call a 'claim right' that she will do *x*. When *S* expressively consents to *x*, she at most grants *A* a Hohfeldian 'privilege' that he may do *x* until she changes her mind.[77]

Nor is expressive consent a declaration that brings about in law the very state of affairs it declares, *e.g.*, a bailiff's uttering 'This court is now in session'[78] (though *non*-consent in the form of a 'No' can, indeed, be such a declaration). A distinctive feature of declarations is that they imply no sincerity condition.[79] A bailiff can bring a court into session by merely uttering, 'This court is now in session', without necessarily representing that he possesses a psychological state of belief in, or desire for, or commitment to bring about what he is uttering. The same cannot be said of a subject *S* who expressively consent's to *A*'s doing something to her by saying 'yes'. When *S*'s utterance of 'yes' operates in law to constitute legal consent, it is not *despite* what it represents about *S*'s mental state, but *because* of what it represents about her mental state—which is why it is commonly and rightly observed, 'Yes does not always mean yes'.[80] Furthermore, if consent were a declaration, it would have to consist of a verbal locution the saying of which 'makes it so' (*e.g.*, 'This court is in session').[81] Yet a woman *S* can utter words that constitute expressive consent to sexual intercourse, both factually and legally, without 'making it so', *e.g.*, when a woman consents to sexual intercourse by saying, literally, 'Make love to me!' or saying, figuratively, 'Take me to the moon!'

A more promising class of illocutions for expressive consent is the class that Searle calls 'directives'. A directive is an utterance by *S* the illocutionary point of which is to get *A* to do something or to remove an antecedently existing restriction on *A*'s doing it. Thus, an utterance that has the illocutionary point of granting permission is a directive, because when *S* uses words to grant *A* permission to do something that *A* would otherwise be prohibited from doing, *S* removes a restriction on *A*'s doing it.[82] Directives are a promising class because acts of consent by a subject *S*, whether factual or legal, often consist either of efforts by *S* to get *A* to do x or efforts by *S* to grant *A* permission to do *x*; and, when they do so, directives are efforts by which *S* represents herself as having the sincerity condition appurtenant to directives, that is, a psychological state of *wish* or *desire*.[83] Thus, women who expressively consent to sexual intimacy are often attempting (and appear to be attempting) either to get their partners to engage in sexual intimacy or to grant their partners permission to engage in such intercourse, and they do so by representing themselves as desiring sexual intimacy. When they do, they are, by definition, performing illocutionary directives. Moreover, when a speech act by *S* suffices to constitute *legal* consent to *x*, the effect of her speech act is to grant *A* legal permission—or, in Hohfeld's taxonomy, a legal 'privilege'—to do what *A* would otherwise be prohibiting from doing.[84] Because speech acts of legal consent in criminal law all have the effect of granting Hohfeldian privileges, and because speech acts of granting permission are Searlean directives, it is tempting to conclude that all speech acts of legal consent in criminal law consist of Searlean directives.

Nevertheless, although some acts of expressive consent are, indeed, directives, it is a mistake to conclude that all are, and a further mistake to conclude that, because acts of legal consent have the effect of granting Hohfeldian privileges, acts of legal consent must also be Searlean directives. *S* can expressively consent to *x* without necessarily attempting or appearing to attempt to get *A* to do *x* by conveying a desire for *x*. Consider a woman who expressively, but begrudgingly, consents to sexual intercourse with her husband in the middle of the night because she suspects that he will otherwise pout. She clearly consents to sexual intercourse, both factually and legally, because she prefers sexual intercourse to the alternative of her husband's pouting; but she can hardly be said to be trying to get him to initiate sexual intercourse when she clearly prefers—and by her begrudging manner lets him know that she prefers—that he go to sleep and stop pouting. In addition, a subject can expressively consent to *x* without experiencing (or conveying) the sincerity condition of desiring to grant *A* permission to engage in *x*. Consider a woman in New York who eagerly and lovingly responds to her husband sexual overtures without knowing—and without caring—that in New York women have a legal right to deny their husbands sexual access. The New Yorker consents to sexual intercourse, both factually and legally, because she unconditionally desires it; but she can hardly be said to trying to grant her husband permission, because the notion of granting him permission never occurs to her. The legal effect of both women's expressive consent is to grant their husbands legal privileges to do something that they would otherwise be prohibited from doing. But it is a fallacy to think that because these women's expressive acts have the effect of granting their husbands privileges, their expressive acts must reflect a psychological desire on their parts to grant their husbands permission.[85]

Now it might be thought that because some acts of expressive consent are directives while others are not, no single category of illocutionary performatives can encompass them all. Yet that is also a mistake. Every speech act of consent, whether it is factual or legal, and whether it is an illocutionary directive or not, is Searlean assertive, though it may take the form of an indirect or figurative assertive. An assertive is an utterance by *S* the illocutionary point of which is to commit *S* to the truth of the proposition that *S* is directly, indirectly or figuratively uttering. A subject who performs a speech act of consent to *x* may or may not be trying to get *A* to perform *x*; and she may or may not be trying to grant *A* permission to do *x*. But regardless of whether she is also performing the latter illocutionary acts, she performs an illocutionary assertive, because she represents herself as having the sincerity condition of believing the truth of what she is directly, indirectly, or figuratively uttering—namely, that she either prefers *x* to the alternatives that she believes she would otherwise face or is so indifferent as to whether *x* occurs as to be willing to delegate its occurrence to *A*.[86]

Notes

1. Oliver Sacks gives the following description of a substantial number of the patients:

   > Patients who . . . survived . . . often failed to recover their original aliveness. They would be conscious and aware—yet not fully awake; they would sit motionless and speechless all day in their chairs, totally lacking energy, impetus, initiative, motive, appetite, affect or desire; they registered what went on about them without active attention, and with profound indifference. They neither conveyed nor felt the feeling of life; they were as insubstantial as ghosts, and as passive as zombies. . . . Such patients, in neurological parlance, showed 'negative' disorders of behavior, *i.e.*, no behavior at all. They were ontologically dead, or suspended, as 'asleep'—awaiting an awakening which came (for the tiny fraction who survived) fifty years later.
   >
   > One thing, and one alone, was (usually) spared amid the ravages of this otherwise engulfing disease: the 'higher faculties'—intelligence, imagination, judgment, and humour. These were exempted—for better or worse. Thus, these patients, some of whom had been thrust into the remotest or strangest extremities of human possibility, experienced their states with unsparing perspicacity, and retained the power to remember, to compare, to dissect and to testify. Their fate, so to speak, was to become unique witnesses to a unique catastrophe.

   Sacks, *Awakenings*, pp. 14-15, 19. For descriptions of the relationships between some of the patients and their families, *see id.* pp. 67-79 (Rose R.); pp. 128-36 (Lucy K.); and pp. 188-201 (Leonard L.).
2. For discussion of silence and passivity as expressions of acquiescence, *see* Feinberg, *Harm To Self*, p. 183-84; McGregor, 'Force, Consent, and the Reasonable Woman', pp. 242-43; and Malm, 'The Ontological Status of Consent', p. 148.
3. *See, e.g.*, Brooks v. Alabama, 555 So. 2d 1134, 1136 (1989) ('communicate' a 'lack of consent'); California v. Coleman, 48 Cal. 3d 112, 143, 768 P.2d 32, 49, 255 Cal. Rptr. 813, 830 (1989) ('words or conduct...manifesting consent to [a] sexual act'); Ozenna v. Alaska, 1999 Alas. App. LEXIS 54 (1999) (complainant had capacity to 'express her consent');

California v. Benn, 2002 Cal. App. Unpub. LEXIS 732, *32 (2002) ('valid consent' was 'conveyed').

4. *See, e.g.*, Nebraska v. Koperski, 254 Neb. 624, 637, 578 N.W.2d 837, 846 (1998) (there was evidence that the complainant 'affirmatively consented'); Louisiana v. Parish, 405 So. 2d 1080, 1089 (1981) (Watson, J., dissenting) (the complainant 'verbally consented'); Bryant v. Indiana, 644 N.E.2d 859, 860 (1994) (the complainant did not 'explicitly consent'); California v. Vargas, 2001 Cal. App. Unpub. LEXIS 275, *50 (2001) (the jury could not have found that the complainant 'expressly consented'); New Jersey v. Sorge, 123 N.J.L. 532, 534, 10 A.2d 175, 176 (1939) (the issue in the case is whether the complainant 'expressly or tacitly consented' to the sexual intercourse that occurred); Royal v. Alabama, 447 S.2d 834, 836 (1983) (defendant testified that the complainant 'gave her consent to have sexual intercourse').
5. Wisconsin Statutes § 940.225(4) (2000) ('"Consent", as used in this section, means words or overt actions by a person . . . indicating a freely given agreement to have sexual intercourse or sexual contact'). *See* also Minnesota Statutes §609.341(4) (2000) ('"Consent", as used in this section, means words or overt actions by a person . . . indicating a freely given agreement to have sexual intercourse or sexual contact'); Washington Rev. Code § 9A.44.010 (2000) ('As used in this chapter . . . (7) "Consent" means that at the time of the act of sexual intercourse or sexual contact there are actual words or conduct indicating freely given agreement to have sexual intercourse or sexual contact').
6. Wisconsin v. Lederer, 99 Wis. 2d 430,434, 299 N.W.2d 457, 460 (1980):

   > We reject defendant's contention that a defendant could be convicted . . . for engaging in consensual sexual relations. The plain terms of the statute require that the state must prove that the act of sexual intercourse must be without consent.
   >
   > Defendant contends that two parties may enter into consensual sexual relations without manifesting freely given consent through words or acts. We reject this contention as we know of no other means of communicating consent.

   The state of Connecticut has held to the same effect. *See* Connecticut v. Richard T. Smith, 210 Conn. 132, 140, 554 A.2d 713, 717 (1989):

   > [W]hether a complainant has consented to intercourse depends upon her manifestations of such consent as reasonably construed. If the conduct of the complainant under all the circumstances should reasonably be viewed as indicating consent to the act of intercourse, a defendant should not be found guilty because of some undisclosed mental reservation on the part of the complainant.
   >
   > [We hold] that the crux of the inquiry on the issue of consent was not the subjective state of mind of the complainant but rather her manifestations . . . of consent by words or conduct as reasonably construed.

7. *See, e.g.*, Brett, 'Commentary', p. 257 (embracing a 'performative account of consent'); Brett, 'Sexual Offenses and Consent', pp. 76-80; McGregor, 'Force, Consent, and the Reasonable Woman', p. 242 ('Consent is performative, it is something that an agent does'); Sherwin, 'Infelicitous Sex', p. 209 ('Consent is a social act . . . an act designed for the expression of a subjective choice'); Malm, 'The Ontological Status of Consent', p. 147 ('I think there are strong pragmatic reasons for thinking that "consent" is best defined as the signification of a particular mental state, rather than as the mental state itself'); McGregor, 'Why When She Says No She Doesn't Mean Maybe', p. 196 ('consent [is] something the agent has to perform that grants permission to do that which would otherwise be impermissible'); Vandervort, 'Mistake of Law and Sexual Assault', p. 267 (citing Austin):

   > The social act of consent consists of communication to another person, by means of verbal or nonverbal behaviour, of permission to perform one or more acts which that person

would otherwise have a legal or non-legal obligation not perform. Consenting, like promising, is thus performative.

Wertheimer, 'What Is Consent?' p. 557 (2000) ('I shall argue [that] . . . consent is best understood as a performative or action, not as a subjective phenomenon').

8. Archard, *Sexual Consent*, p. 4.
9. Archard, *Sexual Consent*, p. 3.
10. Malm, 'Ontological Status of Consent', pp. 147-64.
11. Malm, 'Ontological Status of Consent', pp. 147-48.
12. Malm, 'The Ontological Status of Consent', pp. 150-51, 153.
13. Louisiana v. Parish, 405 So. 2d 1080 (1981).
14. 405 So. 2d at 1089-90 (Justice Watson, dissenting on the ground that even if Parish was guilty of attempted rape before he fell, he abandoned the attempt thereafter).
15. *See, e.g.*, Scherzer v. New Jersey, 301 N.J. Super. 363, 694 A.2d 196 (1997), holding the defendants guilty of having sexual intercourse with a 'mentally defective', *i.e.*, a retarded teenage girl, on the ground that, though the girl 'consented' in the sense that she used 'words or . . . actions that, when viewed in the light of all the surrounding circumstances, would demonstrate to a reasonable person affirmative and freely-given authorization for the specific act of sexual penetration'—'freely' meaning not the product of intimidation or coercion—the defendants knew or should have known that she was 'temporarily or permanently incapable of understanding the nature of [her] conduct'.
16. See generally Searle, The Construction of Social Reality.
17. *See* Brett, 'Sexual Offenses and Consent', p. 73 ('To consent is to act in a way that has conventional significance in communicating permission').
18. For accounts of the trial, *see* Giraldo Rivera ('Wife Confronts Her Husband And Charges Rape'), 18 August 1994, 2:50 PM; Larry King Live ('A Controversy Over Marital Rape'), CNN, 15 May 1992, Transcript # 562-1. For a case in which the police concluded on the basis of a videotape that two men had sexual intercourse with a woman who was too intoxicated to know what was happening but in which the woman herself insisted that she had consented, *see* Garcia, 'Rape, Lies, and Videotape', p. 732 (1992).
19. *See* Husak and Thomas, 'Date Rape, Convention, and Reasonable Mistake', pp. 102-03. Nevertheless, although what silence communicates is largely a matter of social convention, social conventions do not necessarily constitute the standards of prescriptive consent. For example, the fact that a person is silent in settings in which social convention suggests that silence means acquiescence does not mean that person necessarily 'consents' for purposes of the law; because the law is free to reject social convention by imposing standards of prescriptive consent that exceed what social convention dictates.
20. The Antioch College Sexual Offense Policy was adopted in February 1991 and consists of an introduction (entitled 'Sexual Violence and Safety') and the Sexual Offense Policy itself. It is reprinted as Appendix 1 in Francis, *Date Rape*, pp. 136-41.
21. Goodman, 'The Struggle on College Campuses To Create a Standard of Sexual Equality', *The Boston Globe*, 19 September 1993, page 75 (emphasis added). *See* also Jane Gross, 'Even The Victim Can Be Slow To Recognize Rape', *New York Times*, 28 May 1991, section A, page 14, col. 3 ('[C]ounselors encourage women to take the position that sex without an explicit "yes" is not consensual, even between people who have had sexual intercourse in the past').
22. Cowling, *Date Rape and Consent*, p. 92 n.21 (quoting Liz Kelly, author of *Surviving Sexual Violence*).

23. Austin, *How To Do Things With Words*. The later chapters of *How To Do Things With Words* were adopted from notes Austin used for the lectures and from notes of lectures he delivered at Oxford.
24. Austin, *How To Do Things With Words*, pp. 98-100, 109. Austin also identified a third speech act, which is not relevant here, which he called the 'perlocutionary' act that a speaker can perform. 'Perlocution' refers to the effects that illocutionary speech acts have has on the actions, thoughts, beliefs, etc. of a listener. *See id.* at 101 et seq.
25. Austin, *How To Do Things With Words*, p. 6. Unfortunately, because of the particular examples of performatives that Austin invokes, and because of the different ways his student John Searle uses it, the term 'performative' is not as perspicuous a term as it might be. Austin created some of the ambiguity himself by drawing the bulk of his illustrations of performatives from a single subset of performatives (*i.e.*, what he called 'explicit performatives' and what his student John Searle later called 'declarations'), while simultaneously using 'performatives' more broadly as a synonym for 'illocutions'. *See* Austin, *How To Do Things With Words*, pp. 6, 12, 32-33, 58, 68, 74, 87, 99; Austin, 'Performative Utterances', pp. 243-45; Searle, *Expression and Meaning*, pp. 7, 17 (commenting upon the extent to which, for Austin, the class of performatives is broader than the particular illustrations he tended to invoke). Searle also contributed to the ambiguity by, first, following Austin and using 'performatives' broadly as a synonym for illocutionary acts in general and, then, later using 'performatives' as a synonym for 'declarations' alone. Compare Searle, *Expression and Meaning*, pp. 7, 17-18 (using 'performatives' broadly), and Searle, 'Austin On Locutionary and Illocutionary Acts', pp. 403-04 (using 'performatives' broadly), with Searle, 'How Performatives Work', pp. 376-77 (suing 'performatives' as a synonym for declarations).
26. *See* Searle, *Expression and Meaning*. Searle, *Speech Acts*. I do not mean to suggest that Searle's exposition of Austin is beyond criticism but, rather, that it is a paradigm within which philosophy of language is currently done. For critical analysis of Searle, *see* essays by Jennifer Hornsby, Tsohatzidis, Rod Bertolet, and David Holdcroft in *Foundations of Speech Act Theory*.
27. The two categories of illocutionary acts that are not relevant to consent in criminal law are 'commissives' and 'expressives'. A 'commissive', as Austin and Searle both define it, is an illocutionary act—of which promises are paradigmatic examples—whose point is to commit the speaker to some future course of action. *See* Austin, *How To Do Things With Words*, pp. 157-60; Searle, *Expression and Meaning*, p. 14. A speaker *S* who consents to *A*'s conduct *x* within the meaning of the criminal law may, rarely, also 'promise' not to change his mind and/or not to do anything in the future to interfere with *A*'s doing *x*. But neither the existence of *S*'s consent to *x* nor its efficacy in law depends in any way upon the existence or efficacy of the promise that accompanies it, because the defense consent in criminal law does not depend upon an accompanying promise. Consent in criminal law is a Hohfeldian privilege that authorizes *A* to engage in conduct *x* that *S* would otherwise have a claim-right to prevent *A* from performing—not a claim right by *A* to engage in *x*. In contrast, a promise by *S* gives *A* precisely what *S*'s consent in criminal law does not give *A*, namely, a claim right to engage in *x*. *See* generally Thomson, *Realm of Rights*, pp. 349-51; Wellman. *A Theory of Rights*. But *see* Archard, *Sexual Consent*, p. 6 (treating the defense of consent to sexual offenses as an Austinian 'commissive').

    In turn, an 'expressive', as Searle defines it, is an illocutionary act the point of which is 'to express the psychological state specified in the sincerity condition about a state of affairs specified in the propositional content', *e.g.*, to 'congratulate' or 'apologize' to someone. Searle, *Expression and Meaning*, p. 15. The distinctive feature of expressives is that the speaker is trying neither to get his words to 'fit' the world nor to get the world to fit his words, but, rather, to state a proposition the truth of which is presupposed. Thus, the purpose of a person who 'apologizes' for stepping on another's toe is not to claim that the toe was stepped on but to express the very feeling that he is stating. *Id.* The consent defense in criminal law is not an 'expressive' (as Searle defines it), because a speaker who verbally consents is, indeed, trying get his words to 'fit' the world, in that he is trying to get his words to fit what his subjective preferences happen to be under the circumstances.

28. Searle, *Expression and Meaning*, pp. 1-8, 12-20.
29. *See* Searle, *Expression and Meaning*, pp. 30-57, 76-116. For criticism of Searle's analysis of 'indirect' and 'figurative' speech, *see* Bertolet, 'Are There Indirect Speech Acts', pp. 335-49; and , and Tsohatzidis, 'Speaker Meaning, Sentence Meaning and Metaphor', pp. 364-73.
30. Searle, *Expression and Meaning*, p. 30. For Searle's discussion of what a speaker implicitly means by saying 'yes' to a question, *see* Searle, *Speech Acts*, p. 19.
31. A person who says 'I want to make love' may be performing several illocutionary acts. For, in addition to expressing his wishes under the circumstances (*i.e.*, an assertive act), he may also be seeking to get the hearer to respond by making love (*i.e.*, a directive act). In that event, he is speaking literally with respect to the assertive act and indirectly with respect to the directive act. Searle, *Expression and Meaning*, p. 30.
32. Austin took the position early on that illocutionary acts can be performed nonverbally. *See* Austin, *How To Do Things With Words*, pp. 87, 121. *See* also Hornsby, 'Illocution and Its Significance', pp. 187-207, at 197 ('there can be non-verbal performances of illocutionary acts'). In contrast, others take the position that 'speech acts' must be verbal. *See, e.g.*, Searle, *Expression and Meaning*, p. 7. The latter position, however, seems to have less to do with how direct nonverbal statements are capable of being than with how 'speech acts' are defined. *See, e.g.*, Bertolet, 'Are There Indirect Speech Acts?' pp. 338-39:

    > Let us start with some simply physical acts. Morgan notes that if upon being asked my opinion of a spinach souffle I have been served I shovel the contents of my plate into the dog's dish, I have rendered my judgement as clearly as if I had said, 'It's awful', though less directly.
    >
    > While I am not sure that this is less direct than an utterance, it does seem clear that Morgan is right to say that judgment has been clearly rendered. Presumably, no one would want to claim that Morgan had performed any speech act at all, since he did not speak.

33. *See, e.g.*, Malm, 'The Ontological Status of Consent', pp. 160-63 (arguing that it is inappropriate for the law of rape to require that consent be verbal); Remick, 'Read Her Lips', pp. 1139-44 (arguing that a verbal 'yes' ought not to be required if a defendant can show beyond a reasonable doubt that his sexual partner expressed her acquiescence in other ways). Cf. Estrich, 'Rape', p. 1181('we are not [yet] . . . at the point where it is appropriate for the law to presume non-consent from silence'). But *see* Schulhofer, 'The Gender Question in Criminal Law', p. 133:

    > The usual feminist position [that 'no' means 'no'] does not go far enough [in allowing convictions for rape]. Why should there have to be a 'no'? . . . Citizens may not presume a privilege to intrude upon the rights of others, but rather must respect the autonomy of each person and stand clear in the absence of a direct, affirmative manifestation of consent. On this basis, anything less than an explicit 'yes' should not count as consent.

    Sanday, *A Woman Scorned*, p. 284 (nothing less than a verbal 'yes' should count as legal consent to sexual intercourse); Archard, *Sexual Consent*, p. 146 (with respect to 'first sexual encounter[s]' among 'strangers', a man should, indeed, be required to elicit a verbal 'yes' before engaging in sexual intercourse).

34. Olsen, 'The Supreme Court, 1988 Term' p. 130:

 If one accepts a state goal to reduce abortion, there are alternative means to consider, apart from limiting access. The most obvious are for the state to provide more social support for pregnant women . . . and to eliminate rape and other forms of male domination that disable women from preventing conception. A less obvious, but heuristically important, means to reduce abortion would be for the state to outlaw the act of impregnating women who do not wish to become pregnant. State could require a man to obtain informed consent from a woman before he risked impregnating her, and could consider whether to impose a mandatory waiting period before such consent would become effective. This approach would seem no less practical than banning abortions except for the male domination of our society.

35. Alabama provides, for example, that before an actor may perform a lawful abortion upon a minor, he must first secure the 'written consent' of one of the minor's parents or legal guardians. Alabama Code § 26-21-3 (1994).

36. *See, e.g.*, North Carolina v. Alston, 310 N.C. 399, 401-03, 312 S.E.2d 470, 471-73 (1984) ('no' by itself possesses no legal significance, except as evidence that the speaker is submitting to sexual intercourse for fear of death or grievous bodily injury); Goldberg v. Maryland, 41 Md. 58, 395 A.2d 1212 (1979) (same).

37. *See, e.g.*, Wisconsin v. Lederer, 99 Wis. 2d 430, 299 N.W.2d 457 (1980) (defendant is guilty of rape for having sexual intercourse with a woman who protested by saying 'no', where it appears from the circumstances that she not only said 'no', but meant it—that is, that she said it wishing to bring sexual intercourse to a halt). *See* generally Bryden, 'Redefining Rape', p. 377. For a commentator who takes essentially the same position as Wisconsin, *see* Dressler, 'Where We Have Been', pp. 433-34.

38. *See, e.g.*, Revised Statutes of Canada, 1985, c. C-46, § 153.1(3) ('No consent is obtained, for the purposes of this section, if . . . (d) the complainant expresses, by words or conduct, a lack of agreement to engage in the activity'); Queen v. Ewanchuk, [1999] 1 S.C.R. 330, 356 ('[A]n accused cannot rely upon his purported belief that the complainant's expressed lack of agreement to sexual touching in fact constituted an invitation to more persistent or aggressive contact. An accused cannot say that he thought 'no meant yes'). *See* also Nebraska Revised Statutes § 28-318 (2000) ('"Without consent" means (a) . . . (ii) the victim expressed a lack of consent through words'); New Hampshire Revised Statutes § 632-A:2(I)m (2000) ('A person is guilty of the felony of aggravated felonious sexual assault if he engages in sexual penetration with another person . . . [w]hen at the time of the sexual assault, the victim indicates by speech or conduct that there is not freely given consent to performance of the sexual act'); Utah Code § 76-5-406 (2001) ('An act of sexual intercourse . . . is without consent of the victim under any of the following circumstances . . . (1) the victim expresses lack of consent through words or conduct').

 Interestingly, no commentator argues that no man can *ever* have lawful sexual intercourse with a woman who has *ever* said 'no' to him in the past. Rather, they implicitly assume that events can occur after a woman stops saying 'no' and before an actor engages her in sexual intercourse that have the effect of legitimating the intercourse. Yet there has thus far been little analysis of what suffices (or ought to suffice) in law to negate the legal effect of a 'no'. *See* Schulhofer, 'The Feminist Challenge in Criminal Law', p. 2175 (the maxim 'no means no' does not help 'sort out whether the things that happen after the "no" are legitimate or abusive'); Dressler, 'Where We Have Been', p. 426 ('Another issue not resolved by the no-means-no principle is what the male is supposed to do after the "no" (other than not to proceed immediately to intercourse). May the male continue his sexual overtures, albeit more slowly, in order to convince the female to change her mind, or does there have to be some cooling-off period?').

39. This is not to say that a 'yes' is unambiguous in a way that 'no' is not. On the contrary, a speaker who says 'yes' can intend to be performing—and, hence, understood to be performing—many of the same distinct and contrary illocutionary acts as a speaker who says 'no'. As we shall see, what distinguishes 'yes' from 'no' is that no commentator seriously contends that 'yes' ought to be treated in law as an illocutionary 'declaration', while numerous commentators argue that the law ought, indeed, to treat a 'no' as an illocutionary declaration.
40. Leo, 'Don't Oversimplify Date Rape', p. 17.
41. Estrich, 'Palm Beach Stories', pp. 10-11, 32.
42. The incident was widely reported in the Los Angeles papers. *See* 'Pomona: Judge OKs College Hearing for Student Accused of Rape', *Los Angeles Times*, 25 May 1994, pt. B, p. 2, col. 1; Sullivan, 'Date Rape Allegation Ignites a Furor at Pomona College', *Los Angeles Times*, 21 May 1994, pt. B, p.1, col. 2. Because of the degree of detail she reports, however, I rely principally on Estrich's report of the case. *See* Estrich. 'This Case Demeans Real Date-Rape Victims', p. 15A.
43. If the woman is speaking literally when she says 'no' to the question, 'Do you want to make love', she is, at the very least, performing an *assertive* illocutionary act, because she is at the very least committing herself to the truth of what she is implicitly stating. (Moreover, if she is doing so for the purpose of getting the man to stop his sexual advances, she is also performing a directive illocutionary act, though, in that event, she is performing the directive illocutionary act 'indirectly'). If the woman is speaking literally when she says 'no' to the question, 'Is this all right with you?', she is, at the very least, performing a *directive* illocutionary act, because she is at the very least denying the man permission. *See* Searle, *Expression and Meaning*, p. 22 (to 'permit' a person to do something 'has the syntax of directives', because 'it consists in removing antecedently restrictions on his doing it, and is therefore the illocutionary negation of a directive with a negative propositional content').
44. Searle, Expression and Meaning, p. 30.
45. Heidi Malm wagers that 'virtually no man . . . has responded to hearing a "No" with the thought, "Oh good, she's finally consented."' Malm, 'The Ontological Status of Consent', p. 159. Yet a man may well come away with the latter thought if he focuses, not solely upon the locution 'no', but also upon the illocutionary force with which it is uttered—that is, upon what it is reasonable for him to understand his partner to be using the locution 'no' to *do*. Indeed, Malm herself recognizes that 'words cannot be understood in isolation and "No's" directed at particular means of sexual interaction (and certain "Oh no!'s") can be quite common in consensual sex'. *Id.*
46. *See* Husak and Thomas, 'Date Rape, Social Convention, and Reasonable Mistake', p. 122 (citing a 1988 study that 39% of Texas female college undergraduates reported that they had said 'no' when they wanted to have sex, and that 60.8% of sexually experienced women in the study stated that they had said 'no' when they intended to have sex). Estrich published her essay, 'Palm Beach Stories', in the same symposium in which Husak and Thomas cited the Texas study.
47. As Searle puts it, the successful performance of a declaration does not entail a 'sincerity condition', that is, it does not inherently express that the speaker *believes* or *intends* or *desires* what he is saying. Searle, *Expression and Meaning*, pp. 5-6, 19.
48. *See* note 41. *See* also Estrich, 'Rape', p. 1104:

But even if reasonableness is defined—as I argue it should be—according to a rule that 'no means no', it is not unfair to hold those men who violate the rule criminally responsible, provided that there is fair warning of the rule.

Estrich argues that it is enough to show that a man is guilty of having sexual intercourse with a woman without her 'consent' that he proceeded in the face of her saying 'no' to sexual intercourse. Estrich. 'Rape: A Question of Force', p. 13A.

49. In most states, it is not a crime to pressure a woman who is saying 'no' into having sexual intercourse unless the pressure independently amounts to 'force'. *See* Schulhofer, *Unwanted Sex*, p. 255; Remick', Read Her Lips', pp.1116-17; Dripps. 'Beyond Rape', p. 1785 (observing that despite reforms in other areas of rape law in the 1980s, 'the gravamen of rape remains the conjunction of force and non-consent '). For an illustrative case in which 'no' did not suffice to prohibit sexual intercourse, *see* North Carolina v. Alston, 310 N.C. 399, 401-03, 312 S.E.2d 470, 471-73 (1984), where the defendant's rape conviction was reversed on the ground that, although the woman cried and said she did not want to have sexual intercourse, the defendant did not use 'force'.
50. Stephen Schulhofer makes the same point when he says, 'To resolve legal disputes about consent, we must inevitably *assign* some meaning to the word "no".... Whatever "no" means as a matter of the English language, ... "no" should be *treated as* meaning no when we have to resolve legal disputes about consent'. Schulhofer, *Unwanted Sex*, pp. 266-65. Some authorities conceptualize the legal effect of 'no means no' somewhat differently. They say that if a man has intercourse in the face of a 'no', he 'proceeds at his own risk'. *See, e.g.*, Massachusetts v. Lefkowitz, 20 Mass. App. 513, 521, 481 N.E.2d 227, 232 (1985) (Brown, J., concurring); Thomas and Edelman, 'Consent To Have Sex: Empirical Evidence About "No,"' p. 616. However, to speak of a man's proceeding 'at his own risk' is misleading, for it fallaciously implies that the 'risk' in law is less than a certainty; that is, it fallaciously implies that a man who proceeds in the face of a woman's "no" in a jurisdiction in which 'no means no' will be deemed to be innocent in law in the event the woman *did not really mean it*.
51. Searle, *Expression and Meaning*, pp. 16-17.
52. In his later writing, Searle uses the term 'performative', not as he does earlier as a synonym for all illocutionary acts, but as a synonym for declarations alone. *See* note 25.
53. Searle, 'How Performatives Work', pp. 384-85.
54. Searle, 'How Performatives Work', pp. 384-85. Searle, *Expression and Meaning*, pp. 18 ('[A]n extra-linguistic institution [is] a system of constitutive rules in addition to the constitutive rules of language . . . It is only given such institutions as the church, the law, private property, the state and a special position of the speaker and hearer within these institutions that one can excommunicate, appoint, give and bequeath one's possessions or declare war').
55. *See* note 38.
56. In Estrich's words, the woman's complaint to Pomona College 'should be thrown out', not because 'uh-uh' is never sufficient, and not because the woman subjectively desired to have sexual intercourse, but because for purposes of 'no means no', she 'never said no'. Estrich, 'Real Date Rape Victims,' *USA Today*, May 26, 1994.
57. According to the hypothetical, Louise says 'no' for two illocutionary purposes, namely, (i) to assert her preference not to have sexual intercourse under the circumstances, and (ii) to get her partner to desist. However, I do not believe that anything significant turns upon the presence of the second purpose. Imagine, for example, that Nancy is uncertain about how she wants her partner to react once he learns what her preference, and yet, nevertheless, wants him to know beforehand what her preference is in the event that it makes a difference to him. In that event,

Nancy's action of saying 'no' cannot be said to constitute factual consent to sexual intercourse, because believing that her assertion may influence her partner to desist, and making the assertion for the purpose of subjecting him to that influence, her uttering 'no' cannot be said to be a choosing of sexual intercourse under the circumstances.

58. Cf. Oberman, 'Turning Girls Into Women', p. 55 (citing the case of 'Rochelle', who 'avoided boys early on, in order to avoid getting a bad reputation, but began to feel she "had to get a boyfriend" during her sophomore year in high school. "I felt as though I had to conform to everything he said. . . . When the sex came . . . I did it without thinking . . . I wish I would have waited. . . . I did it because, maybe because he wanted it, and I was always like trying to please him"'); Gross, 'Even the Victim Can Be Slow to Recognize Rape', p. 14, col. 3 (referring to K. Kaufman, 'a 38-year-old freelance writer, who allowed a man to sleep in the same bed after he promised not to "bother" her. Later that night, he forced her to have sex, she said. Ms. Kaufman noted that calling what happened to her rape was likely to prompt disdain. "But what people don't understand is powerlessness," she said. "They don't understand the amount of sex women submit to because it's easier than saying no"').
59. Compare Alabama Code § 26-21-3 (1994) (providing that before an actor may perform a lawful abortion upon a minor, he must first secure the 'written consent' of one of the minor's parents or legal guardians), with In re M.T.S.,129 N.J. 422, 444, 609 A.2d 1266, 1277 (1992) (requiring as a defense to rape that actors obtain verbal or non-verbal consent to sexual intercourse).
60. Compare In re M.T.S.,129 N.J. 422, 444, 609 A.2d 1266, 1277 (expressive consent to sexual intercourse for purposes of sexual assault must be 'affirmative' as opposed to passive), with Regina v. R.J.S. [1994] 123 Newfoundland & P.E.I.R. 317 (a person may consent to sexual intercourse for purposes of rape by remaining wholly passive and silent under circumstances in which passivity and silence connotes acquiescence), *apparently overruled by* Queen v. Ewanchuk, [1999] 1 S.C.R. 330, 356 (' a belief that silence, passivity or ambiguous conduct constitutes consent is a mistake of law, and provides no defence'). Compare also Schulhofer, *Unwanted Sex*, p. 271 (an actor should be required to obtain 'positive . . . affirmative permission' as a defense to sex; 'silence . . . is evidence that affirmative consent [is] absent'), with Dressler, 'Where We Have Been', p. 429 ('[P]roof of affirmative permission should not be required in order for the male to avoid conviction. The burden should be on the Government to prove her lack of consent despite her silence, rather than to require the defendant, as a practical matter, to prove that she gave permission'). But *see* Wertheimer, 'Consent and Sexual Relations', p. 100 (the difference between requiring 'affirmative' expressive consent and allowing passive expressive consent 'is of little practical import').
61. Brett, 'Commentary', p. 256.
62. *See* notes 25, 52.
63. Interestingly, having used consent in a factual sense, Brett wrote a later article in which he uses consent in a factual sense. *See* Brett, 'Sexual Offenses and Consent', p. 69 ('Giving consent involves autonomously making changes in a prevailing pattern of rights and obligations').
64. Brett, Commentary, pp. 255, 256, 257.
65. Speech-act theories differ as to whether 'speech acts' are confined to verbal locutions or whether they extend to certain nonverbal equivalents of verbal locutions, *e.g.*, nodding and shaking one's head. *See* note 32.
66. Malm, 'Ontological Status of Consent', pp. 162-63. *See* also Sherwin, 'Infelicitous Consent', pp. 217, 220-21 (referring to consent as both a 'performative' and a 'speech act' and, yet,

intending it to apply to any conduct by which *S* invokes existing social conventions to expresses permission).

67. Nathan Brett is quite explicit, for example, in distinguishing 'actions that communicate permission' that are *also* 'speech acts' from actions that communicate permission 'which are *not* speech acts (for example, in the sexual context touching, undoing clothing, moving to a bedroom)'. Brett, 'Commentary', p. 256 (emphasis added).
68. *See* note 25. For a commentator who uses 'performative' ambiguously to refer sometimes to declaratives alone and sometimes to illocutionary acts generally, *see* Brett, 'Sexual Offenses and Consent', pp. 74 (declaratives alone), 75 (assertives).
69. Strawson, 'Intention and Convention in Speech Acts'.
70. Austin, *How To Do Things With Words*, pp. 116-17. Although Austin also discusses the 'intent' that accompanies performatives as if it were a prerequisite, *id.* at 9, he makes it clear that intent is not indispensable, by taking the position that a speaker can perform an illocutionary act 'unintentionally'. *Id.* at 106-07.
71. Searle, *Speech Acts*, pp. 25, 42-45, 60-62.
72. *See* Archard, *Sexual Consent*, pp. 4-5 (arguing that, because consent is a 'performative', it must be intentional on the performer's part).
73. See Austin, How To Do Things With Words, pp. 98-99, 147.
74. Searle, Expression and Meaning, pp. 4-5.
75. *See, e.g.*, Archard, *Sexual Consent*, p. 6 ('It does seem to be true that if I know what I am doing when I say "I consent", then I put myself under an obligation to honour the commitments that are normally made by a sincere utterance of these words'); Soble, 'Antioch's Sexual Offense Policy', p. 31:

    Antioch also cuts back on the power of consent by making it not binding; one can withdraw consent at any time during any act or sub-act.... This is a difference between Antioch's policy and Belliotti's libertarianism, according to which breaking a sexual promise is at least a *prima facie* moral fault.... My guess is that Belliotti is right, that withdrawing consent to an act to which one has consented is *prima facie* wrong'.

76. The so-called marital exemption in the law of rape is no exception. The marital exception was not based upon the fiction that, by virtue of marrying, a woman made her husband a promise of sexual intercourse that he could go to court to enforce. Rather, it was based upon the fiction that, by virtue of marrying, a woman thereafter consented to each and every separate act of sexual intercourse with her husband at the time it occurred.
77. *See* Feinberg, *Harm To Self*, pp. 178-79. *See* also note 27.
78. But *see* Sherwin, 'Infelicitous Sex', p. 217.
79. See Searle, Expression and Meaning, p. 19.
80. *See* Soble, 'Antioch's Sexual Offense Policy', p. 25 ('yes' does not always mean 'yes'). Cf. Balos and Fellows, 'A Matter of Prostitution', p. 1224 (noting that laws criminalizing prostitution demonstrate 'that "yes" does not mean "yes"'). But *see* Brett, 'Sexual Offenses and Consent', p. 76 (arguing that it is meaningless to say to someone who says, 'I consent', 'That's not true').
81. See Austin, How To Do Things With Words, p. 7.
82. Searle, Expression and Meaning, p. 22.
83. Searle, Expression and Meaning, p. 14.
84. *See* note 27.
85. See text accompanying notes 79.
86. Cf. Feinberg, *Harm To Others*, p. 178 ('Strong consent ("please do") trivially implies weak consent ("you may"), although the opposite is not true. I may reluctantly agree to your

proposal, thus giving you permission, without making any request that you do it, indeed while even preferring that you would not do what you propose'); Malm, 'The Ontological Status of Consent', pp. 147-49.

PART II
LEGAL CONSENT

Introduction

We have seen that the term 'consent' is commonly used in law in a manner that I call 'factual'. That is, it is used in a non-normative sense in law to refer to instances in which a subject *S* subjectively acquiesces in her mind to an actor *A*'s conduct in doing *x* to her or objectively expresses such acquiescence—without necessarily connoting that *S*'s subjective or objective acquiescence constitutes a criminal defense to *A*'s doing *x* to *S*. Thus, criminal courts use consent in a factual sense when they state that a woman's consent to sexual intercourse is a defense to rape *if* her consent is shown to be 'free', 'informed', 'competent', 'voluntary'—and that her consent is *not* a defense if her consent is shown to be 'coerced', 'forced', 'fraudulent', 'incompetent', or 'involuntary'.[1] These references to consent are factual in nature because they are references to instances of attitudinal or expressive acquiescence to sexual intercourse that are not in themselves defenses to rape but, rather, depend for their legal import upon the accompanying circumstances under which they occur.

We have seen, too, though not in as much detail, that consent can also be used quite differently in law than in ordinary language. It can be used 'legally' to refer to instances of attitudinal or expressive acquiescence by *S* to *A*'s conduct x (or to actions by *S* from which legal fictions of such attitudinal or expressive acquiescence are constructed) that *constitute* complete or partial criminal defenses to *A* for doing *x*. Thus, the State of Colorado uses consent in a legal sense when, having stated that 'Unlawful Sexual Contact' is the offense of having sexual contact with a person without that person's 'consent', it defines what such consent must be to negate the offense: '"Consent",' it states, 'means cooperation in act or attitude pursuant to an exercise of free will and with knowledge of the nature of the act. ... Submission under the influence of fear shall not constitute consent.'[2] Similarly, Donald Hubin and Karen Haely use consent in a legal sense when they say: '[T]he relevant defining element of rape is lack of consent. ... Consent involves both knowledge and freedom. The phrase, "informed, voluntary consent," is a useful reminder of this, but it is, strictly speaking, redundant.'[3]

Legal consent, in turn, comes in two distinctive forms that will be explored in greater detail in the chapters of Part II: 'prescriptive consent' and 'imputed consent'. The difference between these two forms of legal consent is that prescriptive consent to *x* presupposes attitudinal or expressive acquiescence to *x*, while imputed consent to *x* does not. 'Prescriptive consent' to *x* consists of the very same elements of attitudinal or expressive acquiescence to *x* that constitute *S*'s factual consent to *x plus* such conditions as are deemed to be sufficient for *S*'s acquiescence to constitute a complete or partial defense to *A*'s doing *x*. 'Imputed consent' to *x*, in turn, consists of *legal fictions* of prescriptive consent to *x* of three kinds—'constructive consent', 'informed consent', and 'hypothetical consent':

'Constructive' consent to *x* is a legal fiction to the effect that, by virtue of *S*'s prescriptively acquiescing to certain conduct *other than x*, *S* also prescriptively consents to *x* itself.

'Informed' consent is a fiction that, by virtue of *S*'s being informed of a *risk* of *x*, and by virtue of *S*'s consciously proceeding despite the risk of *x*, *S* also prescriptively consents to *x* in the event that *x* occurs.

'Hypothetical' consent is a fiction that, because *S* *would* prescriptively acquiesce to *x* *if* she were competent to make the choice, she, therefore, *does* prescriptively consent to *x*.

This is not to say that legal consent exists in both prescriptive and imputed forms with respect to every species of conduct to which consent is a defense. On the contrary, there are some forms of conduct *x*, *e.g.*, *A*'s subjecting *S* to in vitro fertilization, to which *S*'s consent is a defense only if *S*'s consent is prescriptive in nature—that is, only if *S* actually acquiesces to *x* in mind or expression. Similarly, there are others forms of conduct x, *e.g.*, *A*'s rendering *S* a paraplegic, to which *S*'s consent is typically a defense only if consent is imputed to *S*, as when *A* inadvertently paralyzes *S* in the course of a lawful football game, boxing match, or surgical operation. Finally, there are still other forms of conduct *x*, *e.g.*, *A*'s administering an emergency blood transfusion to *S*, to which *S*'s consent can be a defense whether it is prescriptive in nature or imputed to *S*. Historically, a woman's consent to sexual contact could be a defense if it was either prescriptive in nature or imputed to her as a consequence of her having previously married the actor. We will explore the extent to which the law continues to impute consent to sexual contact not only to persons who are married to each other, but also to persons who are not.

The purpose of Part II is not to take positions on the justice or injustice of the particular definitions of legal consent. Jurisdictions differ, and will continue to differ, in their judgments of right and wrong, including their judgments as to what ought and ought not to constitute consent to particular kinds of conduct. The purpose, rather, is to analyze the conceptual elements that contested judgments of legal consent possess in common. By 'conceptual elements', I mean the forms of thought and language through which people formulate and express contested judgments of right and wrong, regardless of what those judgments may be. Jurisdictions differ, for example, in their judgments as to when young women become legally competent to consent to sexual intercourse with older men, though every jurisdiction regards very young girls as legally incompetent to consent to sexual intercourse. Whether fifteen or sixteen or even eighteen is the correct age is a contestable question that jurisdictions can resolve through practical reason and persuasion. In contrast, how rules regarding 'incompetence' differ from rules regarding 'force' and 'fraud', and how incompetence, force, and fraud bear on legal consent, are conceptual questions that lend themselves to analysis.

Chapter 3 draws principally upon the law of rape to illustrate features that are common to prescriptive consent and imputed consent. Chapter 4 examines whether the normative force of prescriptive consent derives from prescriptive consent being a subjective attitude, or an objective expression, or either of them, or both of them. Chapter 5, on prescriptive attitudinal consent, discusses what *more* is required, beyond factual attitudinal acquiescence, to transform such acquiescence into a defense. Chapter 6, on non-contemporaneous prescriptive consent, discusses instances in which a person who does not prescriptively consent to *x* at the time *x* occurs may nevertheless prescriptively consent to it by acquiescing to it either prospectively or retrospectively. Chapter 7, on imputed consent, discusses what *else* suffices, apart from factual acquiescence to *x*, to support fictions of prescriptive consent to *x*.

Notes

1. *See* Introduction to Part I, notes 14-15.
2. Colorado Revised Statutes §§ 18-3-401, 18-3-404 (2000).
3. Hubin and Haely, 'Rape and the Reasonable Man', pp. 115-16.

[illegible] Chapter [illegible]

Notes

1 [illegible]

Chapter Three

Offenses to Which Consent is a Defense

Legal consent by a subject *S* to conduct by an actor *A* is acquiescence by *S*, whether actual or imputed, that changes *S*'s criminal relationship to *A* from that of a victim to a non-victim and, hence, satisfies whatever the criminal law requires to bring about such changes. Legal consent in the context of rape, in turn, transforms *S*'s act of sexual intercourse with *A* from an act of criminal sexual assault into a non-criminal act. To clarify these requirements of criminal law, we shall discuss, (A) why acquiescence by *S*, whether actual or imputed, is a defense to the crime of rape against *S* and, yet, is not a defense to other criminal offenses against *S*; (B) why, among the many offenses to which acquiescence by *S* is *not* a defense, some can be defined without reference to consent, while others cannot; (C) why the requisites of legal consent are contestable in ways that the requirements of factual consent are not; and (D) how the requisites of legal consent render it variable in ways that factual consent is not.

Offenses to Which Acquiescence is Not a Defense: Offenses of Third-Party Harm

When people say that consent is a 'defense' to rape, they do not mean that consent is an issue on which defendants bear the burden of proof; for the prosecution invariably bears the risk of nonpersuasion regarding legal consent in rape cases.[1] Nor do people mean that every instance of attitudinal or expressive acquiescence to sexual intercourse has the legal effect of exonerating actors of rape. Rather, when people say that consent is a defense to rape, they mean that certain kinds of attitudinal or expressive acquiescence—or in their absence, perhaps, certain other mental states or forms of conduct by persons from which legal fictions of actual acquiescence can be imputed to them—can operate to negate the offense of rape. They mean that by virtue of actually or imputedly acquiescing to sexual intercourse in certain ways, certain persons can authorize others to engage in acts of sexual intercourse that would otherwise constitute rape. Conversely, to say that consent by certain persons is *not* a defense to rape means that no instance of attitudinal or expressive acquiescence to sexual intercourse on their part can have the legal effect of exonerating others of criminal responsibility for subjecting them to sexual intercourse, and no legal fiction of such acquiescence may be imputed to them. It means that those persons have no legal authority to privilege others to subject them to sexual intercourse with impunity.

Rape is not the only offense to which consent is a defense in that sense. Most offenses are offenses of non-consent. Thus, larceny is not the taking of another's property as such, but the forcible taking of another's property *without his consent.* Kidnapping is not the forcible removal or confinement of a person as such, but the forcible removal or confinement of a person *without his consent.* So, too, with offenses of trespass, theft, and assault. Legal consent by *S* vis-à-vis *A* transmutes what would otherwise be 'larceny' by *A* into charity; 'kidnapping' into companionship; 'trespass' into hospitality; 'assault' into sport; 'maiming' into surgery; and 'rape' into intimacy. As Rollin Perkins gracefully puts it,

> What is called a 'fond embrace' when gladly accepted by a sweetheart is called 'assault and battery' when forced upon another without her consent; and the act of one who grabs another by the ankles and causes him to fall violently to the ground may result in a substantial jail sentence under some circumstances, but receive thunderous applause if it stops a ball carrier on the gridiron'.[2]

Acquiescence (whether actual or imputed) is not, however, a defense to all offenses. It is not a defense to blackmail or bribery, for example. Nor is it ordinarily a defense to homicide. With the exception of persons on life support who acquiesce to its removal, and with the exception of singular jurisdictions like the Netherlands in which voluntary euthanasia is not an offense, a person cannot exonerate or mitigate a killer's criminal responsibility by acquiescing to his own homicide, regardless of how much he may wish to.[3] Thus, in contrast to a person's power to authorize sexual intercourse, a person is not ordinarily able, by virtue of her desire for it, to permit others to kill her with impunity.

The question is, why? Why is it that acquiescence by *S*, whether actual or imputed, can be a defense to some offenses by *A*, and not to others? We shall see in this and the following sections, respectively, that there are two independent conditions that preclude acquiescence by *S* from being a defense to conduct by *A*: (1) where *A*'s conduct threatens to inflict criminal harm or offense upon persons *other* than *S*, including, perhaps, upon *A* himself; or (2) where *A*'s conduct threatens to inflict criminal harm or offense upon *S herself*. The distinction between grounds 1 and 2 is significant because although each ground suffices to prevent *S*'s acquiescence from constituting a defense, the distinction controls the way in which criminal offences can be formulated. Specifically, offenses that are predicated upon ground 1 *cannot* be formulated as offenses of 'non-consent', while offenses that are predicated upon ground 2 *can* be formulated as offenses of non-consent'.

To address ground 1, consider the difference between rape and adultery. Rape and adultery are both crimes involving sexual intercourse. The difference is that while acquiescence by both participants to sexual intercourse can be a defense to rape for each of them, it is not a defense to adultery. A married person *A* who has sexual intercourse with a person *S* to whom he is not married with *S*'s actual acquiescence, or even with *A*'s own spouse's acquiescence, may or may not be guilty of rape depending upon the conditions under which *S* acquiesces. But in jurisdictions in which adultery is a crime, a married person *A* who has sexual intercourse with a person *S* to whom he is not married with *S*'s actual acquiescence is guilty of adultery, because *S* has no legal authority to exonerate *A* of 'adultery' by acquiescing in the sexual intercourse:

> 'Rape' is the crime of having sexual intercourse with a person without the latter's legal consent.[4] 'Adultery' is the crime of having sexual intercourse with a person while being the spouse of another.[5]

The reason that rape is defined in terms of *S*'s non-consent, while adultery is not, is that the two offenses differ with respect to whom the acts of sexual intercourse are regarded as wrongfully harming and offending. Ordinarily, sexual intimacy is regarded in law as conduct that does not criminally harm or offend anyone, except, perhaps, the sexual participants themselves—and then only when (i) the participants fail actually to choose the conduct for themselves under conditions that the law regards as appropriate to leaving the choice to them, and (ii) the law further fails to impute such choices to them. Accordingly, when two people, *A* and *S*, choose sexual intercourse for themselves by actually acquiescing to it, and when they do so under conditions that the law deems to be normatively sufficient to protect their interests, their acquiescence ordinarily negates all harms of which the criminal law takes cognizance. In contrast, when a married person *A* has sexual intercourse with a person *S* to whom he is not married, the act of intercourse is regarded in law as wrongfully harming the absent spouse, the general institution of marriage, and perhaps even *A* himself.[6] Obviously, in so far as the intercourse by *A* and *S* is regarded in law as wrongfully harming the absent spouse or the institution of marriage, it inflicts wrongful harms that *A* and *S* themselves cannot negate by virtue of choosing it for themselves. By the same token, in so far as the intercourse is regarded in law as inflicting wrongful harm upon *A* despite his desire for it, it inflicts a wrongful harm that *S* herself cannot negate by choosing it for herself.

Whether *S*'s acquiescence is a defense to criminal conduct, therefore, depends in part upon whether the law regards the conduct as wrongfully harmful or offensive either to persons other than *S* herself or to society at large. Determinations of wrongful 'harm' and 'offense' to persons other than *S*, in turn, are more than empirical judgments that conduct imposes burdens on them. They are legal judgments that, all things considered, the burdens that the conduct imposes on others are unjustified. Acquiescence by *S* is not a defense to conduct when in the judgment of the law, the burdens that the conduct imposes upon others are unjustified by the benefits, if any, of leaving the choice to *S* herself. Conversely, acquiescence by *S* can be a defense to conduct when, in the judgment of the law, the benefits of leaving the choice to *S* justify the burdens, if any, that the chosen conduct imposes upon others.

Massachusetts v. Stowell (1983)[7] illustrates the mutually exclusive relationship that exists between the value of participant autonomy that underlies the consent defense, on the one hand, and the recognition of third-party harm that defeats the consent defense, on the other. Judith Stowell, a married woman, was arrested in Worcester, Massachusetts, in the course of having sexual intercourse in the back of a van with a man other than her husband. They were both charged with adultery and convicted. Stowell appealed on federal constitutional grounds, arguing that punishing her for engaging in sexual intercourse that she and her adult partner each chose for themselves infringed upon her federally protected interest in sexual autonomy. The court rejected her federal claim, holding that neither hers nor her lover's consent to sexual intercourse was a federal defense to the state crime of adultery. At the same time, the court reserved for future litigation the question whether the Massachusetts state constitution accorded persons in Stowell's position greater sexual autonomy than the federal Constitution.

The *Stowell* court's opinion is instructive, for the court did not hold that Stowell and her lover had no federal constitutional interest *at all* in sexual autonomy. Nor, on the other hand, did the court hold that the burdens that adultery imposes on absent spouses and the institution of marriage are too great to justify a constitutional defense of *any kind* to adultery. Rather, the court held that the federal constitutional interest in sexual autonomy was too weak under the circumstances, and the burdens on third parties too strong, to create a *federal* defense of consent to the state crime of adultery. At the same time, however, the court reserved the question whether the people of Massachusetts in their *state* constitution had recognized a sufficiently greater interest in sexual autonomy to tip the balance the other way and thereby establish a state constitutional defense of consent to the crime of adultery. *Stowell* thus illuminates what legal consent in criminal law *is*. Legal consent by *S* exists in criminal law only with respect to conduct by *A* that, at most, is wrongfully harmful or offensive to no one except to *S* herself, and that is wrongfully harmful or offensive to *S* only if she fails to choose the conduct for herself under the conditions that the law deems sufficient to satisfy her interests in the matter.

Offenses to Which Acquiescence is Not a Defense: Offenses of Participant Harm

We just concluded examining one class of offenses to which *S*'s acquiescence is no defense, namely, offenses that consist of conduct by *A* that wrongfully harms or offends persons or groups *other* than *S*. We now turn to another class of offenses to which *S*'s acquiescence is no defense, namely, offenses in which *S* is so situated that *A*'s conduct wrongfully harms or offends *S herself*, regardless of her acquiescence to it. Nevertheless, despite the fact that both classes consist of offenses for which *S*'s acquiescence leaves victims wrongfully harmed or offended, the two classes differ significantly. The difference lies in *why S*'s acquiescence leaves victims wrongfully harmed or offended. The reason that *S*'s acquiescence is no defense to offenses against others or society at large is that even though *S*'s acquiescence may occur under conditions sufficient to prevent *A*'s conduct from wrongfully harming *S*, it does nothing to prevent *A*'s conduct from wrongfully harming or offending others. In contrast, the reason that *S*'s acquiescence is no defense to offenses against *S* herself is that *S* is so situated that *S*'s acquiescence fails to occur under conditions sufficient to prevent *A*'s conduct from wrongfully harming or offending her.

To illustrate, compare the offense of adultery and the offense of having sexual relations with underage minors. Like adultery, the latter makes it an offense to have sexual relations with certain persons, regardless of their desire for it.[8] In both cases, the reason the participants' acquiescence to sexual intercourse is no defense is that it fails to negate the criminal harm or offense that the sexual intercourse is regarded as causing. The difference lies in whom the sexual intercourse is deemed to wrongfully harm or offend and why. Adultery is deemed wrongfully to harm or offend absent spouses and members of society as a whole who, not being party to it, do not acquiesce to it. In contrast, sexual intercourse with an underage minor is deemed to wrongfully harm the participating minor herself because, although the minor may acquiesce to sexual intercourse, she does so under conditions of immaturity that are deemed insufficient to prevent her from suffering harms from which the state seeks to protect her.[9]

The Latin maxim *Volenti non fit injuria* ('To a person who consents, no harm is done') captures the conditions under which a person's acquiescence does or does not leave her wrongfully harmed. The maxim, which dates back to Roman civil law, and perhaps to Aristotle, is now applied in civil and criminal cases alike.[10] As a maxim of criminal law,[11] the *volenti* maxim derives its truth from the meaning of its terms. To say that a subject *S* who consents to conduct suffers 'no harm' (*non . . . injuria*) does not mean that by virtue of consenting, *S* suffers no burdens or setbacks *of any kind* from the conduct. If the maxim meant that, it would be patently false; for it is patently false to say that a person who consents to conduct, *e.g.*, a medical patient who consents to surgical amputation of an eye or limb or a breast, suffers no burdens or setbacks to her interests of any kind from it. Rather, to say that *S* suffers 'no harm' (*non . . . injuria*) means that she suffers no burdens or setbacks of a *particular kind*—namely, no *criminally wrongful* burdens or setbacks.[12] Similarly, to say that the criminality of *A*'s conduct is negated by *S*'s 'consent' (*volenti*) does not mean that its criminality is negated by virtue of *S*'s consciously choosing to submit to it, regardless of the conditions of coercion or deception or incompetence under which *S* does so. If the maxim meant that, it would be patently false; for it is patently false to say that a person can suffer no criminal harm from conduct to which she is forced or deceived into consciously submitting, just as it is patently false to say that persons who are incompetent to assess their own interests in sexual intercourse (*e.g.*, underage girls) suffer no criminal harm from engaging in it.[13] Rather, to say that the criminality of *A*'s conduct is negated by *S*'s 'consent' (*volenti*) means that the criminality of the burdens or setbacks that *A* imposes upon *S* is negated by virtue of *S*'s consciously choosing the burdens or setback for herself under such conditions as the law deems sufficient to satisfy her interests in the matter (or, alternatively, by virtue of *S*'s engaging in conduct or possessing a state of mind from which the law deems it appropriate to impute to her a fiction of her having so chosen them). In short, for purposes of the criminal law, the *volenti* maxim, as spelled out, is a truism: 'To a person who [*lawfully*] consents, no [*criminal*] harm is done.' It follows, therefore, that the important work the maxim performs is done in advance of invoking it. The important work consists of making legal determinations as to (i) which burdens upon *S* cease to be of criminal concern when *S* chooses them for herself under appropriate conditions, and (ii) which conditions of choice on *S*'s part, if acted upon, suffice to satisfy her interests in the matter. The two determinations are mutually dependent. For a jurisdiction cannot decide which burdens upon *S* are negated by *S*'s choosing them without making reference to the conditions under which *S*'s choices are made. And it cannot decide which conditions of choice on *S*'s part suffice to negate a burden upon her without making reference to the nature of the burden.

To summarize what we have said thus far, there are two grounds upon which *S*'s actual acquiescence to conduct by *A* is no defense to *A*: (1) where *A*'s conduct threatens to inflict criminal harm on persons or groups other than *S*; and (2) where *A*'s conduct threatens to inflict criminal harm upon *S* herself. This difference between offenses of third-party harm and participant harm helps illuminate a certain paradox about consent. The paradox is that although both classes of offenses *can* both be defined without reference to consent, offenses of third-party harm *must* be defined without reference to consent.

To illustrate the paradox, consider the offenses of adultery and sexual intercourse with underage minors, both of which can both be defined *without* reference to consent, but only one of which can be defined *by* reference to consent. Thus, adultery and sexual intercourse with an underage minor can both be framed without reference to consent:

> ***Adultery.*** It is a criminal offense to have sexual intercourse with a person while being the spouse of another.
>
> ***Corruption of Minors.*** It is an offense to have sexual intercourse with a child who is under the age of sixteen.

These two offenses are not the only ones that can be framed without reference to consent. Every offense to which a participant's acquiescence is no defense, including many subsets of rape, *e.g.*, sexual intercourse with insane or retarded persons and sexual intercourse by means of certain kinds of fraud, can be formulated in the same economical way, making no reference to consent.

Significantly, however, while sexual intercourse with an underage minor can thus be framed without reference to consent (as in Corruption of Minors above), it can *also* be framed in terms of the broader offense of nonconsensual sexual intercourse, namely, as 'statutory rape'. Consider, for example, the way Montana frames the offense of having sexual intercourse with an underage minor. Montana defines it within a broader offense of nonconsensual conduct:

> ***Rape.*** It is an offense to have sexual intercourse with a person without the latter's consent.
>
> ***Statutory Rape.*** A child who is under the age of sixteen is incapable of consent for purposes of this section.[14]

The difference between Corruption of Minors and Statutory Rape is not in *what* they punish, for they both punish the same range of conduct, namely, sexual intercourse with a child under the age of sixteen. The difference is the form in which they frame that range of conduct. Corruption of Minors eliminates all references to consent—including both the statement (which is implicit in Statutory Rape) that consent is a defense to rape, and the statement (which is explicit in Statutory Rape) that minors are legally incapable of consenting to sexual intercourse—and simply makes it an offense for a person to have sexual intercourse with a minor. In contrast, Statutory Rape frames the prohibited harm more circuitously: Statutory Rape first classifies sexual intercourse with minors as a subset of a broader offense of sexual intercourse to which consent *is* a defense, *i.e.*, 'rape', and then eliminates the defense of consent by stating that children under the age of sixteen are 'incapable of consent[ing]' to sexual intercourse. Nevertheless, by virtue of its detour through consent, Statutory Rape serves a purpose that Corruption of Minors does not: Statutory Rape conveys that the criminal harm of statutory rape is part and parcel of a larger class of criminal harm that all rapes possess in common. The wrongful harm that all rapes share in common is the wrongful harm that *A* causes *S* by having sexual intercourse with *S* without her legal consent, that is, without *S*'s having chosen sexual intercourse for herself under conditions that the law deems sufficient to justify leaving the choice to her. If *S* chooses sexual intercourse for herself under such conditions, the law does not regard anyone as having been criminally harmed, including *S* herself. If, however, *S* does not choose sexual intercourse for herself under such conditions, the law regards *S* herself as wrongfully harmed. Similarly, the wrongful harm that is inflicted by having sexual intercourse with a minor—and the one that statutes like Montana's capture by formulating the offense in terms of 'rape'—is the wrongful harm that sexual intercourse itself is deemed to inflict upon a minor when he or she acquiesces to sexual intercourse at an age that the law deems inadequate to justify leaving decisions regarding sexual intercourse to minors.

Now consider the offense of adultery. Like the offense of having sexual intercourse with an underage minor, adultery is also an offense of sexual intercourse to which the parties' acquiescence is not a defense. Paradoxically, however, and in contrast to sexual intercourse with an underage minor, adultery *cannot* plausibly be defined as an offense of non-consent. To see why, suppose for a moment that it were defined in that way. That is, suppose that adultery were denominated 'adulterous rape' and treated as a subset of the crime of sexual intercourse 'without consent':

> ***Rape.*** It is a crime to have sexual intercourse with a person without the latter's consent.
>
> ***Adulterous Rape.*** A person who has sexual intercourse with the spouse of another is incapable of consent for purposes of this section.

The problem with 'Adulterous Rape' is not in what it punishes, for it punishes precisely the same conduct as the crime of Adultery. The problem is that its classification, 'Adulterous Rape', is a misnomer. To classify an offense to which acquiescence is *not* a defense within a larger class of conduct to which consent *is* a defense is to imply that the participants are *victims* whom society wishes to protect. The offense of having sexual intercourse with a child under the age of sixteen can, indeed, be subsumed within the larger offense of sexual intercourse without consent, because the wrongful harm that sexual intercourse with a child under sixteen inflicts is wrongful harm from which society wishes to protect participating children themselves, regardless of their acquiescence to it. The offense of adultery, however, cannot plausibly be subsumed within a larger crime of sexual intercourse without consent, because the wrongful harm that a married person inflicts by having sexual intercourse with a person to whom he is not married is a harm that he inflicts upon innocent spouses, society at large, and perhaps even himself, not a harm that he inflicts upon a participating sexual partner.

To be sure, some crimes are regarded as wrongfully harming both participants and third parties alike. Statutory rape, for example, is deemed by some jurisdictions to constitute both a wrongful harm to the underage participant and a wrongful offense to the public's moral sensibilities.[15] Crimes that are deemed to wrongfully harm participants and third parties alike can be framed either with or without reference to consent. The crime of sexual intercourse with minors, for example, is commonly framed in alternative ways—sometimes in terms of rape, sometimes as an independent crime of sexual abuse of minors.[16] One cannot infer, therefore, from an offense's being framed without reference to consent that the prohibited conduct is deemed wrongfully to harm either third parties alone or participants alone (or both together).[17] Nonetheless, one can infer something from an offense's being framed in terms of consent, namely, that the harm from which the society wishes to protect people is a wrongful harm that in the society's eyes falls at least in part upon the participants themselves.

Now it might be thought that the foregoing account overlooks an alternative explanation as to why certain offenses to which acquiescence is not a defense can be framed as offenses of non-consent, while others cannot. Specifically it might be thought that the real difference between adultery and sexual intercourse with an underage minor is not in the class of persons whom the offenses seek to *protect*, but in the class of persons whom the offenses seek to *punish*. The reason that sexual intercourse with an underage minor can be framed as an offense of non-consent and adultery cannot, so the argument goes, is that society regards underage persons as not only sexually vulnerable, foolish, and immature, but also immune from punishment. Indeed, a number of courts and commentators contend that a jurisdiction's decision to treat certain persons as too vulnerable or immature or foolish to be capable of legally consenting to conduct is also an implicit decision to exempt them from punishment.[18] They contend that it is legally 'inconsistent'[19] for a jurisdiction to punish a person for engaging in conduct with respect to which the jurisdiction deems him too vulnerable or immature or foolish to assess his own interests. There is nothing, however, that is inconsistent in a jurisdiction's blaming a person for conduct with respect to which it deems him to be incapable of assessing his own interests. Jurisdictions do so all the time, as when they punish teenagers for drinking or when they punish bare-fisted pugilists for the serious injuries they inflict and suffer in engaging in mutual combat.[20] And jurisdictions do so because standards of legal competence to consent differ from standards of criminal responsibility. The measure of a person's legal competence to consent is his capacity to know and act upon what is in his interests, while the measure of a person's criminal responsibility is his capacity to know and obey society's prohibitions. Accordingly, a person may lack the former capacity and yet fully possess the latter capacity, provided that he understands and is able to obey the prohibition.[21]

Assume, for example, that two fifteen-year-olds, being infatuated with each other, secretly engage in mutually enthusiastic sexual intercourse within a jurisdiction that regards teenagers under the age of sixteen to be too immature to be capable of legally consenting to sexual intercourse. Assume further that although the jurisdiction has taken the view that the fifteen-year-olds are too young to adjudge whether sexual intercourse is in their interests, it also believes that fifteen-year-olds are old enough to understand and obey its rule that they not engage in sexual intercourse until they are sixteen. If so, the jurisdiction may without contradiction regard the teenagers as simultaneously both victims of offenses of non-consent and perpetrators of offenses of non-consent (as well as accomplices in offenses of non-consent upon themselves).[22] Of course, the jurisdiction also may choose as a matter of prosecutorial policy to exempt the teenagers from prosecution.[23] But there is nothing in the standards that govern legal consent and non-consent that precludes the jurisdiction, if it so wishes, from prosecuting one, or the other, or both of the teenagers, provided that the jurisdiction deems them capable of understanding and obeying its prohibition.[24]

The Contestability of Legal Consent

Courts occasionally refer to instances of legal consent as 'true consent' or 'actual consent'.[25] Thus, the Indiana Court of Appeals used 'true consent' in that way in reviewing Billie Joe Stafford's 1983 conviction for raping a moderately retarded twenty-five year-old woman called 'A.B'. The prosecution proved that A.B., who lived with her mother and had the I.Q. of a six- or seven-year-old child, would complaisantly submit to the sexual requests of any man who tried to seduce her. The jury convicted Stafford under a statute prohibiting sexual intercourse with a person who is 'so mentally disabled or deficient that consent to sexual intercourse cannot be given'. Stafford argued on appeal that the evidence showed that A.B. consented to the sexual intercourse. In rejecting his appeal, the court of appeals distinguished A.B's. factual acquiescence from what it called the 'true consent' required by the statute, holding that 'though A.B. could verbally consent to sexual intercourse, her general judgment level would interfere with a true consent'.[26]

Ironically, courts also use 'true consent' and 'actual consent' in the opposite way—to refer not to instances of legal consent, but to instances of factual consent.[27] A New York court used 'true consent' in that way in 1990 in reviewing a charge against Oran Gonzales for statutory rape. Gonzales, an older man, was charged with having sexual intercourse with boys under the age of seventeen. Gonzales challenged the charge, arguing that the boys consented to the intercourse. The court rejected his challenge, holding that although the boys may have factually acquiesced, they were not old enough legally to consent. However, the court did not frame its holding in the language of 'factual' and 'legal' consent. Rather, referring to the boys' attitudinal and expressive acquiescence as 'true consent', the court declared the boys' true consent to be irrelevant, holding that 'the lack of true consent of those under seventeen is not an element of the substantive offense [of statutory rape]'.[28]

In reality, of course, factual consent and legal consent are each *true* and *actual* forms of consent. Yet they are true and actual forms of consent that also differ from each other. They differ in that legal consent is contestable in ways that factual consent is not. Factual consent to sexual intercourse is largely empirical in nature, the empirical question being whether S, whether in mind or expression, actually chose sexual intercourse under the circumstances under which she believed herself to be—whether by virtue of unconditionally welcoming sexual intercourse, conditionally preferring it to the alternatives she believed she otherwise faced, or by being so indifferent toward sexual intercourse as to be willing to delegate its occurrence to her partner.[a] Observers may of course disagree as to whether such empirical events have occurred on particular occasions, because they may disagree as to what particular persons subjectively desired or objectively communicated. Moreover, because observers realize that the empirical conclusions they reach regarding their own or others' factual consent can affect their own or others' legal relationships, they may allow their personal views of those legal relationships to influence their empirical conclusions. Nonetheless, factual consent is not *defined* by reference to such legal relationships in the way that legal consent is. Legal consent consists of a legal judgment that by virtue of the conditions under which *S* actually or imputedly acquiesced to *x*, S was not wrongfully harmed by *x*. Being a normative judgment, legal consent is contestable in ways that factual consent is not.

Consider, for example, the disagreement between Minnesota and New Mexico as to whether patients who become infatuated with their psychotherapists are capable of legally consenting to sexual intercourse with them. A Minnesota woman whose initials were 'J.A.J.' went to Robert Dutton in 1985 for marital and sexual counseling. In the intimacy of the patient-therapist relationship, J.A.J. became infatuated with Dutton, leaving him a note that stated: 'I have given Robert E. Dutton control of my life—my future—out of my abiding love for him'. The two of them had sexual intercourse several times in a motel and in Dutton's office. Eventually, J.A.J. became disenchanted with Dutton and filed criminal charges against him. Dutton was convicted of having sexual intercourse with J.A.J. without her consent under a Minnesota statute that provided that psychotherapy patients who are emotionally dependent upon their therapists are incapable of consenting to sexual intercourse with them.[29] A similar case arose a year later in New Mexico, involving psychologist Waldemar Leiding and three adult patients. The jury convicted Leiding of having sexual intercourse with his patients without their consent, based on jury instructions to the effect that patients who become emotionally dependent upon their therapists through the dynamics of psychoanalysis are incapable of consenting to sexual intercourse. Leiding appealed, arguing that although his patients were, indeed, emotionally dependent upon him, they nonetheless consented for purposes of New Mexico law because New Mexico deems emotionally dependent patients to be legally capable of consenting to sexual intercourse with their therapists. Agreeing with Leiding, the New Mexico Court of Appeals reversed his convictions, holding that Leiding's patients were not victims of rape under New Mexico law.[30]

The disagreement between Minnesota and New Mexico is not a disagreement as to whether the patients in the two cases *factually* consented to sexual intercourse with their therapists. The patients in both cases factually consented to sexual intercourse because they either unconditionally desired to have sexual intercourse with their therapists or preferred sexual intercourse to the alternatives. Rather, the disagreement turns on the differing legal views of Minnesota and New Mexico regarding the

---

[a] For discussion of the extent to which normative elements enter into determinations of factual consent, see Chapter 1 at nn. 61-67, and Chapter 2, pp. 39-42.

conditions under which the patients empirically consented. Minnesota deemed J.A.J. to be criminally harmed by the sexual intercourse because in Minnesota's judgment, her emotional dependence upon Dutton materially impaired her ability to make appropriate choices for herself regarding sexual relations with Dutton. In contrast, New Mexico did *not* deem Leiding's patients to be criminally harmed because in New Mexico's judgment, the emotional dependence of psychotherapy patients upon their therapists does *not* materially impair their ability to make appropriate choices for themselves regarding sexual relations with their therapists.

Judgments of legal consent are contestable because they represent legal judgments that, by virtue of the conditions under which *S* actually or imputedly acquiesced to *A*'s conduct, *S* was not criminally harmed by the conduct. As such, they are the product of underlying considerations that are themselves matters of empirical and normative dispute, including: the extent to which *S* is vulnerable to exploitation; the harm that *A*'s conduct can cause *S*; the value in allowing people to make self-regarding decisions for themselves; the social consequences of criminalizing *A*'s conduct; the effectiveness of criminalization; alternative ways of regulating *A*'s conduct; and the seriousness of the criminal penalty at issue. Consider, for example, the recent debate in Texas as to whether psychotherapy patients should be deemed legally capable of acquiescing to sexual intercourse with their psychotherapists.[31] It was the law in Texas until 1995 that, like other adults who are emotionally dependent upon other persons, psychotherapy patients are capable of legally consenting to sexual intercourse with their therapists. However, a bill was introduced in 1995 to change the state's legal position. The 1995 bill provided that sexual intercourse between a therapist and a present or former patient who is emotionally dependent upon the therapist is 'without consent' for purposes of the crime of sexual assault and is punishable by up to twenty years in prison. The debate on the bill turned, in part, upon empirical considerations regarding (i) the extent to which patients are emotionally dependent upon their therapists; (ii) the frequency with which therapists sexually exploit that dependency; (iii) the degree to which sexual intercourse harms patients; and (iv) the effectiveness of alternative regulation in the form of tort remedies and licensing. The debate on the bill also turned, in part, on normative considerations regarding (i) the gravity of therapist-patient intercourse in comparison with other criminal harms of sexual assault; (ii) the value of leaving decisions regarding sexual intercourse to the patients themselves; and (iii) the social value of leaving the regulation of therapist-patient interactions to civil rather than criminal law. In the end, the legislature made a normative decision that the benefits of criminalizing the therapists' conduct with sentences of up to twenty years in prison outweighed the social costs.[32]

Judgments of imputed consent are similarly contestable. For many years, for example, it was not an offense in California for husbands to coerce their wives into sexual intercourse because wives, by virtue of marriage, were deemed to have constructively consented to sexual intercourse with their husbands. The law was changed in 1979, but only in part. A man who had sexual intercourse with a woman other than his wife was liable for rape, and punishable as a felon, if he committed the act in any of nine forbidden ways. But a man who had sexual intercourse with his wife was liable only for the lesser offense of 'spousal rape', punishable in the prosecutor's discretion as only a misdemeanor, and then only if he committed the act in one of two forbidden ways, namely, by (i) force or threat of bodily harm, or (ii) threat of future retaliation.[33] Thus, until 1992 it would not have been an offense for husbands to have sexual intercourse with their wives by means of 'duress', 'menace', fraud, or under conditions in which their wives were drugged, drunk, unconscious, or mentally disabled. A bill was introduced in 1993 to remove all the differences between rape and spousal rape, including the differences in penalty. Yet a number of groups opposed it: the district attorneys association opposed the bill on the ground that prosecutors needed discretion to charge the offense at a misdemeanor level in order to persuade juries to convict; the ACLU opposed it on the ground that it would make it an offense for husbands to have sexual intercourse with wives who had Alzheimer's disease; and conservative rights groups opposed it on the ground that it would enable vindictive wives and ex-wives to bring false charges of rape. Ultimately, the district attorneys failed, the ACLU succeeded, and conservatives had a mixture of success and failure: the penalties for rape and spousal rape were made identical; the prohibitions for rape and spousal rape were also made identical (except in not making it an offense for husbands to have sexual intercourse with wives with debilitating mental disorders like Alzheimer's disease); and to discourage false accusations of spousal rape, complainants were required to bring complaints of spousal rape within one year rather than six years.[34]

The Variability of Legal Consent

We have seen that whether a person's actual acquiescence functions as legal consent in law ultimately depends upon whether doing so satisfies the jurisdiction's normative principles. The same is true of imputed consent. Whether a person's conduct is treated as a legal fiction of actual acquiescence ultimately depends upon whether doing so protects what the jurisdiction regards as the person's legitimate interests in the matter at hand. However, a jurisdiction's normative views regarding a person's actual acquiescence and conduct may vary from one context to another, depending, among other things, upon whether the consequences are civil or criminal and, if criminal, upon whether the punishments are harsh or mild.[35] It follows, therefore, that in contrast to factual consent, which either does or does not exist, legal consent is variable: a given instance of empirical acquiescence or conduct may both *constitute* and *not constitute* legal consent within a jurisdiction, depending upon the legal context in which it occurs.

Consider Kenneth Jackson of Alaska. Jackson was accused in 1990 of forcing a mentally retarded, 25-year-old woman, 'TYJ', into having sexual intercourse with him without her legal consent. The existence of their intercourse came to light when TYJ's doctor discovered that TYJ was pregnant. The evidence at trial showed that TYJ, who had an I.Q. of between 51 and 55, functioned at the level of a kindergartner. She had attended special-education classes and completed high school, and she held a job at a restaurant clearing tables. But she could not do simple arithmetic, and she lacked all but the most rudimentary reading and writing skills. She could write nothing except her name; and apart from being able to recognize her address, telephone number, and certain 'survival words', she was unable to read. She had 'a rudimentary awareness of the mechanics of sexual intercourse' and 'was aware that babies came from "sex".' But she

> did not understand birth control, how to prevent pregnancy, or what sexually transmitted diseases are or how to prevent them. She did not know the meaning of words such as IUD, condom, rubber, syphilis, gonorrhea, or AIDS. Apart from her awareness that pregnancy resulted in the birth of a baby, she did not understand any of the practical consequences or potential complications of pregnancy.

Jackson was tried in an Alaskan court on two counts of having sexual intercourse with TYJ without her consent: first-degree sexual assault, which carries a maximum sentence of up to twenty years in prison; and second-degree sexual assault, which carries a maximum sentence of ten years in prison. 'First degree' assault differs from 'second degree' assault in the way in which consent is negated. First-degree sexual assault is the offense of having sexual intercourse with a person without her legal 'consent', meaning without her legal consent having been negated by force or threat. Second-degree sexual assault is the offense of having sexual intercourse with a person who the defendant 'knows' to be 'mentally incapable' of consenting.[36] The jury acquitted Jackson of first-degree sexual assault, finding that TYJ had legally consented to sexual intercourse within the meaning of that statute by consciously acquiescing to it without being forced. At the same time, however, the jury convicted Jackson of second-degree sexual assault, finding that he knew TYJ could not understand the nature or consequences of her conduct. The court of appeals affirmed, ruling that 'there was ample evidence to support a reasonable conclusion that the state met its burden of proving beyond a reasonable doubt that TYJ was mentally incapable of meaningfully consenting to sexual intercourse'.[37] The consequence was that TYJ both *did* and *did not* legally consent to sexual intercourse with Jackson: she did legally consent for purposes of the norm of consent contained in the prohibition of first-degree sexual assault, *i.e.*, actual acquiescence free from 'force'; but she did not legally consent for purposes of the norm contained in the prohibition of second-degree sexual assault, *i.e.*, actual acquiescence free from 'mental incapacity'.

What is true of legal consent that is based upon actual acquiescence, *i.e.*, prescriptive consent, is also true of imputed consent: a person's conduct or state of mind that may justify imputing a legal fiction of acquiescence to her for one purpose may not justify imputing a fiction of acquiescence to her for another purpose. Consider the Virginia law of rape which distinguishes for purposes of rape between 'threats', on the one hand, and 'intimidation', on the other. The difference is that 'threats' are reserved for explicit expressions of intent to inflict bodily harm, while 'intimidation' includes 'psychological pressure' of 'domination and control' that an actor brings to bear upon a subject, causing her to fear some bodily harm even in the absence of explicit threats.[38] It is an offense in Virginia for a man to compel any woman, including his wife, to have sexual intercourse with him 'against [her] will by

... threat'. And it is also an offense in Virginia for a man to compel any woman, including his wife, to have sexual intercourse with him 'against [her] will by . . . intimidation'.[39] But it is not an offense for a man use intimidation to compel his wife with whom he is living in the same household to have sexual intercourse, because by virtue of marrying and living with a man, a woman in Virginia is deemed to give 'implied consent' to certain kinds of pressure to have sexual intercourse, including psychological pressure that induces a fear of some bodily harm.[40] Thus, by marrying and living with a man, a woman in Virginia both is and is not imputed to consent to have sexual intercourse with him: she is imputed to have consented to sexual intercourse by means of intimidation, but she is not imputed to have consented to sexual intercourse by means of threats.

Conclusion

'Consent' is used in law in a *legal* sense, as opposed to a *factual* sense, when it is used in criminal statutes to refer to events that constitute complete or partial defenses to crime. We shall see in later chapters that events that constitute such defenses can take various forms, depending upon the way the statutes are framed. Thus, the events may consist of certain mental states of acquiescence on a subject *S*'s part, certain expressions of certain mental states of acquiescence on *S*'s part, or certain acts or states of mind on *S*'s part from which the law imputes such mental states or expressions of acquiescence to her. Regardless of the form they take, however, such events on *S*'s part constitute complete or partial defenses to crime when two conditions are present: (1) when the jurisdiction at hand believes that an actor *A*'s conduct threatens no legitimate interests other than those, perhaps, of *S* herself; and (2) when these events on *S*'s part completely or partially protect whatever interests the jurisdiction at hand deems *S* to possess with respect to *A*'s conduct.

This means that before a jurisdiction can treat a mental state, expression, or other act on *S*'s part as legal consent to *A*'s conduct *x*, the jurisdiction must resolve a number of normative issues for itself. Specifically, it must decide (1) whether *A*'s conduct harms or offends any person or group *other* than *S* herself; (2) whether the harms or offenses that *A* inflicts upon such persons or groups are justified by the benefits that *S* derives for herself if she is *S* to choose *x* under conditions that suffice to protect her interests; (3) whether *A* wrongfully harms or offends *S* herself by subjecting her to *x without* her subjective or expressive acquiescence; (4) whether the wrongfulness of the latter harms or offenses to *S* can be completed or partially negated by *S*'s choosing *x* for herself under certain conditions of competence, knowledge, freedom, and motivation; and (5) whether the wrongfulness of harms or offenses that *A* inflicts upon *S* can be completely or partially negated by something that *S* can do or feel *other* than to choose *x* under those conditions. If a jurisdiction answers either 'no' to Question 1 or 'yes' to Question 2, and if it answers 'yes' to Questions 3 and 4, it commits itself to giving *S* the authority to legally consent to *x* by choosing it for herself under certain conditions of competence, knowledge, freedom, and motivation. By the same token, if a jurisdiction answers either 'no' to Question 1 or 'yes' to Question 2, and if it answers 'yes' to Questions 3 and 5, it can invoke the legal fiction of treating *S* *as if* she had legally consented to *x* by acquiescing to it in certain ways, while knowing full well that she did not. In theory, of course, jurisdictions could end up agreeing in the answers they give to Questions 1-5, yielding no normative differences among them. In practice, however, answers to such questions tend to be contested, and, hence, jurisdictions tend to differ among themselves as to when mental states, expressions, or other acts on *S*'s part constitute defenses to crime. Also in theory, a given jurisdiction could end up deciding that the conditions of competence, knowledge freedom, and motivation that protect *S*'s interests in choosing *x* for herself are constant, regardless of *what S* happens to be choosing for herself. In practice, however, jurisdictions require greater competence, knowledge, freedom, and motivation for some choices (*e.g.*, life-threatening surgery) than for others (*e.g.*, gifting property), thereby causing a person's legal consent to be a function of what she is consenting to.

Despite the normative differences that exist among them in the way they answer Questions 1-5, Anglo-American jurisdictions nevertheless possess much in common, something that can be illustrated by contrasting what they *do* with what John Stuart Mill in his 1859 essay *On Liberty* argues jurisdictions *ought* to do. Mill devotes much of *On Liberty* to the exposition of a moral and political contention that has come to be called the 'harm principle'.[41] The harm principle is commonly said to be the contention that no valid reason exists for imposing social or legal constraints upon an actor's conduct, including constraints in the form of criminal penalties, except to protect *others* from being wrongfully harmed or offended. Thus, Joel Feinberg, who traces his magisterial *Moral Limits of the Criminal Law* to Mill's essay,[42] claims that the harm principle for Mill was the principle that 'the need to prevent harm (private or public) to parties other than the actor' is 'the only valid [reason]' for invading an actor's liberty.[43] Indeed, Feinberg goes so far as to state that the term 'the harm principle' is an abbreviation for 'the harm to *others* principle'.[44]

It is understandable that commentators would take Mill's harm principle to be a harm-to-others principle, because Mill himself frames it in terms of 'harm to others'[45] and because Mill devotes the great bulk of his discussion of harm to instances of harm to others. Nevertheless, Mill makes it clear that he does not mean to confine society to the prevention of harm to others, because he repeatedly says that society has legitimate authority to prevent certain persons from inflicting self-regarding harm upon *themselves*, namely, those who are unaware of what they are about to do (*e.g.*, a person who is about to 'cross a bridge' without realizing it is 'unsafe'); 'children' and other 'young persons' who are not yet in the 'maturity of their faculties'; people who are 'delirious, or in some state of excitement or absorption incompatible with the full use of the reflecting faculty'; people who lack an 'ordinary amount of understanding'; and, generally, people who lack a 'capacity of being guided to their own improvement by conviction or persuasion'.[46] As Mill says of children, but would presumably also say of others such as the insane, retarded or senile, 'Those who are . . . in a state to require being taken care of by others must be protected against their own actions as well as against external injury'.

The question thus becomes: how does one make space within Mill's harm principle—that is, how does one conceptualize Mill's harm principle—to accommodate Mill's view that the state can prevent certain persons from harming themselves? One possibility is to follow Feinberg and confine Mill's harm principle to being a 'Harm-to-Others' principle. If one does that, however, then in order to make room for what Mill says about persons who are 'in a state to require being . . . protected against their own actions', one is obliged to deny what Mill wishes to maintain, namely, that the harm principle is the *exclusive* basis upon which the state may rightly abridge a person's liberty. One becomes obliged to treat Mill's harm principle as only one of *two* legitimate grounds for abridging a person's liberty, the other being a 'Harm-to-Self' principle. Admittedly, any such Harm-to-Self principle would be limited in scope, because it would be qualified by the maxim, '*Volenti non fit injuria*'. ('To a person who acts voluntarily, no wrongful harm is done.') That is to say, such a Harm-to-Self principle would not allow the state to prevent persons from 'voluntarily' inflicting self-regarding harms. It would extend only to cases in which the state seeks to prevent self-regarding harms by persons, such as children and the mentally infirm, who are incapable of acting voluntarily. Yet, significantly, the same is true of Feinberg's Harm-to-Others principle. The Harm-to-Others principle is *also* limited by the *volenti* maxim. The Harm-to-Others principle does not allow the state to prevent all other-regarding harms. It does not allow the state to prevent harms that are inflicted on others with what Mill calls their 'free, voluntary, and undeceived consent'.[47] Rather, it extends only to cases in which a person harms another '*against his will*'.[48]

Significantly, there is also a second way to reconcile Mill's harm principle with what Mill says about persons who are in need of protection against themselves. The second way is functionally equivalent to the first, but it is conceptually more economical. Instead of requiring *two* harm principles, *i.e.*, a Harm-to-Others principle and a Harm-to-Self principle, each of which is qualified by the *volenti* maxim, the second posits a single Harm-to-Anyone principle, qualified by a single *volenti* maxim:

> ***A Harm-to-Anyone Principle.*** The Harm-to-Anyone principle is simply a combination of the Harm-to-Others principle and the Harm-to-Self principle, namely: 'No valid reason exists for imposing social or legal constraints upon an actor's conduct, including constraints in the form of criminal penalties, unless the constraints are necessary to prevent the actor from wrongfully harming or offending either himself or others'.[49]
>
> ***The Volenti Maxim.*** Like the Harm-to-Others and Harm-to-Self principles, the Harm-to-Anyone principle is qualified by the principle, volenti non fit injuria. The volenti maxim qualifies the Harm-to-Anyone principle by defining a class of persons whom conduct neither wrongfully harms nor wrongfully offends. The maxim tends to be translated differently, depending upon whether an actor A is inflicting harm upon himself, or whether he is inflicting harm upon another, S. With respect to persons who suffer self-regarding harm, it can be translated: 'To a person who acts voluntarily, no wrongful harm is done'. With respect to persons who suffer other-regarding harm, it can be translated: 'To a person who consents, no wrongful harm is done'.[50]

This two-part formula has the advantage of reconciling what Mill says about harm to others with what he says about persons who need protection against themselves. Thus, the *volenti* maxim negates the wrongfulness of any harm or offense which an actor *A* may 'voluntarily' inflict upon himself, and it negates the wrongfulness of any harm or offense that *A* may inflict upon *S* with *S*'s 'consent'.[51] And because no such harms or offenses are 'wrongful', the aim of preventing *A* from inflicting them is not a valid reason under the Harm-to-Anyone principle to interfere with *A*'s liberty. Conversely, however, the *volenti* maxim does not negate the wrongfulness of harms that *A involuntarily* inflicts upon himself, or harms or offenses that *A* imposes on *S without S*'s consent. Accordingly, the state retains a legitimate interest under the Harm-to-Anyone principle in using constraints, including criminal penalties, to prevent an actor *A* from inflicting harms or offenses upon himself, provided that *A* acts involuntarily;[52] and the state retains a legitimate interest in using constraints, including criminal penalties, to prevent *A* from inflicting harms and offenses upon *S*, provided that *A* inflicts them without *S*'s consent.[53]

This two-part formula also has the virtue of emphasizing the pivotal role that the *volenti* maxim plays in defining the scope of the harm principle. Like the maxim, 'Likes should be treated alike', the *volenti* maxim is both a formal truism and a receptacle of substantive and controversial content. As a formal truism, the maxim derives its validity from the conclusory meaning of its terms. Thus, when the *volenti* maxim speaks of the mutually exclusive relationship between 'wrongful harms', on the one hand, and what a person does 'voluntarily' or with another's 'consent', on the other, the maxim is not using 'voluntary' and 'consent' in factual senses to refer to anything the person consciously chooses for himself, however coerced or defrauded or incompetent he may be. Rather, the maxim is using 'voluntary' and 'consent' to refer to choices, whether actual or imputed, that are deemed to be sufficient under the circumstances to satisfy whatever society deems to be the person's legitimate interests in the matter at hand.[54] As a precept of criminal law, the *volenti* maxim withstands the test of time, because it is truism: with respect to other-regarding conduct, it declares, 'To a person who [*lawfully*] consents'—that is, regarding a person who acquiesces to conduct under conditions sufficient to satisfy what society deems to be his legitimate interests in the matter at hand—'no [criminal] harm is done'.[55]

While the *volenti* maxim is, indeed, a truism, it is also a receptacle into which commentators and jurisdictions can introduce normative (and contestable) judgments regarding the supposed *conditions* under which a person's choice of conduct satisfies his legitimate interests in it. Such judgments regarding choice conditions depend, in turn, upon *why* a person's choice of conduct may satisfy his interests in it. Moral philosophers have advanced two distinct reasons as to why a person's choice of conduct may suffice to satisfy his interest in it—the first of which concerns what is *good* for him, and the second of which concerns his *rights*:

A Person's Overall Good. Mill labors to locate the normative force of what a person chooses for himself, not in any notion of 'abstract right', but in the relative consequences to his overall 'well-being' of letting him as opposed to others decide what is ultimately good for him.[56] The reason that society should respect the choices that a person makes for himself, Mill argues, is that 'with respect to his own feelings and circumstances, the most ordinary man or woman has means of knowledge immeasurably surpassing those that can be possessed by anyone else'.[57] A person's 'voluntary choice is evidence that what he so chooses is desirable . . . to him, and his good is on the whole best provided for by allowing him to take his own means of pursuing it'.[58] To be sure, a person may make a mistake as to what is good for him; but 'all errors which he is likely to commit . . . are far outweighed by the evil of allowing others to constrain him to do that they deem his good'.[59]

A Person's Rights. In contrast, other commentators locate the normative force of what a person chooses for himself, not in its instrumental effectiveness in maximizing his well-being, but in a person's right of autonomy, *viz.*, his deontological right to govern himself with respect to his exclusive well-being.[60] Feinberg is an exponent of the latter view. The reason that society should respect the choices that a person makes for himself, Feinberg says, is that '[t]he life that a person threatens by his own rashness is after all *his* life; it *belongs* to him and to no one else.'[61] To be sure, people also tend to know what is good for them. But even when they do not, society may not intervene, because 'autonomy is even more important than personal well-being', and his 'right of self-determination . . . takes precedence even over his own good'.[62]

Each of the aforementioned views lends itself to stronger and weaker interpretations. Thus, a person might take a strong position that people in the 'maturity of their faculties' *always* know what is good for them, or a weaker position that people in the maturity of their faculties *often* know what is good for them. The strong position, which Mill himself rejects, seems empirically implausible, given that the controlling predicate, *i.e.*, that persons are in the 'maturity of their faculties', is itself a judgment of degree.[63] Moreover, because the strong position does not appear to be a product of experience, it may disguise a deontological right of autonomy under a mask of consequentialism. Mill himself adopts the weaker position that people in the mature possession of their faculties *nearly* always know what is good for them, for he concedes that with respect to at least one decision that people may wish to make for themselves, *i.e.*, selling themselves into slavery, people are mistaken if they think it is good for them, and they can rightly be restrained from doing so.[64] Similarly, with respect to autonomy, a person can take a strong position that rights of autonomy are absolute, or a weaker position that rights of autonomy have to be balanced against other considerations. Feinberg himself adopts the strong position that rights of autonomy are absolute and 'should reign supreme'.[65] However, once rights of autonomy are decoupled from what is good for persons, one must wonder why they are confined to persons who are mature adults rather than extending to all willful persons, including children.

We will return in Chapter 6 to these two principal views about what accounts for the normative force as to what a person chooses for himself because we shall see that one particular conception of legal consent, *i.e.*, retrospective consent, may depend upon which view is correct. In the meantime, we can conclude by contrasting the way Anglo-American jurisdictions answer Questions 1-5, which determine the scope of legal consent, with the way Mill answers them. Anglo-American law and Mill agree that, regardless of the quality of *S*'s factual consent to *A*'s conduct, *S*'s factual consent can never amount to a defense for *A* in so far as *A* threatens to inflict wrongful harm or offense upon third persons or groups *other* than *S*. Anglo-American law and Mill also agree that *S*'s factual consent to harms or offenses that *A* imposes upon *S* can never amount to a defense for *A* unless *S*'s consent is sufficiently competent, informed, and free to enable *S* to take responsibility for them.

Anglo-American law and Mill differ, however, in two basic respects. First, in contrast to Mill, Anglo-American criminal law regards it as entirely just to punish an actor for conduct that violates the jurisdiction's shared morality, even if the conduct does not otherwise wrongfully harm or offend any particular person (*e.g.*, criminal laws that make it an offense to engage in cannibalism or otherwise mistreat dead bodies, regardless of the deceased's wishes).[66] Second, and more significantly for our purposes, Anglo-American criminal law differs from Mill with respect to the substantive requirements of 'consent' under the *volenti* maxim—that is, the substantive conditions of competence, knowledge, freedom, and motivation that a person must possess in order for her acquiescence to conduct to satisfy her legitimate interests in the matter. For in contrast to Mill, who believes that all persons in the maturity of their faculties are competent to allow any harm (other than enslavement) to be inflicted upon themselves, Anglo-American criminal law takes the position that there are numerous harms that all persons are incompetent to inflict or allow to be inflicted upon themselves, regardless of how much they consciously desire them. Thus, in contrast to Mill, Anglo-American law makes it an offense for *A* to kill *S* in a game of Russian roulette, to kill *S* as an act of mercy, to maim *S* for perverse aesthetic reasons, to purchase *S*'s body parts, to engage *S* in gambling or prostitution, or to supply *S* with hallucinogenic drugs to use alone at home—regardless of how much *S* may desire those things.[67] It is difficult to determine whether Anglo-American law bases the prohibitions upon the view that the underlying conduct is not good for *S* (despite the fact that *S* may mistakenly think it is), or upon the view that the conduct violates shared morality (regardless of whether it is good for *S*). However, as long as the prohibitions exist, they are an implicit rejection of the contention of Feinberg's that mature adults have an absolute right to govern their own lives. And in so far as the prohibitions are based upon the view that the conduct is not good for *S*, they implicitly reject Mill's contention that, with the exception of voluntary enslavement, persons in the maturity of their faculties know best what is good for them.

Notes

1. As far as I have been able to determine, only two jurisdictions, the State of Washington and the District of Columbia, purport to place the burden of persuasion as to legal consent on defendants. *See* Russell v. United States, 1997 D.C. App. LEXIS 178, 698 A.2d 1007 (D.C. Ct. App., 1997); Washington v. Camara, 113 Wash.2d 631, 781 P.2d 483 (1989). However, in both jurisdictions the prosecution simultaneously bears the burden of proving 'force' beyond a reasonable doubt. Since 'force' negates legal consent in both jurisdictions, judges have no choice in practice but to leave juries with contradictory instructions as to which party bears the burden of persuasion. The English Law Commission has presented a case for obliging defendants to prove consent by a

preponderance of the evidence and has invited comments as to whether its proposal should be adopted. *See* Law Commission, *Consent and the Criminal Law*, para. 4.41-4.45, pp. 44-46.

2. Perkins, *Criminal Law*, p. 962.
3. *See* LaFave and Scott, *Substantive Criminal Law*, vol. 1, § 5.11, p. 687.
4. When I say 'consent' is a defense to rape, I am not referring to the language in which rape statutes are explicitly stated. Every jurisdiction defines the crime of rape in its own distinctive way. Some statutes define rape explicitly in the language of 'consent'; others make no mention of 'consent'. I mean, rather, that regardless of the language they use in defining rape, every jurisdiction provides that it is a defense to rape that the victim either actually acquiesced to sexual intercourse under appropriate conditions of competence, knowledge, freedom, and motivation or is imputed to do so under circumstances justifying a legal fiction of prescriptive consent, or both.
5. The common-law definition of adultery is sexual intercourse by a man, married or single, with a married woman who is not his wife. In most jurisdictions, however, the common-law definition has been enlarged by statute to include sexual intercourse by a married person with some person who is not his or her spouse. *See* Brazener, 'Annotation'. Adultery is an offense in almost half of the states and the District of Columbia, as well as in the U.S. Armed Forces. *See* Coughlin, 'Sex and Guilt', pp. 22-24 and nn. 80-81, 86-87. Criminal penalties range from a maximum fine of ten dollars to several years in jail. Although criminal prosecutions are not common outside the military, it has been said that 'numerous adultery prosecutions occur'. Note, 'Constitutional Barriers to Civil and Criminal Restrictions on Pre- and Extramarital Sex'.
6. Note, 'Constitutional Barriers To Civil and Criminal Restrictions on Pre- And Extramarital Sex', p. 1677:

   > The impact of extramarital sex on the marital relationship, however, provides a state interest unique to adultery laws. In the absence of spousal consent, extramarital intercourse often violates important promises, results in lies and deception, inflicts emotional pain, and can terminate or severely disrupt a marriage.

   See also Iowa v. Ronek, 176 N.W.2d 153, 154-55 (1970) (holding that because of the effect adultery has on the injured spouse, a state may make it a condition of prosecution that the injured spouse actually complain):

   > Adultery is an offense against the husband or wife of the guilty party, and it is also an offense against the public. . . . The provision in section 702.1 that 'no prosecution for adultery shall be commenced but on the complaint of the husband or wife' does not fix the character of the offense. Iowa v. Corliss, 85 Iowa 18, 20, 51 N.W. 1154. The provision is grounded in the regard which the law has for the marital relation and the rights of the husband and wife to condone the wrongs of either toward the other. That the offender cannot be prosecuted except at the instance of the injured husband or wife does not render his crime any the less an offense against the public.
7. 389 Mass. 171, 449 N.E.2d 357 (1983).
8. Different jurisdictions use different terms to describe the underlying conduct of having sexual relations with an underage child, including 'corruption of minors', 'carnal knowledge of a juvenile', 'indecent liberties with a child', 'lewd and lascivious conduct with a child', and 'statutory rape'. *See* Kole, 'Annotation', *2a.
9. For the harms of sexual intercourse from which the state seeks to protect minors, *see* Jones v. Florida, 640 So. 2d 1084 (1994); Goodrow v. Perrin, , 119 N.H. 483, 403 A.2d 864 (1979); Vermont v. Barlow, 160 Vt. 527, 630 A.2d 1299 (1993). *See* also Phipps, 'Children, Adults, Sex and the Criminal Law', pp. 34-41.

10. For a history of the maxim in Roman civil law and, subsequently, in English civil law, *see* Ingman, 'A History Of The Defence of *Volenti Non Fit Injuria*'. For the statements in Aristotle's *Nichomachean Ethics* to which the maxim is sometimes attributed, *see* Aristotle, *Nichomachean Ethics*, V, 1129a32-b1, 1136a10-1137a4, 1138a-b14. For the application of the maxim to criminal cases, *see* Kleinig, 'Consent As A Defence In Criminal Law'.
11. Because this book is a study of the defense of consent in criminal law, I confine my discussion of the *Volenti* maxim to (i) its operation in law, and (ii) its application with respect to other-regarding conduct by *A* vis-à-vis another *S*. In reality, the *Volenti* maxim is a broader precept that operates in ethics as well as law, and applies to self-regarding conduct by *A* as well as to other-regarding conduct by *A*. For discussion of the *Volenti* maxim as a ethical precept, *see* Feinberg, *Harm To Others*, pp. 115-117, 215, 220. For the maxim's application to self-regarding conduct, *see* the text accompanying notes 41-55.
12. Kleinig, 'Consent As A Defence In Criminal Law', p. 329 (stating the maxim as, 'To the one who consents no *wrong* is done') (emphasis added).
13. Feinberg, *Harm To Others*, p. 116:

    Volenti is most plausible when it denies title to complain only to him whose consent was *fully voluntary*, and a person's consent is fully voluntary only when he is competent and unimpaired adult who has not been threatened, misled, or lied to about relevant facts, nor manipulated by subtle forms of conditioning.
14. I am paraphrasing the laws of Montana for heuristic purposes. The Montana law consists of two sections. The first, Montana Code section 45-5-503, defines the larger offense of 'Sexual intercourse without consent':

    A person who knowingly has sexual intercourse without consent with another person commits the offense of sexual intercourse without consent.

    The second section, Montana Code section 45-5-501, defines sexual intercourse with children under sixteen to be 'without' their consent as a matter of law:

    (1) As used in 45-5-503, the term 'without consent' means:
    (a) the victim is compelled to submit by force against himself or another; or
    (b) the victim is incapable of consent because he is:
    (iii) less than 16 years old.
15. *See* Cromeans v. States, 59 Tex. Crim. 611, 129 S.W. 1129 (1910). *See* also Phipps, 'Children, Adults, Sex and the Criminal Law', pp. 37-38.
16. Compare the Louisiana statute, below, with the Alaska statute that follows. Both statutes make it a crime to have sexual intercourse with a minor. The difference is that Louisiana does so with explicit reference to consent, while Alaska does so without any reference to consent:

    Louisiana Rev. Stat. § 14:42(A) (1995) ('Aggravated rape') (emphasis added):

    Aggravated rape is a rape . . . where the anal or vaginal sexual intercourse is deemed to be *without lawful consent of the victim* because it is committed under any one or more of the following circumstances: . . . (4) When the victim is under the age of twelve years.

    Alaska Stat. § 11.41.434(a) (1994) ('Sexual abuse of a minor'):

    An offender commits the crime of sexual abuse of a minor in the first degree if . . . being 16 years of age or older, the offender engages in sexual penetration with a person who is under 13 years of age.

    For other statutes like Alaska's that define the offense without reference to consent, *see* Cal. Penal Code § 261.5 (1994) ('Unlawful sexual intercourse with a minor'). Indiana Code Ann. § 35-42-4-9 (1994) ('Sexual misconduct with a minor'); and Ohio Rev. Code § 2907.04 (2000) ('Corruption of a minor).

17. Sometimes, by virtue of pointedly *excepting* a particular offense from a large category of offenses that are defined by reference to consent, a legislature seems to imply that the offense is predicated on harm to third-parties alone rather than to participants alone or to participants and third parties alike. Thus, New York makes 'consent' a defense to all sexual offenses in New York—all, that is, except one; and, having done so, it further provides that a person shall be deemed not to consent for purposes of any of those crimes when he engages in sexual intercourse or sexual contact by virtue of:
    (1) Forcible compulsion, or
    (2) Incapacity to consent [including by virtue of his being]
    (a) less than seventeen years old; or
    (b) mentally defective; or
    (c) mentally incapacitated; or
    (d) physically helpless.

    New York Penal Law § 130.05 (1994). The one exception is the crime of 'sodomy', which is defined as a crime without reference to the defense of consent. That is, instead of, first, stating that consent is a defense to *all* sexual offenses in New York and, then, providing that a person shall be deemed not to consent when he engages in sodomy, the New York legislature pointedly *excepts* sodomy from the crimes to which consent is a defense—thus implying that sodomy in New York is regarded as being based on harm or offense to the public alone, rather than on harm to the participants.
18. *See, e.g.*, Coughlin, 'Sex and Guilt', pp. 27, 30, 35, 38 (where the author fallaciously assumes that it would be contradictory for a jurisdiction to punish a woman as an adulterer or a fornicator for engaging in sexual intercourse to which she did not 'consent' for purposes of the jurisdiction's law of rape—leading the author fallaciously to conclude that because 18th - and 19th-century jurisdictions wished to punish women for submitting to adultery or fornication as a result of coercion that fell short of common-law 'duress', those jurisdictions had no choice but to confine a woman's non-consent for purposes of the law of rape to coercion that sufficed to constitute common law duress). *See* also Feinberg, *Harm To Self*, p. 15 (making the same mistake).
19. *Model Penal Code*, pt. 1, vol. 1, § 2.06, p. 324 ('[T]o hold the female as an accomplice in a statutory rape upon her person would be inconsistent with the legislative purpose to protect her against her own weakness in consenting, the very theory of the crime'); California v. Tobias, 25 Cal. 4th 327, 334, 21 P.3d 758, 764 (2001) (it is legally 'inconsistent' to treat an underage adolescent as both a victim of sexual intercourse and a perpetrator). But *see id.* ('An exception to this rule might exist where two minors engage in consensual sexual intercourse, and thus both are victims of the other's crime').
20. *See* Bogart, 'On the Nature of Rape', p. 130 n.40 (discussing the possibility in law of 'mutual battery'). *See* also *id.* at 130 ('[W]here there is intoxication, the capacity to give effective consent is compromised and, consequently, [sexual intercourse] may pass over from seduction to rape. Indeed, . . . it is entirely proper to speak of mutual rape where (at least) two individuals engage in sexual relations while intoxicated').
21. *See* Brown, v. Heidreich, 62 N.D. 85; 241 N.W. 599 (1932) ('In our statute, it is expressly provided that she is guilty of violating the law even though she be under the age of consent prescribed in another statute which punishes the male for rape. It is not possible, under this statute, to regard her as legally innocent. . . . In light of this statute, the rape statute must be read as fixing the age of consent merely for the purpose of penalizing the male perpetrator and not for the purpose of establishing the legal innocence of a consenting female').
22. *See, e.g.*, In re P.M., Juvenile, 156 Vt. 303, 592 A.2d 864 (1991) (nothing prevents the state from treating a fifteen-year-old boy, whom it regards as too young to legally consent to

sexual intercourse, as both a 'perpetrator' and a 'victim' for engaging in sexual intercourse with an underage girl who was infatuated with him); In re G.T., Juvenile, 758 A.2d 301, 309 (2000) (nothing prevents the legislature, if it so chooses, from making it an offense for an underage person to have sexual intercourse with another underage person, thereby treating underage sexual partners as both 'perpetrators' and 'victims'). *See* generally Kole, 'Annotation', *2a:

> [C]ourts have specifically addressed in a growing number of cases the applicability of age-specific sex offense statutes to defendant minors who fall within the protected age range. In a majority of those cases, the courts have held that such a defendant can be prosecuted for violating a statute prohibiting sexual activity with a minor in a specified age group even if the defendant himself falls within those age limitations.

To be sure, when states prosecute underage persons for having sexual intercourse, they typically prosecute them for having sexual intercourse with *other* underage persons, in large part because states typically use statutory-rape statutes as vehicles for punishing conduct they believe to have been actually coercive. But nothing prevents a statute from prosecuting an underage person, *A*, for aiding and abetting his sexual partner, *B*, in having sexual intercourse with *A himself*. *See* Kole, 'Annotation', *5 ('Because a child can be held criminally liable for voluntarily engaging in a prohibited sexual act that the child knew to be wrong, such a child may be found to be an accomplice to another person who engages in a prohibited sexual act with the child'). *See* also Michael M. v. Superior Court, 450 U.S. 464, 477 (1981) (Stewart, J., concurring) (in a jurisdiction in which it is a crime for a male to have sexual intercourse with an underage girl, the underage girl may be prosecuted for aiding and abetting her own violation). The English Law Commission originally took the view that a victim of nonconsensual conduct cannot also be a perpetrator, but it thereafter reversed itself. *See* Law Commission, *Consent and the Criminal Law*, para. 1.20-1.23, pp. 9-10. The English Home Office currently takes the view that underage teenagers who have mutually agreeable sex with one another can in theory both be punished for it. *See* Home Office, *Setting the Boundaries: Reforming the Law on Sex Offences*, vol. 1, ch. 3, para. 3.9.14, pp. 55-56 (July 2000).

23. *See* Planned Parenthood Affiliates v. Van de Kamp, 181 Cal. App. 3d 245, 226 Cal. Rptr. 361 (1986) (a state statute, which makes it an offense for any person to engage in sexual intercourse with persons under the age of 14, should not be construed to apply to defendants who are themselves under 14, for if it were so construed, it would discourage sexually active teenagers under the age of 14 from seeking reproduction-related health care).
24. *See, e.g.*, In re Gladys R. 1 Cal. 3d 855, 869, 464 P.2d 127, 83 Cal. Rptr. 671 (1970) (a 12-year-old girl, who is too young to consent to sexual intercourse, can be held criminally liable for sexually molesting another minor if it can be shown that she understood the wrongfulness of her conduct). Hildebrant v. Hildebrant, 216 Mich. App. 384, 548 N.W.2d 715 (1996) (upholding a judgment of criminal delinquency against a pregnant, 15-year-old girl for having sexual intercourse with her 14-year-old brother, while stating, in dictum, that it would not have violated state policy to hold both children criminally responsible for the intercourse). Victims of nonconsensual conduct are entitled to all of the criminal defenses that other defendants possess, such as duress, lack of *mens rea*, insanity, etc. However, they possess no additional defense by virtue of being victims of offenses of non-consent, unless the jurisdiction, as a matter of prosecutorial policy, decides to grant them immunity.
25. *See* Connecticut v. Brown, 59 Conn. App. 243, 251, 756 A.2d 860, 865 (2000) ('consent must have been actual and not simply acquiescence brought by force or fear').

26. Stafford v. Indiana, 455 N.E.2d 401 (1983). But compare New York v Gonzales, 148 Misc 2d 973, 561 NYS2d 358 (1990) (using 'true consent' to refer to an instance of factual consent that, because of the victim's age, was a legally incompetent consent).
27. *See, e.g.*, Glover v. State, 518 So. 2d 247, 248 (1987) (contrasting 'actual consent' with 'legal consent', and stating that 'actual consent' does not suffice to constitute a legal defense to sexual intercourse with an underage girl).
28. New York v. Gonzales, 148 Misc. 2d 973, 979, 561 N.Y.S.2d 358, 362 (1990).
29. Minnesota v. Dutton, 450 N.W.2d 189 (1990). The Minnesota statute (Minn. Stat. § 609.344(1) (1993)) provides:

    A person who engages in sexual penetration with another person is guilty of criminal sexual conduct in the third degree if any of the following circumstances exists:
    (I) the actor is a psychotherapist and the complainant is a patient . . . of the psychotherapist and the patient . . . is emotionally dependent upon the psychotherapist.

    'Sexual penetration', in turn, is defined as 'sexual intercourse . . . committed without the complainant's consent' (Minnesota Statutes 1992, section 609.341(12) (1993).
    An 'emotionally dependent' patient is a patient who is 'unable to withhold consent to sexual contact or sexual penetration by the psychotherapist' (Minn. Stat. § 609.341(19) (1993)).
30. New Mexico v. Leiding, 112 N.M. 143, 812 P.2d 797 (1991). The New Mexico statute that was in effect at the time of Leiding's conduct was defined in terms of 'force' rather than in terms of 'consent' (N.M. Stat. Ann. § 30-9-11 (1995)); but the New Mexico Supreme Court had interpreted the term 'force' to mean 'force *and without consent*' and required that juries be instructed accordingly. *See* New Mexico v. Bell, 90 N.M. 134, 140, 560 P.2d 925, 931 (1977) (emphasis added):

    The applicable rule of criminal procedure . . . requires . . . that '[t]he court must instruct the jury upon all questions of law essential for a conviction of the crime or crimes submitted to the jury'.
    The 'questions of law essential to a conviction' of rape, which was the common law precursor of the statutory offense of criminal sexual penetration, traditionally have been three: (a) carnal knowledge or intercourse, (b) force, and (c) commission of the act *without the consent* or against the will of the victim. It is clear that the jury must be properly instructed on the law relative to each of these three essential elements of the crime.

    In response to the *Leiding* decision, the New Mexico legislature in 1993 amended its law of rape to provide that 'force' for purposes of the law includes:

    (5) the perpetration of criminal sexual penetration or criminal sexual contact by a psychotherapist on his patient, with or without the patient's consent, during the course of psychotherapy or within a period of one year following the termination of psychotherapy.

    New Mexico Code § 30-9-10(A) (1994).
31. John Whitmire, D-Houston, introduced Senate Bill No. 15 into the Texas Senate in 1995 to amend the Texas penal code in several respects, including an amendment to the sexual assault statute (Tex. Penal Code § 22.011(b)). The amendment added subsection (9), below, stating that 'a sexual assault is without the consent of the other person' under section 22.011(b) if:

    (9) the actor is a mental health services provider who causes the other person, who is a patient or former patient of the actor, to submit or participate by exploiting the other person's emotional dependency on the actor.

The bill was debated and passed by both houses of the Texas Legislature and signed into law by the Governor on June 7, 1995.

32. In contrast to Texas, most jurisdictions thus far do not punish sexual intercourse between therapists and patients. *See* Schulhofer, *Unwanted Sex*, pp. 215, 218, 231. Among those that do, the statutes vary. Some punish sexual intercourse only if it is with a present patient, as opposed to a former patient. *See* Colo. Rev. Stat. § 18-3-405.5 (1994). Some punish sexual intercourse with emotionally dependent former patients but only if the therapist has not taken precautions to ensure that the patient has the advice of a third party. Cal. Bus. and Prof. Code § 729(a) (1995). Others punish the same range of conduct as Texas but provide for considerably different penalties. Compare Oregon Code § 16-6-5.1 (1995) (up to three years in prison) with Texas (up to twenty years in prison).
33. As of 1992, it was a crime of rape in California for a man to have sexual intercourse with a woman other than his wife (i) by force or threat of bodily harm, (ii) by threat of future retaliation; (iii) by duress, (iv) by menace, (v) where the woman was mentally incapacitated; (vi) where the woman was unconscious; (vii) by administering intoxicants; (viii) by fraud, including impersonating her husband; or (ix) by extortion. Cal. Penal Code § 261. At the same time, it was a crime of 'spousal rape' for a man to have sexual intercourse with his wife only (i) by force or threat of bodily harm, or (ii) by threat of future retaliation. *See* the History notes to Cal. Penal Code § 262 (1995).
34. Representative Hilda Solis (D-El Monte) introduced AB 187 in 1993; and, as amended, it was signed into law by the Governor later that year. For debate on the bill, *see* Wilkie, 'Wilson OKs Expanding of Spousal Rape Law', *San Diego Union-Tribute*, 1 October 1993, p. A-3 (position of the California District Attorneys Association); Wilkie, 'Definition of Spousal Rape Being Rewritten', *San Diego Union Tribune*, 15 June 1993, p. A-1 (position of the ACLU and of conservative rights groups).
35. *See* Wertheimer, 'Consent and Sexual Relations', p. 95.
36. The Alaska first-degree sexual assault statute, section 11.41.410(a), provides:

    An offender commits the crime of sexual assault in the first degree if . . . (1) the offender engages in sexual penetration with another person without consent of that person.

    Section 11.41.470(8) provides that for purposes of first-degree sexual assault 'without consent' means that a person:

    with or without resisting, is coerced by the use of force against a person or property, or by the express or implied threat of death, imminent physical injury, or kidnapping to be inflicted on anyone.

    The second-degree sexual assault, section 11.41.420(a), provides:

    An offender commits the crime of sexual assault in the second degree if . . . (3) the offender engages in sexual penetration with a person who the offender knows is (A) mentally incapable.

    Section 11.41.470(4) provides that 'mentally incapable' means:

    suffering from a mental disease or defect that renders the person incapable of understanding the nature or consequences of the person's conduct, including the potential for harm to that person.

    For sentences for first and second degree sexual assault, *see* section 12.55.125(d),(h).
37. Jackson v. Alaska, 890 P.2d 587, 593 (1995).
38. Morse v. Virginia, 17 Va. App. 627, 629, 634-35, 440 S.E.2d 145, 147, 149-50 (1994).
39. As of 1984, the Virginia penal code declared it to be a crime of rape for a person to compel any 'female' to engage in sexual intercourse by means of 'force' or 'intimidation'. *See*

Virginia Code § 18.2-61, quoted in Weishaupt v. Virginia, 227 Va. 389, 396 n.3, 315 S.E.2d 847, 850 n.3 (1984). Similarly, the Virginia Code of today declares it to be a crime of rape for a person to compel any 'complaining witness', including 'his or her spouse', to have sexual intercourse by means of 'threat' or 'intimidation'. *See* Virginia Code § 18.2-61 (A and B) (2000).

40. The Virginia Supreme Court held in 1984 that the term 'female' within the Virginia rape statute included wives but that a wife who chooses to live with her husband thereby gives 'implied consent' to having sexual intercourse with her husband. *See* Weishaupt v. Virginia, 227 Va. 389, 404, 315 S.E.2d 847, 855 (1984); Kizer v. Virginia, 228 Va. 256, 321 S.E.2d 291 (1984). The Virginia legislature codified the Court's 1984 rulings by amending the Virginia penal code to make it clear that, while it is a crime for a husband to use 'force' to compel his wife with whom he is living to engage in sexual intercourse, it is not a crime for a husband to use 'intimidation' to compel his wife with whom he is living to engage in sexual intercourse. *See* Virginia Code § 18.2-61, 18.2-67.2:1 (2000).

41 *See* Mill, *On Liberty*. The 19th century debate in England between Mill and his principal adversary regarding the harm principle, Lord James Stephen, was replicated in the mid-20th century in a debate between an advocate of the harm principle, H.L.A. Hart, and his adversary, Lord Patrick Devlin, over the criminal status in England of homosexual conduct. For histories of the harm principle, and the Hart-Devlin debate, *see* Grey, *The Legal Enforcement of Morality*; Harcourt, 'Criminal Law: The Collapse of the Harm Principle'.

42. Feinberg, *Harm To Others*, p. 15 ('This work will be an effort to vindicate the traditional liberalism derived from Mill's *On Liberty*, not by slavishly adhering to its every contention and argument, but by salvaging a central part of it, qualified and reformulated in the light of the many accumulated difficulties and criticisms. The highly qualified view presented here will be at the very least faithful to Mill's liberal motivating spirit').

43. Feinberg, *Harm To Others*, p. 11.

44. Feinberg, *Harm To Others*, p. 11.

45. Mill, *On Liberty*, p. 68 ('The object of his essay is to assert one very simple principle. . . . That principle is . . . [t]hat the only purpose for which power can be rightfully exercised over any member of a civilized community, against his will, is to prevent harm to others').

46. Mill, *On Liberty*, p. 166 ('If either a public official or anyone else saw a person attempting to cross a bridge which [was] unsafe, and there were no time to warm him of his danger, they might seize him and turn him back, without any real infringement of his liberty; for liberty consists in doing what one desires, and he does not desire to fall into the river'); p. 69 ('[T]his doctrine is meant to apply only to human beings in the maturity of their faculties. We are not speaking of children or young persons . . . '); p. 166 (the state may legitimately restrain a person from risks to his life or health if he is 'a child, or delirious, or in some state of excitement or absorption incompatible with the full use of the reflecting faculty'); p. 142 ('ordinary amount of understanding'); and p. 69 ('capable of being guided . . .').

47. Mill, *On Liberty*, p. 71.

48. Mill, *On Liberty*, p. 68.

49. Although Mill's thesis has come to be known as the 'harm' principle, Mill intended to extend to encompass conduct that personally 'offends' members of the public, *e.g.*, acts of public indecency. *See* Mill, *On Liberty*, p. 168:

> [T]here are many acts which, being directly injurious only to the agents themselves, ought not to be legally indicted, but which, if done publicly, are violation of good manners and, coming thus within the category of offences against others, may rightly be prohibited. Of this kind are offences against decency.

Moreover, despite its references to 'harm', the harm principle must be understood as a principle, not against all harms, but against *wrongful* harms and offenses. *See* Feinberg, *Harm To Others*, p. 105:

> Up to this point, we have examined the notion of harm as it is expressed in language by the nominative 'a harm', because we have been interested primarily in a condition or state of a person to which the noun 'harm' refers, namely the state that results when one's interests are affected adversely by events. The condition of set-back interest, however, is only one of the components of harm in the special narrow sense employed by the harm principle. In that sense, we have seen, a harm is a *wrongfully* set-back interest.

See also Dworkin, 'Devlin Was Right', p. 930 ('[T]he term ['harm'] itself is a normative one. Not every setback to a person's interests counts as harmful for the purposes of justifying coercion. Only those that are "wrongs" count').

50. *See* Feinberg, *Harm To Self*, pp. 172-73 (a person 'voluntarily' harms himself, but he 'consents' to being harmed or offended by others).
51. *See* Feinberg, *Harm To Self*, p.100 ('[T]he *Volenti* maxim is most plausibly interpreted as applying not simply to harms in the sense of set-back interests but only to harms in the sense of personal wrongs or injustices. A person may be harmed by what he consents to, in the sense that his interests may be set back, but he cannot be wronged'.).
52. Mill does not discuss whether the state can justly use the criminal law to punish incompetents, such as children, for harming themselves. In contrast, Feinberg baldly states, as if it were obvious, that it would be 'absurd' for the state to punish an incompetent person for the harms they inflict or allow to be inflicted upon themselves. *See* Feinberg, *Harm To Self*, p. 15. Feinberg is correct with respect to persons whose incompetence is such as to preclude them from being able either to assess their interests or to exercise criminal responsibility. But it is not at all absurd, or uncommon, for the state to punish persons for the harms they inflict or allow to be inflicted upon themselves when their incompetence is such as to preclude them from being able to assess their interests *but not* from being able to appreciate their criminal obligations. *See* text accompanying notes 20-24.
53. *See* Mill, *On Liberty*, p. 71 ('[T]here is a sphere of action in which society . . . has, if any, only an indirect interest: comprehending all of that portion of a person's life and conduct which . . . if it . . . affects others, only with their free, voluntary, and undeceived consent and participation'). *See* Feinberg, *Harm To Self*, pp. 13-15, 124, 126, 132.
54. *See* Feinberg, *Harm To Self*, pp. 113-14, 100, 188.
55. *See* text accompanying notes 10-13.
56. *See* Mill, *On Liberty*, pp. 69-70 ('It is proper to state that I forgo any advantage which could be derived to my argument from the idea of abstract right as a thing independent of utility. I regard utility as the ultimate appeal on all ethical questions; but it must be utility in the largest sense, grounded on the permanent interests of man as a progressive being'). This is not to say that Mill was agnostic about the ultimate goods that liberty maximizes. On the contrary, he argues that '[nothing] more or better can be said of any condition of human affairs than that it brings human beings themselves nearer to the best thing they can be'. *Id.* at 128. *See* also *id.* at 120 (the 'end' is 'well-being'). For the argument that Mill takes liberty as an end in itself rather than a means toward 'well-being', *see* Gertrude Himmelfarb, 'Editor's Introduction', in Mill, *On Liberty*, p. 30-33.
57. *Id.* at 143, 150-51.
58. *Id.* at 173.

59. *Id.* at 143. *See* also *id.* at 151 ('[T]he strongest of all the arguments against the interference of the public with purely personal conduct is that, when it does interfere, the odds are that it interferes wrongly and in the wrong place').
60. *See, e.g.*, Brock, *Life and Death*, pp. 30-33.
61. Feinberg, *Harm To Self*, p. 59 (original emphasis).
62. Feinberg, *Harm To Self*, pp. 59, 61.
63. Feinberg, *Harm To Self*, pp. 58-59.
64. Mill, *On Liberty*, p. 173.
65. *See* Feinberg, *Harm To Self*, pp. 25, 61 ('I cannot conceal my own preference for position (3)'). The only exception that Feinberg envisages—and one that Feinberg believes the harm principle can be reformulated to accommodate—is the justice of punishing persons who deliberately conceive and give birth to a child who possesses serious and permanent impairments that the parents know they could easily prevent. Feinberg, *Harmless Wrongdoing*, pp. 325-28.
66. For Mill's view that society has no rightful authority to enforce morality, except in so far as it implicitly does so in the course of preventing harms and offenses, *see* Mill, *On Liberty*, pp. 71, 149-62.
67. For Mill's view that the state has no business preventing a competent adult from killing himself, maiming himself, gambling, or using addictive or deleterious drugs, *see* Mill, *On Liberty*, pp. 147, 149, 165, 166. Anglo-American criminal law also punishes persons for engage in other kinds of conduct that Mill does not discuss but that Mill would presumably also immunize, *e.g.*, prostitution, bigamy, adult incest, and adultery.

Chapter Four

Prescriptive Consent: An Attitude or an Expression?

Legal consent comes in two distinct forms: prescriptive consent; and imputed consent. A given subject *S* 'prescriptively consents' to *x* when she actually chooses *x* in certain ways as that which she desires for herself under the circumstances—whether she does so subjectively in her mind under such conditions of competence, knowledge, freedom and motivation as the jurisdiction deems sufficient to satisfy *S*'s legitimate interests regarding *x*, or she does so objectively by expression under such conditions of communication and such apparent conditions of competence, knowledge, freedom and motivation as the jurisdiction deems sufficient to cause observers reasonably to believe that *S*'s legitimate interests in *x* are satisfied. And a subject *S* is 'imputed' to consent to *x* when she engages in conduct or possesses a state of mind from which the jurisdiction deems it appropriate to construct a fiction of her having prescriptively consented to *x*.

Yet we have refrained thus far from addressing what may constitute the most controversial question today regarding legal consent. The question goes to the basic nature of prescriptive consent on *S*'s part (and, hence, it goes to the basic nature of what fictions of imputed consent 'impute' to *S*). The question concerns the source of the power of prescriptive consent to negate criminal responsibility. What is it about *S*'s choosing *A*'s conduct that negates *A*'s criminal responsibility for subjecting *S* to *x*? Is it something that *S* subjectively experiences in her mind? And, if so, how can something that *S* subjectively experiences operate to negate the criminal responsibility of a third person, *A*, whose perceptions are confined to what he can observe? Or is it something that *S* objectively performs? What, in other words, lies at the core of prescriptive consent? Is it a subjective experience on *S*'s part of choosing conduct for herself? Or is it an objective act on *S*'s part of communicating her choice? Or both? Or either?

To be sure, it makes no practical difference which position a jurisdiction adopts in instances in which *S* acquiesces in *both* mind and expression or in *neither* mind nor expression. However, it does make a difference in the event that a person acquiesces in one respect but not the other. Such cases are rare but nevertheless real. In the case of *California* v. *Burnham*, a woman engaged in sexual intercourse in a subjective state of great physical fear and, yet, objectively expressed unfettered desire to her partners.[1] Rebecca Burnham was married to a man who severely beat her until she agreed, under a threat of further beating, to stand on the street in front of their house and do her best to seduce motorists into having sex with her while her husband photographed her. Rebecca's husband was tried and convicted of spousal rape on the ground that he caused Rebecca to have sexual intercourse by virtue of inducing in her a fear of physical injury that she both subjectively experienced and objectively expressed to him. Yet the motorists whom Rebecca seduced were not prosecuted for having sexual intercourse with her, because, although Rebecca subjectively feared that she would be beaten unless she tried to seduce the motorists, she masked her fear under feigned expressions of desire. The opposite situation, in which a person acquiesces in his or her mind but not in expression, can also occur. The complainant in *New York v. Bink*[2] was a young inmate in a New York city jail whom fellow inmate, Howard Bink, coerced into engaging in sodomy by threats of personal violence. The young inmate reported the incident to jail authorities who offered to isolate him from Bink, but he preferred instead to collaborate with jail authorities in catching Bink in the act. Accordingly, the young inmate returned to his cell, where—while being watched by jail authorities through a one-way mirror—he engaged in sodomy with Bink under a pretense of fear. Bink was tried and convicted of forcible sodomy. But the New York courts reversed Bink's conviction on the ground that, although the young inmate's objective behavior expressed fear of violence, the young inmate knew all along that he was being watched and, hence, subjectively, was not actually in fear of violence.

Cases like *Burnham* and *Bink* force jurisdictions to identify the source of a subject *S*'s power to exculpate by means of consent. Does it lie in *S*'s mind? Or in *S*'s expressive acts? Or in *both* *S*'s mind and *S*'s expressive acts? Or in *either* *S*'s mind *or* *S*'s expressive acts? Interestingly, jurisdictions differ over whether prescriptive consent consists of a subjective mental state of acquiescence on *S*'s part, an objective manifestation by her of such subjective acquiescence, or *either* a mental state of acquiescence *or* a manifestation of it. (Significantly, no jurisdiction regards it as consisting of *both*.) Thus, Canada takes the position that consent in rape cases is a 'state of mind' on a putative victim's part.[3] The State of Wisconsin takes the contrary position that consent to sexual contact consists of 'actual words or conduct indicating freely given agreement to have sexual intercourse or sexual contact'.[4] And Colorado appears to take the position that prescriptive consent to sexual intercourse consists of *either* a mental state of acquiescence or objective manifestation of it on *S*'s part; for Colorado provides that for purposes of sexual assault 'consent' means cooperation in act or attitude pursuant to an exercise of free will and with knowledge of the nature of the act.

More interesting still is the position that moral philosophers take on the question. All appear to take the view that there is a single correct answer to the question. One group of philosophers believes that because prescriptive consent should be regarded as an exercise of autonomy on *S*'s part, it ought to be defined to consist of a 'subjective mental state' that she 'wills', and not an expressive act that she performs.[5] Another group of commentators argues that because prescriptive consent negates what would otherwise be a crime on *A*'s part, it ought to be defined to consist of an objective act by *S* that *A* is capable of perceiving, and *not* a subjective mental state on *S*'s part.[6] Still another group embraces what Alan

Wertheimer calls the 'hybrid' view that prescriptive consent ought to be defined to consist of both a mental state that *S* subjectively experiences and an expressive act that she performs.[7]

I believe that this moral dispute among commentators is misconceived. There is no single, morally correct answer to the question whether prescriptive consent ought to be defined as a subjective mental state, or an objective expression, or both, or either. Instead, each of the aforementioned definitions of prescriptive consent can serve a legitimate function in criminal law, depending upon what a jurisdiction concludes is the purpose of punishment (except, perhaps, for 'hybrid' definitions that define prescriptive consent as *both* a mental state *and* an expression). The choice, therefore, is not between morally correct and morally incorrect definitions of prescriptive consent, but between legitimate and contrasting conceptions of criminal punishment. Jurisdictions that define prescriptive consent as an objective expression on *S*'s part are choosing to predicate an actor's punishment for offenses of non-consent solely upon the harms that he believes or ought to assume he is inflicting upon *S*, and not upon whether he succeeds in actually inflicting them. In turn, jurisdictions that define prescriptive consent as a subjective mental state on *S*'s part are choosing to predicate an actor's punishment for offenses of non-consent in part on whether *S* actually suffers the harms that the offenses are designed to prevent. Whichever decision a jurisdiction makes, it is embracing a tradition in criminal law that is both well-established and morally defensible.

This chapter is a functional analysis of the respective purposes that are served by defining prescriptive consent as a mental state of acquiescence, an expression of a mental state of acquiescence, or a combination thereof. It consists of three parts, each of which proceeds by reference to an argument or position advanced by Joel Feinberg. Part A examines the function performed by defining a person's prescriptive consent as an expressive act on her part, namely, that of protecting defendants from wrongful blame by defining a person's prescriptive consent in terms of objective conduct that defendants are capable of perceiving. Part B examines the function performed by defining a person's prescriptive consent as a subjective mental state on her part, *i.e.*, that of predicating criminal punishment upon the occurrence of actual harm to the person. Part C examines the *justice* of predicating criminal punishment upon the occurrence of actual harm to the person.

The Function Performed by Defining Prescriptive Consent as an Expressive Act

Joel Feinberg is a solid representative of those who favor framing prescriptive consent as an expressive act. Feinberg, relying upon earlier work by John Kleinig, states that, as between objective expressions of acquiescence and subjective mental states of acquiescence, only objective expressions possess the legal power to exculpate persons of crime:

> As John Kleinig points out, the word 'consent' sometimes refers to a mental state rather than an act, in which case it means passive and unspoken acquiescence, but Kleinig rightly insists on the much greater social importance of consent in the sense of a public act, 'in which a person explicitly facilitates the initiative of the other ... '. *Acts* of consent are especially important when our attention centers on the criminal liability of the actor *A* . . . and [upon] the exculpatory effect of his reasons for action. . . . When *A* acts so as to harm or endanger an interest of *S*'s, the consent which . . . transfers to *S* part of the responsibility for *A*'s act is ... an *act* of *S*'s, not merely a silent psychological state. . . . What kind of act then is 'active consent'? It is either a statement in language, or a communication by gesture or conduct understood by a symbolic convention to express consent.[8]

Feinberg advances two arguments in favor of privileging expressions of acquiescence over subjective acquiescence in criminal law, the first of which I will address here and the second of which I will address in sections B and C. Feinberg's first argument is that defining consent as an expressive act is necessary to protect defendants from a form of strict liability, namely, being held strictly liable for subjective feelings of non-acquiescence that their victims possess but do not express. Feinberg supports his argument by hypothesizing a case like *California* v. *Burnham*, that is, a case in which an actor has sexual intercourse with a woman who explicitly and seemingly voluntarily grants him permission and, yet, who grants him permission only because she is secretly and subjectively in fear that she will be beaten or killed by a third person of whom the actor is unaware unless she does her best to seduce the actor. To punish such an actor on the basis of the mental state of a woman of which he had no reason to be aware, Feinberg says, is to subject the actor to strict liability. Yet strict liability—that is, the punishment of actors who have 'no reason to know' that they are committing wrongful acts—'is so unjust that it can hardly ever be justified'.[9] To protect actors from such injustice, a subject's *S*'s prescriptive consent must be defined in terms of her acts rather than her subjective mental states. 'An actor *A*' Feinberg says, 'does not have any direct insight into *S*'s mental states, so the question of his responsibility must be settled by reference to the presence . . . of explicit authorization by *S*, not what *S*'s secret desires or hopes might have been.'[10]

Feinberg is right to be concerned about the injustice of strict liability in criminal law, because criminal law is inherently condemnatory in nature. One can hypothesize imaginary societies that impose criminal sanctions much in the way societies today impose taxes, namely, without expressing any resentment or indignation toward offenders.[11] But in reality, penal regimes are 'blaming' institutions.[12] They are institutions that, in the course of inflicting purposeful suffering upon actors whom they adjudge to have engaged in undesirable conduct, officially blame actors by expressing society's indignation or collective resentment of them for what they have done.[13] Resentment, in turn, is a 'reactive emotion', an emotion that people experience in reaction to conduct that they perceive to be motivated in certain ways.[14] It is the emotion people experience in perceiving an actor's conduct to be motivated by self-seeking malevolence toward, self-indulgent callousness of, or heedlessness regarding the legitimate interests of others.[15] To officially blame an actor for conduct that a jurisdiction endeavors to suppress by means of condemnation and purposeful suffering, then, is to hold the actor out to be blameworthy for the conduct—that is, to hold him out to have brought it about in conscious or inadvertent disregard of the legitimate interests of others.[16] To *justly* blame an actor, in turn, is to blame him only if he is, indeed, blameworthy—that is, only if he has indeed revealed himself to have been motivated by disregard of the legitimate interests of others.[17]

Consider again the passing motorists in *Burnham* who responded to Rebecca Burnham's invitations by having sexual intercourse with her. California could perhaps justly reproach the motorists for committing acts of fornication or adultery with Rebecca. But unless California believes that the motorists should have realized that Rebecca was terrorized into making a show of seduction, California cannot justly condemn them for the wrongful harm they unwittingly inflicted upon her by accepting sexual overtures that she was terrorized into making but secretly hoped they would refuse. For to condemn them would be to attribute to them guilty minds of malice, disinterest, or inadvertence toward Rebecca's sexual wishes that they did not possess. To be sure, to say that it is unjust for California to punish the motorists does not mean that the motorists should be lauded for what they did. Nor does it mean that they showed sensitivity to Rebecca Burnham's wishes. Nor does it mean that they did everything humanly possible to ascertain her true feelings. Nor does it mean that they owe her no financial compensation for her trauma. It merely means that unless California believes that the motorists had so little concern for Rebecca's wishes that they ought to suffer for it, California cannot rightly condemn them for the wrongful harm[18] they unwittingly inflicted upon her.

Anglo-American jurisdictions share Feinberg's strong aversion to strict liability in criminal law, particularly with respect to serious offenses.[19] Nevertheless, some commentators contend that American jurisdictions make an exception in rape cases by imposing strict liability for rape. Thus, Susan Estrich, using '*mens rea*' as a synonym for 'guilty mind', writes that 'American courts have altogether eschewed the *mens rea* or mistake inquiry as to consent, opting instead for a definition of the crime of rape that is so limited that it leaves little room for men to be mistaken, reasonably or unreasonably, as to consent.'[20] When examined in context, however, the judicial assertions of strict liability upon which Estrich and other commentators rely appear to be dicta.[21] That is, they are assertions that courts indeed make, but not in the context of convicting defendants who reasonably believed they were respecting their sexual partners' voluntary choices. Thus, some are assertions that courts make for reasons having nothing to do with whether a defendant had a guilty mind regarding his victim's failure to voluntarily choose sexual intercourse.[22] Others are assertions that courts make in the context of ruling that, in so far as the law requires that a defendant possess a guilty mind, the law does not require that a defendant *know* that sexual intercourse is without his victim's voluntary acquiescence—as opposed, say, to being either reckless or negligent regarding his victim's wishes.[23] Others are assertions that courts make in the context of ruling that, regardless of whether a defendant is entitled to jury instructions on *mens rea*, a defendant cannot rightly demand such instructions without having requested them at trial and without having introduced sufficient evidence at trial to support such instructions.[24] Still others are assertions that courts make in the course of holding that, with respect to a defendant who knew or should have known the *facts* of what he was doing, it is no defense that the defendant did not know that his conduct was against the *law*.[25] Massachusetts is frequently said to be a jurisdiction that punishes rape on a strictly liable basis, but its judicial assertions to that effect are also distinguishable.[26]

The cases that have probably come the closest to imposing strict liability for offenses of non-consent are statutory-rape cases in which actors are convicted of having sexual intercourse with underage girls without regard to how old the actors reasonably believed the girls to be.[27] Some of the cases can be explained, if not justified, on the ground that prosecutors used statutory-rape charges to pursue what they believed were instances of unlawful coercion, *i.e.*, instances in which defendants may have reasonably believed that girls were overage but, nonetheless, knew or should have known that the girls were submitting to sexual intercourse due to force or fear.[28] Other cases can be justified on the ground that, although defendants may have reasonably believed that girls were older than a certain minimum age, *e.g.*, that girls were fully ten years old within a jurisdiction in which it is an offense to have sexual intercourse with a girl who is 'under ten', the defendants, nonetheless, knew or should have known that their actions inflicted the real harm that the state was trying to suppress by using calendar ages as a proxy, *i.e.*, the harm of having sexual intercourse with prepubescent girls.[29] Nevertheless, cases may exist in which defendants have been convicted of statutory rape despite the fact that they reasonably believed their partners to be adults of the age of majority of 18 years or more.[30] If so, those cases both depart from and subvert the fundamental principle upon which Feinberg implicitly relies in his first argument, namely, that persons ought not be punished for serious offenses on a strictly liable basis.[31]

Feinberg is also right that defining prescriptive consent as an expressive act suffices to protect actors from being held strictly liable for their putative victims' mental states. Expressive acts are interpersonal in nature; and accordingly, defining *S*'s prescriptive consent to be an expressive act on her part serves the function of basing *A*'s criminal responsibility upon information about *S*'s wishes that is readily available to *A*—namely, interpersonal conduct by *S* that leads reasonable observers in *A*'s position to believe that *S* in her mind voluntarily chooses the conduct to which he is subjecting her. Nevertheless, it is a fallacy to conclude that, because defining prescriptive consent as an expressive act is *sufficient* to protect actors from strict liability for offenses of non-consent, it is also *necessary* to protect them from strict liability. Indeed, jurisdictions commonly employ an alternative that is at least as effective as Feinberg's in protecting defendants from wrongful blame. Consider what Canada does in the context of rape. Canada, having defined rape to be an offense of non-consent, defines 'consent' to be a mental state on a putative victim's part.[32] Yet Canada protects an actor against the injustice of strict liability by means of supplemental rules of *mens rea*—rules to the effect that an actor is guilty of rape only if he intends, knows, is recklessly unaware, or is willfully blind to the fact that his putative victim is not voluntarily acquiescing to sexual intercourse in her mind.[33] Indeed, this practice of defining consent in rape cases as a mental state on a subject's part while requiring *mens rea* on the actor's part is, if anything, a more precise measure of an actor's guilty mind than Feinberg's. It is more precise because it rightly inculpates a set of malicious actors whom Feinberg's proposal would exonerate, namely, actors who satisfy two criteria: (1) they have sexual intercourse with subjects whose communicative conduct reasonably but falsely conveys that the subjects are voluntarily acquiescing; and (2) they act with the *intent* that the sexual intercourse be *without* the subjects' voluntary acquiescence. Feinberg would exculpate such actors because Feinberg defines consent by reference to communicative conduct that reasonably conveys that a subject is voluntarily acquiescing in her mind, and, hence, Feinberg would rule that the subject 'consents'. In contrast, Canada would punish such actors, because the actors fulfill both of the two requirements for rape: the actors perform the bad acts of having sexual intercourse with women without the women's consent ('consent' in Canada being a state of mind of voluntary acquiescence); and the actors possess guilty minds of acting with the intent to have sexual intercourse with women without the women's consent.

If this analysis is sound, it means that Feinberg is correct in most respects but mistaken in one. He is correct that strict liability in criminal law is presumptively unjust; correct that defining consent to be an expressive act prevents defendants from being held strictly liable for their victims' secret mental states; and correct that defining consent to be a mental state does not itself prevent defendants from being held strictly liable. But he is mistaken in assuming that jurisdictions that define consent to be a mental state cannot do anything *else* to protect defendants from strict liability. They can, and they invariably do. They define consent to be a mental state of acquiescence; and, yet like Canada, they provide that a defendant who subjects a person to conduct without her voluntarily acquiescing in her mind is not guilty unless he has a guilty mind regarding her subjective non-acquiescence. Feinberg favors defining consent as an expressive act because of the function it performs in protecting defendants from strict liability. Yet the same function can be performed as well, if not better, by requiring, as a condition of criminal liability, that actors possess guilty minds of recklessness or negligence regarding their victims' subjective non-acquiescence.

The Function Performed by Defining Prescriptive Consent as a Mental State: The Case of Rape

Feinberg does not discuss the alternative of requiring *mens rea* regarding a victim's mental state, and, hence, we do not know whether he would agree that it protects blameless actors at least as effectively as defining consent to be an expressive act. However, we do know from what Feinberg says in the *second* of his two arguments that he has an independent objection to statutes like Canada's that define consent to be mental state. Feinberg's second argument is the converse of the first. The second argument is not that defining consent to be a mental state will cause blameless actors to be convicted, but that defining consent to be a mental state will cause certain *blameworthy* actors to be *exonerated*—namely, actors who engage in conduct with persons whose expressive acts lead the actors reasonably to believe that they are *not* voluntarily acquiescing in their minds but who, fortunately and secretly, *are* voluntarily acquiescing in secret in their minds. Feinberg believes that such actors ought to be punished on the same basis as actors whose subjects' expressive acts accurately reflect their mental states, because he believes that the fortuity of selecting a putative victim who secretly acquiesces in her mind has no bearing upon an actor's culpability. To illustrate the point, Feinberg imagines a case much like *New York v. Bink*, that is, a case of an actor who has objective reasons to believe that his putative victim *is not* voluntarily acquiescing to his conduct and, yet, nevertheless proceeds, only to discover afterwards that his putative victim *did* voluntarily acquiesce in his mind. If such an actor (who clearly possesses no defense based upon his putative victim's expressive acts) is, nonetheless, exculpated on the basis of what his putative victim secretly felt, Feinberg says, the actor will be exculpated for reasons that are 'quite irrelevant to [his] responsibility'. 'If *A* deliberately rapes *S*', Feinberg writes, 'it is no defense either in a court of law or in "the court of heaven" that *S* "secretly consented to what he did, though she gave no sign."'[34]

Feinberg's second argument raises several issues, including his invocation of the 'court of heaven' to assert that it is fundamentally *unjust* to exculpate defendants on the basis of their putative victims' secret mental states. To lay a foundation for discussing what Feinberg says about the injustice of departing from the 'court of heaven', I shall postpone discussing it until section C and shall focus here on Feinberg's statement that exculpating defendants on the basis of their putative victims' mental states is unheard of in 'courts of law'. We will see that contrary to Feinberg, there is indeed a practice of defining consent as a state of mind, and the practice exists because defining consent as mental state serves an important function: it serves the function of predicating offenses of non-consent on the occurrence of actual harm to victims, because the harms of offenses of non-consent are a function of their mental states.

The Practice of Defining Consent as a Mental State

Feinberg may be right about the court of heaven, but he is mistaken about courts of law. Jurisdictions do define consent to be a mental state, and they do acquit defendants of offenses of non-consent on the basis of such mental states. Indeed, we have already seen that the New York courts are a counterexample to Feinberg's assertion that it is 'not a defense' in 'courts of law' that a putative victim 'secretly consented'. The defendant in *New York v. Bink*, it will be recalled, engaged in an act of sodomy with a fellow prisoner who he believed was submitting out of fear but who, in reality, was secretly cooperating with prison authorities to entrap the defendant. The State of New York prosecuted Bink for rape under a statute that made it an offense to 'force' a person to submit to sodomy. Bink argued that he did not use force because, unbeknownst to him, his putative victim was secretly and voluntarily acquiescing and, thus, 'consenting' to everything he did. The New York courts agreed with Bink and ruled that what his putative victim secretly desired was, indeed, a defense to the crime of forcible sodomy.[35]

The courts of New York are not alone in treating a putative victim's mental state as a defense. Though it is often unclear how jurisdictions mean to define consent,[36] some jurisdictions clearly define it as a mental state on a putative victim's part. The *Model Penal Code* takes the position that the inquiry into consent in rape cases 'is an inquiry into the victim's subjective state of mind'.[37] Canada explicitly states that 'for purposes of the *actus reus* [of the offence of sexual assault], . . . "consent" means that the complainant in her mind wanted the sexual touching to take place':[38]

> Confusion has arisen from time to time on the meaning of consent as an element of the actus reus of sexual assault. Some of this confusion has been caused by the word 'consent' itself. A number of commentators have observed that the notion of consent connotes active behaviour. While this may be true in the general use of the word, for the purposes of determining the absence of consent as an element of the actus reus, the actual state of mind of the complainant is determinative.[39]

Like Canada, California explicitly holds that a putative victim's 'consent' and a defendant's lack of a guilty mind regarding her non-consent are distinct and independent defenses to rape. 'Consent', it says, is a defense to the *actus reus* of rape and obtains when a putative victim voluntarily acquiesces to sexual intercourse in her mind ('When asserting the defense of consent, the defendant focuses on the victim's state of mind alone'). A lack of 'wrongful intent' regarding a victim's non-consent is a defense of *mens rea*, and it obtains when a victim's conduct is such as to cause a defendant reasonably 'to assume' that she is voluntarily acquiescing to sexual intercourse in her mind even if she is not.[40] Other jurisdictions implicitly do what Canada and California do explicitly.[41] Estrich, in her influential analysis of the law of rape, asserts that criminal defendants may defend themselves against charges of rape by showing that their putative victims possessed acquiescing states of mind. The 'disputed issue' in rape trials, she says, is 'her [the complainant's] state of mind'. 'Her intent . . . is disputed; and . . . her state of mind is key'.[42] Stephen Schulhofer, in his authoritative study *Unwanted Sex*, says the same thing.[43]

This is not to say that every jurisdiction defines consent to be a mental state. Some jurisdictions do precisely the converse: they explicitly state that consent is an expressive act. The penal codes of Minnesota, Wisconsin, and the District of Columbia, for example, define consent in rape cases to consist of 'words or overt actions'; the Washington penal code defines it to consist of 'actual words or conduct'; and the courts of New Jersey have held that 'any act of sexual penetration engaged in by [a] defendant without the affirmative and freely-given permission of the victim to the specific act of penetration constitutes the offense of sexual assault', regardless of the victim's 'state of mind'.[44] In addition, jurisdictions that do not explicitly define consent to be an expressive act nonetheless provide that certain kinds of expression *negate* the defense of consent. Thus, after stating that consent is a defense to rape, Utah declares that sexual intercourse shall be deemed to be 'without consent' if a victim 'expresses lack of consent through words or conduct', presumably by saying 'no'.[45] Nevertheless, the tendency to define consent in terms of mental states remains strong, even in jurisdictions that purport to define it as an expressive act. Consider, for example, the contrast between the terms with which Washington and the terms with which the District of Columbia define consent in rape cases and the way their respective courts have interpreted those definitions. The Washington statute defines 'consent' to consist of 'words or overt actions', while the District of Columbia statute defines 'consent' to consist of 'actual words or conduct'. Yet the Washington and District of Columbia courts have both held that it is a defense to rape to show that putative victims possessed acquiescing states of mind—thereby implying, at the very least, that 'consent' must *also* consist of a mental state.[46]

The Function Performed by Defining Consent as a Mental State

We have seen, contrary to what Feinberg says, that the practice of defining consent to be a mental state is commonplace in 'courts of law'. It is commonplace, moreover, because it serves an important function that cannot be performed by defining consent to be an expressive act. To ascertain what that function is, we must inquire into the relationship that exists between mental states of acquiescence, on the one hand, and the harms that offenses of non-consent inflict upon their victims, on the other. And to do that, we must examine the harms that offenses of non-consent inflict upon their victims.

The harms that offenses of non-consent inflict upon their victims obviously vary in kind and in degree. The harms of larceny differ from those of trespass, and the harms of physical assault differ from those of rape. Now it might be possible to abstract from all offenses of non-consent a single, generic harm they all share. But the resulting formulation is likely to be too generalized to be revealing. To provide context for the inquiry, therefore, we shall proceed by reference to a single offense of non-consent and ask, 'What is the wrongful harm from which the law of rape seeks to protect its victims?' Unfortunately, the answer to even the latter question is harder than one would think, because it depends upon whether the question is confined to wrongful harms associated with subjecting a person to sexual intercourse without her *prescriptive* consent, or whether it also extends to wrongful harms associated with subjecting a person to sexual intercourse without her *imputed* consent. If the question extends to sexual intercourse without imputed consent, it becomes impossible to identify any single harm from which the law of rape seeks to protect victims, because in creating fictions of consent, the law treats persons *as if* they suffered no harms from sexual intercourse in order to protect them from *other* harms that it fears would ensue if it did not create the fiction. If, however, the inquiry is confined to sexual intercourse without prescriptive consent—as we shall confine it for the remainder of this chapter—it is, indeed, possible to identify the harms that laws of rape seek to prevent.[47]

Criminal acts of rape inflict two kinds of wrongful harm that the law seeks to prevent. One of the wrongful harms is *dignitary*, rather than material, in nature. Most criminal acts inflict dignitary harms, at least most criminal acts that require *mens rea*.[48] Dignitary harms are the indignities that an actor *A* inflicts upon *S* by manifesting that he has so little regard for *S* that he is ready to abridge *S*'s legitimate interests in order to aggrandize himself. As Jeffrie Murphy observes:

> One reason we so deeply resent moral injuries done to us is not simply that they hurt us in some tangible or sensible way: it is because such injuries are also messages—symbolic communications. They are ways a wrongdoer has of saying to us, 'I count but you do not', 'I can use you for my purposes', or 'I am here up high and you are there down below'. Intentional wrongdoing *insults* us and attempts (sometimes successfully) to degrade us—and thus it involves a kind of injury that is not merely tangible and sensible. It is a moral injury, and we care about such injuries.[49]

The magnitude of dignitary injuries varies, depending upon the species of disregard an actor manifests. Thus, the indignity that *A* inflicts upon *S* by manifesting a *purpose* or *desire* to kill her is greater than the indignity he inflicts by manifesting a *willingness* to kill her; the indignity he inflicts by manifesting *indifference* as to her life is greater than the indignity he inflicts by manifesting *inadvertence* to her life. The magnitude of dignitary harms is also a function of the nature of legitimate interest on *S*'s part that *A* manifests himself as ready to abridge. Thus, because people possess greater legitimate interests in life than in property, an actor who manifests an intent to kill *S* inflicts a greater indignity upon *S* than an actor who manifests an intent to destroy her property. However, because the magnitude of dignitary harms is a function of the readiness of a person to act with *mens rea*, it does not depend upon whether *A* commits a completed crime or attempts to commit a completed crime. The indignity harm that *A* inflicts upon *S* by attempting and failing to kill her is as great as the indignity he inflicts by attempting and succeeding in killing her.

The dignitary harm of rape is the harm that an actor *A* inflicts upon a subject *S* by acting in disregard of her sexual integrity, that is, by proceeding to have sexual intercourse without his having reason to believe that she is subjectively choosing it as that which she desires for herself under conditions of choice to which she is legally entitled. Like all dignitary harms, the magnitude of the dignitary harm of rape is a function of the extent of the actor's disregard of a victim's interests—an intent to violate a person's sexual integrity being worse than recklessness regarding her sexual integrity, and recklessness being worse than negligence. Moreover, like all dignitary harms, the magnitude of the dignitary harm of rape is the same whether an actor with a *mens rea* of rape *succeeds* in having sexual intercourse with *S* without his having reason to believe that *S* is subjectively and voluntarily choosing it for herself, or *fails* in his attempt to do so. For regardless of how *S* may secretly feel about having sexual intercourse with *A*, she suffers an indignity when *A* proceeds to have sexual intercourse without his having reason to believe that *S* is subjectively and voluntarily choosing it for herself—the indignity of *A*'s having manifested contempt toward *S*'s sexual integrity and, hence, toward *S* herself. Consider, for example, the young inmate in *Bink* who engaged in sodomy with fellow inmate Bink under the pretense of submitting out of fear. Although the young inmate secretly initiated the encounter in order to entrap Bink, he would have the right to be indignant about Bink's *willingness* to prey upon his fear in order to subject him to sodomy.

Nevertheless, dignitary harms are not the primary harms that criminal laws seek to prevent. Dignitary harms are derivative of primary, material harms that victims suffer when criminal laws are not observed. Dignitary harms are derivative of the harms an actor *A* inflicts upon *S* by actually abridging her legitimate interests (as opposed to merely manifesting a *willingness* to abridge her legitimate interests). Moreover, because primary harms consist of material harms that victims actually suffer, they are harms that actors do not inflict by merely *attempting* to commit crimes. Primary harms are harms that actors inflict only by *succeeding* in committing crimes and, then, only by succeeding in committing crimes that by their terms are predicated on the occurrence of material harms. The primary harm of murder, for example, is not the indignity *A* inflicts upon *S* by manifesting a willingness to kill her but the more serious material harm he inflicts by actually depriving her of life. The material harm that *A* inflicts by depriving *S* of life is 'primary', and the dignitary harm secondary, because the magnitude of the indignity *A* inflicts upon *S* by manifesting a willingness to deprive *S* of life is a function of the magnitude of the more serious loss *S* suffers in being deprived of life itself.

The primary harm that laws of rape seek to prevent is not the indignity *A* inflicts upon *S* by manifesting a willingness to have sexual intercourse with *S* without her having subjectively and voluntarily chosen it for herself, but the more serious material harm *A* inflicts by actually *having* such intercourse with *S*—that is, sexual intercourse that she does not subjectively choose for herself under conditions of choice to which she is entitled. To illustrate the difference between the primary and derivative harms of rape, suppose that a police officer becomes aware that crimes are about to be committed in cases identical to the two we discussed earlier: *Burnham*, in which a woman subjectively feared that her husband would severely beat her unless she did her best to seduce unwitting motorists into having sexual intercourse with her; and *Bink*, in which a prison inmate, whom a fellow inmate had previously terrorized into an act of sodomy, arranged with prison authorities to ensnare the bully by submitting to an act of sodomy with him under the pretense of being terrorized into it, while knowing all along that prison authorities had them under protective surveillance. A police officer would be professionally obliged to intervene early in a case like *Burnham* to prevent sexual intercourse from occurring, despite the fact that the motorists were not inflicting a dignitary harm upon the woman of disregarding what she expressed her voluntary desires to be. For if an officer waited until intercourse occurred in a case like *Burnham*, the victim would suffer the very primary harm from which the law seeks to protect her, namely, the harm of being subjected to sexual intercourse without having subjectively chosen it for herself under appropriate conditions of freedom. In contrast, an investigating officer in a case like *Bink* might well delay making an arrest until sexual intercourse has occurred. For even though delaying arrest permits a bully to inflict the dignitary harm of disregarding the undercover inmate's expressions of terror, delay does not cause the undercover inmate to suffer the primary harm from which the law seeks to protect him, namely, the harm of being subjected to sodomy that he has not subjectively chosen for himself under appropriate conditions of freedom.

This is not to say that the wrongful harms of rape are necessarily identical by every measure. Rapes can inflict harms that differ from one another on various dimensions, depending upon whether victims are physically beaten until they submit to sexual intercourse, physically frightened into intercourse without actually being beaten, coerced into intercourse without being physically threatened, deceived into intercourse without being physically threatened or coerced, or seduced while being underage but without otherwise being threatened, coerced, or deceived. And jurisdictions may rightly decide to grade the severity of penalties for rape in accord with such differences in harm. But despite their differences, all rapes possess one wrongful harm in common, namely, the wrongful harm of subjecting a person to sexual intercourse without her having subjectively and voluntarily chosen it for herself.

To say that the wrongful harm of rape can be *negated* by a subjective experience is not to say, as some commentators do,[50] that the wrongful harm of rape *consists* of subjective experience on a victim's part. It does not. The primary harm of rape is not a subjective experience of fear or abhorrence, because crimes of rape include acts of sexual intercourse by means of fraud during which victims experience neither fear nor abhorrence (*e.g.*, women who are defrauded into sexual intercourse by means of sham marriages). Nor is it a subjective experience of regret on the victim's part, because crimes of rape include acts of sexual intercourse with minors who often experience no regret at all. Nor, indeed, is it a subjective experience of *any* kind, because crimes of rape include acts of sexual intercourse with persons who are unconscious at the time and who continue to remain unconscious for the duration of their lives.[51] Rather, the primary harm that the law of rape seeks to prevent is the material harm an actor *A* inflicts upon a subject *S* by subjecting *S* to a genital invasion for *A*'s own sexual gratification without *S*'s having subjectively chosen it for herself under the conditions of choice to which she is lawfully entitled.[52] The primary harm of rape is a function of a putative victim's mental state: if a putative victim subjectively and voluntarily chooses an act of sexual intercourse, she does not suffer the primary harm of rape; if she does not subjectively and voluntarily choose an act of sexual intercourse, she does suffer the primary harm of rape. As the *Model Penal Code* puts it with respect to all offenses of non-consent generally, prescriptive consent is a defense because it is a 'state of mind'[53] that 'precludes the infliction of the harm or evil sought to be prevented by the law defining the offense'.[54]

Now that we have identified the relationship between mental states of acquiescence and harm, we can identify the function that is performed by defining consent as a mental state. Defining consent as a mental state on a person's part enables jurisdictions to do something that they cannot do by defining consent as an expressive act. It enables them to grade the gravity of criminal conduct based upon whether actors actually inflict the primary harms that offenses of non-consent seek to prevent. Specifically, it enables jurisdictions to distinguish between *completed* offenses of non-consent and *attempts* to commit such offenses based upon whether or not actors actually cause victims to suffer the harm of being subjected to conduct that they do not subjectively and voluntarily choose for themselves. As among actors who all manifest a readiness to subject persons to conduct without the latter having subjectively and voluntarily chosen it, an actor *A* is guilty of a completed offense of non-consent if he actually harms *S* by actually subjecting her to conduct *x* without her having so chosen it for herself; otherwise, *A* is guilty of nothing more than an attempt to commit the offense.

It is commonly said that because prescriptive consent brings about important changes in a person's legal relationship to others, her prescriptive consent cannot possibly consist of 'private or subjective facts'[55] on her part. As Brett puts it, 'there is simply no way that a purely subjective fact concerning [a person's] attitude can . . . make any change in [her] normative relations to [other] persons.'[56] We now see the fallacy in that view. A person's private and subjective feelings can affect her legal relationship to others, because her feelings determine whether she suffers the primary harm that an offense of non-consent seeks to prevent. And whether a person suffers such harms can determine, in turn, whether others are guilty of the offense.

The Justice of Predicating Criminal Punishment Upon the Occurrence of Actual Harm

We have reached three conclusions thus far. We have seen that defining consent as an expressive act on *S*'s part performs the function of protecting an actor *A* from being unjustly punished on the basis of secret mental states on the part of *S* to which he has no access, and that it does so by predicating *A*'s criminal responsibility instead upon his willingness to proceed in the face of objective evidence that *S* does not subjectively and voluntarily acquiesce to his conduct. We have also seen that the very same function can be performed equally well, if not better, in jurisdictions that define consent as a mental state on *S*'s part, by their requiring as a condition of punishment that A possess *mens rea* regarding *S* non-consent. Finally, we have seen that defining consent as a mental state performs a function that cannot be achieved in any other way, namely, the function of predicating *A*'s criminal responsibility upon his actually bringing about the primary harm that offenses of non-consent seek to prevent.

What remains is to address the *justice* in predicating offenses of non-consent upon the function performed by defining consent as a mental state–that is, the justice in basing an actor's criminal responsibility in part upon whether he actually brings about the primary harm that such offenses seek to prevent. Feinberg, it will be recalled, addresses the issue in his second argument. Feinberg argues that it is unjust to acquit defendants like Howard Bink simply because they happen by chance to select putative victims who secretly and voluntarily acquiesce in their minds; and Feinberg expresses the injustice by imagining how an actor like Bink would be treated in the 'court of heaven': 'If *A* deliberately rapes *S*', he says, 'it is no defense . . . in the court of heaven that *S* secretly consented to what he did, though she gave no sign.'

Feinberg is in good company in thinking that it is unjust to exculpate actors like Bink based upon their putative victims' states of mind. Susan Estrich takes the same position in rape cases, though for different reasons. Estrich argues that defining the offense of rape in terms of *S*'s state of mind has two adverse effects on victims, most of whom are women: (1) it puts women themselves 'on trial', and when trials end in defendants being acquitted, it stigmatizes women by 'signal[ing] that the prosecution has failed to prove [a woman's] sexual violation—"her innocence"'; and (2) it degrades women by enabling defendants to introduce evidence of their prior sexual conduct.[57]

Estrich is a useful counterpoint to Feinberg—both because Estrich has different objections to defining consent in the law of rape in terms of a victim's mental state and, more importantly, because Estrich proposes a different solution. Feinberg and Estrich both want to prevent courts from inquiring into whether complainants actually possessed acquiescent states of mind about sexual intercourse, but they would prevent it in different ways. Feinberg would prevent it by defining consent to be an expressive act on a complainant's part. In contrast, because Estrich takes it for granted that consent is a mental state for purposes of rape, she proposes instead to eliminate non-consent as an element of the offense. The offense of rape, it will be recalled, typically consists of three underlying elements, regardless of the technical terms in which rape statutes are drafted: (1) that the defendant have sexual intercourse with the complainant; (2) that the defendant act with one of several attitudes toward the complainant, *i.e.,* purpose or knowledge that she is not subjectively and voluntarily choosing the sexual intercourse for herself, or, alternatively, recklessness or negligence as to whether she subjectively and voluntarily chooses it; (3) that the complainant did not legally consent to the sexual intercourse. Estrich, in taking it for granted that 'consent' is a mental state for purposes of element 3, proposes to eliminate the third element altogether by proposing that the offense of rape be reformulated to consist of elements 1 and 2 alone. She proposes, that is, that defendants be guilty of rape if (1) they have sexual intercourse with complainants, and (2) they do so while possessed of a guilty mind of a certain sort—regardless of how the complainants themselves may subjectively feel about the intercourse. As she puts it, the offense of rape should consist of 'having sexual intercourse with a woman under circumstances in which one believes, or should reasonably conclude, that the woman is not properly acquiescing in her mind.'[58]

Estrich's proposal is significant for two reasons. First of all, Estrich's proposal does not expand the criminal responsibility of actors as much as she assumes it does. She assumes that if jurisdictions eliminated one of three existing elements of rape, they could punish defendants who now escape punishment. But she is mistaken, at least with respect to jurisdictions that possess criminal attempt statutes like the *Model Penal Code*'s. Actors who now engage in elements 1 and 2—that is, actors like Howard Bink—do not escape punishment in jurisdictions that possess attempt statutes like the *Model Penal Code*'s.[59] Nor in most cases are they punished any less than actors who engage in elements 1 to 3.[60] Rather, such actors remain fully responsible for the offense of attempted rape, and in most cases they are subject to being punished at the very same level as actors who engage in elements 1 to 3. The *Model Penal Code* provision on attempt, like Estrich's proposal, is designed to punish actors on the basis of the wrongful harms that actors believe or should believe they are inflicting as opposed to the wrongful harms that they succeed in inflicting.[61] Indeed, Estrich's proposal is functionally equivalent to replacing the existing offense of rape with the *Model Penal Code* offense of attempted rape, with two additional changes: Estrich would change the name of the new offense from 'attempted rape' to 'rape' with respect to actors who actually engage in sexual intercourse with complainants; and she would punish *all* such actors (as opposed to punishing most of them) at the same level at which actors are presently punished for rape.

Estrich's proposal also casts significant light on Feinberg's proposal that consent be defined as an expressive act. For although Estrich's and Feinberg's proposals differ in form, they, too, are nearly identical in *function*. They differ in form, because they differ with respect to which of the three elements of rape they would eliminate. Estrich, because she takes it for granted that 'consent' is a mental state for purposes of element 3, would eliminate element 3. Feinberg, by virtue of defining 'consent' as an expressive act for purposes of element 3, would render element 2 largely superfluous. He would render it superfluous because when 'consent' is defined as an expressive act under element 3, the presence or absence of such communications of subjective and voluntary acquiescence on *S*'s part nearly always determines whether an actor *A* does or does not possess a guilty mind for purposes of element 2. Thus, by failing to express subjective and voluntary acquiescence in sexual intercourse, *S* leaves *A* in a position in which *A* either knows or should realize that *S* is not subjectively and voluntarily acquiescing; conversely, by expressing such acquiescence, *S* negates the possibility that *A* knows about or is reckless or negligent regarding *S*'s non-acquiescence, thereby precluding *A* from having a guilty mind regarding *S*'s non-acquiescence (unless *A* is the rare actor who, despite all the evidence that *S* is subjectively and voluntarily acquiescing, nevertheless acts for the purpose of having sexual intercourse without *S*'s subjective and voluntary acquiescence). The consequence is that with the exception of such rare actors, Feinberg's proposal to define consent as an expressive act is functionally identical to Estrich's proposal to define consent as a mental state but to eliminate non-consent as an element of rape; for both proposals result in convicting actors of rape who, as Estrich puts it, 'hav[e] sexual intercourse with a woman under circumstances in which one believes, or should reasonably conclude, that the woman is not properly acquiescing in her mind.'

In light of these relationships, let us consider Estrich's argument that inquiring into women's mental states in rape cases imposes unjustified burdens on women. Let us also assume, for purposes of argument, that Estrich is right when she says that inquiring into such mental states imposes burdens on women. The problem with Estrich's proposal to eliminate consent as an element of rape is that it is not clear that her proposal would do anything to reduce those burdens. Estrich's proposal, like the *Model Penal Code* provision on attempted rape, with which it shares many similarities, allows a defendant to argue that he reasonably *believed* that a complainant voluntarily acquiesced in her mind. Yet defenses of reasonable *belief* may have substantially the same effect on complainants as a state-of-mind defense. Consider Estrich's first argument, *i.e.*, that the state-of-mind defense stigmatizes complainants by putting them 'on trial' as to whether they subjectively acquiesced to sexual intercourse. In saying that the state-of-mind defense put complainants 'on trial', Estrich does not mean that the state-of-mind defense produces an explicit verdict as to whether a complainant had an acquiescing mind. Estrich knows that a rape trial can result in only two basic verdicts, both of which are directed solely toward the defendant, namely, 'guilty' or 'not guilty'.[62] Rather, Estrich means that by making the woman's state of mind a salient issue in rape cases, the conventional law of rape enables a jury to base its verdict (and, hence, appear to base its verdict) upon an implicit finding as to whether the woman possessed an acquiescing mind. Yet Estrich's proposal permits essentially the same thing to occur because her proposal also permits defendants to focus attention upon the woman's state of mind. Under Estrich's proposal, evidence of a woman's state of mind ceases to be relevant as direct evidence of an element of the offense, but it continues to be relevant as circumstantial evidence of the defendant's *belief* as to the woman's state of mind. For the measure of whether the defense's evidence is relevant is whether the evidence, if true, renders the defendant's version of events more probable than his version would be without it. Evidence that a woman actually possessed an acquiescing state of mind is relevant to a defendant's assertion that he reasonably believed that she possessed an acquiescing state of mind, because the evidence, if true, makes the defendant's version of events more probable than it would be without the evidence. Therefore, as long as a defendant's beliefs regarding a woman's state of mind remain a defense, as they do under Estrich's proposal and under the *Model Penal Code* provision on attempt, trials will continue to focus upon, and make implicit judgments about, the complainant's state of mind.

The same is also true of Estrich's further argument that the state-of-mind defense degrades complainants by enabling defendants to inquire into the complainants' prior sexual conduct. Jurisdictions differ widely as to when prior sexual conduct evidence is admissible in rape cases, just as courts and commentators differ as to whether rules that exclude such evidence are constitutional.[63] In so far as evidence of a complainant's prior sexual conduct is admissible in rape cases, however, it is almost always admitted as circumstantial evidence rather than direct evidence. That is to say, when a woman's prior sexual conduct comes into evidence in a rape trial, it is rarely because a woman's prior sexual conduct (or lack thereof) is an explicit element of the offense of 'rape',[64] but rather because evidence of prior sexual conduct allegedly alters the probability that an element of the offense is true. Although Estrich's proposal is designed to reduce the admissibility of prior sexual-conduct evidence, it cannot affect the extent to which a woman's prior sexual conduct is currently admissible as circumstantial evidence of elements *other* than her state of mind, *e.g.*, as evidence of a complainant's 'motive' for falsely testifying that sexual intercourse occurred in the first place. Repealing the state-of-mind defense would, indeed, eliminate the use of a woman's prior sexual conduct as circumstantial evidence that she possessed an acquiescing state of mind. However, as long as a defendant is allowed to defend himself on the ground that he reasonably believed a woman to possess an acquiescing state of mind, repealing the state-of-mind defense may not reduce the overall admission of prior-sexual-conduct evidence, because prior sexual conduct of which a defendant is aware is as probative of what he *believed* a woman's state of mind to be as it is of what her state of mind actually *was*.

Now let us assume, contrary to what I have just contended, that Estrich is correct that the state-of-mind defense imposes burdens on complainants that they would not suffer under an expressive-act defense. Even if she is correct, it is not obvious that those unique burdens are unjustified. Whether the burdens are justified depends upon the strength of Feinberg's second argument. As we now know, however, the gist of Feinberg's second argument is not that defining consent as a mental state exculpates defendants like Howard Bink altogether; for defendants like Bink are guilty and fully punishable for attempted rape under attempt statutes like the *Model Penal Code*'s. The gist of Feinberg's argument is that because defining consent as a mental state renders defendants like Bink responsible for attempted rape rather than rape, it unfairly results in defendants like Bink being punished *less* than rapists simply because they had the luck to select victims who secretly acquiesced in their minds. The question, therefore, is whether the criminal law is justified in drawing that distinction—that is, whether it is justified in distinguishing punishments for 'completed' crimes of non-consent (*i.e.*, crimes that are predicated upon the actual occurrence of the primary harms that the criminal laws against them seek to prevent) from punishments for 'attempted' crimes of non-consent (*i.e.*, crimes that are predicated upon an actor's willingness or readiness to inflict such wrongful harms, rather than upon his success in bringing the wrongful harms about).

Feinberg may be right that the 'court of heaven' would not draw that distinction. Like Feinberg, St. Thomas Aquinas believed that God bases his punishment of sinners, not on any harm they succeed in inflicting, but on their willingness to turn away from God.[65] But divine justice and worldly justice are not necessarily the same. The ideal attributes of divine justice may be inappropriate standards for assessing the mundane justice that human beings render to themselves.[66] Mundane courts of law may be justified in grading the punishment of persons who demonstrate a readiness to cause wrongful harm on the basis of whether the persons actually bring about the wrongful harms they intend. Indeed, the criminal law from the time of Plato has distinguished 'murder' from 'attempted murder' on precisely that basis.[67] What distinguishes murder from attempted murder is not that a murderer necessarily possesses a guiltier state of mind or that he necessarily demonstrates a greater willingness to act upon it. The difference often lies in events that are largely outside an actor's control, namely, what philosophers call his 'moral luck' in whether the wrongful harm of homicide actually occurs.[68] Within jurisdictions that provide a state-of-mind defense, the happenstance of *S*'s subjectively acquiescing possesses the same significance for offenses of non-consent as the happenstance of a victim's surviving a homicide attempt possesses for offenses of homicide: they both operate to reduce a person's punishment from the level of suffering that actors with their motivation deserve to the reduced level of a criminal attempt. Conversely, the happenstance of *S*'s *not* subjectively acquiescing possesses the same significance for offenses of non-consent as the death of an intended homicide victim possesses for offenses of homicide: they both deny a person any reduction in punishment from the level of suffering that actors with their motivation deserve. Accordingly, whatever justifies decisions to grade the punishment of homicides based upon whether or not death occurs also justifies grading the punishment of crimes of non-consent based upon whether or not putative victims properly acquiesce in their minds.

Commentators since Plato have disputed whether there is a justification for such reductions in sentence based upon happenstance. Like Feinberg, some commentators contend that courts of law ought to make a greater effort to mimic the 'court of heaven', by looking solely to the willingness of offenders to commit wrongful harm and not to the contingencies of results.[69] In contrast, other commentators defend the use of resulting wrongful harm to grade offenses.[70] Plato himself sided with those who defended the practice of basing penalties on resulting wrongful harm. And he did so, not because he thought that criminal courts were *incapable* of mimicking what Feinberg calls the 'court of heaven', and not because he thought actors who fail are *less deserving* of punishment than those who succeed, but for quite the opposite reason. Plato believed that a society's refusal to grant any reduction at all to actors who fail is sacrilegious as well as immoral—not because the actors deserve reductions in sentence—but because the refusal signals something inappropriate about society's attitude toward *its* undeserved but good fortune. The refusal signals that the society is unaware of its own good fortune, for it signals that the society feels as much resentment over failed crimes (for which it ought, instead, to feel and signal a measure of relief) as over successful crimes (for which it is right to feel and signal full righteous resentment).[71] If Plato and other commentators are right that it is not unjust to base criminal penalties on whether defendants actually succeed in inflicting the wrongful harms that they know or should know they are risking, then it is not unjust to distinguish completed crimes of non-consent from attempted crimes of non-consent based upon whether or not putative victims voluntarily acquiesce in their minds. For putative victims who voluntarily acquiesce in their minds do not suffer the primary harms from which offenses of non-consent seek to protect them.

Before we conclude, however, we should consider several further arguments against defining prescriptive consent as a state of mind. We have focused thus far upon Feinberg's arguments that, because mental states on *S*'s part are subjective, they are too private to affect *A*'s criminal responsibility toward *S*. David Bryden and Heidi Malm present two additional arguments. Bryden argues that because *S*'s subjective attitudes toward *x* can be equivocal, they can be too indeterminate to govern *A*'s criminal responsibility:

> In legal discourse, one either consents or doesn't consent; equivocation is not a legal category. But consent, as a legal construct, [cannot be] synonymous with subjective desire, which is often equivocal. One may desire something in one sense but not in another. For example, one with no physical desire for sex may nevertheless accede to a companion's wishes in order to preserve a relationship, to make a loved one happy, to avoid a scene, or because one is weary of the ordeal of refusal and recrimination. On any given occasion, some combination of these ulterior motives may or may not outweigh one's purely sexual feelings, which of course may also be mixed. Conversely, one's affirmative sexual feelings may be outweighed by negative, ulterior feelings ('he's married', 'it's too soon', etc.). . . . Given the many possible combinations of mixed desires, the law's yes/no answer to the question, 'Did she consent to have sex?' is, as a description of subjective desire, grossly simplistic: Yes/no answers do not take account of mixed or half-conscious feelings. No purely subjective approach to consent can solve this problem.[72]

Bryden is right that people often have equivocal feelings about sexual intercourse of the kind he describes. But it is a fallacy to think that because feelings are equivocal in that way, they are also *indeterminate*. There is nothing indeterminate about the feelings Bryden describes. The people whom Bryden describes all know exactly how they feel. Thus, they know exactly what they wish to do under the circumstances that actually obtain (*e.g.*, that their companions are 'married', or that they cannot abstain from sex without triggering a 'scene'). They also know exactly what they would wish to do if circumstances were different (*e.g.*, if they could abstain from sex without triggering a scene; or if their companions were not married). The equivocation that Bryden describes is not a product of their having indeterminate feelings. It is a product of assessing their feelings under equivocal standards. It is a product of ambivalence about whether to ask them, 'What are your preferences under the circumstances that actually obtain?' or 'What would your preferences be if circumstances were different?' To be sure, if the criminal law were similarly ambivalent about which question to ask, the law could not make determinate judgments about subjective consent. However, the criminal law is not ambivalent about the standards that govern subjective consent. As we have seen, a person factually consents to conduct in her mind if she subjectively chooses the conduct under the circumstances she believes exist. As we will see in Chapter 5, she prescriptively consents to conduct if she factually consents under conditions of competence, knowledge, freedom, and motivation that the jurisdiction deems sufficient to enable her to take responsibility for her choice for purposes of the criminal statute at issue. As measured by those standards, the feelings Bryden describes are not equivocal. They are a basis upon which the law can make determinate judgments as to whether people do or do not subjectively consent.

Malm, in turn, argues that *S*'s subjective attitudes toward *x* are too ephemeral to govern *A*'s criminal responsibility for his conduct toward *S*.[73] The problem with consent as a mental state, Malm says, is that 'mental state of willingness may come and go. I may change my mind intentionally or I may vacillate about whether I am willing to accept something.'[74] Malm is right, of course, that people often subjectively vacillate about the choices they face. Indeed, they can experience vacillation of two distinct kinds. Sometimes their vacillation takes the form of complete *indecisiveness*, that is, a conflict of feelings so profound as to prevent them from coming to any decision at all, even momentarily, regarding their preferences under the circumstances. At other times their vacillation takes the form of a *change of mind*, that is, a decision, promptly followed by a change of mind and a contrary decision. However, there is nothing in either form of vacillation that precludes a jurisdiction from defining prescriptive consent as a mental state. Consider indecisiveness. Indecisiveness precludes a person from *possessing* a mental state of acquiescence, but it does not preclude a jurisdiction from *requiring* that a person possess such a mental state in order to 'consent'. Thus, imagine that because of paralyzing panic or indecisiveness, *S* simply cannot decide whether to submit to *x* as the best she can do for herself under the circumstances or to try to prevent *x*. *S*'s indecisiveness precludes her from choosing *x* as that which she desires for herself under the circumstances; and, hence, it precludes her from possessing a mental state of acquiescence. But *S*'s indecisiveness does not prevent a jurisdiction from deciding a person must possess such a mental state in order to consent. *S*'s indecisiveness simply means that she does not consent within a jurisdiction that requires such a mental state. Now consider a person who is able to make choices for herself but changes her mind by deciding, first, to resist *x* and, then, to go along with *x* and, then again, to resist *x* again. Changes of mind do not preclude a jurisdiction from defining consent as a mental state. They simply focus attention on the state of mind *S* possesses at the moment *x* commences. If she resolves at that moment to resist *x*, she does not subjectively consent to x; if she resolves at that moment to go along with *x*, she does subjectively consent to it; and if she changes her mind while *x* is transpiring, the jurisdiction must decide whether persons in her position may terminate their consent to *x* once *x* commences but before it concludes. To be sure, ephemeral changes of mind on *S*'s part may leave an actor, *A*, in the dark as to *S*'s feelings. But as we have seen, jurisdictions that define consent as a mental state of acquiescence can fully protect *A* against unanticipated mental states of non-acquiescence on *S*'s part, by requiring as a condition of *A*'s criminal responsibility that he possess *mens rea* regarding a victim's mental state of non-acquiescence.

Conclusion

Moral philosophers disagree about the nature of prescriptive consent in criminal law. Specifically, they disagree about whether *S*'s prescriptive consent to conduct *x* ought to be defined as a mental state on *S*'s part, as an expressive act on *S*'s part, or a 'hybrid' of both. (Interestingly, none of them appears to take the position that *S*'s prescriptive consent consists of *either* a mental state *or* an expressive act on *S*'s part). Moreover, they believe that only one of these positions is morally correct, and that commentators and jurisdictions that take contrary positions are mistaken. Thus, they all implicitly disavow jurisdictions, like Colorado, that define consent to consist of either a mental state or an expressive act on *S*'s part.

I believe that the entire controversy is misconceived. There is no exclusively correct way to define prescriptive consent in criminal law. With one exception, all of the aforementioned definitions of prescriptive consent perform legitimate functions in criminal law, depending upon the respective purposes of that jurisdictions choose to adopt. The choice between defining consent as a mental state or an expressive act (or as *either* a mental state *or* an expressive act) is not a choice between morally correct and morally incorrect positions; it is a choice between competing conceptions of criminal punishment. The sole exception is the position that Feinberg and several others adopt (*i.e.*, that consent consists of *both* a mental state *and* an expressive act on *S*'s part), for that serves no legitimate function at all.

Defining consent as an expressive act performs an important function, though it is not the only device that exists that is capable of performing it. Defining consent as an expressive act performs the function of protecting a blameless actor from being criminally punished on the basis of his victim's secret mental state, by basing an actor's criminal responsibility on his victim's objective communicative conduct. Indeed, an actor ought to be judged on the basis of information to which he has fair access, because to judge an actor solely on the basis of another's subjective feelings is a form of strict liability. Within jurisdictions that define consent as a mental state, however, an alternative device exists that can perform the very same function equally as well as, if not better than, defining consent as an expressive act. It is a supplemental device that most commentators[75] and jurisdictions invoke in the course of defining consent as a mental state, *i.e.*, the device of requiring as an additional condition of criminal responsibility that an actor possess *mens rea* regarding a complainant's failure to subjectively and voluntarily acquiesce in his conduct. Thus, a jurisdiction can require that an actor is guilty of acting without his victim's subjective and voluntary acquiescence only if he acted with purpose, knowledge, recklessness or negligence regarding his victim's lack of acquiescence. *Mens rea* requirements of the latter kind protect blameless actors just as effectively as the device of defining consent as an expressive act. In addition, *mens rea* requirements possess the benefit of enabling a jurisdiction to inculpate certain actors who elude punishment within jurisdictions that define consent as an expressive act—actors whom I call 'purposeful assailants'—namely, actors who reasonably infer from their putative victims' expressions that the latter are subjectively and voluntarily acquiescing to conduct but who, nevertheless, act with the malicious purpose that the conduct be without the victims' subjective and voluntary acquiescence.

Defining consent as a mental state also serves a legitimate function, though it is a function that jurisdictions and commentators may or may not choose to embrace depending upon their views of criminal punishment. Within jurisdictions that embrace it, it is a function that can only be performed by defining consent as a mental state on a person's part. Defining consent as a mental state performs the function of basing an actor's criminal responsibility for an offense of non-consent on his actually imposing the primary harm that offenses of non-consent seek to prevent, *i.e.*, the harm of subjecting persons to conduct that they do not subjectively choose for themselves under conditions of choice to which they are legally entitled. To be sure, defining consent as a mental state does not perform the separate important function that is performed by defining it as an expressive act. To perform the function of protecting a blameless actor from being criminally punished on the basis of his victim's secret mental states, a jurisdiction must adopt a supplemental rule. Two such rules exist. One, as previously mentioned, requires as an additional condition of criminal responsibility that actors also possess *mens rea*, whether in the form of purpose, knowledge, recklessness, or negligence, regarding their victims' lack of subjective and voluntary acquiescence. The alternative is what Colorado does in its rape statute: provide that an actor has a defense of consent if his putative victim either voluntarily acquiesces in her mind or expresses such acquiescence, thereby punishing an actor only in the event that he acts act in the absence of both a mental state and expressive act of voluntary acquiescence on his victim's part. The two rules are functionally equivalent to one another, except that 'purposeful assailants' escape punishment under statutes like Colorado's that define consent as consisting of either mental states or expressive acts of acquiescence, while they do not escape punishment under rules of *mens rea*.

The principal objection to defining consent as a mental state is that it provides a defense to actors like Howard Bink merely because they have the undeserved good fortune to select victims who secretly acquiesce in their minds. Yet contrary to what some commentators assume,[76] defining consent as a mental state does not allow defendants like Bink to escape punishment altogether. Rather, it grades the level of their punishment in accord with the wrongful harms they inflict, at least in jurisdictions that also possess attempt statutes like the *Model Penal Code*'s. Defendants can inflict two kinds of wrongful harms upon victims of offenses of non-consent: the primary harm of subjecting them to conduct without their having subjectively and voluntarily chosen it for themselves; and the lesser, dignitary harm of manifesting a *readiness* or *willingness* to subject them to that primary harm. Defendants like Bink do not inflict primary harms upon their victims; and, hence, they are not guilty of committing offenses of non-consent in jurisdictions that define consent to be a mental state. But they do inflict lesser, dignitary harms, and, hence, they are guilty of offenses that seek to prevent such harms, namely, offenses of attempt. Therefore, the essential objection to defining consent as a mental state is not that it enables defendants like Bink to elude punishment altogether, but that it often results in their being punished *less* than they would be punished if they had inflicted the primary harms they were ready to inflict. Whether such lesser sentences are justified depends upon whether it is appropriate for jurisdictions to grade criminal offenses based upon whether or not feared harms actually occur. Some commentators and jurisdictions believe it is not justified.

Others believe it is, indeed, justified, including every jurisdiction that distinguishes between murder and attempted murder based upon whether the person whom a murderous actor shoots actually dies from his wounds.

It follows, therefore, that jurisdictions can legitimately define prescriptive consent in any of three ways: as an expressive act; as a mental state; or, as Colorado does, as either an expressive act or a mental state. However, some commentators argue that jurisdictions ought to do what no jurisdiction thus far appears to do, namely, to combine elements of the first two definitions in the form of 'hybrid' definitions of prescriptive consent. Commentators propose two sorts of hybrids: a true hybrid and a modified hybrid. A true hybrid is a simple combination of consent as a mental state and consent as an expressive act. According to its proponents, a person ought to be regarded as prescriptively consenting to an actor's conduct if and only if two things obtain: (1) she performs an expressive act that objectively conveys to the actor that she is subjectively and voluntarily acquiescing in his conduct; and (2) she actually experiences the subjective and voluntary acquiescence that she is objectively expresses. The two elements are both necessary, it is said, because element 1 is necessary to protect blameless actors from being punished on the basis of their victims' secret feelings, and element 2 is necessary to ensure that a person's acquiescence is genuine and voluntary from her standpoint.[77]

Elements 1 and 2 do, indeed, perform the two respective functions ascribed to them (though, as we have seen, element 1's function can be performed equally well by requiring that actors possess *mens rea*). But it is a fallacy to assume that because elements 1 and 2 each perform useful functions, they can, therefore, be combined to produce a useful definition of prescriptive consent. On the contrary, because the true hybrid treats 1 and 2 as necessary elements of prescriptive consent, it treats each element as insufficient by itself to constitute prescriptive consent, and, hence, it prevents each element from performing its respective function. Thus, by treating element 1 as insufficient to constitute prescriptive consent, the true hybrid prevents element 1 from performing the function of protecting defendants who lack *mens rea*, because the true hybrid denies a defense of consent to *A* when *A* reasonably infers from *S*'s expressive conduct that *S* is voluntarily acquiescing in her mind, whenever *S* for some reason does not voluntarily acquiesces in her mind. By the same token, by treating element 2 as insufficient to constitute prescriptive consent, the true hybrid prevents element 2 from performing the function of predicating punishment upon *S*'s suffering the primary harm that the offense seeks to prevent, because the true hybrid denies a defense of consent to *A* when *S* subjectively and voluntarily acquiesces (and, hence, does not suffer the primary harm that the offense seeks to prevent), whenever *S* does not engage in conduct that expresses such acquiescence. Of course, the injustice of punishing blameless actors can be prevented if the true hybrid's definition of consent as consisting of elements 1 and 2 is supplemented with a rule that actors not be punished for acting without consent if they lack *mens rea*. Yet to supplement a true hybrid definition of consent with requirements of *mens rea* is to render element 2 of the definition superfluous. For in a jurisdiction that supplements a true hybrid definition of consent with requirements of *mens rea*, an actor's criminal responsibility will depend entirely upon whether his putative victim *S* satisfies element 1 by expressing voluntary acquiescence of a kind that would lead a reasonable person in the actor's position to believe that she is acquiescing in her mind, and not at all upon whether or not *S* also satisfies element 2 by actually possessing such an acquiescent state of mind. For regardless of whether *S* actually possesses the state of mind required by element 2, an actor in such a jurisdiction will be guilty whenever *S* fails to satisfy element 1, because he will then have acted both without *S*'s 'consent' and *with mens rea*; and regardless of whether *S* fails to possess the state of mind required by element 2, an actor in such a jurisdiction will be innocent whenever *S* satisfies element 1, because, although he will then have acted without *S*'s 'consent', he will also have acted *without mens rea*.

Most commentators who advocate defining consent as an expressive act argue in favor of what I call a 'modified hybrid'. Thus, Feinberg and others argue that *S* ought to be regarded as prescriptively consenting to *A*'s conduct *x* if and only if two things obtain: (1) she performs an expressive act that objectively conveys to *A* that she is subjectively and voluntarily acquiescing in his conduct; and (2) her *expressive act* is subjectively voluntary on her part.[78] In most cases, of course, the subjective voluntariness or involuntariness with which *S* acts to express acquiescence to *x* will mirror the subjective voluntariness or involuntariness with which *S* chooses *x* in her mind. To the extent it does, a modified hybrid is identical to a true hybrid, and it suffers from the same principal defect: unless a modified hybrid is supplemented with requirements of *mens rea*, it threatens to convict actors who lack guilty minds; and yet if a modified hybrid is supplemented with requirements of *mens rea*, its requirement that expressive acts be voluntary becomes superfluous.

Cases can arise, however, in which *S* voluntarily choose to express acquiescence to *x* without necessarily voluntarily choosing *x* in her mind. In that event, modified hybrids and true hybrids produce different results. Thus, a person 'Jane' may voluntarily express acquiescence to *x* while secretly hoping and expecting an actor *A* to regard her expressed acquiescence as a joke.[79] Or Jane may voluntarily express acquiescence to *x* and then, moments before *x* occurs, change her mind without being able to express her change of mind. Or Jane may voluntarily express acquiescence to *x* and then, before *x* occurs, subjectively come to fear that she will be killed if she resists *A*. In each such case, Jane prescriptively consents for purposes of modified hybrids but not for purposes of true hybrids, because although she voluntarily expresses acquiescence, she does not voluntarily acquiesce in her mind. To the extent the two definitions of consent differ, the modified hybrid possesses an disadvantage that true hybrids do not possess. True hybrids exclude from the class of prescriptively 'consenting' persons all individuals who suffer the very primary harms that offenses of non-consent seek to prevent (though, in doing so, they also exclude from the class of prescriptively 'consenting' persons some individuals who do not suffer those harms). In contrast, modified hybrids treat as 'consenting' individuals who do not voluntarily acquiesce in their minds and, hence, *do* suffer the very primary harms that offenses of non-consent seek to prevent. Thus, modified hybrids leave courts in the position of having to say of individuals like Jane, who suffer the very harms from which the state wishes to protect them, 'They fully consented in the eyes of the law.'

Notes

1. For Victor Burnham's appeal, resulting in a partial reversal of his conviction, *see* California v. Burnham, 176 Cal. App. 3d 1134, 222 Cal. Rptr. 630 (1985). For an account of the trial, *see The San Diego Union-Tribune*, 30 January 1986, p. B-17.
2. New York v. Bink, 84 App. Div. 2d 607, 44 N.Y.S.2d 237 (1981). The New York statute speaks of 'force' rather than 'non-consent', but the New York courts have construed 'consent' to be a defense to 'force'. *See* New York v Smolen, 166 App. Div. 2d 248, 564 N.Y.S.2d 105 (1990), *appeal denied*, 77 N.Y.2d 844 (1991).
3. *See* Regina v. Olugboja, [1982] 1 Q.B. 320, 331 (consent is a 'state of mind').
4. Washington Rev. Code § 9A.44.010 (2000). *See* also the statutes cited in Chapter 2, note 5.
5. *See* Hurd, 'The Moral Magic of Consent', pp. 124-25:

   > By consenting to another's touch, one puts that person at liberty to do what it was antecedently obligatory of her not to do. . . . To have the ability to create and dispel [such] rights and duties is what it means to be an autonomous moral agent. . . . To recognize this capacity is one way to give meaning to the historical philosophical claim that persons are free inasmuch as they will their own moral laws.
   >
   > * * *
   >
   > If autonomy resides in the ability to will the alteration of moral rights and duties, and if consent is normatively significantly precisely because it constitutes an expression of autonomy, then it must be the case that to consent is to exercise the will. That is, it must be the case that consent constitutes a subjective mental state.

   See also Alexander, 'The Moral Magic of Consent (II)', p. 165 ('I agree entirely with Professor Hurd that consent, to be an expression of autonomy, must be the exercise of will and, thus, a subjective mental state').
6. *See, e.g.*, Archard, *Sexual Consent*, p. 4 ('Consent is an act rather than a state of mind. Consent is something I do rather than think or feel'); Brett, 'Sexual Offenses and Consent', p. 73 ('Consent is not a "self-perceived attitude;" it is not an attitude at all. To consent is to *act* in a way that has conventional significance in communicating permission'); Feinberg, *Harm To Self*, p. 173; Kleinig, 'The Ethics of Consent', pp. 93-96; Joan, 'Force, Consent, and the Reasonable Woman', p. 242 and n.33 ('Consent is performative, it is something that an agent does. . . . Consent has sometimes been construed in the "attitudinal" sense of having an attitude of approval toward something. Even if this is a true sense of consent, it is not what we would want to say generates rights, that is, grants permission, to do what is otherwise impermissible'); Malm, 'The Ontological Status of Consent', p. 150; Wertheimer, 'What Is Consent? And Is It Important?', p. 568:

   > [W]e begin by reminding ourselves that we are interested in consent because it renders it permissible for A to engage in sexual relations with B, and we ask 'what could do that?' From that perspective, a suitably qualified - that is, moralized - performative view is, I think, closest to the truth. It is hard to *see* how B's mental state - by itself - can render it permissible for A to proceed. The fact that B actually

desires sexual relations with A or would like A to proceed does not authorize A to have sexual relations with B if A proceeds before B has indicated her agreement.

7. Alan Wertheimer coins the phrase 'hybrid view' for the view that 'a mental state and an act token are necessary and jointly sufficient for consent'). Wertheimer, 'What Is Consent? And Is It Important?', p. 566. For exponents of hybrid views, *see*, *e.g.*, Sherwin, 'Infelicitous Sex', p. 209-10:

   Consent is a social act . . . . At the same time, it is an act designed for the expression of a subjective choice. If. . .the process of choice is constrained, the act of consent is 'infelicitous'.
8. Feinberg, *Harm To Self*, pp. 173, 176 (quoting Kleinig, 'The Ethics of Consent', p. 93. Feinberg uses the letters '*A*' and 'B' to refer to actors and subjects of consent, respectively. In contrast, I have used the letters '*A*' and '*S*' throughout this work to refer to actors and subjects of consent, respectively. Accordingly, to avoid confusion, I have redacted the original passages from Feinberg's book, *Harm To Self*, to conform to my usage.
9. Feinberg, *Harm To Self*, p. 176.
10. Feinberg, *Harm To Self*, p. 173 (emphasis added).
11. Thus, Barbara Wooten imagines a state that removes all condemnation and reproof from its administration of criminal law. *See* Wooten, *Crime and the Criminal Law*, p. 51; Wooten, Social Science and Social Pathology, ch. 8.
12. *See* Schopp, 'Justification Defenses and Just Convictions', pp. 1258-62.
13. *See* Duff, *Trials and Punishments*, pp. 39-73. For an analysis of the concept of 'blame', *see* Cohen, 'Distinctions Among Blame Concepts'.
14. *See* Strawson, 'Freedom and Resentment', pp. 62-72.
15. Some students of reactive emotions draw a distinction between a victim *V*'s 'resentment' of *A* (which they maintain is a nonmoral reactive emotion that *V* feels in response to *A*'s callous or malevolent attitudes toward *V* himself) and a bystander *B*'s 'indignation' toward *A* (which they maintain is a moral reactive emotion that *B* feels in response to *A*'s callous or malevolent attitudes toward *V*). *See* Wallace, *Responsibility And The Moral Sentiments*, pp. 18-23. For a commentator who draws a different distinction between 'resentment' and 'indignation', *see* Hampton, 'Forgiveness, Resentment, and Hatred', pp. 35, 54-60.
16. *See* Wallace, *Responsibility*, pp. 66, 74-83.
17. *See* Scanlon, *What We Owe Each Other*, pp. 103-07, 158-60, 271-72.
18. Rebecca's husband threatened to beat her unless she *tried* to seduce motorists into having sexual intercourse with her. What the motorists unwittingly did was a wrongful harm to her, because although she was terrorized into appearing to want to have sexual intercourse with them, she secretly hoped they would refuse. The situation would have been different if Rebecca's husband had threatened to beat her unless she *succeeded* in having sexual intercourse with her. For in that event, she would have wanted the motorists to have sexual intercourse with her. And by doing what she wanted, the motorists would not have inflicted a wrongful harm on her, because being neither responsible for her dilemma nor capable of relieving her of it, they would have done what she believed was best for her under the circumstances. *See* Chapter 5, note 26 and accompanying text.
19. A fundamental organizing principle of the *Model Penal Code* is that strict liability in criminal law is unjust. *See Model Penal Code* §§ 2.01, 2.05; Simons, 'Criminal Law: When is Strict Liability Just?', p. 1136 ('[T]he basic *Model Penal Code* position [is] that strict liability should be excluded from criminal punishment . . . '.). The U.S. Supreme

Court, in its interpretation of both the Constitution and federal criminal statutes, applies a strong presumption against strict liability in criminal law. *See* Singer, 'The Resurgence of *Mens Rea*: III - The Rise and Fall of Strict Criminal Liability', pp. 397-403 (1989); Wiley', Not Guilty By Reason of Blamelessness'.

20. Estrich, 'Rape', p. 1096. In contrast, however, other commentators disagree with Estrich over whether rape is criminalized on a strict-liability basis. Catharine MacKinnon contends, contrary to Estrich, that 'rape, like many other crimes, requires that the accused possess a criminal mind (*mens rea*) for his acts to be criminal. The man's mental state refers to what he actually understood at the time or to what a reasonable man should have understood under the circumstances'). MacKinnon, *Toward a Feminist Theory of the State*, p. 180. Stephen Schulhofer takes a similar position. Schulhofer, *Unwanted Sex*, p. 238 ('the great majority [of American courts] now accept' the rule that a defendant is guilty of rape only if he was 'negligen[t]' regarding the woman's wishes).
21. *See* Hubin and Haely, 'Rape and the Reasonable Man', p. 122-23 n.15:

    Douglas Husak has pointed out to us that some jurisdictions—Massachusetts, for example—apparently construe rape as a strict liability crime. However, it is not clear that this view would be maintained were it tested by actual cases having the facts we describe (hypothetically) below [namely, cases involving actors who are entirely in good faith as to their sexual partner's desires].

    See also Kinports, 'Rape and Force, p. 782.
22. *See, e.g.*, Michigan v. Hammack, 63 Mich. App. 87, 234 N.W.2d 415 (1975) (the assertion made in the context of a ruling that, where a defendant pleads insanity, the testimony of witnesses as to the defendant's behavior immediately prior to the event in question is relevant to his state of mind).
23. *See, e.g.*, Sherry v. Massachusetts, 386 Mass. 682, 693, 437 N.E.2d 224, 233 (1982) ('Whether a reasonable good faith mistake of fact as to the fact of consent is a defense to the crime of rape has never, to our knowledge, been decided in this Commonwealth. We need not reach the issue whether a reasonable and honest mistake to the fact of consent would be a defense, for even if we assume it to be so, the defendants . . . requested instruction would have required the jury to "find beyond a reasonable doubt that the accused had actual knowledge of [the victim's] lack of consent"'); Maine v. Reed, 479 A.2d 1291 (1984).
24. *See, e.g.*, Kansas v. Cantrell, 234 Kan. 426, 673 P.2d 1147 (1983) (assertion made in the context of a case in which the defendant failed to request a jury instruction on *mens rea*); Grant v. Massachusetts, 391 Mass. 645, 464 N.E.2d 33 (1984) (assertion made in the context of a case in which there was no factual basis for an instruction that a defendant is guilty only if he reasonably believed that his victim was not voluntary acquiescing); Massachusetts v. Williams, 439 A.2d 765, 769 (1982) (assertion made in the context of a case in which—according to Massachusetts v. Fischer, 721 A.2d 1111, 1114-18 (1998), appeal dismissed, 745 A.2d 1214 (2000)—a factual basis for an instruction on reasonable belief was lacking). For a thorough discussion of whether a court in a rape case is obliged to instruct a jury on the defendant's *mens rea* in the absence of a factual basis in the record for the defendant's having made a reasonable mistake of fact, *see* California v. Williams, 4 Cal. 4th 354, 841 P.2d 961 (1992).
25. Kansas v. Cantrell, 234 Kan. 426, 673 P.2d 1147 (1983) (assertion made in the context of a case in which the defendant was mistaken not about the facts but about the law defining rape). Gerald Leonard argues that an actor's mistake as to a victim's consent is a mistake of *law* rather than a mistake of *fact*—and, hence, non-exculpatory in

jurisdictions that regard mistakes of law as non-exculpatory—whenever the mistake is one that a jurisdiction regards as 'unreasonable'. Leonard, 'Rape, Murder, and Formalism', pp. 567-75. However, that seems incorrect. Suppose that an actor, *A*, is a legal authority as to what constitutes an unreasonable mistake as to a woman's consent in a particular jurisdiction—indeed, that he is the very author of the jurisdiction's statute defining 'unreasonable mistakes'. Suppose further that *A* is guilty of making such a mistake himself as to whether a particular woman with whom he is having sexual intercourse voluntarily desires it. It is fallacious to say that *A*'s mistake is a mistake of law rather than fact. For although *A* does, indeed, regard himself as innocent at the time he acts, the ***reason*** he regards himself as innocent is not that he is mistaken about the content of the legal norms of the jurisdiction that he himself drafted but that he so misperceives what the woman actually desires that he does not realize that he is violating those norms.

26. Joshua Dressler and Catharine MacKinnon both cite ***Massachusetts*** v. ***Ascolillo***, 405 Mass. 456, 541 N.E.2d 570 (1989), and ***Massachusetts*** v. ***Simcock***, 31 Mass. App. Ct. 184, 575 N.E.2d 1137 (1991), as instances of strict liability. ***See*** Dressler, 'Where We Have Been', p. 432, MacKinnon, *Sex Equality: Rape Law*, p. 832. However, *Ascolillo* was a case in which there was no evidence to support the defendant's claim that he reasonably believed that the complainant was legally consenting; and *Simcock* was a case in which, if the jury accepted the complainant's account as to the force the defendants used against her (as the jury did), there was no evidence to support an instruction that they reasonably believed otherwise.
27. ***See*** Campbell, 'Annotation'.
28. Fritsch, 'The Law That Made Amy Fisher a Victim', *The New York Times*, 18 April 1993, section 4, p. 2, col.1 ('[P]rosecutors say [that] they sometimes add a charge of statutory rape when they believe an underage girl was really forcibly raped, in case the use of force cannot be proved').
29. This is the argument that Justice Bramwell makes in ***Regina v. Prince***, 2 L.R.-Cr. Cas. Res. 154, 174-75 (1875) to justify holding a defendant culpable for abducting a girl who was 'under 16' though he reasonably believed she was 18. It is an argument that Meir Dan-Cohen further develops, persuasively, in 'Decision Rules and Conduct Rules: On Acoustic Separation in Criminal Law', p. 657, by arguing that society's real concerns in statutory rape can be defined only in morally lumpy terms (*e.g.*, 'infants', young children, 'children', 'young adolescents', 'adolescents'), and not in fine-grained and, therefore, morally artificial markers of '10 years old', '11 years old').

The reason a defendant who has intercourse with a ten-year-old cannot defend himself by claiming that he reasonably believed her to be eleven is not that his mistake could not have been reasonable, but rather that it is irrelevant: regardless of his belief about the victim's age, he still must have perceived himself to be having intercourse with an infant. In our culture, the prohibition of intercourse with children is a nearly indisputable moral norm that the laws defining the offense of statutory rape embody and seek to preserve from violation.

Kenneth Simons proposes two additional arguments in support of punishing actors on an aggravated level for having sexual intercourse with girls whom they reasonably but mistakenly believe to be older than a proscribed age, *e.g.*, the proscribed age, say, of 'under 10', within a jurisdiction that makes it a lesser offense to have sexual intercourse with a girl under 16: (1) an actor who reasonably but mistakenly believes that a girl is 11 years old is, by his own admission, at fault for being willing to commit the lesser wrong of having sexual intercourse with a girl under 16; (2) even if an actor reasonably believes that the victim is 10 or older, he displays substantial fault merely by risking that the victim might be under 10. Simons, 'Criminal Law: When Is Strict Liability Just?', pp. 1092-93. Notice that both of Simons' arguments assume, contrary to Dan-Cohen, that having sexual intercourse with a girl of 9 is truly a greater moral wrong than having sexual intercourse with a girl of 10 or 11. However, if that is so, then an actor who reasonably believes a girl is 10 or 11 should be punished at the level of the blameworthiness he actually possessed, namely, for *attempting* to have sexual intercourse with a girl under 16, rather than for the greater moral wrong that he had no reason to believe he was committing. To be sure, Simons asserts in his second argument that such an actor can be justly blamed for his fault in taking a 'risk' that the girl was under 10. However, if Simons means that actors are at fault any time they engage in conduct that presents a mathematically provable risk of wrongful harm, Simons is mistaken, because all conduct involves mathematical risks of wrongful harm. If Simons means that the law conclusively presumes fault on the part of an actor who takes a mathematically provable risk that a girl he reasonably believes to be 11 will turn out to be under 10, Simons is simply stating a rule of strict liability, not justifying it. Finally, if Simons means that, despite an actor's reasonable efforts to ensure that he is not having intercourse with a girl under 10, he is nonetheless morally at fault for any mathematically provable risk that a girl who reasonably appears to be 11 will turn out to be under 10, Simons must explain how an actor can be morally at fault for doing his best to ensure that, as between two moral wrongs, he not inflicting the greater moral wrong.

30. *See, e.g.*, Rhode Island v. Yanez, 716 A.2d 759 (1998), criticized in Bejma, 'Protective Cruelty'. But compare Idaho v. Dennard, 102 Idaho 824, 642 P.2d 61 (1982) (after the jury found a defendant guilty for having sexual intercourse with a girl who was under 18, the judge set aside the verdict on the grounds that (I) the girl 'had the attributes and appearance of a 25 year old', and (ii) the jury had accompanied its verdict with the statement that it had 'arrive[d] at this decision based strictly on the law' and without reference to 'extenuating circumstances' that it 'did not have the opportunity to apply under the law').

31. *See* Dressler, 'Where We Have Been', p. 432 ('There is simply no more principled basis for dispensing with the *mens rea* requirement in rape cases than there is in regard to any other serious crime'). Notice that the previous argument (*i.e.*, that a state is justified in punishing on a strictly liable basis offenders who have sexual intercourse with girls who happen to fall within a legally arbitrary age limit, *e.g.*, 14, which the state demarcates for administrative reasons within a broader range of ages within which it regards sexual intercourse with girls as equally problematic) does not apply to the age of majority, *i.e.*, 18. For the age of majority is not regarded by the community as legally arbitrary but, rather, as itself having moral significance. *See* Dan-Cohen, 'Decision Rules and Conduct Rules', p. 657:

> [W]hen the statutory age is set at eighteen (the actual situation confronted by the Hernandez court [California v. Hernandez, 61 Cal.2d 529, 393 P.2d 673 (1964)]), the criminal provision no longer corresponds to a viable moral prohibition. In such circumstances, the statutory age of consent conclusively determines the scope of the relevant conduct rule, and thus knowledge by the defendant that the female is below the age is indeed required by the principle of *mens rea*.

See Oregon v. Hoehne, 78 Oregon App. 479, 717 P2d 237 (1986) (although an actor's reasonable mistake as to a girl's age is no defense to the three offenses of (I) having sexual intercourse with a girl who is under 12, (ii) having sexual intercourse with a girl who is between 12 and 14, and (iii) having sexual intercourse with a girl who is between

14 and 16, an actor's reasonable mistake that a girl is 18 or older is a defense to the offense of having sexual intercourse with a girl who, though at least 16, is under 18).

32. Criminal Code, Revised Statutes of Canada,1985, c. C-46, § 265(1)(a). *See* Queen v. Ewanchuk, [1999] 1 S.C.R. 330, 348:
The absence of consent, however, is subjective and determined by reference to the complainant's subjective internal state of mind towards the touching, at the time it occurred. . . . A number of commentators have observed that the notion of consent connotes active behaviour. . . . [F]or the purposes of determining the absence of consent as an element of the actus reus, the actual state of mind of the complainant is determinative. . . . [T]he trier of fact is only concerned with the complainant's perspective. The approach is purely subjective.
33. *See* Criminal Code, Revised Statutes of Canada, 1985, c. C-46, § 273.2; Queen v. Ewanchuk, [1999] 1 S.C.R. 330, 346. England takes much the same position as Canada. The English courts have held that 'consent' in rape cases is a mental state on the putative victim's part. *See, e.g.*, Regina v. Olugboja, [1982] 1 QB 320, 331 (consent is a 'state of mind'). Yet the English courts have also held that a defendant who has sexual intercourse with a woman who lacks a state of mind of consent is not guilty of rape unless he 'knew' or recklessly disregarded the woman's lack of consent. *See* Regina v. Morgan, [1976] A.C. 182. Parliament responded to the *Morgan* decision by enacting a statute, section 1 of which provides:
A man commits rape if
(a) he has unlawful sexual intercourse with a woman who at the time of the intercourse does not consent to it; and
(b) at the time he knows that she does not consent to the intercourse or he is reckless as to whether she consents to it.
Sexual Offenses (Amendment) Act of 1976, section 1. For the current statute, which is the same except that it is gender-neutral with respect to victims, *see* Sexual Offences Act, 1956 §1, as substituted by the Criminal Justice and Public Order act, 1994, § 142.
34. Feinberg, *Harm To Self*, p. 173.
35. *See* note 2.
36. Most penal codes that refer to consent fail to specify whether they are referring to expressions of acquiescence, to mental states of acquiescence, to either, or to both. And courts rarely address the issue because defendants rarely ask courts to decide whether *S*'s possession of an acquiescing mental state is a defense regardless of whether *A* has a guilty mind about *S*'s mental state. To do so, a defendant would have to take the position, at least *arguendo*, that he possessed a guilty mind at the time he acted. Defendants are understandably reluctant to do so because although they might thereby escape being convicted of crimes of non-consent, they run the risk of being found guilty of *believing* that complainants possessed non-acquiescing states of minds and, hence, of being convicted of *attempting* to commit offenses of non-consent.
37. *See* the Comment to *Model Penal Code* § 213.1, pt. II, vol. 1, p. 303. *See* also the authorities cited in Chapter 1, notes 21-29.
38. Queen v. Ewanchuk, [1999] 1 S.C.R. 330 para. 48 (opinion of Major, J.) ('There is a difference in the concept of "consent" as it relates to the state of mind of the *complainant* [in respect of] the *actus reus* of the offence and the state of mind of the *accused* in respect of the *mens rea*. For the purposes of the *actus reus*, "consent" means that the complainant in her mind wanted the sexual touching to take place. In the context of *mens rea*—specifically for the purposes of the honest but mistaken belief in

consent—"consent" means that the complainant had affirmatively communicated by words or conduct her agreement to engage in sexual activity with the accused').

39. Queen v. Ewanchuk, [1999] 1 S.C.R. 330 para. 27 (opinion of Major, J.).

40. *See, e.g.*, California v. Vasquez, 7 Cal. App. 4th 1691, 1701, 281 Cal. Rptr. 661, 667 (1991) (citations omitted):

    There are two types of 'consent' defenses which relate to the elements of the offense [of rape]. The first type involves 'actual consent'. Lack of consent is an element of rape . . . . When the defendant claims that the victim consented and the victim testifies that she did not, the jury must weigh the evidence and decide which of the two witnesses is telling the truth. 'When asserting the defense of consent, the defendant focuses on the victim's state of mind alone'. [T]his 'defense' focuses on whether the defendant committed the sexual act against the will of the victim....The [second type of consent] is based on the defendant's reasonable belief that the victim consented. A defendant who entertains both a reasonable and bona fide belief that the victim voluntarily consented to engage in sexual intercourse does not have the necessary wrongful intent to be convicted of the crime. In contrast to actual consent, [this second defense] 'permits the jury to conclude that both the victim and the accused are telling the truth. The jury will first consider the victim's state of mind and decide whether she consented to the alleged acts. If she did not consent, the jury will view the events from the defendant's perspective to determine whether the manner in which the victim expressed her lack of consent was so equivocal as to cause the accused to assume that she consented where in fact she did not'.

41. Courts regularly describe the offense of rape, for example, as a crime consisting of two distinct elements: (1) 'non-consent' on the part of the victim, and (2) a culpable mind by the defendant regarding the victim's non-consent. If the 'non-consent' to which they refer consisted solely of what putative victims either express or fail to express (as opposed either, or also, to their states of mind), the requirement of a culpable mind would be largely superfluous, especially in jurisdictions in which defendants are deemed to possess culpable minds if they either 'knew' or 'should have known' that the putative victim was not consenting. For in finding that the putative victim did not do or say anything that could reasonably be understood to be an expression of acquiescence for purposes of element (1), a court would necessarily find that the defendant 'should have known' that she was not consenting for purposes of element (2). In contrast, the distinction between 'non-consent' and a 'culpable mind regarding non-consent' makes considerable sense if 'non-consent' refers to a state of mind on the victim's part. For in that event, 'rape', indeed, consists of two distinct elements—a requirement that the victim not possess a state of mind that negates the harm that the law defining the offense seeks to prevent, and an independent requirement that the defendant possess a culpable mind regarding her lack of an acquiescing state of mind.

42. Estrich, 'Rape', p. 1099 and n.25.

43. *See* Schulhofer, *Unwanted Sex*, p. 63 ('It might seem too obvious for discussion that consent means consent in the mind of the person who is supposed to be giving it—in this case, the woman')

44. Wis. Stat. § 940.225(4) (1994) ('"Consent" as used in this section means words or overt actions by a person who is competent to give informed consent indicating a freely given agreement to have sexual intercourse or sexual contact'); Minn. Stat. § 609.341 (1998) ('"Consent" means words or overt actions by a person indicating a freely given present agreement to perform a particular sexual act with the actor'); D.C. Code § 22-4101 (1998) ('"Consent" means words or overt actions indicating a freely given agreement to

the sexual act or contact in question'); Rev. Code Wash. § 9A.44.010(7) (1994) ('"Consent" means that at the time of the act of sexual intercourse or sexual contact there are actual words or conduct indicating freely given agreement to have sexual intercourse or sexual contact'); In re M.T.S., 129 N.J. 422, 444, 609 A.2d 1266, 1277 (1992) ('any act of sexual penetration engaged in by [a] defendant without the affirmative and freely-given permission of the victim to the specific act of penetration constitutes the offense of sexual assault').

45. *See*, *e.g.*, Utah Code Ann. § 76-5-406(1) (1994).
46. *See* Russell v. United States, 698 A.2d 1007 (D.C. Ct. App., 1997); Washington v. Craig, 91 Wash. App. 1004 (1998).
47. For analysis of the harm of offenses of non-consent, and particularly rape, *see* Baber, 'How Bad Is Rape?'; Foa, 'What's Wrong With Rape?'; Murphy, 'Some Ruminations on Women, Violence, and the Criminal Law'; Harrison, 'Rape—A Case Study in Political Philosophy'.
48. Criminal acts do not inflict dignitary harms if they are offenses solely against the public and not at all against individuals, *e.g.*, treason, tax evasion, bribery.
49. Murphy, 'Forgiveness and Resentment', p. 25. *See* also Duff, *Criminal Attempts*, p. 338:

    If a friend has been raped . . . my sympathy for her is not just for the physical and psychological harm she has suffered; . . . but for the *wrongful attack* she has suffered. That is to say, the 'harm' suffered by the victim of a deliberate, wrongful attack is moral as well as material. Similarly, if the attack fails, I share her relief at its failure, but also feel sympathy for her as the intended victim of an attack; not (just) because she was frightened by it, but because she was wronged by it.
50. *See* Harman, 'Harm, Consent, and Distress', pp. 297-301 (arguing that the harm of rape is the 'distress' the victim suffers); California Penal Code § 263 (2001) ('The essential guilt of rape consists in the outrage to the person and feelings of the victims of the rape').
51. *See* 'Women, 29, Still in a 10-Year Coma, Is Pregnant by a Rapist', *New York Times*, 25 January 1996, section B, page 1, col. 2 (reporting the pregnancy of a woman with whom a hospital worker had sexual intercourse while she was in an irreversible coma); 'Death of a Comatose Rape Victim Told', *Los Angeles Times*, 19 March 1997, part A, page 11 (reporting the death of the comatose woman whose assailant had, in the meantime, been convicted of rape). *See* Bogart, 'On the Nature of Rape', p. 122 ('I do not think there is an experiential element intrinsic to the harm of rape notwithstanding the factual connection between the harm and often seriously destructive experiences of victims. . . . It is certain that there is no common experience temporarily extensional with the rape').
52. *See Model Penal Code*, pt. II, vol. 3, § 213.1 cmt. p. 346 (the harm of rape is 'achievement of a particularly degrading kind of unwanted intimacy'. *See* Dressler, 'Where We Have Been', p. 424 ('consent' functions to exculpate an actor because, 'if the victim concurs in mind and spirit [with the act], [her] interests are not violated by the accused's acts. In essence, she is not a victim at all') (quoting Fletcher, 'The Right Deed For the Wrong Reason', 23 *U.C.L.A. Law Review* 293, 300); Hubin and Haely, 'Rape and the Reasonable Man', p. 129 n.25 ('[I]t is the absence of consent [defined as a mental state on the putative victim's part] that results in most of the harm essential to rape').
53. Comments to *Model Penal Code* §§ 2.11, 213.1, in pt. I, vol. 1, p. 393, and pt. II, vol. 1, p. 303 (describing consent as a 'state of mind').

54. *Model Penal Code* § 2.11(1) (stating that prescriptive consent 'precludes the infliction of the harm or evil sought to be prevented by the law defining the offense').
55. Brett, 'Commentary', p. 255.
56. Brett, 'Sexual Offenses and Consent', p. 82.
57. Estrich, 'Rape', pp. 1099-1100.
58. Estrich does not state the proposal in so many words, but it is what I infer Estrich to be proposing when she states (i) that the law of rape ought to focus on the defendant's state of mind, rather than upon the woman's subjective experience, and (ii) that it ought to suffice to constitute a guilty mind on a defendant's part that he believed, or ought to have believed, that he was having sexual intercourse with a woman who lacked an acquiescing mind. *See* Estrich, Rape, pp. 1095, 1098, 1103-04, 1182-83. *See* also Bronitt, 'Rape and Lack of Consent', p. 309.
59. Most jurisdictions provide that a person is not guilty of an 'attempt' to commit crime *x* unless he *intends* to commit all the elements of crime *x*. In jurisdictions of that kind, a person who has sexual intercourse with a woman under circumstances in which he did not realize that she was not properly acquiescing in her mind but should have realized it would not be guilty of attempted rape. For to be guilty of attempted rape, he would have to have acted with intent regarding her nonacquiescence. However, other jurisdictions provide that a person is guilty of an attempt to commit crime *x* if he acts with whatever *mens rea* is required for the completed crime of *x*. See the jurisdictions cited in Kadish and Schulhofer, *Criminal Law and Its Processes*, pp. 590-91. *See* also *See* Regina v. Khan, 1 W.L.R. 813 [1990]. Similarly, the *Model Penal Code* provides that a person is guilty of an attempt to commit crime *x* if acts with whatever *mens rea* is required for 'circumstance elements' of the completed crime of *x*, including the circumstance element of consent. *See Model Penal Code*, pt. 1, vol. 2, pp. 301-04. Since most jurisdictions provide that a person is guilty of the completed crime of rape if he knew *or should have known* that the woman was not properly acquiescing in her mind, *see* Schulhofer, *Unwanted Sex*, p. 258, and because a putative victim's consent is a circumstance element, defendants who are negligent with respect to a putative victim's voluntary consent would be guilty of attempted rape in jurisdictions with attempt statutes like the *Model Penal Code*'s.
60. Under the *Model Penal Code*, sexual assault ranges in gravity, from a first-, second-, and third-degree felony to a misdemeanor, depending upon the circumstances under which it occurs. *See Model Penal Code* §§ 213.1-.3. Estrich would concur with the provisions of the *Model Penal Code* that declare crimes of *attempted* sexual assault to be generally punishable at the same level as completed sexual assaults. *See Model Penal Code* § 5.05(1). However, she would presumably disagree with the exception that the Code makes with respect to attempts to commit rape of the first degree, because the Code declares attempts to commit felonies of the first degree to be punishable at the lesser level of second-degree felonies. *See Model Penal Code* § 5.05(1).
61. Donald Dripps proposes to replace existing rape statutes with two graded offenses that, like Estrich's proposal, would have the effect, he says, of rendering 'the victim's psychology irrelevant' and causing 'liability [to] hinge exclusively on the defendant's conduct and mental state'. Dripps, 'Beyond Rape'. Dripps' two proposed offenses are: (1) an aggravated offense of 'sexually motivated assault', *i.e.*, the offense of knowingly putting a putative victim to the choice between either submitting to sexual intercourse or suffering personal violence; and (2) a lesser offense of 'sexual appropriation', *i.e.*, having sexual intercourse with a person (a) who is unconscious, mentally incompetent, or helpless, (b) who expresses refusal to engage in sexual intercourse, or (c) who

refrains from expressing refusal because of threats of personal violence of a kind that constitute sexually motivated assault. Despite Dripps' representation that responsibility under the two offenses turns solely upon the actor's conduct and state of mind, and not upon the victim's state of mind, Dripps' proposal does not negate the importance of the victim's state of mind, because Dripps expressly allows a defendant charged with either offense to defend on the ground that the putative victim *consented* to the use of force to elicit sexual intercourse. *See id.* at 1797.

62. Of course, some jurisdictions go further and authorize verdicts of 'not guilty by reason of insanity', or 'guilty but insane'. But, like the two basic verdicts of 'guilty' and 'not guilty', the former verdicts are also directed solely toward defendants.
63. *See* Weinstein and Berger, *Weinstein's Federal Evidence*, vol. 2, § 412, and esp. § 412.03[4] pp. 412-1 to 412-24; Wright and Graham, *Federal Practice and Procedure*, vol. 23, § 5387, pp. 563-90, supplemented in 2000 Supplement, pp. 231-54.
64. Prior-sexual-conduct evidence is direct evidence when a defendant seeks to introduce it to show that a putative victim was not previously 'chaste', under rules that declare it to be a defense to have sexual intercourse with a woman who was not previously chaste. *See, e.g., Model Penal Code* § 213.6, providing that it is a defense to having sexual intercourse with a girl who is under the age 16 that 'the alleged victim had, prior to the time of the offense charged, engaged promiscuously in sexual relations with others').
65. Aquinas, *Summa Theologiae*, vol. 27, Question 86 ('The Stain of Sin) and Question 87 ('The Guilt of Punishment').
66. Duff, *Criminal Attempts*, p. 344.
67. Plato, in *The Laws*, defends laws that, while punishing both the murderer and the attempted murder, nonetheless grade respective punishments on the basis of resulting harm, by giving the attempted murderer a penalty less than death. Speaking through the 'Athenian Stranger', Plato says:

    > Let the enactment about wounding be in the following terms:—If anyone has a purpose and intention to slay another who is not his enemy, and whom the law does not permit him to slay, and he wounds him, but is unable to kill him, he who had the intent and has wounded him is not to be pitied—he deserves no consideration, but should be regarded as a murderer and be tried for murder. Still having respect to the fortune which has in a manner favored him, and to the providence which in pity to him and to the wounded man saved the one from a fatal blow, and the other from an accursed fate and calamity—as a thank-offering to this deity, and in order not to oppose his will—in such a case the law will remit the punishment of death, and only compel the offender to emigrate to a neighboring city for the rest of his life, where he shall remain in the enjoyment of all his possessions. But if he have injured the wounded man, he shall make such compensation for the injury as the court deciding the cause shall assess.

    Plato, *Laws* 9.876-9.877. For more on Plato's views of punishment, *see Protagoras* 323-24; *Gorgias* 523-27; *Phaedo* 114; *Laws* 5.735; 9.835 and 855, 860, 864, and 873; 11.934; and *Republic* 2.363, 2.380, 10.614.
68. Thomas Nagel appears to have coined the term 'moral luck'. *See* Nagel, 'Moral Luck'. *See* also Williams, 'Moral Luck'.
69. For the view that the contingencies of resulting harm ought not to affect levels of criminal punishment, *see* Alexander, 'Crime and Culpability', p. 27; Ashworth, 'Taking the Consequences', pp. 110-12; H.L.A. Hart, *Punishment and Responsibility*, pp. 129-31; Schulhofer, 'Harm and Punishment'; Sverdlik, 'Crime and Moral Luck'.

70. For the view that it is not unjust to grade criminal punishment upon the basis of whether resulting harm occurs, *see* Duff, *Intention, Agency, and Criminal Liability*, pp. 189-92; Moore, 'The Independent Moral Significance of Wrongdoing'; Fletcher, *Rethinking Criminal Law*, pp. 481-83.
71. Plato does not deny that the successful and failed murderer are equally deserving of condemnation. They should both be 'considered' as murderers, he says, and both 'tried for murder', because the failed murderer deserves 'no 'consideration' for having failed to kill his victim. Nonetheless, Plato argues that the law ought to reduce the failed murder's sentence to less than death as an expression of respect and gratitude to the god of 'fortune' for taking pity on the malefactor and his victim by deflecting the fatal flow. For the state to do otherwise—that is, for the state to disregard that the malefactor failed in his homicidal purpose and to treat him as if he had succeeded—would be to 'offend the will' of the 'deity' who saw to it that the malefactor did *not* succeed. Despite the demonological terms in which he expresses himself, Plato should be understood to be making a moral assertion. For Plato is attributing to the 'gods' the attitude he believes one *ought* to have toward a community that fails to appreciate it when a malefactor misses his intended target. A community should value human life over human comfort; and, hence, it should be less upset, less angry, at a miss than a hit. Accordingly, a community that uses criminal penalties to express its righteous indignation *ought* to distinguish between a miss and a hit. For to do otherwise is to express the callous view that the community is just as outraged, just as upset, just as angry, at a miss as over a hit. For a similar argument that it is wrong for a person to feel as angry about crimes that do not result in harms as about crimes that do result in harms, *see* Duff, *Criminal Attempts*, pp. 335-38. *See* also *id.* at 345 (contending, in partial contrast to Plato, that taking resulting harms into attack is justified not because of the righteous anger and grateful relief a society thereby expresses *itself* as feeling, but because of the repentance and relief it thereby seeks on instrumental grounds to elicit from the *defendant*).
72. Bryden, 'Redefining Rape', pp. 382-83.
73. Malm, 'The Ontological Status of Consent', p. 149. As part of her argument that mental states are too ephemeral to constitute legal defenses, Malm argues that, if consent were a mental state, it would prevent a person from prospectively consenting—that is, from consenting at Time1 to something that occurs at Time2 when she is unconscious or otherwise oblivious to it. I shall address prospective prescriptive consent in Chapter 6.
74. Malm, 'The Ontological Status of Consent', p. 149.
75. Thus, Larry Alexander and Heidi Hurd both argue that consent ought to be defined as a mental state on *S*'s part; and, yet, they both make it clear that their definitions of consent should not be deemed to preclude an actor from defending himself on the basis of lack of *mens rea*. *See* Alexander, 'The Moral Magic of Consent (II)', p. 168; Hurd, 'The Moral Magic of Consent', p. 127 n.7.
76. *See, e.g.*, Husak and Thomas, 'Date Rape, Social Convention, and Reasonable Mistakes', p. 102, in which the authors, having hypothesized a case like *New York* v. *Bink* in which an actor with a guilty mind has sexual intercourse with a putative victim only to discover afterwards that the putative victim was secretly and voluntarily consenting in her mind, contend that 'for better or worse', the conduct of such an actor is 'beyond the reach of the criminal law' because to punish him would violate the 'principle of legality'.
77. *See, e.g.*, Sherwin, 'Infelicitous Sex', p. 209-10.

78. *See* Feinberg, *Harm To Self*, pp. 189-343. *See* also Archard, *Sexual Consent*, pp. 39-67; Brett, 'Sexual Offenses and Consent', pp. 85-86; McGregor, 'Why When She Says No She Doesn't Mean Maybe and Doesn't Mean Yes', pp. 189-96.
79. *See* Archard, *Sexual Consent*, p. 6.

Chapter Five

Prescriptive Attitudinal Consent

We have seen that prescriptive consent to conduct consists of actual acquiescence to the conduct—whether attitudinal or expressive—under such conditions as jurisdictions prescribe. The prescribed conditions can vary enormously from one jurisdiction to another and within jurisdictions from one offense to another. Prescribed conditions also vary in accord with whether the prescriptive consent is essentially attitudinal or essentially expressive in nature, because attitudinal acquiescence performs a different legal function than expressive acquiescence and, accordingly, demands different accompanying conditions:

> ***Attitudinal Acquiescence.*** The legal function of attitudinal acquiescence on a subject *S*'s part is to determine whether *S* suffered the primary harm that offenses of non-consent are designed to prevent, namely, the harm of subjecting *S* to conduct without her having chosen the conduct for herself under circumstances that are consistent with her well-being. In order for *S*'s subjective choice of the conduct to be consistent with her well-being, her choice must be 'voluntary', that is, it must be the product of such freedom, knowledge, and competence as the jurisdiction deems sufficient to enable *S* to assume responsibility for her choice.
>
> ***Expressions of Acquiescence.*** The legal function of expressions of acquiescence on *S*'s part, in turn, is to determine whether an actor *A* deserves to be blamed for an offense of non-consent, and, specifically, to be blamed for disregarding or neglecting *S*'s interests in being able subjectively to choose conduct for herself under conditions sufficient to enable her to assume responsibility for her choice. In order for *S*'s expression of acquiescence to relieve *A* of blame, the expression must occur under conditions that the jurisdiction deems sufficient to cause a conscientious person in *A*'s position to believe that *S* is subjectively choosing the conduct and that she is choosing it voluntarily.[1]

The conditions that jurisdictions prescribe to transform *S*'s actual subjective acquiescence into prescriptive attitudinal consent will, therefore, differ from the conditions that they prescribe to transform *S*'s expressions of acquiescence into prescriptive expressive consent. For the former are conditions regarding both the *content* of *S*'s subjective choice and the *context* in which she makes it, while the latter are conditions regarding what is *expressed* to *A* as to the content and context of S's choice. Despite their differences, however, the conditions of prescriptive expressive consent are, in large part, normatively derivative of the conditions of prescriptive attitudinal consent. This is so, because the state's purpose in prescribing conditions as to what must be expressed to *A* regarding *S*'s subjective acquiescence is to ensure that *A* possesses sufficient information in order to reasonably conclude that *S* subjectively acquiesced in the conduct at issue and that *S* did so voluntarily (even if it should later turn out that *S* did not).

To illustrate the normatively derivative nature of the conditions of prescriptive expressive consent, consider the provisions of the Oregon 'Death With Dignity Act' (DWDA).[2] The Oregon DWDA is an elaborate statutory regime designed to make painless, lethal medication available to terminally ill patients who may wish to commit suicide. The DWDA does so by providing a defense to a crime of assisted suicide to a physician who prescribes the medication in the good-faith belief that he is acting in accord with his patient's voluntary choice.[3] The DWDA devotes some of its provisions to conditions that are unique to rules regarding prescriptive expressive consent, *viz.*, conditions to ensure that channels for communicating the content and context of patient choices are *accurate*. Thus, the statute requires that a patient personally present the attending physician with two or more oral requests for lethal drugs plus a written request upon a form that the statute prescribes, and that the attending physician personally examine and advise the patient.[4] Nevertheless, the great bulk of the DWDA conditions that define a physician's good faith derive their content conditions that are also the focus of rules of prescriptive attitudinal consent. They are conditions that concern not *how* a physician must learn of the content and context of a patient's choice to accept lethal drugs but *what* he must learn of the content and context of a patient's choice to accept lethal drugs, namely, that the patient is making her request under the conditions of subjective choice that the State of Oregon believes necessary to enable patients to take responsibility for choosing to accept lethal drugs. Thus, DWDA requires that physicians be assured that their patients are 'capable', 'informed', and 'acting voluntarily'[5] in requesting lethal drugs for possible suicide. Specifically, it requires that the attending physician (1) examine his patient for mental competency, both at the time of the patient's initial request and before drugs are prescribed, and seek confirmation of the patient's competency from a consulting physician; (2) inform the patient of (i) the patient's terminal condition, (ii) the risks of taking the drugs, and (iii) the alternatives to suicide; (3) obtain statements from two witnesses that the patient is acting freely; and (4) impose waiting periods of 15 days following the first oral request and 48 hours following the written request to ensure that the patient is not responding to pressures of the moment.[6] In large part, therefore, a patient's request for lethal drugs under the DWDA derives its legal sufficiency as a defense to a crime of assisted suicide from its conveying to the physician that the patient subjectively chose to request lethal drugs and that the patient did so with the competence, knowledge, freedom, and motivation that Oregon believes a patient must possess for her subjective choice to be consistent with her well-being (even if it should later turn out that the patient did not).

Given then that the conditions of prescriptive expressive consent are largely derivative of the conditions of prescriptive attitudinal consent, we shall focus in this chapter on the latter, that is, the conditions that are required to transform actual subjective acquiescence into prescriptive attitudinal consent. We shall address six analytical questions: (A) How does the requirement that subjective acquiescence be 'voluntary' relate to its being 'competent', 'knowing', and 'free'? (B) How do the requirements of 'competence', 'knowledge', and 'freedom' relate to the statutory forms in which offenses of non-consent are drafted? (C) What considerations govern the 'knowledge' required for prescriptive attitudinal consent? (D) What is the relationship between wrongful force on a subject to acquiesce, on the one hand, and a subject's consent to be forced, on the other? (E) What is the relationship between wrongful force on a subject to acquiesce, on the one hand, and the necessity of the subject's offering 'resistance', on the other? (F) What is prescriptive consent? An affirmative state of affairs? Or the absence of negative states of affairs?

The Relationship Between Subjective Acquiescence Being 'Voluntary', and its Being 'Competent', 'Knowing', and 'Free'

The particular conditions that individual jurisdictions prescribe in order to transform *S*'s subjective acquiescence into prescriptive attitudinal consent vary enormously from one context to another depending upon the jurisdiction's legal view of what the person is consenting *to*. Thus, jurisdictions require physicians to provide patients with far more information regarding the risks of surgery as a condition of prescriptive consent to surgery than they require prospective sexual partners to provide each other regarding the risks of sexual intercourse as a condition of prescriptive consent to sexual intercourse. The question nevertheless remains: Is it possible to reduce the multifarious conditions that enter into judgments of prescriptive attitudinal consent to a set of essential categories?

Some authorities make no effort to classify the conditions that enter into judgments of prescriptive attitudinal consent but instead use terms that are entirely conclusory, such as requiring that subjective acquiescence be 'valid', 'genuine', 'effective', 'lawful', or 'legal'.[7] These terms are conclusory because they refer to prescribed conditions by reference to their legal effects, but they do not reveal anything of their content. Others use 'voluntariness' in this same conclusory fashion. In reality, of course, 'voluntariness' is ambiguous. It can be used in a purely factual sense to refer to any conscious exercise of will on a person's part, regardless of how wrongfully pressured a person may be to exercise his will in a certain way. Aristotle, for example, uses it in that way when he states that a prisoner who complies with a ruthless tyrant's demands in order to prevent his parents and children from being wrongfully killed, nonetheless, acts 'voluntarily'.[8] Or alternatively, 'voluntariness' can also be used in a legally conclusory fashion to refer to such additional conditions as are necessary to transform a subject's conscious and willed acquiescence to conduct into a criminal defense on an actor's part. Courts use 'voluntariness' in the latter fashion when they say that a woman's conscious and willed acquiescence to sexual intercourse is a defense to rape only if her acquiescence is 'voluntary'.[9]

The purpose of this section is to clarify conceptually what legislatures and courts mean when they say that a subject's attitudinal acquiescence to conduct is a criminal defense only if it is 'voluntary'. Rather than try to enumerate the many different conditions that different jurisdictions prescribe for attitudinal consent under different offenses or to recommend conditions that jurisdictions *should* prescribe, I shall try to classify such conditions in accord with the ways in which they bring subjective acquiescence about. Specifically, I shall argue that the conditions can be conceptualized as falling within three functional but mutually exclusive categories—freedom, knowledge, and competence—that together constitute what legislatures and courts mean in requiring that attitudinal consent be 'voluntary'.

I shall proceed by reference to the conditions that Joel Feinberg says are necessary to render acts of consent 'fully voluntary', that is, sufficiently voluntary to constitute defenses to crime. '[A] person's consent is fully voluntary', Feinberg says, 'only when he is a competent and unimpaired adult who has not been threatened, misled, or lied to about relevant facts, nor manipulated by subtle forms of conditioning'.[10] As we shall see, these conditions of Feinberg's can be conceptualized as falling into three categories, each characterized by a distinctive manner in which acquiescence is induced in persons. Admittedly, Feinberg is speaking of consent as a public act of communicating acquiescence to conduct, rather than a subjective act of choosing conduct, but the conditions of voluntariness that Feinberg enumerates apply to acts of both kinds of consent.[11] Following Feinberg, I shall address the conditions that are necessary for acquiescence to be voluntary by reference to factors that *negate* voluntariness.

'Freedom' (Or the Absence of 'Wrongful Force')

One of the factors that negates the voluntariness of *S*'s subjective acquiescence to *x*, Feinberg says, is 'threats'. 'Threats' are conditional propositions, whether explicit or implicit, witting or unwitting, that an actor *A* puts to *S* that structure *S*'s options in such a way as to pressure *S* to acquiesce to *x* with either *A* himself or a third person, by causing *S* to believe that unless she does, *A* will leave her in a worsened position as measured by certain baselines.[12] The respective baselines by which threats are measured differ depending upon whether 'threat' is being used normatively or descriptively. A 'normative threat' is a threat to leave *S* in a worsened position as measured by the normative baseline in which law or morals require that an actor leave her. A 'descriptive threat' is a threat to leave *S* is a worsened position as measured by a baseline *other* than the position in which law or morals require that an actor leave her.

Feinberg himself uses 'threat' descriptively; for the baseline by which Feinberg measures threats is not the position in which law or morals require that *A* leave *S* but, rather, *the position in which S can statistically expect a person who possesses A's abilities (albeit not A's morals) to leave S under the circumstances.*[13] Definitions like Feinberg's that measure threats by reference to descriptive baselines are useful in identifying conditional propositions that tend to be regarded as sufficient to invalidate acquiescence. And in doing so, they help illuminate deeper ethical reasons why jurisdictions tend to regard those conditions as sufficient to invalidate acquiescence.

Unfortunately, descriptive definitions like Feinberg's are not useful for the task at hand. Our purpose is not to explain or to justify why jurisdictions tend to regard some conditions as valid and others invalid, but rather to define a class of threats that is coextensive with the threats that jurisdictions regard as sufficient to invalidate acquiescence as a defense to crimes of non-consent. Descriptive definitions are not useful for that purpose because they are over-inclusive, under-inclusive, or both. They are over-inclusive because they invariably define as threats conditional propositions that do *not* invalidate acquiescence. Consider, for example, two of the most commonplace descriptive baselines:

> ***Feinberg's Baseline.*** Feinberg's baseline, which consists of the position in which a person in *S*'s position statistically expects a person with the *A*'s abilities to leave her; and
>
> ***Zimmerman's Baseline.*** David Zimmerman's baseline, which consists of the position that *S* occupied before *A* made his proposal.[14]

Measured by those baselines, however, not all proposals to leave a subject worse off necessarily invalidate resulting acquiescence. For it is possible for *A* to propose to *S* that unless she acquiesces to *x*, *A* will leave *S* *both* worse off than *S* statistically expects persons with *A*'s abilities to leave her *and* worse off than *S* was beforehand—yet without *A*'s proposal necessarily invalidating *S*'s acquiescence as a defense to the crime of subjecting her to *x*. Suppose, for example, that a judge who rarely gives first-offenders maximum jail sentences nevertheless proposes to a first-time wealthy offender that unless the offender agrees to contribute $10,000 to charity, the judge will exercise his discretion to give the offender a jail sentence. The judge's proposal is a 'threat' for both Feinberg's and Zimmerman's purposes. Yet surely the judge's proposal does not operate to invalidate the offender's acquiescence in paying the $10,000 in the event the judge is charged with depriving the offender of $10,000 without the latter's consent.

By the same token, descriptive definitions of threats are under-inclusive for our purposes because they fail to define as 'threats' conditional propositions that can invalidate acquiescence. To illustrate, suppose that the state of 'Vermonia' possesses two pertinent criminal offenses: (1) a Rape Law that makes it a felony, punishable by up to life in prison, for a person to have sexual intercourse with another without the latter's prescriptive attitudinal consent; and (2) a Bad Samaritan Law, which makes it a criminal misdemeanor, punishable by a $500 fine, for a bystander to fail to rescue a person who is in mortal danger if the bystander can do so without risk or substantial inconvenience to himself. Suppose, too, that the following event occurs within Vermonia:

> ***The Bad Samaritan.*** Mary is driving on a stretch of isolated and non-patrolled highway in which motorists are notoriously unwilling to help stranded drivers. Mary's car overturns, leaving her child sufficiently injured that he will die unless immediately taken

> to a hospital. After precious minutes pass, Mary flags down a motorist, Jack, and pleads with him to drive her and her child to the nearest hospital. Jack agrees to do so, but only if Mary first has sexual intercourse with him. Mary, realizing that Jack is the only driver who is likely to come along the road for some time, reluctantly agrees. Jack has sexual intercourse with Mary and then drives her and her child to the hospital. When the state prosecutor later learns of Jack's behavior, he charges Jacks with having sexual intercourse with Mary without her consent.

Measured by most descriptive baselines, Jack's conditional proposition to Mary—'I will drive you and your child to the hospital if, but only if, you have sexual intercourse with me beforehand'—is not a threat. It is not a threat because it does not lead Mary to believe that unless she subjectively chooses to acquiesce to sexual intercourse, she will be left worse off than what most descriptive baselines specify. After all, Jack does not propose to leave Mary either worse off than she statistically expects to be left by persons with Jack's abilities, or worse off than she was before Jack appeared on the scene. Nevertheless, just as a number of moral philosophers maintain that actors such as Jack are guilty of criminal sexual assault,[15] the courts of Vermonia might well conclude that Jack's proposal is an illicit one that invalidates her acquiescence as a defense to rape.

The present task is to define what may be called 'wrongful threats', that is, a class of threats that is coextensive with the threats that jurisdictions regard as sufficient to invalidate acquiescence as defenses to crimes of non-consent. To identify such a class, one must not only define 'wrongful threats' by reference to a *normative* baseline, but also confine the definition to a *particular* normative baseline. Some normative baselines are both too narrow and too broad. Consider, for example, the normative baseline that Alan Wertheimer proposes for defining illegal coercion, namely, the baseline *of the worst position in which the law allows a person lawfully to leave another.*[16] On the one hand, Wertheimer's normative baseline is too narrow, because it would preclude a jurisdiction from doing what it may legitimately wish to do – namely, to make it a criminal offense of non-consent for an actor to elicit sexual intercourse from a woman by telling her that he will otherwise refuse to leave her *better* off than the worst position in which the law allows him to leave her. Thus, it would prevent a jurisdiction from making it an offense of non-consent for an employer to elicit sexual intercourse from a woman by telling her that he will otherwise deny her an employment position that he has a legal right to deny her.[17]

At the same time, however, Wertheimer's normative baseline is too broad, because it would require a jurisdiction to make it a criminal offense for an actor to elicit sexual intercourse from a woman by telling her that he will otherwise leave her worse off than the worst position in which he has a legal right to leave her, regardless of how trivial the latter right may be. Thus, by reference to Wertheimer's baseline, Jack's proposal in 'The Bad Samaritan' is a threat; for the law of Vermonia requires Jack to save Mary's child, and hence by proposing *not* to save the child unless Mary has sexual intercourse with him, Jack is proposing to leave Mary worse off than the worst position that the criminal law of Vermonia allows him to leave her. Yet Jack's proposal is not one that every jurisdiction would regard as sufficient to invalidate Mary's acquiescence as a defense to rape. There are many crimes, after all, that when threatened may induce sexual intercourse and, yet, do not result in rape. It is criminal, for example, to destroy another's property, to appropriate another's property, or to touch a person without her consent. It does not necessarily follow, however, that an actor who elicits sexual intercourse from a woman by threatening otherwise to 'kill her goldfish', or deprive her of '$50', or 'pinch her' without her consent, is guilty of rape.[18] On the contrary, just as the Vermonia courts are free to follow philosophers who maintain that persons like Jack are guilty of rape, they are free to follow other commentators who maintain that persons like Jack are *not* guilty of rape.[19] The Vermonia courts may well decide that although Jack is guilty of being a bad Samaritan, and although he therefore made a 'threat' as measured by the normative baseline Alan Wertheimer proposes, the Vermonia legislature did not intend to impose a sentence of life imprisonment on a person who elicits sexual intercourse by threatening to do something that carries a penalty of no more than a $500 fine.[20]

I think Wertheimer is correct to define 'wrongful threats' by reference to a normative baseline but incorrect in the baseline he selects. It is more appropriate to define a 'wrongful threat' as a conditional proposition, whether explicit or implicit, and whether witting or unwitting, that *A* puts to S that brings pressure to bear upon *S* to acquiesce to *x* with either *A* himself or third person, by causing *S* to believe that unless she acquiesces to *x*, *A* will leave her in a worsened position *as measured by the worst position in which the criminal offense at issue allows a person to leave another as a result of the latter's refusal to acquiesce to x.* Accordingy, *S* acquiesces to *x* by means of a wrongful threat when *A*, whether explicitly or implicitly, and whether unwittingly or unwittingly, causes *S* to believe that if she fails to acquiesce to *x* with *A* or a third person, *A* will leave her worse off than the criminal offense at issue allows a person to leave another as a result of the latter's refusal to acquiesce to *x*. This normative baseline has advantages over Wertheimer's because it enables jurisdictions that wish to do so to punish employers who elicit sexual intercourse from prospective employees by threatening otherwise not to hire them, and it enables jurisdictions that wish to do so to refrain from punishing persons who elicit sexual intercourse by threatening otherwise to inflict trivial wrongs (*e.g.*, depriving persons of small amounts of money).

This does not mean that an actor who is unaware of a wrongful threat he is making, or a third party who is unaware of the threat, is necessarily guilty of an offense whenever *S* acquiesces to *x* as a result of the threat. Defenses of consent are only one of several defenses that criminal law provides. A person who subjects *S* to *x* as a result of a wrongful threat of which he is unaware may be entitled to an acquittal on independent grounds that he lacked *mens rea* regarding *S*'s non-consent.[21] A wrongful threat negates only one defense, namely, the defense of prescriptive attitudinal consent with respect to a subject *S* who acquiesces as a result.

Significantly, 'wrongful threats' as defined above are not the only kind of pressure on *S*'s exercises of will that invalidates acquiescence for purposes of offenses of non-consent. Wrongful threats are a subset of a larger set of illicit, acquiescence-inducing pressures that, for want of a better term, I shall call 'wrongful force'. Wrongful force consists of two subsets: (i) wrongful threats that, as we have seen, are conditional in nature; and (ii) 'wrongful oppression', which is unconditional in nature. Wrongful threats are conditional, because they exert pressure on *S* to acquiesce to *x* by causing *S* to believe that she can prevent *A* from worsening her position *if* and *only* if she acquiesces to *x*, however repugnant she may otherwise find *x*. In contrast, 'wrongful oppression' exerts pressure upon *S*, not by causing *S* to believe that she can prevent her position from worsening by acquiescing to *x*, but rather by causing *S* to believe that her position is such that given the circumstances in which she finds herself, engaging in *x* is preferable to the alternative of forgoing *x*.

Like wrongful threats, 'wrongful oppression' is a normative concept that, for purposes of offenses of non-consent, derives its meaning from a particular normative baseline, namely, the worst position in which the criminal offense at issue allows a person to reduce a subject *S* as a basis for inducing *S* to acquiesce to *x* with himself or with a third person. In turn, a subject *S* acquiesces to *x* by means of wrongful oppression, when (i) *A*, whether wittingly or unwittingly, reduces *S* to a certain position; (ii) the position is worse than the positions in which the criminal offense at issue allows a person to reduce *S* as a basis for inducing her to acquiesce to *x* with himself or a third person; (iii) given the position in which *S* believes herself to be, *S* prefers to acquiesce to *x* rather than not. Again, this does not mean that an oppressor who is unaware of the wrongful oppression to which he is subjecting *S* or who is unaware that the oppression is inducing *S* to acquiesce to *x* is necessarily guilty of an offense. An actor who unwittingly causes *S* to acquiesce to *x* with himself or another as a result of wrongful oppression to which he has subjected her may be entitled to an acquittal on independent grounds that he lacked *mens rea* regarding *S*'s non-consent. Wrongful oppression negates only one defense that an accused might otherwise possess, namely, the defense that *S* prescriptively consented to *x* in her mind.

To illustrate the unconditional nature of wrongful oppression, consider the way Cameron Hooker elicited sexual intercourse from his victim Colleen in *California v. Hooker*.[22] Cameron and his wife abducted Colleen at knife point and held her as a captive, naked, bound, gagged, and blindfolded, for many months. After a year, Cameron and his wife lessened the restraints on Colleen so that she could move freely about the house while they were there but could not escape. Colleen's captivity continued for another two years, during which she was chained to a bed whenever Hooker and his wife were absent or asleep. By the end of the three years, Colleen began having sexual intercourse with Cameron. Significantly, however, Cameron did not elicit sexual intercourse from Colleen by means of a threat; he did not say to her, 'I will beat you or intensify the conditions of your confinement, unless you have sexual intercourse with me.' Rather, Cameron elicited sexual intercourse from Colleen by means of a different kind of wrongful force, though one that the *Hooker* court found equally criminal: by rendering Colleen a longterm captive, Cameron caused her to acquiesce to sexual intercourse by unconditionally placing her in a position in which she preferred captivity *with* sexual intercourse to captivity *without* sexual intercourse—a position that was worse than the position in which the California offense of rape allows a man to place a woman as a basis upon which to elicit acquiescence to sexual intercourse with himself or another.

Interestingly, there is an important respect in which wrongful threats tend to differ normatively from wrongful oppression. The difference concerns the criminal responsibility of *third persons* who engage in the conduct at issue with subjects whom they know to be acquiescing as a result of wrongful force at the hands of others. A third person, *P*, is criminally responsible for engaging in conduct with a subject, *S*, when *P* knows that *S* is being wrongfully threatened that *S* will be harmed unless *S* endeavors to engage in the conduct[23] (as opposed to when *P* knows *S* is being wrongfully threatened that *S* will be harmed unless *S* *succeeds* in engaging in the conduct). Yet *P* is not criminally responsible for engaging in conduct with *S* when *P* knows that *S* is acquiescing only because of existing oppression, provided that *S* remains competent to assess her interests[24] and provided that *P* is neither the source of the oppression nor legally obliged to remedy it.[25] (For the same reason, *P* ought not to be criminally responsible for engaging in conduct with *S* when *P* knows that *S* is acquiescing only because *S* is being wrongfully threatened that *S* will be harmed unless *S* succeeds in engaging in the conduct with *P*).[26] The normative difference is that when *P* declines *S*'s acquiescence in instances in which *S* is being wrongfully threatened with harm unless she *endeavors* to engage in conduct, *P* leaves *S* in the same rightful position *S* occupied before the wrongful threat was made, *i.e.*, the position in which *S* avoids both engaging in sexual intercourse and suffering wrongful harm for failing to do so. In contrast, when *P* turns his back on the acquiescence of *S* when *S*'s acquiescence is the product of wrongful oppression by another, or when *P* declines *S*'s in instances in which *S* is being wrongfully threatened with harm unless *S* *succeeds* in engaging conduct with *P*, *P* not only leaves *S* in the same wrongful position of oppression and threat that *S* occupied beforehand, but denies *S* the benefit of the conduct that *S* prefers under the circumstances.

Now it might be thought that this definition of wrongful force omits an essential species of illicit pressure, namely, what some commentators call 'compulsion'.[27] Compulsion is raw physical power by which *A* succeeds in subjecting S to *x* not by virtue of inducing *S* to believe that submitting is preferable to resisting, but by virtue of her lacking the power to prevent it. Thus, an actor subjects *S* to sexual intercourse by means of compulsion when she is comatose, paralyzed, or otherwise unable to mount any resistance at all; or when he surprises her with an act of sexual penetration before she has a preference about it; or when she does everything within her power to fight him off until the very end but he overwhelms her efforts with superior physical strength. Each is an instance of compulsion, and compulsion is a kind of force, broadly speaking. Nevertheless, compulsion is not part of what is referred to here as 'wrongful force'. The term 'wrongful force' is an effort to identify from within the entire class of instances in which *S* subjectively acquiesces to *x* those instances in which *S* is wrongly *pressured* into exercising her will in favor of acquiescing to *x*. Compulsion can play no role in identifying wrongful pressures because compulsion brings about *x* not by pressuring *S* to exercise her will in favor of acquiescing in *x*, but by bringing *x* about *without regard* to any exercise of will on *S*'s part.

This is not to say that compulsion is irrelevant to whether *S* has been subjected to *x* without having prescriptively consented to it in her mind. Compulsion provides a context in which issues of prescriptive consent arise. The issue in cases of compulsion is: 'Did *S* voluntarily and subjectively choose *x* as that which she desired for herself under the circumstances?' If the answer to the question is no, it follows that *S* did not prescriptively consent to *x* in her mind. If the answer is yes, it follows that *S* did prescriptively consent to *x* in her mind, even though she was powerless to prevent it. In contrast to wrongful force, which undermines prescriptive consent by pressuring *S* to choose *x*, the exercise of compulsion does not affect the legal criteria by which the above question is answered. Of course, where compulsion is brought to bear upon *S* in a context in which she is incapable of voluntarily choosing *x* for herself (say, where *S* is asleep), *S* will not prescriptively consent to *x*. But the reason *S* does not prescriptively consent to *x* is not that she is subjected to compulsion, but that she cannot voluntarily choose *x* and, hence, *does not* voluntarily choose *x*. By the same token, where compulsion is brought to bear upon *S* in a context in which she *is* capable of voluntarily and subjectively choosing *x* for herself (say, where she is conscious of *x* but lacks physical strength to prevent *x* from occurring), her prescriptive consent will be a function of whether or not she exercises her capacity by choosing *x*, and not upon the fact that *x* will occur regardless. To illustrate, consider the English case, *Director of Public Prosecutions v. Morgan*,[28] in which an English air force officer invited fellow airmen to have sexual intercourse with his wife by falsely telling them that his wife wanted him to bring home strangers who would forcibly subject her to rough sex despite her overt resistance. The airmen did as they were invited, using superior physical strength to overwhelm the fervent resistance of a woman who in reality abhorred being overcome. *Morgan* was controversial because the airmen defended themselves on the ground that although they later learned that the woman did not desire or consent to be forcibly overcome, they honestly thought that she did. Now suppose for a moment that the woman's husband had been telling the truth. Suppose that the woman had secretly and subjectively welcomed everything the airmen did at the time they did it, including being subjected to overwhelming physical compulsion that she fought but failed to thwart. In that event, far from having to defend themselves on ground that they lacked *mens rea* as to the woman's nonconsent, the airmen would have defended themselves on grounds of consent. They would have argued that by virtue of voluntarily welcoming the compulsion of being physically compelled to engage in sexual intercourse, the woman prescriptively consented to it in her mind, even though she was not physically capable of preventing it.

To summarize, *S*'s acquiescence to *x* is induced by means of 'wrongful force' (and, hence, is invalid as a defense to the offense of subjecting *S* to *x* without *S*'s prescriptive attitudinal consent) if *S* acquiesces to *x* as a result of either a 'wrongful threat' by anyone or 'wrongful oppression' by the accused. Conversely, *S*'s actual acquiescence to *x* is valid as a defense to an offense of subjecting her to *x* without her prescriptive attitudinal consent only if *S*'s acquiescence is 'voluntary'. And *S*'s acquiescence is 'voluntary' only if it is 'free', that is, only if it is *not* the product of either a wrongful threat by anyone or wrongful oppression by the accused.

Knowledge' (Or the Absence of 'Fraud')

Another of Feinberg's factors that negates the voluntariness of a subject *S*'s subjective acquiescence to *x* is being 'misled, or lied to about relevant facts'. In addressing the kinds of disinformation that deprive empirical acquiescence of normative effect, Feinberg does not include all lies and deceptions by which acquiescing persons are 'misled', but rather confines himself only to certain lies and deceptions, namely, lies and deceptions about facts that are 'relevant' to *S*'s acquiescence to *x*. Relevance, of course, is a derivative concept that presupposes external criteria of reference. Facts are relevant if, and only if, they bear upon, connect up with, or advance determinations that have previously been adjudged by independent criteria to be of significance. Feinberg does not clarify the external criteria by which he believes facts are to be adjudged relevant to acquiescence. However, he seems to be using 'relevance' in a normative sense to refer solely to such facts regarding *A* and *x* that, were *S* 'lied to' or 'misled' about them, would preclude *S*'s acquiescence from being sufficiently 'voluntary' to validate *A*'s conduct in subjecting *S* to *x*. In other words, when Feinberg states that 'a person's consent is fully voluntary only when he . . . has not been . . . misled, or lied to about relevant facts', Feinberg appears to be confining the discussion to lies and deceptions that society regards as too significant to enable a person who relies upon them to decide whether engaging in *x* with *A* is truly in his or her interests. In that spirit, we, too, shall confine our discussion to lies, deceptions, and nondisclosures—or what we shall collectively call 'fraud'—that undermine the legal validity of actual acquiescence. However, because we shall be discussing fraud in the limited context of offenses of non-consent, we shall further confine our discussion to those frauds that, when relied upon, undermine the legal validity of actual acquiescence for purposes of *criminal law*, that is, frauds that are sufficiently serious to prevent a person's actual acquiescence from negating the primary harms that the offenses of non-consent are designed to prevent.

To be sure, by confining his discussion to 'lies' and other acts by which persons are 'misled', Feinberg implicitly confines his references to acts of active *deception*. But the mental states of ignorance on *S*'s part that undermine her prescriptive attitudinal acquiescence sufficiently to cause her harm are not confined to ignorance that is the product of active deception on A's part. Rather, they extend to all instances of ignorance on *S*'s part that prevent her from being able to make a responsible decision about whether to engage in *x*, regardless of whether her mistaken assumptions are conscious or unconscious,[29] and regardless of whether they are the product of deception or nondisclosure on *A*'s part.[30] Consider, for example, two women who both have unprotected sexual intercourse with HIV-positive men who consciously conceal their HIV-positive status: a woman to whom a man lies by telling her that he is HIV-negative; a woman who, without being lied to, simply assumes from the man's silence that he is HIV-negative. The two cases may differ with respect to whether the men possessed *mens rea* regarding the women's unwitting acquiescence.[31] But the cases are identical with respect to whether the women suffered *harm* that offenses of non-consent seek to prevent, *i.e.*, the harm of their engaging in conduct that they do not realize is not in their interests.[32]

Wrongful force and fraud, as defined here, both operate to undermine prescriptive attitudinal consent, but they do so in distinct ways. Wrongful force undermines *S*'s prescriptive attitudinal consent by causing *S* to believe that her position has so changed for the worse that she is induced, illicitly, to subjectively acquiesce to *x* where otherwise she would not. In contrast, fraud undermines *S*'s prescriptive attitudinal consent, not by causing her to believe that her position has thus changed for the worse, but by otherwise illicitly misleading *S* into believing that subjective acquiesce to *x* is more beneficial than it really is. To illustrate, consider the provision of the *Model Penal Code* that makes it an offense for a man to elicit sexual intercourse from a woman by means of a sham marriage ceremony.[33] A man who induces a woman into having sexual intercourse by misleading her into thinking that they have just become lawfully married does not elicit intercourse from her by causing her to believe that her position has so changed for the worse that having sexual intercourse is preferable to not having it, but rather by falsely causing her to believe that her position has so changed for the better that having sexual intercourse advances her well-being more than it does.

This distinction between fraud and wrongful force is of more than academic interest. By classifying impairments of prescriptive attitudinal consent by reference to the way they impair judgments of self-interest, the distinction highlights respective ways in which victims are harmed. To illustrate the usefulness of the distinction by reference to a case in which a court conflated wrongful force with fraud to the victim's disadvantage, consider *Boro v. Superior Court*.[34] The defendant, Daniel Boro, devised a cruel and devious scheme for eliciting sexual intercourse from Ms. R, whom he had not previously met. Having learned through a local hospital that Ms. R had recently undergone a blood test, Boro telephoned Ms. R under the pretense of being a 'Dr. Stevens' from the hospital. Boro told Ms. R that she had tested positive for a potentially fatal venereal disease for which there were only two known courses of treatment: painful and invasive surgery at an uninsured cost of $9000 and requiring a hospital stay of six weeks; or sexual intercourse at a cost of $1000 with an anonymous donor who had been injected with a serum that would cure the disease. Fearing for her life and unable to afford invasive surgery, Ms. R agreed to go to a hotel where Boro, presenting himself as an anonymous donor, took Ms. R's $1000 and had sexual intercourse with her. Boro was arrested and charged with having sexual intercourse with Ms. R without her consent. Surprisingly, however, the appellate court dismissed the charges against Boro, in part by analyzing the case solely in terms of fraud. Instead of focusing upon the fact that Boro conditionally placed Ms. R in fear for her life, the *Boro* court analyzed Boro's scheme as if Boro had simply deceived Ms. R as to the future benefits of having sexual intercourse, comparing his scheme to one in which a man elicits sexual intercourse from a woman by falsely holding out the promise of 'travel, fame, [or] celebrity'.[35] In reality, of course, the harm Boro inflicted on Ms. R is better classified as—and indeed may be what the California legislature[36] regarded as—sexual intercourse by 'force' or 'threat'. After all, Boro did not simply mislead Ms. R regarding the future benefits of having sexual intercourse; rather, he instilled fear in her by causing her to believe that her position had conditionally so changed for the worse that she was induced, illicitly, to acquiesce to sexual intercourse that she would otherwise have eschewed. Boro deceived Ms. R about the curative effects of sexual intercourse, just as he deceived her about being fatally ill. But a man who elicits sexual intercourse from a woman by falsely threatening that he will otherwise kill her imposes precisely the same harm upon her as a man who elicits sexual intercourse from a woman by truthfully threatening that he will otherwise kill her; for the harm of rape by 'wrongful threat' consists of the harm that a woman believes will befall her if she refuses to have sexual intercourse, not the harms that subsequent events reveal would actually have befallen her.[37] Ms. R acquiesced to sexual intercourse with Boro because, based upon what he told her, she believed, as she put it, that 'my life' was 'threatened'.[38]

To summarize, *S*'s acquiescence to *x* with *A* is induced by 'fraud' and, hence, is invalid as a defense to the offense of subjecting her to *x* without her prescriptive attitudinal consent, if *S* is induced by *A* or a third person to acquiesce to *x* as a result of such false beliefs regarding *A* or x (other than false beliefs that constitute wrongful force to acquiesce to *x*) that preclude a person who relies upon them from being able to decide whether engaging in *x* with *A* is truly in his or her interests. Conversely, *S*'s subjective acquiescence to *x* with *A* is valid as a defense to an offense of subjecting her to *x* without her prescriptive attitudinal consent only if it is 'voluntary'. And *S*'s acquiescence is voluntary only if it is 'knowing'—that is, only if it does *not* result from *S*'s acquiescing to *x* with *A* on the basis of such false beliefs about *x* or *A* (other than false beliefs which amount to wrongful force to acquiesce to *x*) that preclude a person who relies upon them from being able to decide whether engaging in *x* with *A* is truly in her interests.

'Competence' (Or the Absence of 'Legal Disability')

We have thus far discussed two categories of conditions necessary to render actual acquiescence voluntary—'freedom' and 'knowledge'. Interestingly, some commentators are ambivalent as to whether any third conceptual category exists over and above those two. Larry Alexander, for example, tentatively classifies prescribed conditions for prescriptive attitudinal consent under the three categories of (i) freedom from threats, (ii) knowledge, and (iii) 'capacity'. Yet having done so, Alexander confesses that the third category, 'capacity', may be capable of being fully 'cashed out in the currency' of freedom from threats and knowledge.[39]

Similarly, Feinberg, in classifying factors that negate the voluntariness of acts of acquiescence, vacillates as to whether a third conceptual category of 'incapacity' exists over and above the categories of 'force' and 'defective belief'. On the one hand, Feinberg believes that force (which constrains exercises of will) and lack of knowledge (which deludes it) together encompass all the factors that negate voluntariness:

> From a theoretical point of view, incapacity appears to be less fundamental a category than force and defective belief. Instead of being a third independent type of voluntariness-reducing factor, incapacity is derivative from the other two. If we ask *which type* of incapacities tend to defeat voluntariness, the answer is—the volitional and cognitive ones; and if we ask how incapable a person must be to lack the power of valid consent, the answer is—incapable of fully understanding the agreement in question, or incapable of choosing otherwise. Ultimately the grounds for dismissing an expression of assent as insufficiently voluntary to be valid reduce, as Aristotle claimed, to two: 'He couldn't help it' and 'He didn't really know (or understand) what he was doing'.[40]

On the other hand, Feinberg goes on to employ the same three categories that Alexander adopts, *viz*., 'force', 'defective belief', and 'incapacity', though the supporting reason that Feinberg gives for doing so is a *non sequitur*. Feinberg argues that 'incapacity' is needed to account for the involuntariness of acquiescence by persons who are incapable of forming preferences, such as persons in comas. Yet the instances of which he feels a need to take account are a null set. Persons who are incapable of forming preferences are not persons who acquiesce to conduct under conditions that render their acquiescence involuntary but, rather, persons who do not acquiesce at all. Nor is 'involuntariness' needed to invalidate defenses of consent in such cases. The defense of prescriptive consent fails in such cases not because the victim actually acquiesced to the conduct under such conditions as render her acquiescence invalid, but because the victim did not in any way actually acquiesce to the conduct in either mind or expression.

Paradoxically (and despite his *non sequitur*), Feinberg may be right that incompetence both *is* and *is not* a superfluous category. Feinberg is probably right that all voluntariness-reducing factors can be reduced to two categories—'He couldn't help it', and 'He didn't really know what he was doing.' Yet he may also be right that three categories are more useful than two (though not for the reason he gives). The solution to the paradox lies in the last of the considerations that Feinberg enumerates as necessary for *S*'s actual acquiescence to be 'fully voluntary', namely, that *S* be an 'adult', that she be 'unimpaired', and that she not be 'manipulated by subtle forms of conditioning'. Subjects who are immature, impaired, or conditioned by manipulation are, indeed, subjects about whom one could say, 'She couldn't help it', 'She didn't really know what she was doing', or both. Yet they also possess something essential in common: they are persons whose disabilities are too fundamental to be negated by relieving them of particular pressures or providing them with particular information. Regardless of how much one may endeavor to free them or inform them with respect to the conduct at issue, they lack the competence to decide whether the conduct is in their long-term interests.

To illustrate, consider young children. Young children may, indeed, be vulnerable to pressure and deception due to their youth. But the legal disability that disqualifies all underage children from prescriptively consenting to sexual intercourse cannot be removed by freeing them from particular pressures or providing them with specific information. They are disqualified because, regardless of how much independence and information one seeks to give them, they are too young to be able to assess their long-term interests. The same thing is true of persons whose judgment is 'impaired' by intoxicants, or mental disorders, and persons who are 'manipulated by subtle forms of conditioning', such as patients in psychotherapy relationships.[41] They are disabled from prescriptively consenting to sexual intercourse because despite the options and information one happens to give them, they lack a third condition of prescriptive attitudinal consent: they lack the 'competence' to assess their options with respect to their long-term interests.

These three conceptual categories—freedom, knowledge, and competence—illuminate the normative judgments that transmute actual subjective acquiescence into prescriptive attitudinal consent. However, they do not reduce the need to make difficult normative judgments. On the contrary, in order to determine whether *S* is 'freely' acquiescing to *x*, one must still do the legal work of deciding whether the pressures that induce *S* to acquiesce are legitimate, given the nature of x and the criminal penalties that attach to subjecting *S* to *x* without her prescriptive attitudinal consent. By the same token, to determine whether *S* is 'knowingly' acquiescing to *x*, one must still do the legal work of deciding whether *S*'s ignorance about *A* or *x* is a legitimate basis upon which to allow *S* to acquiesce to *A*'s subjecting *S* to *x*. The same is true of 'competence'.[42] What counts as legitimate influences on acquiescence will differ from culture to culture, era to era, and context to context. Nevertheless, although freedom, knowledge, and competence are conceptual categories that do not replace the need for making difficult legal judgments, they facilitate the judgments by helping to distinguish among the diverse factors that enter into judgments of 'voluntariness'. Thus, they help reveal that 'compulsion' (in contrast to 'threats') is not a species of force that impairs *S*'s freedom to prescriptively consent to *x*, and that force undermines prescriptive consent in fundamentally different ways than fraud does.

The Relationship of 'Freedom', 'Knowledge', and 'Competence' to the Forms in Which Offenses of Non-Consent are Drafted

Freedom, knowledge, and competence, as defined here, are conceptual categories designed to organize the factors that enter into judgments regarding whether subjective acquiescence is legally voluntary. They are categories that can be superimposed upon statutes and judicial decisions to illuminate issues of prescriptive consent. Nevertheless, they do not necessarily track the categories in which criminal laws are explicitly drafted. Criminal laws are framed in categories of their own.

Frequently, for example, statutes employ single provisions for multiple ends. Consider the Utah statute on rape. The statute makes it an offense to have sexual intercourse with a person without her consent. The statute further specifies that sexual intercourse is 'without consent' if:

> (1) the actor overcomes the victim through the actual application of physical force or violence, or . . . coerces the victim to submit by threatening to retaliate in the immediate future against the victim or any other person;
>
> (2) the actor knows that the victim submits or participates because the victim erroneously believes that the actor is the victim's spouse;
>
> (3) the victim is younger than 14 years of age; or
>
> (4) the victim is younger than 18 years of age and at the time of the offense the actor was the victim's . . . teacher . . . or employer.[43]

The first three subsections can be conceptualized, respectively, in terms of freedom, knowledge, and competence—and their conceptual counterparts of wrongful force, fraud, and incapacity. Thus, subsection (1) addresses instances in which wrongful force deprives a person of the freedom to prescriptively consent; subsection (2) addresses an instance in which fraud deprives a person of the knowledge required to prescriptively consent; and subsection (3) addresses instances in which, regardless of force or fraud, and regardless of the age of her partner, a child's age deprives her of competence to assess her long-term interests regarding sexual intercourse. It is not clear, however, that subsection (4) is wholly based on any of the norms of freedom, knowledge, or competence alone. It is not clear, for example, that the ban on sexual intercourse by 'employers' with persons under 18 is solely based on the same concern with lack of competence that underlies the ban on sexual intercourse with persons under 14. Rather, considering the force and fraud that employers can bring to bear upon vulnerable minors, it is likely that Subsection (4) constitutes a statutory category of persons who are regarded as sufficiently susceptible to *combinations* of force, fraud, and incapacity to justify treating them as a separate group.

For administrative reasons, statutes also create categories of victims who invariably include persons who are not victims of wrongful force, fraud, or incapacity. A good example is the Idaho statute that makes it an offense for any 'officer, employee, or agent' of a jail to have 'sexual contact' with an inmate.[44] The statute is not designed to further the state's interest in *punishing* inmates by depriving them of sexual partners, because jail inmates consist significantly of pretrial detainees who have not been convicted and, hence, cannot be said to deserve any punishment at all. Rather, the Idaho statute is designed to protect inmates from being coerced by staff members into having sexual contact that they would otherwise eschew. The statute creates a class of victims, however, that inevitably includes persons who experience no coercion of the kind the statute seeks to prevent. Thus, the statute would prohibit a jail secretary from having sexual contact with her boyfriend in the privacy of her office while he is being held overnight on drunk-driving charges.[45] The legislature prohibits such conduct, not because it believes the boyfriend is a victim of coercion, but because distinguishing victims from nonvictims is administratively so difficult, and because sexual contact between jail staff and inmates is typically so coercive and invariably of so little social value, that the legislature feels justified in categorically prohibiting it.[46]

The 'Motivation' Required for Prescriptive Attitudinal Consent

We have seen that a subject's motivation in factually acquiescing to conduct is relevant to whether her factual acquiescence is legally 'competent', 'knowing', and 'free'. Assume, for example, that a jurisdiction possesses statutes that together (1) make it an offense for a guardian to use his official position to induce a ward into having sexual intercourse with him; (2) make it an offense for a person to induce another to have sexual intercourse by misrepresenting his HIV status; and (3) make it an offense for a person to elicit sexual intercourse from another by threats of serious bodily harm. Now assume further that a subject *S* is motivated to acquiesce in sexual intercourse with her guardian because *S* blindly believes that her guardian knows what is best for her; or because, being otherwise competent, *S* believes her HIV-positive partner when he falsely tells her that he is HIV-negative; or because, being competent and informed, *S* fears that if she does not submit to sexual intercourse with her partner, he will severely beat her. Obviously, *S*'s motivation is relevant to the issue of her prescriptive consent, because her motivation reveals her not to possess the competence, knowledge, and freedom that the jurisdiction requires for her factual acquiescence to constitute prescriptive consent.

At the same time, we have also assumed that a subject's motivation in factually acquiescing is relevant *only* in so far as it bears upon whether she did so competently, knowingly, and freely. That is, we have assumed that a subject's motivation in factually acquiescing to conduct ceases to be of legal interest once we know that she acquiesced under appropriate conditions of competence, knowledge, and freedom. To illustrate, suppose that a man asks a woman whom he has just met to have sexual intercourse with him. Suppose further that the woman possesses all the competence, knowledge and freedom that the jurisdiction requires for her to take responsibility for her sexuality. Based upon what we have assumed thus far, the law of consent ought to be indifferent as to whether the woman acquiesces and as to the motivation with which she does so. It has not seemed to matter to the issue of her prescriptive consent whether she is motivated by sexual desire, sexual altruism, sexual curiosity, or financial gain.

In most cases, our assumptions are justified; for once a subject possesses the competence, knowledge, and freedom needed to render her factual acquiescence valid, the law of consent tends to be indifferent as to whether she acquiesces and as to the motivation with which she does so. Depending upon how offenses of non-consent are drafted, however, it is possible for a subject's motives to possess independent significance. Indeed, it has been suggested that rape statutes themselves ought to be redrafted so that motivations do matter. Lois Pineau has argued that regardless of whether a woman otherwise possesses the competence, knowledge, and freedom that are needed for her acquiescence to sexual intercourse to be valid as a defense to rape, the woman's motivation in acquiescing ought to matter in one and, perhaps, two independent respects: first, she says, if the sexual act occurs under conditions in which the woman cannot be expected to derive 'sexual enjoyment' and 'pleasure' from it, the law ought to presume that the woman did not prescriptively consent; and second, she says, once the law rebuttably presumes that the woman did not prescriptively consent, the law ought to conclusively presume that the woman did not prescriptively consent, unless the defendant can prove that the woman had 'good reasons' for acquiescing to sexual intercourse that she did not expect to find 'enjoyable'.[47] Unfortunately, because Pineau does not say what she thinks count as 'good reasons' for engaging in sexual intercourse that is not 'enjoyable', it is impossible to know how much a woman's motivations ultimately matter under Pineau's proposal. Pineau may mean to confine 'good reasons' to a few, select and specific motivations (*e.g.*, to become pregnant, to give sexual pleasure to an intimate partner, to be richly paid).[48] If that is what Pineau means, then the motivation with which a woman acquiesces in sexual intercourse plays a significant and independent role under Pineau's proposal. On the other hand, Pineau may mean to leave it to courts and jurors to define 'good reasons' in ways they choose, provided they do not run afoul of the state's standards of competence, knowledge, and freedom. If that is what Pineau means, then the motivation with which a woman acquiesces in sexual intercourse plays no independent role other than to shift the burden of proof from the state to the defendant with respect to sexual encounters that women are not expected to find pleasurable.

In the end, rape statutes may not be good candidates for motivational definitions of consent, because it means taking the position that women may not lawfully consent to sexual intercourse unless they do so for certain enumerated reasons. Nevertheless, there are areas of criminal law in which motivational definitions of consent may be appropriate. Assume, for example, that a jurisdiction is of the view that while it is otherwise an offense for a physician to knowingly administer life-threatening drugs to a patient, it ought not to be an offense for a physician to administer life-threatening doses of painkillers to patients who are suffering from pain that cannot be relieved with doses that are any less, provided that (1) the physician administer the painkiller for the purpose of relieving pain and not to for the purpose of killing, *and* (2) the patient consent to it for the same purpose, *viz.*, to relieve pain and not to die. The jurisdiction can achieve much of the patient protection it seeks by defining prescriptive consent as we have thus far defined it—that is, by requiring that patients personally acquiesce in the treatments, and that they do so with certain levels of competence, knowledge, and freedom. However, the jurisdiction cannot achieve its purpose of confining prescriptive consent to patients who are motivated by desire for pain relief by the way in which it formulates its standards of competence, knowledge, and freedom. To do that, the jurisdiction must make specific reference to that particular motivation. It must refer either to patients who are subjectively motivated by a desire for pain relief or to patients who objectively express themselves to be so motivated, depending upon whether it employs a rule of prescriptive attitudinal consent or prescriptive expressive consent.

The 'Knowledge' Required for Prescriptive Attitudinal Consent

We have seen that a subject *S*'s prescriptive attitudinal consent to conduct *x* consists of two steps: (1) *S* must factually consent to *x* in her mind by subjectively choosing *x* as that which she either prefers for herself under the circumstances or is so indifferent about that she is willing to delegate its occurrence to the actor; and (2) *S*'s factual consent must be the product of sufficient freedom, knowledge, and competence on her part to enable her to take responsibility for her choice (or be indistinguishable from the choice she would have made had she made it under such conditions of freedom, knowledge, and competence). Nevertheless, from a conceptual standpoint, the *freedom* that is required for prescriptive attitudinal consent differs from the *knowledge* that is required in a fundamental way. The difference helps explain the distinctive and puzzling doctrine in criminal law to the effect that frauds 'in the factum' negate prescriptive attitudinal consent, while frauds 'in the inducement' do not.

The difference between prescribed freedom and prescribed knowledge is one we identified in Chapter 1, namely, that *S* can factually consent to *x* in her mind without possessing any freedom *not* to do *x*, but *S* cannot factually consent to *x* without at least being aware of *x*:

> ***Freedom not to do x***. In discussing the fable of Snow White in Chapter 1, we saw that there is no deprivation of freedom not to do *x*—no threat, no oppressive condition, and no compulsion that an actor might bring to bear on *S* in order to induce her to engage in conduct *x*—that precludes *S* from factually consenting to *x* in her mind, that is, from subjectively choosing *x* for herself under the circumstances.
>
> ***Knowledge of x***. In contrast, we also saw in Chapter 1 that there is one kind of ignorance that does, indeed, preclude *S* from factually consenting to *x* in her mind, namely, ignorance that it is *x* itself to which she is being subjected.

This difference is significant. For it means that when a jurisdiction comes to make normative decisions as to the kinds of freedom that persons must possess in order to prescriptively consent to *x*, its decisions are reserved for step 2, because normative disputes regarding freedom arise only with respect to persons who have already factually consented to *x* under step 1. In contrast, when a jurisdiction comes to make normative decisions as to the kinds of knowledge a person must possess in order to prescriptively consent to *x*, its decisions are not confined to step 2, because a person cannot factually consent to *x* under antecedent step 1 without already having knowledge of the existence of *x*. This means that simply by virtue of making it an offense to subject *S* to *x* without her consent, a jurisdiction commits itself to requiring that *S* possess knowledge of a certain kind—namely, knowledge of the existence of what the jurisdiction indisputably means by '*x*'.

To illustrate the difference, suppose that a jurisdiction makes it an offense of rape for an actor to have 'sexual intercourse' with a person without the latter's consent, while defining 'consent' to mean prescriptive attitudinal consent. Suppose further that two cases arise within the jurisdiction: Case 1, in which an actor induces 'Dora' to submit to sexual intercourse by threatening otherwise to harm her in certain ways, *e.g.*, a threat to publish nude photographs of her;[49] and Case 2, in which a physician engages in sexual intercourse with 'Flora' by deluding her into thinking that he is performing a gynecological examination when in fact he is engaging her in coitus. Absent conclusive evidence as to what the legislature intended, judges and lawyers can dispute whether Dora prescriptively consented for purposes of the statute, because, even though she factually consented to sexual intercourse under step 1, they can dispute whether a threat to publish nude photographs is the kind of lack of freedom that renders factual consent invalid under step 2. In contrast, judges and lawyers cannot plausibly contend that Flora prescriptively consented for purposes of the statute, because they cannot plausibly contend that Flora even factually consented under step 1; for Flora lacked knowledge of the existence of the one thing to which the statute indisputably requires consent and without knowledge of which a person cannot factually consent—namely, that she was being subjected to *sexual intercourse*.

To be sure, a jurisdiction that does not wish to treat persons such as Flora as victims of rape can do so in a variety of ways. The jurisdiction can redefine the statutory term 'consent' to include a fiction of imputed consent (*e.g.*, a fiction that by prescriptively consenting to a medical examination, a patient also prescriptively consents to sexual intercourse, regardless of whether she is aware of it). Or it can amend the statute to exclude from punishment all cases in which sexual intercourse occurs because of mistaken belief on a putative victim's part. Or it can amend the statute by adding additional elements to the offense, such as requiring that sexual intercourse occur not only without consent but also by means of certain kinds of force. However, once a jurisdiction commits itself to defining an offense as sexual intercourse with a person 'without the latter's [prescriptive attitudinal] consent', as some jurisdictions do, it is committed to treating persons such as Flora as victims of sexual assault.

Notice that this difference between the freedom and the knowledge that is required for prescriptive consent arises only with respect to step 1. That is, it arises only when deciding whether *S* has factually consented in her mind to conduct to which the law indisputably requires prescriptive attitudinal consent. Once *S* has factually consented under step 1, any and all *further* conditions of knowledge that may be required to satisfy step 2 remain normatively contestable, just as all conditions of freedom are normatively contestable. Nevertheless, this similarity in the way conditions of freedom and knowledge are ascertained at step 2 can be masked by the way required conditions of knowledge are conceptualized. For with respect to conduct *x* to which the law indisputably requires prescriptive attitudinal consent, there are at least two alternative ways to conceptualize the additional facts of which *S* must have knowledge if her factual consent to *x* is to constitute a defense:

> ***Conception 1—Additional facts of which S must be aware if her factual consent to x is to be valid.*** One alternative is to conceptualize the additional facts of which it is adjudged *S* must have knowledge in the same way that we currently conceptualize the freedom that *S* must possess, namely, to conceptualize them as facts of which *S* must be aware if her factual consent to x under step 1 is to be *valid* under step 2. Suppose, for example, that a jurisdiction makes it an offense 'To have sexual intercourse with a woman without her consent', while defining consent to mean prescriptive attitudinal consent. Suppose, too, that a dispute arises as to whether or not a woman must be aware that an actor is not her husband if her subjective acquiescence to sexual intercourse with him is to constitute a defense to rape. Suppose, finally, that a court within the jurisdiction concludes (as the English courts in the late 19th century eventually concluded after much debate)[50] that a woman must, indeed, possess such knowledge if her acquiescence is to constitute a defense. Having reached that conclusion, the court can conceptualize its decision by saying, '*S*'s factual consent to sexual intercourse is not valid unless *S* realizes that her sexual partner is not her husband'.[51]
>
> ***Conception 2—Facts that are inherent in x itself.*** The other alternative is to conceptualize the additional facts of which it is adjudged *S* must have knowledge as constituent features of the very conduct, *x*, to which the statute indisputably requires prescriptive attitudinal consent. Thus, instead of conceptualizing *S*'s knowledge as a necessary condition of her factual consent to *x* being valid—*e.g.*, instead of conceptualizing a woman's knowledge that her sexual partner is not her husband as a necessary condition of her factual consent to sexual intercourse being valid—the court in our hypothetical case can say, 'The marital status of one's sexual partner is a constituent feature of the "sexual intercourse" to which a person must prescriptively consent in her mind; consequently, because *S* was unaware that her sexual partner was not her husband, *S* did not even factually consent to "sexual intercourse" within the meaning of the statute'.[52]

Conceptions 1 and 2 are functionally equivalent ways of conceptualizing the normatively contestable judgments that underlie them, *e.g.*, the judgment that *S*'s knowledge that an actor is not her spouse is necessary for *S*'s subjective acquiescence to constitute a defense to rape. Yet Conception 2 tends to mask the contestability of that judgment by conceptualizing the marital status of *S*'s sexual partner as a constituent element of conduct to which the statute indisputably requires prescriptive attitudinal consent ('sexual intercourse') and, hence, conduct of which the statute indisputably requires knowledge.

The interplay between Conceptions 1 and 2 helps explain the persistence of the puzzling criminal-law doctrine regarding 'fraud in the factum' and 'fraud in the inducement'.[53] The doctrine, which is particularly common in rape cases, purports to identify the relevant factors that distinguish deceptions that preclude defenses of prescriptive consent from deceptions that do not preclude such defenses. To deceive a subject *S* about the *act itself*—that is, to mislead *S* into believing that she is not in fact engaging in the very harm that the law seeks to prevent—constitutes 'fraud in the factum' and precludes *S* from prescriptively consenting. Yet deceptions that cause *S* to be fully informed that she is engaging in an act but, nevertheless, mislead her about the benefits of engaging in it constitute 'fraud in the inducement' and do not vitiate prescriptive consent.[54]

The doctrine derives its rhetorical force from the apparent transparency of the distinction between 'factum' and 'inducement'. Yet in reality the distinction between factum and inducement is ambiguous about the very thing that distinguishes Conception 1 from Conception 2, namely, the standard for identifying the criminal 'act' that the offense seeks to prevent. Conception 1 adopts a narrow standard for identifying the criminal act: it is solely the named conduct to which the law *indisputably* requires that a subject *S* prescriptively consent, such as the fact of 'sexual intercourse' in rape cases. In contrast, Conception 2 adopts a broad standard for identifying the criminal act: it is not only the fact of the conduct to which the law indisputably requires prescriptive consent, but also any additional facts that normative inquiry leads courts to conclude *S* must be aware of if *S*'s subjective acquiescence is to constitute a defense.

Conception 1's narrow standard for defining the acts that the criminal law seeks to prevent has both strengths and weaknesses as a standard for distinguishing 'factum' from 'inducement'. Its strength is that the acts that it identifies are acts of which subjects must indisputably be aware because such awareness is required by what the statute indisputably describes to be the offense. Its weakness is that it defines such acts so narrowly as to be normatively untenable—indeed, so narrowly as to exclude all accompanying facts that courts regard as necessary for a person's acquiescence to constitute a defense. By the same token, Conception 2's broad standard also has strengths and weaknesses as a standard for distinguishing factum from inducement: the strength of identifying precisely the facts of which subjects must possess knowledge if their subjective acquiescence is to constitute a defense, but the weakness of doing so in a manner that masks disputable judgments seem as if they were indisputable judgments.

To avoid reaching normatively untenable results, courts and commentators tend implicitly to adopt a broad standard of Conception 2 for distinguishing 'factum' from 'inducement'.[55] Yet by failing to make explicit the standard that underlies their definition of factum, courts are able to pass off judgments that are normatively contestable as if they were conceptually indisputable. The interchangeability of Conception 1 and Conception 2 enables courts and commentators to conceptualize *any* fraud that they regard as sufficient to invalidate acquiescence as a fraud in the factum.[56] And having done so, they are able to frame their conclusions in the strongest rhetorical form, for they are able to say that, in contrast to victims of wrongful force (who, they say, *do* 'consent' albeit 'involuntarily'), victims of fraud do 'no[t] consent at all'.[57]

Consider, for example, the way the California courts apply the doctrine in so-called impersonation cases, that is, in cases in which an actor engages a woman in sexual intercourse by impersonating her husband. California makes it an offense of rape for an actor to have sexual intercourse with another without the latter's consent, and California defines consent to mean prescriptive attitudinal consent.[58] California also adheres to the doctrine that fraud in the factum vitiates prescriptive consent to rape while fraud in the inducement does not.[59] Whether impersonating a woman's husband constitutes fraud in the factum in California, however, depends upon the standard by which the facts that constitute 'factum' are defined. If California were to choose the narrow standard of Conception 1, factum would be confined solely to the conduct to which the statute indisputably requires prescriptive consent (*i.e.*, the fact of sexual intercourse), and California would have to exonerate spouse-impersonators because spouse-impersonates deceive their victims about the benefits of engaging in sexual intercourse, not about the fact that they are engaging in sexual intercourse. If, on the other hand, California were to conclude after normative inquiry that spouse-impersonators ought to be punished, California could punish them by adopting the broader standard of Conception 2 and defining the facts of 'factum' to include the victim's spousal relationship to the actor. In the end, California has concluded, as most jurisdictions have, that spouse-impersonators ought to be punished, and it has done so by stating that victims of spouse-impersonation are victims of fraud in the factum.[60] By framing the issue in terms of fraud in the factum, California succeeds in exploiting an ambiguity in the standard that defines 'factum' to present a normatively contestable decision as something indisputable.

Ultimately, of course, and regardless of how they may conceptualize them, jurisdictions must make normatively contestable judgments as to the additional knowledge, if any, that subjects must possess if their subjective acquiescence to conduct to which the law requires prescriptive acquiescence is to constitute a defense. Some judges and commentators take the position that although a subject *S* is not required to know everything about an actor and the circumstances of the conduct, *S*'s subjective acquiescence is not a valid defense if she is mistaken about anything that causes her to acquiesce when she would otherwise not do so. Justice l'Heureux-Dub of the Canadian Supreme Court took that position in ***Regina v. Cuerrier*** (1998).[61] The defendant in *Cuerrier* was convicted of having sexual intercourse with a woman without her prescriptive consent by engaging her in intercourse without disclosing that he was HIV-positive. In contrast to judges below, who had held that a woman's acquiescence to sexual intercourse with an actor who conceals that he is HIV-positive is valid as a defense to sexual assault, the Justices of the Canadian Supreme Court concurred that knowledge of life-threatening venereal diseases is a condition of valid acquiescence to sexual intercourse. Among them, Justice l'Heureux-Dub took the broadest view, namely, that with respect to all assaults, including sexual assault, fraud as to a fact that makes a difference to a victim vitiates her consent:

> [T]he assault scheme is also about protecting and promoting people's physical autonomy, by recognizing each individual's power to consent, or to withhold consent, to any touching. . . . In my view, . . . fraud is simply about whether the dishonest act in

> question induced another to consent to the ensuing physical act . . . . Where fraud is in issue, the Crown would be required to prove beyond a reasonable doubt that the accused acted dishonestly in a manner designed to induce the complainant to submit to a specific activity, and that absent the dishonesty, the complainant would not have submitted to the particular activity . . . .[62]

This view produces a rule that is easily understood and applied, but it would also produce results that most judges and commentators—as well as all jurisdictions of which I am aware—find normatively untenable. For it would mean that an actor, who entices a woman to engage in sexual intercourse by falsely telling her that he is a high-ranking executive, or a low-ranking employee, or wealthy, or poor, or sexually experienced, or sexual inexperienced, or married, or single, or younger than he is, or older than he is, would thereby be subjecting her to sexual intercourse without her prescriptive attitudinal consent and, absent other defenses on his part, would be guilty of rape.[63]

In contrast, Susan Estrich favors a rule in rape cases that, while also easy to apply, is narrower than Justice l'Heureux-Dub's. Estrich argues that because interests in sexual autonomy are more important than interests in property, the law ought to treat any mistake on a woman's part that suffices to negate consent defenses to deprivations of property as also sufficient to negate consent defenses to sexual intercourse.[64] Estrich is right, of course, that rape is universally regarded as a more serious harm than theft of property. But it is a fallacy to infer that valid acquiescence to sexual intercourse requires at least as much knowledge as valid acquiescence to transfers of property, unless one knows *why* jurisdictions regard rape as such a serious offense. One possible explanation is that rape laws are designed in part to protect persons from being deceived into exchanging sexual intercourse for less value than they think the intercourse is worth. However, another possible explanation, and a more plausible one given the high criminal penalties that attach to rape, is that rape laws are designed to protect persons from being pressured or deceived into surrendering something that they prize more highly than property, something that they carefully safeguard as integral to their sense of identity, and essential to their emotional and spiritual well-being—namely, sexual intimacy.[65] Estrich's proposal may be tenable in jurisdictions that embrace the first explanation because by embracing that explanation, a jurisdiction commits itself to valuing sexual intercourse in part for its exchange value. As Jeffrie Murphy has pointed out, however, proposals like Estrich's are less plausible in jurisdictions that embrace the second rationale. Jurisdictions that enact rape laws in order to protect persons who safeguard sexual intimacy as being integral to their identity and well-being will not want to invoke rape laws to protect persons who value sexual intimacy so little that they are willing to trade sexual intercourse for goods or status.[66] Instead, such jurisdictions will respond as Vivian Berger does when she says that she has 'minimal sympathy for the idea that the law should protect, via criminal sanctions, the cheated expectations of women who sought to sleep their way to the top but discovered, too late, that they were dealing with swindlers'.[67]

To illustrate, consider, *Regina v. Linekar*,[68] an English case that simultaneously involved deception about marketplace services and sexual intercourse. The defendant Linekar, intending all the while to break his word, promised a prostitute in England, where prostitution is legal,[69] that he would pay her £25 in return for a sexual act. The woman performed the specified act; but after she had, Linekar fled without paying, as he had intended to do all along. On the woman's complaint, Linekar was arrested and prosecuted not for defrauding the woman of £25 but for rape. If Linekar had been charged with defrauding the woman of her services, he presumably would have been found guilty.[70] But it does not necessarily follow—and the English court of appeal held that it did not follow—that Linekar was also guilty of rape. While the English court reversed Linekar's conviction on grounds that reveal little of the court's underlying reasoning, the court may well have reasoned that the English rape statute was designed to protect persons who prize sexual intimacy highly and, by that measure, that Linekar's victim did not suffer a harm that the English rape statute was designed to prevent.

Proposals like Justice l'Heureux-Dub's and Estrich's are seductive because they are rules that adjudicators can apply without having to make contestable normative judgments. Realistically, however, there is no way to avoid making such judgments. In the end, having identified the harms that offenses of non-consent are designed to prevent, one must weigh the extent to which ignorance causes people to suffer such harms against the burden on the state of punishing those who take advantage of it–all in light of alternative regulatory and civil devices for protecting victims.[71] Those are judgments about which reasonable people tend to disagree,[72] as evidenced by the division among the judges in *Regina v. Cuerrier*, the Canadian case in which a defendant was found to have withheld from his sexual partner that he was HIV positive. While seven Justices of the Canadian Supreme Court agreed that the defendant was guilty of sexual assault, they disagreed among themselves by votes of 4-2-1 as to why his nondisclosure sufficed to invalidate his partner's acquiescence to sexual intercourse. And all seven Justices disagreed with all five lower-court judges who took the opposite view that the defendant's nondisclosure did not suffice to invalidate his sexual partner's acquiescence.[73]

The Relationship Between Wrongful Force to Acquiesce and Consent to be Forced to Acquiesce

We have seen that *S*'s mental acquiescence to conduct *x* does not constitute prescriptive attitudinal consent to *x* unless *S*'s exercise of will in acquiescing to *x* is free from pressure; that subjective acquiescence is free from pressure if, and only if, it is not the product of 'wrongful force'; and that wrongful force, whether it consists of 'wrongful threats' or 'wrongful oppression', is defined by reference to certain normative baselines. Nevertheless, the discussion has thus far left unresolved a certain paradox about the normative baseline by which the lawfulness of pressures on *S*'s exercise of will is measured. The paradox goes to the relevance of whether *S* *subjectively consents to be pressured to subjectively acquiesce to x*. Now on the one hand, it would seem that because the very purpose of the baseline is to define the unlawfulness of pressures on *S*'s exercises of will in subjectively acquiescing to *x*, the baseline itself ought not to be dependent upon whether or not *S* subjectively consents to be subjected to pressures. Yet, on the other hand, it would seem that, because the very purpose of adjudging pressures on *S*'s exercises of will to be unlawful is to protect her interests, *S*'s subjective preferences regarding the pressures ought to have a bearing on the baseline by which such judgments are made. Thus, the paradox is that it seems to be both true and untrue that *S* ought to be allowed to acquiesce to otherwise wrongful pressures upon herself to subjectively acquiesce to *x*.

The solution to the paradox, I believe, lies in recognizing the steps involved in identifying the conditions of freedom that are deemed to be necessary if a person's subjective acquiescence to *x* is to constitute prescriptive attitudinal consent to *x*. The process by which jurisdictions set normative baselines for defining wrongful force—and, hence, the process by which they identify required conditions of freedom—inherently involves two steps, not one. The first step alone leaves unresolved whether *S* can prescriptively consent to being subjected to otherwise wrongful force to acquiesce to *x*. Whether she can, and the extent to which she can, depend upon the normative judgments that jurisdictions choose to make in executing the second step.

The first normative judgment that a jurisdiction must make is to identify from within the total range of pressures that may induce subjects to acquiesce to *x* those pressures that the jurisdiction does *not* regard as criminal means for inducing subjects to acquiesce, regardless of how much subjects themselves might wish to be protected from such pressures. Pressures can range from imminent death, injury, and pain, on the one hand, to promises of wealth, power, status, and love, on the other. A person can induce another to subjectively acquiesce to sexual intercourse, for example, by conditionally proposing to worsen her situation by killing her, or beating her, or discharging her from employment, or giving her a low grade, or shaming her in public, or beginning to date other women; or, alternatively, by conditionally proposing to improve her position by refraining from dating other women, or taking her to the prom, or giving her a public prize, giving her a Fortune 500 company, or marrying her. No jurisdiction chooses to protect women from all pressures that others can bring to bear on them to have sexual intercourse, even if it were feasible to do so.

Consider the provision of the *Model Penal Code* that makes it an offense to elicit sexual intercourse by means of 'any threat that would prevent resistance by a woman of ordinary resolution'.[74] Despite its sweeping language, the latter provision is not intended to encompass *every* conditional proposition that would induce an average woman to acquiesce to sexual intercourse, or even every conditional proposition that, if rejected, would harm her in ways that the *Model Penal Code* regards as 'substantial'.[75] Thus, the provision does not extend to a wealthy man who 'threatens to withdraw financial support from his unemployed girlfriend', or a man who 'threatens to withhold an expensive present unless his girlfriend permits his advances'. Although the commentaries to the Code concede that 'it is a task of surpassing subtlety' to distinguish noncriminal pressures from criminal pressures, the commentaries clearly take the position that some pressures on women to engage in sexual intercourse are matters of private 'bargain[ing]' that are 'plainly outside the appropriate reach of criminal sanctions'.[76]

In deciding which acquiescence-inducing pressures to exclude from criminal sanction, jurisdictions typically take into account (i) the conduct to which *A* is pressuring *S* to acquiesce, (ii) the gravity of the pressure to acquiesce that *A* is bringing to bear on *S*, (iii) the legitimacy of *A*'s interests being able to bring such pressure to bear, (iv) the gravity of the criminal sanction at issue, and (v) the availability of noncriminal mechanisms for addressing such pressures. Consider, for example, the factors that enter into *Model Penal Code* provisions:

> (i) The extent to which the *Model Penal Code* criminalizes pressures (and, by the same token, the extent to which it leaves pressures noncriminalized) depends upon the particular interests that are being pressured. Thus, the Code makes it an offense of 'extortion' for *A* to induce *S* to surrender *S*'s *property* by threatening to inflict any of six enumerated harms on *S*. And the Code simultaneously makes it an offense of 'criminal coercion' for *A* to induce *S* to restrict *S*'s *liberty* by threatening to inflict certain harms on *S*.[77] Yet, in enumerating the threatened harms that constitute criminal coercion when directed by *A* against *S*'s liberty, the Code omits two of the six threatened harms that constitute extortion when directed by *A* against *S*'s property—namely, (1) the harms of *A*'s testifying or not testifying regarding *S*'s legal claims or defenses, and (2) 'any other harm[s] which would not benefit [A]'. Because of the differences that the Code perceives between liberty interests and property interests, the Code frees *A* to bring certain kinds of pressures to bear upon *S*'s liberty that, if brought to bear against *S*'s property, would constitute criminal extortion.
>
> (ii) The extent to which the *Model Penal Code* leaves pressures noncriminalized also depends on the gravity of the threatened harm. Thus, in making it an offense of 'gross sexual imposition' for a man to induce a woman to engage in sexual intercourse by means of threats 'that would prevent resistance by a woman of ordinary resolution', the Code means to exclude threatened harms that it regards as 'trivial', *e.g.*, the harm that a policeman threatens by proposing to give a parking ticket, or the harm that a man threatens by proposing to destroy an inexpensive object, unless a woman acquiesces to sexual intercourse.[78]
>
> (iii) The legitimacy of *A*'s interests in being able to bring certain pressure to bear on *S* also has a bearing upon whether the pressure is criminalized. Assume, for example, that a man is engaged to marry a woman who wishes to remain chaste until she is lawfully married. Assume, however, that the man is unwilling to marry until he is certain that he and his intended wife are sexually compatible. Assume, finally, that the man conditionally proposes to the woman that, if she does not acquiesce to having sexual intercourse within the following six months, he will begin dating other women. The man's proposal may impose enormous pressure on the woman—more pressure, indeed, than many proposals that jurisdictions currently define as criminal. Yet, in deciding whether to criminalize the man's proposal, a jurisdiction might consider the legitimacy

of a person's being able to condition a decision to marry upon evidence of sexual compatibility.

(iv) The extent to which a jurisdiction leaves certain pressures noncriminalized depends, too, upon the level at which it punishes prohibited pressure. The *Model Penal Code*, for example, contains two grades of offenses for persons who pressure women into sexual intercourse: the offense of 'rape', which is punished by up to life in prison; and the offense of 'gross sexual imposition', which is punished by up to five years in prison. Because rape carries such grave sanctions, the Code reserves it for persons who induce sexual intercourse by threatening the most fearful harms—namely, 'imminent death, serious bodily injury, extreme pain, or kidnapping'. With respect to threats of lesser harms, the Code either does not punish them at all, or punishes them at the lower level of 'gross sexual imposition'. In contrast, other jurisdictions like Montana possess only one grade of offense for persons who induce sexual intercourse by means of threat; and because Montana punishes the offense severely, it confines it to persons who elicit sexual intercourse by means of threats of the most fearful harms, like threats of death, bodily injury, and kidnapping, leaving unpunished persons who elicit sexual intercourse by threats of lesser harms.[79]

(v) Finally, the extent to which pressures remain noncriminalized depends in part on the availability of alternative mechanisms for regulating them. Thus, many jurisdictions today refrain from making it an offense for an employer to elicit sexual intercourse from an applicant by threatening otherwise not to hire or promote her. The reason that they refrain from criminalizing such conduct is not that they are indifferent to it. Rather, they believe that victims possess alternative remedies that are sufficient, namely, tort suits for back pay and punitive damages under Title VII of the Civil Rights Act of 1964.[80]

To recapitulate, then, the first step in resolving the relationship between the wrongfulness of force and *S*'s consent to be subjected to such force is to exclude from consideration the set of acquiescence-inducing pressures that the jurisdiction classifies as noncriminal means for inducing a subject to acquiesce to *x*, regardless of how much subjects may wish to be protected from such pressures. The acquiescence-inducing pressures that remain are 'conditionally criminal', meaning that they are acquiescence-inducing pressures that the jurisdiction *necessarily* regards as criminal methods for inducing acquiescence from subjects who wish to be free of them but that the jurisdiction *does not* necessarily regard as criminal means for inducing acquiescence from subjects who welcome them.

The second normative step is to identify, from within the range of acquiescence-inducing pressures that the jurisdiction defines as conditionally criminal, those pressures that the jurisdiction deems to be *unconditionally* criminal, that is, pressures that the jurisdiction regards as invalidating subjective acquiescence for purposes of the offense at issue, regardless of how much alleged victims may actually welcome the pressures. Alleged victims typically abhor being subjected to the pressures upon subjective acquiescence that jurisdictions define as conditionally criminal. Yet some subjects may welcome them. A sexual masochist, for example, might welcome being subjected to pressures to engage in sexual intercourse that would be criminal if applied to persons who abhorred such pressures. The purpose of the second step is to identify, from within the kinds of pressures that sadists, for example, bring to bear on masochists to acquiesce to sexual acts, the pressures that a jurisdiction believes ought to deprive sadists of the criminal defense of consent, regardless of how much masochists may welcome such pressures.

To illustrate, consider by analogy the English case of *Regina v. Brown*.[81] The defendants in *Brown* were a group of sadomasochistic men who, for mutual sexual pleasure, enthusiastically engaged in various forms of bondage and mortification of the flesh. The sadomasochistic activities caused no permanent injuries or infection, and none of the participants complained. But a videotape of the activities fell into the hands of the police, causing England to prosecute the defendants for inflicting 'bodily harm' upon one another. The defendants appealed their convictions, arguing that the participants had all welcomed the infliction of pain. The House of Lords rejected the appeal, holding that, just as acquiescence is no defense to murder or permanent maiming or loss of limb, it is no defense to the kinds of bloody and painful injuries that the defendants inflicted upon one another in *Brown*, at least not when done for purposes of sexual gratification.

To be sure, *Brown* was not a case in which pressure was used to induce subjective acquiescence to further conduct. The sadists in *Brown* did not employ torture as pressure to induce the masochists to acquiesce to sexual intercourse, for there was no evidence that the masochists engaged in sexual intercourse with anyone. Nor did the sadists pressure the masochists into acquiescing to torture; the masochists remained free to terminate the activities through the use of 'code' words whenever they wished. The masochists in *Brown* knowingly and enthusiastically submitted to mortification of the flesh, not in order to pressure themselves into acquiescing to further activity, but for the sexual gratification they received from the mortification itself. Nevertheless, *Brown* is a useful analogy to cases involving pressure to acquiesce because courts are likely to decide the cases identically. Thus, given that the House of Lords prohibited the defendants in *Brown* from mortifying the genitals of persons who welcomed mortification for its own sake, the House of Lords is also likely to prohibit defendants from mortifying the genitals of persons who welcome it as means of pressuring themselves into engaging in sexual intercourse with others.

The House of Lords decision in *Brown* is controversial. Some observers contend that the House of Lords went too far in the direction of prohibiting force in spite of the parties' wishes, just as others probably believe that the House of Lords went too far in limiting its decision to instances of sexual gratification. Because *Brown* was controversial, however, it is a vehicle for exploring the relationship between the wrongfulness of force and a subject's consent to be subjected to force that would exist if the House of Lords had gone further in each direction. As a thought experiment, therefore, let us imagine two societies, 'Puritana' and 'Liberale', that take the relationships to their extremes in each respective direction:

> ***Puritana.*** Puritana goes much further than *Brown*. Puritana resolves *every* issue of force in the way in which *Brown* resolved the issue of genital torture. Puritana takes the

position that, if pressure to acquiesce to *x*, whether in the form of threats or oppression, is sufficiently fearful to justify being *conditionally* criminalized as a means for inducing acquiescence to *x*, the pressure is also sufficiently fearful to justify being *unconditionally* criminalized for that purpose. That is to say, Puritana takes the normative view that if a pressure that *A* brings to bear on *S* in order to induce *S* to acquiesce to *x* intrudes sufficiently upon *S* to justify invalidating *S*'s acquiescence in the event that *S* does not welcome it, the pressure is also sufficiently intrusive to justify invalidating *S*'s acquiescence in the event that *S does* welcome it.

Liberale. Liberale goes to the opposite extreme. In all areas in which consent is a defense to criminal conduct, Liberale takes the position that, even though pressure upon *S* to acquiesce to *x* is regarded as sufficiently intrusive to justify invalidating *S*'s acquiescence in the event *S* does not welcome the pressure, pressure never invalidates *S*'s acquiescence in the event *S* welcomes it. In other words, Liberale thus takes the normative view that pressure to induce *S* to acquiesce never suffices by itself to vitiate her acquiescence, regardless of her wishes to be subjected to the pressure.

Significantly, by taking relationships to their respective extremes, Puritana and Liberale eliminate the paradoxical relationship between the wrongfulness of force and a subject's consent to it. Consider Puritana, where wrongful force on a subject to acquiesce to *x* is always wrongful, regardless of the subject's desire to be subjected to the force. Definitions of 'wrongful force' in Puritana remain as impervious to a subject's wishes as its definitions of 'legal disability'. A person who suffers from a legal disability regarding *x* cannot prescriptively consent to *x*, regardless of how much she may welcome her disability.[82] Thus, an underage girl cannot prescriptively consent to sexual intercourse with an older person, even though she may relish being an underage lover, because the very purpose of the legal incapacity is to protect girls from their own wishes. Similarly, in Puritana, where criminal prohibitions of pressures on acquiescence are unconditional, a person who is subjected to wrongful force to acquiesce to sexual intercourse cannot prescriptively consent to the sexual intercourse, regardless of how much she may desire to be pressured into acquiescing to it. The purpose of the unconditional prohibition of force is to protect her from being pressured into acquiescing to sexual intercourse, despite her desire to be pressured into acquiescing to it.

By the same token, there is nothing paradoxical in Liberale about the relationship between otherwise wrongful force and a subject's consent to the force, albeit for opposite reasons. In Liberale, otherwise wrongful force on a subject to acquiesce to *x* ceases to be wrongful if the subject desires to be subjected to it. For regardless of how much force *A* may bring to bear on *S* to subjectively acquiesce to *x*, *S*'s subjective acquiescence to *x* is valid as a defense in Liberale, *provided that S prescriptively acquiesces to A's application of the force.* In order for *S* prescriptively to acquiesce to the force that *A* brings to bear on her, *S* must actually acquiesce to the force, and she must do so as a consequence of possessing such conditions of competence, knowledge, freedom, and motivation as the jurisdiction deems necessary. But the kinds and degrees of force which *A* brings to bear on *S* to acquiesce to *x* do not themselves preclude such conditions of competence, knowledge, freedom, and motivation from existing.

In reality, of course, no jurisdiction approaches the respective extremes of Puritana and Liberale. Like the House of Lords in *Brown*, every jurisdiction is a blend of the two societies. Every jurisdiction unconditionally prohibits some pressures on acquiescence, while only conditionally prohibiting others. This blending of unconditional and conditional prohibitions, in turn, creates a paradoxical relationship between the wrongfulness of force and *S*'s desire to be subjected to it–a paradox that does not exist between either legal disability or fraud, on the one hand, and *S*'s desire to be subjected to them, on the other.[83] In so far as jurisdictions prohibit pressures conditionally, they *allow* subjects to negate the wrongfulness of force on acquiescence by consenting to the force. In so far as jurisdictions prohibit pressures unconditionally, they *refuse* to allow subjects to negate the wrongfulness of force by consenting to it. By prohibiting some pressures unconditionally and others conditionally, jurisdictions both do and do not allow subjects to negate the wrongfulness of force on acquiescence by means of consenting to the force.

The reason jurisdictions are ambivalent about otherwise wrongful force, of course, is that they are ambivalent about legal paternalism. While they feel obliged to protect people, paternalistically, from certain injuries that they might be willing to inflict upon themselves, they also feel obliged to let people decide for themselves what they do to themselves. To see why jurisdictions are ambivalent, imagine social relationships under either of the two extremes. Consider, first, the consequences of allowing any kind of force to induce acquiescence as long as the victim acquiesced to the force, as in Liberale. In that event, jurisdictions that now make it an offense for *A* to kill *S* with *S*'s consent, *e.g.*, voluntary euthanasia, dueling, and Russian roulette, would then have to make an exception for cases of homicide in which *A* kills *S* as a result of executing a threat of death that *S* welcomes as an inducement to acquiesce to something, such as masochistic sexual intercourse. And jurisdictions that currently make it an offense for *A* to maim or permanently disable *S* with *S*'s consent, *e.g.*, gladiatorial combat, would have to make an exception for cases of serious bodily injury in which *S* permanently maims *S* as a result of executing a threat that *S* welcomes as an inducement to acquiesce to sexual intercourse.

Now consider the consequences of making all prohibitions of force unconditional, as in Puritana. Consider, for example, its impact on activities such as collegiate wrestling. Wrestlers typically apply physical pressure to their opponents, including strength that they expect their opponents will find too painful to resist, in the hope of inducing their opponents to resort to uncomfortable and disadvantageous positions from which they can be 'pinned'. Wrestlers are allowed to apply such pressure because wrestlers would rather be subjected to them than be prohibited from wrestling and because jurisdictions believe that the competitive values of collegiate wrestling outweigh the ignominy and discomfort of being painfully induced to succumb to uncomfortable and vulnerable positions on the mat. Yet if a wrestler applied such physical pressure to his roommate without his roommate's welcoming it—or even to a fellow wrestler who was no longer willing to participate—the wrestler would be guilty of assault. It follows, therefore, that jurisdictions that regard welcomed force as being just as criminal as unwelcomed force must make one of two alterations in their rules in order to be consistent: either they must *cease* to make it an offense for the wrestler to assault his roommate; or they must *begin* to make the sport of collegiate wrestling an offense.

Significantly, this analysis of the relationship between the wrongfulness of force and a subject's consent to force may help to illuminate a persistent debate among commentators as to how reforms in the law of rape ought to be framed. Although feminist reformers all seek to protect women from certain pressures to acquiesce to sexual intercourse, they differ about how to do it. Some argue that women are better protected by laws against 'force', while others argue that women are better protected by laws against 'non-consent'.[84] In reality, the debate rests on false conceptual premises. Concepts of non-consent and force are each capable of incorporating whatever views a jurisdiction may wish to codify regarding the wrongfulness of pressures on subjective acquiescence:[85]

> ***Conceptions of Non-Consent.*** The concept of consent is broad enough to encompass any view of wrongful pressures that a jurisdiction may wish to adopt. Thus, Puritana can frame its view of wrongful pressure in terms of non-consent, by making it clear that, just as disability and fraud vitiate subjective acquiescence regardless of an acquiescing party's desires to be subjected to them, and just as certain kinds of harms to persons are criminal regardless of a person's wishes, *e.g.*, homicide, so, too, wrongful pressures vitiate subjective acquiescence regardless of the acquiescing party's desires to be subjected to them. Liberale, too, can frame its view of wrongful pressure in terms of non-consent by making it clear that, just as certain bodily invasions are criminal only in so far as they are unwelcome, *e.g.*, sexual intercourse, medical surgery, so, too, pressures on persons to acquiesce are criminal only in so far as acquiescing parties do not welcome them. And finally, because Puritana and Liberale can both frame their views in terms of non-consent, so, too, jurisdictions whose views of wrongful pressure are a mixture of the two approaches can do so.

> ***Conceptions of Force.*** The concept of 'force'—that is, the concept of inducing subjective acquiescence by means of illicit threats or oppression—is also broad enough to encompass any normative view of wrongful pressures that a jurisdiction may wish to adopt. Thus, Puritana can frame its views of pressure in terms of 'force' by making it clear that it encompasses any criminally wrongful pressure, regardless of whether the acquiescing party welcomes the pressure. At the same time, Liberale can also frame its views of wrongful pressure in terms of force, by making it clear, as some jurisdictions do,[86] that wrongful pressure ceases to be 'force' if it is welcomed by the acquiescing party. And finally, because Puritana and Liberale can both frame their views in terms of force, so, too, jurisdictions whose views of wrongful pressures are a mixture of the two approaches can do so.

This analysis also resolves a question that was reserved in Chapter 3. We saw there that offenses of non-consent can often be reformulated to prohibit precisely the same conduct but without explicitly or implicitly referring to non-consent, but we reserved the question whether offenses of non-consent can *always* be reformulated in that way. The answer is that offenses of non-consent can be reformulated by omitting all references to consent in cases in which conditions either preclude a person from even factually consenting or unconditionally invalidate her factual consent as a defense. Recall the Canadian rape statute discussed in Chapter 1. Using consent factually, the statute proceeds in two steps: sections 143(a) and 143(b)(ii)-(iii) make it an offense for a man to have sexual intercourse with a woman other than his wife without her having actually acquiesced to having sexual intercourse with a man other than her husband; and section 143(b)(i) makes it an offense for a man to have sexual intercourse with a woman other than his wife *with* her actual acquiescence to sexual intercourse with a man other than her husband, in the event that the man elicits her acquiescence by means of certain kinds of force or fraud:

> ***Canadian Criminal Code Section 143.*** A male person commits rape when he has sexual intercourse with a female person who is not his wife,
> (a) without her consent, or
> (b) with her consent if the consent
> (i) is extorted by threats or fear of bodily harm,
> (ii) is obtained by personating her husband, or
> (iii) is obtained by false and fraudulent representations as to the nature and quality of the act.[87]

Significantly, Canada could have achieved most of its goals by omitting all references to consent. Thus, without mentioning consent or non-consent, Canada could have duplicated most of the prohibitions in sections 143(a) and 143(b)(ii)-(iii) by identifying conditions that render a woman *incapable* of acquiescing to sexual intercourse with a man other than her husband (*e.g.*, unconsciousness, ignorance that she is having sexual intercourse, and ignorance that she is having it with a man other than her husband), and simply prohibiting a man from having sexual intercourse with a woman other than his wife under those conditions. Similarly, without mentioning consent or non-consent, Canada could have duplicated many of the prohibitions in section 143(b)(i) by taking the factors that the section explicitly or implicitly enumerates as *unconditionally invalidating* a woman's acquiescence to sexual intercourse with a man other than her husband (presumably threats of death or serious bodily injury), and simply prohibiting a man from eliciting sexual intercourse from a woman other than his wife by those means.

Nonetheless, there are two things that Canada could not do without referring at least implicitly to a woman's non-consent. First, there is a subset set of cases under section 143(a) in which a man has sexual intercourse with a woman other than his wife without her even factually consenting that cannot be captured without making at least implicit reference to non-consent, namely, cases in which he uses overwhelming physical compulsion to subject a woman to sexual intercourse against her wishes. For the reason the woman does not factually consent in such cases is not that she is incapable of acquiescing, but that she chooses not to acquiesce—an event that a jurisdiction can render relevant only by making reference to the fact of her nonacquiescence. Second, there is a subset of cases under section 143(b)(i) in which a man has sexual intercourse with a woman other than his wife with her factual consent but by means of force that cannot be captured without making at least implicit reference to non-consent, namely, cases in which he elicits her acquiescence by means of force that is *conditionally* criminal and to which she does not prescriptively acquiesce. For the feature that causes such pressures to invalidate a woman's acquiescence to sexual intercourse is precisely that she does not prescriptively acquiesce to the pressures—again, a feature that can only be identified by making statutory reference to the fact of her non-acquiescence.

To illustrate the latter point, let us assume for a moment that Canada takes the legal position that, although a man ought to be punished for rape if he induces a woman to acquiesce to sexual intercourse by threatening to inflict moderate pain that she does not welcome, he ought not to be punished for rape if he does so by threatening to inflict moderate pain to which she does prescriptively consent (*e.g.*, spanking). In that event, Canada not only *can* frame the rule by reference to consent, it *must* frame the rule by reference to consent, because the prohibition on having sexual intercourse by means of moderate pain is predicated upon the pain's not being prescriptively consented to. Canada could frame such a prohibition in the language of 'force', using 'force' to encompass wrongful pressure only in so far as it is not prescriptively consented to. But even then it is making implicit reference to consent as that which negates force.

The Relationship Between Wrongful Force and a Subject's 'Resisting'

The relationship of consent to wrongful force is only one of the paradoxes of prescriptive attitudinal consent. Another concerns the relationship between an actor's pressuring *S* into subjectively acquiescing to *x* by means of wrongful force, on the one hand, and *S*'s 'resistance' to the threats, on the other.

The latter paradox is particularly common in rape cases. All jurisdictions regard it as rape for an actor to subject a person to sexual intercourse by either *unwanted compulsion* or *wrongful threat*—that is, by either subjecting her to unwelcome sexual intercourse by means of overwhelming physical strength or inducing her to submit to sexual intercourse by wrongfully threatening her with certain harms. Now suppose that a woman finds herself confronted by a man who, although he is not subjecting her to overwhelming physical strength, demands that she submit to sexual intercourse under circumstances in which she feels she has only three options: (1) to submit to an act of sexual intercourse that she abhors, (2) to refuse to submit and suffer the very harm, *e.g.*, a brutal beating, with which she is being wrongfully threatened, or (3) to resort to evasions by which she can successfully avoid both the burden of unwanted sexual intercourse and the burden of any of the threatened harms from which the statute seeks to protect her. Clearly, if the woman ultimately decides to submit to sexual intercourse as the least of three evils, she cannot attribute her submission to compulsion, because she is not being subjected to superior physical strength. Nor can she attribute her submission to the pressure of a wrongful threat, because she knows all along that she possesses an alternative to sexual intercourse that does not entail her suffering any of the threatened harms from which the statute seeks to protect her—namely, the alternative of option 3. Paradoxically, however, in defining rape, many jurisdictions state that alleged victims are not required to 'resist' their assailants in any way. The paradox, then, is to reconcile these 'no resistance' rules with definitions of rape that make it an offense to elicit sexual intercourse by means of compulsion or enumerated threatened harms.

The laws of Florida and Virginia are good examples. Like most jurisdictions, Florida and Virginia previously adhered to the so-called utmost resistance rule, the rule that a man who subjects a woman to sexual intercourse is not guilty of rape, unless *either* the woman resists to the utmost until her resistance is overcome by superior physical strength *or* she is prevented from resisting by threats of certain harm. Then in 1974 and 1981, respectively, Florida and Virginia did what nearly all jurisdictions by now have done: they abolished the utmost-resistance rule in rape cases.[88]

Significantly, however, while Florida and Virginia both abolished the utmost-resistance rule, they differed as to what to insert in its place:

> ***Florida.*** The Florida legislature abolished all resistance requirements and provided that 'consent shall not be deemed or construed to mean the failure by the alleged victim to offer physical resistance to the offender'.[89]
>
> ***Virginia.*** The Virginia legislature was more ambivalent than Florida. Like Florida, it abolished all resistance requirements. Yet, unlike Florida, Virginia provided that evidence of nonresistance on the alleged victim's part remained relevant to whether she prescriptively consented: 'The Commonwealth need not demonstrate that the prosecuting witness cried out or physically resisted the accused in order to convict the accused of an offense under this article, but the absence of such resistance may be considered when relevant to show that the act alleged was not against the will of the prosecuting witness'.[90]

These conflicting approaches raise fundamental questions about the relationship of resistance to non-consent and compulsion. Is resistance *constitutive* of compulsion and non-consent, as the utmost-resistance rule suggests? Or is resistance *irrelevant* to compulsion and non-consent, as Florida suggests? Or is resistance *contingently related* to compulsion and non-consent in some way, as Virginia suggests? Significantly, the answer is that there *is* no single answer because 'resistance' means different things in different jurisdictions. 'Resistance' stands in different relationships to compulsion and non-consent in different jurisdictions, because 'resistance' possesses two distinct meanings. These distinct meanings are not the product of different views as to what constitutes rape; for each understanding of resistance is conceptually compatible with any legal view a jurisdiction may elect to adopt. Rather, the various meanings represent different ways of conceptualizing the relationship between compulsion and wrongful force.

We shall begin with the meaning of 'resistance' that underlies the rule that nearly all jurisdictions have by now rejected—the utmost-resistance rule. Despite the extent to which it has been repudiated, the rule that a woman must resist to the utmost can be regarded as a logical corollary of what it means to 'force' a woman to submit to sexual intercourse by means of either compulsion or wrongful threats. When use of the utmost-resistance rule was at its height, most jurisdictions held the view that a person was guilty of rape only if he either subjected a woman to sexual intercourse *without* any exercise of will on her part, *e.g.*, by doing so while she was unconscious or by overpowering her with superior physical strength, or *induced her to acquiesce* to sexual intercourse by threatening her with certain kinds of wrongful harm, namely, death or serious bodily injury.[91] (We shall see in a moment that the logic of the utmost-resistance rule does not depend upon what wrongful harms are prohibited.) Contrary to what is often said of it,[92] the utmost-resistance rule did *not* require a woman who was threatened with death or serious bodily injury to struggle until she suffered the very harms of death or grievous bodily injury from which the law sought to protect her.[93] Nor did the rule require a woman to continue to struggle even after discovering that her assailant possessed such superior strength that further struggle would be futile.[94] Nor did the rule require resistance of a woman who lacked the capacity to resist, such as persons who were unconscious or too 'frozen' or paralyzed with shock to react.[95] Rather, the rule provided that a woman who possessed the capacity to resist, who did not believe that countermeasures would be futile, and who could resort to countermeasures without risking the wrongful harms of death or grievous bodily injury, could not be heard to complain about rape without first 'resisting to the utmost'—that is, without *resorting to such countermeasures as she had the capacity to invoke without risking any of the enumerated harms from which the law of rape* sought to protect her (*i.e.*, the harms of death or serious bodily injury).

Given this understanding of 'resistance', the utmost-resistance rule is a logical corollary of rules that make it an offense to subject a person to sexual intercourse by means of compulsion or wrongful threats. It is obviously a corollary of rules against eliciting sexual intercourse by means of 'compulsion'; because a person who, believing she may have the capacity to thwart an actor's use of physical strength, exercises her will by choosing to acquiesce to sexual intercourse rather than attempt to thwart it is *not* someone who is subjected to sexual intercourse by being overwhelmed with superior physical strength without any exercise of will on her part.[96] More significantly, the utmost-resistance rule is also a corollary of rules against causing a person to submit to sexual intercourse by mean of wrongful threats; because a person who submits to sexual intercourse when she can escape it by resorting to countermeasures that she believes she can invoke without suffering any of the wrongful harms from which the law seeks to protect her is *not* one who is being induced to acquiesce to sexual intercourse by fears of such harms. Rather, she is someone who is induced to acquiesce by fears of harms that, though real, are less than those from which the law seeks to protect her.

To illustrate, consider *Louisiana v. Powell* (1983).[97] Louisiana law provides that a man is guilty of aggravated rape if *either* he subjects a woman to sexual intercourse without an exercise of will on her part by overcoming her utmost resistance with superior physical strength *or* he prevents her from resisting to the utmost by threatening her with 'death' or 'great and immediate bodily harm'.[98] The defendant and the putative victim in *Powell* were social acquaintances. While waiting to get a ride home in the evening, the putative victim saw the defendant parked in a car nearby, walked to the car, and got in to talk. The defendant offered to drive her home, and she accepted. But instead of driving her home, the defendant took her to a secluded area where he slapped her several times to intimidate her into acquiescing to sexual intercourse. Rather than try to run or struggle, the putative victim went along with his demands by removing her pants as he removed his, and yielding to sexual intercourse. The putative victim testified that she did so because she was afraid, and the Louisiana Court of Appeal conceded that 'certainly, she was afraid.' Yet the court reversed the defendant's conviction on the ground that he did neither of the two things that the Louisiana statute prohibited: (1) because the putative victim preferred to acquiesce than physically resist, the defendant did not achieve sexual intercourse without an exercise of will on her part by overcoming her with superior physical strength; and (2) because the physical harms with which the defendant threatened the woman were harms less than 'death' and 'great and immediate bodily harm', the defendant did not achieve sexual intercourse by threatening her with either of the harms that a woman in Louisiana must fear to vitiate her acquiescence for purposes of aggravated rape.[99] A critic of Louisiana law would argue that a woman who has been repeatedly slapped should not have to relinquish the protection of the law of aggravated rape merely because the further pain and discomfort she fears she will suffer if she continues to struggle happen to be less than death and great bodily harm. But given the norm that Louisiana has elected to adopt—namely, that the onerous penalty of life imprisonment without the possibility of parole ought to be reserved for persons who induce acquiescence to sexual intercourse by threats of 'death' or 'great and immediate bodily harm'—it follows that a woman who acquiesces in lieu of resorting to countermeasures that involve less serious harms is not a victim of aggravated rape.

The fact that the utmost-resistance rule is a corollary of the norms of rape means that it is superfluous: a jurisdiction can abolish the utmost-resistance rule without in any way altering the judgments that it would otherwise reach in rape cases. To illustrate, compare the *Powell* case with *Montana v. Thompson* (1990).[100] Much like Louisiana, Montana provided that a man is guilty of rape if he either subjects a person to sexual intercourse by means of compulsion or induces the person to acquiesce by means of threat of 'death', 'bodily injury', or 'kidnapping'.[101] The defendant in *Thompson* was a Montana high-school principal who was charged with inducing a female student to acquiesce to sexual intercourse by warning her that if she did not, he would see that she did not graduate from high school. If *Thompson* had arisen in Louisiana, the Louisiana courts would have acquitted the principal on ground that he neither used superior physical strength to overcome the woman's utmost resistance nor prevented her from resisting by threatening her with death or great bodily harm. That is, they would have ruled that the student failed to resort to countermeasures that she could have invoked without fear of any of the harms from which the law sought to protect her, *i.e.*, the countermeasure of saying 'no' and walking away. Yet the Montana court in *Thompson* reached the identical result, and for essentially the same reasons, without mentioning resistance.[102] The *Thompson* court held that, although the principal's conduct was 'disgusting', and although the principal 'intimidated' the student into having sexual intercourse, he was not guilty of rape, because he neither resorted to physical compulsion nor induced her to acquiesce to sexual intercourse by the kinds of threats of death, bodily injury or kidnapping that Montana law requires to constitute rape.[103]

One can rightly criticize Louisiana and Montana for defining wrongful force too narrowly, and some commentators do.[104] What is significant, however, is that the utmost-resistance rule remains a corollary of wrongful force, regardless of how broadly a jurisdiction defines wrongful force. Assume, for example, that, in the aftermath of *Thompson*, Louisiana and Montana both amend their definitions of wrongful force by providing that it also constitutes rape to elicit sexual intercourse by means of a threat that amounts to criminal extortion when property is at issue, including threats of any wrongful physical pain. Assume further that two identical cases thereafter arise in Louisiana and Montana, both involving high school principals who induce students to engage in sexual intercourse by threatening otherwise to kill themselves. Despite their new and broad definitions of rape, Louisiana and Montana would both dismiss charges for reasons that, however different they may appear on the surface, are essentially the same. Montana would dismiss charges on the ground that the actor did not induce the student to acquiesce to sexual intercourse by threatening the student with any of the harms that are prohibited by the Montana rape statute, *i.e.*, death, serious bodily injury, kidnapping, or harms that amount to criminal extortion when property is at issue, including any physical pain. Louisiana would dismiss charges on the ground that the student did not resist to the utmost, that is, she did not resort to a countermeasure by that she could have avoided both sexual intercourse and the kinds of wrongful threats that the Louisiana rape statute prohibits. The latter rationale appears different from the former but, in reality, is a corollary of the former.

In contrast, the law of Florida exemplifies a second meaning of 'resistance'. Florida, like Montana, rejects the utmost-resistance rule.[105] Yet, unlike Montana, Florida goes further and affirmatively provides that 'consent shall not be deemed or construed to mean the failure by the alleged victim to offer physical resistance to the offender'.[106] What does Florida mean in saying that alleged victims need not physically resist? Does Florida mean that it regards persons as victims of rape by compulsion or wrongful threat even though they fail to resort to countermeasures that they can invoke without having to suffer either sexual intercourse, on the one hand, or any of the harms from which the Florida rape law seeks to protect them, on the other? Clearly not. Florida is using 'resistance' to mean the contrary of what Louisiana means by it. In stating that alleged victims need not 'resist', Florida means that alleged victims may rightly complain of rape even though they do not resort to countermeasures that, if invoked, *would, indeed*, cause them to suffer the very harms from which the law seeks to protect them.

This second meaning of resistance has implications much like the first meaning. Just as the utmost-resistance rule is superfluous, the 'need-not-resist' rule is equally superfluous, because given what it means by 'resistance', the need-not-resist rule produces the same results that would exist in its absence. To be sure, a jurisdiction like Florida could give substantive content to a need-not-resist rule if it wished. Thus, shortly after Florida had repealed its resistance requirement, a Florida court in *Hufham v. Florida (1981)*[107] interpreted the repeal as evidence of the kinds of threats of physical harms that the legislature regarded as sufficient to taint a woman's acquiescence to sexual intercourse. The defendant in the Florida case invited a woman he met at a dance to go to his car to share cocaine. The woman went, thinking her dance partner was right behind her. When they got in the car, the defendant drove to a secluded spot behind the dance hall and, hearing the woman's partner calling her, cupped his hands over her mouth to prevent her from shouting for help. When the calling subsided, he shook her to induce her to submit; and she, preferring to go along rather than suffer the physical pain and stress of struggling to free herself, submitted. The defendant argued at trial that the woman had resisted too little to be able to complain of sexual assault by means of 'physical force and violence' under Florida law. The court rejected the argument. Among other things, the court interpreted the 1974 repeal of the resistance requirement as a legislative policy that the physical pain and stress that the woman feared in the event she resisted did, indeed, constitute a threat of 'physical force and violence' sufficient to taint her acquiescence for purposes of Florida law.

Nevertheless, even though Florida has interpreted the 1974 need-not-resist statute as implicitly expanding the meaning of 'physical force and violence' under the Florida law, the logical relationship between its norms of prohibited force and the 'resistance' to which alleged victims need not resort remains the same. Alleged victims in Florida must still show that they acquiesced to sexual intercourse by virtue of pressures that Florida means to prohibit. And to do that, they must still show that there were no countermeasures to which they could have resorted without suffering the very baseline harms from that Florida means to protect them. The only difference is that, by virtue of treating the 1974 need-not-resist rule as an implicit expansion of 'physical force and violence', the Florida courts have simply set a new baseline from which to determine whether alleged victims, by physically resisting, would suffer the very harms from which Florida seeks to protect them. For it is only in order to avoid *those* harms that they need not 'resist'. Thus, if the victim in *Hufham* had realized she could thwart the defendant without physical harm to herself by triggering a car alarm that would bring people running and had deliberately refrained from doing so for fear of social embarrassment, the Florida court would not have held her to be a victim of sexual intercourse by means of 'physical force and violence'. Instead, the Florida court would have held that when the law states that alleged victims have no need to resort to 'physical resistance', the law means only that they have no need to resort to physical resistance that would cause them to suffer the very 'physical force and violence' from which Florida seeks to protect them.

These two meanings of resistance also explain the diverse ways in which rape statutes are occasionally framed. Some jurisdictions define the wrongful force they mean to criminalize by referring to a victim's 'resistance'. However, they do so in diverse ways, depending upon whether they adopt the first or second meanings of resistance. Compare, for example, the way West Virginia and Ohio define sexual assault:

> ***West Virginia*** makes it an offense for a person to elicit sexual intercourse by means of 'physical force that overcomes such earnest resistance as might reasonably be expected under the circumstances'.[108]
>
> ***Ohio*** basing its statute upon a *Model Penal Code* provision, makes it an offense for a person to elicit sexual intercourse by 'any means that would prevent resistance by a person of ordinary resolution'.[109]

West Virginia and Ohio both distinguish the countermeasures that they *do* require of victims, on the one hand, from the countermeasures that they do *not* require, on the other hand. But they draw the distinction by referring to two different kinds of resistance. Thus, in prohibiting actors from eliciting sexual intercourse by force that 'overcomes such earnest resistance as might reasonably be expected under the circumstances', West Virginia adopts the first meaning of resistance: West Virginia uses 'earnest resistance' to refer to the countermeasures to which it expects victims to resort precisely because they do not involve harms from which West Virginia seeks to protect victims (*i.e.*, the harms that persons suffer by resorting to earnest resistance); for West Virginia punishes actors only if they 'overcome' such resistance by causing victims to submit to sexual intercourse for fear of harms from which West Virginia *does* seek to protect them, *i.e.*, the harms that victims suffer by resorting to *more* than earnest resistance. In contrast, in prohibiting actors from eliciting sexual intercourse by means 'that would prevent resistance by a person of ordinary resolution', Ohio adopts the *second* meaning of resistance: Ohio uses 'resistance' to refer to countermeasures to which it does *not* expect victims to resort precisely because they *do* involve harms from which Ohio seeks to protect them, *i.e.*, the harms of resorting to resistance to which even 'persons of ordinary resolution' are understandably reluctant to resort; for Ohio punishes actors who cause persons of ordinary resolution to submit to sexual intercourse for fear of the harms they will otherwise suffer. Of course, regardless of whether they enact statutes in terms of 'non-consent', or 'force', or conduct 'overcoming resistance', or conduct 'preventing resistance', jurisdictions must decide what kinds of acquiescence-inducing pressures they do and do not mean to prohibit. Once a jurisdiction makes that judgment for itself, however, the two meanings of 'resistance' enable the jurisdiction to frame its prohibition in the language of resistance. The first meaning of resistance (which refers to alternatives to sexual intercourse to which jurisdictions expect people to resort in defense of their sexual autonomy) enables a jurisdiction to frame its prohibition in terms of pressures that *overcome* victims who fully resort to such 'resistance'. The second meaning of resistance (which refers to alternatives to sexual intercourse to which jurisdictions do *not* expect people to resort in defense of their sexual autonomy) enables a jurisdiction to frame its prohibition in terms of pressures that *prevent* victims who understandably wish to avoid such 'resistance' from doing anything but submit to sexual intercourse.

We have thus far addressed two contrary meanings of 'resistance'. Yet one puzzle remains, namely, the puzzle presented by statutes such as that of Virginia. The Virginia statute states that the prosecution 'need not demonstrate that the prosecuting witness cried out or physically resisted the accused in order to convict the accused'; and yet the statute also states that the 'absence of such resistance' is admissible to show that the alleged victim consented. The Virginia statute is puzzling because if evidence of non-resistance is admissible, then instructing juries on the exculpatory significance of such evidence ought also to be permissible. Yet if a jury may be instructed that evidence of non-resistance exculpates, the prosecution will, indeed, 'need' evidence of resistance to convict defendants of rape in cases in which non-resistance is at issue. One possible solution to the puzzle is to assume that Virginia's two references to 'resistance' are identical to Louisiana's, and that Virginia merely means to be placing the burden of non-persuasion regarding non-resistance upon defendants. That solution is unlikely, however, because making a defendant bear the burden of non-persuasion regarding non-resistance is functionally equivalent to making him bear the burden of non-persuasion regarding the dispositive issue as to whether he subjected the alleged victim to wrongful pressure. The more likely solution is that Virginia's two references to 'resistance' are not consistent with each other. It is more likely, that is, that Virginia is using 'resistance' in two different senses. When Virginia states that no resistance is 'need[ed]' to convict a defendant of rape, it is using 'resistance' in the way Pennsylvania does to mean that alleged victims need not resort to countermeasures that would subject them to the very harms from which the law seeks to protect them. Yet when Virginia states that evidence of non-resistance is admissible to prove the alleged victim consented, it is using 'resistance' in the way Louisiana uses it, to mean that a person cannot rightly complain of rape without resorting to countermeasures that she could invoke without suffering harms from which the law seeks to protect her. The puzzle of the Virginia statute is, not that it is contradictory, but that it uses the same word, 'resistance', to refer to two different things.

Before we conclude this analysis of the relationship between prescriptive consent and resistance, we should consider a very different rationale that some commentators have advanced for rules regarding resistance in the law of rape. Some commentators have argued that the law of rape requires resistance not only to determine whether putative victims prescriptively consent to sexual intercourse in their minds, but also to provide a 'substitute for *mens rea*'.[110] The law of rape requires resistance, these commentators say, in order to provide 'notice' to an actor that a victim is not prescriptively consenting to sexual intercourse in her mind. Thus, Susan Estrich writes:

> [C]ourts have demanded that the victim demonstrate her non-consent by engaging in resistance that will leave no doubt as to nonconsent. The definition of non-consent as resistance—in the older cases, as utmost resistance, while in some more recent ones, as 'reasonable' physical resistance—functions as a substitute for *mens rea* to ensure that the man has notice of the woman's nonconsent.[111]

The force of this argument depends upon what commentators mean by it. If commentators mean that an absence of resistance can provide notice of prescriptive attitudinal consent because an absence of resistance can *constitute* prescriptive attitudinal consent, they are correct. By the same token, if commentators mean that the presence of resistance can provide notice of a lack of prescriptive attitudinal consent because the presence of resistance can *constitute* a lack of prescriptive attitudinal consent, they are also correct. Commentators who mean the above, however, are implicitly conceding that the notice-giving functions of resistance and non-resistance are epiphenomenal of their function in constituting non-consent and consent, respectively. That is, the commentators are implicitly conceding that, while resistance and non-resistance both possess the side-effect of providing notice, rules regarding resistance derive their content exclusively from their function in defining prescription consent.

In point of fact, however, commentators appear to mean something quite different when they say that requiring resistance is a substitute for ensuring that actors possess *mens rea*. They appear to believe that even *after* actor *A* has reduced subject *S* to a state of prescriptive non-consent, the law requires resistance on *S*'s part in order to provide notice to *A* and to any trier of fact in a later trial that *S* has not consented. Thus, David Bryden writes, 'Whatever one may think of the [resistance requirement], . . . it can be defended as an effort to corroborate the woman's testimony that she did not consent'.[112] Unfortunately, this view manifests a profound confusion about the essential nature of prescriptive consent. The law does not require resistance by *S* in order to give *A* or others notice of a state of non-consent on her part that already independently exists. On the contrary, the law of rape requires resistance only when, by resorting to it, *S* can avoid both sexual intercourse and the alternative harms from which the statute seeks to protect her. Accordingly, when *S* refuses to resort to such resistance, she precludes herself from ever *being* in a state of non-consent in the first place. Indeed, if a law of rape required that *S* resist even after *A*'s wrongful threats of force reduced her to a state of prescriptive non-consent, the law would be contradicting itself. Suppose, for example, that a jurisdiction makes it an offense for an actor to subject a person to sexual intercourse by threats of death, kidnapping, or bodily injury. Suppose further that *A* threatens *S* with bodily injury in order to induce her to submit to sexual intercourse. Suppose finally that *S* chooses to submit to sexual intercourse with *A* rather than suffer bodily injury. If the jurisdiction acquitted *A* on the ground that, although *A*'s threats reduced *S* to a state of prescriptive non-consent, *S* should nevertheless have resisted in order to give *A* notice of her non-consent, the jurisdiction would be contradicting itself, because by requiring *S* to resist, it would be requiring *S* to subject herself to the precise harm of bodily injury from which the jurisdiction seeks to protect her.

Prescriptive Consent–An *Affirmative* State of Affairs? Or the *Absence* of *Negative* States of Affairs?

We have assumed thus far that prescriptive consent consists of an *affirmative* choosing of conduct on a subject *S*'s part–a choosing that can consist of an unconditional desire for the conduct, a conditional preference for the conduct, all things considered, or, in some jurisdictions, such an indifference toward the conduct that *S* is willing to delegate its occurrence or nonoccurrence to others. Accordingly, we have assumed that with respect to jurisdictions that define prescriptive consent as a mental state on *S*'s part, an actor *A* who subjects *S* to conduct *x* lacks a defense of prescriptive consent in the event that *S* possesses any of the following mental states of non-acquiescence to *x*:

> (1) ***A subjective choice not to acquiesce to x.*** *S* is capable of making a choice, and she makes one; but her choice is a subjective choice *not* to acquiesce to *x*. Example: *S* regards *x* as abhorrent and she is willing to do anything she can to prevent *x*; but either she concludes from the outset that she is helpless to prevent *x*, or she eventually discovers from the futility of her efforts that she was mistaken in originally thinking she could prevent it.
>
> (2) ***A subjective choice to acquiesce to x but an unlawful one.*** *S* is capable of making a choice, and she makes one by subjectively choosing to acquiesce to *x*; but the choice occurs under conditions that invalidate *S*'s acquiescence as a defense. Example: *S* chooses to submit to *x* but only because she is unlawfully forced to do so, or because she is unlawfully defrauded into doing so, or because she is legally incompetent to make the choice.
>
> (3) ***An incapacity to subjectively choose to acquiesce to x.*** *S* is incapable of subjectively choosing whether to acquiesce to *x* or not. Example: *S* is subjected to *x* while she is asleep or unconscious or otherwise unaware that it is *x* to which she is submitting.
>
> (4) ***A capacity to acquiesce subjectively to x but a failure to make a decision regarding x.*** *S* is capable of deciding whether or not to acquiesce to *x*; but, without feeling indifferent toward *x*, she fails to exercise her capacity to choose—that is, she fails either to choose to acquiesce to *x* or to choose *not* to acquiesce to *x*. Example: *S*, being frozen by panic or racked by indecisiveness or merely distracted, does not decide in time how she feels about *x*.

By the same token, we have also made similar assumptions thus far with respect to jurisdictions that define prescriptive consent as an *expressive* act. That is, we have assumed that prescriptive expressive consent consists of an expression of an affirmative choosing of conduct on *S*'s part—an expression that can take the form of an expressed unconditional desire for the conduct, an expressed conditional preference for the conduct, all things considered, or an expression of such indifference to the conduct that *S* is willing to delegate its occurrence or nonoccurrence to others. Accordingly, we have assumed that *A* lacks a defense of prescriptive expressive consent if *S*'s behavior or non-behavior expresses that she possesses any of the mental states 1 to 4, described above.

Commentators largely agree with this taxonomy—with one notable exception. They agree that mental states 1 to 3, or expressions thereof, all suffice to negate the existence of any prescriptive consent on *S*'s part. They also agree that mental state 4 or expression thereof *ought* to negate prescriptive consent with respect to all offenses of nonconsent. And they agree that, with one exception, mental state 4 or expression thereof *does* negate prescriptive consent with respect to all offenses of non-consent. The singular exception, they say, is the offense of rape. When it comes to the current law of rape, they say, 'consent' does not consist of an affirmative choice on *S*'s part. Rather, they say, the law of rape currently presumes that persons consent to sexual intercourse unless they either choose *not* to submit (mental states 1 and 2) or are incapable of choosing to submit to it (mental state 3). The consequence, they say, is that persons who possess or express mental state 4—that is, persons who, while possessing the capacity to acquiesce to sexual intercourse, fail to make any choice at all regarding sexual intercourse, including failing to choose to delegate its occurrence to others—are nevertheless treated as consenting to sexual intercourse for purposes of the law of rape. Thus, Heidi Malm writes, '[I]n all but a few jurisdictions, . . . a woman is presumed to have consented unless she has provided a *clear* expression of *dissent*. [The] utter absence of any positive sign of consent would not be enough . . . .'[113] Christina Tchen claims that there is a 'presumption' in the law of rape that victims 'consent' to sexual intercourse.[114] And Lani Anne Remick writes that 'Only under the law of rape [is] the person whose rights may potentially be violated burdened with the obligation of conveying her non-consent affirmatively':

> Although there are other crimes for which non-consent is an element or consent is a defense, only in rape is proof of a lack of consent insufficient to prove nonconsent. . . . In rape law, however, the 'default' position is consent. Proof of the absence of affirmative indications of consent by the victim is not enough to defeat a consent defense; instead, the prosecution must show that the alleged victim indicated to the defendant through her overt actions and/or words that she did not wish to participate in sexual activity with him. . . . Consequently, a woman's right to control sexual access to her body is not absolute, but attaches only upon her affirmative assertion of a desire to deny that access on a given occasion.[115]

I believe these commentators are mistaken about the existence of a so-called negative definition of consent[116] in the law of rape. More importantly, I believe their mistake reflects a further fallacy about the nature of prescriptive consent itself. Persons cannot lawfully 'consent' to sexual intercourse unless they affirmatively choose sexual intercourse for themselves. And they cannot affirmatively choose sexual intercourse if they possess and express mental states of type 4—that is, mental states in which they fail to choose to acquiesce, fail to choose *not* to acquiesce, and fail to choose to delegate the issue to others. The reason commentators think otherwise is that they mistakenly believe that a person who submits to *x* because she is reluctant to resist *x* and suffer the consequences is a person who is *not* freely and affirmatively choosing *x*–when, in reality, she is a person whose refusal to resist and suffer the consequences can *constitute* a free and affirmative choosing of *x*. As a result, when courts rule that rape complainants prescriptively consent to sexual intercourse by virtue of failing to resist, Malm and others mistakenly infer that courts have changed the very definition of 'consent' from a requirement of a free and affirmative choice (*i.e.*, a mental state or expressive act of freely choosing of sexual intercourse) to a mere absence of negative choice (*i.e.*, the absence of resistance to sexual intercourse).

To understand the fallacy in these claims about 'negative consent', one must distinguish the claim that Malm and others are making from claims they are *not* making. When Malm and other commentators contend that the law of rape is distinctive in applying a 'presumption of consent', they are not referring to a burden of proof. The prosecution does, indeed, bear the burden of proving non-consent beyond a reasonable doubt in rape cases. But, as Malm and the others recognize, the prosecution bears the same burden with respect to all offenses of non-consent. The prosecution's burden to prove non-consent is not distinctive to rape cases. Moreover, Malm and the others emphasize that the central question is not 'Who bears the burden of proof when consent is contested in rape cases? but 'What precisely is in dispute when consent is contested in rape cases?'[117] It is their contention that while the dispute with respect to other offenses of non-consent is 'Did the complainant affirmatively choose *x*?', the dispute in rape cases is 'Did the complainant affirmatively negate or dissent to *x*?'

By the same token, the claim about 'negative' consent in rape cases is not an argument against permitting *non-verbal* acquiescence to sexual intercourse. Nor is it an argument against inferring acquiescence from *passivity* or *silence*. Commentators do, of course, differ as to whether prescriptive consent to sexual intercourse ought to be verbal rather than non-verbal, just as they differ as to whether prescriptive consent to sexual intercourse ought to be active rather than passive. But when Malm and other commentators complain that prescriptive consent in rape cases is 'negative' rather than 'affirmative', their contention is not that prescriptive consent ought to be verbal rather than non-verbal, or active rather than passive. Malm herself believes that prescriptive consent to sexual intercourse ought to be defined broadly enough to include not only non-verbal expressions of acquiescence but also passive and silent expressions of acquiescence.[118] Rather, their contention goes to the state of mind that expressions of acquiescence should be required to express a person to possess. The contention is that regardless of whether prescriptive consent to sexual intercourse is expressed verbally or non-verbally, actively or passively, prescriptive consent ought to consist of an affirmative choice of sexual intercourse rather than a mere failure to resist it.

The key to this claim regarding negative consent is the supporting evidence that its exponents cite–and also *fail* to cite. Significantly, they do not provide evidence in the form of statutes or cases that equate prescriptive consent with mental state 4 or expressions thereof. That is, although they claim that the law of rape presumes that women prescriptively consent to sexual intercourse unless women actively disavow it, they do not cite statutes or cases that equate prescriptive consent with mental states of non-acquiescence such as frozen panic, indecisiveness, or distraction. Rather, they cite statutes and cases that equate prescriptive consent with failure to *resist*. Thus, Malm states that 'this negative definition of consent . . . allows the requirements of force and (or) resistance to be returned covertly to the definitions that dropped them (for what is resistance but a showing of dissent)'.[119] Peter Tiersma states that '[r]equiring resistance to prove non-consent effectively redefine[s] the crime of rape. Rather than being analyzed as sexual intercourse without the woman's consent, it [is] viewed as sexual intercourse without physical resistance'.[120] Remick states:

> [I]n the context of sexual activity the law presumes consent. For example, proving both that a woman did not verbally consent and that her actions consisted of lying still and not moving does not raise a presumption of nonconsent, but of consent. Only through evidence of some sort of overt behavior such as a verbal 'no' or an attempt to push away the defendant can the prosecution meet its burden of proving nonconsent. . . . [R]efusing to treat a lack of consent as non-consent raises yet another problem. By requiring affirmative manifestations of nonconsent, courts have essentially kept the resistance requirement alive despite its widespread statutory repeal . . . .[121]

In short, these commentators assume that because the law equates prescriptive consent with failure to resist, the law must be defining prescriptive consent *negatively*.

However, it is a mistake to think that a person cannot affirmatively and freely choose *x* if she submits to it for fear of resisting it. Moreover, it is a mistake that comes from misunderstanding what it is to choose *x affirmatively* and *freely* for purposes of the criminal law:

> ***An Affirmative Choice of x.*** A person affirmatively chooses *x* for purposes of the criminal law if she (1) unconditionally desires it, (2) conditionally prefers it to what she believes to be the alternatives under the circumstances, or (3) is so indifferent toward *x* it that she is willing to delegate its occurrence or non-occurrence to others. Accordingly, a person who submits to sexual intercourse in order to avoid the consequences of resisting it *does* affirmatively choose sexual intercourse, because she prefers sexual intercourse to what she believes to be the alternative consequences.

> ***A Free Choice of x.*** A person's choice to submit to *x* to avoid the evil of *y* is a free choice for purposes of the criminal law, *provided* that the evil of *y* is not among the threatened harms from which the criminal statute at hand seeks to protect persons with respect to choices of *x*. Accordingly, a person's choice to submit to sexual intercourse to avoid the consequences of resisting *is* a free choice of sexual intercourse for purposes of the law of rape, provided that the consequences to her of resisting are not among the

threatened harms from which the statute at hand seeks to protect persons with respect to choices of sexual intercourse.

To illustrate, recall the *Thompson* case in which a high-school principal pressured a high-school senior into having sexual intercourse by threatening to prevent her from graduating. The principal was charged with rape under a Montana statute that made it an offense to elicit sexual intercourse by forcing another to choose between submitting to sexual intercourse, on the one hand, or resisting and suffering consequences of 'death', 'bodily injury', or 'kidnapping', on the other.[122] The court acquitted the principal on the ground that, as 'disgusting' as the principal's conduct was, he did not put the student to any of the choices from which the Montana statute sought to protect her. He did not force her to choose between submitting to sexual intercourse or resisting and suffering 'death', 'bodily injury', or 'kidnapping'. Rather, he forced her to choose between submitting to sexual intercourse or resisting and suffering something *less* than 'death', 'bodily injury', or 'kidnapping'—namely, the shame of not graduating. The high-school student prescriptively consented *for purposes of the Montana statute*, because (1) she 'affirmatively' chose sexual intercourse, by actively preferring it to the alternatives of resisting and suffering the consequences, and (2) she chose sexual intercourse 'freely', because, although her choice was conditioned by circumstances, the alternatives she faced were not among the threatened harms from which the Montana statute sought to protect her.

One can criticize the Montana rape statute for adopting too broad a view of conditions that suffice to render choices of sexual intercourse 'free' (*i.e.*, any condition other than threats of death, bodily injury, or kidnapping). Indeed, the Montana legislature amended the statute in the aftermath of *Thompson*[123] to expand the list of threatened harms from which the statute protects persons—thereby restricting the conditions that suffice to render choices of sexual intercourse free, and restricting (but not eliminating) the kinds of resistance that, when not resorted to, constitute free and affirmative choices of sexual intercourse. Nevertheless, criticisms of rape statutes like Montana's ought to be conceptualized accurately. The normative flaw in rape statutes is not that they replace definitions of affirmative consent with definitions of negative consent. The normative flaw, if anything, is that rape statutes define too broadly the conditions of 'free' choice that render a person's affirmative choice of sexual intercourse a defense to rape.

Now one might think it hardly matters how one conceptualizes criticisms of statutes like Montana's. But it does matter, because references to 'negative consent' confuse what critics mistakenly *think* disturbs them about rape statutes with what *really* disturbs them. Critics mistakenly think that what disturbs them is the real or expressed mental state that rape statutes equate with prescriptive consent (*i.e.*, supposedly a negative mental state of *not dissenting*). In reality, what really disturbs critics is that, although rape statutes actually equate prescriptive consent with affirmative choosing, statutes define the accompanying conditions of freedom, under which such affirmative choices are lawful, so broadly that they deprive persons of the protections that critics believe persons ought to possess with respect to sexual intercourse. This mistake has two important consequences. First of all, if jurisdictions truly equated prescriptive consent to sexual intercourse with an absence of active dissent to it, they would have to exculpate many rapists whom they currently convict; because they would have to exculpate rapists who have sexual intercourse with victims who, being unconscious, underage, defrauded, frozen by panic, distracted, or simply indecisive, do not actively dissent to the sexual intercourse. Second, if jurisdictions were prohibited from equating a person's prescriptive consent with her failure to resist in certain ways, jurisdictions could not define rape by reference to submission to threats of certain harms; because, as explained in the previous section, to define a person's non-consent to *x* by reference to her submission to *x* for fear of harms *a*, *b*, or *c* is *itself* to define her consent to *x* by reference to her refusal to resort to resistance by which she could elude *x* *without* fear of harms *a*, *b*, or *c*.

Conclusion

We have seen that if *S*'s mental acquiescence to conduct *x* is to constitute a criminal defense within a jurisdiction in which subjecting *S* to *x* is otherwise an offense, two things are necessary:

> ***Step 1.*** *S* must subjectively choose *x* either as that which she prefers for herself under the circumstances or as that toward which she is so indifferent as to be willing to delegate its occurrence to the actor; and
>
> ***Step2.*** *S*'s choice must be the product of such (i) competence to assess her interests, (ii) knowledge of the circumstances, and (iii) freedom from pressure as the jurisdiction deems necessary to enable her to take responsibility for her choice for purposes of the offense at issue (or otherwise be indistinguishable from the choice she would have made if she made the choice under such conditions of freedom, knowledge, and competence).

This two-step framework is a way of conceptualizing the issues of prescriptive attitudinal consent, not a way to resolve issues that remain normatively contestable. Jurisdictions and commentators will continue to differ normatively as to the conditions of competence, knowledge, freedom, and motivation that are needed to validate *S*'s subjective acquiescence to *x* as a defense to *x*. Nevertheless, given that the two-step framework is fundamental to conceptualizing issues of prescriptive attitudinal consent, one might assume that in so far as jurisdictions and commentators have difficulty with prescriptive consent, it must be normative difficulty with underlying issues of dispute, not conceptual difficulty with the framework itself.

In reality, however, jurisdictions and commentators have conceptual difficulties of two kinds. First, they sometimes confuse the existence of step 1 alone with its existence under the additional conditions of step 2. That is, they treat *S*'s mere subjective acquiescence to *x* as if it were identical to *S*'s subjectively acquiescing to *x* under appropriate conditions of competence, knowledge, freedom, and motivation. Second, with respect step 2, they fail to distinguish the kinds of pressure that invalidate acquiescence from the kinds of pressure—the kinds of 'force'—that do not affect its validity.

The first conceptual mistake, *i.e.*, confusing the existence of step 1 alone with its existence under the additional conditions of step 2, occurs with some frequency. Courts and commentators make the mistake, for example, when they say that the offense of 'statutory rape' is 'misnamed'—or that statutory rape is 'not really "rape" at all'—given that underage girls can be victims of statutory rape even though they freely and knowingly 'consent' to sexual intercourse.[124] The California Supreme Court's decision in *Michael M. v. Superior Court* is a good illustration.[125] Michael M., a 17-and-a-half-year-old boy, was convicted of having sexual intercourse with a 16-year-old girl under a California statute that made it an offense for an actor to engage in sexual intercourse with a 'female' under the age of 18. Michael M. challenged his conviction on equal protection grounds, arguing that in singling out 'females' as victims, the statute infanticized underage girls by implying that, in contrast to underage boys, underage girls alone are incapable of consenting to sexual intercourse. The California Supreme Court rejected the argument, by contrasting the offense with which Michael M. was charged ('sexual intercourse with a minor') with the independent offense of rape. A person in California is guilty of 'rape', the court said, if he induces any woman, including an underage girl, to acquiesce to sexual intercourse by means of wrongful pressure or wrongful fraud. A person in California is guilty of the independent offense of having 'sexual intercourse with a minor', however, merely by having sexual intercourse with an underage girl, regardless of whether he wrongfully pressured or defrauded her for purposes of the offense of rape—that is, regardless of whether her decision to engage in sexual intercourse was 'volitional' and 'intelligent' for purposes of the offense of rape. It therefore follows, the court said, that when California made it an offense independent of 'rape' for an actor to have sexual intercourse with a 'minor [girl]', California assumed that underage girls were 'fully capable of freely and voluntarily consenting to sexual relations':

> We emphatically reject defendant's contention that to uphold the constitutionality of section 261.5 [sexual intercourse with a minor] necessarily creates adverse inferences concerning the capacity of minor females to make intelligent and volitional decisions. By its adoption of section 261.5 the Legislature necessarily acknowledged the obvious truism that minor females are fully capable of freely and voluntarily consenting to sexual relations. If this was not so, the charge brought in these cases would uniformly be one of rape [under section 261].[126]

The persuasiveness of the California Supreme Court's argument in *Michael M.* depends upon what it means in saying that underage girls are 'fully capable of freely and voluntarily consenting to sexual relations'. If the court means that underage girls are capable of acquiescing in accord with step 1, that is, capable of subjectively choosing sexual intercourse as that which they prefer under the circumstances, the court is, of course, correct. But the court must mean something more than that. After all, adult women who acquiesce to sexual intercourse at the point of a gun, or in the mistaken belief that they are with their husbands, also acquiesce to accord with step 1. In order to dismiss Michael M.'s claims that California infanticizes underage girls, the court compares them, not with adult women victims, but with adult women who acquiesce 'freely', 'intelligent[ly]', and 'voluntarily'. This suggests that when the court says that underage girls are fully capable of freely and voluntarily consenting to sexual relations, it means to equate underage girls with adult women who, being competent to assess their interests regarding sexual intercourse, acquiesce to it under appropriate conditions of freedom and knowledge—that is, women who not only acquiesce to accord with step 1 but do so under conditions sufficient to satisfy step 2. If that is what the court means, however, the court is patently mistaken because in contrast to adult women, underage girls are deemed to lack competence to assess their interests regarding sexual intercourse and, hence, are incapable of acquiescing under conditions sufficient to satisfy step 2.

To be sure, an underage girl who chooses to have sexual intercourse with her boyfriend may satisfy two of the three conditions of step 2, *i.e.*, the conditions of freedom from wrongful pressure and knowledge. And if she does, her acquiescence suffices to exonerate a boyfriend of 'rape' as California defines it. But it is also true of most adult victims of sexual intercourse without prescriptive consent that they satisfy two of the three conditions of step 2. Most adult women who are induced to acquiesce to sexual intercourse by means of wrongful threats not only subjectively choose sexual intercourse in accord with step 1, but do so as a consequence of possessing competence and knowledge sufficient to satisfy step 2. Similarly, most adult women who are defrauded into acquiescing to sexual intercourse not only subjectively choose sexual intercourse in accord with step 1, but do so while in possession of sufficient competence and freedom from pressure to satisfy step 2. An underage girl who acquiesces to sexual intercourse under only two of the three conditions required by step 2 is as much a victim of sexual intercourse without prescriptive consent as any adult woman who does so. By implying otherwise–that is, in dismissing Michael M.'s claim that the California statute infanticized underage girls with the statement that underage girls are 'fully capable of freely and voluntarily consenting to sexual relations'—the California Supreme Court treated acquiescence under step 1 alone as if it were equivalent to acquiescence under the additional conditions of step 2.

This tendency to confuse the mere existence of step 1 with its existence under the additional conditions of step 2 is not confined to cases involving conditions of competence, such as cases of statutory rape. It also extends to cases involving conditions of freedom from pressure and knowledge. David Bryden, in his exhaustive critique of the American law of rape, reveals this confusion in addressing an actor's use of extortion and fraud to elicit sexual intercourse. Bryden criticizes a proposal to reform rape statutes that currently punish sexual intercourse 'by force and without consent', by replacing them with simpler statutes that punish any sexual intercourse 'without consent'. Bryden assumes that the consent to which the proposal refers is prescriptive attitudinal consent, that is, a mental state of acquiescence to sexual intercourse formed under conditions sufficient to constitute a defense to rape.[127] Based on that assumption, he acknowledges that the reason the proposed reform punishes actors who elicit sexual intercourse by wrongfully threatening victims with physical harm is that conscious submission to sexual intercourse as a result of such threats is not 'consent'.[128] Having said that, however, Bryden also criticizes the proposed reform, arguing that statutes that punish sexual intercourse 'without consent' fail to punish actors who induce victims to acquiesce to sexual intercourse by means of wrongful extortion or wrongful fraud; because, he says, when victims submit to sexual intercourse as a result of extortion or fraud, they *do* consent:

> Sexual extortion is a complicated problem in its own right, and requires a separate statutory provision. Indeed, since the victim of extortion 'consents' to sex, extortion would require special treatment even under a statute . . . prohibiting all nonconsensual sex. [The same is true of] sex obtained by fraud . . . Like extortion, sexual fraud should be covered by a separate statutory provision, even in a jurisdiction [that prohibits all nonconsensual sex].[129]

Bryden's argument exhibits the same confusion as the California Supreme Court's argument in *Michael M*, *i.e.*, the mistake of assuming that a person who subjectively acquiesces to sexual intercourse under step 1, and under only *two* of the three conditions required by step 2, nonetheless prescriptively acquiesces to it sufficiently to satisfy her interests for purposes of the offense at issue. In reality, a person does not prescriptively acquiesce to sexual intercourse in her mind unless she satisfies steps 1 and 2 in their entirety. Accordingly, any statute that makes it an offense to have sexual intercourse with a person without her prescriptive attitudinal consent is just as capable of punishing actors who induce acquiescence to sexual intercourse by means of wrongful extortion or fraud as it is of punishing actors who induce such acquiescence by means of wrongful physical force, and for precisely the same reason. The statute punishes them all because, although their victims subjectively choose sexual intercourse as that which they prefer for themselves under the circumstances (and, hence, satisfy step 1), the victims do not do so under conditions sufficient to validate their acquiescence as defenses under step 2. Victims of sex by wrongful extortion, like victims of sex by wrongful threats of physical force, acquiesce under conditions of wrongful pressure, while victims of sex by fraud acquiesce under conditions of wrongful ignorance. Bryden makes the mistake of thinking that victims of sex by extortion and fraud nonetheless consent for purposes of statutes that require prescriptive attitudinal consent, because Bryden mistakenly conflates acquiescence under step 1 with acquiescence under the additional conditions of step 2.

The tendency to fall prey to this confusion is not the only conceptual difficulty surrounding prescriptive attitudinal consent. A second and more serious conceptual difficulty involves step 2 alone. Jurisdictions and commentators misunderstand the relevance of force to prescriptive consent. The basic problem is that they fail to distinguish the kinds of pressure that affect the validity of acquiescence from the kinds of pressure (or 'force') that do not. And as a consequence, they run the risk of either criminalizing conduct that they do not wish to punish, or decriminalizing conduct that they do wish to punish.

The confusions regarding force fall into at least four categories. One is the tendency to confuse *compulsion*, which has no bearing on the validity of acquiescence under step 2, with *pressure to acquiesce*, which directly affects it. Compulsion is a means by which an actor brings about *x*, not a means of inducing acquiescence to *x*. It is the power to bring about *x* without regard to *S*'s acquiescence to it. Thus, an actor uses compulsion to bring about *x* with respect to subjects who lack an opportunity to acquiesce (*e.g.*, subjects who are asleep or unconscious or penetrated by 'surprise' before they can react); subjects who have an opportunity to acquiesce but do not acquiesce (*e.g.*, subjects who, despite their repugnance and utmost physical resistance, are eventually overwhelmed by superior physical strength); and subjects who have an opportunity to acquiesce but whose acquiescence has no bearing upon whether *x* occurs (*e.g.*, subjects who are paralyzed but who nonetheless subjectively welcome *x*). In itself, however, compulsion is neither a wrongful nor rightful way of bringing about *x*. Rather, its wrongfulness depends entirely upon whether *S* prescriptively consents under steps 1 and 2 to the event, *x*, that she cannot stop. If she does not prescriptively consent to *x*, she is a victim. If she does prescriptively consent to *x* (as a subject does, for example, when she subjectively welcomes the impetuous kiss of a lover whose impassioned embrace she could not fend off even if she wanted to), she is not a victim. In both cases, the lawfulness of *x* depends upon whether a subject acquiesces and upon the conditions under which she acquiesces, neither of which is controlled by the fact that *x* is brought about by compulsion.

Jurisdictions and commentators alike make the mistake of assuming that because pressure to acquiesce to *x* can invalidate acquiescence as a defense, compulsion to engage in *x* must invalidate *x*.[130] Several jurisdictions, for example, make it an offense to have sexual intercourse with persons who, they say, lack the 'capacity to consent' by virtue of being 'physically helpless'[131]—as if persons who are physically incapable of stopping sexual intercourse must also be incapable of welcoming it.[132] Feinberg makes the same mistake in drawing a distinction between actors who induce acquiescence to *x* from subjects who are intoxicated, on the one hand, and actors who bring *x* about through overwhelming physical strength, on the other. Feinberg states that, although drunken acquiescence may under certain circumstances be sufficiently competent for purposes of prescriptive consent, 'brute force . . . compulsively employed . . . renders an act just about as nonvoluntary as it possibly can be, and an act that is *totally involuntary* cannot be "voluntary enough" for *any* purpose'.[133] The common fallacy in these illustrations is the assumption that if conduct is involuntary in the sense of being unpreventable, it must also be involuntary in the sense of being unwelcomed.

A related confusion arises under rape statutes of two kinds: statutes that make it an offense to elicit sexual intercourse by 'force' or 'threats'; and statutes that, having made it an offense to have sexual intercourse 'without consent', then define sexual intercourse 'without consent' to include sexual intercourse by 'force' or 'threats'. The confusion under both types of statutes concerns the meaning of the term 'force' in contradistinction to the meaning of the term 'threats'. The term 'force' in these statutes can be used in two different ways: (i) it can be used to refer to an actor's infliction of certain kinds of pain, injury, or physical pressure on a subject for the purpose of achieving sexual intercourse, eventually causing *S* to submit to sexual intercourse for fear that if she does not, the pain, injury, or physical pressure will continue if not worsen; or (ii) it can be used to refer an actor's use of raw physical strength to achieve sexual intercourse in ways that *S* cannot stop. If 'force' has the former meaning, it is either redundant upon, or supplemental to, the term 'threat'. For like other threats, the infliction of pain upon *S*, which induces *S* to give in to sexual intercourse for fear that the pain will otherwise continue, is pain that brings about sexual intercourse in the same way as threats—namely, by causing *S* to believe that she is better off acquiescing than not.[134] Alternatively, if 'force' has the latter meaning, it is a synonym for 'compulsion', and as such it is vulnerable to the criticism that it punishes an actor for the ways in which he brings sexual intercourse about, regardless of whether his putative victim prescriptively consents to it in her mind.

A second confusion is a tendency to conflate physical contact that is *incident to the act of x itself* with physical contact that constitutes *wrongful pressure to acquiesce to x*. Stephen Schulhofer illustrates this in discussing the relationship between physical force and rape. Schulhofer argues that much as one might wish to do so, it is impossible to fashion rape laws that prohibit all forms of physical force, because physical force is inherent in sexual intercourse:

> The problem [of distinguishing permitted from prohibited force] can't be solved by . . . prohibiting *all* uses of force. That approach won't avoid the vagaries of distinguishing permitted from impermissible force, because physical activity, some of it forcible, is inherent in sexual intercourse. And many of the other physical aspects of sexuality, though not inherent in intercourse, are expected and pleasurable, provided that there is consent. . . . Getting physical—hugging, lifting a woman up, pushing her backward, removing her clothes, and physically penetrating her body—all can be unobjectionable, and even wonderful, when a woman has given her consent.[135]

Schulhofer is right, of course, that it is inherently impossible to prohibit parties from having physical contact with one another while simultaneously permitting them to engage in consensual sexual intimacy. But he is mistaken in thinking that students of the law of rape must regard this impossibility as 'frustrating'.[136] The wrongful force with which the law of rape is concerned, including wrongful force in the form of physical contact, consists of wrongful pressure to acquiesce to the physical contact of sexual intercourse, not the physical act of sexual intercourse itself. The act of 'physically penetrating [a woman's] body' is precisely that to which the woman must prescriptively consent, not a factor that vitiates her consent. If a woman freely, knowingly, and competently acquiesces to the physical act of sexual penetration, the penetration is not an offense. If she does not so acquiesce—if, for example, she is wrongfully pressured into acquiescing—sexual penetration is an offense. However, the physical act of penetration does not constitute physical pressure to acquiesce in the selfsame physical act of penetration *itself.* To think that it does is to confuse what is being prescriptively consented to with the kinds of pressures that invalidate the consent.

Schulhofer appears, on the surface, to have a stronger claim with respect to the physical preludes to sexual intercourse, *e.g.*, 'hugging, lifting a woman up, pushing her backward, removing her clothes'. For physical preludes of that kind are, indeed, common incidents of sexual intercourse. And unlike sexual intercourse itself, they can have the effect of pressuring a subject into submitting to sexual intercourse. They can pressure her the same way that threats do—by causing her to believe that, if she does not submit, she will be left worse off, whether by virtue of being physically harmed or by virtue of having to engage in physical or verbal resistance. Nevertheless, the fact that physical preludes to sexual intercourse *can* constitute pressure on acquiescence does not mean that they *inherently* constitute pressure on acquiescence. Nor does it mean that when they do constitute pressure, they must constitute *wrongful* pressure on acquiescence. Physical preludes to sexual intercourse only constitute pressure when subjects perceive that they must either submit or be left worse off. Subjects do not perceive physical preludes to sexual intercourse as pressure when they welcome the pressures either for their own sake or as preludes to sexual intercourse. Moreover, even when subjects do perceive physical preludes to sexual intercourse as pressure to acquiesce, the pressure is not wrongful with respect to subjects who welcome it qua pressure.

Of course, subjects will remain who do perceive physical preludes to sexual intercourse as pressure and who do not welcome it. How should the law treat them? Should rape laws be changed to make it an offense for an actor to use physical contact to pressure a subject into acquiescing to sexual intercourse, provided, presumably, that the actor knows or should know that the subject perceives the physical contact as pressure to acquiesce and does not welcome it? Or would that change in the law be too dramatic a departure from socially accepted sexual mores? Those are normatively contestable questions about which reasonable people can differ. But regardless of how one chooses to resolve them, they remain genuine questions, not inherent contradictions. The fact that the most commonplace preludes to consensual sexual intercourse are inherently physical does not preclude a jurisdiction from making it an offense for an actor knowingly to use such preludes to pressure a subject for whom they are unwelcome into acquiescing to sexual intercourse.

A third confusion involves the *baseline* for measuring the wrongfulness of pressure in the form of threats against *S* to acquiesce to *x*. The confusion consists in the failure to distinguish threats to which *S* prescriptively consents from threats to which she does *not* prescriptively consent. The confusion is evident in responses by Robin West and Joan McGregor to Donald Dripps' proposal for reforming existing rape laws.[137] Dripps proposes to replace laws that currently make it an offense for an actor to have sexual intercourse with *S* without her *consent* with two separate offenses: (1) an aggravated offense of *threatening S* with certain harms unless she submits to sexual intercourse; and (2) a lesser offense of having sexual intercourse with *S* without her factual consent or despite her saying 'no'. With respect to the aggravated offense, however, Dripps does not propose to eliminate considerations of *S*'s prescriptive consent altogether. Instead, he means to retain them by conditioning the unlawfulness of *A*'s threats upon *S*'s *not having prescriptively consented to the threats*:

> The gist of the new offense would be purposely or knowingly facing the victim with the alternatives of sexual submission or physical violence; whether she chooses Scylla or Charybdis is immaterial. Such an approach would not forbid rough sex; just as with football, individuals would be able to consent to violence. But the consent must be to the violence, not to the sex.[138]

McGregor and West both claim to embrace Dripps' proposal with respect to the aggravated offense,[139] but, in reality, they misunderstand it. They believe that Dripps' aggravated offense eliminates considerations of *S*'s prescriptive consent altogether—while, in reality, the aggravated offense moves *S*'s prescriptive consent from one place to another. They embrace Dripps' proposal because they mistakenly believe that Dripps would make it an offense for *A* to make certain threats to induce *S* to acquiesce to elicit sexual intercourse, regardless of whether *S* prescriptively consents to the threats.[140]

What explains this misunderstanding? Why do McGregor and West take Dripps to be eliminating consent defenses when he means to preserve them? One possibility is that they give undue significance to Dripps' statement that, although he means to retain *S*'s consent as a defense to the 'violence' by which *A* induces her to submit to sexual intercourse, he eliminates *S*'s consent as a defense 'to the sex' that occurs as a result. In reality, the two are functionally equivalent ways to exculpate actors who make consented-to threats to obtain sexual intercourse. Thus, a jurisdiction can declare it to be an offense to make nonconsented-to *threats*. Or a jurisdiction can declare it to be an offense to threaten to elicit nonconsented-to *sex*, while simultaneously defining 'nonconsented-to sex' to mean sex elicited by nonconsented-to threats. Dripps prefers the former (which is framed in terms of nonconsented-to 'threats') to the latter (which is framed in terms of nonconsented-to 'sex'). But the statutes are identical in exculpating actors of extorting sex with respect to persons who prescriptively consent to be subjected to the extortion. For regardless of whether or not statutes are framed in terms of a victims' 'non-consent to *sex*', persons who prescriptively consent to be subjected to sexual extortion also prescriptively consent to the sex to which they submit as a result of the extortion. They prescriptively consent to both, because in submitting to sexual intercourse, they not only choose it as that which they prefer under the circumstances, but, having consented to the threatened pressure, they also base their choice on appropriate conditions of competence, knowledge, freedom, and motivation.

Another, and perhaps more interesting, explanation as to why McGregor and West fail to recognize the role of prescriptive consent in Dripps' aggravated offense is that they unwittingly conflate threats that are conditionally criminal with threats that are unconditionally criminal. The two classes of threats are easy to conflate. Both kinds constitute pressure on acquiescence. Both can induce a subject who would not otherwise do so to acquiesce to sexual intercourse. Both can work to invalidate sexual intercourse that they induce. And many threats that are used to induce sexual intercourse are, indeed, unconditionally criminal. The difference is that threats that are conditionally criminal work to invalidate *S*'s acquiescence to sexual intercourse as a defense to rape only if *S* does not prescriptively consent to the threats (*e.g.*, threats of mild pain as part of sado-masochistic sex), while unconditionally criminal threats invalidate *S*'s acquiescence as a defense regardless of whether she prescriptively consents to them (*e.g.*, threats of death). McGregor and West may possess the normative view that any threat that is sufficiently grave to invalidate acquiescence if *S* does *not* consent to it must also be sufficiently grave to invalidate acquiescence if she *does* consent to it.[141] But if so, they face a dilemma over certain threats, such as threats of moderate physical pain. For they must either criminalize such threats even when the subjects do consent to them, or they must decriminalize threats of moderate physical pain even when subjects do not consent to them.

Ultimately, Dripps is just as guilty as McGregor and West of failing to distinguish between wrongful threats, though in a different respect. McGregor and West treat all wrongful threats as unconditionally criminal and, hence, fail to distinguish among wrongful threats based upon whether or not they are consented to. In contrast, Dripps treats all wrongful threats as conditionally criminal and, hence, fails to distinguish among wrongful threats based upon whether they are grave or moderate in nature. The consequence is that McGregor and West would treat consented-to threats against *S* as wrongful ways to elicit sexual intercourse, regardless of how mild the threats may be, while Dripps would treat consented-to threats against *S* as lawful ways to elicit sexual intercourse, regardless of how grave the threats may be.

The final confusion is also the most pervasive, at least in the context of rape scholarship. It consists of the tendency to think that controversial questions regarding requirements of 'force' in rape cases can be eliminated by, instead, making it an offense to act without the subject's 'consent'. Thus, Lynne Henderson argues that '"force" should not be a necessary requirement to transform heterosexual intercourse into rape, because it should go without saying that if a woman is not consenting, the man has to force her into the act'.[142] McGregor, hoping to eliminate contested issues of force, argues rape should consist of sexual intercourse without consent, regardless of any accompanying force. Why, she asks, 'should the *actus reus* of rape include force as a necessary element? . . . Why not merely nonconsensual sexual intercourse?'[143] Vivian Berger wonders '[a]t what point . . . an element of "force" came to be added to the notion of lack of consent . . .'.[144] Craig Byrnes asserts that 'force need not and should not be an element of rape', because the sole issue ought to be 'the woman's willingness to engage in intercourse'.[145]

These efforts to avoid making contested judgments regarding 'force' by replacing it with 'nonconsent' are premised upon the fallacy that, in cases in which subjects feel they have been pressured into sexual intercourse, judgments regarding force are *independent* of prescriptive consent—as opposed to their being *constitutive* of prescriptive consent. A subject prescriptively consents to *x* in her mind if, (1) she subjectively chooses *x* either as that which she prefers for herself under the circumstances or that toward which she is so indifferent that she is willing to delegate its occurrence to the actor, and (2) her subjective choice is the product of sufficient freedom from pressure, knowledge, and competence to enable her to take responsibility for her choice (or is indistinguishable from the choice she would have made if she had possessed such freedom, knowledge, and competence). It follows, therefore, that to determine whether a subject's actual acquiescence to *x* under step 1 is sufficiently free from pressure under step 2 to constitute a defense to an actor's subjecting her to *x*, a jurisdiction must make contestable normative judgments as to the kinds of pressure on acquiescence, *i.e.*, the kinds of force, that do and do not invalidate such acquiescence. Jurisdictions can be rightly criticized for the judgments they ultimately make, but jurisdictions cannot avoid the task of making judgments as to which pressures are wrongful and which are not by replacing inquiries into 'force' with inquiries into 'non-consent'.[146]

What accounts for this fallacy? Why do commentators mistakenly assume that ascertaining whether a person prescriptively 'consents' to something to which she reluctantly submits can be separated from whether she is 'forced' to acquiesce to it? They do so, I believe, because they mistakenly assume that it is possible to know something that is in fact unknowable of a person who reluctantly chooses to submit to *x* as a lesser evil under the circumstances: they mistakenly assume it is possible to know whether the person really *does* or really *does not* wish to engage in *x*. They maintain that a person prescriptively 'consents' to something to which she reluctantly submits only if she really 'wants' to engage in it.[147] As Joshua Dressler expresses it for himself and others, 'the bottom line' in rape cases is, 'Did the female want the intimacy to occur at this time or not?'[148] In reality, however, a subject *S* who reluctantly submits to conduct, *x*, both *does* and *does not* want x. On the one hand, she really wants *x*, in that she consciously chooses *x* for herself under the circumstances, 'all things considered'. On the other hand, she really does not want *x*, in that she would not choose *x* if, counterfactually, she were not being subjected to pressures from which she wishes she were free. Nothing in *S*'s preference set is capable of resolving which wish is real, because both are real. Of course, the law can resolve the impasse between *S*'s all-things-considered wish and her counterfactual wish by determining whether the pressures that produced the two wishes were *lawful* pressures or *wrongful* pressures. But, of course, that is precisely the inquiry into 'force' that commentators think they can avoid by futilely searching for what *S* really wanted.

Notes

1. *See* Washington Revised Code § 9A.44.010 (1994) ('"consent" means that at the time of the act of sexual intercourse there are actual words or conduct indicating freely given agreement to have sexual intercourse'); In re M.T.S., 129 N.J. 422, 448-49, 609 A.2d 1266, 1278-79 (1992) (defining 'consent' as 'words or . . . actions that, when viewed in

the light of all the surrounding circumstances, would demonstrate to a reasonable person affirmative and freely-given authorization for the specific act of sexual penetration'). Jurisdictions are not obliged to punish every person who is blameworthy. Instead, they can elect to punish only the most blameworthy actors, such as those who *know* that their victims are not voluntarily acquiescing in their minds. *See, e.g.*, Arizona Revised Statutes § 13-1406(A) (2001) ('A person commits sexual assault by intentionally or knowingly engaging in sexual intercourse or oral sexual contact with any person without consent of such person').

2. The Oregon electorate enacted the 'Oregon Death With Dignity Act' as an initiative ('Measure 16') on Nov. 8, 1994. The federal courts thereupon enjoined it from going into effect, until the U.S. Supreme Court denied review three years later. *See* Lee v. Oregon, 869 F. Supp. 1491 (D. Ore., 1994), Lee v. Oregon 891 F. Supp. 1439 (D. Ore. 1995), rev'd, 107 F.3d 1382 (9th Cir., 1997), cert. denied sub nom. Lee v. Harcleroad, 522 U.S. 927 (1997). Meanwhile, the Oregon legislature required that the Death With Dignity Act be re-submitted to the Oregon electorate as a referendum. The electorate reaffirmed the Act on Nov. 4, 1997. *See* Egan, 'Right To Die: In Oregon, Opening a New Front in the World of Medicine', *The New York Times*, 6 November 1997, section A, p. 27, col. 1. For the text of the Act, *see* Ore. Rev. Stat. §§ 127.800-897 (1997).
3. Oregon Rev. Stat. § 127.885 (1977).
4. Oregon Rev. Stat. §§ 127.835, 127.897 (1977).
5. Oregon Rev. Stat. § 127.820 (1997).
6. *See* Oregon. Rev. Stat. §§ 127.805 ('voluntarily'): 127.815 (attending physician determines competency); 127.820 (consulting physician confirms competency); 127.815 (attending physician informs the patient); 127.805 (two witnesses); and 127.850 (waiting periods).
7. *See* Chapter 1, notes 14-15.
8. Aristotle, *Nichomachean Ethics*, III, 1110a:

   > Actions are regarded as involuntary when they are performed under compulsion or through ignorance. An act is compulsory when it has an external origin of such a kind that the agent or patient contributes nothing to it; *e.g.*, if a voyager were to be conveyed somewhere by the wind or by men who had him in their power. But sometimes the act is done through fear of something worse . . . *e.g.*, if a tyrant who has a man's parents and children in his power were to order him to do something dishonorable on condition that if he did it their lives would be spared, and if he did not they would be put to death. . . . Such actions . . . seem more voluntary than involuntary ones; because at the time that they are performed they are matters of choice.

9. *See, e.g.*, Regina v. Olugboja, [1982] QB 320, [1981] 3 All ER 443, [1981] 3 WLR 585 (June 17, 1981).
10. Feinberg, *Harm to Others*, p. 116. Unfortunately, in his four-volume study of *The Moral Limits of the Criminal Law*, Feinberg uses the term 'fully voluntary' in two distinct ways. In *Harm to Others* (volume 1), which I quote here, Feinberg uses 'fully voluntary' as a term to describe conditions that are necessary to render acts of consent sufficiently voluntary to constitute a criminal defense—or what he later calls 'voluntary enough' to constitute a defense. *See* Feinberg, *Harm to Others*, p. 118. In contrast, in *Harm to Others* (volume 3), Feinberg uses 'fully voluntary' to refer to conditions that go beyond what is necessary to constitute a defense by coming close to the unattainable ideal of 'perfectly voluntary' consent. *See* Feinberg, *Harm to Others*, p. 104.

11. Feinberg regards consent as a communicative act that, in order to perform its exculpatory function in criminal law, must be assessed from the standpoint of a reasonable observer in the actor's position. *See* Feinberg, *Harm To Self*, pp. 198, 273. Nevertheless, he also believes that, to constitute consent, the act by which *S* expresses acquiescence must not only appear to be voluntary on *S*'s part, but also *be* voluntary on her part. *See id.* at 176, 195-96. The conditions that he enumerates as necessary for *S*'s public act of expressing acquiescence to be a voluntary act are identical to the conditions that are necessary for a subjective act on *S*'s part of acquiescing in her mind to be voluntary.
12. Although Feinberg does not define 'threats' in precisely this way, I believe his views are consistent with it. *See* Feinberg, *Harm To Self*, pp. 193-94, 217-32.
13. Feinberg, *Harm To Self*, p. 215.
14. *See* Zimmerman, 'Coercive Wage Offers'.
15. *See, e.g.*, Archard, *Sexual Consent*, pp. 55-60; McGregor, 'Why When She Says No She Doesn't Mean Maybe and Doesn't Mean Yes', p. 197; Wertheimer, *Coercion* p. 218.
16. Wertheimer, *Coercion*. pp. 217-21.
17. Compare Wertheimer, 'Consent and Sexual Relations', pp. 102-05, with Schulhofer, *Unwanted Sex*, pp. 137-68 (who argues that it ought to be a sexual offense of non-consent for an employer to condition discretionary employment on sexual intercourse).
18. *See, e.g.*, Malm, 'The Ontological Status of Consent', p. 153 ('Have sex with me or I will kill your goldfish'); Alexander, 'The Moral Magic of Consent (II)', p. 173 (Have sex with me or I will pinch you or not pay you the $50 I owe you). Wertheimer subsequently qualifies his earlier position by arguing that *A*'s threat does not invalidate *S*'s consent unless it is 'reasonable' to expect *S* to succumb to the threat. *See* Wertheimer, 'Consent and Sexual Relations', pp. 102, 104. However, the term 'reasonable' is simply a stand-in to account for the fact that there is no necessary correspondence between threats to violate *S*'s rights and threats that taint *S*'s consent.
19. *See, e.g.*, Feinberg, *Harm To Self*, p. 303; Zimmerman, 'Coercive Wage Offers'. *See* also authorities cited in note 18.
20. Cf. Hubin and Haely, 'Rape and the Reasonable Man', p. 116:

    > A bank teller confronted by a would-be robber obviously armed only with a squirt gun filled with distilled water can hardly claim coercion if he gives the robber money upon being squirted. And the threat, 'Give me all the money in your cash drawer or I'll let the air out of your car's tires', would hardly be counted as a coercive threat in ordinary circumstances. Turning over the funds, if done, is done voluntarily in these cases. It is an act consented to despite the use of [illegal] force or the threat of [illegal] force.
21. *See* Feinberg, *Harm To Self*, pp. 195-96.
22. *See* California v. Hooker, 244 Cal. Rptr. 337 (Ct. App. 1988).
23. *See* Massachusetts v. Therrien, 383 Mass. 529, 538-39, 420 N.E.2d 897, 902 (1981) ('If the victim appears to consent to intercourse because of a threat of a third person or because of fears arising from actions of a third person, and a defendant knew of those threats or of the circumstances causing those fears, such a defendant [can] properly be found guilty of rape'). *See* also Feinberg, *Harm To Self*, p. 196.
24. For discussion of the argument that women in contemporary society are too oppressed to be able to consent to sexual intercourse, *see* Burgess-Jackson, *Rape*, pp. 54-55.
25. *See* Feinberg, *Harm To Self*, pp. 196, 244, 246. But *see* Burgess-Jackson, *Rape*, p. 101 (arguing that just as a third person is responsible for taking advantage of a threat made by another, he is responsible for taking advantage of oppression caused by another).

26. *See* the discussion of the *Burnham* case in Chapter 4, note 1.
27. *See* Feinberg, *Harm To Self*, p. 190.
28. [1976] App. Cas. 182 (House of Lords). The House of Lords, ruling that it is a defense to rape that an actor neither knew nor was reckless about a woman's non-consent to sexual intercourse, nonetheless affirmed the defendants' conviction on the ground that the defendants must have known or been reckless about the woman's non-consent.
29. For discussion of the difference between conscious and unconscious assumptions that are false, *see* Law Commission, *Consent in the Criminal Law*, para. 6.29–.30, pp. 69-70.
30. *See* Law Commission, *Consent and the Criminal Law*, para. 6.24, p. 68.
31. Some jurisdictions appear to confine an actor *A*'s liability to instances of active deception, probably in the belief that an actor who deceives is more likely to possess a guilty mind about *S*'s non-consent than an actor who merely fails to disclose. *See, e.g.*, Alabama Code § 13A-6-65(a) (1) (2001). However, in order to separate the question of consent, *i.e.*, 'Has *S* suffered a harm that we wish her to be spared?', from the question of *mens rea*, 'Did *A* inflict the harm with a guilty mind?' jurisdictions ought (1) to recognize that *any* mistake on *S*'s part that prevents her properly assessing her interests taints her consent, regardless of whether it results from deception or nondisclosure, and (2) to account separately for *A*'s *mens rea* by separately providing that he is criminally responsible for the harm he inflicts on *S* only if he possessed a guilty mind about it. *See* Papadimitropoulos v. Regina, (1957) 98 Criminal Law Reporter 249, 261 (Australian High Court) ('[I]n considering whether an apparent consent is unreal it is the mistake or misapprehension that makes it so. It is not the fraud producing the mistake which is material so much as the mistake itself. [I]f the mistake or misapprehension is not produced by the fraud of the man, there is logically room for the possibility that he was unaware of the woman's mistake so that a question of his *mens rea* may arise. . . . For that reason it is easy to understand why the stress has been on the fraud. But that stress tends to distract the attention from the essential inquiry, namely, whether the consent is no consent because [of the victim's misapprehension]').
32. For a jurisdiction that distinguishes the question 'Did the defendant's conduct inflict the *harm* of an offense of non-consent?' from the question 'Did the defendant possess *mens rea* regarding his conduct?', *see* Law Commission, *Consent in the Criminal Law*, para. 6.25-.26, pp. 68-69.
33. *See Model Penal Code* § 213.1(2) (c):

> A male who has sexual intercourse with a female not his wife commits a felony of the third degree if . . . he knows that . . . she submits because she mistakenly supposes that he is her husband.

See also *Model Penal Code*, pt. 2, vol. 2, pp. 332-33 (section 213.1.(2) (c) extends to a person who 'stages a mock marriage to create the false supposition that they are man and wife'). But *see* Papadimitropoulos v Regina, 98 CLR 249, [1958] Argus LR 21 (Australian Supreme Court).

34. 163 Cal. App. 3d 1224, 210 Cal. Rptr. 122 (1985). We shall return to *Boro* in Chapter 8 as an example of conceptual confusion even within the confines of fraud.
35. 163 Cal. App. 3d at 1230 n.5, 210 Cal. Rptr. at 126 n.5.
36. The prosecuting attorney in *Boro* elected to charge Boro under California Penal Code section 261(4) with having had sexual intercourse with Ms. R. while she was 'unconscious' of what he was doing, rather than charging him under California Penal Code section 261(2) with having had sexual intercourse with her 'by means of force or fear of immediate and unlawful bodily injury'. This is not to say that the prosecutor was wrong to charge Boro under section 261(4) rather than section 261(2). The prosecutor

may well have correctly concluded that fear of 'immediate and unlawful bodily injury' under section 261(2) means fear of bodily injury which a victim will imminently suffer at the hands of the defendant himself, and not fear of bodily injury which a victim will suffer in the indefinite future through self-contracted illness. Nevertheless, even if the prosecutor was correct to charge Boro under section 261(4), the appellate court, in ascertaining the scope of section 261(4), failed to recognize the distinctive thing of which Ms. R. was 'unconscious', namely, that she could refuse to have sexual intercourse without dying as a consequence.

37. *See* Feinberg, *Harm To Self*, pp. 198, 301-02. *See* also Massachusetts v. Caracciola, 409 Mass. 648, 652-53, 569 N.E.2d 774, 777 (1991) (a man who masquerades as a policeman and, while doing so, elicits sexual intercourse from a woman by falsely threatening to jail her unless she submits, is guilty of eliciting sexual intercourse by means of 'force').
38. 163 Cal. App. 2d at 1227, 210 Cal. Rptr. at 123.
39. Alexander, 'The Moral Magic of Consent (II)', pp. 166-67.
40. Feinberg, *Harm To Self*, p. 316. Interestingly, in discussing capacity to consent, Feinberg is ambivalent as to whether he is discussing a capacity needed for even factual acquiescence (*see id.* at 188, 317-18) or a capacity needed for such acquiescence to be prescriptively valid (*see id.* at 320-22, 31).
41. Schulhofer, *Unwanted Sex*, pp. 215, 218, 231.
42. *See, e.g.*, Buchanan and Brock, *Deciding for Others*, pp. 18-19, 23-25.
43. Utah Code Ann. §§ 76-5-406 and 76-5-404.1(3) (h) (1998). For convenience, I have renumbered, as subsections '1-5', provisions that in section 76-5-406 are subsections '2' and '4(i)', '7', '9', and '10'. And I have interpolated into subsection '5' provisions of section 76-5-404.1(3) (h) that section 76-5-406(10) incorporates by reference.
44. Idaho Code § 18-6110 (1998).
45. Thus, in Robert Altman's movie, *Cookie's Fortune*, the statute would have prohibited Emma (Liv Tyler) from having sexual intercourse with her boyfriend, deputy-sheriff Jason (Chris O'Donnell), while she was being held in jail with Willis (Charles Dutton).
46. *See* Schulhofer, *Unwanted Sex*, p. 223:

> A few exceptional [psychotherapy] patients might know just what they are doing and choose freely to initiate an affair. But working rules about competency inevitably generalize. Most states automatically consider 15-year-olds too immature to consent to sex, though a few might not be. In the same way, patients are best treated as incapable of giving valid, adequately informed consent to sex with their therapists, though in rare cases they might not be.

See also Meir Dan-Cohen, distinguishing between 'basic offenses', *i.e.*, offenses which classify persons precisely in accord with the jurisdiction's underlying policies, and 'secondary' or 'derivative' offenses, *i.e.*, offenses that classify persons in accord with administratively-useful categories. *See* Dan-Cohen, 'Basic Values and the Victim's State of Mind', p. 761.

47. Pineau, 'Date Rape', p. 231 ('sexual enjoyment', 'sexual pleasure'), p. 224 ('good reasons'), p. 239 ('enjoyable').
48. The only qualifying motivations Pineau mentions are the 'pay-off' of 'money' or 'opera tickets', and the dynamics of sado-masochism. *See* Pineau, 'Date Rape', pp. 224, 231.
49. *See, e.g.*, North Carolina v. Lester, 321 S.E.2d 166 (Ct. App., 1984), *affirmed*, 330 S.E.2d 205 (1985).
50. *See* Regina v. Dee, 15 Cox CC 579 (Ireland, 1884), disavowing Regina v. Jackson, 168 ER 911 (1822), and Regina v. Barrow, LR 1 CCR 158 (1868).

51. Cf. Regina v. Cuerrier, [1998] 2 S.C.R. 371, sec. 243 (Cory, J.) (concluding, in a rape case in which the defendant failed to disclose that he was HIV-positive, that an actor's 'fail[ure] to disclose that he is HIV-positive can constitute fraud which may vitiate consent to sexual intercourse').
52. *See* Regina v. Linekar, [1995] 3 All ER 69, [1995] 2 WLR 237 ('An essential ingredient of the offence of rape is the proof that the woman did not consent to the actual act of sexual intercourse with the particular man who penetrated her. . . . [T]hat ingredient is proved in the husband impersonation cases because the victim did not consent to sexual intercourse with the particular man who penetrated her'). Cf. Regina v. Cuerrier, [1998] 2 S.C.R. 371, sec. 191 (McLachlin, J.) (concluding, in a rape case in which the defendant failed to disclose that he was HIV-positive, that '[w]here the person represents that he or she is disease-free, and consent is given on that basis, deception on that matter goes to the very act of assault. The complainant does not consent to the transmission of diseased fluid into his or her body').
53. For accounts of the doctrine, *see* Archard, *Sexual Consent*, pp. 46-50; Feinberg, *Harm To Self*, pp. 291-300.
54. For a description of the doctrine, *see* Feinberg, *Harm To Self*, pp. 291-300.
55. *See* Archard, *Sexual Consent*, pp. 49-50 ('Our intuition is that to be deceived in the *factum* is to be completely misled about an important, indeed probably crucial, aspect of the act. To be deceived in the inducement is to be less than completely misled about the act'); Falk, 'Rape By Fraud and Rape By Coercion', p. 158 ('the predictive utility of the [factum-inducement] distinction has been seriously undermined by its elastic application in rape cases'). We shall see in Chapter 8 that when courts fail to adopt a broad standard for defining factum, it may be because they mistakenly conflate factual attitudinal consent with prescriptive attitudinal consent.
56. *See* Feinberg, *Harm To Self*, pp. 294, 304-05; Kleinig, 'The Ethics of Consent', pp. 102-05; McGregor, 'When She Says No', pp. 200-01.
57. *See* Feinberg, *Harm To Self*, p. 292 (stating that the difference between acquiescence based on fraud in the inducement as opposed to acquiescence based fraud in the factum is that the former is 'involuntary consent', while the latter is 'no consent at all'). *See* also *id.* at 295 (stating that while fraud in the inducement renders sexual intercourse 'involuntary in degree', fraud in the factum renders it 'wholly involuntary').
58. *See* Chapter 4, note 40.
59. *See* California v. Cicero, 157 Cal. App. 3d 465, 485-86, 204 Cal. Rptr. 582, 596-97 (1984).
60. *See* Boro v. California, 163 Cal. App. 3d 1224, 1229, 210 Cal. Rptr. 122, 125 (1985).
61. [1998] 2 S.C.R. 371.
62. [1998] 2 S.C.R. 371, para. 12.
63. For Justices in *Cuerrier* who criticize Justice l'Heureux-Dub's position on these *reductio* grounds, *see* [1998] 2 S.C.R. 371, sec. 47 (McLachlin, J.); sec. 134-35 (Cory, J.). *See* also Dripps, 'Beyond Rape', p. 1803 (arguing, rightly, that to treat all material frauds as sufficient to invalidate acquiescence to sexual intercourse would have the effect of treating acts of adultery, which are no longer crimes in most jurisdictions, as rapes whenever such acts are predicated on fraud).
64. *See* Estrich, 'Rape', p. 1120.
65. As Joan McGregor puts it:

    Much of our personal identity is tied to our gender and sexual expression and hence to our sexual self-determination. In our society, sexual interactions are regarded as personal, private, intimate relationships. . . . Moreover, it is commonly believed that sexual relationships are imbued with significance and meaning beyond the physical act.

McGregor, 'Force, Consent, and the Reasonable Woman', p. 235. Ironically, having argued that sex is *different* from property, McGregor then concludes that fraud that taints acquiescence with respect to surrenders of property ought, at the very least, to constitute a baseline for determining fraud that taints acquiescence to sexual intercourse. *Id.* at 237-38.

66. *See* Murphy, 'Some Ruminations on Women, Violence, and the Criminal Law', in Jules L. Coleman and Allen Buchanan, *In Harm's Way: Essays in Honor of Joel Feinberg* (Cambridge, England: Cambridge University Press, 1994), 209-229, pp. 213-28, 221-22.
67. Berger, 'Not So Simple Rape', p. 76.
68. [1995] 3 All ER 69, [1995] 2 WLR 237, [1995] 2 Cr App Rep 49.
69. *See* Chuang, 'Redirecting the Debate Over Trafficking in Women', p. 104 n.123; Chamallas, 'Consent, Equality, and the Legal Control of Sexual Conduct,' p. 826 n.209.
70. *See Model Penal Code* § 223.3(1) (a person who, in return for something of value, promises to perform a future action is guilty of theft if he does not intend to fulfill his promise at the time he makes it); Dripps, 'Beyond Rape', p. 1803 (most jurisdictions regard personal services as things of value for purposes of the law of theft).
71. For overview of the issues of fraud that have arisen in the context of sexual intercourse, *See* Falk, 'Rape By Fraud And Rape By Coercion', pp. 39, 48-79, 108-113.
72. Compare Dripps, 'Beyond Rape', pp. 1802-03, Feinberg, *Harm To Self*, pp. 300-05, and Schulhofer, *Unwanted Sex*, pp. 152-59, all of whom argue that the class of wrongful frauds that suffice to constitute rape ought to be defined more narrowly than the class of frauds that suffice to constitute theft, with Estrich, 'Rape', p. 1093, 1120; Larson, 'Women Understand So Little', pp. 438-53; McGregor, 'When She Says No', p. 188, 199-203; and West, 'Legitimating the Illegitimate', p. 1450 (all of whom argue that the class of wrongful frauds that suffice to constitute rape ought to be at least as large as the class of frauds that suffice to constitute theft).

    The English Law Commission originally took the position that any fraud that actually induces consent also illegally taints it. *See* Law Commission, *Consent and Offences Against the Person*, para. 26.1. After considerable criticism, *see, e.g.*, Leng, 'Consent and Offences Against the Person, pp. 480-88, the Law Commission withdrew its proposal and put, in its place, a recommendation that the law remain as it was, namely, that only fraud as to the 'nature of the act' or the 'identity' of the person involved taints consent. *See* Law Commission, *Consent in the Criminal Law*, para. 6.79.
73. Justices Cory, Major, Bastarache, and Binnie held for the majority that a person elicits sexual intercourse by fraud if he intentionally induces a person to engage in sexual intercourse by withholding information that involves a 'significant risk of serious bodily harm'. *See* Regina v. Cuerrier, [1998] 2 S.C.R. 371, sec. 139. Justices McLachlin and Gonthier took the view that an intentional withholding of information constitutes 'fraud' only if the information would have revealed that the actor was infected with a contagious venereal disease. *See id.* sec. 72. Justice l'Heureux-Dub took the view that intentionally withholding information constitutes fraud if revealing it would have changed one's sexual partner's mind. *See id.* sec. 16. The four judges on the intermediate court of appeals below, and the single trial judge, all took the view that a person elicits sexual intercourse by fraud only if either he misleads his partner into believing that he is not engaging her in sexual intercourse for purposes of sexual gratification, or he misleads her about his identity by impersonating someone else she

knows. *See* Regina v. Cuerrier, 141 D.L.R. 4th 503 (British of Columbia Court of Appeal, 1997).

74. MPC § 213.1(2).
75. *See Model Penal Code*, pt. 2, vol. 2, § 213.1, p. 314.
76. *Id.*
77. *Model Penal Code* §§ 212.5, 223.4.
78. *Model Penal Code*, pt. 2, § 213.1, p. 313.
79. *See* Montana v. Thompson, 243 Mont. 28, 792 P.2d 1103 (1990) (acquitting a high school coach of rape despite findings that he threatened to prevent a student from graduating unless she had sexual intercourse with him, on the ground that threats of nongraduation are not threats of imminent 'death, bodily injury, or kidnapping' as required by Montana law). *See* also W. Va. Code § § 61-8B-1(1), 61-8B-4(a) (1) (1999).
80. For articles on the so-called 'tort/crime distinction', including grounds for regulating social harms by means of tort law rather than criminal law, *see* Symposium 'The Intersection of Tort and Criminal Law'.
81. Regina v. Brown, [1993] 2 All Eng. Rep. 75 (House of Lords).
82. This is not to say that a person who possesses legal incapacity at Time 1 cannot prospectively consent, prescriptively, to conduct that occurs at Time 2 at which he lacks legal competence. For an analysis of prospective consent, see the discussion later in this chapter.
83. Just as prescriptive consent is incompatible with legal incapacity, prescriptive consent is also incompatible with fraud—though for a different reason. The reason that prescriptive consent by *S* is incompatible with legal incapacity by *S*, regardless of how much *S* may desire the incapacity, is that *S*'s legal incapacity itself precludes *S*'s desire from carrying any legal weight. In contrast, the reason that prescriptive consent by *S* is incompatible with fraud upon *S*, regardless of how much *S* may desire to be defrauded, is that *S*'s desire to be defrauded itself precludes the misrepresentation from constituting fraud. To illustrate, imagine that a woman, *S*, has a boyfriend, *A1*, who has an identical twin brother, *A2*, and that *S* makes a wager with *A2* that *A2* cannot successfully deceive her into kissing him in the belief that he is actually her boyfriend, *A1*. Assume, too, that *A2* accepts the wager and succeeds in eliciting a kiss from *S*. In that event, one of two things must be true: either *S* is indifferent as to whether she kisses *A2*, in which event she is not truly defrauded into engaging in conduct that she seeks to avoid; or *S* endeavors to avoid kissing *A2*, in which event she does not truly desire be defrauded (although she may desire to run the 'risk' of kissing *A2*). Joel Feinberg asserts that, just as an otherwise competent subject *S* can prescriptively consent to be forced to do *x*, *S* can prescriptively consent to be defrauded into doing *x*. *See* Feinberg, *Harm To Self*, pp. 311-12. However, in so stating, Feinberg conflates *S*'s consent to a *risk* of *x*—and the consequent fictional *imputation* of prescriptive consent to *x*—with prescriptive consent to *x*.

    To be sure, although a person cannot grant prescriptive *contemporaneous* consent to conduct with respect to which she is legally disabled or defrauded at the time, despite her desire thus to consent, we shall see in Chapter 6 that a person is often able to grant prescriptive *prospective* consent to conduct that she expects to occur in the future at a time when she will lack the competence and knowledge necessary to contemporaneously consent to it.

84. Compare Robin West, 'Legitimating the Illegitimate', pp. 1445, 1447-48 (preferring that rape laws be predicated on force rather than non-consent) with Henderson, 'Getting To Know', p. 64 (preferring that rape laws be predicated on non-consent rather than force).
85. This discussion of force is confined to the goal protecting women from one of the factors that negates the validity of acquiescence in sexual intercourse, namely, wrongful pressure to acquiesce to it; and, accordingly, 'force' is defined as being confined to pressures on acquiescence. This does not prevent the language of 'force' from being used to protect women from incompetence and fraud in acquiescing to sexual intercourse. In order to do so, however, 'force' must be defined—as it is, indeed, defined in some jurisdictions (*see, e.g.*, McNair v. Nevada, 108 Nev. 53,58, 825 P.2d 571, 573 (1992); Illinois v. Borak, 13 Ill. App. 3d 815, 820, 301 N.E.2d 1, 5 (1973)–as consisting of the force inherent in a sexual act to which prescriptive consent has not been given.
86. *See, e.g.*, Hawaii v. Lima, 624 P.2d 1374 (1981).
87. Criminal Code, R.S.C., 1970, c C-34, Section 143 (repealed 1980-81).
88. The Florida Supreme Court adopted the utmost-resistance rule in 1891. *See* Hollis v. Florida, 27 Fla. 387, 9 So. 67 (1891). Cf. Bailey v. Florida, 76 Fla. 213, 79 So. 730 (1918). The Florida legislature, in 1974, repealed the statute upon which the utmost-resistance rule rested. *See* Act of Oct. 1, 1974, ch. 74-121, § 1, 1974 Fla. Laws 371, 372, *as construed in* Hufham v. Florida, 400 So. 2d 133, 134 (Fla. 5th DCA 1981). The utmost-resistance rule was in effect in Virginia in 1980, *see* Snyder v. Virginia, 220 Va. 792, 263 S.E.2d 55 (1980), and repealed in 1981, *see* Farish v. Virginia, 2 Va. App. 627, 346 S.E.2d 736, 738-39 (1986).
89. *See* Florida Laws 1995, c. 95-348, § 2, eff. July 1, 1995, now codified at Florida Statutes § 794.011(1) (a) (1999). *See* also Kentucky Revised Statutes § 510.010(2) (1998) ('physical resistance on the part of the victim shall not be necessary to meet this definition [of forcible compulsion]'); Maine Revised Code, tit. 17, § 251(E) (1999) ('"Compulsion" as defined in this paragraph places no duty upon the victim to resist the actor'); Ohio Revised Statutes § 2907.02(C) (2000) ('A victim need not prove physical resistance to the offender in prosecutions under this section').
90. Virginia Code Ann. § 18.2-67.6 (1998).
91. For a statement and history of the utmost-resistance rule, *See* Wisconsin v. Plitcha, 135 N.W.2d 768 (1965); New York v. Yanik, 43 N.Y.2d 97; 371 N.E.2d 497; 400 N.Y.S.2d 778 (1977).
92. *See, e.g.*, McGregor, 'When She Says No', p. 177 ('Historically, rape was defined as "carnal knowledge of a woman forcibly and against her will". . . . The result was that to prove "forcibly" and "against her will," the courts . . . required victim resistance, expressed first as "utmost resistance." This requirement reflected the view that it was better for a woman to die than be "dishonored"'); West, 'A Common on Sex and Rape', p. 237 ('To be a rape victim, one had to be so vigilant about protecting one's honor that one would truly fight to the death to protect it').
93. *See* Missouri v. Stamps, 569 S.W.2d 762, 767 (1978):

    The prosecutrix testified directly and convincingly that she was accosted by defendant, that her life was threatened and that he achieved penetration against her will. Defendant has the temerity to suggest that the victim did not use her utmost efforts to resist the attack upon her. Under the circumstances in which this crime occurred, defendant's argument that there was no showing of 'utmost resistance' is fatuous. . . . Defendant told her he had a knife and would kill her if she did not cooperate. Where, as here, a victim is put in such fear of physical violence that her will is overcome the utmost resistance doctrine is inapplicable.

The Wisconsin Supreme Court explicitly stated as much in the most famous and frequently cited of the utmost-resistance cases. *See* Brown v. Wisconsin, 106 N.W. 536, 538 (1906) ('[Utmost resistance is not required] where the power of resistance is overcome by unconsciousness, threats, or exhaustion'). Accord Wisconsin v. Herfel, 49 Wis. 2d 513, 517, 519, 182 N.W.2d 232, 235 (1971) ('Common sense and the experience of mankind must be used to determine when a person's will is overcome by threats of imminent physical violence which if carried out would cause great bodily harm. . . . . The law does not require a woman to become a martyr to test by resistance the sincerity of a threat to rape at gunpoint).

94. *See, e.g.*, Illinois v. Defrates, 33 Ill. 2d 190, 194, 210 N.E.2d 467, 469 (1965) ('useless... acts of resistance are not necessary'); Illinois v. Williams, 23 Ill. 2d 295, 299, 178 N.E.2d 372, 375 (1961) ('Inasmuch as the law does not require a useless act, if the superiority of strength of the defendant was so great that effectual resistance might be impossible, there need be no showing of any struggle; similarly, if the defendant and the victim are so remote from human help that an outcry might be unavailing, there need be no outcry'); Illinois v. Scott, 407 Ill. 301, 306, 95 N.E.2d 315, 317 (Ill. Sup. Ct., 1950) ('If the account of the prosecuting witness be taken as true, the vital question is whether she ceased resistance because it was useless or . . . because she ultimately consented').
95. *See, e.g.*, Illinois v. Jones, 28 Ill. App. 3d 896, 899, 329 N.E.2d 855, 858 (1975) (resistance not necessary where victim is paralyzed by fear); Illinois v. Defrates, 33 Ill. 2d 190, 195, 210 N.E.2d 467, 469 (1965) ('there is nothing in the evidence which supports the conclusion that the prosecutrix was gripped by a paralyzing fear'); Illinois v. Scott, 407 Ill. 301, 305, 95 N.E.2d 315, 317 (1950) (the utmost resistance rule does not require resistance on the part of a person who is 'paralyzed by fear').
96. This is what David Bryden appears to mean when he says that 'force and resistance are two sides of the same coin'. Bryden, 'Redefining Rape', p. 356. And it appears to be what the Washington legislature thought when it defines 'forcible compulsion' as 'physical force which overcomes resistance'). *See* Wash. Rev. Code 9A.44.010 (2001).
97. Louisiana v. Powell, 438 So. 2d 1306 (Ct. of App., 1983). The complainant testified that the defendant threatened to kill her if she did not acquiesce; but the court found that, in light of evidence that he also said that he would not hurt her and that he displayed no weapon, there was insufficient evidence to conclude that she believed him, even if he said it.
98. La. Rev. Stat. 14:42 (1998). The statute prohibits threats of death by prohibiting threats by means of weapons that can cause death. *See* Louisiana v. Robertson, 454 So.2d 204 (1984). The penalty for aggravated rape is life imprisonment without the possibility of parole.
99. The defendant in *Powell*, having been charged with both aggravated rape and forcible rape, was convicted of forcible rape. However, because the two offenses are substantively identical and differ only in the sentencing discretion they give jurors, *see* Louisiana v. Parish, 405 So.2d 1080, 1086-87 (1981), the *Powell* court reversed the conviction as if the defendant had been convicted of aggravated rape. *See* 438 So.2d at 1309-10 (Stoker, J., dissenting).
100. Montana v. Thompson, 243 Mont. 28, 792 P.2d 1103 (1990). A LEXIS search of Montana cases for the word 'utmost' within three words of 'resistance', 'resisted', or 'resist' produces no cases.

101. Montana law makes it an offense for a person to 'knowingly ha[ve] sexual intercourse without consent with another person'. Montana Code Annotated § 45-5-503 (1998). At the time *Thompson* was decided, Montana law further provided that 'the term "without consent" means' either that the victim was subjected to compulsion or that she was forced to acquiesce 'by threat of imminent death, bodily injury, or kidnapping to be inflicted on anyone'. *See* Montana v. Thompson, 243 Mont. 28, 31, 792 P.2d 1103, 1105 (1990).
102. A LEXIS search of Montana cases for the word 'utmost' within three words of 'resistance', 'resisted', or 'resist' produces no cases.
103. 243 Mont. 28, 33, 792 P.2d 1103, 1107 (1990).
104. *See* Schulhofer, *Unwanted Sex*, pp. 2-4 (criticizing the Montana case); Bryden, 'Redefining Rape', p. 360 (same).
105. Pennsylvania, having embraced the 'utmost' resistance rule by both common-law decision and statute, repealed the rule in 1972. *See* Pennsylvania v. Mlinarich, 518 Pa. 247, 257-59, 542 A.2d 1335, 1340-41 (1985).
106. Florida Statutes § 794.011(1) (a) (1999).
107. Hufham v. Florida, 400 So. 2d 133 (Ct. App., 1981).
108. *See* West Virginia Code §§ 61-8B-1(1) (a), 61-8B-2(a)-(b) (1) (2001).
109. *See* Ohio Code § 2907.03(A) (1) (2001).
110. Estrich, 'Rape', p. 1101 (citations omitted). *See* also Note, 'The Resistance Standard in Rape Legislation', p. 685.
111. Estrich, 'Rape', p. 1099.
112. Bryden, 'Redefining Rape', p. 371. *See* also *id.* at 377 ('Another function of the FRR is to corroborate other evidence that the victim did not consent, and that the perpetrator had a culpable *mens rea*'.); Estrich, 'Rape', p. 1101.
113. Malm, 'The Ontological Status of Consent', p. 155.
114. Tchen, 'Rape Reform and a Statutory Consent Defense', p. 1554.
115. Remick, 'Read Her Lips', pp. 1111-12.
116. Malm, 'The Ontological Status of Consent', p. 155 (referring to 'this negative definition of consent').
117. *See* Malm, 'The Ontological Status of Consent', p. 157.
118. *See* Malm, 'The Ontological Status of Consent', pp. 160-63 (verbal versus non-verbal consent), pp. 163-64 ('positive' consent versus 'tacit' consent).
119. Malm, 'The Ontological Status of Consent', p. 156.
120. Tiersma, 'The Language of Silence', p. 66.
121. Remick, 'Read Her Lips', pp. 1111, 1113.
122. *See* note 103.
123. At the time *Thompson* was decided, Montana law, having made it an offense to have sexual intercourse with a person 'without consent', defined the term 'without consent' to mean either that the victim was subjected to compulsion or that she was forced to acquiesce 'by threat of imminent death, bodily injury, or kidnapping to be inflicted on anyone'. *See* Montana v. Thompson, 243 Mont. 28, 31, 792 P.2d 1103, 1105 (1990). In the aftermath of *Thompson*, the legislature expanded the term 'without consent' to include 'the threat of substantial retaliatory action that causes the victim to reasonably believe that the offender has the ability to execute the threat.' Montana Code Annotated § 45-5-501(1) (b) (1998).
124. *See, e.g.*, Drake v. Georgia, 239 Ga. 232, 233, 236 S.E.2d 748, 750 (1977) ('Statutory rape is not really "rape" at all').

125. 25 Cal. 3d 608, 601 P.2d 572 (1979), 159 Cal.Rptr. 340 (1979), affirmed, 450 U.S. 464 (1980).
126. 25 Cal. 3d at 614, 601 P.2d at 576.
127. *See* Bryden, 'Redefining Rape', p. 355 ('We will consider first the simplest proposal: Define the act of rape as nonconsensual sexual penetration, omitting any reference to force. For present purposes, we will define "nonconsensual" subjectively, without requiring, by rule of law, any particular manifestation of the victim's non-consent'); *id.* at 359 (submission to sexual intercourse elicited by means of wrongful threats of physical force is 'non-consent').
128. Bryden, 'Redefining Rape', p. 359.
129. Bryden, 'Redefining Rape', pp. 361, 373.
130. *See, e.g.*, Cowling, *Date Rape*, p. 107 ('There are several ways of depriving someone of free choice. One way . . . is simply to physically overpower the person: in that case there is nothing to discuss, and we are plainly dealing with rape').
131. *See, e.g.*, Alabama Code § 13A-6-70 (2000); New York Penal Code § 130.05 (2000); West Virginia Code § 61-8B-4 (2000).
132. *See, e.g.*, Hawaii v. Oshiro, 5 Haw. App. 404, 407 n.3, 696 P.2d 846, 850 n.3 (1985) (consent is not a defense to sexual intercourse with a woman who has been rendered helpless by the administration of nitrous oxide) (dictum). Not all jurisdictions make this mistake. *See, e.g.*, Utah Code § 76-5-406(5) (2000) (it is a crime to have sexual intercourse with a person who is 'physically unable to resist', but only if the person has 'not consented' to it). It might be argued that the former jurisdictions, which make it a crime to have sexual intercourse with a person who is physically unable to resist, are not making a mistake at all but, rather, are legislating prophylactically. That is, it might be argued that the former jurisdictions may recognize that they are criminalizing a range of conduct in which some putative victims are not harmed at all but that they prefer to do so in order to prevent the risk that cases of harmful intercourse will go unpunished. But given the alternative of statutes like Utah's, it is hard so see why the former jurisdictions would enact such laws unless they were mistaken.
133. Feinberg, *Harm To Self*, p. 340 (original emphasis).
134. *See* Feinberg, *Harm To Self*, pp. 194-95 (the application of pain to which a person yields for fear that, otherwise, the pain will continue is 'properly described' as a threat, not as 'compulsion').
135. Schulhofer, *Unwanted Sex*, pp. 279-80.
136. Schulhofer, *Unwanted Sex*, p. 279.
137. *See* Dripps, 'Beyond Rape'; McGregor, 'When She Says No', pp. 175-208; West, 'Legitimating the Illegitimate'.
138. Dripps, 'Beyond Rape', p. 1797.
139. *See* McGregor, 'When She Says No', p. 189 ('Dripps . . . [is] on to an important insight about rape: that forceful compulsion to secure sex should be a sufficient condition for rape. The use of violence, including overwhelming compulsion or threats of violence, to secure sex is wrongful and should be sufficient for liability for rape'); West, 'Legitimating the Illegitimate', p. 1445 ('The most important practical consequence of [Dripps'] reconstruction . . . is to rid the law of sexual assault of its present insistence on both force and non-consent as conditions of culpability. This dual requirement . . . cannot be justified); *id.* at 1447-48 ('[Dripps] is also right to insist that the dual requirement of non-consent and force in many jurisdictions' definitions of rape is unjustified and results in serious underenforcement of laws against violent sexual assault').

140. McGregor, 'When She Says No', p. 189 ('Dripps and [Catharine] MacKinnon before him are on to an important insight about rape: that forceful compulsion to secure sex should be a sufficient condition for rape. . . . We should not need to inquire further about consent'); West, 'Legitimating the Illegitimate', p. 1445 ('[U]nder Dripps' proposed law, a woman's "consent" to sex is not the determinative line between rape and sex, and indeed is virtually irrelevant. . . Dripps' proposed reform statute takes the strikingly different tactic of dropping the issue of consent (even as a defense) and defining the wrong entirely by reference to the defendant's conduct and state of mind.... The victim's "consent" need never enter the picture').
141. This, for example, seems to be Simon Bronitt's view. *See* Bronitt, 'Rape and Lack of Consent', pp. 309-10.
142. Henderson, 'Rape and Responsibility', p. 158.
143. McGregor, 'Force, Consent, and the Reasonable Woman', p. 239. Admittedly, when McGregor speaks of 'consent', she is referring to prescriptive ***expressive*** consent, not prescriptive *attitudinal* consent. But for the purpose of the present question—*i.e.*, whether, in cases where a subject is pressured into submitting to sexual intercourse, it should be necessary to prove that she was 'forced'—it makes no difference whether one is speaking of prescriptive attitudinal consent or prescriptive expressive consent.
144. Berger, 'Man's Trial, Woman's Tribulation', p. 8.
145. *See* Byrnes, 'Putting the Focus Where it Belongs', pp. 292, 300.
146. *See* Dripps, 'Beyond Rape', p. 1788 n.30 ('We cannot escape the need to inquire into the pressures brought to bear by the defendant simply by restating the naive view of consent in the statutory language').
147. *See, e.g.*, Benedet, 'Hostile Environment Sexual Harassment Claims and the Unwelcome Influence of Rape Law', p. 137 (the issue in rape cases ought to be, not whether there is 'force', but whether the sex is 'wanted').
148. Dressler, 'Where We Have Been', p. 429. *See* also Byrnes, 'Putting the Focus Where It Belongs', pp. 293, 299 (the issue in rape cases ought to be, not whether there was 'force', but whether the woman 'manifest[ed]' a 'a subjective, inward willingness' to engage in sexual intercourse).

Chapter Six

Non-contemporaneous Prescriptive Consent

We have focused thus far on instances of prescriptive consent on a subject *S*'s part, whether attitudinal or expressive in nature, that are *contemporaneous* with the conduct *x* to which *S* is prescriptively consenting. *S*'s prescriptive attitudinal consent to *x* is 'contemporaneous' with *x* when (i) *S* factually consents to *x* by subjectively choosing *x* as that which she prefers for herself under the circumstances or that about which she is so indifferent as to be willing to delegate its occurrence to others; (ii) *S* makes her subjective choice under conditions of voluntariness sufficient to enable her to take responsibility for her choice; and (iii) *S* makes her subjective choice *at the very time x occurs*. In turn, *S*'s prescriptive expressive consent to *x* is 'contemporaneous' with *x* when (i) *S* factually consents to *x* by expressing that she is subjectively choosing *x* as that which she prefers for herself under the circumstances or that about which she is so indifferent as to be willing to delegate its occurrence to others; (ii) *S* expresses her choice under conditions sufficient to convey that her choice is voluntary; and (iii) *S*'s expression conveys that she is acquiescing up to and including the time at which *x* occurs.

Frequently, however, in lieu of factually consenting to conduct at the time it occurs, people factually consent to conduct only *prospectively*, or only *retrospectively*, and *not* contemporaneously. The most common examples of such prospective and retrospective factual consent are changes of mind. Thus, people choose beforehand, whether subjectively or expressively, to engage in conduct at a future time at which they expect the conduct to occur; and, yet, as the time approaches, and as people learn more about the conduct and about themselves and their values, they change their minds and reject the conduct in mind or expression. Or conversely, people reject conduct at the time it occurs, and yet, as time passes, they regret their prior disavowals and come to embrace the conduct as something they are glad occurred.

Such instances of prospective and retrospective acquiescence are commonplace. They are also true instances of *factual* consent, because they are instances in which persons truly choose conduct—albeit prospectively or retrospectively—as that which they prefer for themselves under the circumstances they envisage or that about which they are so indifferently as to be willing to delegate its future occurrence to others. Yet, with respect to whether such instances of factual consent are also valid as defenses to crime—that is, with respect to whether factual acquiesence can ever constitute *prescriptive* consent—prospective and retrospective factual consent differ significantly from contemporaneous factual consent. For as a legal matter, Anglo-American criminal law tends strongly to privilege a subject's contemporaneous assessments of her interests over her non-contemporaneous assessments.[1] Thus, other things being equal, in the event of conflict between *contemporaneous consent* on the one hand, and prospective or retrospective non-consent on the other, the criminal law tends to privilege contemporaneous consent.[2] Similarly, other things being equal, in the event of conflict between *contemporaneous non-consent* and prospective or retrospective consent, the criminal law tends to privilege contemporaneous non-consent.[3] One can imagine fictional legal regimes that privilege mental states and expressions by reference to *when* they occur rather than *what* they consist of—that is, by privileging any *prior* mental state and expression (whether of acquiescence or non-acquiescence) over any *later* ones—or vice versa. By the same token, one can imagine fictional legal regimes that privilege mental states and expressions of *acquiescence* (whenever they may occur) over mental states and expressions of *non-acquiescence* (whenever they may occur)—or vice versa. Other things being equal, however, ours is a legal world that tends to privilege *contemporaneous* choices (whether the choices consist of acquiescence or non-acquiescence) over *non-contemporaneous* choices.

Occasionally, however, criminal law does recognize prospective factual consent as a valid defense to crime, despite the absence of contemporaneous prescriptive consent. Occasionally, too, the criminal law also recognizes retrospective factual consent as a defense to crime, despite the absence of contemporaneous prescriptive consent. Nevertheless, as between the two, the criminal law recognizes the existence of *prospective* prescriptive consent far more often than the existence of *retrospective* prescriptive consent.

Prospective Prescriptive Consent in the Face of Contemporaneous Non-acquiescence

Ordinarily, *S*'s failure prescriptively to acquiesce to conduct at the time at which the conduct occurs negates any prior acquiescence. Occasionally, however, prior acquiescence trumps even the most blatant failures of contemporaneous prescriptive consent. Thus:

> ***'Living Will'.*** *S*, having witnessed her mother's lingering death while on life support, executes a so-called Living Will within a jurisdiction that requires living wills for lawful termination of life support. *S*'s Living Will states that if *S* ever finds herself in a situation in which her life can be sustained only by means of a respirator with little or no chance of permanent recovery, and *S* is unconscious or otherwise incapable of making a decision, it is her wish that she not be assisted by a respirator, and that if such assistance has already commenced, it be disconnected. *S* is involved in an automobile accident that leaves her comatose. *S*'s physician initially connects *S* to a respirator in the hope of her recovering consciousness. But when it appears that she will not recover, the physician disconnects the respirator and *S* dies. Ruling: The courts rule that, because of

S's prior Living Will, the physician has a defense of consent to criminal charges of having caused *S*'s death.[4]

'The Skydiver'. *S* enrolls in two successive skydiving programs. But upon each flight, as the time comes for her to jump, *S* freezes at the open door and, to her later chagrin, refuses to move. Having enrolled in a third program, *S* directs her instructor that in the event she freezes again, she wishes him to push her out the door. When the moment on the third flight arrives for *S* to jump, she freezes again. But this time, despite *S*'s gasps of 'No, please don't', her instructor pushes her out the door. Although her parachute opens, *S* sustains a broken wrist on landing. Ruling: The courts rule that, because of *S*'s prior instructions, the instructor has a defense of consent to criminal charges of assault for pushing *S* out the door.

The 'Living Will' and 'Skydiver' possess several normative features in common, as we shall see. Nevertheless, they also differ from one another in an important respect. The two subjects both acquiesce beforehand in conduct that, if it occurs at all, will occur at a future time when the subjects do not expect to acquiesce to it. Yet the subject of the 'Living Will' acquiesces to future conduct on the understanding that she will be incapable of making any decision at all at that future time, while the skydiver acquiesces to future conduct on the assumption that she *will* be capable of making a decision at that future time and will *object* to it at that time. To be effective, therefore, not only must the skydiver's consent be prospective, it must also be irrevocable. The difference is significant, because irrevocability involves additional normative considerations that are absent in cases like the 'Living Will'. For that reason, we shall begin with cases like the 'Living Will' in which subjects prospectively acquiesce to conduct that, if it takes place at all, will take place at times when they are incapable of acquiescing to anything.

Prospective Prescriptive Consent to Conduct That Will Occur When a Subject is Incapable of Consenting to it

Instances of living wills are not the only context in which the criminal law allows subjects to consent beforehand to conduct that, if it takes place at all, will take place at a future time when they are unconscious. The criminal law does so routinely. Thus:

'Surgery'. A Christian Scientist *S*, who is suffering from acute appendicitis, agrees with her physician *A* that *A* may place her under general anesthesia and remove her appendix in the event it is diseased. *A* places *S* under general anesthesia, discovers that *S*'s appendix is diseased, and removes it. Ruling in response to a complaint from *S*'s clergyman, the prosecutor rules that because of *S*'s advance agreement, *A* has a defense of consent to criminal charges of maiming *S*.

'Sexual Skeptic'. A married woman *S*, who is skeptical that a man can have sexual intercourse with a sleeping woman without her being aware of it and who seeks novel forms of intimacy with her husband, challenges her husband *A* to see if he can succeed within a fortnight in consummating sexual intercourse with her while she is asleep

> without her realizing it. *S* falls asleep. *A* has sexual intercourse with *S* while she is asleep. Ruling: The courts rule that because of *S*'s advance agreement, *A* has a defense of consent to criminal charges of sexually assaulting his wife.[5]

> ***'Generous Sister'.*** A young woman, *S*, has a collection of vintage champagne of which her brother *A* likes to partake when he goes on a date. Ordinarily, *A* asks *S* if he can take a bottle as he is leaving on a date. In this instance, *A* knows that *S* will be out of town at a conference during a weekend on which *A* hopes to have date. Accordingly, *A* asks *S*, 'Can I take a bottle of your champagne in the event I have a date this weekend?' *S*, realizing that she may not be thinking about it when the time arrives, says, 'Sure. If you want a bottle, just take it and don't bother trying to reach me.' Ruling: in a jurisdiction that defines consent as a mental state on *S*'s part, the district attorney rules that because of *S*'s subjective acquiescence beforehand, *A* has a defense to larceny for taking a bottle of *S*'s champagne at a time when *S* was not conscious of the taking.

In each of these cases, *A* inflicts a harm upon *S* that is a criminal harm if inflicted upon her without her prescriptive consent (*i.e.*, removing *S* from life support, excising a portion of *S*'s body, engaging *S* in sexual intercourse, taking *S*'s property). In each case, *A* inflicts the harm upon *S* without *S*'s having prescriptively consented at that time. Yet in each case, *S*'s prospective acquiescence negates the offense by constituting a form of prospective prescriptive consent that authorizes *A* to inflict a harm that would otherwise constitute an offense against *S*.

These examples—'Living Will', 'Surgery, Sexual Skeptic', and 'Generous Sister'—possess two significant features in common. First, in contrast to persons who choose future conduct knowing that they retain the capacity to change their minds immediately before it occurs, each of the subjects chooses future conduct knowing that it will occur at a time when she will not be able to make a decision. Thus, in Surgery the patient *S* does more than choose to be subjected to conduct at a future time; she chooses beforehand to be operated upon at a future time, knowing that when the time arrives, she will be unconscious and, hence, incapable of making any decision on her behalf. Second, the three examples all occur within jurisdictions which possses an underlying norm in common: they occur in jurisdictions that take the view that allowing subjects to commit themselves in advance to conduct that will occur when they are incapable of agency enhances their overall well-being.[6] Indeed, every Anglo-American jurisdiction takes the same view, most notably in medical cases. For if medical patients were not allowed to prospectively consent to surgery when they are unconscious, one of two things would follow: either doctors would be prohibited from operating upon patients under general anesthesia, or doctors would be allowed to operate upon patients without regard to their prior consent.

Prospective Prescriptive Consent to Conduct That Will Occur When a Subject Refuses to Consent to it

'Skydiver' possesses certain elements in common with the previous hypothetical cases. The subjects in each hypothetical case prospectively consent to conduct that they know will take place at a future time when they are not acquiescing to it, and they all do so within jurisdictions that treat the prospective consent as legally valid. Yet, despite their similarities, 'Skydiver' possesses a distinctive feature of which jurisdictions must take account in deciding whether to treat prospective consent as valid. The distinction is that, in contrast to the previous subjects who realize that the reason they will not be acquiescing to future conduct at the time it occurs is that they will lack the capacity even factually to consent at that time, the skydiver realizes that the reason she will not be acquiescing to being pushed out the airplane door is that she will be emphatically objecting to it. In attempting prospectively to consent to being pushed out the door, she seeks to relinquish a legal privilege, a privilege to grant or withhold consent to be pushed, that she otherwise possesses at the moment she freezes at the airplane door. She asks that her prospective consent be treated in law as irrevocable.

'Skydiver' thus raises a normative question that the previous cases do not: given the criminal law's general preference for contemporaneous decisionmaking, what is the justification for privileging the skydiver's prospective acquiescence over her contemporaneous objection? To address the question, let us add several hypothetical cases to the mix:

> ***'Plea Bargain'.*** As part of a guilty plea, a defendant *S* agrees beforehand that, if she fails to cooperate with the prosecution in gathering evidence against accomplices, a state officer *A* may seize her and commit her to prison, regardless of how emphatically she may object to being imprisoned at the time. *S* thereafter fails to cooperate. *A* seizes *S* and commits her to prison despite her heated objections at that time. Ruling: The prosecutor refuses to prosecute *A*, stating that, based on *S*'s agreement beforehand, *A* has a defense of consent to criminal charges of assaulting and kidnapping *S*.

> ***'Consumer Purchase'.*** As part of installment purchase of an automobile, a consumer *S* agrees beforehand that if she does not make monthly payments for the car, the seller *A* may peaceably enter upon her land and seize the car, regardless of how much she may object to *A*'s entry at that future time. *S* thereafter fails to make the monthly payment. *A* enters upon *S*'s land and seizes *S*'s car despite *S*'s heated objections at that time. Ruling: The courts rule that, based on *S*'s prior agreement, *A* has a defense of consent to criminal charges of trespassing upon *S*'s land.

> ***'Spendthrift'.*** A spendthrift *S* agrees beforehand that a friend *A* may hold the spendthrift's money and not return it to her for a year, regardless of how emphatically the spendthrift may demand during the year that *A* return her money.[7] *S* delivers her money to *A* and thereafter demands its return. *A* refuses to return *S*'s money to her, despite *S*'s fervent insistence that he do so. Ruling: The courts rule that, based on *S*'s prior agreement, A has defense of consent to criminal charges of appropriating *S*'s money.

> ***'Alcoholic'.*** An alcoholic *S* agrees beforehand that, if she has more than five drinks during the evening, her friend *A* may physically seize her car keys from her, including by means of minor force if necessary, regardless of how much *S* may protest at the time.[8] *S* has more than five drinks. *A* uses minor force to seize *S*'s car keys from her

despite her heated objections at that time. Ruling: The courts rule that, based upon *S*'s prior agreement, *A* has a defense of consent to criminal charges of assault against *S*.

Like the skydiver, the subjects in these hypothetical cases not only acquiesce beforehand to what *A* will thereafter do to them, they also acquiesce to their advance preferences being *irrevocable*: they acquiesce to binding themselves to their advance preferences, regardless of any contrary preferences they may thereafter have.[9] Thus, in 'Spendthrift', *S* not only acquiesces beforehand to *A*'s holding her money for a year, *S* also acquiesces beforehand to her *not being able to change her mind* about *A*'s holding her money for a year. Moreover, like 'Skydiver', these are hypothetical cases in which jurisdictions typically allow subjects to bind themselves to their advance preferences. Nevertheless, significant normative differences exist between the first two examples, on the one hand, and the remaining examples, on the other. 'Plea Bargain' and 'Consumer Purchase' are instances of reciprocal commitment: they are instances in which subjects bind themselves vis-à-vis their future preferences in return for the restraint their counterparts are exercising, under circumstances in which all parties hope to gain from the exchange. In short, they are instances of contract.[10] Thus, when the defendant in 'Plea Bargain' acquiesces beforehand to being incarcerated in the event that she does not cooperate with the prosecution in the meantime, it is not because *S* believes beforehand that she will benefit from being incarcerated; rather, it is because she believes at the prior time that the benefits of what she obtains from *A* in return for binding herself more than outweigh the burdens of what she is binding herself to, though she realizes that she may feel differently about the bargain in the event she is incarcerated. In contrast, 'Skydiver', 'Spendthrift', and 'Alcoholic' are instances of nonreciprocal commitment: they are instances in which parties bind themselves vis-à-vis the future because they believe that binding themselves will itself benefit them, without their having derived anything from *A* in exchange.[11] Thus, when the spendthrift acquiesces beforehand to having no access to her money at times when she may want it, she does so because she believes beforehand that she will benefit in the future from having no access to her money at that future time, though she realizes that she may feel differently when the time comes.

The difference between reciprocal and nonreciprocal commitments is normatively significant, because reciprocal commitments provide a benefit to *S* that justifies allowing *S* to bind herself irrevocably to her preferences beforehand—namely, the benefit to *S* of the enforceable promise on *A*'s part that *S* receives in exchange for her commitment. In contrast, where such benefits are lacking, jurisdictions are understandably reluctant to allow subjects to bind themselves irrevocably to their advance preferences on nothing but their personal pleas that binding themselves will itself benefit them in the future. Significantly, jurisdictions tend to do so only with respect to subjects who reasonably believe beforehand that, though they may retain some competence to assess their own interests by the time of the event, their competence at that time will be substantially diminished, whether because of fear (*e.g.*, 'Skydiver'), psychological pressure (*e.g.*, Spendthrift), or other perceptual impairment (*e.g.*, 'Alcoholic').[12]

Indeed, nonreciprocal irrevocable commitments are sufficiently rare that the paradigm for it comes not from law but from Homer's account of Odysseus' encounter with the Sirens. Odysseus had learned from Circe that the Sirens' songs were so irresistible that, once he had heard them, he would want to sail to them, even though doing so would bring him death.[13] Yet, in his curiosity about the world, Odysseus wanted to hear the Sirens. So after putting wax in the ears of his sailors and directing them to sail toward the Sirens' island, Odysseus ordered his men to bind him to the mast of his ship and not to release him until the ship had cleared the island, despite any intervening pleas by him to the contrary. Odysseus' sailors did as he directed and refused to release Odysseus until they had cleared the island. Odysseus' case is an easy one for enforcing prospective acquiescence because, once the sailors had tied Odysseus to the mast (as Odysseus had ordered while he was fully competent), the principal features of the case all militated in favor of enforcing his prospective acquiescence to not being released from the mast: (1) Odysseus was competent, well-informed, and free at the time he ordered his men to bind him to the mast; (2) the risk to Odysseus and his men of complying with his future preferences was death; (3) the wrong to Odysseus of his sailors' disregarding his future preferences was a wrong not of commission, but of omission, *i.e.*, the wrong of their failing to release him from the mast; and (4) Odysseus' competence to assess his interests at the time he actually called upon his men to release him was substantially impaired.

These four factors are controlling normative considerations with respect to nonreciprocal prospective prescriptive consent. The less any one of them is present, the less likely jurisdictions will be to enforce a person's prospective acquiescence. To contrast Odysseus' case with a harder case for enforcing prospective acquiescence in the face of contemporary non-acquiescence, consider the following:

> ***'Borderline Personality'.*** Janet is a young, educated woman who functions relatively well in both her private and professional spheres of her life. Yet she suffers from periodic bouts of depression and panic that cause her and others great distress. In one of her better moments, Janet agrees with her analyst and in writing that he may commit her for treatment for a compulsory period of 60 days if at any time he concludes that she is suffering from an episode for which institutionalization would be helpful; that he may do so even though her condition would not otherwise justify involuntary commitment; and that he may do so over her objections at the time. A time comes when the analyst concludes that he should commit Janet in accord with her written agreement. Yet when he endeavors to do so, Janet protests, claiming that she feels fine, that does not need institutionalization, and that she wishes to rescind her prior agreement.[14]

'Borderline Personality' is a harder case than Odysseus'. Indeed, Janet's prospective acquiescence is acquiescence that courts might decline to validate[15] because (1) Janet suffers from a borderline personality and, hence, may have been less competent when she signed the written agreement than Odysseus was when he ordered his men to tie him to the mast; (2) the risks to Janet of complying with her contemporaneous desire to remain at liberty are smaller than the risks to Odysseus and his men of complying with his contemporaneous desire to be released from the mast; (3) the wrong to Janet of institutionalizing her for 60 days against her will is greater than the wrong to Odysseus of not releasing him from the mast until the ship clears the island; and, most importantly, (4) Janet, not being a candidate for involuntary commitment, is more competent to assess her interests when she protests her institutionalization than Odysseus was when he fell under the Sirens' spell. Factors 1 to 3 all have a bearing upon how severely diminished a subject's competence must be at the time of an event if the subject's prospective acquiescence is to be enforced. But regardless of how favorable factors 1 to 3 may be for purposes of enforcing a subject's prior nonreciprocal acquiescence, jurisdictions are not likely to enforce it in the face of a subject's contemporaneous objections unless the jurisdiction believes that the subject has diminished competence under factor 4 to assess his interests at the time he objects.[16]

Retrospective Prescriptive Consent in the Face of Contemporaneous Non-acquiescence

A subject *S* retrospectively consents to conduct *x* in a *factual* sense when, although *S* does not choose *x* as that which she wishes for herself at the time at which *x* occurs, she later embraces *x* as that which she has wished for herself. In turn, *S*'s retrospective consent is *prescriptive*—that is, it constitutes a defense to an actor who subjects *S* to *x*—when the law treats it as sufficient to enable *S* retrospectively to take responsibility for conduct that occurred earlier. Consider:

> ***'Awakened Lover'.*** *S* and *A* are lovers who, having made love earlier in the evening, both fall asleep. *A* awakens at 3:00 a.m. and finding *S* still asleep, initiates an act of sexual intercourse with her while she is sleeping. During the course of the act, *S* awakens, embraces *A*, saying, 'This is nice—we should do it this way again.' Ruling: The courts rule that, based on *S*'s subsequent ratification of what *A* did while she was asleep, *A* has a defense of consent to a criminal charge of rape.[17]

The notion of prescriptive retrospective consent has an ancient pedigree. The Statute of Westminster of 1285 made it a crime to 'ravish a woman . . . where she neither assented before nor *after*'.[18] Nevertheless, despite its pedigree, the concept of retrospective prescriptive consent remains paradoxical in ways that prospective prescriptive consent is not. Joel Feinberg illustrates the paradox in the ambivalence with which he discusses what he calls 'subsequent consent'. On the one hand, Feinberg says that 'very little can be done . . . to extract coherence from the strange notion of "subsequent consent"'. Subsequent consent by *S* is 'actual consent' by *S*, Feinberg says, but it is actual consent that comes too late because 'it cannot have the effect of retroactively warranting' conduct to which *S* has not contemporaneously consented.[19] Yet on the other hand, Feinberg says that subsequent consent 'expresses, after the fact . . . [a] lack of a sense of grievance in the "consenter" for a harmless invasion of h[er] sovereignty'.[20] Donald Dripps expresses similar ambivalence with respect to cases in which *S* is subjected to sexual intercourse over her objections but in which the intercourse operates to cause her to change her mind and to welcome what she originally found repugnant. Dripps says that *S*'s 'retroactive approval' does not exonerate an actor whose initial, non-consented-to sexual conduct 'would still be criminal'. Yet Dripps concedes that 'retroactive approval' of the intercourse renders it 'unlikely to be prosecuted'.[21]

What accounts for this ambivalence? If Feinberg is right that *S*'s retrospective acquiescence to *A*'s conduct can render the conduct 'harmless', what is so 'strange' about allowing it to 'retroactively warran[t]' conduct that would otherwise be an offense? Indeed, if retrospectively acquiesced-to conduct is harmless, why does voluntary, retrospective acquiescence *not* exonerate *A* of harm-based offenses in the same way and for the same reason that voluntary contemporaneous acquiescence exonerates *A* of harm-based offenses? Conversely, if Dripps is right that retrospectively acquiesced-to conduct is 'still . . . criminal', then why is it 'unlikely to be prosecuted'? To be sure, prosecutors may believe that conduct to which subjects ultimately acquiesce, even retrospectively, is not sufficiently serious to warrant prosecution. Or prosecutors may believe that *jurors* may feel that retrospectively acquiesced-to conduct is not sufficiently serious to warrant conviction. But if prosecutors and jurors are correct that retrospectively acquiesced-to conduct is not serious, then why is it 'still . . . criminal'? Why, in other words, are rulings like the ruling in 'Awakened Lover' so rare in criminal law?

Let us begin by examining whether voluntary, retrospective acquiescence does, indeed, cause conduct to have been harmless. Whether it does, and the extent to which it does, depend very much upon what one *means* by 'retrospective acquiescence'. Feinberg imagines a case in which *A* violently rapes a woman *B* who initially charges *A* with rape but who thereafter falls in love with *A*:

> Suppose *A* violently forces his attention on *B* without her consent, and she then prefers rape charges against him. But between the time of *A*'s indictment for the crime, and the scheduled date of his trial, he is visited constantly by *B* who gradually falls in love with him, and in the nick of time drops charges against him, leading to his release. 'If I had known him then as well as I know him now', she says, 'I would surely have consented.'[22]

Unfortunately, Feinberg's hypothetical case is not a good example of retrospective acquiescence, at least not the kind of retrospective acquiescence that renders conduct 'harmless'. The hypothetical victim, *B*, is a woman who no longer wishes her assailant to be punished; who in Feinberg's words 'forgives' her assailant for what he did;[23] who feels she 'would have consented' to sexual intercourse if she had known then what she now knows; and who may even now be glad that *A* assaulted her—glad, in the sense that the assault led to something that would not otherwise have occurred, namely, her visiting *A* in jail and eventually falling in love with him. Yet none of those dispositions or actions on *B*'s part precludes *B* from continuing to feel that *A* wrongfully harmed her when he violently assaulted her. A victim like *B* may possess reasons for wishing that her assailant not go to prison without necessarily feeling that he did not harm her. Likewise, she may feel that she *would have* acquiesced to what her assailant did without necessarily feeling she *did* acquiesce to what he did. Likewise, she may be glad that events eventually ensued in the way they did, without denying that they ensued in that way because of a serious harm to her. Finally, in order to forgive her assailant, she not only *may* concede that he wrongfully harmed her, she *must* concede that he wrongfully harmed her, because forgiveness presupposes harm; forgiveness is a decision to desist in resenting an actor for conduct that one recognizes to have been wrongful.[24]

A better example of retrospective consent is the famous scene in the film 'Gone With The Wind' in which Rhett Butler, after years of alternating passion and strife, seizes his wife Scarlett O'Hara during a squabble and carries her struggling up the grand stairway of their mansion to her bedroom, presumably to ravish her. Even apart from what thereafter transpires in the bedroom (about which viewers are left to their imaginations), it is clear that Rhett's seizure of Scarlett at the stairway is a physical assault to which Scarlett does not even factually consent. Nevertheless, when Scarlett's maid enters Scarlett's bedroom the next morning, she finds Scarlett to be radiant, benevolent, and full of renewed love for Rhett. To say that Scarlett declines to press 'charges' against Rhett, or that Scarlett 'forgives' Rhett, or that Scarlett 'would have consented' if she had known what she now knows, or that Scarlett is glad that everything including the harm to her of the assault eventually worked out as they did—none of these accurately captures Scarlett's feelings. Instead, Scarlett appears not to feel assaulted at all. She seems to feel that Rhett knew better than she did what she wanted for herself. Like other people who are forced into situations they later come to embrace, Scarlett seems pleased in retrospect that Rhett disregarded her opposition, pleased that Rhett did something that she now embraces as a furthering of her interests, though she failed to realize it at the time.

Scarlett's story is analogous to that of a religious cult member who is kidnapped by his parents and subjected to professional 'deprogramming' to rid him of the cult's influence. Admittedly, Scarlett is not analogous to a cult member who, though he wishes to drop charges against his parents, nevertheless continues to resent them for what they did to him. Nor is she analogous to a cult member who, though he forgives his parents by ceasing to resent them for what they did, nevertheless feels that they harmed him. Nor is she analogous to a cult member who, though he is glad that events have worked out as they have—perhaps because of acquaintances he has made in the process—nonetheless feels that his parents mistreated him. Rather, Scarlett is analogous to a cult member who, after everything is over and done with, says 'Thank you!' to his parents, 'Thank you for knowing me better than I did'.[25] Such a person who voluntarily and *retrospectively* acquiesces to *x* in his mind is very much like a person who voluntarily and *contemporaneously* acquiesces to *x* in his mind. A person who voluntarily and contemporaneously acquiesces in *x* in his mind (*e.g.*, a bout of wrestling with *A*) may suffer harms in the form of touching and bruising at *A*'s hands; but such harms are not *wrongful* harms to him because he voluntarily chooses them for himself. Similarly, a person who voluntarily and retrospectively acquiesces in *x* in his mind may suffer the harms of touching and bruising at *A*'s hands; but they are not wrongful harms to him, because he voluntarily and subjectively chooses them for himself at a time when he is best able to assess whether they are in his interests, namely, afterwards.[26]

To be sure, retrospective consent differs from prospective and contemporaneous consent in one respect: when *S*, whether prospectively or contemporaneously, voluntarily acquiesces to *A*'s conduct in her mind, there is no period of time during which she suffers wrongful harm at his hands; but when *S* retrospectively acquiesces to *A*'s conduct in her mind, there is, indeed, a period of time during which she suffers wrongful harm at his hands, *viz.*, the period from the occurrence of the conduct to the time at which *S* retrospectively acquiesces to it. Thus, when Odysseus acquiesced in advance to being bound and held to the mast, he placed himself in a position in which, though he suffered the harm of being bound to the mast, he at no time suffered it as a *wrongful* harm. In contrast, Scarlett suffered a wrongful harm from the moment Rhett seized her at the base of the stairway until she subsequently came to welcome the assault. Nevertheless, although the two cases differ significantly *until S* retrospectively acquiesces to the relevant conduct in *S*'s mind, they do not differ *once S* voluntarily and retrospectively acquiesces to it. For at the moment at which *S* voluntarily and retrospectively acquiesces to the conduct, the conduct is something that *S* chooses for herself and, hence, something that not only is *no longer* a wrongful harm to *S* but that is no wrongful harm to *S at all*. Thus, when Scarlett decides after the fact that she wants Rhett to have done to her what he did to her, Rhett's actions not only cease to *be* a wrong to Scarlett, but cease to *have been* a wrong to her.

If this analysis is correct, it supports Feinberg assertion that *S*'s voluntary and retrospective acquiescence renders *A*'s conduct 'harmless' to her: if *S*'s voluntary retrospective acquiescence consists of a mental state on her part, her acquiescence constitutes a negation of the primary harm that offenses of non-consent seek to prevent (and if *S*'s voluntary retrospective acquiescence takes the form of an expression, it is strong evidence of the negation of the primary harm that offenses of non-consent seek to prevent). Unfortunately, the analysis also reaffirms the paradox with which we began: If retrospective acquiescence can negate the wrongfulness of harm, why is it not a defense to offenses of non-consent in the same way that contemporaneous acquiescence and prospective acquiescence are? Why, with rare exceptions, do jurisdictions tend to deny retrospective acquiescence the normative role they routinely grant to contemporaneous and prospective acquiescence, namely, the role of being a formal defense to offenses of non-consent?[27]

Several explanations come to mind. First, it might be argued that even though *S*'s voluntary, retrospective subjective acquiescence precludes *A*'s conduct *x* from constituting a wrongful harm to *S*, it does not negate *A*'s culpability in subjecting her to *x* at a time when *A* knew or should have known that *S* was not prescriptively consenting. *A* can be rightly blamed for subjecting *S* to *x*, so the argument goes, because he knew *S* was not voluntarily acquiescing to it, regardless of whether *S* later voluntarily acquiesced to it. One problem with that argument is that it assumes that *A*'s blameworthiness—his *mens rea*—is measured exclusively by what he knows or has reason to know of *S*'s subjective wishes at the time at which he subjects her to *x*. However, if it is true that retrospective acquiescence negates the wrongfulness of *A*'s conduct, it follows that assessment of *A*'s *mens rea* ought to take account of not only what *A* knows or has reason to know *S* is choosing for herself at the time of the conduct, but also what *A* knows or has reason to know *S* will choose for herself in the future. *A* may have a difficult time showing that he reasonably believed at the time of the conduct that *S* would acquiesce to *A*'s conduct at a later time. But if *A* can make such a showing, he ought to be acquitted of having *mens rea* because, given that *A* reasonably believed at the time of *x* that *S* would voluntarily and retrospectively acquiesce to *x* at a later time, he must have reasonably believed that he was not subjecting her to a harm that would wrong her. Another problem with the aforementioned argument is that it conflates *A*'s responsibility for *being willing* to subject *S* to a wrongful harm with his responsibility for *actually subjecting S* to a wrongful harm. *A* is guilty of a crime of wrongful harm if, and only if, he (i) performs the *actus reus* of subjecting *S* to the wrongful harm, and (ii) he does so with the *mens rea* of believing or having reason to believe that he is subjecting *S* to the wrongful harm. An actor who possesses the *mens rea* of being willing to inflict a wrongful harm but does not do so is, at most, guilty of *attempting* to inflict a wrongful harm. Accordingly, an actor who, while having no reason to believe that *S* will ever voluntarily acquiesce to it, subjects *S* to conduct to which she *does* voluntarily and retrospectively acquiesce in her mind, ought at most to be punished for attempting to subject *S* to conduct without her consent.

Second, it can be argued that, even if jurisdictions wished to recognize retrospective acquiescence as a defense, they would have difficulty distinguishing a subject's retrospective acquiescence from two dispositions on a victim's part that jurisdictions rarely wish to treat as defenses to criminal misconduct: namely, a victim's desire that her assailant not be prosecuted and a victim's decision to forgive her assailant. This argument has some force, for it is true that jurisdictions rarely choose to delegate to victims the formal power to drop charges or to pardon offenders.[28] The problem with the argument is its premise—that courts are incapable of distinguishing retrospective acquiescence from desires to forgive or excuse. Retrospective acquiescence, after all, is very different from the latter desires. *S* retrospectively acquiesces to conduct when she comes to believe that the conduct itself was in her interest, though she did not believe so at the time. In contrast, *S* 'forgives' when she decides to cease resenting an actor for conduct she continues to regard as wrongful; and *S* seeks to 'excuse' when she no longer wishes that an actor be punished.[29] Given the variety of subtle states of mind that courts are accustomed to scrutinizing in criminal cases, and given the circumstantial evidence that is likely to accompany genuine instances of retrospective acquiescence, it is doubtful that courts are incapable of identifying it.

Third and perhaps most interestingly, it can be argued that retrospective consent is arbitrary in a way that prospective consent is not, because retrospective consent is unbounded by time. To illustrate this arbitrariness, contrast retrospective consent with prospective consent. We have seen that the feature that justifies allowing *S* to prescriptively consent beforehand to conduct that occurs thereafter is *S*'s lack of capacity or diminished competence at the time the conduct occurs. Accordingly, a person who prospectively consents is presumably able to rescind his consent at any time up to and until the period of his incapacity or diminished competence begins. Thus, Odysseus would presumably have been able to rescind his consent to remain bound to the mast if he had changed his mind *before* coming within range of the Sirens' voices. By the same token, a person's prospective consent remains valid only as long as his incapacity or diminished competence persists. Thus, Odysseus' prospective consent to remain bound to the mast would presumably have lapsed if he had prospectively consented to remain bound even after he and the ship were no longer in danger. In contrast, there is no natural limit to retrospective consent apart from the lives of both participants. Scarlett O'Hara happened to acquiesce to Rhett's conduct the next morning. What if she had not done so until the next month, or the next year? What if she acquiesced the next morning but then changed her mind the following month? At each moment she retrospectively acquiesces in her mind, Rhett's conduct ceases to be a harm. At each moment she changes her mind, it becomes a harm again. Of course, a jurisdiction can designate the date of trial as the time at which a subject must decide once and for all whether retrospectively to consent to conduct that is otherwise criminal. But that is precisely what makes retrospective consent appear arbitrary in a way that prospective consent and contemporary prescriptive consent are not.

Ironically, while *officially* prospective prescriptive consent is more acceptable and widespread than retrospective prescriptive consent, *unofficially* retrospective prescriptive consent may be at least as common, if not more so. Prosecutors, after all, are reluctant to pursue reported criminal charges on behalf of alleged victims who presently believe that defendants acted in their interests.[30] More importantly, even if they wished to, prosecutors cannot pursue criminal charges that are not reported to them; and persons who no longer feel aggrieved by criminal conduct tend not to report it. Rhett may have criminally assaulted Scarlett by seizing her against her will. But no prosecutor ever knew, because Scarlett had no inclination to report it.

Now it might be thought that the concept of retrospective prescriptive consent is vulnerable to an argument *ad absurdum*. The argument goes as follows:

> ***'Retrospective Non-consent'.*** The justification for allowing *S* to retroactively decriminalize conduct to which she did not contemporaneously consent is that *S* supposedly possesses superior knowledge of her interests at the later time. However, if *S*'s superior knowledge afterwards justifies allowing her to retroactively decriminalize

> conduct to which she did not prescriptively consent at the time, then her superior knowledge afterwards should also justify allowing her to retroactively criminalize conduct to which she did prescriptively consent at the time. Yet it is absurd to think that a person who voluntarily says 'yes' to conduct when it occurs can retrospectively render it criminal it by saying 'no' after the fact.

This analogy is flawed, to be sure. But the flaw does not lie in equating retrospective non-consent to retrospective consent with respect to the primary harm that offenses of non-consent seek to prevent. In each case, *S* acknowledges the events that occurred contemporaneously with *x* and, yet, contends that her retrospective mental state controls the extent to which those events caused her to suffer the primary harm that the offense of non-consent seeks to prevent. Thus, with respect to retrospective consent, *S* acknowledges that she was subjected to *x* without her contemporaneous prescriptive consent. Yet *S* rightly contends that because her retrospective change of mind alters the meaning of that event to her, and because her retrospective change of mind consists of her now choosing *x* as that which she believes to have been in her interests *all along*, her retrospective mental state of acquiescence precludes her *all along* from having suffered the primary harm that the offense of non-consent seeks to prevent. Similarly, with respect to retrospective non-consent, *S* acknowledges that she was subjected to *x* with her contemporaneous prescriptive consent. Yet *S* rightly contends that because her retrospective change of mind alters the meaning of that event to her, and because her retrospective change of mind consists of her now repudiating *x* as that which she believes to have been contrary to her interests all along, her retrospective mental state of acquiescence causes her to have suffered all along the primary harm that the offense of non-consent seeks to prevent.

The flaw in the analogy is to assume that because retrospective acquiescence arguably suffices to validate conduct that would otherwise be criminal, retrospective non-consent must also suffice to invalidate conduct that would otherwise be non-criminal. The assumption is a *non sequitur*, because it ignores that within jurisdictions that define consent as a mental state, offenses of non-consent consist of *two* elements only one of which is arguably controlled by a subject's mental state. *S*'s retrospective attitudinal consent arguably suffices to decriminalize conduct that would otherwise be criminal, because within jurisdictions that define consent as a mental state, *S*'s retrospective attitudinal consent negates the primary harm that offenses of non-consent seek to prevent and thereby arguably negates one of the two elements that are necessary to render an actor guilty of an offense of non-consent—namely, that he have subjected *S* to *x* without her voluntarily acquiescing to it in her mind (although *S*'s retrospective consent does not exonerate an actor of *attempting* to commit an offense of non-consent). In contrast, *S*'s retrospective attitudinal non-consent does not suffice to criminalize conduct that would otherwise be non-criminal, because it at most supplies one of the two elements that are necessary to render an actor guilty and does nothing to supply the other element—namely, that an actor act with *mens rea*. Regardless of how *S* may thereafter feel about choices she voluntarily made at the time, an actor cannot be justly punished for subjecting *S* to conduct without her prescriptive attitudinal consent if, at the time he acted, he reasonably believed that she was voluntarily acquiescing in her mind. He must be acquitted not because he has not wrongfully harmed her, but because he neither knew nor had reason to know that he was wrongfully harming her.

Conclusion

A subject *S* consents to *x* in a *factual* sense when *S* chooses x, whether subjectively or expressively, as that which she prefers for herself under the circumstances or that about which she is sufficiently indifferent as to be willing to leave its occurrence to others. *S* can make such choices at various times with reference to the occurrence of *x*. Thus, *S*'s factual consent to *x* is 'prospective' if she chooses *x* for herself only in advance of the occurrence of *x* and not at the time *x* actually occurs; her factual consent is 'contemporaneous' if she chooses *x* at the time it occurs; and her factual consent is 'retrospective' if she chooses *x* for herself only after the occurrence of *x* and not at the time *x* actually occurs. Needless to say, factual consent alone does not suffice by itself to constitute a defense to an actor who subjects *S* to *x*. Factual consent is a defense only if it occurs under such conditions of competence, knowledge, freedom, and motivation as the jurisdiction at hand deems to be necessary to enable (or appear to enable) *S* to take responsibility for her choice for purposes of the offense at issue.

Significantly, however, one of the conditions of competence that determines whether *S*'s factual consent is a valid defense—that is, one of the conditions of *S*'s factual acquiescence that determines whether it constitutes prescriptive consent—is the *timing* with which it occurs with reference to *x*. Anglo-American criminal law adopts a strong presumption in favor of the necessity of contemporaneous factual consent. The law typically requires as a condition of prescriptive consent to *x* that *S* not only choose *x*, and choose *x* competently, knowingly, and freely, but that *S* do so contemporaneously with the occurrence of *x*. This does not mean that the law never treats prospective and retroactive consent as valid defenses to crime. Rather, it means that the law recognizes them only exceptionally. The law officially recognizes prospective consent as a defense only when prospective consent is part of a bargained-for and reciprocal exchange from which *S* is expected to benefit, or when *S*'s prospective consent is predicated upon *S*'s incapacity or diminished competence to make contemporaneous decisions for herself in the future. The law's official recognition of retrospective consent, in turn, is quite rare, though, as an unofficial matter, prosecutors may give effect to retrospective consent (and perhaps rightly) by relying upon it to dismiss charges.

Interestingly, prospective and retrospective prescriptive consent are significant, not only in their own right, but also for what they reveal of the nature of *contemporaneous* prescriptive consent. Consider, for example, the question whether contemporaneous prescriptive consent is best conceptualized as mental state or an expression. We saw in Chapter 4 that contemporaneous prescriptive consent implicates three normative considerations:

> ***An Actor's Mens Rea:*** the culpability, or 'blameworthiness', of an actor *A* who subjects *S* to *x* without reasonably believing that *S* is voluntarily and subjectively choosing *x* for herself under the circumstances (even if *A* later discovers that *S* actually did voluntarily and subjectively choose *x* for herself under the circumstances).
>
> ***An Actor's Lack of a Mens Rea:*** the lack of culpability, or blamelessness, of an actor who subjects *S* to *x*, or tries to subject *S* to *x*, because he reasonably believes that *S* is voluntarily and subjectively choosing *x* for herself under the circumstances (even if *A* later discovers that she was not).
>
> ***Harm:*** the harm that *S* suffers when *A* subjects her to *x* without her voluntarily and subjectively choosing it for herself under the circumstances (regardless of whether *A* possesses or lacks *mens rea* regarding *S*'s lack of consent).

We also saw in Chapter 4 that these considerations can be accommodated by proceeding in three steps: (1) by defining *S*'s prescriptive consent as a mental state of voluntary acquiescence on *S*'s part, thereby highlighting the factor that determines whether *S* suffers the primary harm from which the state seeks to protect her by making it a crime to subject her to *x* without her 'consent'; (2) by punishing *A* for the completed crime of subjecting *S* to *x* without her consent if he subjects her to *x* without her consent *and* does so with *mens rea* regarding *S*'s lack of consent; (3) by punishing *A* for the inchoate crime of 'attempting' to subject *S* to *x* without her consent if he tries, unsuccessfully, to subject her to *x* and do so with *mens rea* regarding *S*'s lack of consent.

Conceptualizing consent as a mental state, while appropriate for contemporaneous acquiescence, works less well for prospective and retrospective acquiescence. Consider prospective consent. The most common instances of prospective prescriptive consent in criminal law are instances of bargained-for exchange, as in 'Plea Bargain' and 'Consumer Purchase'. Bargained-for exchange, in turn, is a form of contracting, and as such it presupposes operative acts of consent that consist, not of mental states of acquiescence, but of expressions of acquiescence. By the same token, to the extent jurisdictions recognize it, retrospective prescriptive consent will tend in practice to take the form of an expression. One can imagine a jurisdiction that opts to treat *any* voluntary and retrospective mental state of acquiescence by *S* as sufficient to validate conduct that occurs without her contemporaneous acquiescence, even if *S* changes her mind by the time trial occurs. In practice, however, in order to be certain that *S*'s retrospective acquiescence is a settled state of mind on her part, jurisdictions are likely to measure it by what *S* expresses her mental state to be at the time of trial. The inquiry at trial is, indeed, an inquiry into what *S* subjectively chooses for herself at that time, because her subjective mental state controls whether she has suffered the primary harm that the statute seeks to prevent. But because the inquiry at trial focuses largely upon what *S*, as a witness, declares her choice at that time to be, the jury's determination of *S*'s mental state at that time will rarely depart from what reasonable jurors would infer it to be from what she declares it to be at that time.

Prospective and retrospect consent also cast light on the debate among commentators as to the justification for allowing a subject *S* to authorize *A* to subject her to conduct *x* that would otherwise be an offense against her. We saw in Chapter 3 that some commentators argue that the justification is *S*'s self-interest: *S* possesses unique knowledge of her own personal goals and values, and, hence, she knows better than others whether *x* is in her interests. In contrast, other commentators argue that the justification is autonomy: *S* should be allowed to control whether she engages in *x* because regardless of whether *x* is in her interests, the conduct affects no one but herself. Oddly enough, prospective prescriptive consent and retrospective prescriptive consent—at least as jurisdictions commonly define them—appear to be based upon opposing justifications. Doctrines of prospective prescriptive consent appear to be based on notions of *S*'s self-interest rather than autonomy. Thus jurisdictions typically allow *S* to bind herself to the mast only when *S*'s relative competence to perceive and assess her self-interests is expected to substantially diminish by the time the future conduct occurs. Indeed, if doctrines of prospective prescriptive consent were based on notions of *S*'s autonomy (as opposed to *S*'s interests), jurisdictions would recognize prospective consent far more widely than they presently do, rather than treating it as an *exception* to a normative presumption in favor of contemporaneous consent; for interests in autonomy apply as much to prospective consent as to contemporaneous consent. Conversely, as between the two of them, autonomy succeeds better than self-interest in explaining the feature that is so distinctive of retrospective prescriptive consent—namely, its striking *rarity* as an official defense. For the one goal that retrospective consent is incapable of achieving—and thus the one goal the unattainability of which would explain the striking reluctance of jurisdictions to recognize retrospective consent as a defense—is the goal of enhancing *S*'s autonomy to engage in *x*, because by the time *S* retrospectively consents to *x*, she can no longer influence whether *x* has occurred in the past.[31] On the other hand, if *S*'s self-interest were the goal that jurisdictions invoked retrospective consent to serve, jurisdictions would recognize the legitimacy of retrospective consent far more often than they presently do, for *S* knows the most about herself after *x* occurs when she is able to place it in the context of her life as a whole. Indeed, if *S*'s self-interest were the controlling consideration, jurisdictions would *always* measure the harm of nonconsensual offenses by what *S* perceives her interests to be afterwards, including appropriate cases in which *S* voluntarily acquiesces at the time only to revoke her acquiescence thereafter, though to avoid strict liability, jurisdictions would also acquit actors who lacked *mens rea* regarding *S*'s non-consent.

Notes

1. For analysis of why prospective acquiescence is less likely to reflect a person's interests than contemporaneous acquiescence, *see* Allen Buchanan, 'Advance Directives And The Personal Identity Problem', *Philosophy and Public Affairs*, Vol. 17, No. 4, pp. 277-302, and esp. 278-79; Buchanan and Brock, *Deciding For Others*, pp. 103-110; Thomas Schelling, *Choice and Consequence* (Cambridge, Mass.: Harvard University Press, pp. 96-98; and John Stuart Mill, *Principles of Political Economy* (W. Ashley ed.), pp. 959-60.
2. Thus, a woman is deemed prescriptively to consent to sexual intercourse if she competently, knowingly, and freely acquiesces to the sexual intercourse at the last moment before intercourse occurs, even if her contemporaneous acquiesce follows upon prior non-acquiescence. *See, e.g.*, State v. Dizon, 47 Haw. 444, 459 n.5, 390 P.2d 759, 768 n.5 (1964) (upholding a jury instruction that 'if you should find that although initially the idea of the act was completely abhorrent to her, but that she did in fact ultimately consent prior to penetration, then you cannot find the defendant guilty of rape'); Hazel v. State, 221 Md. 464, 469, 157 A.2d 922, 925 (1960) ('With respect to the presence or absence of the element of consent, it is true, of course, that however reluctantly given, consent to the act at any time prior to penetration deprives the subsequent intercourse of its criminal character'). Law reformers have proposed that, once a woman says 'no' to sexual intercourse, a man who subsequently has sexual intercourse with her should be deemed guilty of rape, unless he follows special procedures to ensure that she eventually changes her mind before sexual intercourse takes place. *See* Dripps, 'Beyond Rape', pp. 1807-09; Schulhofer, *Unwanted Sex*, pp. 72-74. But even under such proposals, a woman's eventual consent trumps any prior expression of non-acquiescence.

   Conversely, once a woman competently, knowingly, and freely acquiesces to sexual intercourse, and intercourse takes place, her prescriptive consent is not invalidated by a subsequent, negative change of mind. *See* Battle v. State, 287 Md. 675, 684, 414 A.2d 1266, 1270 (1980) ('[If a woman] consents prior to penetration and withdraws the consent following penetration, there is no rape'). One can imagine a fictional society in which woman who acquiesces to sexual intercourse is granted a subsequent 'cooling off' period of hours or days in which to change her mind if she so wishes. Cf. the Federal Trade Commission rule to the effect that, after a customer has agreed to purchase goods from a door-to-door salesman, the customer has three days in which to repudiate the sale (*see* 16 C.F.R. 429.1(a) (1998)). In such a society, a woman's retrospective non-acquiescence would, indeed, trump her contemporaneous acquiescence, and constitute a determination that she had been wrongfully harmed, though the defendant would presumably have a defense of lack of *mens rea*.
3. *See* the discussion in the remainder of this chapter.
4. Cf. Uniform Rights of the Terminally Ill Act, Ohio Code §§ 2133.12(A), 2133.24(A) (2003) (a patient's advance directive provides a physician with a defense to criminal assault).
5. This hypothetical case is based upon Bullington v. Florida, 616 So. 2d 1036, 1038 (Fla. App. Ct., 1993), in which the court held that a man was not guilty of rape for having sexual intercourse with a woman during periods in which she was unconscious, given that the woman had consented in advance to engaging in sexual intercourse while drugged and bound. *See* also Kramer, 'Rule by Myth', p. 126 (footnotes omitted):

   > As early as 1870, the court in Commonwealth v. Burke held that sexual intercourse 'with a woman in a state of unconsciousness at the time, whether that state has been produced by the act of the [defendant] or not, is presumed to be without her consent,

and is rape'. While Burke remains good law, some jurisdictions allow the presumption of non-consent to be rebutted by evidence that the woman consented prior to losing consciousness.

Brown v. State, 138 Ga. 814, 76 S.E. 379 (1912), in which the court stated:

> Carnal knowledge of a woman while she is asleep and unconscious of the act, and her body being penetrated before she awakens, would be against her will and without her consent, and would constitute the offense of rape, unless she had given the party charged with the rape some reason to believe that she consented to the act.

Utah Code Ann. § 76-5-406(5) (1998) ('An act of sexual intercourse . . . is without consent of the victim [if] . . . the victim has not consented *and* the actor knows the victim is unconscious . . '.) (emphasis added).

6. '[A]n individual's rational agreement to be subjected to future coercion is justified if such coercion could reasonably be expected to result in a "net gain" of freedom'. Dresser, 'Ulysses And The Psychiatrists', p. 788. *See* also Van De Veer, 'Paternalism and Subsequent Consent', p. 636 (prospective consent is justified for someone who 'rightly believe[s] that it is the most effective way to maximize his own satisfactions in the long run, given his own less than perfect ability to exercise self-control in particular types of circumstances').
7. This example comes from Lavin, 'Ulysses Contracts'.
8. This example comes from Schelling, *Choice and Consequence*, p. 88.
9. For an analysis of what it means for one to bind oneself in a variety of settings, including one-party settings in which no other actor is involved, *see* Elster, *Ulysses And The Sirens*.
10. Thomas Schelling distinguishes reciprocal commitments from non-reciprocal commitments as follows:

    > Full freedom entails the freedom to bind oneself, to incur obligation, to reduce one's range of choice. Specifically, this is the freedom of contract: and it works through expectations. The behavior of others depends on what they expect of me; by restricting my own freedom of choice, I gain influence over the choices of others. The results can be called 'cooperation', 'immunity', 'bargaining power', or even 'coercion'.

    Schelling, *Choice and Consequence*, p. 98.
11. For an analysis of nonreciprocal commitments, *see* Elster, *Ulysses and the Sirens*, pp. 36-111; Schelling, *Choice and Consequence*, pp. 57-112.
12. *See* Buchanan and Brock, *Deciding For Others*, pp. 171-72.
13. Homer, *The Odyssey*. bk. XII, 180-217.
14. This example is based on a more extended example in Dresser, 'Ulysses and the Psychiatrists', pp. 779-80.
15. Jon Elster states that such binding voluntary commitments are lawful in Norway, though Thomas Schelling believes they are unlawful in the United States. Compare Elster, *Ulysses and the Sirens*, p. 38, with Schelling, *Choice and Consequence*, p. 96.
16. For an analysis of various kinds of incompetence, *see* Schelling, *Choice and Consequence*, pp. 88-91. For the argument that normative judgments enter into a society's views of incompetence, *see id.* at 95-108. But *see* Feinberg, *Harm To Self*, p. 83 (arguing that when a subject is fully and equally competent both prospectively and contemporaneously, her prospective consent ought to prevail over her later objections at the time the conduct occurs).
17. *See, e.g.*, Regina v. Barrow, 11 Cox Crim. Cas. 191 (1868) (reversing the conviction of a man who commenced sexual intercourse with a woman who was asleep but who, upon

awakening, consented to the sexual intercourse); Pollard v. State, 2 Iowa 567, 568, 570 (1856) (implying that, if the '[defendant] was in the act of sexual intercourse with [the prosecutrix]', and if 'she was awakened by the pleasure of sexual enjoyment, and suffered no pain' nor offered further resistance, adultery or seduction would be more appropriate than a charge of rape); Regina v. Clarke, 6 Cox Crim. Cas. 412 (1854) (same). *See* generally Renee Madeleine Horn, '*State v. Moorman*: Can Sex With a Sleeping Woman Constitute Forcible Rape?', 65 *North Carolina Law Review* 1246, 1252 ('[I]f a man began an act of sexual intercourse with a sleeping woman who then awakened and welcomed his advances, consent might be shown').

18. 13 Edward I, c. 34, s. 1.
19. Feinberg, *Harm To Self*, p. 182.
20. Feinberg, *Harm To Self*, p. 187.
21. Dripps, 'Beyond Rape', p. 1809.
22. Feinberg, *Harm To Self*, p. 182.
23. Feinberg, *Harm To Self*, p. 182.
24. *See* generally Robert Karen, *The Forgiving Self: The Road From Resentment To Connection* (New York, New York: Doubleday, 2001).
25. Cf. Peterson v. Sorlien, 299 N.W.2d 123, 128-29 (Minn. Sup. Ct., 1980) (after three days of detention and deprogramming that the plaintiff resisted, she 'assented' to the regimen for purposes of the law of torts, thereby 'affirm[ing', after the fact, the initial three days of detention and deprogramming).
26. *See* Rosemary Carter, 'Justifying Paternalism', *Canadian Journal of Philosophy*, vol. 7, no. 7, 133-45, p. 140 ('It is highly unlikely that anyone will subsequently consent to a paternalistic act which will not harmonize with his permanent aims and preferences').
27. For the proposition that victims of rape have no power to authorize sexual intercourse by consenting after intercourse takes place, *see* Battle v. Maryland, 287 Md. 675, 681, 414 A.2d 1266, 1269 (1980) ('The authorities are unanimous in the view that consent subsequent to the act of intercourse will not prevent its being rape').
28. For discussion of the state's reluctance to empower victims to 'condone' offenses, *see* Wayne LaFave and Austin Scott, *Criminal Law* § 57, pp. 410-11 (St. Paul, Minnesota: West Publishing Co.) (2d ed., 1986). *See* also New York v. Brim, 22 Misc. 2d 335, 338, 199 N.Y.S.2d 744, 749 (1960) (citations omitted) ('[F]orgiveness . . . has no proper place in the criminal law. The interest of the state is paramount and controls prosecutions. For it is the public, not a complainant, that is injured by the commission of a crime'); Wisconsin v. Lederer, 99 Wis. 2d 430, 444, 299 N.W.2d 457, 465 (1980) (a rape victim's express wish that her assailant not be sent to jail is irrelevant).

    To be sure, some jurisdictions, in limited circumstances, do officially delegate to victims the power to forgive or condone crimes. Thus, some jurisdiction have enacted 'misdemeanor compromise' statutes that provide that, if an injured party to a misdemeanor appears in court and acknowledges that he has received satisfaction for an injury, the prosecution is to be terminated. *See, e.g.*, Cal. Penal Code § 1378 (1999). However, these statutes are designed to assist victims in receiving compensation for their injuries and, hence, are predicated on findings that victims no longer wish offenders to be prosecuted—not on findings that a victim retrospectively believes that a defendant's actions were actually in the victim's interests.
29. Cf. Va. Code § 18.2-66 (1995) (allowing a girl who comes of age to exonerate a person whom she marries who had sexual intercourse with her when she was underage).
30. See Miller, The Decision To Charge A Suspect With a Crime, p. 173.

31. Consider Scarlett O'Hara's encounter with Rhett Butler. By allowing Scarlett to consent after-the-fact to Rhett's assault, a jurisdiction does nothing to enhance Scarlett's autonomy to engage in sexual intercourse that has already occurred. A doctrine of retrospective prescriptive consent enhances a subject's autonomy only in rare cases in which, by making it clear that subjects such as Scarlett will be allowed to give defenses of consent to actors like Rhett, the doctrine induces actors like Rhett to engage in risk-taking actions that they would otherwise eschew and, hence, induces such actors to provide subjects like Scarlett with subsequently welcomed experiences that they would otherwise lack.

Chapter Seven

Imputed Consent

Perry Kingwell, an amateur hockey player in Saskatchewan, did not prescriptively consent to the foul that put him in the hospital for three days. He did not even see it coming. Kingwell, in an attempt to retrieve the puck from an area behind the net, was facing the boards with his back to the playing ice when Roger Cey, an opposing player, fouled Kingwell from behind by cross-checking him in the neck with his stick. Cey's blow with the stick smashed Kingwell's face into the boards, resulting in injuries to Kingwell's mouth, nose, and neck, and causing him to be hospitalized for three days with concussion. In addition to receiving a five-minute penalty from the referee, Cey was charged by a prosecutor for the Crown with the crime of 'assault causing bodily harm' in violation of section 245.1(1)(b) of the Canadian Penal Code.[1] A person 'assaults' another person for purposes of section 245.1(1)(b) when he intentionally applies force to another person without the latter's consent. An assault, in turn, causes 'bodily harm' for purposes of section 245.1(1)(b) when it causes 'any hurt or injury calculated to interfere with [a person's] health or comfort'.[2] In his defense, Cey argued that, while he may have assaulted Kingwell, causing him bodily harm, Kingwell 'consented' to the assault for purposes of section 245.1(1)(b).

The judge in a bench trial acquitted Cey on the ground that Kingwell legally consented to the assault. The trial judge did not find that Kingwell *prescriptively* consented to the assault. That is, the judge did not find that Kingwell contemporaneously acquiesced in mind or expression to a vicious cross-checking that he did not even see coming. Nor did the judge find that Kingwell personally made a conscious decision in advance that he preferred to be cross-checked in that manner rather than not play hockey. Rather, the trial judge held that Kingwell was personally aware of the risks of being cross-checked in the course of play; that cross-checking, though a major foul under amateur hockey rules, 'has . . . been the standard of play in [amateur] hockey for a long time'; that Cey did not intend the cross-checking to cause the injuries that ensued; and that by virtue of agreeing to play hockey with knowledge of the risks of such cross-checking, Kingwell 'consent[ed]' to the blow he received.[3]

The Saskatchewan Court of Appeal agreed that hockey players can *legally* 'consent' to assaults under section 245.1(1)(b) without *prescriptively* consenting to the assault, namely, by means of 'implicit' or 'implied'consent. Nevertheless, the Court of Appeal reversed Cey's acquittal on the ground that the trial judge's interpretation of implied consent under section 245.1(1)(b) was both too narrow and too broad. The interpretation was too narrow, the court said, because the trial judge predicated Kingwell's implied consent on Kingwell's being subjectively aware—actually informed—of the risk of the kind of cross-checking he suffered. The court reasoned that the standards of implied consent that govern assaults that occur in the course of play and that cause non-intentional injuries do not depend entirely upon a player's subjective awareness of risk. Rather, they depend in part upon 'objective criteria' applicable to all players at Kingwell's level:

> [W]hen it comes to implied consent in the context of a team sport such as hockey, there cannot be as many different consents as there are players on the ice, and so the scope of implied consent, having to be uniform, must be determined by reference to objective criteria. . . . It is clear that in agreeing to play the game, a hockey player consents to some forms of intentional bodily contact and to the risk of injury therefrom. Those forms sanctioned by the rules are the clearest example. Other forms, denounced by the rules but falling within the accepted standards by which the game is played, may also come within the scope of consent.[4]

At the same time, however, the Court of Appeal also held that the trial court's interpretation of implied consent under section 245.1(1)(b) was too broad. The trial court had held that, by virtue of being subjectively aware of the risks that they will occur, a hockey player consents to all assaults that are 'customary in the game' and that are not intended to cause injury. The Court of Appeal agreed that subjective awareness of risk can play a role in consent. Thus, the court said, a player who subjectively accepts a risk of assault by willingly engaging an opposing player in a fistfight after play has ended may be deemed to consent to resulting injuries.[5] Nevertheless, the court held that, regardless of whether a player subjectively accepts risks of assault, and regardless of how customary the assaults may be, a hockey player cannot lawfully consent to assaults that are too 'inherently dangerous' to be lawful.[6]

In short, the court of appeal in *Cey* held that legal consent under section 245.1.(1)(b) encompasses two distinct levels of implied consent. The basic level applies to all players who agree to engage in amateur hockey, regardless of the particular risks of which they may be subjectively aware. By virtue of agreeing to engage in the sport, hockey players all implicitly consent—or, in my terminology, 'constructively consent'—to assaults that either accord with the rules of amateur hockey or 'are inherent in and reasonably incidental to the normal playing of the game',[7] regardless of their wishes at the time. In addition, a further level of assault applies to players who are consciously aware of certain risks, *e.g.*, players who willingly engage in fistfights with specific opponents after play is suspended. By virtue of possessing conscious awareness of risks, individual players may implicitly consent—or, in my terminology, give 'informed consent'—to additional levels of assault, over and above the assaults to which all players implicitly consent, regardless of their wishes to parry or avoid particular punches at the time they are thrown.[8] In either event, however, the further an assault is removed from the nature of the game, and the more dangerous the assault is, the less the law will allow players to lawfully consent to it by virtue of risking it, regardless of how much the players may wish to do so.[9]

'Constructive consent' and 'informed consent' are two species of a larger subset of legal consent that we shall call 'imputed consent'—'imputed' because it consists of attributing prescriptive consent to persons who do not possess it. A third species of imputed consent is 'hypothetical consent', or what some commentators call 'dispositional consent',[10] namely, prescriptive consent that is attributed to incompetent persons on the basis of what they *would have* prescriptively consented to if they had been able to do so. All three species are legal in nature because by virtue of possessing them, *S* authorizes *A* to engage in conduct that would otherwise constitute a crime against *S*. All three species are instances of 'imputed' consent because in all three, the law attributes to persons incidents of prescriptive consent that they do not in fact possess:

> ***Constructive Consent.*** Based upon *S*'s prescriptive acquiescence to something else, *e.g.*, participation in amateur hockey, the law treats *S* as if he prescriptively consents to the conduct that is at issue, *e.g.*, *A*'s conduct in cross-checking *S* in the neck from behind.

> ***Informed Consent.*** Based upon *S*'s voluntary acquiescence to running a risk of *x*, *e.g.*, the risk of being punched in the face in the course of a fistfight, the law treats *S* as if he prescriptively consents to *x* itself, *i.e.*, being punched in the face.[11]

> ***Hypothetical Consent.*** Based upon findings that *S* would prescriptively acquiesce to *x* if *S* were competent at the time, the law treats *S* as if he did prescriptively consent to *x*.

To be sure, to impute prescriptive consent is to create a legal fiction—a fiction that *S* actually acquiesced to *x* in mind or expression under appropriate conditions of competence, knowledge, freedom, and motivation. Being a fiction, the imputation can consist of any of the various forms of prescriptive consent that constitute defenses to *x*. Thus, jurisdictions that define prescriptive consent as a mental state can impute fictions of prescriptive *attitudinal* consent to *S*, while jurisdictions that define prescriptive consent as an expression can impute fictions of prescriptive *expressive* consent to *S*. Moreover, in cases in which time elapses between *S*'s voluntary activity or assumption of risk and the occurrence of the conduct to which *S* is deemed to give constructive or informed consent, the imputation can be of either prospective prescriptive consent or contemporaneous prescriptive consent. Thus, courts can conceptualize the constructive consent of hockey players in two alternative ways: they can adopt the fiction that in stepping on the ice, hockey players *prospectively* consent to non-intentional injuries that may occur during the course of play, much as Odysseus prospectively and prescriptively consented to remain tied to the mast; or, alternatively, they can adopt the fiction that, having stepped on the ice, hockey players *contemporaneously* consent to every non-intentional injury at the moment it occurs, much as medical patients under local anesthetic contemporaneously and prescriptively consent to surgical incisions at the moment they occur. Some courts prefer fictions of prospective prescriptive consent, while others prefer fictions of contemporaneous prescriptive consent.[12] The two approaches are functionally equivalent because they are alternative ways to conceptualize the fact that by virtue of *S*'s taking the ice, *A* has a defense to non-intentional injuries he may inflict upon *S* in the course of play.

Like all legal fictions, fictions of prescriptive consent can be replaced with functionally equivalent rules that make no reference to consent. Thus:

> Fictions of constructive consent to harms of certain kinds can be replaced with substitute rules to the effect that harms that are inherent in, and reasonably incidental, to certain *activities* (*e.g.*, body-checking in the sport of amateur hockey) are lawful in so far as they befall persons who voluntarily participate in those activities.
>
> Fictions of informed consent to harms of certain kinds can be replaced with substitute rules to the effect that certain harms, which are otherwise criminal, are lawful if directed against persons who voluntarily assume the *risks* of such harms.
>
> Fictions of hypothetical consent can be replaced with substitute rules to the effect that it is lawful to subject incompetent persons to certain harms to which they do not prescriptively consent if the persons would have prescriptively consented to those harms it if they had been competent at the time.

Nevertheless, the fact that legal fictions of prescriptive consent can be replaced does not mean that they serve no function. We shall see that in addition to possessing features in common with one another, fictions of prescriptive consent come into play precisely because they further some of the same values of personal agency that underlie acts of prescriptive consent.

Constructive Consent

The most notorious example of constructive consent in criminal law—though hardly the most common example today—is Lord Matthew Hale's conception of the 'marital exemption' to the law of rape, the rule that husbands cannot be convicted of raping their wives. Hale, in his 17th-century treatise on criminal law, conceptualized the exemption in terms of the wife's consent. '[A] husband cannot be guilty of a rape committed by himself upon his lawful wife', Hale wrote, 'for by their mutual matrimonial consent and contract, the wife hath given up herself in this kind unto her husband, which she cannot retract.'[13]

The English marital-rape case *Regina v. Miller*[14] is a good illustration of the way Hale's conception of imputed consent worked. Gwendoline May Miller left her husband Peter in 1953 and filed for divorce, but without obtaining a judicial separation order or agreement to separate. While her divorce petition was pending, Peter attacked Gwendoline May, threw her down three times, and then forced her to have sexual intercourse with him, leaving her in a state of nervous hysteria. Peter Miller was charged with two criminal offenses: (i) rape, and (ii) assault occasioning actual bodily harm. He defended against the charge of rape by arguing, based on Hale, that by consenting to marry him, Gwendoline had consented to his engaging in acts of sexual intercourse with her that would otherwise constitute rape. And he defended against the charge of assault by arguing that because his wife had consented to having sexual intercourse with him, she also implicitly consented to his using such force as was necessary to elicit sexual intercourse if she resisted. The English court disagreed with Peter about the crime of assault, but it agreed with him about the crime of rape. It held that, by consenting to marry him, Gwendoline May consented in criminal law to his having carnal knowledge of her, that is, to his being sexually intimate with her:

> Rape is unlawful carnal knowledge of a woman without her consent by force, fear or fraud, and it is an essential ingredient of that particular offence that it must be without the woman's consent. It is argued that, in the case of a married woman, by the contract of matrimony she gives her consent to acts of intercourse with her husband and that that consent cannot subsequently be revoked.
>
> * * *
>
> Can I say that, because the wife has left her husband and has brought a petition for divorce, that amounts to a termination of the marriage, or that one should infer a revocation of the wife's implied consent? I have considered the matter very carefully, and I cannot see that the fact that a petition for divorce has been presented has any effect in law on the existing marriage.
>
> * * *
>
> Therefore, I must apply the law as it stands, there being no evidence which enables me to say that the wife's implied consent to marital intercourse has been revoked by an act of the parties or by an act of the courts. The result is that, as the law implies consent to what took place so far as intercourse is concerned, . . . the defendant cannot be guilty of the crime of rape, and I shall direct the jury that there is no evidence on which they can convict him of rape.[15]

At the same time, however, the *Miller* court rejected Peter's argument about assault. By marrying Peter, Gwendoline May consented to his being sexually intimate with her; but she did not surrender her right to complain about his assaulting her or about his assaulting her in such a way as to cause her bodily injury in the form of nervous hysteria. She consented to the *sexual* component of 'sexual assault', but she did not consent to the force that was used to obtain it:

> It seems to me . . . that although a husband has a right to marital intercourse and the wife cannot refuse her consent, and although, if he does have intercourse against her actual will, it is not rape, nevertheless, he is not entitled to use force or violence for the purpose of exercising that right. If he does so, he may make himself liable to the criminal law, not for the offence of rape, but for whatever other offence the facts of the particular case warrant. If he should wound her, he might be charged with . . . causing

actual bodily harm, or he may be liable to be convicted of common assault. The result is that in the present case I am satisfied that the second count is a valid one and must be left to the jury for their decision.[16]

Unfortunately, the term that the *Miller* court used to describe Gwendoline May's consent to her husband's carnal knowledge of her—'implied' consent—is ambiguous. Like the term 'tacit consent', the phrase 'implied consent' is sometimes used to refer, not to the legal fiction of imputed consent, but to what is called 'consent implied in fact'.[17] Specifically, it is used to refer to a subset of prescriptive expressive consent that John Simmons calls a 'sign' of consent.[18] As Simmons points out, there are three ways in which a person can express to others that he possesses a mental state of acquiescence to *x*:

> ***Express Verbal Consent.*** A person can make verbal statements that under prevailing linguistic conventions directly express to others that he possesses a mental state of acquiescence to *x*.[19] (A dental patient, for example, can verbally express his actual acquiescence to having a tooth pulled by telling the dentist, 'You may pull it now.').
>
> ***Express Nonverbal Consent.*** A person can use *nonverbal* gestures that, given social conventions of communication, directly express to others that he possesses a mental state of acquiescence to *x*.[20] (A dental patient, for example, can nonverbally express his actual acquiescence to having a tooth pulled by nodding his head vigorously, up and down, when the dentist asks, 'Do you want me to pull the tooth now?').
>
> ***A 'Sign' of Consent.*** A person can make verbal statements or use nonverbal gestures that under linguistic and social conventions *indirectly* express to others—or, in the ambiguous language of consent, 'tacitly' or 'impliedly' express to others—that he possesses a mental state of acquiescence to *x*, namely, by directly expressing a mental state of acquiescence to something *other than x* that under linguistic and social conventions conveys acquiescence to *x* itself. (Assume, for example, a dental patient who verbally directs the dentist to begin administering the laughing-gas that the dentist uses as an anaesthetic in pulling teeth by saying, 'Okay, doc, start the laughing gas.' In one respect, the patient is directly expressing a desire to be anaesthetized. In another respect, however, given linguistic and social conventions, the patient is indirectly expressing to the dentist a willingness to have his tooth pulled, because that is the state of mind that a dentist, who is a member of the linguistic community, would understand the patient to be expressing.).

The three expressions differ in the way they prescriptively express acquiescence. But all of them, including 'signs' of consent, are genuine instances of prescriptive expressive consent because they all convey that the dental patient possesses a mental state of acquiescence to having his tooth pulled.

In contrast, however, the terms 'implied consent' and 'tacit consent' can also be used very differently. They can be used to refer not to signs of mental states of acquiescence, but to what courts call 'consent implied in law'; that is, they can be used to refer not to evidence of competent, knowing, and free acquiescence, but to fictions of such acquiescence that are imputed to persons on the basis of related things to which they have prescriptively consented.[21] Recall, for example, what the *Miller* court meant when it said that Gwendoline May 'impliedly' consented to her husband Peter's having carnal knowledge of her whenever he wished. The court did not mean that, when Peter threw her down three times and forced her into sexual intercourse, Gwendoline made verbal or nonverbal statements that under linguistic and social conventions prescriptively conveyed to him that she acquiesced in her mind to his having carnal knowledge of her. Nor did the court mean that when Gwendoline May originally married Peter, she prescriptively consented in advance to his having carnal knowledge of her at his pleasure for the duration of their marriage by virtue of thinking or expressing the thought 'Yes, I mean to bind myself to being sexually intimate with this man at his future pleasure, no matter how strong my objections at the time may be.' Rather, the court meant that by virtue of her marrying Peter, the court was going to treat Gwendoline May *as if* she had prescriptively acquiesced in mind or expression to being sexually intimate with him at his pleasure, regardless of whether she had actually done so.[22] The court meant that Gwendoline May prescriptively acquiesced to a social practice from which she expected to benefit (*i.e.*, marriage to Peter) that rendered it appropriate in the judgment of English lawmakers to treat her in the same way she would have been treated if she had prescriptively acquiesced to something else, *i.e.*, sexual intimacy with Peter at his future pleasure.[23]

In reality, the marital exemption is no longer as widespread as it was in Hale's time. Many jurisdictions, like England itself, have abolished the marital exemption altogether, treating spouses and non-spouses identically for purposes of the law of rape.[24] Nevertheless, although the marital exemption has been at least partially abolished in every Anglo-American jurisdiction, a number of jurisdictions continue to retain it in one form or another.[25] Thus, a number of jurisdictions take the position that for a husband's carnal knowledge of his wife to constitute rape, his wife must first take steps to distance herself from the marriage, steps ranging from filing for divorce, obtaining a personal protective order, executing a formal separation agreement, or moving out of the household.[26] Other jurisdictions define the rape of a spouse more narrowly than rape of a non-spouse. Thus, some jurisdictions, having made it an offense for a man to have sexual intercourse with a woman other than his wife *either* by means of force *or* under conditions in which the woman is mentally disabled, intoxicated, unconscious, or senile, nevertheless provide that it is a criminal offense for a man to have sexual intercourse with his wife *only* if he does so by means of force, thereby exempting from liability for rape actors who have sexual intercourse with their wives under conditions in which their wives are mentally disabled, intoxicated, unconscious, or senile.[27] Other jurisdictions define marital rape still more narrowly, making it a criminal offense for a man to rape his wife by means of force only if he causes bodily injury.[28]

That some jurisdictions retain a marital exemption, however, does not mean that they also frame it in the form of constructive consent. Jurisdictions that retain the marital exemption have a choice as to how to frame it. They can eschew the fiction of prescriptive consent by defining the *actus reus* of the offense in such a way as to exempt spouses from the class of victims whom the law protects against nonconsensual sexual intercourse. Or, alternatively, they can invoke a fiction of prescriptive consent by, first, defining the *actus reus* of the offense in such a way as to protect everyone from nonconsensual sexual intercourse and, thereafter, providing that certain acts of sexual intercourse between an actor and his wife shall be regarded as being with her prescriptive consent. To illustrate the difference, consider the contrasting ways in which Connecticut treats 'married' persons and 'cohabiting' persons with respect to the offense of sexual assault in the fourth degree. Connecticut, while generally making it an offense for an actor to have 'sexual contact' with another 'without' the other's 'consent',[29] nevertheless grants a defense to actors who have sexual contact with spouses and cohabiting persons. Yet Connecticut uses contrasting statutory models to frame the two defenses. With respect to married persons, Connecticut defines the *actus reus* of sexual assault in such as way as to exempt spouses from the class of victims who are entitled to complain about nonconsensual sexual contact, because Connecticut stipulates that 'sexual contact' includes only contact for purposes of sexual gratification with the 'intimate parts of a person *not married to the actor*'.[30] With respect to cohabiting persons, however, Connecticut defines the exemption in terms of constructive consent. It does so by proceeding in two steps. First, Connecticut makes it an offense for *A* to have sexual contact with any person other than *A*'s spouse without the latter's consent—including a person with whom *A* is cohabiting. Then, having made it an offense for *A* to have sexual contact with any person other than *A*'s spouse without her consent, Connecticut exonerates an actor who can show that at the time of the alleged offense he and the alleged victim were 'living together by mutual consent'.[31] Thus, the cohabitant's consent in living with *A* negates a charge that the sexual contact was without her consent.

Why, then, would a jurisdiction like Connecticut choose to frame its law in the form of fictions of constructive consent when it could eschew the fiction altogether? To address the question, let us examine two rules—one of which is typically framed in terms of a fiction of constructive consent, and one of which is not.

Unwanted Life-Saving Treatment. The law governing unwanted life-saving medical treatment has changed considerably over the past half century. Fifty years ago, it was common for states to compel persons to accept life-saving treatment over their objections, including persons who were terminally ill and persons whose objections to treatment were religiously grounded. Today, most if not all states allow competent, terminally ill persons to reject life-saving treatment either in person or by advance medical directives ('living wills');[32] and most states allow otherwise healthy persons to reject life-saving blood transfusions if their rejections are religiously grounded.[33] Despite those changes, however, states continue to impose life-saving medical treatment on persons, over their objections, when (i) persons are otherwise medically healthy, (ii) they themselves induce the need for treatment through efforts to commit suicide, (iii) they are brought to the state for treatment, (iv) their objections are not religiously based, and (v) the medical treatment carries no dangerous side-effects or long-term discomfort.[34]

Accordingly, imagine a case of an 'Overdosed Student' in Maryland who, having read too much Arthur Schopenhauer, decides to kill himself in order to make a philosophical statement about death. Before swallowing sleeping pills, the student executes a written statement, explaining why he is committing suicide and objecting to any life-saving intervention. Shortly thereafter and before the pills have taken effect, his college roommate discovers him and calls an ambulance. At the hospital the student explains to the attending physicians why he wants to die and hands them copies of his written statement. Despite his continuing objections, however, the attending physician straps the student to a hospital bed, pumps the student's stomach, and saves his life. When the student recovers, he urges the district attorney to charge the attending physician with assaulting him without his consent. The district attorney, relying on Maryland case law on the state's overriding 'interest in sustaining life',[35] refuses.

Unwanted Blood-Alcohol Test. The law governing drunk driving has also changed considerably over the past 50 years. States are increasingly concerned about alcohol-related accidents. Most states, if not all of them, now employ mechanisms to compel drivers who are involved in traffic accidents to submit to blood-alcohol tests. New Mexico is a good example. The New Mexico 'Implied Consent Act' provides that if a police officer has reason to think that a driver involved in an accident is guilty of drunk driving, and is unconscious, the officer may direct that blood be taken from the unconscious driver to test for blood alcohol.[36]

Now imagine a 'Libertarian Driver' in New Mexico who, for political reasons, carries written instructions in his wallet that, under no conditions, does he wish any officer of the state to take blood from him in the event he is unconscious. The driver is involved in an automobile accident that causes him to lose consciousness. A police officer places the unconscious driver under arrest for suspected drunk driving and, despite the driver's written statement, directs that the driver's blood be drawn for blood-alcohol testing. The test is negative. However, when the driver recovers and learns that blood was drawn over his written objection, he urges the district attorney to charge the police officer with having bodily assaulted him without his consent. The district attorney, relying on the New Mexico statute, refuses.

The Overdosed Student and Libertarian Driver possess several features in common. In both cases, they suffer bodily intrusions without their prescriptive consent and, indeed, over their explicit objections. In both cases, the bodily intrusion would ordinarily constitute criminal assault. In both cases, the state legitimizes the bodily intrusion because of its special interest in life and safety. Yet the two cases differ in the way in which the respective states conceptualize the lawfulness of the bodily intrusions. The State of Maryland in the Overdosed Student treats the bodily intrusion as an *exception* to its general rule that nonconsensual bodily intrusions are unlawful. Thus, despite what it concedes to be the student's non-consent, the state justifies the bodily intrusion on the basis of the state's countervailing 'interest in sustaining life'. In contrast, New Mexico does the opposite. New Mexico treats the bodily intrusion as being *consistent* with its general rule that nonconsensual bodily intrusions are unlawful: New Mexico, invoking the language of 'implied consent', justifies the bodily intrusion on the ground that, by driving on New Mexico highways, drivers consent to blood-alcohol tests.

It is no accident that New Mexico frames its drunk-driving rule in the language of consent, while jurisdictions with rules regarding compulsory medical treatment do not. Most jurisdictions with blood-alcohol rules characterize them in terms of consent, yet no jurisdiction that is willing to compel competent patients to submit to life-saving medical treatment over their objection appears to do so in the name of consent. What explains the difference? The answer cannot be that the Libertarian Driver has voluntarily done something, *i.e.*, operating a motor vehicle on public highways, while the Overdosed Student has not. For the Overdosed Student *has* voluntarily acted—he has voluntarily overdosed on sleeping pills. If voluntary action suffices to justify constructions of consent, it should suffice as much for the Overdosed Student as for the Libertarian Driver. Indeed, it should suffice to justify whatever the state wishes to do to any person over the person's objections because every person takes voluntary actions at some time in his or her life. Nor can the answer be that the Libertarian Driver did something that *normatively* justifies a bodily intrusion over his objection because the Overdosed Student also did something that justifies a bodily intrusion over his objection—he put his life in danger by attempting to commit suicide. If the student had not put his life in danger or done something else that triggered a comparable state interest, the state would not have been justified in pumping his stomach over his objection.

What supports the imputation of consent to the Libertarian Driver is *what* he did, and not merely that he did it voluntarily. He voluntarily participated in a social practice in the expectation of benefiting from it, *i.e.*, operating a motor vehicle on the public highways, the benefits of which depend upon the willingness of participants to make certain personal sacrifices, including complying with traffic rules and submitting to blood-alcohol tests when circumstances suggest drunk driving. He chose to take advantage of the benefits of a social practice that, in the state's judgment, could not justly exist and otherwise might not exist in its present form without the concomitant burdens of blood-alcohol testing. In contrast, the Overdosed Student, by attempting to commit suicide, did not seek the benefits of a social practice that the state facilitates by imposing concomitant burdens on its participants. Suicide is not a social practice that the state seeks to facilitate. Nor is stomach-pumping a burden that the state imposes in order to enable people justly to resort to suicide.

Admittedly, New Mexico was not obliged to conceptualize its statute in terms of constructive consent. Like states with suicide prevention rules, New Mexico could have framed its law without reference to consent. Still, in contrast to states with suicide-prevention rules, New Mexico was able to conceptualize the statute in terms of constructive consent because the principle that underlies rules regarding compulsory blood-alcohol testing shares a family resemblance to the principle that underlies defenses of prescriptive consent. The principle that underlies defenses of *prescriptive* consent is that persons can validate conduct *x* that would otherwise violate their interests by voluntarily choosing *x* for themselves. The principle, in turn, that underlies the rule regarding compulsory blood-alcohol testing, as well as other rules of *constructive* consent, is that persons can validate *x* that would otherwise violate their interests by choosing to participate in a social practice that is deemed by the state to depend for its operation upon the ability to subject them to *x*. The feature that prescriptive and constructive consent share is that they both serve to enable persons to choose for themselves what would otherwise be unlawful. The norms that underlie prescriptive consent enable persons to choose *x* where they otherwise could not, while the norms that underlie constructive consent enable persons to choose a social activity where they otherwise could not.

Ultimately, whether and when prescriptive acquiescence to a social practice ought to be treated as constructive consent to *x* is a normative issue. In some instances, the normative issue is noncontroversial. Every jurisdiction takes the view, for example, that by voluntarily choosing to engage in certain social activities, persons constructively consent to allow others to impose certain physical contact upon them, regardless of their objections (*e.g.*, a certain amount of touching that occurs on subway platforms, athletic stadiums, and crowded buses):[37]

> Generally speaking, consent is a defense to battery; and most of the physical contacts of ordinary life are not actionable because they are impliedly consented to by all who move in society and so expose themselves to the risk of bodily contact. So nobody can complain of the jostling which is inevitable from his presence in, for example, a supermarket, an underground station, or a busy street; nor can a person who attends a party complain if his hand is seized in friendship, or even if his back is, within reason, slapped.[38]

With similar uniformity, every jurisdiction repudiates the view that, by voluntarily walking in dark alleys, people constructively consent to have sexual intercourse with any stranger who forces them to do so.

In other cases, however, jurisdictions differ in their normative judgments as to whether prescriptive acquiescence to a social activity should be treated as constructive consent to related conduct. Thus, to return to sexual intercourse, consider a situation in which a woman, having prescriptively consented to an act of sexual intercourse, seeks to rescind her consent after sexual penetration has occurred, but the man refuses to withdraw. Some jurisdictions take the normative position that sexual autonomy is a sufficiently high value that a man is guilty of rape if he continues in an act of sexual intercourse after learning that the woman wishes him to withdraw.[39] Other jurisdictions, however, disagree and take the normative position that, given the difficulty of regulating copulation once penetration has occurred, a woman is deemed to consent to the completion of an act of sexual intercourse once she prescriptively consents to its commencement.[40] Although the latter position has its critics, framing it in the language of consent serves a heuristic purpose. It expresses the jurisdiction's view that the reason a woman can be subjected to the unwanted continuation of an act of sexual intercourse that has begun with her consent is that she voluntarily chooses the whole act for herself by virtue of voluntarily choosing a part to which the jurisdiction deems the whole to be inextricably linked for purposes of the criminal law.[41]

Informed Consent

The Libertarian Driver, as described above, happened to be aware of the risk that he might be subjected to blood-alcohol testing while unconscious. However, New Mexico does not rely upon the fact that drivers are aware of the risk when it imputes prescriptive consent to them. New Mexico treats drivers as having authorized blood-alcohol testing merely by virtue of driving on the public highways, and in that respect it treats drivers in the same way Canada treats hockey players. Just as Canada treats persons who play hockey as having authorized certain kinds of physical assaults that occur within the course of play, regardless of whether they are subjectively aware of the risks, so, too, New Mexico treats persons who drive on public highways as having authorized blood-alcohol testing, regardless of whether they are subjectively aware of the risk of blood-alcohol testing.

Frequently, however, the state treats a person as legally consenting to conduct that would otherwise criminally infringe upon his interests, not by virtue of his prescriptively consenting to it, and not by virtue of his constructively consenting to it, but by virtue of his knowingly accepting the risk that it will occur. An example is the way Canada treats HIV-positive actors who have sexual intercourse with others. An HIV-positive actor who does not intend to kill his sexual partner but who nonetheless infects his sexual partner by failing to disclose his HIV-positive status is guilty of assault in Canada, for infecting with his sexual partner without the latter's 'consent'. However, an HIV-positive actor who does not intend to infect his sexual partner but who nonetheless infects his sexual partner after fully disclosing his HIV-positive status is *not* guilty of assault in Canada, because his sexual partner is deemed to have 'consented' to the infection merely by virtue of consciously taking the risk of the infection.[42]

Unfortunately, in discussing the relationship between risk-taking and consent, courts and commentators tend to conflate two significantly different cases: cases in which consciousness of the risk of *x* is inherent in run-of-the-mill prescriptive consent to *y*; and cases in which consciousness of the risk of *x* is, at most, a predicate for imputing fictions of prescriptive consent to *x*. To illustrate, consider the following hypothetical cases:

> ***'Inflammation'.*** A patient Joan has 20-30 vision in one eye but only 20-100 vision in the other. In order to correct her vision, Joan seeks out a laser surgeon, *A*, who informs her that, in order to correct vision in the one eye, he must operate on both. *A* also

informs Joan that while there is only a small risk that she will go blind in both eyes, there is a larger, but still less than 15%, risk that she will suffer inflammation in one or both eyes for as much as a week. Joan hopes to escape inflammation, but she would prefer even the certainty of a week of eye inflammation to the alternative of forgoing an opportunity for improved vision and submits to the surgery. To her disappointment, Joan develops a week of inflammation in both eyes. ***Ruling***: In response to a criminal complaint that *A* committed a 'battery' upon Joan by inflicting the 'bodily injury' of an inflammation on her, the state's prosecutor refuses to prosecute *A* for battery, ruling that, because Joan preferred even the certainty of a temporary eye infection to the alternative of forgoing the opportunity for improved vision, and because *A* proceeded with appropriate care, Joan 'consented' to *A*'s conduct in inflicting the bodily injury of an eye inflammation on her.

'Blindness'*.** A patient, Helen, has the same eye conditions as Joan, and she goes to the same doctor for the same treatment. Unfortunately, the worst risks materialize in Helen's case, and to her horror she goes blind in both eyes. Helen complains to the prosecutor, stating that she quite obviously did not prefer the certainty of total blindness to the alternative of forgoing a laser procedure on eyes that were still healthy! ***Ruling: in response to a criminal complaint that *A* committed an 'aggravated battery' upon Helen by inflicting the 'grievous bodily injury' of blindness on her, the prosecutor recognizes that Helen did not submit to the surgery because she preferred the certainty of blindness to the alternative of forgoing an operation on eyes that were still healthy, . Nevertheless, the prosecutor rules that, because the likelihood of improved vision justified the small *risk* of blindness, because Helen preferred a small *risk* of blindness to the alternative of forgoing an opportunity for improved vision, and because *A* proceeded with appropriate care, Helen 'consented' to *A*'s conduct in inflicting the grievous bodily injury of blindness on her.

Joan and Helen have much in common. Neither of them hopes or believes that the events they fear, *i.e.*, inflammation and blindness, respectively, will actually occur. At the same time, however, both of them realize that if *A* does what he proposes to do and certain events occur, inflammation and blindness will result. The difference is that when the prosecutor says that Joan 'consented' to the inflammation, he means that she *prescriptively* consented to it: he means that while Joan hoped and believed inflammation would not occur, she nevertheless preferred even a certainty of temporary inflammation to the alternative of forgoing a chance of improved vision. In contrast, when the prosecutor says that Helen 'consented' to blindness, he does *not* mean that Helen preferred even a certainty of blindness in both eyes to the alternative of forgoing a well-intended operation on eyes that, after all, were still healthy, for that would be absurd. Nor does the prosecutor mean that, regardless of whether Helen was informed or otherwise aware of the risk of blindness, she constructively consented to it merely by proceeding with the surgery. Rather, the prosecutor means that because Helen consciously preferred a justifiable *risk* of blindness to the alternative of forgoing the potential benefits of surgery, she is treated *as if* she had prescriptively consented to the conduct of *A* that resulted in her going blind.

It is important to distinguish the prescriptive consent in 'Inflammation' from the imputed consent in 'Blindness', because they rest on different factual and normative premises. The prosecutor in 'Inflammation' realized that Joan knew that there was merely a risk of inflammation rather than a certainty. But the prosecutor did not base his finding of consent by Joan upon her having opted for a risk rather than a certainty of inflammation. Instead, the prosecutor based his finding of consent upon a finding that Joan preferred laser surgery to even the certainty of inflammation. And the prosecutor did so on the normative premise that the likelihood of improved vision justifies even the certainty of temporary inflammation in a person who prefers inflammation to the alternative of forgoing a likelihood of improved vision. In contrast, the prosecutor in 'Blindness' not only realized that Helen knew that there was a small risk of blindness, he also based his finding of consent upon there *being* merely a risk of blindness. The prosecutor would not have ruled that Helen consented to *A*'s conduct in blinding her if he had been obliged to find that Helen preferred the certainty of blindness to the alternative. For one thing, there was no factual basis for such a finding. But even more importantly, the prosecutor would have had to conclude, absurdly, that a likelihood of improved vision justifies the certainty of blindness. The only reason the prosecutor ruled that Helen consented to the blindness is that he knew the laser surgery involved at most a small *risk* of blindness, and on that basis he imputed prescriptive consent to her.

I am using the term 'informed consent' to distinguish Helen's legal consent from Joan's legal consent. That is, I am using the term to refer to criminal cases like Helen's in which *S* is sufficiently informed about the risks of what a criminal statute states to be a harm *x* that it seeks to prevent (*e.g.*, the 'grievous bodily injury' of blindness) and in which, though *S* does not prescriptively consent to *x* itself—that is, though *S* does not choose *x* as that which she prefers for herself under the circumstances—*S* is treated *as if* she prescriptively consented to *x itself* because of her willingness to run a risk of *x*. I am not using the term to refer to cases like Joan's in which *S* is sufficiently informed about what a criminal statute states to be a harm *y* that it seeks to prevent (*e.g.*, inflammation) and in which *S* prescriptively consents to *y* by choosing it as that which she prefers for herself under the circumstances. This usage of 'informed consent' is consistent with the way the term is *sometimes* used in the law of torts, but not with the way it is *always* used in the law of torts. 'Informed consent' is a term of art in the law of torts for the kinds of educated or 'informed' decisions to submit to medical treatment that medical patients must make if their physicians are not to be liable for harming the patients without their 'consent'. In the law of torts, however, the term 'consent' in the phrase 'informed consent' is used to refer to all forms of legal consent, whether they are prescriptive or imputed. Thus, the law of torts would use 'informed consent' to refer to both Joan's and Helen's cases. In contrast, I draw a distinction between Joan's and Helen's cases by using 'prescriptive consent' to refer to cases like Joan's, and using 'informed consent' to refer exclusively to cases like Helen's.

Such imputations to *S* of prescriptive consent to *x* based upon *S*'s consciously risking *x* involve at least two normative judgments about which jurisdictions can differ.[43] First, an imputation of consent by S rests upon a normative judgment that the risk of which *S* is conscious is a risk that persons are justified in taking. The Canadian court's discussion of fistfights in *Cey* is a good example. It will be recalled that, after addressing conventional assaults to which all hockey players constructively consent, the *Cey* court discusses the additional risks that individual hockey players run by willingly entering into fistfights after play is suspended. When the *Cey* court says that a hockey player who knowingly engages in a fistfight 'consents' to be punched in the face, the court does not mean that he believes or hopes he will be so punched and prefers it to the alternative of not fighting; for there is no factual basis for assuming that all hockey players who engage in fights believe or hope they will be punched in the face. Rather, the court means what the prosecutor meant in 'Blindness': the court means that hockey players knowingly accept the risk of being punched. Whether the state will allow hockey players to accept the risk depends, in turn, upon whether it believes the social benefits of the risky conduct outweigh the harms that occur when the risk materializes. On the one hand, no jurisdiction allows persons to assume the risks of serious bodily injury involved in street fighting because no jurisdiction sees any social value in street brawls.[44] On the other hand, every jurisdiction sees enough social value in competitive boxing, at least at collegiate and amateur levels, to allow persons to assume the risk of assault.[45] With respect to injuries from fistfighting in amateur hockey, however, jurisdictions differ as to the risks that they will allow amateur hockey players to assume, because jurisdictions differ as to the social value of brawling on the ice outside the course of play.[46]

Second, determinations of informed consent rest upon normative judgments as to the amount of information that *S* must possess about a risk if *S*'s decision to face the risk is to constitute a defense to *A* in the event the risk materializes. The amount of information typically depends upon the seriousness of the risk, the importance of the information to persons in *S*'s position, and the opportunity that *A* possesses to acquire and provide the information. Thus, medical patients who are contemplating life-threatening surgery are likely to be entitled to more detailed information about the risks of death than persons exposed to HIV through sexual intercourse; and the latter are likely to be entitled to more information about risks than hockey players who engage in fistfights on the spur of the moment.

Ultimately, of course, rules of informed consent are legal fictions. The fiction is that because persons prescriptively acquiesce to *risks* of *x*, they also prescriptively acquiesce to *x itself*. Moreover, because they are fictions, the norms that underlie them can be stated without reference to fictional consent. Consider, for example, the statute under which Canadian hockey players are prosecuted for engaging in fistfights outside the course of play. The statute is presently framed in terms of fictional consent. It states that a person is guilty of assault if he intentionally applies force to another person without the latter's 'consent'.[47] The Canadian courts, in turn, have construed the statute to mean that hockey players who knowingly take the risk of being punched by engaging in fistfights outside the course of play thereby consent to be punched, provided that the blows are not too inherently dangerous to be permitted.[48] The Canadian courts could have achieved the same results, however, without invoking fictions of consent simply by holding that the assault statute as a whole, including its provision on consent, simply does not apply to hockey players who knowingly take the risk of being punched by engaging in fistfights outside the course of play, provided that the blows are not too 'inherently dangerous' to be permitted.

Framing a law like Canada's in the language of consent has both advantages and disadvantages. One disadvantage is that consent to *x* is a gloss and, hence, a roundabout way of stating an underlying norm for which the presence of prescriptive consent to *x* is irrelevant. Another disadvantage, as we shall see in Chapter 8, is that it enables critics who disagree with the substance of norms framed as fictions to disparage them as 'fictions' and, hence, escape some of the burden of addressing their substance.[49] In contrast, however, the strength of legal fictions of informed consent is the opposite of their weakness. Their weakness, as we have seen, is that they disingenuously transmute what a person *does* do (*i.e.*, prescriptively consent to take a risk of *x*) into something which he does not do (*i.e.*, prescriptively consent to *x* itself). Their strength is that they signal what assumption-of-risk rules possess in common with rules of prescriptive consent. Both rules enhance *S*'s autonomy to submit to conduct on *A*'s part by immunizing *A* from criminal liability for harm, *x*, that *A* inflicts upon *S* in the course of his conduct: rules of prescriptive consent enhance *S*'s autonomy to choose conduct that involves a certainty of harm *x*, while assumption-of-risk rules enhance *S*'s autonomy to choose conduct that involves a mere *risk* of *x*. Because a jurisdiction cannot enable *S* to choose conduct that involves risks of *x* without immunizing *A* from liability for *x* in the event the latter ensues, framing *S*'s assumption of risk of *x* as a fiction of consent to *x* expresses the sense in which by legally choosing to engage in conduct involving a risk of *x*, *S* also legally chooses *x*.

Hypothetical Consent

Constructive consent and informed consent are both based upon a person's voluntarily doing *something*. Thus, New Mexico bases its fiction of prescriptive consent to blood-alcohol testing upon a person's prior voluntary choice to operate a motor vehicle in the state, and Canada bases its fiction of prescriptive consent to HIV-infection upon a person's voluntary choice to run the risk of infection. Hypothetical consent differs in that respect from those two forms of imputed consent because hypothetical consent is not based upon instances of voluntary acquiescence. Rather, hypothetical consent is a fiction of prescriptive consent to *x* that is imputed to *S* based upon a determination that *S* *would* have prescriptively consented to *x* or to a risk of *x* *if* *S* had had the opportunity, which *S* did not.

Hypothetical consent comes in two distinct versions, one of which plays a significant role in moral and political theory, and the other of which plays a doctrinally significant role in criminal law. Both versions are premised on attributing hypothetical features to *S* in order to determine whether *S*, if she were possessed of those features, would prescriptively consent to *x*. But the two versions differ with respect to (i) their purposes; (ii) the identity of *S*; and (iii) the hypothetical features that are attributed to *S*:

> ***Moral and Political Theory.*** The purpose of inquiries into hypothetical consent in moral and political theory is to identify optimal rules of moral and political justice by asking what rules persons in a society would choose for themselves under fair and appropriate conditions. For the latter purpose, *S* is not a particular person in contradistinction to all other persons but, rather, a collection of persons or a composite person who starts out with every trait that persons in society may possess. At the same time, however, to ensure that *S* makes choices under conditions that are appropriate for generating rules for everyone, theorists radically alter and idealize *S*'s existing features by both adding to and subtracting from them. As David Gautier (who employs hypothetical consent to construct moral theory) puts it, the purpose in adding and subtracting features is to identify an 'Archimedean point' that '[a person] must occupy, if one's own decisions are to possess the moral force needed to govern the moral realm.'[50] The most influential example of hypothetical consent in political theory is John Rawls' *A Theory of Justice*, in which Rawls asks what kind of political state *S* and *S*'s counterparts would choose for themselves if they were in an 'original position' in which (i) they possessed a thin conception of the good and a capacity to act on it; (ii) they made their decisions behind a 'veil of ignorance' regarding the accidents of birth and fortune that distinguish them from others; and (iii) they bargained with one another under certain procedural constraints.[51]
>
> ***Criminal Law.*** In contrast, the purpose of inquiries into hypothetical consent in criminal law is to determine, pursuant to existing offenses of non-consent, whether a particular person, who may once have been fully competent but is presently incapable of entertaining or expressing personal wishes, would choose certain conduct for herself given the values to which she has shown herself to be committed. For that purpose, the criminal law accepts everything that is known about *S*, including her distinctive personal values and idiosyncrasies. Moreover, the criminal law attributes only two hypothesized conditions to *S*: (i) that, for a brief moment, *S* either regains the competence she formerly possessed or gains new competence and, during that brief moment, decides how she wishes to be treated when her incompetence reattaches; and (ii) that in making her decision *S* has the benefit of the information about her condition that the persons possess who are presently responsible for her welfare.

Hypothetical consent of the idealized kind employed in moral and political theory may have a role in criminal law because it may help in formulating just rules of criminal responsibility, including rules in which consent and even hypothetical consent are defenses.[52] However, it is at most a conceptual device for *formulating* new criminal offenses, not an interpretive device for *giving meaning* to the term 'consent' under existing offenses. Indeed, one can hardly imagine a criminal offense that defines consent in accord with the way it figures in, say, in Rawls' *A Theory of Justice*, because the rule would be too vague to give actors notice of their rights and obligations. Rather, under existing criminal offenses, hypothetical consent consists of prescriptive consent that presently incompetent subjects *would* give if for a brief moment they were competent (or competent again) and knowledgeable about their long-range conditions.

The *Quinlan* case (1976) from New Jersey is a good example of how hypothetical consent operates in criminal law.[53] Karen Ann Quinlan was an active, vibrant, normal young woman of 21 when she fell unconscious. She was immediately taken by friends to a hospital where, on an emergency basis, physicians performed a tracheotomy, placed her on a tracheal-tube respirator, and commenced feeding her through a nasal-gastro tube. Despite those precautionary measures, Karen never regained consciousness. Although she retained some brain stem functions, *e.g.*, reacting to light, responding to sound and noxious stimuli, blinking her eyes, grimacing, making stereotyped cries, sounds and chewing motions, she remained in chronic and persistent vegetative state with no awareness of her surroundings. Within five months, her father filed a lawsuit against various persons, including the local prosecutor and the attorney general of the state. He sought an order (i) declaring himself guardian for Karen with authority to discontinue extraordinary medical procedures sustaining her, and (ii) enjoining state prosecutors from instituting criminal prosecutions in the event Karen died as a consequence.

The New Jersey Supreme Court assumed for purposes of the lawsuit that because Karen was not 'brain dead', removal of life support *without* her consent might well render Karen's father and her attending physicians criminally responsible for homicide.[54] It held, however, that because persons have a constitutional right to refuse treatment, removal of life support *with* their consent was not a criminal offense.[55] The court then discussed three ways in general in which persons on life support might consent to its removal:

> ***Contemporaneous, Prescriptive Consent.*** First, the court stated that persons who are competent at the time that life support is removed may contemporaneously give their prescriptive consent to its removal. As the court put it: 'We have no doubt . . . that if Karen were herself miraculously lucid for an interval (not altering the existing prognosis of the condition to which she would soon return) and perceptive of her irreversible condition, she could effectively decide upon discontinuance of the life support apparatus, even if it meant the prospect of natural death.'[56]
>
> ***Prospective, Prescriptive Consent.*** Second, the court stated that persons who are incompetent at the time that life support is removed may, nevertheless, prescriptively consent to its removal by prospectively consenting at a time when they are still competent by 'firmly evinc[ing] their "wish[es]" at that time'.[57] (The court later explained that persons can prospectively consent to be removed from life support in a variety of ways, including (i) by means of statutorily authorized, advance medical directives (*i.e.*, 'living wills'); (ii) by executing appropriate powers of attorney; or (iii) by making oral or written statements that are sufficiently 'specific', 'consistent',

'thoughtful', 'mature', and proximate to the effect to 'clearly' and 'convincing[ly]' demonstrate their 'subjective' wishes regarding future life support.)[58]

Hypothetical Consent. Finally, the court said, persons who are incompetent at the time that life support is removed, and who have not prospectively consented, may nevertheless consent in another way. They may exercise their 'right of choice', the court said—or, as I would put it, 'choice' may be imputed to them—if a court-appointed surrogate determines that removal is what they 'would' choose under the circumstances.

Needless to say, the *Quinlan* court dismissed the first possibility, that is, that Karen might be capable of giving contemporaneous consent to the removal of life support. The court also dismissed Karen's father's suggestion that Karen, while previously competent, prospectively consented to be removed from life support. Although Karen's father had introduced evidence of prior statements by Karen regarding her distaste for using extraordinary medical procedures to sustain the lives of comatose patients, the court dismissed the statements as too 'remote' and 'impersonal' to be probative of a 'firmly evinced wish' to be removed from life support.[59] Nevertheless, the court held that Karen's 'right of choice' to be removed from life support could be preserved by permitting her father, as a court-appointed surrogate in consultation with her family, 'to render [his] best judgment . . . as to whether she would exercise it in these circumstances'.[60] As the court explained in a later case, hypothetical consent—or 'substituted judgment' as it is typically called[61]—is designed to 'effectuat[e] as much as possible the decision that the incompetent patient would make if he or she were competent':

> Under the substituted judgment doctrine, where an incompetent's wishes are not clearly expressed, a surrogate decisionmaker considers the patient's personal value system for guidance. The surrogate considers the patient's prior statements about and reactions to medical issues, and all the facets of the patient's personality that the surrogate is familiar with—with, of course, particular reference to his or her relevant philosophical, theological, and ethical values—in order to extrapolate what course of medical treatment the patient would choose.[62]

Quinlan and life-support cases like it are the cases in which hypothetical consent is most frequently litigated, but they are not the arena in which hypothetical consent is most frequently invoked in practice. It is invoked on a daily basis in hospital emergency wards where physicians perform life-saving surgery on unconscious and incompetent patients who have never prescriptively consented. The long-standing justification for such emergency surgery is that, although it occurs without the patients' prescriptive consent, it is performed with their 'implied consent'.[63] When courts speak of 'implied consent' in the context of emergency, life-saving surgery, however, they are not referring to constructive consent, *i.e.*, the imputation of prescriptive consent to a person based on his voluntary participation in a social practice. Nor are they referring to informed consent, *i.e.*, the imputation of prescriptive consent to a person based upon his conscious assumption of risk.

Rather, they are referring to hypothetical consent—that is, to the natural, yet rebuttable, presumption that patients whose lives are in danger and who cannot be consulted in time for their prescriptive consent *would* wish attending physicians to operate on them in the meantime. The courts are referring to hypothetical consent because in contrast to the way they treat constructive and informed consent, courts are prepared to negate a subject's 'implied consent' to emergency surgery when the subject clarifies in advance that the rebuttable presumption of consent does not apply to her and that, in fact, she does not wish to be subjected to life-saving surgery.[64]

The Canadian case *Malette v. Shulman* (1990)[65] is a good example, although it arose in the setting of a civil suit for criminal assault and battery rather than a criminal prosecution for assault. Georgette Malette, 57, a Jehovah's Witness who was carrying a card stating that she objected on religious grounds to receiving blood transfusions under any circumstances, was rushed while unconscious to the hospital after a head-on collision with a truck. Malette was bleeding profusely when she arrived at the emergency ward. The attending physician Dr. Shulman concluded after consultations that Malette had lost so much blood that a blood transfusion was necessary to save her life. Despite being aware of the card she was carrying, he went ahead and performed the transfusion. Malette, after recovering, promptly brought a suit for battery, arguing that Dr. Shulman had violated her person without her consent. Dr. Shulman argued that persons who are unconscious and in need of life-saving surgery are deemed to consent. The Canadian court initially agreed with Dr. Shulman that patients who are unconscious are deemed to give 'implied consent' to emergency, life-saving surgery:

> The emergency situation is an exception to the general rule requiring a patient's prior consent. When immediate medical treatment is necessary to save the life or preserve the health of a person who, by reason of unconsciousness or extreme illness, is incapable of either giving or withholding consent, the doctor may proceed without the patient's consent. The delivery of medical services is rendered lawful in such circumstances on the rationale that the doctor has implied consent from the patient to give emergency aid... [On that] basis, in an emergency the law sets aside the requirement of consent on the assumption that the patient, as a reasonable person, would want emergency aid to be rendered if she were capable of giving instructions.[66]

Nevertheless, the court held Dr. Shulman responsible for assault and battery. Implied consent to emergency surgery, it said, is a rule designed to effectuate what a patient would want under the circumstances. When nothing is known about what a particular patient would want, the law sensibly assumes that, like most people, she would rather have a blood transfusion than die. However, when it is known that a patient would rather die than undergo a transfusion, doctors cannot disregard her wishes by relying upon what most people would want under the circumstances to attribute to her hypothetical consent that they know to be groundless.

> A physician's authority to make decisions for his patient is necessarily a limited authority. If the physician knows that the patient has refused to consent to the proposed procedure, he is not empowered to overrule the patient's decision by substituting his decision for hers, even though he, and most others, may think hers a foolish or unreasonable decision.
>
> * * *
>
> In this case, the patient, in effect, issued standing orders that she was to be given 'NO BLOOD TRANSFUSION!' in any circumstances. . . . Her instructions plainly contemplated the situation in which she found herself as a result of her unfortunate accident. In light of those instructions . . . she cannot be said to have consented to blood transfusions in this emergency. Nor can the doctor be said to have proceeded on the reasonable belief that the patient would have consented had she been in a condition to do so.[67]

The *Quinlan* and *Malette* courts imply that their respective rules of hypothetical consent look solely to what patients themselves would choose rather than relying on socially preferred outcomes. And their rules of hypothetical consent may, indeed, operate in that fashion. However, nothing *requires* that rules of hypothetical consent look solely to what putatively consenting persons would choose for themselves. Jurisdictions may elect to combine rules of hypothetical consent with mild or even strong presumptions in favor of certain preferred outcomes. Indeed, some jurisdictions do precisely that with respect to blood transfusions involving Jehovah's Witnesses. Consider the rule in New Jersey, for example. With respect to patients who are unconscious or otherwise incompetent, New Jersey protects their right of 'self-determination' by 'determin[ing] and effectuat[ing], in so far as possible, the decision that the patient would have made if competent'.[68] Like other jurisdictions, New Jersey reasons that because most people wish to receive blood transfusions when their lives are at stake, it may assume that emergency-ward patients who are incompetent would wish the same thing, and hence that they implicitly consent to receive blood. Moreover, like Canada in *Malette*, New Jersey also takes the view that the forgoing assumption is negated when circumstances reveal that patients would *not* choose life-saving operations for themselves. However, unlike Canada, New Jersey resists allowing the assumption of hypothetical consent to be easily rebutted. Rather, because of New Jersey's social preference for saving lives, New Jersey scrutinizes all cases through the lens of a strong, though rebuttable, presumption that patients wish to live. Therefore, unless a patient makes it 'unequivocal[ly]' clear while she is competent that she is making a 'fully informed and knowing decision to refuse blood', New Jersey courts resolve 'any glimmer of uncertainty as to [her] desires in an emergency situation . . . in favor of preserving life'.[69]

In the end, the scope and role of hypothetical consent are normative decisions that each jurisdiction must make for itself. All jurisdictions appear to agree that determinations of hypothetical consent are appropriate in emergency ward situations in which life is at stake and no opportunity exists to consult with the patient. Most jurisdictions also agree that determinations of hypothetical consent are an inappropriate basis for deciding whether an incompetent patient would wish to be an organ donor.[70] Beyond that, the scope of hypothetical consent is normatively contested even in jurisdictions in which it is most commonly invoked.[71] Thus, judges and commentators differ as to (i) the kinds of interests on *S*'s part that can rightly be made to depend upon *S*'s hypothetical consent,[72] (ii) the kinds of evidence that count toward hypothetical consent,[73] (ii) the standards by which surrogates decide what *S* would wish under the circumstances,[74] (iii) the criteria by which surrogates are selected, and (iv) the extent to which the decisions of surrogates are subject to judicial review.[75] Critics worry that in deciding what *S* would wish under the circumstances, surrogates will tend to attribute their own values to *S* or be influenced by their personal stakes in the outcome.[76]

The sharpest conceptual critique of the use of hypothetical consent in authorizing medical treatment, however, is that it is a 'legal fiction'. Louise Harmon is the leading exponent of that critique, though a number of judges share her view.[77] Harmon argues that in the area of medical intervention, *e.g.*, removal of life support, sterilization, organ transplant, hypothetical consent is a 'dangerous' and 'brutal' fiction.[78] Harmon is right that hypothetical consent is a legal fiction, and she has perceptive things to say about the way legal fictions operate. But she and judges who share her views are mistaken about what the fiction underlying judgments of hypothetical consent *is*.

To clarify what the fiction is, consider cases in which courts authorize the sterilization of retarded women who have been incompetent from birth.[79] Courts which address the issue agree that patients who are retarded from birth present special challenges for rules of hypothetical consent.[80] In contrast to patients like Karen Quinlan who had been competent, patients who have never been competent cannot leave evidence of personal choices or values that they embraced when competent and, hence, cannot reveal what they would now personally choose if they were competent.[81] Accordingly, courts agree that with respect to patients who have never been competent, there is no functional difference between asking 'What choice would this never-competent woman make for herself if, for a brief moment, she were competent to make a personal decision?', and asking 'What choice is in this never-competent woman's personal *best interests*?'[82] Nevertheless, in authorizing retarded women to be sterilized, courts differ as to how to frame the legal standard. They currently adopt one of two approaches, though, significantly, they could just as easily adopt still a third:

> ***Hypothetical Consent.*** Some courts conceptualize the issue in terms of hypothetical consent. The *Moe* case (Massachusetts 1982) is a good example.[83] Mary Moe was a sexually mature adult who, having been retarded from birth, had the mental age of a four-year-old. She was institutionalized in a setting in which it was thought she would likely have sexual encounters with other patients unless she was confined to her room. Mary's physicians testified that she could not tolerate ordinary methods of birth control and was incapable of raising a child. After Mary was discovered to have had a sexual encounter within the institution, her mother petitioned to have her sterilized. The court

established standards for granting approval. The *Moe* court reasoned in three steps: (1) Every person, including retarded persons, has a 'fundamental right' to 'choose' to be voluntarily sterilized, if he or she so desires.[84] (2) In order to assure that an incompetent person has the same rights of 'free choice and self-determination' as competent persons, a court must 'substitute itself as nearly as possible for the individual in the decisionmaking process' by seeking to determine whether she 'would consent to sterilization if [she were] competent to make such a decision'.[85] (3) Because a person who is incompetent from birth leaves no 'prior stated preferences' or prior 'expression[s] of intent', a court must infer what she would prefer from 'objective criteria' regarding what is in her 'interests'.[86]

Best Interests. Other courts, when faced with cases like *Moe*, omit the first two steps of the Massachusetts court's reasoning and move directly to the third step of determining what is in the retarded woman's best interests. The English case *In re F* (1990) is a good example.[87] Ms. F was a retarded adult woman who was identical to Mary Moe in all relevant respects. In response to her mother's petition, three judges on the Court of Appeal and five Law Lords in the House of Lords agreed in granting authority to have Ms. F sterilized. What is significant, however, is the way the various judges framed their opinions. They considered framing them in terms of 'consent'. That is, they considered ruling, (1) that the basic rule is that no woman can be sterilized without her consent; (2) that just as an unconscious patient can give 'implied consent' to emergency surgery, an incompetent woman can give implied consent to sterilization; and (3) that, with respect to a severely retarded woman, her consent to sterilization can be inferred from her 'best interests'.[88] In the end, however, they omitted steps (1) and (2) entirely. Rather than trying to justify sterilization *within* rules of consent, they justified the sterilization of severely retarded women as falling *outside* requirements of consent, ruling that sterilization is lawful when it can be shown to be in the woman's 'best interests'.[89]

Alternative Standard. With respect to severely retarded women for whom sterilization is in their best interests, courts have the alternative of framing their decisions not in one step or in three steps, but in *two steps*. Courts can replicate the results of Hypothetical Consent and Best Interests by taking the following position: (1) in order to treat severely retarded women with respect, sterilization ought to be based upon what the women would choose for themselves if they were competent; and (2) in the absence of other evidence as to what such women would choose for themselves, it ought to be assumed that they would choose in accord with their best interests. 'Alternative Standard' has something in common with each of the other two rules, for like them it ultimately bases sterilization decisions on a woman's best interests. Yet it also differs from the other two rules in significant respects. The Alternative Standard differs from 'Hypothetical Consent' in that it bases its inquiry into what a woman would choose for herself if she were competent upon her right not to 'choose' or to 'consent' to sterilization but to be treated with respect. At the same time, the Alternative Standard also differs from the 'Best Interests' rule in that it looks to a woman's best interests only because they constitute the best available evidence of what the woman would choose for herself if she were competent.

Louise Harmon and others characterize Hypothetical Consent as a 'fiction' by virtue of a feature that Hypothetical Consent and the Alternative Standard possess in common, namely, that each rests upon hypothetical determinations as to what retarded patients would have chosen for themselves if they had been competent.[90] Harmon is correct that Hypothetical Consent is fictional in nature, but she is mistaken about what makes it so. A fiction is a misrepresentation, a statement of something that, on its own premises, is necessarily false. In expressing a legal fiction, a speaker consciously or unconsciously refers to the absence of a certain fact as the occurrence of that very fact. In contrast, when a speaker states what a patient 'would have chosen' under circumstances that do not exist, he is expressing a *counterfactual*, not a *fiction*. A counterfactual statement can never be entirely verified or refuted, though it may be more or less persuasive. But a counterfactual statement is not a fiction because it is not invariably false, and it does not refer to a thing by anything other than what it is, namely, a counterfactual.

To illustrate, consider a driver who is taken unconscious and bleeding to death from an automobile accident to an emergency ward where physicians give her a blood transfusion in the belief that she would want a transfusion. If the driver eventually recovers, she may persuade her physicians that they were mistaken about what she would have wanted.[91] But, even if she does, the driver's position after the fact does not render the physicians' statement a fiction at the time they made it. The same is true of previously competent patients, like Karen Quinlan, who, it is believed, will never recover consciousness and, hence, will never be able to testify as to what they would have wanted. Determining what such patients would have desired under counterfactual conditions may be difficult and, perhaps, unpersuasive. But the difficulty and unpersuasiveness of a determination does not render it a fiction unless it is necessarily false. The same is also true of never-competent patients like Mary Moe. Indeed, if anything, determinations regarding never-competent patients rest on a more persuasive foundation than determinations regarding previously competent patients like Karen Quinlan, because rather than engaging in the problematic task of trying to determine what a particular patient with a particular history of competence would wish under very different circumstances, courts approach never-competent patients on the plausible assumption that if they were competent they would desire what is in their best interests.[92]

In reality, what distinguishes the three elements of Hypothetical Consent from the two elements of the Alternative Standard is not the counterfactual step of determining that *S would have chosen x* (which is common to both) but the additional step of thereupon treating *S* as if she *had, indeed, chosen x*. The *Quinlan* and *Moe* courts both took that latter step in order to bring Karen Quinlan and Mary Moe within the legal framework of rights of 'choice' and 'consent' and 'self-determination' that competent patients possess. Obviously, however, in the absence of prospective consent in the form of advance medical directives, incompetent patients are incapable of actually choosing anything. Therefore, in order to bridge the gap between the rights of choice that the *Quinlan* and *Moe* courts believed incompetent persons ought to possess, on the one hand, and the incapacity of Karen Quinlan and Mary Moe to make any choices at all, on the other, the *Quinlan* and *Moe* courts created fictions: the *Quinlan* and *Moe* courts invoked facts that plausibly *were true* of Karen and Mary, *i.e.*, that the two women 'would have' prescriptively consented to *x*, in order to attribute to them facts that *could not possibly be true*, *i.e.*, that the two women 'did' prescriptively consent to *x*. The attributions are fictions because in explicitly characterizing absences of prescriptive consent as occurrences of prescriptive consent, the two courts made assertions that they conceded to be false.

Harmon may also be mistaken in regarding fictions of hypothetical consent as undesirable in the area of medicine. In themselves, legal fictions are neither pernicious nor benign. A fiction is pernicious only if speakers or listeners are unaware of it and, in their unawareness, are misled into embracing values that they would otherwise reject. Yet it is difficult to see how anyone could be misled by fictions of hypothetical consent on behalf of incompetent or comatose persons because it is obvious that such persons are not actually choosing anything. Thus, people may be misled by emotion, or self-interest, or the interests of third persons, into wrongly believing that Karen Quinlan *would have chosen* to be removed from life support.[93] But they are hardly likely to be misled by the fiction of hypothetical consent into thinking that she *did* choose to be removed from life support.[94]

At the same time, a legal fiction can be beneficial if by transparently associating a thing with something it is not, the fiction reveals underlying values that the two things possess in common. The fiction of hypothetical consent may have a benign effect because, without misleading, it illuminates values that patients like Karen Quinlan share with competent patients on life support. Consider, for example, what would have been lost if the New Jersey court in *Quinlan* had eschewed the fiction of hypothetical consent in framing its decision. The *Quinlan* court could have reached the same result without reference to hypothetical consent by employing the Alternative Standard. That is, the court could have held that, to afford Karen Quinlan the respect to which she was constitutionally entitled, the court was obliged to treat her in accord with what she would have chosen for herself. Yet applying the Alternative Standard fails to convey something that Hypothetical Consent expresses. It fails to convey what the decision regarding Karen Quinlan shares with decisions regarding competent patients on life support, namely, that both are entitled to be treated as much as possible as agents of their own well-being.

Conclusion

Like 'justice', 'equality', 'freedom', 'property', 'responsibility', etc., 'consent' is a major concept by which we organize and express our normative judgments of the world. Like these other concepts, consent has a protean capacity to encompass a broad range of normative judgments. Yet unlike them, consent possesses normative breadth that is difficult to explain. Specifically, consent possesses broader normative scope than its conceptual predicates appear capable of supporting.

'Justice' has broad normative scope because, like concepts of 'right' and 'good' and 'fair', justice is what philosophers call a 'purely normative' concept:[95] it properly applies to any empirical state of affairs or relationship that *ought to be*. 'Equality', 'freedom', 'property', and 'responsibility' also have broad normative scope, though for different reasons. None of them is purely normative in nature because each can be used in two alternative ways. Each can be used factually to refer to certain empirical states of affairs or relationships without regard to whether these states or relationships ought to exist or ought to possess normative effects. Yet each can also be used normatively to refer empirical states of affairs or relationships that ought to exist or ought to possess normative effects. The reason that equality, freedom, property and responsibility possess broad scope when used normatively is that they are minimally constrained by their conceptual predicates as to the actual or supposed empirical states and relationships to which they are capable of applying.

Consent, too, is a concept that can be used both *factually* to refer to certain empirical states of affairs without regard to their legal effects, and *legally* to refer to the identical empirical states under such conditions that suffice to constitute defenses to criminal wrongdoing. Yet in contrast to other concepts that possess broad normative scope, consent, when used legally, would appear to be confined with respect to the empirical states to which it is conceptually capable of applying. After all, when used factually, 'consent' refers to instances in which *S*, in mind or expression, chooses certain conduct for herself under the circumstances, without regard to whether she does so under conditions deemed sufficient to enable her to take responsibility for her choice. In turn, when consent is used in a legal sense to refer to such choices as occur under conditions sufficient to enable *S* to take responsibility for them, consent remains confined to empirical instances in which *S*, whether in mind or expression, actually chooses *x* for herself under the circumstances. To illustrate the narrow normative scope to which consent's conceptual predicates appear to confine it, consider the following hypothetical case:

> ***'Surprise Surgery'.*** Amanda, a resident of the state of 'Vermonia' and a victim of a chronic and uncomfortable hernia, agrees to submit to general anesthesia for purposes of repairing the hernia. Amanda's physician, Dr. John, informs her in advance that there is a .01% risk that the anesthesia will cause paralysis of her extremities. Dr. John also informs Amanda that he will make an incision to reach the hernia, repair it, and close the incision with stitches. However, Dr. John does not bother to tell Amanda that to reach the hernia, he must necessarily cut abdominal muscle, and that to suture the incision, he follows the standard though not necessary practice of using internal stitches that will dissolve over time. Amanda agrees to submit to the operation as described. During the course of the operation, Dr. John discovers a malignant tumor on Amanda's pancreas. Rather than subject Amanda to a second round of anesthesia, Dr. John

> removes the tumor and minor amounts of surrounding pancreas tissue. When Amanda awakens, she discovers to her horror and anger that (i) her legs are permanently paralyzed, (ii) Dr. John first cut abdominal muscle and then used internal stitches that will remain in her body until they are absorbed, and (iii) Dr. John excised a portion of her pancreas. Accordingly, Amanda urges the local prosecutor to indict Dr. John for battery on all three counts—'battery' being defined in Vermonia as the offense of 'touching a person without the person's consent'. Amanda argues that she could not have 'consented' to those three touchings within the meaning of the statute because she did not even factually consent to them.

Amanda is correct that she did not factually consent to the three touchings. Thus, she did not choose, either in mind or expression, to the severing of abdominal muscle or to suturing with internal stitches; for even though surgeons are aware that hernia operations necessarily involve muscle incision and preferably involve the use of dissolvable sutures, Amanda, like most lay people, was not aware of those facts.[96] Nor did Amanda choose in mind or expression to be anesthetized in such a way as to leave herself paralyzed; for, though she was willing to run the risk of paralysis, she was never willing to trade the use of her legs for the benefits of a hernia operation.[97] Nor could Amanda have chosen in mind or expression to have a portion of her pancreas removed; for she scarcely knew that she possessed a pancreas, much less that it was diseased. Nevertheless, Amanda is almost certainly wrong in concluding that she did not consent to the three touchings within the meaning of the Vermonia assault statute. For if the courts of Vermonia are like Anglo-American jurisdictions, they can be expected to dismiss any indictment the prosecutor pursues. And they will do so by making a normative move that accounts for consent's possessing broader normative scope than its conceptual predicates seem to support: *they will impute to Amanda choices that she did not make*. They will hold that (i) Amanda constructively consented to be sutured with internal stitches by prescriptively consenting to a surgery to which such stitching is incidental; (ii) Amanda consented to be anesthetized in a manner that caused paralysis by voluntarily accepting a justifiable risk that paralysis would occur; and (iii) Amanda consented to the removal of the tumor on her pancreas because given the emergency conditions, Dr. John could reasonably assume that Amanda would have wanted him to remove the tumor.[98]

To be sure, like most battery statutes, the Vermonia statute is formulated in such a way that the only possible defense to a touching of *S* is that the touching be with *S*'s 'consent'. Accordingly, unless the Vermonia courts are willing to convict Dr. John of conduct that appears reasonable, they must either read new terms into the statute or interpret the existing term 'consent' to encompass touchings to which Amanda at most only fictionally acquiesced. However, that does not explain why the Vermonia legislature, like most legislatures, would formulate the statute in such a way in the first place. Why wouldn't it spare its courts the need to create fictions of consent by making explicit provisions for the three kinds of touchings that the fictions presently address? Why, in other words, wouldn't it frame the offense of battery along the following lines?

> ***Battery (Revised).*** It is an offense to touch a person, unless (i) the touching is with the person's consent, (ii) the touching is incidental to touching that is with the person's consent, (iii) the person voluntarily accepted the risk of the touching, or (iv) the touching arises in the context of a life-threatening emergency in which the person is incapable of consenting, but in which it is reasonable to assume the person would have consented if he or she had been capable of doing so.

The legal scope of 'consent' would be far narrower than it presently is if, instead of drafting offenses of non-consent as they presently do, jurisdictions drafted offenses of non-consent in the fashion of 'Battery (Revised)'. The superficial reason that jurisdictions do not do so is that they are so accustomed to equating *fictional* prescriptive consent with *actual* prescriptive consent that they rarely think to distinguish the former from the latter. But that simply begs the more fundamental question: *why* is it that jurisdictions are so accustomed to equating fictional prescriptive consent with actual prescriptive consent that it rarely occurs to them to distinguish between them? I am not sure. But it may be that, like people generally, lawmakers find it useful to possess a single, grand organizing concept of 'consent' to encompass all instances in which the reason *A* has a defense to the crime of subjecting *S* to conduct is that the conduct is in *S*'s interest—rather than having to conceptualize them in four distinct categories.

Notes

1. Regina v. Cey, 48 C.C.C. 3d 480 (1989).
2. *See* Regina v. Maloney, 28 C.C.C. 2d 323, 326 (1976). *See* also Regina v. Gray, [1981] 6 W.W.R. 654, 661 (1981) (applying the *Maloney* standard). Criminal Code section 245 is now codified at Criminal Code 265 (*see* R.S.C. 1985, c. C-46, § 265).
3. Regina v. Cey, 48 C.C.C. (3d) 480, 484, 486 (1989).
4. Regina v. Cey, 48 C.C.C. (3d) 480, 490 (1989).
5. Regina v. Cey, 48 C.C.C. (3d) 480, 490 (Gerwing, J., 1989).
6. Regina v. Cey, 48 C.C.C. (3d) 480, 482 (1989).
7. Regina v. Cey, 48 C.C.C. (3d) 480, 489 (1976) (quoting Regina v. Maloney, 28 C.C.C. (2d) 323 (1976).
8. For a discussion of the Canadian courts' view that a hockey player can consent to additional levels of assault by willingly engaging in a fight, *see* White, 'Sports Violence As Criminal Assault', 1986 *Duke Law Journal*, pp. 1045-47. *See* also Regina v. Gray, 6 W.W.R. 654, 656 (1981). For discussion of my usage of 'informed consent' in relationship to its usage in the law of torts, *see* section B, *infra*.
9. The issue of the limits of consent was first raised in Regina v. Maki, [1970] 3 O.R. 780, 783 (1970) (quoting The Queen v. Coney, 8 Q.B.D. 534, 549 (1882) (Stephen, J.)), where the court said:

   > In cases where life and limb are exposed to no serious danger in the common course of things, I think that consent is a defence to a charge of assault, even when considerable force is used, as, for instance, in cases of wrestling, single-stick, sparring with gloves, football, and the like; but in all cases the question whether

consent does or does not take from the application of force to another its illegal character, is a question of degree depending upon circumstances.

10. *See, e.g.*, Feinberg, *Harm To Self*, pp. 173-74, 181, 186-87; Malm, 'The Ontological Status of Consent', p. 149.
11. *See* Feinberg, *Harm To Self*, p. 278 ('informed consent' to *x* really means voluntary assumption of a *risk* of *x*).
12. Compare Warren v. Georgia, 255 Ga. 151, 155, 336 S.E.2d 221, 224 (1985) (conceptualizing the 'marital rape exemption' as prospective consent that, at the moment of marriage, a woman gives to future acts of marital intercourse), with Lane v. Maryland, 348 Md. 272, 703 A.2d 180 (1997) (conceptualizing the marital rape exemption as contemporaneous consent that, by virtue of having married, a woman gives to every act of marital intercourse at the time it occurs).
13. Hale, *The History of the Pleas of the Crown*, vol. 1, p. *629. For a history of the marital rape exemption, including the appropriateness of attributing it to Hale, *see* Barton, 'The Story Of Marital Rape'.
14. [1954] 2 Q.B. 282, [1954] 2 All ER 529.
15. [1954] 2 Q.B. 282, [1954] 2 All ER 529 (opinion of Lynskey, J.).
16. [1954] 2 Q.B. 282, [1954] 2 All ER 529 (opinion of Lynskey, J.).
17. *See* Powell, 'Consent To Operative Procedures', p. 190. For a commentator who unwittingly conflates these two meanings of 'implied consent', *see* Tchen, 'Rape Reform and a Statutory Consent Defense', pp. 1523-24.
18. Simmons, 'Tacit Consent And Political Obligation', p. 286:

    In calling it an act a 'sign of consent', I mean that because of the context in which the act was performed, including the appropriate conventions (linguistic or otherwise), the act counts as an expression of the actor's intention to consent.
19. Simmons, 'Locke's Problem Of Political Consent', p. 168:

    Express consent, on the Lockean account, is consent given by positive action of some direct and explicit sort whose sole conventional point is to give consent—such as an oral or written promise or oath . . .
20. Simmons, 'Locke's Problem Of Political Consent', p. 168:

    Express consent, on the Lockean account, is consent given by positive action or some direct and explicit sort whose sole conventional point is to give consent—such as . . . a positive but nonverbal act that explicitly signifies acceptance or agreement (such as a signal or wave).
21. As Simmons puts it, in the context of consent by an actor to perform a future act (as opposed to consent to the conduct of another):

    An act may be such that it binds the actor morally to the same performance to which he would be bound if he had in fact consented. I may do something which is not itself a [sign] of consent, but which nonetheless binds me as if I had consented; after performing the act, it would be wrong (ceteris paribus) for me not to do those things which my actual consent would have bound me to. Consider a simple case such as joining a game of baseball. Many writers have held that while in joining the game I may do nothing which could be construed as giving my consent (tacit or otherwise) to be governed by the umpire's decisions, nonetheless, by participating in the activity, I may become bound to be so governed, just as if I had in fact consented.

    Simmons, 'Tacit Consent And Political Obligation', at 287.
22. *See* Hasday, 'Contest and Consent', p. 1399 ('Hale's theory generally did not concern itself with a wife's actual state of mind. To be sure, his explanation depended on the

proposition that a woman had actually agreed to her marriage, under circumstances free from legally cognizable force, duress, or fraud. But after a woman had made that decision, Hale's theory no longer turned on what a woman actually wanted or would agree to if asked.')

23. Cf. Regina v. Clarence [1888] 22 Q.B. 23, 2 All E.R. 529 (opinion of Hawkins, J.) ('The intercourse which takes place between husband and wife after marriage is not by virtue of any special consent on her part, but is mere submission to an obligation imposed on her by law').
24. The House of Lords, construing the Sexual Offences (Amendment) Act of 1976, held in 1991 that the common-law exemption of husbands from rape did not survive the 1976 Act. *See* Regina v. R., [1992] 1 AC 599, [1991] 4 All ER 481, [1991] 3 WLR 767. Nevertheless, although the Sexual Offences (Amendment) Act does not formally take account of marriage as a factor bearing upon culpability, criminal courts still take marital relationships into account as a mitigating factor in setting sentences for spousal rape. *See* Regina v. W., reported in The Criminal Law Review, December 1992, pp. 905-06. For American jurisdictions that have likewise abolished the marital exemption, either by statute or by judicial decision, *see* Eskow, 'The Ultimate Weapon', p. 682 n.34.
25. For a list of state statutes, effective 1997, governing sexual assault by one spouse of the other, *see* Connerton, 'The Resurgence Of The Marital Rape Exemption'. *See* also Hasday, 'Contest and Consent', pp. 1484-85.
26. *See, e.g.*, Louisiana Revised Statutes 14:43 (1998):

    A. Simple rape is a rape committed when the anal or vaginal sexual intercourse is deemed to be without the lawful consent of a victim who is not the spouse of the offender because it is committed under any one or more of the following circumstances:

    * * *

    For purposes of this Section, a person shall not be considered to be a spouse if a judgment of separation from bed and board has been rendered, or if the person and the offender are not legally separated but are living separate and apart and the offender knows that a temporary restraining order, preliminary or permanent injunction, or other order or decree has been issued prohibiting or restraining the offender from sexually or physically abusing, intimidating, threatening violence against, or in any way physically interfering with the person.

    For a discussion of such limitations, *see* Sitton, 'Comment, Old Wine In New Bottles', pp. 277-81.
27. *See, e.g.*, Idaho Code §§ 18-6101, 18-6107 (1998); Michigan Compiled Laws Annotation § 750.5201 (1998); Ohio Stat. Ann. § 2907.02 (1998); 21 Oklahoma Stat. Ann. § 1111 (1998); Virginia Code Ann. §§ 18.2-61, and 18.2-67.2:1 (1998); W. Va. Code § 61-8B-6 (1999).
28. *See, e.g.*, Virginia Statutes Annotation § 18.2-61(B) (1998):

    If any person has sexual intercourse with his or her spouse and such act is accomplished against the spouse's will by force, threat or intimidation of or against the spouse or another, he or she shall be guilty of rape.

    However, no person shall be found guilty under this subsection unless, at the time of the alleged offense, (i) the spouses were living separate and apart, or . . . (ii) the defendant caused bodily injury to the spouse by the use of force or violence.
29. Connecticut General Statutes § 53A-73A (1997).

30. Connecticut General Statutes § 53A-65(3) (1997).
31. Connecticut General Statutes § 53A-67(b) (1997).
32. *See* Swartz, 'The Patient Who Refuses Medical Treatment', pp. 162, 177. *See* also Buchanan and Brock, *Deciding for Others*, pp. 94-95.
33. Byrn, 'Compulsory Lifesaving Treatment For the Competent Adult', pp. 25, 29.
34. For a collection of cases, *see* Karnezis, 'Annotation'; Byrn, 'Compulsory Lifesaving Treatment For The Competent Adult', pp. 17-18.
35. The 'Overdosed Student' is a hypothetical case, based upon what Maryland case law implies Maryland would do in such a case. *See, e.g.*, Hamilton v. McAuliffe, 353 A.2d 634 (Maryland 1976). Cf. John F. Kennedy Memorial Hospital v. Heston, 58 N.J. 576, 582, 279 A.2d 670, 673 (1971). The New Jersey Supreme Court, in In re Claire C. Conroy, 98 N.J. 321, 351, 486 A.2d 1209, 1224 (1985), later overruled *John F. Kennedy Memorial Hospital* to the extent that *John F. Kennedy* permitted the state to administer life-saving medical treatment in the absence of consent to an elderly patient with severe and permanent mental and physical impairments and a limited life expectancy. But there is no reason to doubt the validity of *John F. Kennedy* in a case in which the patient is otherwise healthy.
36. New Mexico Statutes Annotated § 66-8-107(A) (1998):

    > Any person who operates a motor vehicle within this state shall be deemed to have given consent . . . to chemical tests of his breath or blood or both . . . for the purpose of determining the drug or alcohol content of his blood if arrested for any offense arising out of the acts alleged to have been committed while the person was driving a motor vehicle while under the influence of an intoxicating liquor or drug.

    New Mexico Statutes Annotated § 66-8-108 (1998):

    > Any person who is dead, unconscious or otherwise in a condition rendering him incapable of refusal, shall be deemed not to have withdrawn the consent provided by Section 66-8-107 . . . and the test or tests designated by the law enforcement officer may be administered.
37. *See, e.g.*, 11 Delaware Code § 451 (1998) ('In any prosecution for an offense, it is a defense that the victim consented to the act done. . . . Any person who enters the presence of other people consents to the normal physical contacts incident to such presence').
38. Collins v. Wilcock, [1984] 1 W.L.R. 1172, 11177 (Goff, J.).
39. *See, e.g.*, McGill v. Alaska, 18 P.3d 77 (2001); Connecticut v. Siering, 35 Conn. App. 173, 644 A.2d 958 (1994); Robinson v. Maine, 496 A.2d 1067 (Maine 1985); Minnesota v. Crims, 540 NW2d 860 (1995); Regina v. Kaitamaki, [1980] 1 N.Z.L.R. 59 (New Zealand); South Dakota v. Jones, 521 NW2d 662 (1994).
40. *See, e.g.*, Regina v. Salmon, [1969] SASR 76 (Australia); California v. Vela, 172 Cal. App. 3d 237, 218 Cal. Rptr. 161 (1985); Battle v. State, 287 Md. 675, 414 A.2d 126 (Md. App. 1980); North Carolina v. Way, 297 N.C. 293, 254 S.E.2d 760 (1979); Regina v. Richardson, [1978] Tas. S.R. 178 (Tasmania).
41. *See* Regina v. Kaitamaki, [1980] 1 N.Z.L.R. 59, 64-65 (Woodhouse, J., dissenting) ('The initiation of intercourse by penetration done with her consent is, in my opinion physically, or legally in terms of the statute itself, quite incapable of separation from the rest of the same uninterrupted occasion of intercourse until withdrawal').
42. *See* Regina v. Cuerrier, [1998] 2 S.C.R. 371.
43. Kenneth Simons, writing about the law of torts, draws a parallel between *A*'s defense of consent by *S* in criminal law to *A*'s defense of 'assumption of risk' by *S* in the law of

torts. *See* Simons, 'Assumption of Risk and Consent in the Law of Torts', p. 233 n.64. However, Simons conceptualizes the defense of assumption of risk in torts in a way different from how I conceptualize the defense of informed consent in criminal law here. Simons argues that *A*'s defense of assumption of risk in torts comes into play with respect to risks that *A* imposes upon *S* that *would be* tortious if *A* imposed them upon persons who prefer that the risks be reduced. With respect to such risks, *A* has a defense of assumption of risk in torts, Simons argues, if *S* consciously undergoes the risks with certain preferences in mind–namely, the preference of preferring to undergo the risks to enjoying the benefits of the reduction in risks to which he has a right under the law of torts. *See id.* at 217. For purposes of criminal law, however, it is not clear that *S*'s personal preferences regarding risks ought to matter. A risky activity that an actor *A* makes available to *S* either does, or does not, possess sufficient potential benefits to users to justify making the activity available to them for purposes of the criminal law. If the risky activity does possess such potential benefits (*e.g.*, the sport of hang-gliding or bungee-jumping as practiced in most places), it ought not to matter that *S* would prefer that *A* undertake to render the activity less risky (*e.g.*, installing enormously expensive fail-safe devices). *See id.* at 247. If, however, the risky activity does not possess such potential benefits to users (*e.g.*, bare-fisted boxing, drag-racing, or Russian roulette), it ought not to matter that *S* prefers the risky activity to ones that would be less risky (*e.g.*, boxing with gloves, drag-racing at a track, or Russian roulette with a paint gun). *See id.* at 250, 274.

44. *See, e.g.*, Attorney-General's Reference (No. 6 of 1980), [1981] Q.B. 715, 719. Cf. The Queen v. Coney, 8 Q.B.D. 534, 549 (1882) (Stephen, J.).
45. *See* generally McCutcheon, 'Sports Violence, Consent, And The Criminal Law' p. 272. Cf. R. v. Brown, [1993] 2 All ER 75 79 (Lord Tempelman) ('Violent sports including boxing are lawful activities').
46. For the differences in the way Canadian courts and courts within the United States treat fistfights that occur in hockey outside the course of play, *see* White, 'Sports Violence As Criminal Assault', pp. 1034-35. *See* also Savoras, 'Fighting: It's All in a Day's Work on the Ice'.
47. R.S.C. 1985, c. C-46, s. 265, formerly R.S.C. 1970, c. C-34, s. 245.1(1)(b).
48. *See* note 6.
49. *See* Chapter 8, at notes 45-50.
50. Gauthier, *Morals By Agreement*, p. 232.
51. *See* Rawls, *A Theory of Justice*, pp. 17-21, 136-42 (describing original position and veil of ignorance); Rawls, *Political Liberalism*, pp. 22-28 (explaining place of original position and veil of ignorance in the theory of political liberalism). For the argument that Rawls' original position is not a procedure for discovering justice but, rather, a procedure for testing the quality of an intuition of justice a person already has, *see* Dworkin, 'The Original Position', pp. 18, 24-26. For a critical discussion of the role of hypothetical consent in political theory, *see* Barry, *Theories of Justice*, pp. 282-92.
52. *See, e.g.*, Alexander, 'Justification and Innocent Aggressors', pp. 1186-88; Thomson, 'The Trolley Problem', p. 195.
53. In re Karen Quinlan, 70 N.J. 10, 355 A.2d 647 (1976).
54. The New Jersey Supreme Court has since held that life support may be removed from an incompetent patient without her consent, if (i) the patient is conscious, and (ii) maintaining her on life support involves 'such unavoidable and severe pain' as to be 'inhumane'. In re Claire C. Conroy, 98 N.J. 321, 366, 486 A.2d 1209, 1232 (1985). A

lower court in New Jersey has also since held that life support may be removed from a comatose patient without her consent if she has never previously been competent. *See* In re Marie Moorhouse, 250 N.J. Super. 307, 593 A.2d 1256 (1991). Nevertheless, the New Jersey Supreme Court continues to hold that, with respect to previously competent but presently comatose patients who are not suffering pain—like Karen Quinlan—life support may not be removed without their consent. *See* In re Hilda M. Peter, 108 N.J. 365, 374, 529 A.2d 419, 424 (1987).

55. 70 N.J. 10, 51, 355 A.2d 647, 669-70 (citations omitted):

> Having concluded that there is a right of privacy that might permit termination of treatment in the circumstances of this case, we turn to consider the relationship of the exercise of that right to the criminal law. We are aware that such termination of treatment would accelerate Karen's death. The County Prosecutor and the Attorney General maintain that there would be criminal liability for such acceleration. Under the statutes of this State, the unlawful killing of another human being is criminal homicide. We conclude that there would be no criminal homicide in the circumstances of this case. . . .
>
> . . . . The termination of treatment pursuant to the right of privacy is, within the limitations of this case, ipso facto lawful. Thus, a death resulting from such an act would not come within the scope of the homicide statutes proscribing only the unlawful killing of another. There is a real and in this case determinative distinction between the unlawful taking of the life of another and the ending of artificial life-support systems as a matter of self-determination.
>
> Furthermore, the exercise of a constitutional right such as we have here found is protected from criminal prosecution. We do not question the State's undoubted power to punish the taking of human life, but that power does not encompass individuals terminating medical treatment pursuant to their right of privacy.

56. 70 N.J. 10. 39, 355 A.2d 647, 663.
57. 70 N.J. at 22. 355 A.2d at 653.
58. *See* In re Nancy Ellen Jobes, 108 N.J. 394, 412, 529 A.2d 434, 443, (1987); In re Hilda M. Peter, 108 N.J. 365, 378, 529 A.2d 419, 425 (1987); In re Clair C. Conroy, 98 N.J. 321, 361, 486 A.2d 1209, 1229-30 (1985).
59. 70 N.J. 10, 21, 355 A.2d 647, 653.
60. 70 N.J. 10, 41-22, 355 A.2d 647, 664:

> If a putative decision by Karen to permit this non-cognitive, vegetative existence to terminate by natural forces is regarded as a valuable incident of her right of privacy, as we believe it to be, then it should not be discarded solely on the basis that her condition prevents her conscious exercise of the choice. The only practical way to prevent destruction of the right is to permit the guardian and family of Karen to render their best judgment, subject to the qualifications hereinafter stated, as to whether she would exercise it in these circumstances. If their conclusion is in the affirmative this decision should be accepted by a society the overwhelming majority of whose members would, we think, in similar circumstances, exercise such a choice in the same way for themselves or for those closest to them.

Some commentators, but not this author, understand the *Quinlan* court to be stating that a decision by Karen's surrogate to remove her from life support is valid only *because* 'an overwhelming majority' of persons in society would make the same decision for themselves. *See* Dresser, 'Life, Death, and Incompetent Patients'.

61. Buchanan and Brock, *Deciding for Others*, p. 94.

62. In re Nancy Elles Jobes, 108 N.J. 394, 414-15, 529 A.2d 434, 444 (1987) (citations and footnotes omitted).
63. *See* Powell, 'Consent To Operative Procedures', p. 199.
64. *See* Byrn, 'Compulsory Life Saving Treatment for the Competent Adult', p. 15 n.64; Swartz, 'The Patient Who Refuses Medical Treatment', pp. 174-79. Cf. American Law Institute, *Restatement of the Law* (2d) Torts, vol. 1, § 62, p. 94, Illustration 5.
65. Malette v. Shulman, 67 D.L.R. 4th 321 (1990).
66. Malette v. Shulman, 67 D.L.R. 4th 321, 328-29 (1990).
67. Malette v. Shulman, 67 D.L.R. 4th 321, 335 (1990).
68. In re Alice Hughes, 259 N.J. Super. 193, 199, 611 A.2d 1148, 1151 (1992).
69. *See* In re Alice Hughes, 259 N.J. Super. 193, 202, 611 A.2d 1148, 1152 (1992). *See* also Swartz, 'The Patient Who Refuses Medical Treatment', p. 177.
70. For the general rule, *see* In re Guardianship of Pescinski, 2d 4, 226 N.W.2d 180 (1975); Harmon, 'Falling Off the Vine', pp. 34-37. But *see* Hart v. Brown, 29 Conn. Supp. 368, 289 A.2d 386 (Super. Ct. 1972).
71. *See, e.g.*, the majority and dissenting opinions within the New Jersey Supreme Court in re Nancy Ellen Jobes, 108 N.J. 394, 529 A.2d 434 (1987), and In re Hilda M. Peter, 108 N.J. 365, 529 A.2d 419 (1987).
72. Compare In re Karen Quinlan, 70 N.J. 10, 355 A.2d 647 (1976), with In re Westchester County Medical Center on behalf of O'Connor, 72 N.Y.2d 517, 531 N.E.2d 607, 534 N.Y.S.2d 886 (1988). Compare the opinion of the court with the dissenting opinion regarding 'substituted judgment' in Cruzan v. Director, Missouri Department of Health, 497 U.S. 261 (1990); and compare the opinion of the court with the dissenting opinion by Judge Jones in In re John Storrar, 52 N.Y.2d 363; 420 N.E.2d 64 (1981). *See* generally Kadish, 'Letting Patients Die, pp. 879-80.
73. Compare In re Karen Quinlan, 70 N.J. 10, 22, 355 A.2d 647, 653 (1976), with In re Claire C. Conroy, 98 N.J. 321, 362, 486 A.2d 1209, 1230 (1985).
74. *See* Cantor, 'Discarding Substituted Judgment And Best Interests', pp. 1208-1211. Cf. Eaton and Larson, 'Experimenting with the 'Right to Die' in the Laboratory of the States', pp. 1281-82(describing inconsistency among courts in the way they apply the requirement that there be 'clear and convincing evidence' evidence of what an incompetent patient would wish for himself).
75. For a discussion as to when judicial review is and is not appropriate, *see* In re Marie Moorhouse, 250 N.J. Super. 307, 593 A.2d 1256 (1991).
76. For criticisms of hypothetical consent in the context of the removal of life support, *see* Burt, *Taking Care Of Strangers*, pp. 152-53; Dresser, 'Life, Death, and Incompetent Patients'; Harmon, 'Falling Off The Vine'; Tribe, *American Constitutional Law*, p. 1368, note 25; Weber, 'Substituted Judgment Doctrine'.
77. *See* Harmon, 'Falling Off The Vine'. *See* also Conservatorship of the Person of William J. Drabick, 200 Cal. App. 3d 185, 208, 333, 245 Cal. Rptr. 840, 854 (1988) (Peterson, J., concurring); Conservatorship of Valerie N. Mildred, 40 Cal. 3d 143, 174, 184-89, 707 P.2d 760, 781, 788-91 (1985) (Bird, C.J., dissenting); In re Estate of Longeway v. Community Convalescent Center, 133 Ill. 2d 33, 55-63, 549 N.E.2d 292, 302-06 (1989) (Ward, J., dissenting); Guardianship of Jane Doe, 411 Mass. 512, 518, 583 N.E.2d 1263, 1268 (1992); *id.* 411 Mass. at 526-35, 583 N.E.2d at 1272-77 (O'Connor, J., dissenting); Airedale NHS Trusts v. Bland, [1993] AC 789, [1993] 1 All ER 821, [1993] 2 WLR 316 (Lord Mustill).
78. Harmon, 'Falling Off The Vine', p. 61.

79. For a discussion of the sterilization cases, *see* Harmon, 'Falling Off The Vine', pp. 66-73.
80. For the argument that discussions of hypothetical consent are philosophically unsound with respect to persons who, by virtue of lacking psychological continuity from birth, must also be deemed to lack personal identity from birth, *see* Buchanan and Brock, *Deciding For Others*, pp. 114-15.
81. *See, e.g.*, Guardianship of Jane Doe, 411 Mass. 512, 518, 583 N.E.2d 1263, 1268 (1992); Superintendent of Belchertown State School v. Joseph Saikewicz, 373 Mass. 728, 751, 370 N.E.2d 417, 431 (1977); In re Nancy Ellen Jobes, 108 N.J. 394, 449, 529 A.2d 434, 462 (1987) (Pollock, J., concurring); Custody of a Minor, 393 N.E.2d 836, 844 (Mass. 1979) ('In the case of a child, however, the substituted judgment doctrine and "the best interests of the child" test are essentially coextensive, involving examination of the same criteria and application of the same basic reasoning').
82. *See* note 81. *See* also Cantor, 'Discarding Substituted Judgment And Best Interests', p. 1215 n.83; Swartz, 'The Patient Who Refuses Medical Treatment', p. 179.
83. In re Mary Moe, 385 Mass. 555, 432 N.E.2d 712 (1982).
84. 385 Mass. at 563, 432 N.E.2d at 719.
85. 385 Mass. at 565, 720; 432 N.E.2d at 572, 724.
86. 385 Mass. at 566, 571, 432 N.E.2d at 720, 723.
87. In re F (Mental Patient, Sterilization), [1990] 2 A.C. 1.
88. For the Court of Appeal, *see* [1990] 2 A.C. 1, 13-16 (Lord Donaldson), 30 (Neill, J.), 37 (Butler-Sloss, J.). For the House of Lords, *see* [1990] 2 A.C. at 72-73 (Lord Goff).
89. For the court of appeals, *see* [1990] 2 A.C. at 17-21 (Lord Donaldson), at 31-34 (Neill, J.), and at 42 (Butler-Sloss, J.) For the House of Lords, *see* [1990] 2 A.C. at 51-52 (Lord Bridge), at 55-57 (Lord Brandon), at 68-70 (Lord Griffiths), at 74-75 (Lord Goff), at 83 (Lord Jauncey).
90. Harmon, 'Falling Off The Vine', pp. 60-69. *See* also Price and Burt, 'Sterilization, State Action, and the Concept of Consent', pp. 61-62.
91. The driver's subsequent testimony may persuade her physicians that they were mistaken in stating that the driver 'would have chosen' a blood transfusion if she had been conscious. But the driver's testimony does not, and cannot, render the physicians' statement invariably false at the time they made it, because the driver's testimony is itself counterfactual, rather than factual, coming as it does after the fact.
92. For the argument that courts are safer to base determinations of hypothetical consent on statistical information about what most people desire, rather than on idiosyncratic inquiries into the values systems of particular persons, *see* Cantor, 'Discarding Substituted Judgment and Best Interests', pp. 1241-72.
93. For the argument that inquiries into what an incompetent patient 'would have chosen' are subterfuges for implicitly taking account of the interests of third person without explicitly acknowledging it, *see* Dresser, 'Life, Death, and Incompetent Patients', pp. 189-90.
94. But *see* Price and Burt, 'Sterilization, State Action, and the Concept of Consent', p. 58, criticizing the use of hypothetical consent in the sterilization context as:

    nothing short of an extended conceit on the proposition of voluntariness. It is a fiction which authorizes the state to intervene because a party other than the subject provides the green light. Often that third party is the parent of the subject individual, but the doctrine is equally applicable when the third party is . . . a guardian ad litem or a conservator. By characterizing the transaction as "consensual" rather than "compulsory" third-party consent allows the truly involuntary to be declared voluntary, thus bypassing constitutional, ethical, and moral questions, and avoiding the violation of taboos. Third-party consent is a miraculous creation of the law—adroit, flexible, and useful in covering the unseemly reality of conflict with the patina of cooperation.

95. *See* Feldman. 'Objectivity in Legal Judgment' p. 1189.
96. Archard asserts that a person who consents to *p* also 'consents' to anything, *q*, that *p* necessarily entails. *See* Archard, 'A Nod As Good As A Wink', p. 278. The statement tends to be true in so far as 'consent' is being used legally, because persons who legally consent to *p* are, indeed, ordinarily deemed to constructively consent to everything that *p* necessarily entails. But the statement is false in so far as 'consent' is being used factually. For persons cannot factually consent to things of which they are unaware. *See* O'Neill, 'Between Consenting Adults', p. 255 ('Consent may not extend to the logical implications, likely results, or the indispensable presuppositions of that which is explicitly consented to').
97. For the distinction in torts between *S*'s assuming a risk of *x*, on the one hand, and *S*'s consent to *x*, on the other, *see* Mansfield, 'Informed Choice In The Law Of Torts', pp. 17-18:

    The inquiry thus far as referred to consent and assumption of risk without any effort to identify them as separate concepts. . . . Consent is the right term to use when the plaintiff was willing that a certain event occur, probably some conduct on the part of the defendant, because he desired an invasion of a normally protected interest. Ordinarily he will believe that the invasion is substantially certain to follow the event, and the term consent focuses on his belief in the certainty of the invasion. Assumption of the risk is the right term to use when the plaintiff was willing that a certain event occur, but he neither desired an invasion of a normally protected interest nor did he suppose that such an invasion was substantially certain to result.
98. *See* Colorado Revised Statutes § 18-1-703(1) (1998):

    The use of physical force upon another person which would otherwise constitute an offense is justifiable and not criminal under any of the following circumstances:...(e) A duly licensed physician, or a person acting under his direction, may use reasonable and appropriate physical force for the purpose of administering a recognized form of treatment which he reasonably believes to be adapted to promoting the physical or mental health of the patient if . . . (II) The treatment is administered in an emergency when the physician reasonably believes that no one competent to consent can be consulted and that a reasonable person, wishing to safeguard the welfare of the patient, would consent.

PART III
THE CONSEQUENCES OF CONCEPTUAL COMPLEXITY

Introduction

All Anglo-American criminal codes are rife with references to 'consent'. Yet most lawmakers would be hard-pressed to state precisely what they mean by it. As Emily Sherwin observes, 'It is in the nature of law that law can and must determine whether consent has occurred, even though no one is sure just what consent is.'[1]

A principal reason why people are uncertain as to what consent means is that when consent is used in a legal sense, its meaning changes, depending upon what is being consented to and the consequences of non-consent. Another factor is that when consent is used in a legal sense, its meaning is contestable, depending upon the legal views of its users. In that respect, people are uncertain about consent in the way they are uncertain about 'justice.' But people are also uncertain about consent for an additional reason that does not apply to justice. Justice has the virtue, at least, of being conceptually transparent: it is, and is universally understood to be, a purely normative concept, a receptacle for what is right and good. Consent is conceptually more complex, being sometimes legal and sometimes factual in nature, and being sometimes solely a state of mind, sometimes solely an expressive act, and sometimes a fiction of one or the other.

Conceptual complexity is not itself a problem. The problem is conceptual complexity dimly grasped. Chapter 8 explores some of the legal confusions that arise when lawmakers only dimly comprehend the conceptual structure of consent.

Note

[1] Sherwin, 'Infelicitous Sex,' p. 229.

Chapter Eight

The Confusions of Consent

The purpose of this chapter is to examine areas in which the conceptual apparatus of consent can mislead people of good faith into making mistakes of judgment. We have seen that consent is a single concept with a multiplicity of competing conceptions. Some conceptions of consent are purely factual, while others are prescriptive. Some conceptions of consent involve mental states of acquiescence, while others involve expressions of acquiescence. Some conceptions of consent either consist of or contain instances of actual acquiescence, while others consist of fictions of actual acquiescence. The confusions of consent arise when one conception or one category of consent is confounded with another. We shall focus below on three types of confusion: (A) the category mistake of confusing consent as a choosing of *x* under the circumstances ('factual consent') with consent as a choosing of *x* under conditions of voluntariness sufficient to render it a defense to the crime of committing *x* ('prescriptive consent'); (B) the mistake of confusing consent as a prescriptive subjective choice ('prescriptive attitudinal consent') with consent as a prescriptive expression of such a choice ('prescriptive expressive consent'); and (C) the mistake of confusing legal consent as an actual choice of *x* ('prescriptive consent') with legal consent as a legal fiction of such a choice ('imputed consent').

I shall draw upon cases that I believe illustrate confusion on the part of decisionmakers. These illustrative cases possess three features in common: (i) they involve rulings that are legally problematic; (ii) the rulings are framed in terms of consent; and (iii) the language of 'consent' that lawmakers invoke creates risks of legal confusion. Admittedly, absent explicit commentary by a decisionmaker, one can never be certain that a legally-problematic decision is conceptually confused as opposed to being perverse. Nevertheless, the rulings below are precisely the sort of legally problematic rulings that decisionmakers would render if they were conceptually confused about consent.

Confusing Factual Consent with Prescriptive Consent

Probably the most common category mistake is the mistake of responding to a question about prescriptive consent with an answer about factual consent. The mistake cannot occur—or, more accurately, it cannot taint the outcome of a trial—when a decisionmaker responds to a judge's question 'Did *S* [prescriptively] consent?' by answering 'No, *S* did not [factually] consent,' because factual consent is a necessary component of prescriptive consent. Suppose, for example, that a woman testifies that the reason she failed to consent prescriptively to sexual intercourse with her husband is that she was asleep at the time and, hence, incapable of even factually consenting. The outcome of such a case turns entirely upon whether the jury believes the woman. If the jury believes that the woman was asleep, it will find that she did not consent in *any* way, either factually or prescriptively; if, on the other hand, the jury finds that the woman was awake, it will presumably find that she consented in *both* ways, given that the jury possesses no credible evidence to the contrary. In contrast, however, the mistake of confounding factual consent with prescriptive consent can taint the outcome of a case in which *S* admits that she factually consented but denies that she prescriptively consented. That is, the mistake can arise when *S* concedes that she '[factually] consented' to *x* but contends that she failed to do so under the conditions of competence, knowledge, freedom, and motivation that are required by law for her factual consent to possess prescriptive effect. If the judge instructs the jury in the language of '[prescriptive] consent' without explicitly distinguishing it from '[factual] consent,' the judge creates a risk that the jury will confuse the former with the latter. Thus, by responding to the judge's question 'Did *S* [prescriptively] consent?' by answering 'Yes *S* did indeed [factually] consent,' a jury exculpates *A* of criminal conduct against *S* without ever determining whether *S* possessed sufficient competence, knowledge, freedom, and motivation for *S*'s factual consent to constitute a defense to *A*.

We shall consider three cases in which consent appears to have been used, whether wittingly or unwittingly, in ways that could mislead decisionmakers into making findings of legal consent merely by virtue of finding that complainants factually consented—without making further determinations as to whether the complainants factually consented under conditions of competence, knowledge, freedom, and motivation sufficient to exonerate their partners of sexual assault.

Blair: Equating the 'Freedom' Required for Prescriptive Consent with the Minimal Criteria of Factual Consent

In the *Texas v. Valdez*, the so-called 'condom case' discussed in the Introduction, a Travis County grand jury appears to have confused a victim's coerced submission to sexual intercourse with prescriptive consent and in doing so unwittingly subverted Texas' requirement that, to constitute a defense to rape, a woman's factual acquiescence to sexual intercourse must be 'free' from fear of death or serious bodily injury. *Valdez* was not a case in which anyone deliberately manipulated the Travis County grand jury into overlooking issues of freedom, but the danger of manipulation nevertheless exists.

Blair v. Wyoming[1] appears to be a case in which defense counsel attempted to confuse the jury. The complainant *S* testified that having met Blair in a bar, she invited him to her apartment where he turned violent and coerced her into submitting to sexual intercourse by threatening to beat her. Blair denied the charges, claiming that *S* had freely acquiesced to sexual intercourse. The trial record suggests that Blair's lawyer exploited the ambiguous language of consent to mislead the jury into overlooking issues of prescriptive freedom. The ambiguity arose because the trial judge used 'consent' in one way, while the investigating police officer used it in another. The trial judge in his jury instructions used consent prescriptively, that is, as a synonym for the kind of lawful acquiescence by *S* to sexual intercourse that exonerates *A* of criminal liability for rape. In contrast, the arresting officer in his report used consent in a factual sense, that is, as a synonym for the kind of mere acquiescence or submission that does not necessarily authorize *A* to do what he seeks to do. Blair's attorney pounced on the ambiguity in an apparent effort to confuse the jury, forcing the officer to repeat over and over again what he said in his report—namely, that *S* 'consented' to sexual intercourse. Sensing the attorney's motives, the police officer responded that though he, indeed, reported that *S* 'consented' to sexual intercourse, he meant instead to write that she 'submitted':

> Q. [The victim] stated to you, and you stated in your report of that interview that, quote, Rich said that he wanted to have sex, and she consented to this; is that correct?
>
> A. The consent part, that was my wording. The report was typed—
>
> Q. Is that correct, the quote that I have stated?
>
> A. That is what I typed in my report. That is not what she told me verbatim, no.
>
> Q. Officer Kaiser, . . . you have here in your report, if I may read it to you, that Rich said that he wanted to have sex and she consented to this. And goes on to state, Rich then commented that he would like to have sex with her daughter. [The victim] became upset at that comment. She left the bedroom, went upstairs to get her daughter, . . . she and [her daughter] left the residence by way of the outside stairs; isn't that correct?
>
> A. Yes.
>
> Q. You don't mention in your report in that area with that sentence, you don't qualify the word 'consent' in any way to mean that she submitted; do you?
>
> A. No, in that—as I say, that was my terminology. That was, I believe, an error on my part. 'I submitted' would have been the proper word, rather than 'consent'.[2]

One must sympathize with the police officer in *Blair*. The defense attorney endeavored to distort the police officer's reported statement about consent, implying that the officer said something that the defense attorney knew perfectly well he did not mean. When the police officer reported that *S* 'consented,' he meant precisely what he said. He was using consent factually to denote that *S* reluctantly acquiesced to sexual intercourse in response to Blair's alleged threats, because she regarded it as the lesser of two evils under the circumstances. Obviously, the police officer did not mean what the trial judge meant by consent; he did not mean that the woman *lawfully* acquiesced, because if he thought she had lawfully acquiesced, he would not have proceeded to arrest Blair and charge him with sexual assault. Yet because the police officer realized that the defense counsel was exploiting the ambiguity to mislead the jury about what he meant, the officer was forced to repudiate a perfectly sensible use of 'consent' on his part by stating that he meant to say 'submitted'.

Boro: Equating the 'Knowledge' Required for Prescriptive Consent with the Minimal Criteria of Factual Consent

We saw in Chapter 1 that in order for *S* to factually consent to *x*—that is, in order for *S* to choose *x*, whether in mind or expression, as that which she prefers under the circumstances or that about which she is sufficiently indifferent to be willing to leave its occurrence to *A*—a person must either possess or express that she knows that it is, indeed, *x* that she is choosing. In addition, we saw in Chapter 5 that, in order for a person to *prescriptively* consent to *x*, a person must possess such additional knowledge as the jurisdiction deems necessary to justify leaving the choice to her for purposes of the criminal law. To be sure, a jurisdiction may consciously take the view that, for purposes of prescriptive consent to *x*, a person is entitled only to as much information as is needed for factual consent to *x*. In that event, equating prescriptive consent with factual consent is hardly a mistake, much less a conceptual mistake. Nevertheless, rulings defining prescriptive 'knowledge' by reference to factual standards are sometimes so anomalous, and leave decisionmakers feeling so uncomfortable, as to suggest that the rulings are products not of clear-headed judgment on the decisionmakers' part, but of their mistakenly conflating legal consent with factual consent.[3]

Recall the *Boro* case from Chapter 5. The defendant, Daniel Boro, masquerading as a physician, deceived the victim, Ms. R., into believing that she was suffering from a fatal illness that could only be cured by sexual intercourse with an anonymous 'donor,' namely, himself now secretly masquerading as a donor. Ms. R., terrified that she would otherwise die, submitted to sexual intercourse with him. Boro was apprehended and charged with rape. He challenged the charge, arguing that by agreeing to the proposed therapy, Ms. R. consented to sexual intercourse within the meaning of the law.[4] The prosecutor, denying that Ms. R. consented, relied upon the following definition of consent in the California statute: '"Consent" shall be defined to mean positive cooperation in act or attitude pursuant to an act of free will. The person must act freely and voluntarily and have knowledge of the nature of the act or transaction involved.' The court rejected the prosecutor's argument and dismissed the rape charge. The court ruled that the statutory definition of consent was not intended to alter the traditional rule that with respect to the various ways in which a woman can be defrauded into sexual intercourse, only fraud 'in the factum,' and not fraud 'in the inducement,' vitiates consent as a defense to rape.

The court's analysis in *Boro* raises two related questions: How does the court distinguish factum from inducement? And how does the distinction bear upon the legal issue as to whether Ms. R. consented for purposes of the law of rape? The *Boro* court answered the first question by defining the 'factum' of rape narrowly to consist solely of that in which the law indisputably requires that a person acquiesce if her acquiescence is to constitute a defense, namely, the fact of *sexual intercourse*.[5] By that definition, a woman is a victim of fraud in the factum if she is defrauded into thinking that she is submitting to something *other* than sexual intercourse, while she is a victim of fraud in the inducement if she is defrauded into thinking that submitting to what she knows to be sexual intercourse will benefit her. To illustrate the difference, the *Boro* court contrasted the fraud in *Boro* with the fraud in the earlier case of *California v. Minkowski* (California 1962).[6] The victims in *Minkowski* were three young girls who suffered from menstrual cramps. Minkowski, the family physician, took advantage of the girls' trust and naiveté by deceiving them into thinking that he was conducting a gynecological examination when in reality he was subjecting them to sexual intercourse. Minkowski asked each of the girls to bend over the examination table with surgical gowns drawn over her head and her feet spread apart. He told them that he would be inserting gynecological instruments for purposes of treatment. Instead, after first inserting a metal instrument, he substituted another, which they said 'felt different' and which they did not realize was his penis. The fraud in *Minkowski* was in the factum, the *Boro* court said, because it deceived the girls about the very 'fact' to which complainants must indisputably acquiesce if their acquiescence is to constitute a defense to rape—the fact of sexual intercourse. In contrast, Ms. R. knew that she was submitting to sexual intercourse. She was deceived, not as to *whether* she was submitting to sexual intercourse, but as to *why*. She was deceived, not about the fact of sexual intercourse, but about its therapeutic value. The fraud upon Ms. R. was in the 'inducement,' the court said, because it falsely induced her to engage in an act that she knew to be sexual intercourse for benefits that turned out to be nonexistent.

The more difficult question, which *Boro* answers less well, is legal in nature. What is the relationship between fraud in the factum, as the *Boro* court defines it, and the legal issue whether Ms. R. 'consented' for purposes of the statute? Why is the distinction between 'factum' and 'inducement' dispositive of the legal question of a defendant's criminal responsibility? Why should a sexual predator like Daniel Boro, who terrified Ms. R. into having sexual intercourse with a stranger for fear that she would otherwise die of disease, be exonerated of sexual assault? Would the legislature be wrong to declare such conduct to be without the victim's prescriptive consent? If not, then why does the *Boro* court hold that it was with Ms. R.'s prescriptive consent?

The court's reasoning is revealing. Besides what it concedes is 'scant authority' on the issue, the court relies on two independent arguments. The first argument is a practical one. The court does not deny that Ms. R. was brutalized. On the contrary, the court repeatedly refers to Ms. R. as a 'victim,' sympathizes with the 'heartless cruelty' she suffered, and even refers once to her travail as 'rape'. The court justifies its judgment, however, by arguing that in cases in which women know they are engaging in sexual intercourse, it is difficult to 'draw' a legal 'line' between egregious cases like Ms. R.'s, on the one hand, and more debatable cases, where women are induced into sexual intercourse by false 'promises of travel, fame, celebrity, and the like,' on the other.[7] In the absence of a clear line between a 'rapist' and a 'seducer,' the court reasons that prudence dictates that it rely on the distinction between fraud in the factum and fraud in the inducement, as the court defines them.

The court's argument possesses some force. California had once had a statute that treated seduction by false promises of marriage as equivalent to rape. But the legislature had repealed the statute shortly before *Boro* arose, thereby indicating that it did not wish to punish all fraud in the inducement as rape. Accordingly, to punish Boro, the court would have had to draw a legal line between criminal rape, on the one hand, and noncriminal seduction, on the other. The weakness in *Boro*'s reasoning, however, is that legally Ms. R.'s case differed dramatically from most deceptive seductions. Daniel Boro did not merely mislead Ms. R. He led her to believe that unless she submitted to sexual intercourse, she would die. He put her in fear for her life, much as if he had directly threatened her life. In terms of 'line drawing,' *Boro* is the easiest case of rape by fraud because it has more in common with rape by threat of force than with rape by fraud. It is a line regarding legal consent that other courts have had no trouble drawing. Indeed, it is a line that the California legislature itself found easy to draw. Shocked by the decision in *Boro*, the legislature responded by providing that fraud in the inducement that causes a woman to fear for her life vitiates consent to sexual intercourse for purposes of the criminal law.[8]

The *Boro* court's second argument is the more interesting because there the court appears to reduce the question 'Did Ms. R. prescriptively consent to sexual intercourse?' to the question 'Did she factually consent to sexual intercourse?' The difference between the fraud in *Minkowski* and the fraud in *Boro*, the court says, is that the girls in *Minkowski* did '*not consent*' to sexual intercourse, while Ms. R. *did* 'consent' to sexual intercourse, albeit because of 'fraud'. What does the court mean in distinguishing the *Minkowski* girls, who did 'not' consent to sexual intercourse, from Ms. R. who gave 'consent induced by fraud'? How does the distinction bear upon whether Ms. R.'s consent counts for purposes of the criminal law? The answer lies in what the court means by consent to sexual intercourse. The court cannot be using consent in a legal sense because if it were, it would be begging the question it purports to be addressing. To say that Ms. R. legally consented to sexual intercourse while the *Minkowski* girls did not is to state a conclusion, not an argument. Rather, the court must be using consent in a factual sense. If so, the court is right in several respects. Using consent in a factual sense, the court is right to say that the *Minkowski* girls did not consent to sexual intercourse. The *Minkowski* girls did not choose sexual intercourse for themselves either in mind or expression, because they were unaware, and the defendant realized they were unaware, that the defendant was going to have sexual intercourse with them. Using consent factually, the *Boro* court is also right that Ms. R. did consent to sexual intercourse, for she deliberately chose sexual intercourse over the alternatives she believed were open to her. Indeed, when Boro, masquerading as a physician, momentarily threatened to cancel the 'therapy,' Ms. R. strove fervently to persuade him to carry on as planned.

More interesting is what the *Boro* court does next or, more accurately, what it does *not* do next. It will be recalled that in contrasting the *Minkowski* girls' *lack* of consent with Ms. R.'s 'fraudulently induced consent,' the *Boro* court uses 'consent' factually. It will be recalled that the *Boro* court further reasons that Ms. R.'s 'consent' amounted to 'legally recognized consent'. One would expect, therefore, that in moving from the factual to the legal—in moving from the 'is' of factual consent to the 'ought' of legally recognized consent—the court would buttress the move with supporting legal argument. One would expect the court to explain why it deems factual consent to sexual intercourse to be legally sufficient in *Boro*, that is, why it concludes that Ms. R. did not suffer an injury that the rape statute was designed to prevent. Instead of providing such reasons, the court seems to think it is not obliged to, because it seems to equate the statute's legal reference to 'consent' to sexual intercourse with the quite distinct existence of factual consent to sexual intercourse.

Salsman: Equating the 'Competence' for Prescriptive Consent with the Minimal Criteria of Factual Consent

Just as jurisdictions typically require additional levels of knowledge over and above the minimal knowledge needed for factual consent, so, too, jurisdictions typically require additional levels of 'competence' over and above the minimal capacities needed for factual consent. Thus, a high-school girl who passionately engages in sexual intercourse with her college-age boyfriend clearly possesses the minimum knowledge and capacity that persons must possess in order to be able to choose sexual intercourse as that which they prefer for themselves under the circumstances, *i.e.*, knowledge that they are engaging in sexual intercourse and a conscious preference for it, all things considered. And such a girl may also possess the additional levels of *freedom, and knowledge* that are required to transmute her factual consent into prescriptive consent. But unless the girl is *of age* for purposes of laws of statutory rape, she lacks the additional levels of *competence* that laws everywhere require for her factual acquiescence to amount to prescriptive consent, that is, for her factual consent to constitute a defense to a charge of statutory rape against her boyfriend. Occasionally, however, jurisdictions reduce the requirements of prescriptive competence to the minimal criteria of factual consent in ways that suggest that rather than making conscious judgments about prescriptive consent, they are unthinkingly conflating the requirements of prescriptive consent with the criteria of factual consent.

The most poignant examples involve persons who are mentally retarded. Every jurisdiction, in one way or another, makes it an offense for an actor to have sexual intercourse with a subject who, because of mental deficiency, is 'incapable' of consent.[9] Needless to say, the consent to which jurisdictions refer is necessarily *legal* in nature because it is consent that jurisdictions deem sufficient to constitute a defense to rape. By the same token, the mental 'capability' that jurisdictions require as conditions of prescriptive consent is also necessarily legal in nature: it is the mental competence that jurisdictions believe suffices to allow a subject to decide for herself whether to engage in sexual intercourse. Some jurisdictions appear to be fully conscious of the difference between the minimal capacities needed for factual consent and the competence required for prescriptive consent. Thus, New York requires as a condition of prescriptive consent that a person possess *more* than the minimal capacities needed for factual consent—that is, more than mere consciousness that she is engaging in sexual intercourse. New York requires that the alleged victim not only understand the 'physiological nature' of 'coitus,' but also understand 'its significance and its consequences,' including its 'moral quality,' that is, 'how it will be regarded in the framework of the societal environment and taboos to which a person will be exposed'.[10]

In contrast, other jurisdictions reduce the prescriptive standard of ability to consent to the same minimal shape it would possess if it were factual in nature, thereby raising the possibility that they may be mistakenly conflating the two standards. *Salsman v. Kentucky* (1978) is a good example.[11] The alleged victim in *Salsman* was a 24-year-old woman with an I.Q. of 56 and a mental age of ten who, because of deafness, had to read lips to be understood. She was home alone on a visit to her mother when David Salsman, a milkman, entered the house. After placing milk and bread in the refrigerator, Salsman asked the woman, who was sitting in a rocking chair, to have sexual relations with him. She refused. Salsman then lifted her up from the chair, removed her clothes, and had vaginal and anal intercourse with her. He testified that he did not threaten her or use physical force against her, and that she did not resist other than saying, 'No.' Salsman was tried for third-degree rape, an offense that Kentucky defined as the crime of having sexual intercourse with a person who, because of a 'mental defect,' is 'incapable of consent,' that is, 'incapable of appraising the nature of her conduct'. Salsman was convicted at trial. But the Kentucky court of appeals reversed, holding that the alleged victim, with her I.Q. of 57 and mental age of ten years, did not suffer from a 'mental defect' that rendered her 'incapable of consent'. The court held that the alleged victim was mentally able to consent to sexual intercourse under Kentucky law because, despite her severe mental retardation, she was able to comprehend the sole thing by which such competence is measured in Kentucky, namely, that 'Salsman was seeking to perform sexual acts upon her'.[12]

To be sure, the alleged victim responded to Salsman's overtures by saying 'no' rather than 'yes'. But, in deciding whether she was competent to consent, the Kentucky court did not focus on whether she exercised her capacities by saying 'no' as opposed to 'yes'. The court held her to be competent to consent to sexual intercourse for purposes of Kentucky law because, regardless of whether she said 'yes' or 'no,' she was not too retarded to realize that she was saying it to *sexual intercourse*. The Kentucky court thus implicitly reduced a prescriptive standard to a factual standard: it reduced the prescriptive standard that governs the competence of *severely retarded* persons *in Kentucky* to consent to sexual intercourse to the minimal factual standard that governs the capacity of *any* person *anywhere* to consent to sexual intercourse, namely, consciousness that one is engaging in 'sexual intercourse' as opposed to other forms of conduct.

Now it is possible that the *Salsman* court was fully aware of the differences between prescriptive consent and factual consent, and that the *Salsman* court reduced the former to the latter because it was firmly of the view that severely retarded persons are entitled to no greater protection against reckless choices than nonretarded persons are. Yet it is hard to believe that a Kentucky court would have taken the same view with respect to a ten-year-old girl who is nonretarded. That is, it is hard to believe that a Kentucky court would have taken the position that a ten-year-old girl who is old enough to know what sexual intercourse is, and old enough to desire it, must also be old enough to know whether it is in her interests. That the *Salsman* court took that position with respect to a retarded girl with the mental age of a ten-year-old suggests that the court mistakenly equated the girl's factual consent with the standards that ought to govern her prescriptive consent.

The *Salsman* court is not the only court that has reduced prescriptive competence to factual capacity in ways that suggest that it may be conceptually confused.[13] Moreover, if the ruling in *Salsman* resulted from confusion, it was confusion that the Kentucky legislature had facilitated by the way it had defined mental incompetence to consent. The Kentucky legislature, it will be recalled, provided that a person is mentally incompetent to consent to sexual intercourse if she is mentally 'incapable of the nature of the conduct'. The problem with the latter standard is that it is ambiguous as to whether 'appraising the nature of the conduct' means merely understanding that the conduct is *sexual intercourse* or whether it means understanding the significance of sexual intercourse sufficiently to justify the state's allowing a retarded person to take responsibility for choosing it for herself.

To illustrate the difference, consider the contrasting ways in which the courts of Virginia and Washington interpret what it means in rape cases for a mentally retarded person to be '[c]apable of appraising the nature of the conduct'. The alleged victim in *Adkins v. Virginia* (1995)[14] was a 16-year-old girl to whom the Virginia court of appeals referred to as 'Teresa'. Teresa, who had been retarded from birth, had an I.Q. of 58 and the mental age of a ten-year-old. Several days before the charged offense, Teresa met the 27-year-old Adkins at the mall and gave him her telephone number. One day before the offense, Teresa's mother heard Teresa talking with Adkins on the telephone and told him, 'Teresa is mentally retarded. Leave her alone.' On the day of the offense, Teresa's mother went shopping, leaving Teresa at home. Teresa knew that her mother did not want her to talk with or to see Adkins. Nevertheless, Teresa called Adkins and asked him to pick her up. The two met and went to Adkins' apartment, where they had sexual intercourse, had dinner, and had intercourse again. When the police arrived, they found Adkins and Teresa hiding in the apartment. Teresa told the police that she was hiding because she did not want to go home. The jury, finding that Teresa suffered a 'mental incapacity' that 'prevent[ed]' her 'from understanding the nature or consequences of the sexual act involved,' found Adkins guilty. Interestingly, the Virginia court of appeals reversed, holding that Teresa possessed the 'mental capacity' to 'understand the nature or consequences of the sexual act involved' because she knew enough to realize that she was 'making love' (as she put it at trial) and that she could become pregnant from 'making love'. The court of appeals thus implicitly held that the prescriptive competence of mentally retarded persons to consent to sexual intercourse in Virginia is no greater than the factual capacity of the non-retarded, namely, awareness that one is engaging in 'sexual' intercourse, *i.e.*, intercourse that can result in pregnancy, together with a desire for it, however 'unwise' the decision may be.[15]

Admittedly, one cannot be certain that the Virginia court, in holding that Teresa was prescriptively competent to consent to sexual intercourse, was misled by the fact that Teresa was capable of choosing sexual intercourse over the alternatives. Nevertheless, it is possible that the Virginia court was confused, particularly when its decision is juxtaposed with the very different way the Washington supreme court construed the identical statutory language the year before. The alleged victim in *Washington v. Ortega-Martinez* (1994)[16] was a 30-year-old woman with an I.Q. in the 40s and a mental age between five and nine. As in *Adkins*, a jury in *Ortega-Martinez* found the defendant guilty of having sexual intercourse with a woman who, because of her 'mental incapacity,' was 'prevented from understanding the nature or consequences of the act of sexual intercourse'. Again, as in *Adkins*, a state court of appeals in *Ortega-Martinez* reversed the conviction, ruling that because the woman knew she was engaging in 'sexual intercourse' and that it could result in pregnancy, she necessarily 'underst[ood] the nature and consequences' of her conduct. In contrast to *Adkins*, however, the prosecutor in *Ortega-Martinez* took a further appeal, arguing that the court of appeals had adopted too narrow a view of prescriptive competence. The Washington supreme court agreed with the prosecutor, holding that the prescriptive purpose of the statutory phrase, *i.e.*, 'understanding the nature and consequences of the act of sexual intercourse,' is to protect the mentally disabled from exploitation. A retarded person, the court said, must possess more than a 'superficial' understanding of the 'physical mechanics of sexual intercourse'. Rather, she must possess a 'meaningful' understanding.[17] Thus, in contrast to the Virginia court in *Adkins*, the Washington court interpreted prescriptive competence by reference to the purposes it serves, *i.e.*, to protect retarded persons from exploitation. And in doing so, it held that prescriptive consent requires levels of competence over and above the capacity needed for factual consent.

Confusing Attitudinal Consent with Expressive Consent

The confusion we previously examined consisted of the category mistake of unwittingly equating one conception of consent with another. However, category mistakes regarding consent are not confined to unwitting substitutions of that kind. They can also consist of unwittingly combining distinct conceptions of consent, (as well as the distinct legal functions they serve) into amalgams that serve neither function. An example is the practice in some jurisdictions of defining the defense of consent to rape to consist of neither prescriptive *attitudinal* acquiescence alone nor prescriptive *expressive* acquiescence alone but, rather, an amalgam of the two.

It will be recalled from Chapters 1 and 2 that *S*'s factual consent to conduct can take two distinct forms: *S*'s subjective acquiescence to the conduct ('factual attitudinal consent'); or *S*'s objective expression of subjective acquiescence ('factual expressive consent'). We also saw in Chapter 4 that in their respective prescriptive forms, attitudinal consent and expressive consent serve distinct functions in criminal law: *S*'s prescriptive attitudinal consent to *A*'s conduct negates the primary harm to *S* from which the criminal offense at issue seeks to protect *S*. In turn, *S*'s prescriptive expressive consent affects whether *A*'s conduct is culpably motivated and, specifically, whether *A* knows or should know that he is subjecting *S* to the primary harm from which the law seeks to protect her. Occasionally, and perhaps unwittingly, jurisdictions amalgamate the two conceptions of consent in ways that serve neither function. The consequence is that they treat *A* as acting with *S*'s prescriptive consent even in cases in which *A* knowingly subjects *S* to the very harms from which the law of rape seeks to protect her.

To begin, consider a case that arises, not in a jurisdiction that falls prey to the mistake, but in a jurisdiction that succeeds in avoiding it. Consider *California v. St. Andrew* (1980).[18] Clifford St. Andrew was a hospital attendant working the night shift in the psychiatric ward of a San Francisco hospital in which the complainant, Mrs. S., was a patient. Clifford St. Andrew had participated a few days before in 'sheeting' Mrs. S., that is, in wrapping her in hospital sheets in order to restrain her from harming herself. Mrs. S. testified that on the night in question, St. Andrew entered and left her hospital room a number of times over a two-hour period, during which he made increasingly overt sexual advances to her, culminating in acts of cunnilingus and sexual intercourse to which she submitted. She testified that, although St. Andrew said nothing during two hours except for an early remark that she had 'good stomach muscles' and that he would return to give her a body rub, she was 'afraid he would strike me', 'afraid he would smother me', and afraid that he would have her 'sheeted' and locked alone in a room with him. Accordingly, she said, feeling too frightened to protest or resist, she silently submitted to St. Andrew's two sexual acts. St. Andrew was charged and convicted of rape, but because of errors at trial, he was ordered to be retried. In reviewing the evidence for purposes of retrial, the California court of appeals identified three features that, it happens, are characteristic of cases in which mistakes occur: (1) the evidence sufficed to show that Mrs. S. genuinely believed that if she did not submit to sexual intercourse with St. Andrew, he would 'strike' her, 'strangle' her, or have her 'sheeted'; (2) the evidence also sufficed to show that Mrs. S's fear, though genuine, had 'no basis in fact' and, hence, was 'unreasonable'; and, finally, (3) the evidence sufficed to show that, despite the unreasonableness of Mrs. S's fears, St. Andrew was fully *aware* of her fears.

Jurisdictions differ in the way they address cases like *St. Andrew*, but they all have two goals in mind: to protect persons such as Mrs. S. from the harm of submitting to sexual intercourse out of fear of death or serious bodily harm, and to protect defendants from being punished for harms that they had no reason to know they were inflicting. Recently, some jurisdictions have addressed those dual goals in the context of closed institutions, *e.g.*, prisons, jails, hospitals, by enacting statutes that operate prophylactically to protect institutionalized persons from abuse by punishing any custodian who has sexual intercourse with any inmate, regardless of the circumstances—that is, regardless of whether the defendant resorted to force, fraud, or exploitation.[19] California, however, possesses no such statute. Instead, it uses more conventional means to address the two goals of protecting victims such as Mrs. S. who submit to sexual intercourse out of genuine fear of death or serious bodily injury, and of protecting defendants who may have no reason to know that they are eliciting sexual intercourse by means of such fears. California does so by addressing the two goals separately. First, California inquires into the alleged victim's state of mind, inquiring whether she submitted to sexual intercourse out of 'fear' that she would otherwise suffer death or unlawful bodily injury.[20] An alleged victim's fears are entirely a function of her subjective state of mind and depend neither upon whether the fears are 'reasonable' nor upon whether reasonable observers in a defendant's position would have been aware of them.[21] Accordingly, once California determines that a woman has submitted to sexual intercourse out of subjective fear that she would otherwise suffer death or unlawful bodily harm, however irrational her fear may be, California recognizes her as having suffered the harm that its rape statutes are designed to prevent.

Second, if California finds that the woman is harmed, it makes further inquiry into what was communicated to the defendant regarding her state of mind, or what would have been communicated to a reasonable observer in the defendant's position. California holds defendants responsible if they knew that their victims submitted out of fear of bodily harm or if reasonable observers in their position would have known. Defendants do not escape liability simply because victims' fears were 'unreasonable'. Rather, a defendant is guilty of having sexual intercourse with a victim who fears bodily injury even if the fear is 'unreasonable', provided that he 'knew' or should have known of the victim's 'subjective fear' and 'took advantage of it'.[22] As the court put it in *St. Andrew*, 'One who takes advantage of a victim's unreasonable fears of violence should not escape punishment any more than the swindler who cheats gullible people by false statements which they should have found incredible . . . .'[23]

Significantly, however, California appears to be among a minority of states that address cases like *St. Andrew* by making separate inquiries into an alleged victim's state of mind, on the one hand, and the defendant's awareness of it, on the other. Most states collapse the two inquiries into one. They take the position that a woman who submits to sexual intercourse out of genuine fear of death or serious bodily harm shall be deemed to prescriptively consent to it as long as her fear is unreasonable.[24] As a consequence, they fail to protect women who suffer the harm of submitting to sexual intercourse out of fear of death or serious bodily harm, and they fail to punish assailants who knowingly cause such harm. The State of Maryland, for example, defines rape as the offense of having sexual intercourse with a person 'without [her] consent' and by 'threat of force,' including the act of inducing a woman to submit to sexual intercourse by fear of death or serious bodily injury.[25] Yet Maryland also takes the position that a woman's submission is without her consent only if it is 'reasonable' for her to fear that she will otherwise be killed or suffer serious bodily injury.[26] Maryland thus exonerates, on grounds of consent, defendants who have sexual intercourse with women who they know are submitting for fear of death or serious bodily injury, provided the women's fears are unreasonable.[27]

One can only speculate as to why Maryland adheres to the 'reasonable fear' test of non-consent. For, like other jurisdictions, Maryland adheres to the test without explaining it. In all likelihood, however, the test is intended to ensure that a woman's subjective fear has sufficient basis in fact to alert reasonable observers in the defendant's position to her fears.[28] If so, the test reduces to a single standard of 'reasonable fear' the two elements for which California makes separate provisions, namely, (1) that the victim have genuine fears of death or serious bodily injury, and (2) that the defendant or reasonable observers in the defendant's position be aware of her fears. The problem with the single standard is that by requiring that a victim's fears be reasonable, it exculpates a defendant who is fully aware of his victim's fears, simply because reasonable observers in his position would not be aware of them.

The more interesting question is, why? Why would Maryland adhere to a rule that acquits defendants who know that their victims are submitting to sexual intercourse out of genuine fear of death or grievous bodily injury? It is possible, of course, that Maryland is fully conscious of what it is doing. Maryland may simply have no sympathy with women who are unreasonably fearful and, hence, no desire to invoke its rape laws to protect such women against men who exploit their fears to ravish them. Yet that seems unlikely, given that Maryland is eager to use its fraud laws to protect the elderly and other unreasonably gullible persons from predators who exploit their credulousness to impoverish them. It is also possible that Maryland uses the test to screen out cases in which women who claim to have submitted to sexual intercourse out of fear are simply lying. Yet that also seems unlikely, given the alternative of instructing jurors under the California test that they shall not convict unless they are persuaded beyond a reasonable doubt that alleged victims are telling the truth about their fears. The more interesting possibility is that in adopting the position that a woman prescriptively consents to sexual intercourse unless (i) she genuinely fears death or serious bodily injury, *and* (ii) her fear is reasonable, Maryland unwittingly falls prey to the conceptual confusion of treating the *separate* legal functions that are served by the *separate* conceptions of attitudinal consent and expressive consent as if they were functions of a conception of consent that is *unitary* in nature.

Confusing Actual Consent with Imputed Consent

We saw in Chapter 7 that consent can be used in a legal sense to refer not to instances of actual acquiescence to x that occur under conditions that suffice to constitute criminal defenses, but to legal fictions of such acquiescence. To recall the difference, consider the way the state of Delaware would treat the following, hypothetical case:

> ***'The Fastidious Football Fan'.*** *S* is a football fan who loves going to high school games but hates being pushed or physically pressed by strangers. To avoid physical contact, *S* makes it a practice to arrive after a game has begun, to sit in an aisle seat, and to leave before the game has ended. Recently, however, he attended a game that was officially halted in the third quarter because of an approaching thunder and lightning storm. As the crowd filled the aisles, *S* repeated loudly what he had announced upon entering the stadium: 'I don't want anyone to touch me, and I will call the police if anyone does.' Despite *S*'s warnings, a number of persons, including *A*, who was being pushed from behind, pressed up against *S*. When later asked about it, *A* admitted that, with effort, he could have held his ground against the crowd behind him and avoided pressing against *S*, but that he did not bother because, as he put it, 'It was a situation that we were all in together.'
>
> *S* took down *A*'s name and formally requested that the Delaware district attorney charge *A* with misdemeanor assault. Assault in Delaware is the offense of 'intentionally touch[ing]' another person, either with a part of one's body or with any instrument, knowing that one is thereby likely to cause offense or alarm to such other person.[29] The district attorney refused, stating that, although *A*'s conduct would have otherwise constituted an assault against *S*, *S* 'consented' to the assault within the meaning of Delaware penal code section 451. Section 451 states: 'In any prosecution for an offense, it is a defense that the victim consented to the act done . . . . Any person who enters the presence of other people consents to the normal physical contacts incident to such presence.'[30]

Notice that, when the district attorney states that *S* consented to being touched, he is using consent in a legal sense to refer to *A*'s defense to assault, but he is not using it prescriptively. The district attorney does not mean that *S* subjectively acquiesced to being touched or that *S* objectively expressed such subjective acquiescence, for *S* did everything he could at the time to avoid being touched. Rather, the district attorney is using consent as a legal fiction to mimic the legal effects that would exist if *S* had prescriptively consented. *S* did something, *i.e.*, he voluntarily attended a crowded football game, that Delaware regards as being legally inconsistent with his being able to complain about crowd pressure. Accordingly, Delaware treats *S as if* he had prescriptively consented to being touched, while knowing full well that there was nothing that *S* could have done, short of not attending the football game, to evade the legal fiction of having consented to being touched.

'The Fastidious Football Fan' is an illustration of imputed consent, not of *confusion* about imputed consent. Nevertheless, the use of legal fictions of consent can lead to conceptual confusion and, specifically, to confusing imputed consent with prescriptive consent. The latter confusion is apparent in cases in which courts have repudiated the so-called 'marital rape exemption'. With one possible exception, the confusion does not appear to have caused courts to repudiate marital exemptions that they would otherwise have retained. But it has misled courts into thinking that the arguments they marshal possess greater validity than they do.

The marital exemption, it will be recalled, is the rule that, although a husband can be guilty of committing other crimes of violence against his wife, he cannot be guilty of raping his wife.[31] The exemption can be framed in two distinct ways. Some jurisdictions frame it as an exception to what otherwise constitutes rape. Thus, until 1984 New York defined first-degree rape as the act of 'engag[ing] in sexual intercourse with a female . . . by forcible compulsion', provided that the 'female' is 'not married to the actor' (meaning that if a female *is* married to him, an actor *may* use forcible compulsion). [32] Similarly, until 1977, rape was defined in Maryland as the act of a man of 'having . . . carnal knowledge of a female over the age of ten years by force without the consent and against the will of the victim', provided that the intercourse was 'unlawful' ('unlawful' being understood to be carnal knowledge of persons who were not married to each other).[33] In contrast, other jurisdictions frame the marital exemption, not as an exception to what otherwise constitutes rape, but as an interpretation of the term 'consent' for purposes of rape statutes. Thus, until 1976, rape was defined in England as a man's having sexual intercourse with a woman 'without her consent', and women were deemed to have 'consented' to have sexual intercourse with their husbands by virtue of marrying them.[34] Regardless of the way in which the exemption is framed, however, its defenders commonly justify it in terms of 'consent'.[35] As Matthew Hale famously put it 1671, 'The husband cannot be guilty of a rape committed by himself upon his lawful wife, for by their mutual matrimonial consent and contract the wife hath given up herself in this kind unto her husband, which she cannot retract.'[36]

Significantly, when Hale asserts that by marrying, women prospectively consent to sexual intercourse with their husbands for purposes of the law of rape, Hale is using consent in the same way Delaware uses it when Delaware states that 'any person who enters the presence of other people *consents* to the normal physical contacts incident to such presence.'[37] Hale's maxim is not a factual assertion about what women subjectively think as they engage in marriage, any more than Delaware law is a factual assertion about what people subjectively think as they 'enter the presence of other people'. Nor is Hale's maxim a factual assertion about what all women implicitly communicate about their subjective thoughts when they marry. For if it were, women would be able to negate any implicit communication by explicitly announcing that they possess no such thoughts, much as the 'Fastidious Football Fan' tried to negate any implicit messages by making it explicit as he entered the stadium that he would take offense at being pressed by the crowd. Rather, much like the Delaware rule, Hale's maxim is an assertion about how the law treats women who engage in marriage, regardless of what the women subjectively think or objectively express at the time they marry. Hale's maxim declares that the law treats women who marry *as if* they had prospectively consent to have sexual intercourse with their husbands whenever their husbands happen to demand it. Women cannot negate the force of the maxim by anything they actually feel or explicitly say about sexual intercourse at the time of marriage or thereafter, because the maxim is not premised on what they actually feel or explicitly say. Like Delaware's rule, Hale's maxim is a legal fiction of prescriptive consent, not an instance of actual prescriptive consent.

The marital exemption has suffered a checkered history since Hale declared it to be part of English common law. No jurisdiction in England or the United States retains it in the stark form in which Hale stated it.[38] Some jurisdictions, including England, have abolished it altogether,[39] while others have abolished it with respect to most varieties of rape, retaining the marital exemption only with respect to the offense of having sexual intercourse with a woman who is underage and/or the offense of having sexual intercourse with a woman who is mentally incompetent.[40] Still others have abolished it with respect to marriages that are in the process of formal dissolution in one way or another, *e.g.*, where a spouse has filed for divorce, obtained a separation agreement, moved out of the family home, or obtained a protection order.[41] The significant cases for our purposes are ones in which courts have either invalidated[42] or disavowed[43] the marital exemption by criticizing the soundness of Hale's maxim. Although the courts in these cases all had independent reasons to reject the marital exemption, they relied on two fallacies: (1) the fallacy that, rather than being a legal fiction of acquiescence by women, Hale's consent is a reference to actual acquiescence by women and, as such, can be discredited by being shown to be empirically inaccurate; and, conversely, (2) the fallacy that, if Hale's consent is revealed to be legal fiction, it can be discredited simply on that ground alone.

The opinion of the English Court of Appeal in *R. v. R.* (1990-91),[44] and that of the Massachusetts supreme court in *Massachusetts v. Chretien* (1981),[45] both illustrate the latter fallacy, *viz.*, the fallacy of assuming that it suffices to discredit a conception of legal consent by revealing that it constitutes a fiction of prescriptive consent. The English and Massachusetts courts both held that, although the marital exemption had once been part of their common law, it had ceased to be so, in part because Hale's assertion about consent had been revealed to be a 'fiction'. Thus, the lower English court in *R. v. R.* reasoned that Hale's notion of consent must be a 'fiction' because it is 'offensive' and 'senseless' to think that when a woman marries, she 'subjectively' commits herself to have sexual intercourse with her husband 'at any time, whether she is willing or not'.[46] The English Court of Appeal, in turn, agreed that Hale's notion of consent was a legal fiction, and it rejected Hale's consent on that ground alone: '[Hale's "consent"] can never have been other than a fiction, and fiction is a poor basis for the criminal law.'[47] Similarly, the Massachusetts court reasoned that because 'there is no reason why agreement to enter a relation of intimacy necessarily means consent to intercourse on demand', Hale's consent is 'essentially fictive'; and that because it is 'essentially fictive', it should be rejected.[48]

The English and Massachusetts courts are right, of course, that Hale's consent is a fiction of prescriptive consent to sexual intercourse. But they are wrong to think that in order to be legally justified, conceptions of consent must be prescriptive in nature. Penal codes are rife with instances of imputed consent that are legally sound, including the Delaware statute referred to in 'The Fastidious Football Fan'. To be sure, because legal fictions are not predicated on acts of actual acquiescence, their underlying rationales are not transparent. Yet it is a fallacy to think that because the rationales that underlie legal fictions are nontransparent, the rationales must be spurious. Every legal fiction is, in effect, a legal rule; and, as with other rules, legal fictions purport implicitly to be grounded upon supporting rationales. It follows, therefore, that one cannot effectively criticize a legal fiction by declaring it to be a fiction, any more than one can effectively criticize a rule by declaring it to be a *rule*. To criticize a legal fiction, one must approach it in the same way one would approach any other rule: one must examine it critically to discover and assess its underlying rationale.

With respect to Hale's maxim, the original rationale is unclear. The most plausible explanation is probably one that Anne Coughlin and others advance.[49] Coughlin argues that the reason that rape was originally regarded as a capital crime at common law was that it involved not only forced sexual intercourse, but also *illicit* sexual intercourse, namely, sexual intercourse of a kind that even when *not* forced was both shameful and criminal for both parties, *e.g.*, adultery and fornication. The sole kind of sexual intercourse that when not forced was neither shameful nor criminal for either party was sexual intercourse between lawfully married spouses. The reason a man could not be guilty of raping his wife, and, hence, the reason to construct a fiction of prescriptive consent, was that a husband who forced his wife to have sexual intercourse was not forcing her to become party to a kind of sexual intercourse that was otherwise shameful and criminal. If Coughlin is right about the original rationale for Hale's maxim, the maxim is anachronistic, for adultery and fornication are no longer punished as criminal offenses in most jurisdictions. And its being anachronistic would have been a good reason for the English and Massachusetts courts to reject it. Instead, the two courts rejected Hale's maxim on the fallacious ground that because imputed consent is a fiction, any justification for imputed consent must also be spurious.

Despite their apparent misconceptions about imputed consent, the English and Massachusetts courts recognized, at least, that Hale's consent was a legal fiction. In contrast, some courts commit the opposite fallacy. They mistakenly confuse Hale's *fiction* of prospective prescriptive consent with being an *assertion* of prospective prescriptive consent, and, having confused them, they fault Hale for misrepresenting women's subjective feelings. They seize a legal fiction that treats married women *as if* they prospectively consented to have sexual intercourse with their husbands and treat it as an assertion that married women *do in fact* prospectively consent to such intercourse. The Maryland supreme court's decision in *Lane v. Maryland* (1997) is an example. The Maryland court reasoned that when Hale stated that women who engage in the act of marriage consent to have sexual intercourse with their husbands, Hale must have meant that they actually consent to marital intercourse in the same way that people today actually consent to 'non-marital sexual intercourse'. The reason courts and legislatures have since changed their views of Hale's maxim, the Maryland court said, is their 'belated recognition' that, while Hale's statement is 'generally true' of married women, 'it is not always so, and when it is not, the justification for the "[marital] exemption" disappears'.[50] The Georgia supreme court in *Warren v. Georgia* (1985) committed the same fallacy of treating Hale's fiction of consent as an assertion of prescriptive consent. The Georgia court held that Hale's 'implied consent theory to spousal rape is without logical meaning', because it is inconsistent with the way 'normal' women feel. No 'normal woman', the court said, would 'knowingly include an irrevocable term to her revocable marriage contract that would allow her husband to rape her'. And because no normal woman would make such consent explicit, the court said, it was 'incredible to think that any state would sanction such behavior by adding an implied consent term to all marriage contracts'.[51]

Interestingly, what misled the Maryland and Georgia courts may have been the common practice of referring to Hale's maxim as a maxim of 'implied consent'.[52] Yet implied consent has two very different meanings. On the one hand, it is used to refer to expressions of subjective acquiescence that are 'implied' in the sense that they are *non-verbal* evidence (rather than verbal evidence) of what a person actually desires under the circumstances. Thus, a woman, who eagerly responds to her boyfriend's invitation to sexual intercourse by smilingly but silently undressing him and leading him into bed, 'implies' consent to sexual intercourse, because she provides non-verbal evidence that she actually desires to engage in sexual intercourse. On the other hand, 'implied consent' is also used to refer, not to expressions that are evidence of what a person actually desires, but to conduct by a person from which the law constructs a fiction of what she actually desires. Thus, a football fan who attends a crowded game in Delaware 'impliedly' consents to be subjected to crowd pressure. In the terminology of the law of contracts, the difference is between consent 'implied in fact', and consent 'implied in law'.[53] The Maryland and Georgia courts were correct that Hale's consent is implied consent because Hale's consent is an imputation to a woman of prescriptive consent to sexual intercourse based upon her conduct in marrying, regardless of her of state of mind at the time. But the Maryland and Georgia courts were wrong in thinking that it was the kind of implied consent that arises from a woman's nonverbal conduct as to what she is actually thinking. The Maryland and Georgia courts took consent that for Hale was implied *in law* and mistakenly analyzed it as if it were implied *in fact*.

Ultimately, the mistakes that Maryland and Georgia made in confusing imputed consent with prescriptive consent were probably harmless; for the two courts had other, sufficient reasons to disavow the marital exemption. But the same mistake also arises in cases in which it is not so obviously harmless, *i.e.*, in cases in which, after interpreting state rape statutes not to include a marital exemption, courts must decide whether to apply their interpretations retroactively to convict defendants who acted before the courts had disavowed the marital exemption. The prevailing rule regarding retroactivity is that a newly announced interpretation can be applied retroactively if, and only if, a defendant with a reasonable understanding of the law would have had notice at the time he acted that his conduct was criminal. Interestingly, some courts, having disavowed the marital exemption, have applied their rulings retroactively for reasons that appear to confuse imputed consent with prescriptive consent. The defendants had notice when they acted that their conduct was criminal, the courts say, because the defendants did precisely what the statutes at the time plainly declared to be a criminal offense, namely, they had sexual intercourse with women without the women's 'consent'.[54] The New Jersey supreme court held in *Smith v. New Jersey* (1981),[55] for example, that the defendant had notice that his conduct constituted an offense because at the time the defendant acted it was the 'plain meaning' of the New Jersey law that sexual intercourse without a woman's consent was a crime.[56] Yet to say, as the New Jersey court did, that the meaning of consent was both 'plain' and 'facially clear' is to beg the very question that was at issue in the case, namely, whether consent under New Jersey law included Hale's fiction of consent or whether it was confined to prescriptive consent. If the meaning of consent was, indeed, 'facially clear' to the New Jersey court, it was only so because the court implicitly and fallaciously assumed that all legal consent must consist of prescriptive consent.

Conclusion

The word 'consent', it is said, '[is] a common word whose meaning [is] known to all English speaking people.'[57] Yet it is also said that we 'encounter difficulties... when we consider what consent is, [because] it is unclear what constitutes consent.'[58] Paradoxically, both statements are true. Everyone knows that to consent to *x* is, in one way or another, to choose or want *x* for oneself. Yet, at the same time, no one is quite certain what consent is because people have different and continually changing conceptions of what it means to choose or to want something for oneself.

This chapter discusses three confusions that occur when people conflate one conception of consent with another: (A) the mistake of confusing 'consent' as a choice of *x*, all things considered, with 'consent' as such a choice under conditions of voluntariness sufficient to render it a defense to the crime of committing *x*; (B) the mistake of confusing 'consent' as a subjective choice with 'consent' as an expression of such a choice; and (C) the mistake of confusing 'consent' as an actual and lawful of *x* with 'consent' as a legal fiction of an actual choice.

Conceptual confusions regarding consent, however, are not confined to such mistakes. They can also arise in cases in which everyone understands that consent is being used prescriptively to refer to *S*'s voluntary acquiescence to *x*. They occur because people mistakenly associate features that are characteristic of one of the two elements that constitute prescriptive consent with features of the other element. Recall that prescriptive consent consists of two elements: (1) a factual element that is constant and invariable; and (2) and certain variable elements. The constant element is that *S*, in mind or expression, actually chooses *x* for herself under the circumstances. The variable elements are the background conditions of competence, knowledge, freedom, and motivation on *S*'s part (or, in the case of expressive consent, the background conditions of *apparent* competence, knowledge, freedom, and motivation on *S*'s part) that jurisdictions believe are necessary to enable *S* to take responsibility for her choice for purposes of the offense at issue. Admittedly, once a jurisdiction identifies the background conditions that it believes must exist for *S*'s acquiescence to constitute a defense for an actor who subjects her to *x*, determining whether *S* possessed or expressed such competence, knowledge, freedom, and motivation is a factual matter. But determining what those conditions ought to be is not a factual matter. It is a normative undertaking that *within* a given jurisdiction will be resolved differently depending upon what *x* is, and that *across* jurisdictions will be resolved differently depending upon their respective normative views.

To illustrate the difference between the constant and variable elements of prescriptive consent, suppose that a jurisdiction makes it an offense for an actor *A* to have sexual intercourse with a subject *S* without her prescriptive attitudinal consent. Suppose further that a third party induces *S* into ingesting a beverage that contains a stupefying drug. And suppose finally that when *S* is so intoxicated as to have slurred speech and a wobbling gait, *A*, who is aware of *S*'s intoxication but not party to the act of drugging *S*, subjects *S* to sexual intercourse that, when the intoxication dissipates, *S* finds abhorrent. *S*'s case presents two questions. The first question (*i.e.*, 'Was *S* conscious that *A* was about to engage her in sexual intercourse and, if so, did *S* consciously choose it as that which she preferred for herself under the circumstances?') is a factual question, the correct answer to which is invariable (though evidence may not clearly reveal it). In contrast, the second question (*i.e.*, 'Does a woman whose unwitting but profound intoxication causes her to consciously submit to sexual intercourse with someone who is not responsible for her intoxication but with whom she would otherwise find the prospect of sexual intercourse abhorrent possess the "competence" to take responsibility for her choice for purposes of the law of rape?') is a normative question about which jurisdictions differ.[59] Moreover, because the latter is a normative question, the overall question in the case—'Did *S* "consent" to sexual intercourse with *A* for purposes of the law of rape?'—is also a normative question about which jurisdictions differ.

Some authorities appear to assume that because the answer to the first question regarding prescriptive consent is objective in nature, the answer to the overall question 'Did *S* prescriptively consent to *x*?' is also objective in nature. Consider the Colorado law governing the offense of 'sexual assault', which makes it an offense for an actor to engage in sexual intercourse with a person under various enumerated conditions. With one significant exception, the conditions that the Colorado statute enumerates appear to fall into two general categories:

> ***(1) Conditions that Preclude Factual Consent.*** The Colorado statute makes it an offense for an actor to engage in sexual intercourse with a person who does not even factually acquiesce to it. Thus, it is an offense under the Colorado statute for *A* to engage in sexual intercourse with *S* when *S* is 'unconscious', 'asleep', 'physically helpless' to resist, or 'incapable of appraising the nature of [her] conduct'.[60]

> ***(2) Conditions that Render Factual Consent Involuntary.*** The Colorado statute also makes it an offense for an actor to engage in sexual intercourse with a person who

> consciously acquiesces to it but who lacks the motivation, freedom, knowledge, or competence that Colorado deems necessary for the person to take responsibility for her choice. Thus, it is an offense under the statute for *A* to induce *S* to submit to sexual intercourse by threats of 'death', 'serious bodily injury', 'kidnapping', or 'extreme pain'; by defrauding *S* into believing that the intercourse is therapeutic; or by prevailing upon *S* at a time when she is underage.[61]

In addition to these enumerated conditions, however, Colorado envisages still a third condition that renders sexual intercourse an offense:

> ***(3) Any Other Condition that Causes a Victim to Submit 'Against' Her 'Will'.*** An actor is also guilty of sexual assault under the statute if he 'causes submission of the victim to sexual penetration by any means other than those [previously] set forth . . . but of sufficient consequence reasonably calculated to cause submission against the victim's will.'[62]

This third condition under the Colorado statute is a puzzle. It cannot refer to victims who do not even factually consent to sexual intercourse—that is, victims who do not in any way choose sexual intercourse as that which they prefer under the circumstances—because if it did, it would be superfluous to condition 1. Nor can it refer to victims who are forced or defrauded into consciously choosing sexual intercourse by such means as the statute enumerates; because if it did, it would be superfluous to condition 2. Nor, finally, can it refer to victims who reluctantly choose sexual intercourse under such conditions as the actor presents but who would not otherwise submit to it; because if it did, it would punish actors who present conditions that are legally acceptable under the statute (*e.g.*, 'I'll take you to Europe, but only if you have sex with me'). To be coherent, therefore, condition 3 must refer to victims who choose to have sexual intercourse under conditions that Colorado implicitly regards as legally illicit but that the statute leaves unspecified. If so, it requires juries to make normatively contestable decisions regarding the conditions of lawful sexual intercourse without providing juries with any guidance as to how to make them.

Indeed, the defendants in *Johnson v. Colorado* (1981)[63] made precisely that argument. *Johnson* was a consolidated appeal on behalf of four defendants who had all been separately convicted of 'causing' women to submit to sexual intercourse 'by . . . means other than those [previously] set forth . . . but . . . reasonably calculated to cause submission against the victim's will.'[64] The defendants challenged their convictions, arguing that the Colorado statute was unconstitutionally vague. Specifically, they argued that, by making it an offense to elicit sexual intercourse 'by any means . . . reasonably calculated to cause submission against the victim's will', the statute was 'so amorphous as to lack any guidelines' for courts and juries 'in determining guilt', and 'so open-ended as to be without meaning'. The Colorado supreme court agreed with the defendants' premise, that a criminal statute violates the Due Process Clause if it 'forbids . . . the doing of an act in terms so vague that men of common intelligence must necessarily guess as to its meaning and differ as to its application.'[65] Nevertheless, the court rejected the defendants' appeal. It ruled that the Colorado statute contains a 'discernible standard' that is 'sufficiently definite and objective' to 'guide a judge and jury in deciding whether a crime has been committed'.[66] The court explained that in making it an offense to engage in sexual intercourse against a person's 'will,' the statute employs the term 'will' as a synonym for a person's prescriptive 'consent'.[67] The court further explained that in making it an offense to use 'any means' to 'cause submission,' the statute employs the term 'submission' as a synonym for the absence of prescriptive consent. As a consequence, the Court said, the statute contains a 'sufficiently precise standard to guide a judge and jury in deciding whether a crime has been committed,' because it distinguishes lawful from unlawful sexual intercourse by reference to whether the alleged victim prescriptively 'consented,' on the one hand, or 'submitted,' on the other.[68]

Now it is possible that rather than being confused, the *Johnson* court knew exactly what it was doing. That is, it is possible that the *Johnson* court fully intended to be delegating to juries open-ended discretion to define the standards of competence, knowledge, freedom, and motivation that distinguish prescriptive consent from mere factual consent. But given the *Johnson* court's language, it seems unlikely. For far from admitting that it was delegating open-ended discretion to juries, the *Johnson* court denied that it was doing so by insisting, instead, that a standard that distinguishes 'consent' from 'submission' is 'definite and objective'. In reality, the distinction between consent and submission is anything but objective. 'Consent' and 'submission' are legal terms of art that Colorado uses to distinguish lawful acquiescence from unlawful acquiescence, and they differ as much as people's normative views about them do. If the *Johnson* court thought otherwise, the court confused the contestedness and variableness of prescriptive consent with the constancy and objectivity of factual consent.

Notes

1. Blair v. Wyoming, 735 P.2d 440 (1987).
2. 735 P.2d at 742-43.
3. See, e.g., Goldenberg v. Massachusetts, 338 Mass. 377, 383, 155 N.E.2d 187, 191 (1959), in which the court dismissed rape charges against a physician who deceived a woman into thinking that engaging in sexual intercourse with him would induce the fetus she was carrying to be aborted, on the ground that 'the phrase ["without her consent"] . . . describes the attitude of a woman who in fact is unconscious', not a woman like the complainant who is 'sensible of what the defendant [is] doing and offer[s] no resistance.'
4. The rape statute that was then in effect in California did not speak of 'consent' but, rather, made it an offense to engage in 'an act of sexual intercourse accomplished with a person not the spouse of the perpetrator . . . [w]here a person is at the time unconscious of the nature of the act . . . .' California Penal Code § 261(4), quoted at 163 Cal. App. 3d at 1229, 210 Cal. Rptr. at 125. Nevertheless, the Boro court analyzed the question 'Did Boro have sexual intercourse with Ms. R when she was unconscious of the nature of the act?', as if it were identical to the question 'Did Boro have sexual intercourse with Ms. Boro without her consent?' See 163 Cal. App. 3d at 1229-30, 210 Cal. Rptr. at 125-26.

5. For alternative ways to define 'factum' in rape cases, see Chapter 5, pp. 195-201.
6. 204 Cal. App. 2d 832, 23 Cal. Rptr. 92 (1962).
7. 163 Cal. App. 3d at 1230 n.5, 210 Cal. Rptr. at 126 n.5.
8. See California Statutes ch. 1056, § 1 (1985), now codified at California Penal Code § 266c (2001) ('Every person who induces any other person to engage in sexual intercourse . . . when his or her consent is procured by false or fraudulent representation or pretense that is made with the intent to create fear [of physical injury or death], and which does induce fear [of physical injury or death] . . . is punishable by imprisonment ... for not more than one year or in the state prison for two, three, or four years').
9. Jurisdictions differ in the precise way they frame the issue of competence, but they all make it an offense to have sexual intercourse with a person who suffers from fundamental weakness of mind. See Larsen, 'Annotation'.
10. New York v. Easley, 42 N.Y.2d 50, 364 N.E.2d 1328, 396 N.Y.S.2d 635 (1977).
11. 565 S.W.2d 638 (Ky. Ct. of App., 1978).
12. 565 S.W.2d at 640.
13. See, e.g., Illinois v. Blunt, 65 Ill. App. 2d 268, 212 N.E.2d 719 (1965) (a 23-year-old woman with an I.Q. of between 68 and 78 and a speech impediment, who, within a few hours, had two acts of sexual intercourse with two strangers whom she had met for the first time that day, was not so 'mentally deficient' as to be 'incapable of consent', because she knew what 'sexual intercourse' was and knew that it might result in pregnancy or disease); Stephenson v. Alabama, 35 Ala. App. 379, 48 So. 2d 255 (1950) (a 27-year-old woman, with the mental age of an eight-year old, who could not read, write, or tell time, was 'mentally capable' of giving 'legal consent' to two acts of sexual intercourse with a man within a few hours, because she knew that she was submitting to sexual intercourse, and knew that it might result in pregnancy); Vermont v. Jewett, 109 Vt. 73, 192 A. 7 (1937) (a 34-year-old woman with the mental age of a seven-year-old was capable of consenting to sexual intercourse because, 'although she may have been a child mentally, she was not a child physically', since a 'child of seven is without desire for such intercourse, whereas we cannot presume that fact in the case of a physically mature woman').
14. Adkins v. Virginia, 20 Va. App. 332, 457 S.E.2d 382 (1995).
15. 20 Va. App. at 345-46, 457 S.E.2d at 388-89.
16. 124 Wash. 2d 702, 881 P.2d 231 (1994).
17. 124 Wash. 2d at 711-12, 881 P.2d at 236-37 (1994).
18. 101 Cal. App. 3d 450, 161 Cal. Rptr. 634 (1980).
19. Statutes of this kind protect victims from being induced to submit to sexual intercourse through force, fraud, or exploitation; and, yet, they do so without requiring specific findings of such harms. Rather, they operate prophylactically to sweep within their terms a class of persons who are particularly vulnerable to such harms, even though not all members of the class necessarily suffer such harms by engaging in sexual intercourse. At the same time, the statutes also protect defendants from being punished for acts for which they acted in good faith, because custodians of closed institutions cannot easily have sexual intercourse with inmates without knowing that they are doing so. See generally Schulhofer, Unwanted Sex, p. 223.
20. California Penal Code § 261(a) (2) ('Rape is an act of sexual intercourse accomplished with a person not the spouse of the perpetrator . . . Where it is accomplished against a person's will by means of . . . fear of immediate and unlawful bodily injury on the person or another'). At the time St. Andrew was decided, section 261 defined rape as

the act of causing a person to submit to sexual intercourse 'by threats of great and immediate bodily harm, accompanied by apparent power of execution . ...'

21. See California v. Iniguez, 7 Cal. 4th 847, 856, 859, 872 P.2d 1183, 1188, 1190 (1994) (a woman who submits to sexual intercourse out of subjective fear that she will otherwise suffer bodily harm suffers the harm of rape, regardless of whether the defendant knew, or should have known, that she feared bodily harm—though whether he is punished for inflicting the harm depends upon whether he knew or should have known that she submitted out of fear).
22. California v. Iniguez, 7 Cal. 4th 847, 857, 872 P.2d 1183, 1188 (1994).
23. California v. St. Andrew, 101 Cal. App. 3d at 466, 161 Cal. Rptr. at 644 (1980), quoting Salsman v. Kentucky, 565 S.W.2d 638, 641 (1978)). See also California v. Barnes, 42 Cal. 3d 284, 304 n.20, 721 P.2d 110, 122 n.20 (1986); Clark v. State, 197 Ga. App. 318, 321, 398 S.E.2d 377, 379-80 (1991).
24. See Maryland v. Rusk, 289 Md. 230, 248, 424 A.2d 720, 727 (1981) ('The vast majority of jurisdictions have required that the victim's fear be reasonably grounded in order to obviate the need for either proof of actual force on the part of the assailant or physical resistance on the part of the victim').
25. See Maryland Code art. 27, § 462 (1999) ('A person is guilty of rape in the first degree if the person engages in vaginal intercourse with another person by force or threat of force against the will and without the consent of the other person and . . . places the victim in fear that the victim or any person known to the victim will be imminently subjected to death, suffocation, strangulation, disfigurement, serious physical injury, or kidnapping'); Maryland Code art. 27, § 463 (1999) ('A person is guilty of rape in the second degree if the person engages in vaginal intercourse with another person by force or threat of force against the will and without the consent of the other person'). Although sections 462-63 define rape as an act that occurs 'against the will' and 'without the consent' of a person, the Maryland courts have declared the two phrases to be 'synonymous'. See Maryland v. Rusk, 289 Md. 230, 241, 424 A.2d 720, 725 (1981) (against will and without consent are 'synonymous'). The Maryland courts have also interpreted 'force' within the meaning of section 463 to include threats of bodily harm. See Robinson v. State, 67 Md. App. 445, 508 A.2d 159, cert. denied, 307 Md. 261 (1986) (All that is required to prove 'force' or 'threat of force' is that in the mind of the victim, the victim was placed in reasonable apprehension of imminent bodily injury of such a nature as to impair or overcome his or her will to resist').
26. See Maryland v. Rusk, 289 Md. at 244, 424 A.2d at 727 (1981).
27. See, e.g., Winegan v. Maryland, 10 Md. App. 196, 202, 268 A.2d 585, 589 (1970) (a stranger who accosted a 17-year-old girl on the street and, while holding his hand in his pocket in a way that caused her to be 'afraid he had a gun', told her to go with her to his apartment or he would 'destroy' her is not guilty of rape for the sexual intercourse to which she submitted for fear that he would shoot her, because the girl's fear was 'unreasonable' under the circumstances). Winegan was decided in 1970, at a time when rape was defined, as it was at common law, as 'the act of a man having unlawful carnal knowledge of a female over the age of ten years by force without the consent and against the will of the victim.' See Lane v. Maryland, 348 Md. 272, 279, 703 A.2d 180, 184 (1997). For purposes of the factual allegation in Winegan, the common law definition was identical to the way Maryland presently defines first-degree rape. See id., 348 Md. at 279-90, 703 A.2d at 184-89.

28. Cf. Mills v. Arkansas, 270 Ark. 141, 144, 603 S.W.2d 416, 418 (1980) ('Subjective feelings of fear of physical injury by the victim must be based on some act of the accused that can be reasonably interpreted to warrant such fear').
29. 11 Delaware Code § 601 (1999).
30. 11 Delaware Code § 451 (1999).
31. See, e.g., Regina v. Miller, [1954] 2 QB 282, [1954] 2 All ER 529, [1954] 2 WLR 138 (a husband, whose relationship to his wife has not been legally severed, cannot be guilty of raping her, but he can be guilty of assault and battery).
32. Liberta v. New York, 64 N.Y.2d 152, 474 N.E.2d 567 (1984) (quoting New York Penal Code §§ 130.00, 130.35). New York Penal Code §§ 130.00 and 130.35 still take the same form today that they took in 1984, but, by virtue of Liberta, the definition of 'female' has been unenforceable since 1984.
33. See Lane v. Maryland, 348 Md. 272, 280, 703 A.2d 180, 184 (1997).
34. Until 1976 in England, rape was defined as it had been at common law, namely, the act of a man in having carnal knowledge of a woman without her consent. See Section 1(1) of the Sexual Offences Act of 1956 ('It is a felony for a man to rape a woman'); Regina v. Miller, [1954] 2 QB 282, [1954] 2 All ER 529, [1954] 2 WLR 138. Moreover, until that time, a woman, by virtue of marrying a man, was deemed to consent to have sexual intercourse with him, at least until she became legally separated from him. See Regina v Steele (1976) 65 Cr App R 22. In 1976, Parliament changed the form of the English rape statute by providing that 'a man commits rape if (a) he has unlawful sexual intercourse with a woman who at the time of the intercourse does not consent to it; and (b) at the time he knows that she does not consent to the intercourse or he is reckless as to whether she consents to it . . . '. See Section 1(1) (a) of the Sexual Offences (Amendment) Act 1976. For the current version of the offense, which is identical to the 1976 version except that it is gender-neutral with respect to victims, see Sexual Offences Act, 1956 §1, as substituted by the Criminal Justice and Public Order Act, 1994, § 14.
35. Even in jurisdictions in which rape is stated to consist of the act of a man of having 'unlawful' sexual intercourse with a woman without her consent, what renders the sexual intercourse 'lawful' when it occurs among persons who are married to each other is, in part, that both parties have consented to the marriage. See Lane v. Maryland, 348 Md. 272, 279-80, 703 A.2d 180, 184 (1997).
   Hale himself gave no further explanation of that statement, but his proposition seems to be that (1) there is implicit in the marriage contract an irrevocable consent of the wife to sexual intercourse with her husband, (2) because such intercourse occurring during the marriage is thus, by law, consented to, it is not unlawful, and (3) because it is not unlawful, it cannot constitute rape.
36. See Hale, The History of the Pleas of the Crown, vol. 1, p. *629. Hale's treatise, though composed in manuscript form as early as 1671, was not published until 1726, 60 years after his death in 1676. Since Hale had left instructions in his will that no amendments to his work were to be made, it seems likely that his published views were of the common law as it existed in the 1670's. See Lane v. Maryland, 348 Md. 272, 281, 703 A.2d 180, 195 (1997).
37. Hale conceptualized the marital exemption as a fiction of prospective prescriptive consent: a woman, in marrying, prospectively consents to marital intercourse at her husband's future pleasure. However, as we saw in Chapter 7, the marital exemption can equally well be conceptualized as a fiction of contemporaneous consent: a woman,

having married, contemporaneously consents to acts of marital intercourse at the time they occur.

38. Indeed, there is reason to doubt that it ever existed, even in England, in the stark form in which Hale stated it. See the opinion of Justice Willis in Regina v. Clarence, (1888) 22 QBD 23, [1886-90] All ER Rep 133.
39. See Regina v. R, [1992] 1 AC 599, [1991] 4 All ER 481, [1991] 3 WLR 767 (House of Lords).
40. See, e.g., Ark. Stat. Ann. § 5-14-103(a) (2) (1999) ('A person commits rape if he engages in sexual intercourse or deviate sexual activity with another person . . . not his spouse who is a patient or resident of a hospital, nursing home, human development center, or other similar facility, and who is incapable of consent because he is mentally defective or mentally incapacitated') (emphasis added); W. Va. Code § 61-8B-5(a) (2) (2000) ('A person is guilty of sexual assault in the third degree when . . . the person, being 16 years old or more, engages in sexual intercourse or sexual intrusion with another person who is less than 16 years old and who is at least four years younger than the defendant and is not married to the defendant') (emphasis added).
41. See, e.g., Maryland Code art. 27, § 464D (1999) (the marital exemption does not apply to spouses who have 'lived separate and apart without cohabitation and without interruption either pursuant to a 'written separation agreement executed by both the person and the person's legal spouse', or 'for at least 3 months immediately before the commission of the alleged rape or sexual offense').
42. See, e.g., Liberta v. New York, 64 N.Y.2d 152, 474 N.E.2d 567, 485 N.Y.S.2d 207 (1984) (the state's statutory version of the marital exemption is unconstitutional under the Equal Protection Clauses of the U.S. and New York Constitutions, because it lacks a 'rational basis'); Massachusetts v. Chretien, 383 Mass. 123, 417 N.E.2d 1203 (1981) (the martial exemption, which had hitherto been part of the common law of the state, was repealed by statute in 1974).
43. See, e.g., New Jersey v. Smith, 85 N.J. 193, 426 A.2d 38 (1980) (the marital exemption in its starkest form was never part of the common law of New Jersey).
44. Regina v. R. [1991] 1 All ER 747 (Crown Court at Leicester), affirmed, [1992] 1 AC 599, [1991] 2 All ER 257, [1991] 2 WLR 1065 (Court of Appeal), affirmed, [1992] 1 AC 599, [1991] 4 All ER 481 [1991] 3 WLR 767 (House of Lords).
45. 383 Mass. 123, 417 N.E.2d 1203 (1981).
46. Regina v. R. [1991] 1 All ER 747 (Crown Court at Leicester).
47. Regina v. R. [1992] 1 AC 599, [1991] 2 All ER 257, [1991] 2 WLR 1065 (Court of Appeal). See also Regina v. R., [1991] 4 All ER 481 (House of Lords) (Lord Kinkel) (referring to 'the absurdity of the fiction of implied consent').
48. 383 Mass. at 128, 417 N.E.2d at 1207 (quoting the Commentaries to the Model Penal Code).
49. See Coughlin, 'Sex and Guilt'; Perkins and Boyce, Criminal Law, p. 203 (arguing that it was 'an element of the crime [of rape] that the sex be unlawful, and marital sex is not unlawful').
50. Lane v. Maryland, 348 Md. at 281, 703 A.2d at 185:

> The law sanctioned sexual intercourse between husband and wife because the law assumed that such intercourse, as an integral part of the marital relationship, was, in fact, consensual, and, to that extent, it stood on the same footing as consensual non-marital sexual intercourse. The change in philosophy with respect to the marital 'exemption', whether marked by courts or by legislatures, arises from the law's belated recognition that, although that assumption may be generally true and well-

justified, it is not always so, and when it is not, the justification for the 'exemption' disappears.

51. Warren v. Georgia, 255 Ga. 151, 155, 336 S.E.2d 221, 224 (1985).
52. See Lane v. Maryland, 348 Md. at 289, 703 A.2d at 189; Warren v. Georgia, 255 Ga. at 154, 336 S.E.2d at 224; Weishaupt v. Virginia, 227 Va. 389, 398, 315 S.E.2d 847, 851 (1984).
53. See Powell, 'Consent To Operative Procedures', p. 190.
54. See, e.g., Warren v. Georgia, 255 Ga. at 157, 336 S.E.2d at 226 (1985); Smith v. New Jersey, 85 N.J. 193, 209-10, 426 A.2d 38, 46 (1981); New York v. De Stefano, 121 Misc. 2d 113, 128, 467 N.Y.S.2d 506, 517 (1983).
55. 85 N.J. 193, 426 A.2d 38.
56. New Jersey v. Smith, 85 N.J. at 209-10, 426 A.2d at 46 (the New Jersey statute is 'facially clear', and its 'plain meaning' gave the defendant notice that his conduct was prohibited). The New Jersey statute in Smith made it a crime for a person to have sexual intercourse with a woman 'against her will', but the phrase 'against her will' had been interpreted to be synonymous with without her 'consent'. See 85 N.J., at 198, 426 A.2d at 40 (citing New Jersey v. Heyer, 89 N.J.L. 187, 98 A. 413 (E. and A., 1916).
57. Louisiana v. Vaughn, 431 So.2d 358, 362 (La. Sup. Ct., 1982) (quoting jury instructions in a rape prosecution).
58. O'Neil, 'Between Consenting Adults', p. 254.
59. Jurisdictions differ as to whether a man is guilty of rape if he has sexual intercourse with a woman whose ability to appraise or control her conduct has been substantially impaired by intoxicants that are administered without her knowledge, if he was not the person who administered them to her. Compare Model Penal Code § 213.1(1) (a man is guilty if 'he has substantially impaired [a woman's] power to appraise or control her conduct by administering or employing without her knowledge drugs . . . for the purpose of preventing resistance') with South Carolina v. Galati, 365 N.W.2d 575 ('[W]e fail to see either a reasonable or a logical basis for protecting [a] defendant from a rape charge' simply 'because the agent which caused the victim's condition was not administered by the defendant or by a person in privity with the defendant'). See generally Kramer, 'Rule by Myth', pp. 124-31 (1994).
60. Colorado Revised Statutes §§ 18-3-401, 18-3-402 (1998). The 1998 version of section 18-3-402 ceased to be effective on November 1, 1998, and was replaced with an amended version. See Colorado Revised Statutes § 18-3-401 (2001).
61. Colorado Revised Statutes § 18-3-402 (1998), repealed effective November 1, 1998.
62. Colorado Revised Statutes § 18-3-403 (2001).
63. 638 P.2d 1 (1981).
64. Colo. Rev. Stat. § 18-3-403(1)(a) (1999) (emphasis added).
65. 638 P.2d at 3 (quoting Connally v. General Construction Co., 269 U.S. 385 (1926)).
66. 638 P.2d at 7.
67. 638 P.2d at 5 n.5.
68. 638 P.2d at 5 n.5.

Conclusion

The English Parliament established a Commission in 1965 to propose revisions to English law, including criminal law. The Commission initially decided in 1992 that rather than taking on the task of proposing legislation regarding the defense of consent in criminal law, it would leave issues of consent to the courts to resolve on a case-by-case basis. Eventually, however, the Commission was persuaded that in order to fulfill its mission to codify the English penal code, it had to confront consent. Accordingly, two years later the Commission issued a 71-page consultation paper, *Consent and Offences Against the Person*, designed to reformulate and clarify offenses of non-consent.[1] The paper was severely criticized by commentators in England for being 'metaphorically as well as literally lightweight', 'short on critical edge', and 'virtually devoid of theoretical depth'.[2] In response the Commission withdrew the paper and, in 1995, after commissioning a philosopher to write a background paper on criminalization, issued a new 290-page consultation paper in 1995 entitled *Consent in the Criminal Law*,[3] which was well received. In addition to being commended for resting upon 'sound theoretical foundations', it was specifically praised for being informed by an awareness of the 'conceptual complexity' of consent in the criminal law.[4]

Significantly, however, despite its efforts to achieve conceptual clarity, the Commission failed to recognize that its references to consent are riddled with the same ambiguities and contradictions that accompany most discussions of consent. The 1995 paper is ambivalent about each of the three conceptual dichotomies that divide discussions of consent in criminal law, namely: (1) whether consent is an inherently *legal* concept, *i.e.*, something that itself *constitutes* a defense to criminal conduct, or whether it is a factual concept, *i.e.*, something that is a defense only if it is independently demonstrated to be 'valid' or 'voluntary'; (2) whether consent by a subject *S* is a mental state on her part, whether it is an expressive act on her part, or whether it is either or both; and (3) whether *S*'s legal consent to conduct *x* is 'prescriptive' in nature or 'imputed'—that is, whether it is confined to actual and voluntary instances of acquiescence to *x*, or whether it extends to legal fictions of such acquiescence.

Among these three dichotomies, the Commission is most ambivalent about whether consent is legal or factual in nature—that is, whether it constitutes a defense to criminal wrongdoing or is at most a component part of such a defense. The ambiguity is embedded in the Commission's definition of 'consent'. For the Commission defines consent in terms of consent: '*Consent* shall mean a valid and subsisting *consent*'. The Commission's first reference to 'consent' is legal in nature, because it refers to something that itself possesses legal 'valid[ity]'. The second mention of consent is factual, because it refers to something that is not a defense unless it is independently shown to be 'valid'. This ambiguity is pervasive throughout the Commission's 1995 paper. Thus, the Commission sometimes uses consent in a wholly factual sense, as in the following paragraph in which the Commission refers to 'valid consent', consent that 'is or may be' a defense, and consent elicited by 'threat':

> We provisionally propose that a person should not be treated as having given a valid consent, for the purposes of any offence to which consent is or may be a defence, if he or she gives such consent because a threat, express or implied, has been made to use non-consensual force . . . against him or another if he or she does not consent, and he or she believes that, if he or she does not consent, the threat will be carried out immediately or before he or she can free himself or herself from it.[5]

At other times, the Commission uses consent in a wholly legal sense, as when the Commission states that 'the intentional causing of any injury to another person other than a seriously disabling injury . . . should not be criminal if, at the time of the act or omission causing the injury, the other person consented to the injury'.[6] Yet at still other times the Commission uses consent in both a legal and a factual sense within the same sentence, as when it states, 'We provisionally propose that a person should be guilty of an offence . . . if he or she does any act which, if done without the consent of another, would be an offence . . . and he or she has procured that other's consent by deception'.

The Commission is also ambivalent about whether consent (whether legal or factual) consists of a mental state on a person's part, an expression of such a mental state, or both. Thus, the Commission sometimes implies that consent is an expressive act, as when it refers to consent as something that is 'given' by a person, and that may be either 'express[ed]' or 'implied'.[7] At other times, the Commission suggests that consent is a mental state, as when the Commission states that a person's consent is not valid if the person is 'unable . . . to make a decision for himself or herself on the matter in question' and, then, defines such inability entirely in subjective terms.[8] This ambivalence of the Commission is significant because mental states perform significantly different legal functions than expressions in the definition of offenses of non-consent: defining offenses of non-consent in terms of the absence of mental states of consent on a victim's part is to define offenses of non-consent by reference to harms that actors *actually* inflict, while defining offenses of non-consent in terms of the absence of expressions of consent on an alleged victim's part is to define them by reference to harms that actors should *assume* they are inflicting.

To its credit, the Commission makes a decided effort to use consent 'prescriptively' to refer to instances of actual and voluntary acquiescence to *x*, rather than using it to refer to legal fictions of acquiescence to *x*. Thus, the Commission repeatedly states that a person has a defense if his alleged victim *either* 'consent[s] to an injury of the type caused' *or* 'consent[s] to the risk of an injury of the type caused'.[9] Yet the Commission also conflates prescriptive consent with imputed consent. Thus, it states that 'a person should be regarded as consenting to an injury of the type caused if he or she consents to an act or omission which he or she knows or believes to be *intended* to cause injury to him or her of the type caused'.[10] To illustrate the conflation, suppose that elementary school students *A* and *S* are playing a game of dodge ball in which *A* succeeds in striking *S* with a rubber ball that *S* is confidently doing everything she can to evade. The Commission would say that because *S* consented to play dodge ball knowing that *A* intended to strike her with the ball, *S* should be regarded as consenting to the blow, even though she at most consented to the *risk* of the blow. By treating *S*'s consent to a risk of *x* as equivalent to *S*'s consenting to *x* itself, the Commission undermines its otherwise consistent effort to use consent prescriptively by using it to refer to a fiction of prescriptive consent.

The Commission's work is not an isolated example. The same ambiguities and contradictions about consent commonly occur in the most thoughtful writing about consent.[11] They also commonly figure in legislative provisions regarding consent. Some rape statutes, for example, use consent in both factual and legal senses, referring sometimes to acquiescence that may or may not be a defense depending upon whether it is voluntary, and referring at other times to acquiescence that occurs under conditions sufficient to constitute a defense. Other rape statutes use 'consent' in a legal sense but fail to specify whether the term refers solely to prescriptive consent or also to legal fictions thereof. Still other rape statutes use consent prescriptively but fail to specify whether the underlying acquiescence to *x* consists of a mental state on *S*'s part or an expression thereof. Thus:

> ***Factual-Legal.*** The Kansas rape statute contains two sections: *section 1*, which states that it is rape to have sexual intercourse with a person who, by virtue of enumerated conditions, 'does not consent to [it]', including when the person is overcome by force or fear; and *section 2*, which states that it is also rape to have sexual intercourse with a person 'when the victim's consent was obtained through a knowing misrepresentation . . . that the sexual intercourse was a medically . . . necessary procedure'. Perhaps unwittingly, the statute uses consent in contradictory ways. 'Consent' in section 1 is legal in nature because, being consent that does not even come into existence in the event that a victim submits because of force or fear, it is consent that is always a defense. In contrast, consent in section 2 is factual, because it is consent that may or may not be a defense, depending upon whether it is induced by misrepresentation.
>
> ***Prescriptive-Imputed.*** For centuries it was a common-law offense in England for a man to have carnal knowledge of a woman 'without her consent'.[12] In 1976 Parliament made it a statutory offense for a man to have sexual intercourse with a woman 'who at the time of the intercourse does not consent to it'.[13] Consent was a defense to both offenses, and, yet, 'consent' was ambiguous as to whether it was confined to prescriptive consent or extended to fictions of prescriptive consent. The English courts ruled that the pre-1976 common-law offense used 'consent' in a legal sense to refer both to a woman's prescriptive consent to sexual intercourse and to fictions of such consent, *e.g.*, the fiction that a woman who married a man prescriptively consented to have sexual intercourse with him at his future pleasure. Yet, after extended litigation, the English courts eventually ruled that the post-1976 statute used 'consent' prescriptively to refer solely to a woman's actual acquiescence to sexual intercourse under appropriate conditions of competence, knowledge, and freedom—and not to fictions of such acquiescence.[14]

Attitudinal-Expressive. The Arkansas penal code makes it an offense to have sexual intercourse with a victim who is 'incapable of consent', and the Arkansas code defines being 'incapable of consent' as being 'physically unable to communicate lack of consent'.[15] The Arkansas code thus implies that to be incapable of 'consent' is to be incapable of 'communicat[ion]'. But if Arkansas really means to define consent as *consisting* of a communication, why does Arkansas refer to being unable to communicate a 'lack of '*consent*', thereby implying that consent and non-consent are states of affairs to be communicate[d]' and, hence, states of affairs that must exist independently of communication? Wouldn't Arkansas be clearer if, like Maryland, it defined 'incapable of consent' as being 'physically unable to communicate *unwillingness* to submit to an act of vaginal intercourse'?[16] But if Maryland, in turn, really means to define consent as a communication, why does it refer to a victim's being unable to communicate 'unwillingness'?[17] Wouldn't Maryland be clearer if, like Colorado, it defined 'incapable of consent' as being 'unable to *indicate* willingness'?[18] But if Colorado, in turn, really means to define consent as a communication, why does it provide that consent is a defense to an actor who has sexual intercourse with a person who is unable to communicate,[19] thereby implying that consent cannot consist of a communication?

Confusions regarding consent result not only from conflating one conception of consent with another, but also from confounding the basic elements that constitute all conceptions of legal consent. Judgments of legal consent in criminal law consist of two distinct steps:

Step 1. *S* must choose *x*—whether actually or fictitiously, and whether in mind or expression—as that which she prefers for herself under the circumstances or that about which she is sufficiently indifferent that she is willing to leave its occurrence to *A*; and

Step 2. *S*'s choice must be the product (or, with expressive consent, it must *appear* to be the product) of such competence to assess *S*'s interests, knowledge of the circumstances, freedom from pressure, and motivation as the jurisdiction deems necessary to enable her to take responsibility for her choice for the purposes of the offense at issue–or, if it is not, it must be (or appear to be) indistinguishable from the choice *S*'s would have made for herself if she had possessed the option of making her choice under such conditions of competence, knowledge, and freedom.

Significantly, every Anglo-American jurisdiction either explicitly defines sexual assault in terms of absence of legal 'consent' or implicitly does so by means that mimic the use of 'non-consent'. Thus, despite the diverse forms in which jurisdictions frame their statutes, every jurisdiction makes it a crime for *A* to have sexual intercourse with *S* without *S*'s having in any way chosen it for herself in accord with Step 1 (*e.g.*, by *A*'s having intercourse with *S* when *S* is unconscious, when *S* is misled into thinking that she is not having sexual intercourse, or when *A* physically overwhelms *S* despite her utmost resistance). Similarly, every jurisdiction also makes it a crime for *A* to have sexual intercourse with *S* by inducing her to choose sexual intercourse without her possessing what the jurisdictions regards as minimum levels of competence, knowledge, freedom, and motivation under Step 2 (*e.g.*, by *A*'s inducing *S* to acquiesce when *S* is underage or mentally incompetent, by *A*'s deceiving *S* into thinking he is her husband, or by *A*'s threatening *S* with serious bodily harm). Although a minority of jurisdictions such as Utah achieve these results with statutes that explicitly define sexual assault as sexual intercourse without legal 'consent'[20] (or 'against' a victim's 'will')[21] the majority of jurisdictions do so in ways that suggest they misunderstand the import of the two steps that constitute legal consent. Rather than defining sexual assault in terms of the law of legal consent alone, some state statutes define the offense as sexual intercourse with a person *both* by 'force' *and* without her legal 'consent' (or by 'force' *and* 'against' her 'will'); other statutes define the offense as sexual intercourse by 'force' alone (or by 'compulsion', or 'coercion' alone) without explicitly mentioning a victim's non-consent; and still other statutes define the offense as sexual intercourse *either* by 'force' *or* without legal 'consent'. In doing so, states replicate in circuitous fashion the results they could achieve more directly by defining rape in terms of the lack of legal consent alone:

> ***By 'Force' and Without Legal 'Consent'.*** Some state statutes (*e.g.*, Ohio's) explicitly define rape as sexual intercourse by 'force' *and* without *S*'s legal 'consent'[22] (or by 'force' *and* 'against' *S*'s 'will').[23] This conjunction of force and non-consent leads some observers to conclude that jurisdictions with such statutes must be exculpating actors who subject victims to nonconsensual intercourse *without* using what is traditionally regarded as force, *e.g.*, actors who have intercourse with victims who are underage, mentally incompetent, or deceived.[24] But that is not so. All jurisdictions with such statutes punish actors who have intercourse with underage or mentally incompetent victims, much as they would if they defined rape solely in terms of non-consent alone. To do so, however, these jurisdictions must proceed in a roundabout fashion. Either they must enact supplemental statutes, making it a crime to have sexual intercourse with persons who are underage, mentally retarded, or victims of fraud.[25] Or they must reduce the meaning of 'force' to the meaning of the companion term 'non-consent' by ruling that an actor who has sexual intercourse with a person whose immaturity, mental incompetence, or ignorance precludes her from consenting shall be deemed to have used 'force'.[26]

> ***By Force Alone.*** Other state statutes appear to do something quite different. They explicitly define rape as sexual intercourse by 'force' alone (or 'compulsion' or 'coercion' alone).[27] In reality, however, all such jurisdictions ultimately treat rape either as a crime of legal non-consent alone (such as Utah's), or as a crime of force and legal non-consent (such as Ohio's). Thus, some jurisdictions simply interpret the term 'force' to ***mean*** 'without legal consent'.[28] Other jurisdictions go through the process of transforming statutes that appear to prohibit force *alone* into statutes that define rape as sexual intercourse by force *and* non-consent—either by means of separate statutes that explicitly state that consent is a defense to sexual intercourse by force,[29] or by judicial rulings that interpret 'force' to mean 'force plus a lack of legal consent'.[30] Having come around to define 'force' to mean 'force plus non-consent', the latter jurisdictions ultimately do what jurisdictions do that start with requirements of force and non-consent: they punish an actor *A* who has nonconsensual sexual intercourse with *S* without *A*'s using what is traditionally regarded as force (*e.g.*, actors who have sexual intercourse with victims who are underage, mentally retarded, or deceived) either by

enacting separate statutes to that effect,[31] or by ruling that nonconsensual intercourse with such victims shall be deemed to be by force.[32]

By 'Force' or Without Legal 'Consent'. Still other state statutes define sexual assault as sexual intercourse ***either*** by 'force' *or* without legal 'consent'.[33] In practice, however, these statutes, too, are reduced to prohibiting sexual intercourse without legal consent. Thus, jurisdictions with such statutes do one of two things. Either they interpret the term 'force' to be superfluous, by ruling that consent is a defense to sexual intercourse by means of force.[34] Or they reserve 'force' for serious sexual offenses and lack of 'consent' for lesser sexual offenses; and having done so, they interpret 'force' to mean 'by aggravated force and without legal consent', while interpreting 'non-consent' to include cases in which lesser kinds of force are used to undermine legal consent, *e.g.*, the force employed to override a 'no'.[35]

In all these cases, defining rape by reference to force is a roundabout way of replicating the results of defining it by reference to a lack of legal consent alone. The common-law definition of rape is an example. English courts until 1976 regarded rape as a common-law offense to be defined by the courts.[36] But English courts differed over how they framed the offense: sometimes they framed it as carnal knowledge of a woman without her legal 'consent'; at other times they framed it as carnal knowledge of a woman both by 'force' *and* without her legal 'consent' (or, alternatively, both 'force' and 'against her will'); and at still other times they defined it in both ways within the same opinion.[37] In the end, however, nothing significant turned upon the term 'force'; for the English courts ruled that it was 'rape' for a man to have sexual intercourse with a woman who was unaware of it at the time, and 'rape' for a man to have sexual intercourse with an underage girl who was eager to engage in it.[38] The prohibition of force was revealed to be either redundant of the kinds of force that already sufficed to negate legal 'consent' or wholly inoperative.[39]

Not surprisingly, many distinguished scholars are critical of jurisdictions that define rape in terms of 'force' plus 'non-consent'. What is surprising, however, is the nature of their criticism, for it reveals a fundamental misunderstanding of the nature and scope of legal consent. Scholars criticize the conjunction of force and non-consent *not* on the ground that the conjunction is redundant, but on the ground that the conjunction is profoundly unjust.[40] Depending upon the particular remedies they favor, these scholars argue that defining rape in terms of force and non-consent fails to give victims the protection victims would enjoy if rape were defined instead solely in terms of force,[41] solely in terms of non-consent,[42] or in the alternative terms of force *or* non-consent.[43] In doing so, however, they misunderstand how jurisdictions treat the conjunction of force and non-consent, and they misconceive the significance of legal consent.

Consider, for a moment, scholars who criticize requirements of 'force' plus 'non-consent' on the ground that the requirement of force is unjust.[44] The contention is that an actor who has non-consensual intercourse with a person ought to be punished for that alone, regardless of whether the actor also used force in doing so. This contention, in turn, takes one of two forms, the first of which rests on a misunderstanding of how jurisdictions actually behave. The first argument is that by exculpating actors who do not use force, jurisdictions fail to punish actors who achieve sexual intercourse with persons without using what is traditionally regarded as force (*e.g.*, by defrauding them, or by exploiting their incompetence to consent).[45] As we have seen, however, that is not so. Jurisdictions that define rape in terms of force plus non-consent either possess supplemental statutes that punish such actors or take the position that such actors shall be *deemed* to have used 'force'.

The second argument against requiring 'force' plus 'non-consent' is more revealing, because it is premised upon a pervasive conceptual fallacy regarding the nature of legal consent. This argument does not focus upon cases in which actors achieve sexual intercourse with victims who are unconscious (for jurisdictions can easily treat those as instances of 'force'). Nor does it focus upon cases in which actors induce acquiescence from victims who are ignorant or incompetent (for as we have seen, jurisdictions commonly deem such actors to have used 'force'). Rather, the argument focuses upon cases that are central to feminist concerns, *viz.*, cases in which actors induce women to submit to unwanted sexual intercourse by means of pressures that, although substantial, do not amount to what jurisdictions regard as 'force'. The argument is that by exculpating actors for failing to use 'force', jurisdictions allow such actors to pressure women into sexual intercourse that is non-consensual on their part. Robin West states the argument in representative fashion, using the example of a professor who pressures a student into sexual intercourse by threatening her with an undeserved low grade:

> [Consider] sex that is concededly nonconsensual, but is not (at least in any of the most obvious ways) *forced.* Whatever falls into this category is, according to still-standard definitions of rape found in most states' rape law, fully legal. . . . [One example] is sex obtained through some sort of coercion. . . . A woman who has sex with a professor in order to guarantee that she will receive the grade she earned in his course has been coerced into sex, which again may concededly be nonconsensual, but she has not been forced, and was therefore not raped.[46]

The key to West's argument lies in what West means in saying that the hypothetical student's decision to submit to sex with her professor can be 'conceded' to be nonconsensual. West means that although the student made a deliberate decision to submit to sexual intercourse, her submission can be 'conceded' to be something she did not really want, in that she *would have refused it if she had not been threatened with an unfair grade*. The fallacy in the argument is the assumption that the student's counterfactual wishes (*i.e.*, what she would have chosen if the circumstances had been as she wished) control whether she legally consented to doing what she deliberately did. The counterfactual wishes of a person who actually chooses *x* as the best she can do for herself under the circumstances, and who does so under conditions of freedom that jurisdictions regard as sufficient to enable her to take responsibility for her choice, are wholly immaterial.[47] What matters is that she actually chooses *x* under conditions that the jurisdiction at hand regards as free of wrongful force. That is what legal consent to *x* *is*.

To be sure, perhaps jurisdictions *should* treat threats such as the professor's as instances of wrongful 'force' for purposes of sexual assault.[48] If they do, sexual intercourse induced by such threats becomes intercourse *both* by force *and* without legal consent. If they do not, however, sexual intercourse remains intercourse *without* force and thus *with* legal consent. For that is what it means for a person legally to consent to sexual intercourse in the context of unwanted pressure: it means she deliberately submitted to sexual intercourse as a result of pressures that she wishes had not been present but that the jurisdiction does not regard as wrongful means for inducing acquiescence to sexual intercourse. Nor is the analysis any different if a woman says 'no' to sexual intercourse. Some jurisdictions regard the pressures that actors bring to bear upon women to induce them to submit to sexual intercourse despite their saying 'no' as wrongful pressures. Others do not. In jurisdictions that do, actors are guilty of sexual intercourse by force and without consent. In jurisdictions that do not, actors are guilty neither of using force nor of having sexual intercourse without consent. In no case, however, can one meaningfully say of a person who reluctantly acquiesces to sexual intercourse in the face of unwanted pressures, 'She is not a victim of sexual intercourse by force, but she is a victim of sexual intercourse without consent'.[49]

Significantly, scholars also criticize jurisdictions that require 'force' plus 'non-consent' on an opposite ground, namely, that it is not the requirement of *force* that is unjust, but the requirement of *non-consent*. Thus, Catharine MacKinnon as well as West argues that an actor's mere use of force to achieve sexual intercourse ought to render him guilty of rape, regardless of whether the woman consents to the intercourse.[50] This criticism also comes in two distinct forms, but both rest on the same fallacy—the fallacy that defining rape solely in terms of non-consent leaves many victims unprotected. West argues that in so far as consent is a defense to sexual intercourse by means of force, it exonerates an actor who so frightens his victim with threats of death or mayhem that she fearfully 'consents' to sexual intercourse rather than risk being killed:

> [T]he recent and notorious Texas case, in which a woman was found to have consented to sex with a man who held a knife at her throat because she pleaded with him to use a condom to avoid the risk of AIDS, was such a case: There was undeniable force, but her rational, articulated attempt to minimize harm to herself demonstrated her desire to acquiesce, rather than risk great harm by fighting, and hence demonstrated her consent.[51]

Unfortunately, West makes the same legal mistake as the Texas grand jury whose refusal to indict the assailant was later overturned: West erroneously assumes that when a jurisdiction makes it a criminal offense to have sexual intercourse by 'force' and without 'consent', the jurisdiction is using 'consent' in a factual sense to refer to acquiescence that satisfies Step 1, regardless of threats of death and harm that may be used to induce the acquiescence.[52] In reality, of course, when jurisdictions make it a crime to have sexual intercourse by force and without consent, they are using 'consent' in a legal sense to refer not only to acquiescence that satisfies Step 1, but also to acquiescence that occurs under conditions of competence, knowledge, freedom, and motivation sufficient to satisfy Step 2. Otherwise, such jurisdictions would be taking the unprecedented position that an actor who beats and maims a woman until she yields by saying 'Just do what you want, but please don't hurt me any more' commits no sexual offense.

MacKinnon's argument against consent is more substantial. She argues that in so far as consent is a defense to pressures to engage in sexual intercourse, consent legitimates a 'sado-masochistic' model of sexual intercourse.[53] That is, for MacKinnon consent effectively legitimates sexual intercourse that is the product of social, economic, and political pressures that cause women to choose sexual intercourse when it is contrary to their interests and, worse yet, to regard the accompanying pressures as acceptable and even desirable.[54] The fallacy in this argument does not lie in MacKinnon's conception of the conditions under which women choose sexual intercourse; rather, it lies in her conception of legal consent. Suppose for a moment that MacKinnon convinces lawmakers that they ought to protect women from pressures to engage in sexual intercourse that women are socialized to regard as acceptable and even desirable. Suppose, further, that lawmakers wish to codify that protection in a traditional way—that is, by prohibiting actors from subjecting women to sexual intercourse by means of such 'force' and without their 'consent'. There is nothing in the two-step nature of legal consent that prevents lawmakers from doing so. On the contrary, in order to comply with Step 2, a woman's acquiescence to sexual intercourse must be sufficiently free, informed, and competent to enable her to take responsibility in the eyes of the law for her choice. A woman's choice is not 'free' under Step 2 if it is the product of pressures that unconditionally taint it, that is, pressures that operate to taint her choice even if she *welcomes* them.[55] Indeed, it is in part because underage girls are subject to such pressures that their acquiescence to sexual intercourse does not constitute legal consent even if it can be shown that they welcome the pressures.

Of course, MacKinnon realizes that jurisdictions today refuse to treat general social pressures on women as sufficient to invalidate the sexual acquiescence of women who welcome the pressures. However, that is a feature not of the concept of consent itself, but of the particular conceptions of consent that jurisdictions currently embrace. No legal change can be won under any banner–whether under the banner of 'force' or 'non-consent'—without first persuading jurisdictions to alter their understanding of the kinds of pressures on women that are wrongful. Once a jurisdiction is persuaded to change its norms, the norms can be fully codified in terms of consent. Indeed, in some ways, employing 'non-consent' is more precise than using 'force'. Both concepts suffice to enable jurisdictions to prohibit an actor from subjecting a victim to *x* without the victim's having in any way chosen it for themselves (*e.g.*, victims who are unconscious or who resist to the utmost). And force and non-consent both suffice to enable jurisdictions to punish an actor for inducing a victim to submit to *x* by means of wrongful pressures to acquiesce in *x*. But force and non-consent do not suffice equally well to prohibit an actor from inducing a victim to acquiesce to *x* by means *other* than pressure (*e.g.*, taking advantage of a victim's ignorance, immaturity, or mental incompetence to induce her to choose *x* where doing so is not in her interests). There is only one way in which jurisdictions can invoke the concept of force to prevent an actor from inducing a victim to choose *x* by wrongful means other than wrongful pressure. It is the same circuitous and disingenuous way in which jurisdictions presently invoke force in such cases: jurisdictions begin with judgments of non-consent and then present them as fictions of force, by declaring that to induce a person to acquiesce to *x* without her possessing the knowledge or competence necessary to take responsibility for her choice is to use 'force'.[56] It would be simpler and more perspicuous to start and finish with legal consent as the controlling standard.

Why, then, does the English Law Commission speak indiscriminately of what are, in essence, distinct conceptions of consent? Why do state legislatures commonly frame rape statutes in terms of force, or force and non-consent, in ways that are redundant, circuitous, or incomplete? Why do commentators conclude that rape statutes, if they are to be just, must be framed in whole or in part in terms of force? Perhaps it is because they only dimly grasp the diverse work that consent does in legal discourse and, dimly grasping it, fail to appreciate its potential scope.

Notes

1. Law Commission, *Consent and Offenses Against the Person*.
2. Roberts, 'The Philosophical Foundations of *Consent in the Criminal Law*', p. 389. *See* also Omerod, 'Consent and Offences Against the Person' (criticizing the 1994 paper for 'superficiality'); Leng, 'Consent and Offences Against the Person' (criticizing the 1994 paper for failure to 'set out its philosophical underpinnings in terms of the proper aims of the law').
3. Law Commission, *Consent and the Criminal Law*. Philosopher Paul Roberts' paper, 'Consent and the Criminal Law: The Philosophical Foundations', was published by the Law Commission as Appendix C to the 1995 Consultation Paper. Roberts subsequently wrote a separate critique of the 1995 Consultation Paper. *See* Roberts, 'The Philosophical Foundations of *Consent and the Criminal Law*'.
4. Roberts, 'The Philosophical Foundations of *Consent and the Criminal Law*', p. 389 ('conceptual complexity'); Shute, 'The Second Law Commission Consultation Paper on Consent', p. 685.
5. Law Commission, *Consent and the Criminal Law*, para. 27.
6. Law Commission, *Consent in the Criminal Law*, para. 5. *See* also *id*. at para. 30:

   > We invite comments on what the law should be in relation to a case where an apparent consent is procured by an offer to avert a consequence of such a kind that, if the apparent consent were procured by the offeror's threat to bring that consequence about, that threat would nullify the consent altogether so as to incur for the offeror liability for the offence to which consent is a defence.

7. Law Commission, *Consent in the Criminal Law,* para. 8(1) ('express or implied'), and para. 12 ('a valid consent may not be given by a person without capacity').
8. Law Commission, *Consent in the Criminal Law,* para. 12-13, and 17. *See* also *id.* at para. 9(a) (distinguishing the defense of 'consent' from the independent defense of 'believ[ing] that the other person consented . . . [where] it would not have been obvious to a reasonable person in his or her position that the other person did not so consent').
9. *See, e.g.*, Law Commission, *Consent in the Criminal Law,* para. 6, 8(1) and 9.
10. Law Commission, *Consent in the Criminal Law,* para. 8(2).
11. For example, Joel Feinberg, having first stipulated that 'consent' is a legal concept for expressions of acquiescence that constitute defenses to crime, not only thereafter uses 'consent' in a factual sense to refer to expressions of acquiescence that do *not* constitute defenses, but also thereafter uses 'consent' to refer *not* to expressions but to what expressions *express, i.e.*, underlying states of mind of acquiescence. Compare Feinberg, *Harm To Self,* pp. 330-31, with *id.* at 262-63, 287, 333. Similarly, Alan Wertheimer, having declared himself to be 'squarely in the camp that maintains that the concept of consent is fundamentally legal', thereafter contradicts himself by asking, '[I]s it permissible for a male to have sexual relations with a woman who consents to sexual relations while voluntarily intoxicated.' Wertheimer, 'Intoxicated Consent To Sexual Relations', p. 373.
12. The Statute of Westminster (Second) of 1285 made it an offense for a man to 'ravish a woman, married, maid or other where she neither assented before nor after'. 13 Edward I, c. 34, § 1. English commentators and courts thereafter generally treated 'assent' as interchangeable with 'consent'. *See* Hale, *The History of the Pleas of the Crown,* vol. 1, p. *629; Regina v. Clarence, 22 Q.B.D. 23, 51 (1888) ('Rape consists in a man having sexual intercourse with a woman without her consent') (opinion of Hawkins, J.); Rex v. Harms, [1944] 2 D.L.R. 61. *See* generally Pollock and Maitland, *The History of English Law,* vol. 2, pp. 490-91.
13. Sexual Offences (Amendment) Act 1976, s 1(1). The House of Lords, construing the 1976 statute, ruled that the word 'unlawful' in the statute was mere surplusage. *See* Regina v. R., [1992] 1 AC 599, [1991] 4 All ER 481, [1991] 3 WLR 767:

    > For the purposes of section 1 of the Sexual Offences Act 1956 (which relates to rape) a man commits rape if—(a) he has unlawful sexual intercourse with a woman who at the time of the intercourse does not consent to it; and (b) at the time he knows that she does not consent to the intercourse or he is reckless as to whether she consents to it. . . .

14. *See* Regina v. R., [1992] 1 AC 599, [1991] 4 All ER 481, [1991] 3 WLR 767 (construing 'consent' to sexual intercourse in 1976 statute as being confined to prescriptive consent).
15. Arkansas Statutes Annotated §§ 5-14-101, 5-14-103 (1999).
16. Maryland Annotated Code art. 27, §§ 461(d), 463 (1999).
17. Maryland Annotated Code art. 27, §§ 461(d), 463(a)(2) (1999).
18. Colorado Revised Statutes § 18-3-401(3) (2000).
19. Colorado Revised Statutes § 18-3-402(4)(3) (2000).
20. *See* Utah Code § 76-5-402 (2001). *See* also Kansas Statutes § 21-3502 (2000); Montana Code § 45-5-502(1) (1995); Wisconsin Statutes § 940.225 (2000).
21. *See* Colorado Revised Statutes § 18-3-402 (2001) ('against the victim's will').
22. Ohio Revised Code § 5924.120(A) (2001) (governing members of the Ohio military) ('Any person subject to this code who commits an act of sexual intercourse with a female not his wife, by force and without her consent, is guilty of rape').

23. *See* California Penal Code § 261(2) (2001); Massachusetts Laws ch. 265, § 22 (2002); North Carolina General Statutes § 14-27.3 (2000); Virginia Code § 18.2-61 (2001). Oddly enough, Maryland defines rape as sexual intercourse by 'force' and without 'consent' *and* 'against' the 'will'. *See* Maryland Code art. 27, § 463 (1999).
24. *See* West, 'A Comment on Consent, Sex, and Rape', p. 239.
25. *See, e.g.*, California Penal Code § 261 (2000).
26. *See, e.g.*, New Mexico Statutes § 30-9-10(A) (2002) ('"force or coercion" means: . . . (4) the perpetration of criminal sexual penetration or criminal sexual contact when the perpetrator knows or has reason to know that the victim is unconscious [or] asleep. . . '.). California v. Cicero, 157 Cal. App. 3d 465, 475, 204 Cal. Rptr. 582, 590 (1984) ('"force" plays merely a supporting evidentiary role', constituting whatever demonstrates that the 'act of intercourse has been undertaken against a victim's will'); Massachusetts v. Burke, 105 Mass. 376, 377 (1870) (finding that where defendant knew that complainant was so drunk as to be incapable of consenting, the requisite force was 'such force as was necessary to effect the purpose'). *See* generally Falk, 'Rape By Fraud and Rape By Coercion', pp. 52-53, 138-40.
27. *See, e.g.*, Arkansas Compiled Acts § 5-14-103L(a)(3) (2001) ('compulsion'); District of Columbia Code § 22-4102(1)-(2) (2001); Idaho Code § 18-6101(3) (2001) ('force or violence'); Indiana Code § 35-42-4-1 (2001); New Jersey Statutes § 2C:14-2c(1) (2001) ('physical force or coercion'); Ohio Code § 2907.02(2) (2001); Oklahoma Statutes, tit. 21, § 1111(3) (2000); South Dakota Codified Laws § 22-22-1(2) (2001).
28. *See, e.g.*, Mosley v. State, 323 Ark. 244, 914 S.W.2d 731 (1996) ('The test for determining whether there was force is whether the act was against the will of the party upon whom the act was committed'); In re M.T.S., 129 N.J. 422, 448-49, 609 A.2d 1266, 1278-79 (1992) (defining 'force' to mean without 'consent').
29. *See, e.g.*, New Hampshire Revised Statutes §§ 632-A:2, 632-A:4, 632-A:7 (2001), as construed in New Hampshire v. Cooper, 135 N.H. 258, 603 A.2d 499 (1992).
30. *See, e.g.*, California v. Haywood, 118 Ill. 2d 263, 515 N.E.2d 45 (1987) (construing an Illinois rape statute, which speaks only of 'force or the threat of force', as implying a defense of consent). *See* generally, Michelle Anderson, 'Reviving Resistance in Rape Law', *University of Illinois Law Review*, pp. 953-1011, pp. 1000-01 ('In twenty-eight states and the District of Columbia, only force appears in the statutory definition, although consent is a defense under the case law').
31. *See, e.g.*, Connecticut Gen. Stat. §§ 53a-70, 53a-71 (2001).
32. *See, e.g.*, Pennsylvania v. Brown, 184 Pa. Super. 494, 498, 136 A.2d 138, 140 (1957) ('Force may be constructive where the female is unconscious from intoxication or the use of drugs or asleep and where, known to the defendant, she is so unsound of mind as to be unable to give legal consent').
33. *See, e.g.*, Iowa Code § 709.1(1) (1999) ('Any sex act between persons is sexual abuse by either of the persons when the act is performed with the other person in any of the following circumstances. The act is done by force or against the will of the other'). *See* also Alabama Code §§ 13A-6-61 (2001) ('by forcible compulsion'), 13A-6-65 ('without her consent'); Pennsylvania Code, tit. 18, §§ 3121 (by force'), 3124.1 ('without the complainant's consent'). Statutes like the aforementioned are to be distinguished from statutes that define rape as sexual intercourse by 'force' or 'without consent' but that use 'without consent' to refer not to absences of legal consent but to absences of factual consent—that is, to instances in which women have not in any way consciously acquiesced in sexual intercourse, whether because they are unconscious or are unaware that sexual intercourse is occurring. Cf. MacKinnon, *Sex Equality: Rape*, pp. 855-56

(misinterpreting the Penal Code of India, which uses 'without consent' to mean 'without *factual* consent', as if it were using 'without consent' to mean 'without *legal* consent').

34. *See, e.g.*, Ledezma v. Iowa, 632 N.W.2d 911 (2001) (consent is a defense to a charge of having sexual intercourse with a woman by 'force' or 'against' her 'will').
35. Massachusetts v. Berkowitz, 537 Pa. 143, 150, 641 A.2d 1161, 1164 (1994) (holding that the defendant did not use sufficient pressure to be guilty of 'forcible' sexual intercourse under Pennsylvania Code, tit. 18 § 3121, but that he did use sufficient pressure to be guilty of indecent assault under Pennsylvania Code, tit. 18, § 3126, by disregarding the victim's 'no').
36. Although rape had been defined and criminalized by the Statute of Westminster (Second) in 1285, the English courts treated it as a common-law offense, scarcely ever making reference to the Statute of Westminster. In the Sexual Offences Act of 1956, Parliament established penalties for rape, but did not define it, leaving it to the courts to define it. *See* Director of Public Prosecutions v. Morgan, [1976] AC 182, [1975] 2 All ER 347, [1975] 2 WLR 913 ('The offence lacks statutory definition. The Sexual Offences Act 1956, s 1(1) merely declares it an offence for a man to rape a woman.' (Lord Simon Glaisdale); *id.* ('section 1 of the 1956 Act does not say that a man who has sexual intercourse with a woman who does not consent to it commits an offence; it says that a man who rapes a woman commits an offence. Rape is not a word in the use of which lawyers have a monopoly and the question to be answered in this case, as I see it, . . . according to the ordinary use of the English language . . . '.) (Lord Cross of Chelsea). Finally, in 1976 Parliament defined the offense by statute. *See* Sexual Offences (Amendment) Act 1976, s 1(1).
37. *See, e.g.*, Rex v. Harling, [1938] 1 All ER 307 (defining rape as 'carnal knowledge of [a woman] . . . without her consent and against her will'); Director of Public Prosecutions v. Morgan, [1976] AC 182, [1975] 2 All ER 347, [1975] 2 WLR 913 ([The trial judge's instruction, describing rape as 'having unlawful sexual intercourse with a woman without her consent and by force'] is 'unexceptional' (Lord Hailsham of St. Marylebone; *id.* ('[It] is my opinion that the prohibited act is and always has been intercourse without consent of the victim') (Lord Hailsham of St. Marylebone).
38. *See, e.g.*, Rex v. Harling, [1938] 1 All ER 307 (underage girls), and Regina v. Flattery, 2 Q.B.D. 410 (1877) (girl, who thought her physician was conducting a gynecological exam, was unaware that he was having sexual intercourse with her). But compare Massachusetts v. Goldenberg, 338 Mass. 377, 155 N.E.2d 187 (1959) (a physician who elicits sexual intercourse from a woman by means of fraud does not do so 'by force and against her will' within the meaning of Massachusetts law, because force is different from fraud), with Massachusetts v. Helfant, 398 Mass. 214, 221 n.5, 496 N.E.2d 433, 439 n.5 (1986) (questioning whether *Goldenberg* is good law).
39. *See* Secretary of State for the Home Office, *Report of the Advisory Group on the Law of Rape*, p. 195 para. 18-20:

    The traditional common law definition, derived from a 17th century writer and still in use, is that rape consists in having unlawful sexual intercourse with a woman without her consent, by force, fear or fraud.

    This definition can be misleading, since the essence of the crime consists in having sexual intercourse with a woman without her consent and it is, therefore, rape to have intercourse with a woman who is asleep or with one who unwillingly submits without a struggle.

    As Smith and Hogan point out in their text book on the Criminal Law: 'Earlier authorities emphasized the use of force; but it is now clear that lack of consent is the crux of the matter and this may exist though no force is used. The test is not 'was the act against her will?' but 'was it without her consent?'

40. *See* West, 'A Comment on Consent, Sex, and Rape', p. 233 ('[I]n most states, sex that is undeniably forced is, nevertheless, not rape if the victim "consented" to it; and, second, sex that is undeniably nonconsensual is, nevertheless, not rape if there was no force used to obtain it. Scores of feminist scholars and reformers, as well as a number of criminal law scholars . . . view this narrow definition as basically indefensible'). Paradoxically, Catharine MacKinnon criticizes the conjunction of force and non-consent on the ground that the requirement of non-consent is both redundant and abusive. *See* MacKinnon, *Toward A Feminist Theory of the State*, pp. 172, 245.
41. *See, e.g.*, MacKinnon, Toward A Feminist Theory of the State, p. 185.
42. *See* Estrich, 'Rape', pp. 1095-96.
43. *See* McGregor, 'When She Says No', pp. 189-203; West, 'A Comment on Consent, Sex, and Rape', pp. 243-46.
44. Joan McGregor and Robin West both argue that a lack of consent ought to suffice by itself to render an actor guilty of rape. *See* McGregor, 'When She Says No', pp. 189-203; West, 'A Comment on Consent, Sex, and Rape', pp. 243-46.
45. *See* West, 'A Comment on Consent, Sex, and Rape', p. 239.
46. West, 'A Comment on Consent, Sex, and Rape', pp. 239-40.
47. *See* the Conclusion to Chapter 5.
48. *See* Schulhofer, *Unwanted Sex*, p. 197.
49. For courts that commit the same fallacy, *see* North Carolina v. Alston, 310 N.C. 399, 408, 312 S.E.2d 470, 475-76 (1984) (dictum); Regina v. Olugboja, [1982] 1 QB 320. Of course, it is not a contradiction for a court to grade sexual offenses by defining a more serious offense as sexual intercourse by force and without consent, while defining the lesser as sexual intercourse without consent alone, provided that it is understood that the force that is needed to taint consent for purposes of the higher offense (say, threats of physical harm) is different from the lesser force that suffices to taint consent for the lesser offense (say, force that overcomes a 'no'). *See* 18 Pennsylvania Compiled Statutes §§ 3121, 3124.1 (2001).
50. *See* MacKinnon, *Toward A Feminist Theory of the State*, p. 245; West, 'A Comment on Consent, Sex, and the Law', p. 244.
51. West, 'A Comment on Consent, Sex, and Rape', p. 238.
52. *See* the discussion of *Valdez* in the Introduction.
53. *See* MacKinnon, *Toward A Feminist Theory of the State*, p. 172.
54. *See* MacKinnon, *Sex Equality: Rape*, pp. 769, 779, 817-18, 839-40, 885-87.
55. *See* Chapter 5, pp. 201-10.
56. *See* notes 26, 28, 32.

Bibliography

Books and Articles

Alexander, L. (1996), 'The Moral Magic of Consent (II)', *Legal Theory*, vol. 2, pp. 165-74.

Alexander, L. (1994), 'Crime and Culpability', *Journal of Contemporary Legal Issues*, vol. 5, pp. 1-30.

Alexander, L. (1987), 'Justification and Innocent Aggressors', *Wayne Law Review*, vol. 33, pp. 1177-89.

American Law Institute. (1980), *Model Penal Code and Commentaries*, American Law Institute, Philadelphia.

American Law Institute. (1965), *Restatement of the Law (2d) Torts*, West, St. Paul.

Anderson, M. (1998), 'Reviving Resistance in Rape Law', *University of Illinois Law Review*, pp. 953-1011.

Anscombe, G.E.M. (1963), 'Two Kinds of Error in Action', *Journal of Philosophy*, vol. 60, pp. 393-401.

Aquinas, T., *Summa Theologiae*, T.C. O'Brien, trans, 1974, Blackfriars, London.

Appleyard, B. (1992), 'Sleazy Legal Dance Round the Minefield of Date-Rape', *Sunday Times*, 2 February 1992.

Archard, D. (1998), *Sexual Consent*, Westview, Boulder.

Archard, D. (1997), 'A Nod's As Good As A Wink: Consent, Convention, and Reasonable Belief', *Legal Theory*, vol. 3, pp. 273–90.

Aristotle, *Nichomachean Ethics* (J.A.K. Thomson, trans, H. Tredennick, rev ed, 1976).

Ashworth, A. (1993), 'Taking the Consequences', in S. Shute, J. Gardner, and J. Horder, eds, *Action and Value in the Criminal Law* , Clarendon, Oxford, pp. 107-24.

Austin, J.L. (1979), 'Performative Utterances', in *Philosophical Papers*, J.O. Urmson & G.J. Warnock, eds, 3rd ed, Clarendon, Oxford.

Austin, J.L. (1962), *How To Do Things With Words*, J. O. Urmson & M. Sbisa, eds, 2nd ed, Harvard, Cambridge, Massachusetts.

Baber, H.E. (1987), 'How Bad Is Rape?', *Hypatia*, vol. 2, no. 2, pp. 125-38.

Barry, B. (1989), *Theories of Justice*, University of California Press, Berkeley.

Barton, J.L. (1992), 'The Story Of Marital Rape', *The Law Quarterly Review*, vol. 108, pp. 260-71.

Bejma, V. (2000), 'Protective Cruelty: State v. Yanez and Strict Liability as to Age in Statutory Rape', *Roger Williams University Law Review*, vol. 5, pp. 499-561.

Benedet, J. (1995), 'Hostile Environment Sexual Harassment Claims and the Unwelcome Influence of Rape Law', *Michigan Journal of Gender & Law*, vol. 3, pp. 125-74 (1995).

Berger, V. (1988), 'Real Rape', *Criminal Justice Ethics*, vol. 7, pp. 69-81.

Berger, V. (1977), 'Man's Trial, Woman's Tribulation', *Columbia Law Review*, vol. 77, pp. 1-103.

Bertolet, R. (1994), 'Are There Indirect Speech Acts?', in S. Tsohatzidis (ed.), *Foundations of Speech Act Theory*, Routledge, New York, pp. 338-39.

Bienen, L. (1977-78), 'Mistakes', *Philosophy and Public Affairs*, vol. 7, pp. 224-45.

Bogart, J.H. (1996), 'Commodification and Phenomenology: Evading Consent in Theory Regarding Rape', *Legal Theory*, vol. 2, pp. 253-64.

Bogart, J.H. (1991), 'On the Nature of Rape', *Public Affairs Quarterly*, vol. 5, no. 2, pp. 117-136.
Bradley, C. (1999), *Criminal Procedure: A Worldwide Survey*, North Carolina, Durham.
Brazener, R. (1972), 'Annotation: Validity of Statute Making Adultery and Fornication Criminal Offenses', *American Law Reports*, 3rd series, vol. 41, pp. 1338-42.
Brett, N. (1998), 'Sexual Offenses and Consent', *Canadian Journal of Law and Jurisprudence*, vol. 11, no. 1, pp. 69-88.
Brett, N. (1988), 'Commentary', in A. Bayefsky (ed.), *Legal Theory Meets Legal Practice*, pp. 253-257.
Brock, D. (1993), *Life and Death: Philosophical Essays in Biomedical Ethics*, Cambridge, New York.
Brock, D. and A. Buchanan. (1990), *Deciding for Others: The Ethics of Surrogate Decisionmaking*, Cambridge University, Cambridge.
Bryden, D. (2000), 'Redefining Rape', *Buffalo Criminal Law Review*, vol. 3, pp. 317- 488.
Byrnes, C. (2001), 'Putting the Focus Where it Belongs: Mens Rea, Consent, Force, and the Crime of Rape', *Yale Journal of Law and Feminism*, vol. 10, pp. 277-305.
Bronitt, S. (1992), 'Rape and Lack of Consent', *Criminal Law Journal*, vol. 16, no.5, pp. 289-310.
Buchanan, A. (1988), 'Advance Directives And The Personal Identity Problem', *Philosophy and Public Affairs*, vol. 17, no. 4, pp. 277-302.
Buchanan, A. and D. Brock. (1990), *Deciding for Others: The Ethics of Surrogate Decisionmaking*, Cambridge University, Cambridge.
Burt, R. (1979), *Taking Care Of Strangers*, Free Press, New York.
Byrn, R. (1975), 'Compulsory Lifesaving Treatment For the Competent Adult', *Fordham Law Review*, vol. 44, pp. 1-36.
Campbell, C. (1997), 'Annotation: Mistake or Lack of Information as to Victim's Age as Defense to Statutory Rape', *American Law Reports* 5th series, vol. 46, pp. 499-522.
Cantor, N. (1996), 'Discarding Substituted Judgment And Best Interests: Toward A Constructive Preference Standard For Dying, Previously Competent Patients Without Advance Instructions', *Rutgers Law Review*, vol. 48, pp. 1193-1272.
Carter, R. (1977), 'Justifying Paternalism', *Canadian Journal of Philosophy*, vol. 7, no. 7, pp. 133-45.
Chamallas, M. (1988), 'Consent, Equality, and the Legal Control of Sexual Conduct', *Southern California Law Review*, vol. 61, pp. 777-862.
Chuang, J. (1998), 'Redirecting the Debate Over Trafficking in Women: Definitions, Paradigms, and Contexts', *Harvard Human Rights Journal*, vol. 11, pp. 65-107.
Cohen, S. (1977), 'Distinctions Among Blame Concepts', *Philosophy and Phenomenological Research*, vol. 38, pp. 149-66.
Connerton, K. (1997), 'The Resurgence Of The Marital Rape Exemption: The Victimization Of Teens By Their Statutory Rapists', *Albany Law Review*, vol. 61, pp. 237-343.
Coughlin, A. (1991), 'Sex and Guilt', *Virginia Law Review*, vol. 84, pp. 1-46.
Cowling, M. (1998), *Date Rape and Consent*, Ashgate, Aldershot.
Dan-Cohen, M. (2000), 'Basic Values and the Victim's State of Mind', *California Law Review*, vol. 88, pp. 759-778.
Dan-Cohen, M. (1992), 'Conceptions of Choice and Conceptions of Autonomy', *Ethics*, vol. 102, no. 2, pp. 221-43.
Dan-Cohen, M. (1984), 'Decision Rules and Conduct Rules: On Acoustic Separation in Criminal Law', *Harvard Law Review*, vol. 97, pp. 625-77.

Didion, J. (1992), 'Sentimental Journeys', *After Henry*, Simon & Schuster, New York, pp. 253-319.

Dresser, R. (1986), 'Life, Death, and Incompetent Patients: Conceptual Infirmities and Hidden Values in the Law', *Arizona Law Review*, vol. 28, pp. 373-405.

Dresser, R. (1982), 'Ulysses And The Psychiatrists: A Legal And Policy Analysis Of The Voluntary Commitment Contract', *Harvard Civil Rights-Civil Liberties Law Review*, vol. 16, pp. 777- 854.

Dressler, J. (1998), 'Where We Have Been, And Where We Might Be Going: Some Cautionary Reflections On Rape Law Reform', *Cleveland State Law Review*, vol. 46, pp. 409-422.

Dripps, D. (1994), 'Panel Discussion: Men, Women, and Rape', *Fordham Law Review*, vol. 63, pp. 125-73.

Dripps, D. (1992), 'Beyond Rape: An Essay on the Difference Between the Presence of Force and the Absence of Consent', *Columbia Law Review*, vol. 92, pp. 1780-1809.

Duff, A. (1996), *Criminal Attempts*, Clarendon, Oxford.

Duff, A. (1993), 'Choice, Character, and Criminal Liability', *Law and Philosophy*, vol. 12, pp. 345-83.

Duff, A. (1990), *Intention, Agency, and Criminal Liability: Philosophy of Action and the Criminal Law*, Basil Blackwell, Oxford.

Duff, A. (1986), *Trials and Punishments*, Cambridge University, Cambridge.

Dworkin, G. (1966), 'The Resistance Standard in Rape Legislation', *Stanford Law Review*, vol. 18, pp. 680-89.

Dworkin, G. (1999), 'Devlin Was Right: Law and the Enforcement of Morality', *William & Mary Law Review*, vol. 40, pp. 927-46.

Dworkin, R. (1975), 'The Original Position', in N. Daniels, ed., *Reading Rawls*, Basic, New York, pp. 16-53.

Eaton, T. and E. Larson. (1991), 'Experimenting with the "Right to Die" in the Laboratory of the States', *Georgia Law Review*, vol. 25, pp. 1253-1326.

Edelman, D. and G. Thomas. (2000), 'Consent To Have Sex: Empirical Evidence About "No"', *University of Pittsburgh Law Review*, vol. 61, 579-628.

Elster, J. (1984), *Ulysses And The Sirens: Studies In Rationality And Irrationality*, Cambridge University, Cambridge.

Eskow, L. (1996), 'The Ultimate Weapon?: Demythologizing Spousal Rape and Reconceptualizing Its Prosecution', *Stanford Law Review*, vol. 48, p. 677.

Estrich, S. (1994), 'Rape: A Question of Force', *USA Today*, 11 August 1994, p. 13A.

Estrich, S. (1994), 'Real Date Rape Victims', *USA Today*, 26 May 1994.

Estrich, S. (1992), 'Palm Beach Stories', *Law and Philosophy*, vol. 11, pp. 5-33.

Estrich, S. (1987), *Real Rape*, Harvard, Cambridge, Massachusetts.

Estrich, S. (1986), 'Rape', *Yale Law Journal*, vol. 95, pp. 1087-1184.

Falk, P. (1998), 'Rape By Fraud and Rape By Coercion', *Brooklyn Law Review*, vol. 64, pp. 39-180.

Feinberg, J. (1988), *Harmless Wrongdoing*, Oxford, New York.

Feinberg, J. (1986), *Harm To Self*, Oxford, New York.

Feinberg J. (1985), *Offense To Others*, Oxford, New York.

Feinberg, J. (1984), *Harm To Others*, Oxford, New York.

Feldman, Heidi. (1995), 'Objectivity in Legal Judgment', *Michigan Law Review*, vol. 92, no. 2, pp. 1187-1255.

Fellows, M.L. and B. Balos. (1990), 'A Matter of Prostitution: Becoming Respectable', *New York University Law Review*, vol. 74, pp. 1220-1303.

Fletcher, G. (1978), *Rethinking Criminal Law*, Little Brown, Boston.

Foa, P. (1977), 'What's Wrong With Rape?', in M. Vetterling-Braggin, F. Elliston, and J. English, *Feminism and Philosophy*, Rowman and Littlefield, Totowa, pp. 346-59.

Francis, L. (1996), *Date Rape: Feminism, Philosophy, and Law*. Pennsylvania State, University Park.

Fritsch, J (1993), 'The Law That Made Amy Fisher a Victim', *The New York Times*, 18 April 1993, section 4, p. 2, col. 1.

Garcia, R. (1992), 'Rape, Lies, and Videotape', *Loyola of Los Angeles Law Review*, vol. 25, pp. 711-56.

Gauthier, D. (1986), *Morals By Agreement*, Clarendon, Oxford.

Goodman, E. (1993), 'The Struggle on College Campuses To Create a Standard of Sexual Equality', *The Boston Globe*, 19 September 1993.

Grey, T.C. (1983), *The Legal Enforcement of Morality* , Knopf, New York.

Grogan, D. 'The Six Faces of Sarah Bear Witness to a Sexual Assault', *People*, November 26, 1990, section: crime, page 107 et seq.

Gross, J. (1991), 'Even The Victim Can Be Slow To Recognize Rape', *New York Times*, 28 May 1991, section A, page 14, col. 3.

Haji, I. (1997), 'Multiple Selves and Culpability', *Legal Theory*, vol. 3, pp. 249-276.

Hale, M. (1736), *The History of the Pleas of the Crown*, R.H. Small ed., 1847, Philadelphia.

Hampton, J. (1988), 'Forgiveness, Resentment, and Hatred', in J. Murphy and J. Hampton, *Forgiveness and Mercy*, Cambridge University, New York, pp. 35-87.

Harcourt, B. (1999), 'Criminal Law: The Collapse of the Harm Principle', *Journal of Criminal Law and Criminology*, vol. 90, pp. 109-94.

Harman, J. (1981), 'Harm, Consent, and Distress', *Journal of Value Inquiry*, vol. 15, pp. 293-309.

Harmon, L. (1990), 'Falling Off the Vine: Legal Fictions And The Doctrine Of Substituted Judgment', *Yale Law Journal*, vol. 100, pp. 1-71.

Harrison, R. (1986), 'Rape—A Case Study In Political Philosophy', in S. Tomaselli and R. Porter (eds), *Rape*, Basil Blackwell, Oxford, pp. 41-56.

Hart, H.L.A. (1968), *Punishment and Responsibility: Essays in Philosophy of Law*, Oxford, New York.

Hart, H.L.A. (1957), 'Analytical Jurisprudence in Mid-Twentieth Century: A Reply To Professor Bodenheimer', *Pennsylvania Law Review*, vol. 105, pp. 953-75.

Hasday, J.E. (2000), 'Contest and Consent: A Legal History of Marital Rape', *California Law Review*, vol. 88, 1375-1505.

Henderson, L. (1993), 'Getting To Know: Honoring Women in Law and in Fact', *Texas Journal of Women and the Law*, vol. 2, pp. 41-73.

Henderson, L. (1992), 'Rape and Responsibility', *Law & Philosophy*, vol. 11, nos. 1-2, pp. 127-78.

Hohfeld, W. (1919), *Fundamental Legal Conceptions*, Yale, New Haven.

Hom, R.M.. (1987), '*State v. Moorman*: Can Sex With a Sleeping Woman Constitute Forcible Rape', *North Carolina Law Review*, vol. 65, pp. 1246-66.

Home Office. (2000), *Setting the Boundaries: Reforming the Law on Sex Offences*, HMSO, London.

Homer, *The Odyssey*, R. Fagles, trans, 1996, Penguin, New York.

Hornsby, J. (1994), 'Illocution and Its Significance', in S. Tsohatzidis (ed.), *Foundations of Speech Act Theory*, Routledge, New York, pp. 187-207.

Hubin, D. and Haely. (1999), 'Rape and the Reasonable Man', *Law and Philosophy*, vol. 18, pp. 113-39.

Hurd, H. (1996), 'The Moral Magic of Consent', *Legal Theory*, vol. 2, no. 2, pp.121-46.

Ingman, T. (1981), 'A History Of The Defence of *Volenti Non Fit Injuria*', *Juridical Review New Series*, vol. 26, no. 1, pp. 1-28.

Karen, R. (2001), *The Forgiving Self: The Road From Resentment To Connection*, Doubleday, New York.

Karnezis, K. (1979), 'Annotation: Patients Right To Refuse Treatment Allegedly Necessary To Sustain Life', *American Law Reports*, 3rd series, vol. 93, pp. 67-85.

Kadish, S. (1992), 'Letting Patients Die: Legal and Moral Reflections', *California Law Review*, vol. 80, pp. 857-88.

Kadish, S. and S. Schulhofer. (1995), *Criminal Law and Its Processes*, 6th ed., Little, Brown, Boston.

Kinports, K. (2001), 'Rape and Force: The Forgotten Mens Rea', *Buffalo Criminal Law Review*, vol. 4, pp. 755-99.

Kleinig, J. (1979), 'Consent As A Defence In Criminal Law', *Archiv Fur Rechts und Sozialphilosophie*, vol. 65, pp. 329-46.

Kole, S. (1994), 'Annotation: Statute Protecting Minors In A Specified Range From Rape Or Other Sexual Activity As Applicable to Defendant Minor Within Protected Age Group', *American Law Reports*, vol. 18, 5th series, pp. 856-91.

Kramer, K. (1994), 'Rule by Myth: The Social and Legal Dynamics Governing Alcohol-Related Acquaintance Rapes', *Stanford Law Review*, vol. 47, pp. 115-160.

LaFave, W. and A. Scott. (1986), *Criminal Law*, 2nd ed., West, St. Paul.

LaFave, W. and A. Scott (1986), *Substantive Criminal Law*, 2nd ed., West, St. Paul.

Larsen, K., 'Rape or Similar Offense Based on Intercourse With Woman Who Is Allegedly Mentally Deficient', *American Law Reports*, 3rd series, vol. 31, pp.1227-76.

Larson, J. (1993), 'Women Understand So Little, They Call My Good Nature Deceit', *Columbia Law Review*, vol. 93, pp. 374-472.

Lavin, M. (1986), 'Ulysses Contracts', *Journal of Applied Philosophy*, vol. 3, no. 1, pp. 89-101.

Law Commission. (1995), Consultation Paper No. 139: *Consent and the Criminal Law*, HMSO, London.

Law Commission. (1994), Consultation Paper No. 134: *Consent and Offenses Against the Person*, HMSO, London.

Leng, R. (1995), 'Consent and Offences Against the Person: Law Commission Consultation Paper No. 134', [1994] *Criminal Law Review*, pp. 480-88.

Leo, J. (1991), 'Don't Oversimplify Date Rape', *U.S. News and World Report*, 11 February 1991, p. 17.

Leonard, G. (2001), 'Rape, Murder, and Formalism: What Happens If We Define Mistake of Law?', *Colorado Law Review*, vol. 72, pp. 507-94.

MacKinnon, C. (2001), *Sex Equality: Rape Law*, Foundation, New York.

MacKinnon, C. (1988), *Toward A Feminist Theory of the State*, Harvard, Cambridge, Massachusetts.

MacKinnon, C. (1983), 'Feminism, Marxism, Method and the State: Toward Feminist Jurisprudence', *Signs: Journal of Women in Culture and Society*, vol. 8, no. 4, pp. 635-658.

Malm, H.M. (1996), 'The Ontological Status of Consent and Its Implications for the Law on Rape', *Legal Theory*, vol. 2, pp. 147-64.

Mansfield, J. (1961), 'Informed Choice In The Law Of Torts', *Louisiana Law Review*, vol. 22, pp. 17-76.

McCutcheon, P. (1994), 'Sports Violence, Consent, and the Criminal Law', *Northern Ireland Legal Quarterly*, vol. 45, no. 3, pp. 267-84.

McGregor, J. (1996), 'Why When She Says No She Doesn't Mean Maybe and Doesn't Mean Yes', *Legal Theory*, vol. 2, pp. 185-208.

McGregor, J. (1994), 'Force, Consent, and the Reasonable Woman', in J. Coleman and A. Buchanan (eds), *In Harm's Way: Essays in Honor of Joel Feinberg*, Cambridge University, Cambridge, pp. 231-54.

Mill, J.S. (1848), *Principles of Political Economy*, Ashley ed., 1909, Kelley, Fairfield, 1987.

Mill, J.S. (1859), *On Liberty*, G. Himmelfarb ed., 1974, Penguin Books, London.

Miller, F. (1969), *Prosecution: The Decision To Charge A Suspect With a Crime*, Little Brown, Boston.

Moore, M. (1999), 'The Independent Moral Significance of Wrongdoing', in *Placing Blame: A General Theory of the Criminal Law*, Clarendon Press, Oxford, pp. 104-52.

Moore, M. (1993), 'Foreseeing Harm Opaquely', in S. Shute, J. Gardner, and J. Horder (eds), *Action and Value In Criminal Law*, Clarendon, Oxford, pp. 125-55.

Murphy, J. (1994), 'Some Ruminations on Women, Violence, and the Criminal Law', in J.L. Coleman and A. Buchanan, *In Harm's Way: Essays in Honor of Joel Feinberg*, Cambridge University, Cambridge, pp. 208-229.

Nagel, T. (1979), 'Moral Luck', in *Mortal Questions*, Cambridge University, Cambridge, pp. 24-38.

Note. (1991), 'Constitutional Barriers to Civil and Criminal Restrictions on Pre- and Extramarital Sex', *Harvard Law Review*, vol. 104, pp. 1660-80.

Note. (1988), 'Focusing on the Offender's Forceful Conduct: A Proposal for the Redefinition of Rape Laws', *George Washington Law Review*, vol. 56, pp. 399-430.

Note. (1966), 'The Resistance Standard in Rape Legislation', *Stanford Law Review*, vol. 18, pp. 680-89.

Note. (1952), 'Forcible and Statutory Rape: A Review of the Operations and Objectives of the Consent Standard', *Yale Law Journal*, vol. 62, pp. 54-83.

Oberman, M. (1994), 'Turning Girls Into Women: Re-Evaluating Modern Statutory Rape Law', *J. Criminal Law and Criminology*, vol. 85, pp. 15-79.

Olsen, F. (1988), 'The Supreme Court, 1988 Term: Comment: Unraveling Compromise', *Harvard Law Review*, vol. 103, pp. 105-35.

Omerod, D. (1994), 'Consent and Offences Against the Person: Law Commission Consultation Paper No. 134', *Modern Law Review*, vol. 57, pp. 928-40.

O'Neill, O. (1985), 'Between Consenting Adults', *Philosophy and Public Affairs*, vol. 14, pp. 252-77.

Perkins, R. and R. Boyce. (1982), *Criminal Law*, 3rd ed., Foundation Press, Mineola.

Perkins, R. (1969), *Criminal Law*, 2nd ed, Foundation Press, Mineola.

Phipps, C. (1997), 'Children, Adults, Sex and the Criminal Law: In Search of Reason', *Seton Hall Law Journal*, vol. 22, pp. 1-66.

Pineau, L. (1989), 'Date Rape: A Feminist Analysis', *Law and Philosophy*, vol. 8, pp. 217-43.

Plato, *The Collected Dialogues of Plato*, E. Hamilton and H. Cairns, eds, 1963, Princeton University, Princeton.

Pollock, F. and F. W. Maitland. (1911), *The History of English Law*, 2nd ed, Cambridge University Press, reissued, 1968, London.

Powell, R. (1961), 'Consent To Operative Procedures', *Maryland Law Review*, vol. 21, no. 3, pp. 189-218.

Price, M. and R. Burt. (1975), 'Sterilization, State Action, and the Concept of Consent', *Law and Psychology Review*, vol. 1, pp. 57-78.

Radden, J. (1996), *Divided Minds and Successive Selves: Ethical Issues In Disorders of Identity and Personality*, MIT, Cambridge.

Rawls, J. (1993), *Political Liberalism*, Columbia University, New York.

Rawls, J. (1971), *A Theory of Justice*, Harvard University, Cambridge, Massachusetts.

Remick, L.A. (1993), 'Read Her Lips: An Argument For A Verbal Consent Standard In Rape', *University of Pennsylvania Law Review*, vol. 141, pp. 1103-1151.

Roberts, P. (1997), 'The Philosophical Foundations of *Consent in the Criminal Law*', *Oxford Journal of Legal Studies*, vol. 17, no. 3, 389-414.

Sanday, P.R. (1996), *A Woman Scorned*, Doubleday, New York.

Scanlon, T. (1998), *What We Owe Each Other*, Harvard University, Cambridge, Massachusetts.

Schelling, T. (1984), *Choice and Consequence*, Harvard University, Cambridge, Massachusetts.

Shute, S. (1996), 'The Second Law Commission Consultation Paper on Consent', [1996] *Criminal Law Review*, pp. 684-93.

Simons, K. (1997), 'Criminal Law: When is Strict Liability Just?', *Journal of Criminal Law & Criminology*, vol. 87, pp. 1075-1137.

Simons, K. (1987), 'Assumption of Risk and Consent in the Law of Torts: A Theory of Full Preference', *Boston University Law Review*, vol. 67, pp. 213-87.

Singer, R. (1989), 'The Resurgence of Mens Rea: III - The Rise and Fall of Strict Criminal Liability', *Boston College Law Review*, vol. 30, pp. 337-408.

Russell, D. E.H. (1990), *Rape In Marriage*, 2nd ed., Indiana, Bloomington.

Ryle, G. (1949), *The Concept of Mind*, Hutchinson, New York.

Sacks, O. (1983), *Awakenings*, E.P. Dutton, New York.

Saks, E. (1977), *Jekyll On Trial: Multiple Personality Disorder and the Criminal Law*, New York University, New York.

Savoras, B. (1997), 'Fighting: It's All in a Day's Work on the Ice: Determining the Appropriate Standard of a Hockey Player's Liability to Another Player', *Seton Hall Journal of Sports Law*, vol. 7, pp. 487-511.

Schulhofer, S. (1998), *Unwanted Sex: The Culture of Intimidation and the Failure of Law*, Harvard, Cambridge, Massachusetts.

Schulhofer, S. (1995), 'The Feminist Challenge in Criminal Law', *University of Pennsylvania Law Review*, vol. 143, pp. 2151-2207.

Schulhofer, S. (1990), 'The Gender Question in Criminal Law', in E. Paul, F. Miller, and J. Paul, eds, *Crime, Culpability, and Remedy*, pp. 105-37.

Schulhofer, S. (1974), 'Harm and Punishment: A Critique of Emphasis on the Results of Conduct in Criminal Law', *University of Pennsylvania Law Review*, vol. 122, pp. 1497-1607.

Schopp, R. (1993), 'Justification Defenses and Just Convictions', *Pacific Law Journal*, vol. 24, pp. 1233-1321.

Searle, J. (1995), *The Construction of Social Reality*, Free Press, New York.

Searle, J. (1991), 'How Performatives Work', *Tennessee Law Review*, vol. 58, pp. 371-92.

Searle, J. (1985), *Expression and Meaning: Studies in the Theory of Speech Acts*, Cambridge University, Cambridge.

Searle, J. (1969), *Speech Acts: An Essay In the Philosophy of Language*, Cambridge University, Cambridge.

Searle, J. (1968), 'Austin On Locutionary and Illocutionary Acts', *The Philosophical Review*, vol. 77, no. 4, pp. 405-24.

Secretary of State for the Home Office. (1975), *Report of the Advisory Group on the Law of Rape*, Cmnd. 6352, Stationery Office, London.

Sherwin, E. (1996), 'Infelicitous Sex', *Legal Theory*, vol. 2, pp. 209-31.

Simmons, J. (1998), 'Locke's Problem Of Political Consent', *Social Theory And Practice*, vol. 24, no. 2, pp. 161-82.

Simmons, J. (1976), 'Tacit Consent And Political Obligation', *Philosophy And Public Affairs*, vol. 5, 1975-76, pp. 274-91.

Sitton, J. (1993), 'Comment, Old Wine In New Bottles: The 'Marital' Rape Allowance', *North Carolina Law Review*, vol. 72, pp. 261-289.

Smolowe, J. (1990), 'The 21 Faces of Sarah', *Time*, 12 November 1990, p. 87.

Soble, A. (1997), 'Antioch's Sexual Offense Policy: A Philosophical Exploration', *Journal of Social Philosophy*, vol. 28, No. 1, pp. 22-36.

Stevenson, C.L. (1944), *Ethics and Language*, Yale, New Haven

Strawson, P. (1971), 'Intention and Convention in Speech Acts', reprinted in J. Rosenberg & C. Traces, eds, *Readings in the Philosophy of Language*, Prentice-Hall, Englewood Cliffs, pp. 599-614.

Strawson, P. (1962), 'Freedom and Resentment', *Proceedings of the British Academy*, vol. 48, pp. 1-25.

Sullivan, T. (1992), *Unequal Verdicts: The Central Park Jogger Trials*, Simon & Schuster, New York.

Sverdik, S. (1988), 'Crime and Moral Luck', *American Philosophical Quarterly*, vol. 25, pp. 79-86.

Swartz, M. (1985), 'The Patient Who Refuses Medical Treatment: A Dilemma For Hospitals and Physicians', *American Journal of Law and Medicine*, vol. 11, no. 2, pp. 147-94.

Symposium. (1996), 'The Intersection of Tort and Criminal Law', *Boston University Law Review*, vol. 76, pp. 1-333.

Tchen, C. (1983), 'Rape Reform and a Statutory Consent Defense', *Journal of Criminal Law and Criminology*, vol. 74, pp. 1518-55.

Thomas, G. and D. Edelman. (2000), 'Consent To Have Sex: Empirical Evidence About "No"', *University of Pittsburgh Law Review*, vol. 61, pp. 579-628.

Thomson, J. (1990), *The Realm of Rights*, Harvard, Cambridge, Massachusetts.

Tiersma, P. (1995), 'The Language of Silence', *Rutgers Law Review*, vol. 48, pp. 1-99.

Tribe, L. (1988), *American Constitutional Law*, 2nd ed, Foundation, New York.

Tsohatzidis, S. (1994), 'Speaker Meaning, Sentence Meaning and Metaphor', in *Foundations of Speech Act Theory: Philosophical and Linguistic Perspectives*, Routledge, New York, pp. 364-73.

Tsohatzidis, S.(ed.), (1994), *Foundations of Speech Act Theory: Philosophical and Linguistic Perspectives*. Routledge, New York.

Vandervort, L. (1987-88), 'Mistake of Law and Sexual Assault: Consent and Mens Rea', *Canadian Journal of Women and the Law*, vol. 2, no. 2, pp. 233-309.

Van De Veer, D. (1979), 'Paternalism and Subsequent Consent', *Canadian Journal of Philosophy*, vol. 9, no. 4, pp. 631-642.

Wallace, R.J. (1994), *Responsibility And The Moral Sentiments*, Harvard University, Cambridge, Massachusetts.

Weber, W. (1985), 'Substituted Judgment Doctrine: A Critical Analysis', *Issues in Law and Medicine*, vol. 1, pp. 131-56.

Weinstein, J. and M. Berger. (2001). *Weinstein's Federal Evidence*, 2nd ed., Matthew Bender, New York.

Wellman, C. (1985), *A Theory of Rights: Persons Under Laws, Institutions, and Morals*, Rowman & Allanheld, Totowa.

Wertheimer, A. (2001), 'Intoxicated Consent To Sexual Relations', *Law and Philosophy*, vol. 20, pp. 373-401.

Wertheimer, A. (1999), 'What Is Consent? And Is It Important?', *Buffalo Criminal Law Review*, vol. 3, pp. 557-583.

Wertheimer, A. (1996), 'Consent and Sexual Relations', *Legal Theory*, vol. 2, pp. 89-112.
Wertheimer, A. (1987), *Coercion*, Princeton University, Princeton.
West, R. (1996), 'A Comment on Consent, Sex, and Rape', *Legal Theory*, vol. 2, pp. 233-51.
West, R. (1993), 'Legitimating the Illegitimate: A Comment on Rape', *Columbia Law Review*, vol. 93, pp. 1442-59.
White, D. (1986), 'Sports Violence As Criminal Assault: Development Of The Doctrine By Canadian Courts', *1986 Duke Law Journal*, pp. 1030-1054.
Wiley, J.S. (1999), 'Not Guilty By Reason of Blamelessness: Culpability in Federal Criminal Interpretation', *Virginia Law Review*, vol. 85, pp. 1021-1162.
Wilkie, D. (1993), 'Wilson OKs Expanding of Spousal Rape Law', *San Diego Union-Tribune*, 1 October 1993, p. A-3.
Wilkie, D. (1993), 'Definition of Spousal Rape Being Rewritten', *San Diego Union-Tribune*, 15 June 1993, p. A-1.
Williams, B. (1994), 'The Actus Reus of Dr. Caligari', *University of Pennsylvania Law Review*, vol. 142, pp. 1661-1673.
Williams, B. (1981), 'Moral Luck', in *Moral Luck: Philosophical Papers, 1973-1980*, Cambridge University, Cambridge, pp. 20-39.
Wooten, B. (1963), *Crime and the Criminal Law: Reflections of a Magistrate and Social Scientist*, Stevens & Sons, London.
Wooten, B. (1959), *Social Science and Social Pathology*, Allen & Unwin, London.
Wright, C.A. and K. Graham. (1980), *Federal Practice and Procedure*, West, St. Paul.
Zimmerman, D. (1981), 'Coercive Wage Offers', *Philosophy and Public Affairs*, vol. 10, No. 2, pp. 125-45.

Cases

Airedale NHS Trusts v. Bland, [1993] AC 789, [1993] 1 All ER 821, [1993] 2 WLR 316.
Arizona v. Bartlett, 171 Ariz. 302, 830 P.2d 823 (1992).
Arizona v. Denton, 101 Ariz. 455, 420 P.2d 930 (1966).
Ash v. Indiana, 455 N.E.2d 965 (Indiana Ct. App. 1983).
Adkins v. Virginia, 20 Va. App. 332, 457 S.E.2d 382 (1995).
Attorney-General's Reference (No. 6 of 1980), [1981] Q.B. 715.
Battle v. Maryland, 287 Md. 675, 414 A.2d 1266 (1980).
Bennett v. Alabama, 31 Ala. App. 435, 18 So. 2d 291 (1944).
Blair v. State, 735 P.2d 440 (Wyoming Sup. Ct., 1987).
Boro v. California, 204 Cal. App. 2d 832, 23 Cal. Rptr. 92 (1962).
Brooks v. Alabama, 555 So. 2d 1134 (Crim. App. , 1989).
Brown v. Georgia, 138 Ga. 814, 76 S.E. 379 (1912).
Brown v. Wisconsin, 106 N.W. 536 (1906).
Brown, v. Heidreich, 62 N.D. 85, 241 N.W. 599 (1932).
Bryant v. Indiana, 644 N.E.2d 859 (Indiana Sup. Ct., 1994).
Bullington v. Florida, 616 So. 2d 1036 (Ct. App. 1993).
California v. Barnes, 42 Cal. 3d 284, 721 P.2d 110, 228 Cal. Rptr. 228 (1986).
California v. Benn, 2002 Cal. App. Unpub. LEXIS 732 (2002).
California v. Boro, 163 Cal. App. 3d 1224, 210 Cal. Rptr. 122 (1985).
California v. Bruce, 208 Cal. App. 3d 1099, 256 Cal. Rptr. 647 (1989).
California v. Burnham, 176 Cal. App. 3d 1134, 222 Cal. Rptr. 630 (1985).
California v. Cicero, 157 Cal. App. 3d 465, 204 Cal.Rptr. 582 (1984).
California v. Coleman, 48 Cal. 3d 112, 768 P.2d 32, 255 Cal. Rptr. 813 (1989).
California v. Haywood, 118 Ill. 2d 263, 515 N.E.2d 45 (1987).
California v. Hooker, 244 Cal. Rptr. 337 (Ct. App., 1988).
California v. Iniguez, 7 Cal. 4th 847, 872 P.2d 1183 (1994).
California v. Kuches, 120 Cal. 566, 52 P. 1002, 1003 (1898).
California v. LaSalle, 103 Cal. App. 3d 139, 162 Cal. Rptr. 816 (1980).
California v. McKellar, 146 Cal. Rptr. 327 (1978)(California Ct. App.).
California v. Minkowski, 204 Cal. App. 2d 832, 23 Cal. Rptr. 92 (1962).
California v. Morehead, 192 Cal. App. 3d 292, 238 Cal. Rptr. 570 (1987).
California v. Rivera, 44 Cal. App. 4th 466, 41 Cal. Rptr. 2d 421 (1995).
California v. St. Andrew. 101 Cal. App. 3d 450, 161 Cal. Rptr. 634 (1980).
California v. Tobias, 25 Cal. 4th 327, 21 P.3d 758 (2001).
California v. Vargas, 2001 Cal. App. Unpub. LEXIS 275 (2001).
California v. Vasquez, 7 Cal. App. 4th 1691, 281 Cal. Rptr. 661 (1991).
California v. Vela, 172 Cal. App. 3d 237, 218 Cal. Rptr. 161 (1985).
California v. Williams, 4 Cal. 4th 354, 841 P.2d 961 (1992).
Clark v. Georgia, 197 Ga. App. 318, 398 S.E.2d 377 (1991).
Coley v. Florida, 616 So.2d 1017 (Florida Ct. App. 1994).
Collins v. Wilcock, [1984] 1 W.L.R. 1172, 1177.
Connecticut v. Brown, 59 Conn. App. 243, 756 A.2d 860 (2000).
Connecticut v. Siering, 35 Conn. App. 173, 644 A.2d 958 (1994).
Connecticut v. Smith, 210 Conn. 132, 554 A.2d 713 (1989).
Conservatorship of the Person of William J. Drabick, 200 Cal. App. 3d 185, 333, 245 Cal. Rptr. 840 (1988).
Conservatorship of Valerie N. Mildred, v. Valerie N., Objector, 40 Cal. 3d 143, 707 P.2d 760 (1985).

Copithorne v. Framingham Union Hospital, 401 Mass. 860, 520 N.E.2d 139 (1987).
Cromeans v. Texas, 59 Tex. Crim. 611, 129 S.W. 1129 (1910).
Cruzan v. McCanse, 760 S. 2d 408, 425-26 (Missouri, 1988), affirmed sub nom, Cruzan v. Director, Missouri Department of Health, 497 U. S. 261 (1989).
Curtis v. Georgia, 236 Ga. 362, 223 S.E.2d 721 (1976).
Custody of a Minor, 393 N.E.2d 836, 844 (Mass. 1979).
Davis v. Missouri, 557 S.W.2d 41 (Missouri Ct. App., 1977).
Director of Public Prosecutions v. Morgan, [1976] App. Cas. 182 (House of Lords).
Dolchok v. Alaska, 763 P.2d 977 (Alaska Ct. App. 1988).
Drake v. Georgia, 239 Ga. 232, 236 S.E.2d 748 (1977).
Farish v. Virginia, 2 Va. App. 627, 346 S.E.2d 736 (1986).
Flannery v. Texas, 676 S.W.2d 369 (Tex. Ct. Crim. App., 1984).
Glover v. State, 518 So. 2d 247 (1987).
Goldberg v. Maryland, 41 Md. 58, 395 A.2d 1212 (1979).
Goldenberg v. Massachusetts, 338 Mass. 377, 155 N.E.2d 187 (1959).
Goodrow v. Perrin, 119 N.H. 483, 403 A.2d 864 (1979).
Grant v. Massachusetts, 391 Mass. 645, 464 N.E.2d 33 (1984).
Guardianship Of Jane Doe, 411 Mass. 512, 583 N.E.2d 1263 (1992).
Hamilton v. McAuliffe, 353 A.2d 634 (Maryland Supreme Court, 1976).
Harley v. United States, 373 A.2d 898 (D.C. Court of Appeals, 1977).
Hartley v. Alaska, 653 P.2d 1052, 1054 (Alaska Sup. Ct., 1982).
Hawaii v. Dizon, 47 Haw. 444, 390 P.2d 759 (1964).
Hawaii v. Lima, 624 P.2d 1374 (1981).
Hawaii v. Lira, 70 Haw. 23, 759 P.2d 869 (1988).
Hawaii v. Oshiro, 5 Haw. App. 404, 696 P.2d 846 (1985).
Hazel v. Maryland, 221 Md. 464, 157 A.2d 922 (1960).
Hollis v. Florida, 27 Fla. 387, 9 So. 67 (1891).
Hufham v. Florida, 400 So. 2d 133 (Fla. 5th DCA 1981).
Idaho v. Dennard, 102 Idaho 824, 642 P.2d 61 (1982).
Idaho v. Gossett, 119 Idaho 581, 808 P.2d 1326 (Ct. App., 1991).
Illinois v. Blunt, 65 Ill. App. 2d 268, 212 N.E.2d 719 (1965).
Illinois v. Borak, 13 Ill. App. 3d 815, 301 N.E.2d 1 (1973).
Illinois v. Defrates, 33 Ill. 2d 190, 210 N.E.2d 467 (1965).
Illinois v. Jones, 28 Ill. App. 3d 896, 329 N.E.2d 855 (1975).
Illinois v. Scott, 407 Ill. 301, 95 N.E.2d 315 (1950).
Illinois v. Williams, 23 Ill. 2d 295, 178 N.E.2d 372 (1961).
In re M.T.S.,129 N.J. 422, 609 A.2d 1266 (1992).
In re Alice Hughes, 259 N.J. Super. 193, 611 A.2d 1148 (1992).
In re Claire C. Conroy, 98 N.J. 321, 486 A.2d 1209 (1985).
In re Estate of Longeway v. Community Convalescent Center, 133 Ill. 2d 33, 549 N.E.2d 292 (1989).
In re F (Mental Patient, Sterilization), [1990] 2 A.C. 1.
In re Guardianship of Pescinski, 67 Wis. 2d 4, 226 N.W.2d 180 (1975).
In re Hilda M. Peter, 108 N.J. 365, 529 A.2d 419 (1987).
In re Karen Quinlan, 70 N.J. 10, 355 A.2d 647 (1976).
In re Marie Moorhouse, 250 N.J. Super. 307, 593 A.2d 1256 (1991).
In re Nancy Ellen Jobes, 108 N. J. 394, 529 A. 2d 434 (1987).
In re P.M., Juvenile, 156 Vt. 303, 592 A.2d 864 (1991).
In re G.T., Juvenile, 758 A.2d 301 (2000).
In re Gladys R., 1 Cal. 3d 855, 464 P.2d 127, 83 Cal. Rptr. 671 (1970).

Iowa v. Sullivan, 298 N.W.2d 267 (Iowa Sup. Ct., 1980).
Iowa v. Ronek, 176 N.W.2d 153, 154-55 (1970).
Jackson v. Alaska, 890 P.2d 587 (Ct. App, 1995).
Jackson v. Georgia, 225 Ga. 553, 170 S.E.2d 281 (1969).
John F. Kennedy Memorial Hospital v. Heston, 58 N.J. 576, 279 A.2d 670 (1971).
Johnson v. Colorado, 638 P.2d 1 (1981).
Jones v. Florida, 640 So. 2d 1084 (Fla. Sup. Ct. 1994).
Kansas v. Cantrell, 234 Kan. 426, 673 P.2d 1147 (1983).
Kizer v. Virginia, 228 Va. 256, 321 S.E.2d 291 (1984).
Lane v. Maryland, 348 Md. 272, 279, 703 A.2d 180, 184 (1997).
Ledezma v. Iowa, 632 N.W.2d 911 (2001).
Lee v. Oregon, 869 F. Supp. 1491 (D. Ore., 1994), Lee v. Oregon 891 F. Supp. 1439 (D. Ore. 1995), reversed, 107 F.3d 1382 (9th Cir., 1997), cert. denied sub nom Lee v. Harcleroad, 118 S. Ct. 328 (1997).
Liberta v. New York, 64 N.Y.2d 152, 474 N.E.2d 567 (1984).
Louisiana v. Collins, 242 La. 704, 138 So. 2d 546 (1962).
Louisiana v. Parish, 405 So. 2d 1080 (1981).
Louisiana v. Powell, 438 So. 2d 1306 (Ct. App., 1983).
Louisiana v. Robertson, 454 So.2d 204 (1984).
Louisiana v. Vaughn, 431 So.2d 358 (La. Sup. Ct., 1982).
McIlwain v. Florida, 402 So. 2d 1194 (Florida. Ct. App. 1981).
Maine v. Reed, 479 A.2d 1291 (1984).
Maine v. Ricci, 507 A.2d 587 (1986).
Malette v. Shulman, 67 D.L.R. 4th 321 (Ont. Ct. App., 1990).
Maryland v. Rusk, 289 Md. 230, 424 A.2d 720 (1981).
Massachusetts v. Ascolillo, 405 Mass. 456, 541 N.E.2d 570 (1989).
Massachusetts v. Bobilin, 25 Mass. App. Ct. 410, 519 N.E.2d 1349 (1988).
Massachusetts v. Burke, 105 Mass. 376 (1870).
Massachusetts v. Caracciola, 409 Mass. 648, 569 N.E.2d 774 (1991).
Massachusetts v. Chretien, 383 Mass. 123, 417 N.E.2d 1203 (1981).
Massachusetts v. Helfant, 398 Mass. 214, 496 N.E.2d 433 (1986).
Massachusetts v. Lefkowitz, 20 Mass. App. 513, 481 N.E.2d 227 (1985).
Massachusetts v. Simcock, 31 Mass. App. 184, 575 N.E.2d 1137 (1991).
Massachusetts v. Stowell, 389 Mass. 171, 449 N.E.2d 357 (1983).
Massachusetts v. Therrien, 383 Mass. 529, 420 N.E.2d 897 (1981).
Mayes v. Maryland. 50 Md. App. 628, 440 A.2d 1093 (1982).
McArtor v. Wyoming, 699 P.2d 288 (Wyoming Sup. Ct., 1985).
McGill v. Alaska, 18 P.3d 77 (2001).
McGuinn v. United States, 191 F.2d 477 (D.C., Cir., 1951).
McNair v. Nevada, 108 Nev. 53, 825 P.2d 571 (1992).
Michael M. v. Superior Ct., 25 Cal. 3d 608, 601 P.2d 572 (1979), 159 Cal. Rptr. 340 (1979), affirmed, 450 U.S. 464 (1980).
Michigan v. Hale, 142 Mich. App. 451, 370 N.W.2d 382 (1985).
Michigan v. Hammack, 63 Mich. App. 87, 234 N.W.2d 415 (1975).
Mills v. Arkansas, 270 Ark. 141, 603 S.W.2d 416 (1980).
Minnesota v. Crims, 540 N.W.2d 860 (1995).
Minnesota v. Dutton, 450 N.W.2d 189 (Ct. App., 1990).
Missouri v. Dighera, 617 S.E.2d 524 (Missouri Ct. App. 1981).
Missouri v. Stamps, 569 S.W.2d 762 (1978).
Montana v. Garn, 274 Mon. 296,871 P.2d 878 (1994).

Montana v. Thompson, 243 Mont. 28, 792 P.2d 1103 (1990).
Morse v. Virginia, 17 Va. App. 627, 440 S.E.2d 145 (1994).
Mosley v. State, 323 Ark. 244, 914 S.W.2d 731 (1996).
Nebraska v. Koperski, 254 Neb. 624, 578 N.W.2d 837 (1998).
New Hampshire v. Cooper, 135 N.H. 258, 603 A.2d 499 (1992).
New Jersey v. Harris, 70 N.J. Super. 9, 174 A.2d 645 (1961).
New Jersey v. Johnson, 68 N.J. 349, 346 A.2d 66 (1975).
New Jersey v. Martin, 235 N.J. Super. 47, 561 A.2d 631 (1989).
New Jersey v. Olivio, 123 N.J. 550, 589 A.2d 597 (1991).
New Jersey v. Sorge, 123 N.J.L. 532, 10 A.2d 175 (1939).
New Jersey v. Smith, 85 N.J. 193, 426 A.2d 38 (1980).
New York v. Brim, 22 Misc. 2d 335, 199 N.Y.S.2d 744(1960).
New York v. Bink, 84 App. Div. 2d 607, 44 N.Y.S.2d 237 (1981).
New York v. De Stefano, 121 Misc. 2d 113, 467 N.Y.S.2d 506 (1983).
New York v. Easley, 42 N.Y.2d 50, 364 N.E.2d 1328, 396 N.Y.S.2d 635 (1977).
New York v. Gonzales, 148 Misc 2d 973, 561 NYS2d 358 (1990).
New York v. Hough, 159 Misc. 2d 997, 607 N.Y.S.2d 884 (1994).
New York v. Smolen, 166 App. Div. 2d 248, 564 N.Y.S.2d 105 (1990), *appeal denied*, 77 N.Y.2d 844 (1991).
New York v. Yanik, 43 N.Y.2d 97, 371 N.E.2d 497, 400 N.Y.S.2d 778 (1977).
New Mexico v. Bell, 90 N.M. 134, 560 P.2d 925 (1977).
New Mexico v. Leiding, 112 N.M. 143, 812 P.2d 797 (Ct. of App., 1991).
North Carolina v. Alston, 310 N.C. 399, 312 S.E.2d 470 (1984).
North Carolina v. Anthony, 351 N.C. 611, 528 S.E.2d 321 (2000).
North Carolina v. Brown, 332 N.C. 262, 420 S.E.2d 147 (1992).
North Carolina v. Carter, 265 N.C. 626, 144 S.E.2d 826 (1965).
North Carolina v. Lester, 321 S.E.2d 166 (1984), *affirmed*, 330 S.E.2d 205 (N.C. 1985).
North Carolina v. Moorman, 320 N.C. 387, 358 S.E.2d 502 (1987).
North Carolina v. Way, 297 N.C. 293, 254 S.E.2d 760 (1979).
Ohio v. Johnson, 1993 Ohio App. LEXIS 3677 (July 21, 1993).
Ozenna v. Alaska, 1999 Alas. App. LEXIS 54 (1999).
Papadimitropoulos v. Regina, (1957) 98 Criminal Law Reporter 249, [1958] Argus LR 21 (Australian High Court).
Paul v. Florida, 110 So. 2d 388 (Florida Sup. Ct., 1959).
Pennsylvania v. Berkowitz, 537 Pa. 143, 641 A.2d 1161 (1994).
Pennsylvania v. Brown, 184 Pa. Super. 494, 136 A.2d 138 (1957).
Pennsylvania v. Fischer, 721 A.2d 1111 (Pa. Super. Ct. 1998), appeal dismissed, 745 A.2d 1214 (Pa. 2000).
Pennsylvania v. Mlinarich, 518 Pa. 247, 542 A.2d 1335 (1985).
Pennsylvania v. Williams, 439 A.2d 765 (Pa. Super. Ct. 1982).
Peterson v. Sorlien, 299 N.W.2d 123/(Minn. Sup. Ct., 1980).
Pierson v. Wyoming, 956 P.2d 1119 (Wyoming Sup. Ct., 1998).
Planned Parenthood Affiliates v. Van de Kamp, 181 Cal. App. 3d 245, 226 Cal. Rptr. 361 (1986).
Pollard v. Iowa, 2 Iowa 567 (1856).
Queen v. Coney, 8 Q.B.D. 534 (1882).
Queen v. Ewanchuk, [1999] 1 S.C.R. 330, 356.
Queen v. Park, 1995 Canadian Supreme Court LEXIS 43, para. 39.
Re: Jordan J., 1992 Conn. Super. LEXIS 2282 (1992).
Regina v. Abraham, (1977) 30 C.C.C. (2d) 332.

Regina v. Barrow, 11 Cox Crim. Cas. 191 (1868).
Regina v. Brown, [1993] 2 All Eng. Rep. 75 (House of Lords).
Regina v. Carmen M., (1992), 11 C.R.R. (2d) 363.
Regina v. Cey, 48 C.C.C. 3d 480 (Saskatchewan Ct. App., 1989).
Regina v. Clarence, [1888] 22 Q.B. 23, 2 All E.R. 529.
Regina v. Clarke, 6 Cox Crim. Cas. 412 (1854).
Regina v. Cuerrier, [1998] 2 S.C.R. 371 (Canadian Supreme Court).
Regina v. Dee, 15 Cox CC 579 (Ireland, 1884).
Regina v. Diggs, 1987 W.C.B.J. 10646, 1 W.C.B. (2d) 429 (Nova Scotia Ct. App.).
Regina v. Flattery, 2 Q.B.D. 410 (1877).
Regina v. Gray, [1981] 6 W.W.R. 654 (Saskatchewan Ct. App., 1981).
Regina v. Kaitamaki, [1980] 1 N.Z.L.R. 59 (New Zealand).
Regina v. Khan, 1 W.L.R. 813 [1990].
Regina v. Leclerc, (1991) 67 CCC (3d) 563.
Regina v. Linekar, [1995] 3 All ER 69, [1995] 2 WLR 237,[1995], 2 Cr App Rep 49.
Regina v. Maki, [1970] 3 O.R. 780 (Ontario Ct. App., 1970).
Regina v. Malone, (1998) 2 Cr App Rep 447Regina v. Maloney, 28 C.C.C. 2d 323 (Ontario, Ct. App., 1976).
Regina v. Miller, [1954] 2 Q.B. 282, [1954] 2 All ER 529.
Regina v. O'Connor, (1998) 159 D.L.R. (4th) 304 (British Columbia Court of Appeal).
Regina v. Olugboja, [1982] 1 Q.B. 320, 332, [1981] 3 All ER 443, [1981] 3 WLR 585 (English Ct. App.).
Regina v. Prince, 2 L.R.-Cr. Cas. Res. 154 (1875).
Regina v. R., [1992] 1 AC 599, [1991] 4 All ER 481, [1991] 3 WLR 767.
Regina v. Richardson, [1978] Tas. S.R. 178 (Tasmania).
Regina v. Salmon, [1969] SASR 76 (Australia).
Regina v. Steele, (1976) 65 Cr App R 22.
Regina v. Stoll, 1999 W.C.B.J. 286, 41 W.C.B. (2d) 54 (Ontario Court, General Division).
Rex v. Harling, [1938] 1 All ER 307.
Rex v. Harms, [1944] 2 D.L.R. 61.
Rhode Island v. Yanez, 716 A.2d 759 (1998).
Robinson v. Maine, 496 A.2d 1067 (1985).
Robinson v. Maryland, 67 Md. App. 445, 508 A.2d 159, cert. denied, 307 Md. 261 (1986).
Royal v. Alabama, 447 S.2d 834 (Alabama Crim. App. 1983).
Russell v. United States, 1997 D.C. App. L1EXIS 178, 698 A.2d 1007 (D.C. Ct. App., 1997).
Salsman v. Kentucky, 565 S.W.2d 638 (Ky. Ct. of App., 1978).
Scherzer v. New Jersey, 301 N.J. Super. 363, 694 A.2d 196 (1997).
Schneckloth v. Bustamonte, 412 US 218 (1973).
Sherry v. Massachusetts, 386 Mass. 682, 437 N.E.2d 224 (1982).
Snyder v. Virginia, 220 Va. 792, 263 S.E.2d 55 (1980).
South Carolina v. Galati, 365 N.W.2d 575 (South Carolina, 1985).
South Dakota v. Jones, 521 N.W.2d 662 (1994).
Stafford v. Indiana, 455 N.E.2d 401 (Ct. App., 1983).
Stephenson v. State, 35 Ala. App. 379, 48 So. 2d 255 (1950).
Superintendent of Belchertown State School v. Joseph Saikewicz, 373 Mass. 728, 370 N.E.2d 417 (1977).
Thomas v. Georgia, 159 Ga. App. 249, 249 S.E.2d 37 (1981).
Vermont v. Barlow, 160 Vt. 527, 630 A.2d 1299 (1993).
Vermont v. Jewett, 109 Vt. 73, 192 A. 7 (1937).

Warren v. Georgia, 255 Ga. 151, 336 S.E.2d 221 (1985).
Washington v. Ferrier, 136 Wash.2d 103, 960 P.2d 927 (1998).
Washington v. Camara, 113 Wash.2d 631, 781 P.2d 483 (1989).
Washington v. Ieremia, 78 Wash. App. 746, 899 P.2d 16/(1996).
Washington v. Ortega-Martinez, 124 Wash. 2d 702, 881 P.2d 231 (1994).
Weishaupt v. Virginia, 227 Va. 389, 315 S.E.2d 847 (1984).
West Virginia v. Pancake, 170 W. Va. 690, 296 S.E.2d 37 (1982).
In re Westchester County Medical Center on behalf of O'Connor, 72 N.Y.2d 517, 531 N.E.2d 607, 534 N.Y.S.2d 886 (1988).
Whittaker v. Wisconsin, 50 Wis. 518, 7 N.W. 431 (1880).
Winegan v. Maryland, 10 Md. App. 196, 268 A.2d 585 (1970).
Wisconsin v. Herfel, 49 Wis. 2d 513, 182 N.W.2d 232 (1971).
Wisconsin v. Lederer, 99 Wis. 2d 430, 299 N.W.2d 457 (Ct. App. 1980).
Wisconsin v. Plitcha, 135 N.W.2d 768 (1965).

Statutes

Alabama Code §§ 13A-2-7(c), 13A-6,61, 13A-6-65(a)(1), 13A-6-70, 26-21-3 (2000).

Alaska Statutes §§ 11.41.410(a), 11.41.420(a), 11.41.434(a), 11.41.470(4,8) (2000).

Arizona Revised Statutes § 13-1406(A) (2001).

Arkansas Stat. § 5-14-101, 103(a)(2)(1999).

California Penal Code §§ 261, 261.5, 266, 1378 (2001).

Revised Statutes of Canada 1970, c. C-34, §§ 143, 158.

Revised Statutes of Canada, 1985, c. C-46, § 153.1(3), 265, 273.1.

Colorado Revised Statutes §§ 18-1-703, 18-3-401, 18-3-402(4)(e), 18-3-404,18-3-405.5 (1994).

Connecticut General Statutes §§ 53A-65(3), 53A-67, 53A-73(A) (1997).

Delaware Code tit. 11, §§ 451, 453, 601, 772 (2001).

District of Columbia Code §§ 22-4101, 22-4102 (1998).

Florida Statutes § 794.011(1) (2000).

Idaho Code §§ 18-6101, 18-6107, 18-6110 (1998).

Indiana Code § 35-42-4-9 (1994).

Iowa Code § 709.1(1) (1999).

Kansas Statutes § 21-3502 (2000).

Kentucky Revised Statutes § 510.010(2) (1998).

Louisiana Revised Statutes §§ 14:42(A), 14:43 (1992).

Maine Revised Statutes tit. 17-A, §§ 252(1), 251 (1980).

Maryland Code art. 27, § 462-64 (1999).

Massachusetts Laws ch. 265, § 22 (2002).

Michigan Compiled Laws Annotated § 720.520d(1), 750.5201 (2000).

Minnesota Statutes §§ 609.341, 609.344 (2000).

Missouri Revised Statutes § 556.061(5)(1999).

Montana Code §§ 45-2-211, 45-5-502, 45-5-503 (2000).

Nebraska Revised Statutes § 28-318 (2000).

(Netherlands), Termination of Life on Request and Assistance with Suicide (Review Procedures) Act, Upper House of the States General, 2000-01, no. 137, 26 691 (28 Nov. 2000).

Nevada Revised Statutes § 200.481, 200.366(10) (2002).

New Hampshire Revised Statutes § 632-A:2(I)m, 632-A:4, 632-A:7 (2000).

New Hampshire Revised Statutes §§ 632-A:2.

New Jersey Statutes § 2C:14-2c(1) (2001).

New Mexico Code §§ 30-9-10(A), 66-8-107, 66-8-108 (1998).

New York Penal Code §§ 130.00, 130.05, 130.20 (2000).

North Carolina General Statutes § 14-27.3 (2000).

Pennsylvania Code, tit. 18, §§ 3121, 3124.1 (2000).

Ohio Rev. Code §§ 2907.02-.04, 5924.120 (2000).

Oklahoma Stat. , tit. 21, § 1111 (1998).

Oregon Code §§§ 16-6-5.1, 127.800-897 (1997).

South Dakota Codified Laws § 22-22-1(2) (2001).

Utah Code §§ 76-5-402, 76-5-404, 76-5-406 (2001).

Virginia Code §§ 18.2-61, 18.2-66, 18.2-67.2:1, 18.2-67.6 (2000).

Washington Revised Code § 9A.44.010(2000).

West Virginia Code § § 61-8B-1(1), 61-8B-2(a)-(b)(1), 61-8B-4(a)(1), 61-8B-5a, 61-8B-6 (2000).

Wisconsin Statutes § 940.225(4)(2000).

Index of Cases

Adkins v. Virginia 317–18
Airedale NHS Trust v. Bland 302 n77
Arizona v. Bartlett 23 n15
Arizona v. Denton 23 n15
Ash v. Indiana 57 n28

Bailey v. Florida 241 n88
Battle v. Maryland 266 n27
Battle v. State 264 n2, 299 n40
Bennett v. Alabama 23 n15
Blair v. Wyoming 310–12
Brooks v. Alabama 93 n3
Brown v. Heidreich 132 n21
Brown v. State 265 n5
Brown v. Wisconsin 241 n93
Bryant v. Indiana 94 n4
Bullington v. Florida 264 n5

California v. Barnes 54 n6, 332 n23
California v. Benn 93 n3
California v.Boro 188–9, 236 n36, 238 n60, 312–15
California v. Bruce 54 n6
California v. Burnham 139–40, 143, 150–1, 164 n1, 165 n18
California v. Cicero 23 n14, 238 n59, 348 n26
California v. Coleman 93 n3
California v. Haywood 348 n30
California v. Hernandez 168 n31
California v. Hooker 184–5, 235 n22
California v. Iniguez 320, 332 n21, 332 n22
California v. Kuches 62 n62
California v. LaSalle 48, 49, 62 n60
California v. McKellar 23 n15
California v. Minkowski 313, 314–15
California v. Morehead 58 n33
California v. Rivera 23 n15
California v. St Andrew 319–20
California v. Tobias 23 n12, 132 n19
California v. Vargas 94 n4
California v. Vasquez 170 n40
California v.Vela 299 n40
California v. Williams 166 n24
Clark v. State 332 n23
Coley v. Florida 26, 54 n7
Collins v. Wilcock 299 n38
Connecticut v. Brown 22 n4, 134 n25
Connecticut v. Richard T Smith 94 n6
Connecticut v. Siering 299 n39
Conservatorship of the Person of William J Drabick 302 n77
Conservatorship of Valerie N Mildred 302 n77
Copithorne v. Framingham Union Hospital 57 n29
Cromeans v. States 131 n15
Cruzan v. Director, Missouri Department of Health 302 n72
Cruzan v. McCanse 8, 11 n12
Curtis v. Georgia 58 n34

Davis v. Missouri 21–2
Director of Public Prosecutions v. Morgan 186, 236 n28, 349 n36, 349 n37
Dolchok v. Alaska 54 n12
Drake v. Georgia 243 n124

Farish v. Virginia 241 n88
Flannery v. Texas 58 n34

Glover v. State 134 n27
Goldberg v. Maryland 98 n36
Goldenberg v. Massachusetts 330 n3
Goodrow v. Perrin 130 n9
Grant v. Massachusetts 166 n24
Guardianship of Jane Doe 302 n77, 303 n81

Hamilton v. McAuliffe 299 n35
Harley v. United States 22 n4
Hart v. Brown 302 n70
Hartley v. Alaska 53 n1
Hawaii v. Lima 241 n86
Hawaii v. Lira 26, 54 n8
Hawaii v. Oshiro 244 n132
Hazel v. State 264 n2
Hildebrant v. Hildebrant 133 n24
Hollis v. Florida 241 n88
Hufham v. Florida 215–16, 241 n88, 243 n107

Idaho v. Dennard 168 n30
Idaho v. Gossett 62 n59
Illinois v. Blunt 331 n13
Illinois v. Borak 241 n85
Illinois v. Defrates 242 n94, 242 n95
Illinois v. Jones 242 n95
Illinois v. Scott 242 n94, 242 n95
Illinois v. Williams 242 n94
In re Alice Hughes 302 n68, 302 n69
In re Claire C Conroy 299 n35, 300 n54, 301 n58, 302 n73
In re Estate of Longeway v. Community Convalescent Center 302 n77
In re F (Mental Patient, Sterilization) 291, 303 n87
In re G T 133 n22
In re Gladys R 133 n24
In re Guardianship of Pescinski 302 n70
In re Hilda M Peter 300 n54, 301 n58, 302 n71
In re John Storrar 302 n72
In re Karen Quinlan 286–7, 292–3, 302 n72, 302 n73
In re M T S 101 n60, 147–8, 170 n44, 233 n1, 348 n28
In re Marie Moorhouse 300 n54, 302 n75
In re Mary Moe 290–1, 292–3
In re Nancy Ellen Jobes 8, 11 n13, 301 n58, 302 n62, 302 n71, 303 n81
In re P M 133 n22
In re Westchester County Medical Center 302 n72
Iowa v. Corliss 130 n6
Iowa v. Ronek 130 n6
Iowa v. Sullivan 54 n12

Jackson v. Alaska 122–3, 135 n37
Jackson v. Georgia 24 n17
John F Kennedy Memorial Hospital v. Heston 299 n35
Johnson v. Colorado 329–30
Jones v. Florida 130 n9

Kansas v. Cantrell 166 n24, 166 n25
Kizer v. Virginia 136 n40

Lane v. Maryland 297 n12, 325–6, 332 n27, 333 n33, 333 n35, 334 n50, 335 n52
Ledezma v. Iowa 349 n34
Lee v. Harcleroad 233 n2
Lee v. Oregon 233 n2
Liberta v. New York 333 n32, 334 n42
Louisiana v. Adkins 23 n15
Louisiana v. Collins 23 n14
Louisiana v. Parish 67, 75, 94 n4, 95 n13, 242 n99
Louisiana v. Powell 213, 242 n97, 242 n99
Louisiana v. Robertson 242 n98
Louisiana v. Vaughn 327, 335 n57

McArtor v. Wyoming 23 n15
McGill v. Alaska 299 n39
McGuinn v. United States 54 n3
McIlwain v. Florida 58 n32
McNair v. Nevada 41–2, 61 n48, 241 n85
Maine v. Reed 61 n51, 166 n23
Maine v. Ricci 54 n12
Malette v. Shulman 288–9
Maryland v. Rusk 321, 332 n24, 332 n26
Massachusetts v. Ascolillo 167 n26
Massachusetts v. Berkowitz 349 n35
Massachusetts v. Bobilin 58 n34

Massachusetts v. Burke 348 n26
Massachusetts v. Caracciola 237 n37
Massachusetts v. Chretien 324, 334 n42
Massachusetts v. Fischer 166 n24
Massachusetts v. Goldenberg 349 n38
Massachusetts v. Helfant 35, 57 n29, 349 n38
Massachusetts v. Lefkowitz 100 n50
Massachusetts v. Simcock 167 n26
Massachusetts v. Stowell 113–14
Massachusetts v. Therrien 235 n23
Massachusetts v. Williams 166 n24
Mayes v. Maryland 54 n12
Michael M v. Superior Court 133 n22, 225–6, 227
Michigan v. Hale 26, 54 n10
Michigan v. Hammack 166 n22
Mills v. Arkansas 333 n28
Minnesota v. Crims 299 n39
Minnesota v. Dutton 120, 134 n29
Missouri v. Dighera 56 n26
Missouri v. Stamps 241 n93
Montana v. Garn 23 n14
Montana v. Thompson 213–14, 223, 240 n79, 242 n100, 243 n101, 243 n123
Morse v. Virginia 135 n38
Mosley v. State 348 n28

Nebraska v. Koperski 94 n4
New Jersey v. Harris 22 n4
New Jersey v. Johnson 56 n25
New Jersey v. Martin 23 n15
New Jersey v. Olivio 56 n23
New Jersey v. Smith 334 n43, 335 n56
New Jersey v. Sorge 94 n4
New Mexico v. Bell 134 n30
New Mexico v. Leiding 120, 134 n30
New York v. Bink 140, 146–7, 150–1, 164 n2, 174 n76
New York v. Brim 266 n28
New York v. De Stefano 335 n54
New York v. Easley 331 n10
New York v. Gonzales 119, 134 n26, 134 n28
New York v. Hough 41, 61 n46, 61 n47
New York v. Smolen 164 n2
New York v. Yanik 241 n91
North Carolina v. Alston 98 n36, 100 n49, 350 n49
North Carolina v. Anthony 23 n15
North Carolina v. Brown 62 n62
North Carolina v. Carter 56 n26
North Carolina v. Lester 237 n49
North Carolina v. Moorman 34, 35, 37, 56 n26, 60 n38
North Carolina v. Way 299 n40

Ohio v. Johnson 58 n34
Oregon v. Hoehne 168 n31
Ozenna v. Alaska 93 n3

Papadimitropoulos v. Regina 236 n31
Paul v. Florida 23 n14
Pennsylvania v. Brown 348 n32
Pennsylvania v. Mlinarich 243 n105
Peterson v. Sorlien 266 n25
Pierson v. Wyoming 23 n15
Planned Parenthood Affiliates v. Van de Kamp 133 n23
Pollard v. State 265 n17

Queen v. Coney 296 n9, 300 n44
Queen v. Ewanchuk 98 n38, 101 n60, 169 n32, 169 n33, 169 n38, 170 n39
Queen v. Park 55 n17

R v. Brown 300 n45
R v. R 324
Re Jordan J 61 n54
Regina v. Abraham 26, 54 n4
Regina v. Barrow 237 n50, 265 n17
Regina v. Brown 205, 240 n81
Regina v. Carmen M 17, 19, 21–2
Regina v. Cey 11 n11, 269–70, 283, 296 n1
Regina v. Clarence 298 n23, 334

n38, 347 n12
Regina v. Clarke 265 n17
Regina v. Cuerrier 23 n15, 199–200, 238 n51, 238 n52, 239 n73, 299 n42
Regina v. Dee 237 n50
Regina v. Diggs 23 n14
Regina v. Donovan 54 n4
Regina v. Gray 296 n2
Regina v. Jackson 237 n50
Regina v. Kaitamaki 299 n39, 299 n41
Regina v. Khan 172 n59
Regina v. Leclerc 7, 11 n11
Regina v. Linekar 201, 238 n52
Regina v. Maki 296 n9
Regina v. Malone 26, 54 n11
Regina v. Maloney 296 n2
Regina v. Miller 272–5, 333 n34
Regina v. Morgan 169 n33
Regina v. O'Connor 23 n14
Regina v. Olugboja 53 n1, 54 n11, 164 n3, 169 n33, 234 n9, 350 n49
Regina v. Prince 167 n29
Regina v. R 298 n24, 334 n39, 334 n44, 334 n46, 334 n47, 347 n13, 347 n14
Regina v. R J S 101 n60
Regina v. Richardson 299 n40
Regina v. Salmon 299 n40
Regina v. Steele 333 n34
Regina v. Stoll 23 n15
Regina v. W 298 n24
Rex v. Harling 349 n37, 349 n38
Rhode Island v. Yanez 168 n30
Robinson v. Maine 299 n39
Royal v. Alabama 94 n4
Russell v. United States 129 n1, 171 n46

Salsman v. Kentucky 316–17, 332 n23
Scherzer v. New Jersey 95 n15
Schneckloth v. Bustamonte 32, 56 n24
Sherry v. Massachusetts 166 n23
Smith v. New Jersey 327, 335 n54
Snyder v. Virginia 241 n88
South Carolina v. Galati 335 n59
South Dakota v. Jones 299 n39
Stafford v. Indiana 119, 134 n26
State v. Dizon 264 n2
State v. Moorman 265 n17
Stephenson v. Alabama 331 n13
Superintendent of Belchertown State School v. Joseph Saikewicz 303 n81

Texas v. Valdez 1–2, 9–10, 11 n3, 310, 344
Thomas v. Georgia 24 n17

Vermont v. Barlow 130 n9
Vermont v. Jewett 331 n13

Warren v. Georgia 297 n12, 326, 335 n51, 335 n52, 335 n54
Washington v. Camara 129 n1
Washington v. Craig 171 n46
Washington v. Ferrier 56 n25
Washington v. Ieremia 23 n14
Washington v. Ortega-Martinez 318
Weishaupt v. Virginia 135 n39, 136 n40, 335 n52
West Virginia v. Pancake 58 n34
Whittaker v. Wisconsin 48–9, 57 n28, 62 n61
Winegan v. Maryland 332 n27
Wisconsin v. Herfel 25, 53 n1, 241 n93
Wisconsin v. Lederer 66, 94 n6, 98 n37, 266 n28
Wisconsin v. Plitcha 241 n91

Index

abortion
and Alabama Code 98 n35, 101 n59
prevention of 98 n34
acquiescence
and adultery 112–15
attitudinal 177
communication of 76–9
conditions precluding use as defense 112, 115–16
and consent 3, 4
consequences of 2
contemporaneous 247, 261
expression of 65–8, 177
and factual consent 20, 22
factual subjective 75
and legal consent 19, 25
and mental states 20–1, 26-9, 51, 52, 274
and offenses of participant harm 114–19
and offenses of third-party harm 111–16
prospective 247, 248–54, 261
and commitments 252–4
and irrevocability 249, 251–2
and mental states 262–3
and rape 26
retrospective 247, 254–61
arbitrariness of 259
and forgiveness 258–9
and wrongful harm 255–8
state of mind of 4
and underage sexual intercourse 17–20, 114–15
see also factual attitudinal consent; factual expressive consent; subjective acquiescence
actual consent 119
adultery 114–19
and acquiescence 112–15
definition 116, 117, 130 n5
and wrongful harm 113, 114
Alabama Code
and abortion 98 n35, 101 n59
and assent 53 n2
and rape 348 n33
Alaska Statutes
and definition of rape 15, 22 n3
and sexual abuse of a minor 131 n16
and sexual assault 135 n36
Alexander, Larry
conditions for prescriptive attitudinal consent 189–90
and consent 31, 32, 55 n20, 164 n5, 174 n75
Altman, Robert 237 n45
Antioch College, policy on student sexual contact 76–7, 102 n75
Aquinas, St Thomas 156
Archard, David
and consent 97 n33, 102 n75, 164 n6
consent as a performative 66
and deception 238 n55
Aristotle 115
and involuntary action 61 n42
and voluntariness 179, 234 n8
Arizona Revised Statutes, and sexual assault 233 n1
Arkansas Statutes
and consent 340
and rape 334 n40
assent 25, 53 n2
and consent 50
attitudes, propositional 40–1
Austin, J L 89, 96 n24, 96 n25
and illocutionary acts 90
and language 77
and performatives 90
authorization, mental states of 31–4
autonomy

and choice 128
and prescriptive consent 140
awareness, and factual attitudinal consent 39–42, 53

Berger, Vivian
and force 232
and rape 200
Bertolet, R, and indirect speech acts 97 n32
Bienen, Leigh, and legal consent 15
Bink, Howard 140, 150, 153, 156, 161
blood-alcohol test, unwanted, and constructive consent 277–9
Bogart, J H, and rape 171 n51
Boro, Daniel 188, 312, 313, 314
Brett, N
and consent 55 n21, 89, 95 n17, 164 n6
and mental states 152
Bryden, David
defining rape 244 n127
and fraud 226–7
and mental states 158
and resistance 218, 242 n96
Burnham, Rebecca 139–40, 143, 165 n18
Burt, R, and sterilization 303 n94
Burundanga 57 n31
Byrnes, Craig, and force 232

California Penal Code
and consent 147, 312
and fraud 331 n8
and impersonation 198–9
and misdemeanor compromise 266 n28
and rape 121–2, 135 n33, 171 n50, 330 n4, 331 n20
and underage sexual intercourse 131 n16
Canada, Revised Statutes of
and consent 98 n38, 140, 147
and imputed consent 7–8
and mental states 169 n32
and rape 25–6, 51–2, 144–5, 209
and sodomy 16
and underage sexual intercourse 17–19
capacity
and factual attitudinal consent 34–9, 53, 56 n27
and prescriptive attitudinal consent 240 n83
Carter, Rosemary, and paternalism 266 n26
Cey, Roger 269–70
Chamallas, M, and consent 62 n56
choice
affirmative 222
and awareness 39
conceptions of 44
and consent 3–4
contemporaneous 248
and factual attitudinal consent 44–9, 53
and freedom 43–4, 222–3
and Mill on 127–8
and retrospective consent 128
and rights of autonomy 128
Colorado Revised Statutes
and assault 304 n98
and capacity 56 n27
and consent 107, 140, 160, 161, 340
and sexual assault 328–9
commitments
non-reciprocal 252
reciprocal 252
common law, and offense of rape 254, 347 n12, 349 n36
competence
and factual consent 315
and form of statute 191–3
legal 118–19
mental 315–17
and motivation 193
and subjective acquiescence 189–91
see also hypothetical consent
compulsion
and force 229

and prescriptive attitudinal consent 191, 228
and subjective acquiescence 184–5
see also force; resistance
concepts
confusion over 3
legal 6
conduct
attitude towards 40–1
choice of 127–8
multiple descriptions of 40–2
Connecticut General Statutes, and sexual assault 276
consciousness, *see* capacity
consent
conceptual confusion 2–3, 8-10, 52, 307, 309, 327–8, 337–40, 346
confusing attitudinal with expressive 318–21
confusing factual with imputed 321–7
confusing factual with prescriptive 309–18
contemporaneous 248
core conception of 4–5
as defense 111–12, 124, 140, 141–2
definition 2, 9, 66, 70–1, 147–8, 169 n36, 337
fictions of 321–2, 324–5
forms of 3–4
generic concept of 3–4
language of 65
Law Commission paper on 337–9
legal competence 118–19
legal use of 294
minimal elements of 27
negative 220–3
non-contemporaneous 248
non-normative conceptions of 16
normative scope of 293–5
as a performative 66, 89–91
and rape 9, 15, 21, 22 n2, 54 n12, 107
and rape reform 3
signs of 274
specific concept of 3–4
and submission 25–6, 50, 330
transformative nature of 15, 22 n2
and *Volenti non fit injuria* 115, 129
see also constructive consent; factual attitudinal consent; factual consent; factual expressive consent; hypothetical consent; implied consent; imputed consent; informed consent; legal consent; prescriptive attitudinal consent; prescriptive consent; prescriptive expressive consent
constructive consent 29, 270, 271, 272–80
and blood-alcohol test 277–9
definition 108
and imputed consent 107
and marital exemption to law of rape 272–6, 323–7
principle of 279
contemporaneous prescriptive consent 247, 261–2, 264 n2
and removal of life support 286
Copithorne, Starr 35
Coughlin, Anne, and the marital exemption 325
Cowling, M, force and rape 244 n130
Crawford, Dale 71–4
Crawford, Trish 71–4, 75
criminal law, condemnatory nature of 142–3
criminal responsibility, and hypothetical consent 285

Dan-Cohen, Meir
and conceptions of choice 44
and freedom and choice 43–4, 46–7
offense classifications 237 n46
and statutory rape 167 n29
Death With Dignity Act (Oregon) 178, 234 n2
deception, *see* fraud
Delaware Code

and assault 322
and definition of consent 9
and social activities 299 n37
description
and conduct 40–2
and criminal law 41
desire, and factual attitudinal consent 29–31, 32–3, 45–6, 53
dignitary harm 171 n48
and rape 148–50, 161
dispositional consent, *see* hypothetical consent
District of Columbia Code, and consent 147, 148, 170 n44
dreaming, and consent 37–8
Dressler, Joshua
and consent 101 n60, 171 n52, 233
and prospective consent 265 n6
Dripps, Donald
and aggravated offense 230–2
and deception 238 n63
and retroactive approval 255
and sexual offenses 172 n61
and wrongful threats 232
Duff, A, and wrongful harm 171 n49
duties, as legal concept 6
Dutton, Robert 120, 121

emotions, reactive 142, 165 n15
Estrich, Susan
and consent 97 n33, 154, 200
and definition of rape 153–4, 155, 172 n58
and legal consent 15
and mental states 147, 153, 155–6
and 'no' 80–1, 82–3, 99 n48
and Pomona College case 84–5
and rape reform 3
and resistance 218
and strict liability 143
euthanasia (Netherlands) 30, 112
expressions, social construction of 68

factual attitudinal consent 4–5, 107, 319
centrality of concept 51
and choice 44–9, 53
definition 51
and legal consent 51
mental nature of 28–9
mental states of authorization 31–4
mental states of desire 29–33, 45–6, 53
mental states of indifference 30
minimum conditions for 27–8, 53
awareness 39–42, 53
and capacity to consent 34–9, 53, 56 n27
freedom 42–8, 53, 195
and 'no' 86
and ranked preferences 45–9
and rape 51–2
and withholding of privileges 31, 32, 33
see also acquiescence; factual expressive consent; subjective acquiescence
factual consent
and awareness 39
and competence 315
confusing with imputed consent 321–7
confusing with prescriptive consent 309–18
definition 16–17, 51, 107
elements of 20–1, 22
and legal consent 16, 52
and mental states 20–1
non-contemporaneous 247
and rape 21, 22
timing of 261
and underage sexual intercourse 18–20
see also factual attitudinal consent; factual expressive consent
factual expressive consent 5, 62 n62, 107
communication of 76–9
definition 51, 88
essential elements of 67–8, 87–8

and factual subjective acquiescence 75
and illocutions 77, 78–82, 90, 91–3, 96 n27, 97 n31
interpretive gap 72–4
and 'no' 79–87, 100 n57
normative judgements of 88
observer's interpretation of 70–1
observer's measurement of 71–5
as a performative 66, 89–91
and point of view 69–71, 90
and promises 91
social context of 68
speaker's intentions 69–71
and speech-act theory 77–9
and 'yes' 76–80, 91
see also acquiescence; factual attitudinal consent; subjective acquiescence
factum, fraud in the 197–8, 199, 312–14
Feinberg, Joel
and consent 102 n86, 154, 235 n11, 347 n11
and deception 187, 238 n57
and the harm principle 125, 126, 137 n49, 137 n51, 138 n65
and incapacity 190, 237 n40
and involuntary action 61 n42
and mental states 145–6, 152–4, 156, 158
and prescriptive consent 141–2, 163
and rights of autonomy 128
and subsequent consent 254–5
and 'the court of heaven' 153, 156, 157
and threats 180, 244 n134
and voluntariness 180, 187, 234 n10
Florida Laws, and resistance 211, 214
force
conceptions of 208
consent to 205–10
and definition of rape 341–5
meaning of 228–9
non-criminal 202–4
and rape reform 3, 208
unconditionally criminal 204–5
wrongful
and compulsion 185–6
definition 229, 241 n84
and oppression 184–5
and prescriptive attitudinal consent 188, 191, 227–33
and resistance 210–19
and threats 180–4
see also compulsion; resistance
fraud
and fraud in the factum 197–8, 199, 312–14
and fraud in the inducement 197–8, 199, 312, 313, 314
and prescriptive attitudinal consent 187–9, 226–7, 236 n31, 240 n83
and rape 201
freedom
and choice 43–4
and factual attitudinal consent 42–8, 53
and form of statute 191–3
and motivation 193
perception of 42–3
and prescriptive attitudinal consent 195–7
and subjective acquiescence 180–7
Fritsch, J, and statutory rape 167 n28

Gautier, David, and hypothetical consent 285
Gonzales, Oran 119
Goodman, Ellen, on Antioch policy 77

Haely, Karen
and consent 107
and harm of rape 171 n52
and strict liability 166 n21
and threats 235 n20
Hale, Lord Matthew, and marital

exemption 272, 323–6, 333 n35, 333 n36, 333 n37
harm, wrongful
and adultery 113, 114
and contemporaneous prescriptive consent 262
and dignitary harm 148–50, 161, 171 n48
and offenses of non-consent 148–51
and primary harm 150–1, 161
and punishment 156–7, 161
and rape 117
and retrospective consent 255–8
and statutory rape 118
and underage sexual intercourse 114–15
harm principle 125–7, 128–9
Harman, John, and legal consent 15
Harmon, Louise, and hypothetical consent 290, 292
Harrison, R, on rape 11 n10
Hart, H L A, on confusion over concepts 3
Hasday, J E, and marital exemption to law of rape 297 n22
Henderson, L
and force 232
and rape reform 241 n84
Hohfeld, Wesley 91, 92
homicide 112
Hooker, Cameron 184–5
Hough, Lamont 41
Hough, Lenny 41
Hubin, Donald
and consent 107
and harm of rape 171 n52
and strict liability 166 n21
and threats 235 n20
Hurd, Heidi
and consent 57 n30, 164 n5, 174 n75
and moral magic of consent 15
hypothetical consent 8, 62 n57, 271, 284–93
and criminal law 285
critiques of 290
definition 108, 284
and fictions of 292–3
and imputed consent 107
and life-saving surgery 288–90
and moral and political theory 285–6
and removal of life support 8, 286–8
and sterilization of retarded women 290–1, 303 n94

Idaho Code, and sexual offenses 192–3
impersonation 198–9
implied consent 269–70
ambiguity of term 274–5, 326
and blood-alcohol test 277–8
and life-saving surgery 287–9
imputed consent 7–8, 196
conditions for 122, 124–5
confusing with actual consent 321–7
contestability of 121–2
definition 139, 271
as a fiction 271–2, 322, 324–5
forms of 107–8, 271
and hypothetical consent 8
variability of 123–4
and wrongful harm 148
see also constructive consent; hypothetical consent; informed consent
indecisiveness
and indifference 30, 55 n15
and mental states 159
indeterminacy, and mental states 158
Indiana Code, and underage sexual intercourse 131 n16
indifference
and factual attitudinal consent 28, 30, 53
and indecisiveness 30, 55 n15
inducement, fraud in the 197–8, 199, 312, 313
informed consent 270, 271, 280–4
definition 108
and imputed consent 107

Iowa Code, and rape 348 n33
irrevocability, and prospective prescriptive consent 249, 251–2

Jackson, Kenneth 122–3
judgement, and factual attitudinal consent 35–6
justice, as normative concept 294

Kansas Statutes, and rape 339
Kelly, Liz, on consent 77
Kentucky Revised Statutes, and resistance 241 n89
Kingwell, Perry 269–70
Kleinig, John 141
knowledge
  conceptions of 197–8
  and form of statute 191–3
  and motivation 193
  and prescriptive attitudinal consent 195–201
  and subjective acquiescence 187–9

Law Commission (England) 129 n1, 133 n22
  consultation paper on consent 337–9
  and fraud 239 n72
legal attitudinal consent, conditions for 53
legal concepts, definition 6
legal consent 6
  and acquiescence 19, 25
  conceptions of 15–16
  conceptual elements of 108
  conditions for 124–5
  contestability of 119–22, 125
  as defense 124
  definition 15, 50, 114
  and factual attitudinal consent 51
  and factual consent 16, 52
  forms of 50, 107, 139
  and the harm principle 128–9
  hypothetical 8
  judgements of 340
  and mental states 28–9
    of acquiescence 21, 26–7
    of authorization 31–4
    of desire 29–33, 45–6
  prescriptive 6–7, 107
  and rape 15, 21, 25, 50
  and submission 25–6
  transformative nature of 15, 22 n2
  and underage sexual intercourse 17–20
  variability of 122–4
  and withholding of privileges 31, 32, 33
  see also imputed consent; prescriptive consent
legal expressive consent 75
Leiding, Waldemar 120, 121
Leo, John, and 'no' 80–2, 83
Leonard, Gerald, and consent 166 n25
L'Heureux-Dub, Justice 199–200, 201
life-saving treatment
  and hypothetical consent 288–90
  unwanted 276–7
life support
  and hypothetical consent 8, 286–8
  removal of 300 n54
living wills 276, 286
  and prospective prescriptive consent 248–50
Louisiana Revised Statutes
  and aggravated rape 131 n16, 213
  and consent 26
  rape and marriage 298 n26

McGregor, J
  and consent 55 n21
  and force 232, 244 n139, 245 n140
  and resistance 241 n92
  and sexual relationships 238 n65
  and wrongful threats 230, 232
MacKinnon, Catharine
  and force 344
  and mental states 166 n20
  and rape reform 3
Maine Revised Code, and resistance 241 n89

Malette, Georgette 288
Malm, H M
and capacity 57 n28
and consent 66–7, 97 n33
and expressive consent 89
and mental states 159, 174 n73
and negative consent 220, 221, 222
and 'no' 99 n45
and subjective consent 62 n56
marital exemption, and rape 272–6, 297 n22, 323–7, 333 n35, 333 n36, 333 n37, 334 n41
marriage, *see* marital exemption
Maryland Code
and consent 340
and marital exemption 323, 334 n41
and rape 320–1, 332 n25
masochism 205
medical treatment
and hypothetical consent 288–90
unwanted 276–7
mens rea
and contemporaneous prescriptive consent 262
and mental states 160
and strict liability 143–5
mental states
and acquiescence 20–1, 26–9, 51, 52, 274
of authorization 31–4
and awareness 39–42
and capacity to consent 34–9, 56 n27
and consent 26–7
of desire 29–33, 45–6, 53
and factual consent 20–1, 22
and freedom 42–8
and indecisiveness 159
and indeterminacy 158
of indifference 28, 30, 53
and legal consent 21
and *mens rea* 143–5, 160
and prescriptive consent 145–52, 159, 160–2, 219, 220
and justice 152–9
and propositional attitudes 40–1
and prospective consent 262–3
Michigan Compiled Laws, and capacity 56 n27
Mill, John Stuart
and choice 127–8
and the harm principle 125–9
Miller, Gwendoline May 272–5
Miller, Peter 272–5
Minnesota Statutes
and consent 88–9, 94 n5, 147, 170 n44
and criminal sexual conduct 134 n29
Missouri Revised Statutes, and assent 53 n2
Model Penal Code
and attempted rape 154, 155, 156, 161, 172 n59
and deception 188, 236 n33
and harm of rape 171 n52
and incapacity 56 n27
and mental states 147
and mental states of acquiescence 26
and prescriptive consent 151, 172 n54
and pressures 202–4
and rape 335 n59
and sexual assault 172 n60
and statutory rape 132 n19
and strict liability 165 n19
and theft 239 n70
and underage sexual intercourse 17, 18, 173 n64
Moe, Mary 290–1, 292, 293
Montana Code
and consent 23 n14, 243 n123
and rape 213, 243 n101
and sexual offenses 131 n14
motivation, and prescriptive attitudinal consent 193–5
multiple personality disorder 36, 37, 59 n37, 60 n39
Murphy, Jeffrie
and moral injuries 149
and rape 200

Nagel, Thomas 173 n68
Nebraska Revised Statutes, and consent 98 n38
need-not-resist rule 214–16
negative consent 220–3
Nevada Revised Statutes, and non-consensual physical contact 42
New Hampshire Revised Statutes, and consent 98 n38
New Mexico Code
  and blood-alcohol test 299 n36
  and force 348 n26
  and rape 134 n30
New York Penal Code
  consent and sexual offenses 132 n17
  and marital exemption 323
  and underage sexual intercourse 17
'no'
  and factual expressive consent 85–7, 100 n57
  and 'no means no' 79–85
Noble, Patricia 34, 37–8, 60 n40
non-consent, offenses of
  formulation of 208–10
  and wrongful harm 148–51
non-contemporaneous prescriptive consent 247–8
  prospective 248–54, 261
    and commitments 252–4
    and irrevocability 249, 251–2
    and mental states 262–3
  retrospective 254–61
    arbitrariness of 259
    and forgiveness 258–9
    and wrongful harm 255–8

Odysseus, and prospective prescriptive consent 253–4
offenses
  classifications 237 n46
  of non-consent 111–12
  of participant harm 114–19
  of third-party harm 112–14
Ohio Revised Code
  and rape 341, 347 n22
  and resistance 241 n89
  and sexual assault 216
  and underage sexual intercourse 131 n16
Olsen, F, and prevention of abortion 98 n34
O'Neill, Onora, and consent 40–1, 327
oppression, wrongful, and subjective acquiescence 184–5
Oregon Revised Statutes, and Death With Dignity Act (Oregon) 234 n6

Parish, Marvin 67, 69
participant harm
  and acquiescence 116
  offenses of 114–19
paternalism, legal 207, 266 n26
penal codes, and consent 169 n36
Pennsylvania Code
  and rape 348 n33
  and resistance 217
perceptions, and freedom 42–3
Perkins, Rollin, and consent 112
permanently vegetative state, and hypothetical consent 8
Pineau, Lois, and motivation 194, 237 n48
Plato 156, 157, 173 n67, 174 n71
Pomona College 81, 84–5, 100 n56
preferences, ranked 47
  and desire 45–6
  and factual attitudinal consent 46–9
prescriptive attitudinal consent
  and capacity 240 n83
  conceptual difficulties with 224–32
  conditions for 177–9, 189–90, 195, 224
  confusing with prescriptive expressive 318–21
  contemporaneous 247, 261
  and Death With Dignity Act (Oregon) 178

and force 201–10, 227–33
resistance to 210–19
and form of statute 191–3
and fraud 226–7, 240 n83
knowledge required for 195–201
conceptions of 197–8
motivation required for 193–5
and subjective acquiescence 179
and competence 189–91
and freedom 180–7, 195–7
and knowledge 187–9
and threats 230–2
see also prescriptive consent; prescriptive expressive consent
prescriptive consent 6–7
and autonomy 140
and conceptual confusion 327–8
confusing with factual consent 309–18
contemporaneous 247, 261–2, 264 n2, 286
and criminal responsibility 139
definition 107, 139, 162
controversy over 140–1, 159–60
hybrid 162–4
elements of 327–8
as expressive act 141–5, 152, 159, 160, 219–20
fictions of 271–2, 324–5
and *mens rea* 143–5, 160
as mental state 145–6, 152, 159, 160–2, 219, 220
function of defining as 148–52
and justice 152–9
practice of defining as 146–8
and negative consent 220–3
prospective 248–54, 261
and commitments 252–4
and irrevocability 249, 251–2
and mental states 262–3
and removal of life support 286–7
and punishment 141, 160
retrospective 254–61
arbitrariness of 259
and forgiveness 258–9
and wrongful harm 255–8
and strict liability 142–4
variability of 123
and wrongful harm 148–51
see also prescriptive attitudinal consent; prescriptive expressive consent
prescriptive expressive consent
conditions for 177–8, 219–20
confusing with prescriptive attitudinal 318–21
contemporaneous 247
and Death With Dignity Act (Oregon) 178
see also prescriptive consent; prescriptive attitudinal consent
Price, M, and sterilization 303 n94
primary harm, and rape 150–1, 161
privilege, withholding of 31, 32, 33
promises, and factual expressive consent 91
propositional attitudes, opaqueness of 40–1
prospective prescriptive consent
and commitments 252–4
and contemporaneous non-acquiescence 248–54, 261
and irrevocability 249, 251–2
and mental states 262–3
and removal of life support 286–7
punishment
and consent as a mental state 152–9, 161–2
grading of 156–7, 161
and prescriptive consent 141, 160

Quinlan, Karen Ann 286, 290, 292, 293

rape
and acquiescence 26
and consent 9, 15, 21, 22 n2, 54 n12, 107
consent as defense 111, 124, 140, 141–2
definition 11 n18, 15, 116, 117, 153, 209, 340–6
and dignitary harm 148–50

and factual attitudinal consent 51–2
and factual consent 21, 22
and legal consent 15, 21, 25, 50
and marital exemption 272–6, 297 n22, 323–7, 333 n35, 333 n36, 333 n37, 334 n41
and mental states 28–34
and motivation 194
nature of 200
and negative consent 220–3
and primary harm 150–1
and resistance 210–19
and submission 25–6
and utmost-resistance rule 211
and wrongful harm 117, 118, 148–51
see also spousal rape; statutory rape

rape reform 241 n84
and conceptual confusion 3
and force 208
stranger 9

Rawls, John 300 n51
and hypothetical consent 285, 286

Remick, L A
and consent 97 n33, 220
and negative consent 222

resentment 165 n15
nature of 142

resistance
and framing of rape statutes 216–17
meanings of 211–12, 216–17
and need-not-resist rule 214–16
as substitute for *mens rea* 217–19
and utmost-resistance rule 211, 212–14
and wrongful force 210–19
see also compulsion; force

retroactivity 326–7

retrospective consent, and choice 128

retrospective prescriptive consent
and contemporaneous non-acquiescence 254–61
arbitrariness of 259
and forgiveness 258–9
and wrongful harm 255–8

rights, as legal concept 6

risk
assumption of 299 n43
and consent 39–40
and informed consent 280–4

Russell, Diana 47, 49

Ryle, Gilbert, and category mistakes 9

Sacks, Oliver 57 n28, 60 n41, 65, 93 n1

sadism 205

Salsman, David 316–17

Sarah, and multiple personality disorder 36, 37, 59 n37

Schelling, Thomas, and commitments 265 n10

Schulhofer, S
and competency 237 n46
and consent 97 n33, 100 n50, 101 n60, 170 n43
and mental states 147
and rape 166 n20
rape and force 229–30
and threats 235 n17

Searle, John 81–2
and declarations 83–4, 99 n47
and directives 92
and illocutionary acts 90
and performatives 90
and sincerity conditions 91
and speech-act theory 78–9

Sherwin, Emily
and consent 31, 32, 165 n7, 307
and willingness 61 n55

Simmons, John, expression of consent 274

Simmons, Kenneth
and assumption of risk 299 n43
and statutory rape 167 n29

Soble, A, and Antioch policy 102 n75

social practices, and constructive consent 278–9

sodomy, and consent 16

Solis, Hilda 135 n34

speech-act theory 101 n65

and consent 66, 77–9
and declarations 82–3, 85
and directives 92
extra-linguistic declarations 83–4
illocutions 77-82, 90, 96 n27, 97 n31
and indirect speech acts 97 n32
and 'no' 80–1
and performative 89, 90
spousal rape 121–2
and marital exemption 272–6, 323–7, 333 n35, 333 n36, 333 n37, 334 n41
St Andrew, Clifford 319
Stafford, Billie Joe 119
state of mind, *see* mental states
statutory rape 116–17, 118, 144, 167 n28, 167 n29
definition 116–17
and Model Penal Code 132 n19
and prescriptive attitudinal consent 224–32
and strict liability 144
and wrongful harm 118
sterilization (retarded women)
Alternative Standard 291–2
and best interests 291
and hypothetical consent 290–1, 303 n94
Stowell, Judith 113–14
stranger rape 9
Strawson, Peter, and illocutionary acts 90
strict liability 143–4
injustice of 142–3, 165 n19
and statutory rape 144
subjective acquiescence 35–6, 39, 47–50, 52, 53, 62 n56, 65, 88, 107, 319
and compulsion 185–6
and force
consent to 205–10
non-criminal 202–4
unconditionally criminal 204–5
and form of statute 191–3
and fraud 187–9
and prescriptive attitudinal consent 179
and threats 180–4, 230–2
and voluntariness 179
and competence 189–91
and freedom 180–7
and knowledge 187–9
and wrongful oppression 184–5
see also acquiescence; factual attitudinal consent; factual expressive consent
submission
and consent 25–6, 50, 330
and mental acquiescence 27
and rape 25–6
substituted judgement, *see* hypothetical consent
suicide, assisted 178

Tchen, Christina, and consent 220
Termination of Life on Request Act (Netherlands) 30, 112
Texas Penal Code
and acquiescence to sexual intercourse 121, 134 n31
and rape 2
third-party harm
and acquiescence 115–16
offenses of 111–14
threats 180, 181, 235 n17, 235 n20, 244 n134
and Model Penal Code 202–4
and prescriptive attitudinal consent 230–2
and resistance 210–19
and subjective acquiescence 180–4, 230–2
wrongful 180–4, 230, 232, 235 n18, 343–4
Tiersma, Peter, and negative consent 222
Travis County grand jury 1–2, 310
true consent 119

underage sexual intercourse 130 n8
and competence 191

and consent 17–20, 114–15
definition 116, 131 n16
and prescriptive attitudinal consent 224–6
and punishment of minors 118–19, 133 n22, 133 n23, 133 n24
and strict liability 144
Uniform Rights of the Terminally Ill Act (Ohio) 264 n4
United States Supreme Court 32
and strict liability 165 n19
Utah Code
and consent 148, 264 n5
and rape 192
and sexual assault 341
utmost-resistance rule 211, 212–14
as corollary of wrongful force 213–14

Valdez, Joel 1–2, 9–10, 310
Virginia Code
and rape 135 n39
rape and marriage 298 n28
and resistance 211, 217
and retrospective consent 266 n29
Volenti non fit injuria 115
and consent 129
and the harm principle 126–7
voluntariness
and competence 189–91
and form of statute 191–3
and freedom 180–7
and compulsion 185–6
threats 180–4
and wrongful oppression 184–5
and knowledge 187–9
and subjective acquiescence 179

Washington Revised Code, and consent 94 n5, 147, 148, 170 n44, 233 n1
Watson, Justice 67, 69, 75, 85
Wertheimer, Alan 10
and consent 101 n60, 140–1, 164 n6, 347 n11
and hybrid view 165 n7
and illegal coercion 182, 183
and wrongful threats 183, 235 n18
West, Robin
and consent 344–5, 350 n40
and rape reform 241 n84
and wrongful threats 230, 232, 343–4
West Virginia Code, and sexual assault 216, 334 n40
Westminster, Statute of (1285) 254, 347 n12, 349 n36
Whitmire, John 134 n31
Whittaker, Samuel 48, 49, 50
Williams, Bernard 58 n35
Wilson, Elizabeth 1–2, 9–10
Wisconsin Statutes, and consent 66, 70, 94 n5, 140, 147, 170 n44
Wooten, Barbara 165 n11
wrongful force, *see* force, wrongful

'yes', and factual expressive consent 76–80, 91

Zimmerman, David
and threats 181